HANDBOOK
OF THE MEDIA
IN ASIA

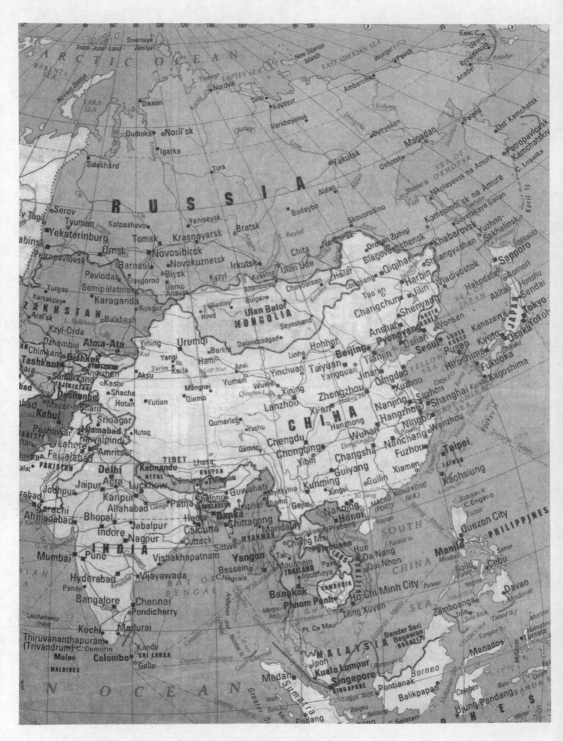

ASIA: POLITICAL
Based on Survey of India map with the permission of the Surveyor General of India.

HANDBOOK
OF THE MEDIA
IN ASIA

Edited by
Shelton A. Gunaratne

Sage Publications
New Delhi * Thousand Oaks * London

First published in 2000 by

Sage Publications India Pvt Ltd
M-32 Market, Greater Kailash, Part 1
New Delhi 110 048

Sage Publications Inc.
2455 Teller Road
Thousand Oaks, California 91320

Sage Publications Ltd
6 Bonhill Street
London EC2A 4PU

Published by Tejeshwar Singh for Sage Publications India Pvt Ltd, lasertypeset by Asian Telelinks, New Delhi, and printed at Chaman Enterprises, Delhi.

Library of Congress Cataloging-in-Publication Data

Handbook of the media in Asia/edited by Shelton A. Gunaratne.
    p.   cm.
    Includes bibliographical references and index.
    1. Mass media—Asia—Handbooks, manuals, etc. I. Gunaratne, Shelton A.
P92.A7 H36   302.23'095—dc21   2000   00–021783

ISBN: 0-7619-9427-0 (US–HB)
          81-7036-901-0 (India–HB)

Sage Production Team: Ritika Prasad, M.S.V. Namboodiri, & Santosh Rawat

This book is dedicated to my parents
Don William (1907–1975)
&
Ariyawathie (1913–)

Contents

Part 2: Southeast Asia

Acknowledgments

For responding to my reasonable requests, ignoring the brash ones, and letting me rewrite their manuscripts: the 36 contributors to this book.

For independently reviewing several of the book chapters: Leonard Chu, Kunda Dixit, Mazharul Haque, Youichi Ito, Srinivas Melkote, Joompol Rodcumdee, Amos Owen Thomas, Chung-Chuan Yang, and Kyu Ho Youm.

For helping to get the resource books on Asian mass communication and tele-communication and building a specialized collection at Minnesota State University Moorhead: Rodney Erickson, retired collection management librarian, and Jean Kramer, technical services librarian.

For his thoroughness in correspondence and attention to detail during the various phases of the project: Tejeshwar Singh, managing director of Sage Publications India Pvt Ltd.

For her thorough editing and tolerance of my suggested improvements: Ritika Prasad, manuscript editor at Sage Publications India Pvt Ltd.

For inviting me to be guest editor of a special issue of *Gazette* on Asian communication media that preceded this book: Cees Hamelink, editor-in-chief of *Gazette*; and Sage Publications London.

For her speed in retrieving electronic mail attachments and mailing hard-copy manuscripts to the publisher: Marian Olson.

For his willingness to assist with his resources: Jacob Arfwedson, research manager, World Association of Newspapers.

For tolerance of my neglect of family duties for many months: Yoke-Sim, my spouse; Junius Asela, my son; and Carmel Maya, my daughter.

Shelton A. Gunaratne

OVERVIEW

Shelton A. Gunaratne

1. WHAT IS ASIA?

This volume[1] follows the customary division of Asia into the South, the Southeast, and the East. It excludes Oceania, as well as the parts of the Asian continent that belong to the Middle East and the former Soviet Union. Yet this book covers an area inhabited by 3.3 billion people or 55 percent of the world's six billion population.[2] They live in 22 countries, two autonomous economies—Hong Kong, which Britain reverted to China in July 1997, and Macau, which Portugal reverted to China in December 1999—and an independent economy—Taiwan, a break-away province of China.

The seven countries in South Asia—excluding Afghanistan, which is more akin to the Middle East—belong to the South Asian Association for Regional Coope-ration (SAARC). They have set up plans to liberalize trade within the region by 2001 through the creation of a South Asian Preferential Trade Agreement (SAPTA). Within SAARC, Bangladesh, India, and Sri Lanka have formed the Bay of Bengal Club. Another offshoot group comprising Bangladesh, Bhutan, India, and Nepal was also in the offing. Excepting the Maldives and Sri Lanka, SAARC belongs to the world's *low-income* countries, which the World Bank has defined as those with a Gross National Product (GNP) per capita of US$ 785 or less. In terms of the Human Development Index (HDI), Sri Lanka, Maldives, India, and Pakistan are in the *medium* category while the others are in the *low* category (Table 1). South Asia accounts for 1.3 billion inhabitants, or 40 percent of Asia's total population.[3]

The 10 countries in Southeast Asia belong to the Association of Southeast Asian Nations (ASEAN). This number excludes East Timor, which separated from

[1] This is a country-specific handbook on the media in Asia. It follows a special double issue of *Gazette, 61* (3 & 4), 1999, which I edited to highlight continental or regional mass media trends and concerns related to Asia. This overview is an updated and expanded version of the essay I wrote for the special *Gazette* issue.
[2] By 2025, Asia would have 53.7 percent of the estimated 7.9 billion world population (US Census Bureau, 1998).
[3] By 2025, South Asia would have 44.2 percent of Asia's estimated population of 4.2 billion (US Census Bureau, 1998).

Indonesia in 1999. They fall into all four income categories as defined by the World Bank. Cambodia, Vietnam, Laos, and Myanmar, comprising a total population of 142 million, are *low-income* countries. Indonesia, Philippines, and Thailand, with a total population of 356 million, are in the *lower middle-income* category—countries with a GNP per capita of US$ 786 to US$ 3,125. Malaysia is the only country in the *upper middle-income* category—countries with a GNP per capita of US$ 3,126 to US$ 9,655. Brunei Darussalam and Singapore, comprising a total population of 3.4 million, belong to the *upper-income* category—economies with a GNP per capita of US$ 9,656 or more. In terms of the HDI, Singapore and Brunei are in the *high* human development category; Malaysia, Thailand, Philippines, Indonesia, Vietnam, Myanmar, and Cambodia are in the *medium* category; and Laos in the *low* category (Table 2). Southeast Asia as a whole has 524 million people, or almost 16 percent of Asia's total population.[4]

East Asia has four of the richest economies in Asia. However, the vast majority of the people are in China, which belongs to the *lower middle-income* category, together with North Korea. The population in these two countries exceeds 1.3 billion. Sparsely populated Mongolia is the only *low-income* country. The other economies fall into the *upper-income* category. In terms of the HDI, China and Mongolia (and possibly North Korea) are in the *medium* human development category while the others are in the *high* category (Table 3). The region as a whole has almost 1.5 billion people, or about 45 percent of Asia's total population.[5]

In Asia, press freedom, as defined by Freedom House, is not significantly correlated with the economic standing of a country.[6] Press freedom is higher in the low-income countries of South Asia (barring the Maldives, Bhutan, and Pakistan, which reverted to military rule in October 1999) than in the middle-income countries of Southeast Asia (barring Thailand, the Philippines, and possibly Indonesia, which became freer under President Wahid in late 1999). However, the upper-income economies of East Asia have greater press freedom than all other Asian countries. South Korea transformed itself into a free and open media system following the overturn of Chun Doo-Hwan's regime in 1987 (Heo, Uhm, & Chang, this volume); and Taiwan transformed itself similarly with the lifting of martial law in 1988 (Wang & Lo, this volume; Vanden Heuvel & Dennis, 1993).

2. PRESS FREEDOM IN ASIA: AN OCCIDENTAL VIEW

Article 19 of the Universal Declaration of Human Rights (UDHR) asserts: "*Everyone* has the right to freedom of opinion and expression; this right includes freedom to hold opinions without interference and to seek, receive and impart information

---

[4] By 2025, Southeast Asia would have 17 percent of Asia's estimated population (US Census Bureau, 1998).
[5] By 2025, East Asia would have 38.8 percent of Asia's estimated population (US Census Bureau, 1998).
[6] The correlation between the per capita GNP and Freedom House PF scores was a negative 0.32 (p = 0.135). Lower scores denoted higher press freedom while higher GDPs denoted higher income. Hence the negative correlation.

and ideas through any media regardless of frontiers." However, more than half a century after the adoption of the Declaration, its practical application leaves much to be desired. Mehra (1986), a South Asian scholar, says, "Publicly, all societies profess to be free. In practice, no society permits absolute freedom; restraints only come in varying degrees. The issue becomes even more complex during interaction among societies with different levels of freedom" (p. xii).

Only two countries in Asia, the Philippines and South Korea, have ratified all eight of the international human rights instruments highlighted by the United Nations (Table 4). Three South Asian countries—Bhutan, Maldives, and Pakistan—and six Southeast Asian countries—Brunei, Indonesia, Laos, Malaysia, Myanmar, and Singapore—as well as China have failed to ratify both of the 1966 international covenants: one on civil and political rights; the other on economic, social, and cultural rights. Brunei has ratified only one instrument, the 1989 convention on the rights of the child.

The annual Freedom House surveys of press freedom worldwide makes Mehra's (1986) point clear. The 1999 survey rated Norway as the freest country. Yet it had a restriction score of 5 on a scale of zero through 100. Nauru came second with a score of 6 and Bahamas third with 7. New Zealand, Marshall Islands, and Switzerland followed with 8 while Belgium and Denmark came next with 9. Australia, Luxembourg, and Sweden trailed with 10, followed by Jamaica with 11, and Austria and Iceland with 12. Only then came the United States with a score of 13 in the company of Germany and St Lucia. Thus the land of the First Amendment was not the freest in press freedom on the Freedom House criteria. Significantly, not a single Asian country came within the first tier of free-press countries scoring 15 or less. Japan, the freest in Asia had a restriction score of 19. Taiwan had a score of 25, South Korea of 28, and the Philippines, Thailand, and Mongolia a score of 30 each. These were the only other Asian nations that qualified as "free" (see Table 6 and Figure 1).

Sussman (1998) asserts that Freedom House measures press freedom worldwide on a set of criteria founded on Article 19, placing emphasis on the singular indefinite pronoun *everyone*. The level of press freedom is measured using four criteria: ● Laws and regulations that influence media *content*; ● political pressures and controls on media *content*; ● economic influences over media *content*; and ● repressive actions. The first three criteria are judged on a scale of 0–15 and the fourth on a scale of 0–5 both for broadcast and print media. Not free (NF) are those countries with scores of 61 to 100; partly free (PF) are those with a score of 31 to 60; and free (F) are those with a score of 0 to 30.

On the basis of these criteria, South Asia has no nation within the "free" category; Southeast Asia has two—Philippines and Thailand; and East Asia has four—Japan, Taiwan, South Korea, and Mongolia. (Freedom House has not rated Hong Kong and Macau, both of which now belong to China.) Five countries in South Asia—India, Sri Lanka, Bangladesh, Nepal, and pre-Musharraf Pakistan—fall into the "partly free" category, together with one country—Indonesia—in Southeast Asia. The "not free" category includes two countries in South Asia—the Maldives and

Bhutan, as well as post-coup Pakistan; seven in Southeast Asia—Cambodia, Malaysia, Laos, Singapore, Vietnam, Brunei, and Myanmar; and two in East Asia—China and North Korea.

The Freedom House survey paints a grim picture of Asia: Only 10.2 percent of Asians (333 million people) enjoy a "free" press, while 45.6 percent (1.5 billion) have access to a "partly free" press, and 44.2 per cent (1.4 billion) to a "not free" press.

Sussman (1998) draws a connection between the authoritarian tendencies and the economic misfortunes that befell Asia in 1997. In his view, "pervasive and institutionalized" press controls had disabled transparency in two Asian nations in particular, Malaysia and Indonesia. People thus remained ignorant of corruption, cronyism, and bad economic policies. In Malaysia, individuals and companies close to the ruling coalition own the broadcast media and the major newspapers. "Conflicts with Malaysian values" can be sufficient reason for the government to withdraw a broadcast license. In Indonesia, the radio network of the government, comprising 49 broadcasting and 309 transmitting stations, provided official news reports that all "private" stations also had to carry. The official journalists' association issued licenses to all journalists thereby ensuring "consensual journalism" or self-censorship[7] (Sussman, 1998, p. 1). In this volume, Safar, Sarji, and Gunaratne have documented the changes taking place in Malaysia, while Idris and Gunaratne draw attention to the post-Suharto *reformasi* in Indonesia.

In South Asia, laws and regulations affecting media content are at a high point in the Maldives, Nepal, and Bhutan (Figure 1). Political pressures and controls on media content are high in all the countries, except on the print media in India. Economic influences on media content are high in Bangladesh (print) and Bhutan (broadcast). Pakistan stands out on repressive action, although Ali and Gunaratne (this volume) see changes for the better—an optimism dashed by another military coup in late 1999. Repressive action on the print media has increased in Sri Lanka, Nepal, Bangladesh, and Bhutan (see Table 2 in the introduction to the section on South Asia). AMIC, the Asian mass media documentation center in Singapore, has published comprehensive compilations of mass media laws and regulations in India (Venkateswaran, 1993), Sri Lanka (Selvakumaran & Edrisinha, 1995), Bangladesh (Gaziul Hoque, 1992), Pakistan (Jabbar & Isa, 1997), and Nepal (Pokhrel & Koirala, 1995).

In Southeast Asia, Myanmar scores almost the maximum on all four criteria of press restrictions (Chadha & Kavoori, this volume). Brunei is ahead of communist Vietnam in overall press restrictions. Laws and regulations affecting media content have reached the zenith in Myanmar, Brunei, and Vietnam, followed closely by Singapore and Laos. Political pressure on both the broadcast and the print media have reached a maximum in Myanmar, Brunei, Vietnam, Cambodia, and Malaysia, again followed closely by Laos and Singapore. Economic influences on broadcast

---

[7] On November 13, 1998, a special session of the People's Consultative Assembly (MPR) adopted a freedom of information declaration (No. 17/MPR/1998) that should create a less stringent environment for the mass media in Indonesia. Earlier, the Habibie government dropped the requirement that all journalists must be members of the government-backed Indonesian Journalists Association.

and print media are the highest in Myanmar, while in Singapore, Indonesia, and Brunei it is dominantly the print media that suffers in this respect. Repressive actions are at their maximum on print media in Myanmar and Cambodia (see Table 2 in the introduction to the section Southeast Asia). Teodoro and Kabatay (1998) and Muntarbhorn (1998) have documented the legislation affecting the mass media in the Philippines and Thailand, the two countries with high press freedom in Southeast Asia. Ang and Yeo (1998), and Faruqui and Ramanathan (1998) have compiled a similar compendium for Singapore and Malaysia respectively.

In East Asia, laws and regulations affecting media content, as well as political pressures, have reached high points in North Korea and China, the two communist countries in the region. Economic influences over content, as well as repressive actions, have reached the maximum points in North Korea, while China is at the maximum in repressive actions on print media even though Yan (this volume) sees a much better future for press freedom. South Korea scores high on political pressures on print media (see Table 2 in the introduction to the section on East Asia).

3. ASIAN VALUES: AN ORIENTAL VIEW

Does the dearth of press freedom in Asia reflect what some identify as "Asian values"? If so, do such values run counter to Article 19 of the Human Rights Declaration? Hsiung (1985) says that human rights in East Asia do not have the same individualistic connotation as in the West: "the individual's flight to freedom and emancipation" (p. 7). He points out that "the Western concept of human rights conceived in the Western *adversarial* democratic tradition has no exact equivalent in East Asia," which inherited a *consensual*, group-oriented tradition (p. 12). Mehra (in Hamelink and Mehra, 1990) states that the holistic, consensual, and communal values of the Orient have expanded the scope of human rights to include an affirmative obligation on the state "to advance the economic, social and cultural well-being of their peoples" (p. viii). The "Asian values" school has used this line of reasoning to equate press freedom with press–government harmony.

Menon (in AMIC, 1994) says:

> It is obvious that indigenous philosophies have a greater bearing on press systems in [South Asia] than any scale of values based on Western communication theories, and there is a real need to re-examine Western theories and practices in the light of Asian cultures and traditions. However, the search for an Asian perspective does not imply rejection of the Western perspective. It should take whatever is useful and put this in the context of that society's social structure, cultural values and religious beliefs (pp. xi–xii).

Vanden Heuvel and Dennis (1993) point out that the media in much of East and Southeast Asia "stand in harmony with Confucian philosophy, which stresses consensus and cooperation" unlike the Western media's "dedication to individual freedom and rights" (p. iii). They say that Asians complain about the "forward, adversarial style of the Western media" and "the sex and violence of some Western entertainment programming," while Western journalists complain about excessive restrictions and inadequate access to information (p. 2).

Is the Occidental view of pluralism at variance with the Asian perspective of press freedom? Some ASEAN journalists have proposed an Asian model of journalism in which the press works with the government to build a national consensus. They contend that the national press, as an instrument of nation building, should support the state's development efforts. They say that the media need scrutiny because journalism is too important to be left to journalists (Masterton, 1996). Latif (1998) says that an Asian journalist "must respect, embrace and voice the authenticity of Asia" (p. 14); and that an Asian journalist cannot be free until he or she repudiates "colonial textuality" (p. 11). Chua Lee Hoong (in Latif, 1998) contends that Singapore editors have bluntly rejected "the 19th century notion of the press as the 'Fourth Estate' " (p. 147).[8]

The notion of press–government harmony is implicit in some definitions of developmental journalism as well. But Hartmann, Patil, and Dighe (1989), in their study of Indian villages, hardly found evidence to support Schramm's (1964) view of the "miraculous" potential of the mass media as "information multipliers." They contended that "mass communications play little part" in the success of government-initiated developmental activities without the involvement of "the people concerned as participants" (p. 266).

Thus the press–government harmony model might merely relegate the press to be the public relations arm of the government, as in the case of the communist model, thereby causing a media credibility gap. People, whether Asian or not, tend to distrust mass media that are too closely associated with the government. Most Asian countries have in place an adversarial political party system inherited from colonial rule. Within such a structure, press freedom must reflect an adversarial press as well.

Locke (1998) says that Western culture "is objectively the best" because it values reason, individual rights, and science and technology (p. A4). He draws attention to John Locke's contention that individuals do not exist to serve governments, but rather that governments exist to protect individuals, who have the unalienable right to life, liberty, and the pursuit of happiness. Thus the Occident emphasizes individual rights, as when Sussman (1998) asserts that the starting point of press freedom "is the smallest, most universal unit of concern: the individual" (p. 14). He says the operative word of Article 19 is *everyone*—meaning the individual. As Mehra (1989) elucidates, the Occident views man as "a rational animal with an inherent dignity" and "sovereignty to determine his acts and destiny" (p. 1). This viewpoint has produced "the individualistic, democratic, egalitarian and liberal tradition of Western political theory" (p. 3). The Orient, on the other hand, does not necessarily accept "the notion of man as purely a rational animal or as an end in himself" (p. 3). The Asians "value their consensual and communal traditions with their emphasis on duties and obligations to the collective and social harmony" (p. 3).

[8] Seow, 1998, however, argues that the Singapore press has become the mouthpiece of the state, using invidious self-censorship to distort the news.

This "epistemological distinction," however, is insufficient to explain the dearth of press freedom in Asia. Press freedom is an abstract concept that the Asian-values school may denigrate in the absence of a clear operational definition. Freedom House has operationalized the obstacles to press freedom within the context of Article 19. The question to resolve is whether the four strands of obstruction—legal, political, and economic obstacles, and repressive actions—are pertinent criteria to measure press freedom even if one were to construe press freedom as a collective right?

The MacBride Commission asserted that:

> Freedom of speech, of the press, of information and of assembly [is] vital for the realization of human rights. Extension of these communication freedoms to a broader individual and collective right to communicate is an evolving principle in the democratization process (cited in Traber & Nordenstreng 1992, p. 60).

Such a collective right to communicate is in harmony with Oriental philosophy—Buddhist, Hindu, Confucian, or Islamic. However, individualism has an Oriental foundation as well. For instance, the Hinayana school of Buddhism places heavy emphasis on individual action and responsibility in treading the "Noble Eightfold Path." The Buddhist approach is consistent with the idea of the rational man so often associated only with Locke and the Enlightenment. Press freedom is an essential ingredient of the right to communicate, both in a collective and individual sense. Chua (in Latif, 1998), however, contends that "press freedom remains distinct from freedom of speech" in Singapore (p. 148).

Are political and economic pressures and repressive actions consistent with maintaining social harmony or the collective right to communicate? A South Asian seminar on communication ethics emphasized the indispensability of "commitment to truth, respect for human dignity and concern for the vulnerable, disadvantaged and oppressed" (AMIC, 1997, p. v). This Asian perspective, in fact, is consistent with the call to remove the four strands of obstacles implicit in the annual Freedom House assessment of press freedom.

Prime Minister Mahathir of Malaysia equates Asian values with "not-so-liberal democracies" that provide "political stability, long-range vision, and consistency" (Mahathir & Ishihara, 1995, p. 84). He says that from an Asian perspective "democracy does not confer a license for citizens to go wild" (p. 83). Mahathir, however, rejects the authoritarian and communist models of the press because within such models wisdom becomes the monopoly of a few, and power becomes the determinant of truth. He also rejects the libertarian model because there are not many remarkably stable countries "where full, free and utter license can be allowed to run riot" (quoted in Mehra, 1989, p. 114). He opts for a socially responsible press that must compete in the economic marketplace "within the bounds of decency and responsibility" (p. 116). Mahathir advocates the greatest media freedom consonant with the vital interests of society; the Freedom House assessment, however, shows a very high degree of political pressure on media content in

Malaysia. The press has to follow the *Rukunegara*, the Malaysian national ideology, which stresses national unity, democracy, social equity, progressive thought, and traditional culture. The distinctions among authoritarian, communist, and social-responsibility models of the press become unclear within Mahathir's Asian perspective.

In a 1984 address to the American Society of Newspaper Editors, Singapore's leader Lee Kuan Yew said the theory of the press as the Fourth Estate did not fit Singapore, which had to build one nation out of four racial groups that had "co-existed in separate segments of the island demarcated by the British for disparate immigrant groups" (quoted in Mehra, 1989, p. 119). He cited India, the Philippines, and Sri Lanka where the practice of "the marketplace contest of ideas" had "ended in less than happy results" (p. 118). In his view, the media in these countries had produced "confusion and dissension" instead of building "enlightenment and consensus" (p. 6).[9] These remarks, however, reflect the absence of a consensus on a collective Asian perspective of a free press. Within ASEAN itself, the Philippines, Thailand, and possibly Indonesia (under Wahid) have opted for the so-called Western model. In East Asia, Mongolia, Taiwan, and South Korea have joined Japan in practicing the free-press model.

Pancasila, the five principles embodied in the preamble of the 1945 Indonesian Constitution determined the limits of media freedom in the archipelago until the post-Suharto developments. Article 1 of the code of ethics of the Indonesian Journalists Association requires its members to be faithful to *Pancasila*: belief in the one and supreme god; a just and civilized humanity; national unity; democracy, led by the wisdom of consensus among representatives; and social justice for the people. Within this national ideology, the Suharto regime closely monitored the mass media for tendentious or sensational writing relating to SARA—*Suku* (ethnic groups), *Agama* (religion), *Ras* (race) and *Antar-golongan* (inter-group relations). The Suharto backers claimed that the *Pancasila* press philosophy was different from the authoritarian or the communist models because it interwove freedom with responsibility.

The long periods of colonialism, marked by a bewildering mix of liberalism and democracy, as well as by ethnic, religious, and other forms of civil strife, have clearly had an impact on the current state of the media in Asia. T.J.S. George (in Latif, 1998) argues that "in Asian countries, historical factors have brought about different realities in different societies," and that it "is neither prudent nor necessary to apply Western yardsticks to this scenario and praise one country or decry another" (p. 21). This school of thought also tends to place greater emphasis on the vitality and importance of the grassroots and on traditional forms of communication, as is evidenced in studies of the information flow in rural communities (see Hartmann

[9] Lee expressed a revised viewpoint in a speech at the Asian Media Conference in Los Angeles in October 1998. Because the new information technology had made it impossible for governments to suppress inconvenient news, he said, the best governments could do was "to require the official view to be carried in the media, along with other views over which they have no control" (*The Straits Times*, October 31 and November 2, 1998).

et al., 1989). B.G. Verghese (in Latif, 1998), however, states adamantly that "freedom of expression is properly a human right" (p. 32) and argues the need for a free flow of information. S.K. Datta-Ray (in Latif, 1998) points out the lack of a common Asian identity and claims that "the state of the Asian press is not far removed from the state of Asian politics" (p. 27).

The media profiles of the 25 Asian countries or economies that the contributors to this volume have developed clearly prove the veracity of George's assertion that "historical factors have brought about different realities in different societies." However, they do not necessarily support his contention that the application of "Western yardsticks," a highly abstract term, might not be prudent or necessary in these societies. These profiles, in fact, show a wide variety of "Asian values," another highly abstract term, across these societies, so that "Asian values" fail to emerge as a viable substitute for "Western yardsticks" for determining media freedom.

The profiles show that countries in Asia broadly fall into the following political categories:

- Communist: Laos (Buddhist), China (Buddhist-Confucian), North Korea (Buddhist-Confucian), and Vietnam (Buddhist).
- Authoritarian (traditional monarchy, non-party presidential and military): Bhutan (Buddhist), Maldives (Islamic), Brunei Darussalam (Islamic), Myanmar (Buddhist), and post-coup Pakistan (Islamic).
- Dominant Party: Cambodia (Buddhist), Malaysia (Islamic), and Singapore (Buddhist-Confucian).
- Type II Parliamentary/Presidential Democracies with a Relatively Free Media System: Mongolia (Buddhist), India (Hindu), Post-Suharto Indonesia (Islamic), Sri Lanka (Buddhist), Bangladesh (Islamic), and Nepal (Hindu). China's two SARs—Hong Kong and Macau—also fit in here.
- Type I Parliamentary/Presidential Democracies with a Large Degree of Media Freedom: Thailand (Buddhist), Philippines (Christian), South Korea (Buddhist-Confucian/Christian), Taiwan (Buddhist-Confucian), and Japan (Buddhist-Shinto).

What is remarkable in this classification is that the political categories cut across Asia's major religions. Buddhist-Confucian countries range from the freest to the most authoritarian. Islamic countries range from moderately free to authoritarian. With Nepal's transition to democracy, the two Hindu countries have occupied the moderately free zone. Thus, the state of Asian politics does not represent a common set of Asian values founded on Asia's principal religions. As Datta-Ray says, the press is a creature of politics. The cry of "Asian Values" has come most vociferously from the two countries in the dominant-party category, as well as pre-reformasi Indonesia, as justification for taming the media. Freedom of expression is a human right, not a Western yardstick.

The first three models of the above classification represent varying degrees of authoritarianism rather than a value system common to all Asians. What is more important is to make the media system of a country more consistent with universal human values. The Universal Declaration of Human Rights and its covenants, as well as the NWICO vision of the MacBride Commission, provide the framework for promoting a socially responsible press in Asia and elsewhere. *Pancasila, Rukunegara,* and similar national ideologies also can provide guidance for journalists within the UDHR framework. Debasing the watchdog function of the mass media as a Western-liberal value will not necessarily bring stability to nations in the long run. Case in point: Indonesia 1998. Masterton (1996) points out the lack of a general agreement on Asian values; and he observes, "News values...are the same everywhere because human curiosity is the same everywhere" (p. 3).

Hamelink (in Hamelink & Mehra, 1990) points out that the universality of human rights could also mean the recognition of the concurrent existence of at least three concepts of those rights—the bourgeois/capitalist, the Marxist, and the Islamic. But, he says, both the universalist and the relativist positions are fraught with risks. He argues: "Universalism may obscure a 'human rights colonialism' [that] abuses human rights as an instrument of foreign policy while relativism may imply an ethical relativism that amounts to moral indifference" (p. xvi). While the UDHR declares that everyone has the right to freedom of opinion and expression, Article 19 of the ICCPR not only attaches special duties and responsibilities to it but also subjects it to legal restrictions related to areas such as defamation, national security, public health or morals, and public order. Are Asian values equivalent to conceding greater restrictions?[10]

Gunaratne (1976) contended that the media-subservience protagonists, who vehemently criticized the libertarian concepts as irrelevant Western norms, conveniently overlooked the Western contribution to authoritarian concepts, which they found so relevant to the Third World. In the contemporary context, one may well ask: Did "Asian values" originate in medieval Europe? Gunaratne (1978) argued that "the democratic Third World governments could promote developmental journalism better through fostering a socially responsible *independent* press rather than through media subservience" (p. 6). Gunaratne (1993) wrote: "Democracy requires the press to point fingers and hurl accusations through thorough investigation. In the process, errors will inevitably occur" (p. 180). The solution, he suggested, was to promote ethics to hold down partisanship and sensationalism. In this sense, the proposal to standardize press ethics on a global scale (Venkateswaran, 1996, p. 10) is more pertinent to promote socially responsible journalism than the forced imposition of so-called "Asian values," which rulers in medieval Europe also practiced.

Xu (1998), on the other hand, has argued that one should interpret Asian values as an idea rather than as a literal term—the idea "to safeguard national identity and cultural distinctiveness in the face of domination or monopoly by Western media, cultures and values" (p. 38). French and Richards (1996) have drawn attention to the greater potential of such domination with the creation of the World Trade

---

[10] Bauer and Bell, 1999, present a collection of essays unmasking Asian values.

Organization (WTO) to dismantle the barriers to free trade and to extend that concept to services covering the audiovisual sector as well. Xu's interpretation of Asian values will provide powerful resistance to global forces that could impose Occidental values through "invasion from the skies" (that is, television) or from cyberspace.

4. THE OLD AND THE NEW MEDIA

Lerner's (1958) theory postulated that urbanization and literacy, followed by media participation and political participation, produced the critical mass of "modernity" that propelled countries to the take off point of self-sustaining economic and social growth. Lerner hypothesized that "in populous societies, urbanization is the intervening variable [that] is crucial for the take-off toward increasing literacy" (p. 66). He said the "critical minimum" of urbanization was about 10 percent and the "critical optimum" was 25 percent, beyond which "literacy continues to rise independently of the growth of cities" (p. 59).

The correlation between *urbanization* and *literacy* for all three regions of Asia, presuming the validity and reliability of data in Table 5, was a statistically significant 0.57 ($p = 0.003$). Within each of the three subregions, however, the correlation was not significant: for South Asia, the least economically developed region, the correlation was 0.39 ($p = 0.38$); for Southeast Asia, it was 0.47 ($p = 0.17$); and for East Asia, the most advanced region, it was 0.08 ($p = 0.86$). In South Asia, urbanization ranged from 7 percent in Bhutan to 35 percent in Pakistan, while literacy ranged from 38.1 percent in Nepal to 95.7 percent in the Maldives. The Lerner paradigm failed to hold for Pakistan, which had the region's highest degree of urbanization but a low literacy rate of 40.9 percent, slightly higher than Bangladesh (38.9 percent) but lower than the least urbanized Bhutan (44.2 percent). On the other hand, Maldives and Sri Lanka stood out as havens of literacy (≥ 90 percent) at the "critical optimum" of urbanization.

No country in South Asia has reached a daily newspaper circulation rate of 10 copies per 100 people that UNESCO recommended in 1962 as a minimum goal. Only two countries in Southeast Asia, Singapore and Malaysia, had reached that goal. All countries in East Asia, except China and Mongolia, have exceeded that target. The "old paradigm" saw literacy as the prerequisite for mass media participation. The data in Table 5 produced an overall correlation of 0.39 ($p = 0.07$) between *literacy* and *newspaper penetration* (that is, circulation per 100 people) with South Asia showing a correlation of 0.49 ($p = 0.32$); Southeast Asia, 0.43 ($p = 0.22$); and East Asia, 0.21 ($p = 0.69$). This provides clear evidence of the existence of intervening variables such as per capita income in relation to price between literacy and newspaper penetration. On the other hand, an overall statistically significant correlation of 0.74 ($p = 0.00$) exists between tertiary enrollment and newspaper penetration—0.53 ($p = 0.27$) for East Asia, 0.77 ($p = 0.01$) for Southeast Asia, but almost a negligible 0.09 ($p = 0.89$) for South Asia.

A basic standard of five radio receivers per 100 people had been set by UNESCO in 1962. Every country in Asia, except Bhutan and Nepal, has achieved this target.

Radio penetration was highest in Sri Lanka in South Asia, Singapore in Southeast Asia, and South Korea in East Asia. The overall correlation between *literacy* and *radio penetration* for Asia was a statistically significant 0.54 (p = 0.01)—with 0.82 (p = 0.02) for South Asia, 0.34 (p = 0.34) for Southeast Asia, and 0.59 (p = 0.17) for East Asia. Thus, literacy has a higher and significant correlation with radio penetration than with newspaper penetration. Literacy has a similar correlation with TV penetration: 0.57 (p = 0.04) overall for Asia—with 0.73 (p = 0.06) for South Asia, 0.42 (p = 0.22) for Southeast Asia, and 0.35 (p = 0.43) for East Asia. Sri Lanka has the highest TV penetration in South Asia, Brunei in Southeast Asia, and Japan in East Asia. All Asian countries, except Bangladesh, Bhutan, Laos, Myanmar, and Nepal, have exceeded the UNESCO minimum standard of two TV receivers per 100 people.

The new electronic media are supplementing, or are in the process of replacing, the old media as the world heads on toward the Third Communication Revolution. An efficient computer network connected to a digitized telecommunication infrastructure is vital for the proliferation of the new media encompassing the World Wide Web, electronic mail, and the like (Gunaratne et al., 1997). Table 5 provides the data for mainline telephone penetration and Internet-host penetration to determine where the three regions of Asia stand in the process of informatization.

Telephone penetration, that is, the number of mainline telephones per 100 people, exceeds 40 in Macau, Japan, and the three "Tigers" in East Asia, where only North Korea, China, and Mongolia are behind with a low penetration of four to six. However, even that low is much better than the telephone penetration of the whole of South Asia, except the Maldives, which has reached seven. The telephone penetration of fewer than three per 100 people reflects South Asia's unsatisfactory economic development. In Southeast Asia, Singapore stands far ahead in telephone density, followed by Brunei and Malaysia. Myanmar, Laos, and Cambodia are in the same category as South Asia. (The 1999 *APT yearbook* provides greater details on telecommunication in Asia.)

East Asia is well ahead in Internet penetration, that is, the number of hosts per 10,000 people, with Hong Kong (357) leading the way, followed by Taiwan (143), and Japan (134). However, China, Mongolia, and North Korea—with less than one host per 10,000—have a long way to go, just as much as does all of South Asia and most of Southeast Asia. Singapore (259) stands next only to Hong Kong in Internet penetration. Brunei (39) and Malaysia (30) are ahead of most other countries in Southeast Asia (Figure 2).

5. FREEDOM AND COMPETITION

Although Naisbitt (1996) extols the economic success of East Asia, Frank (1993), the father of the dependency theory, points out that the "successes" of the four "Tigers"—Hong Kong, Singapore, South Korea, and Taiwan—and Japan was "not associated with much electoral democracy" (p. 19). Three of the "Tigers" had "prospered" under "completely authoritarian regimes, which are only now beginning to yield in response to economic success" (p. 20). Frank explains that these economies were not models of free market capitalism. He says that "in Korea and Taiwan, growth was heavily dependent, and in Singapore less so, on national state intervention and Japanese foreign investment" (p. 8). They "owe their present economic position either to political beginnings born of the Cold War...or to racial/communal problems" (p. 8). As bastions of anti-communism, they benefited enormously from Western economic and political support.

This interpretation of the success of the "Tigers" gives a different twist to the argument that "Asian values" propelled them to economic heights and that political and media freedoms associated with the Western or neo-liberal model are not vital prerequisites. The exceptional conditions under which the "Tigers" prospered do not provide and Asian-values model for the rest of Asia to emulate. However, developing countries worldwide can learn much from the "Tiger" economies' ability to be exceptionally competitive in the world material economy.

If one were to judge global competitiveness on the basis of the share of the world trade, South Asia scores very poorly. Although Asia's share of world trade in 1996 was 25 percent or almost US$ 1.4 trillion (Figure 3), the SAARC countries' exports accounted for less than US$ 50.2 billion (Figure 4). Thus their contribution to Asia's share of world trade was a mere 4 percent—a clear indication of the need for an accelerated program for the education and training of their large population to become more globally competitive. India, the Goliath in SAARC, exported merchandise valued at US$ 33 billion. Pakistan's exports totaled US$ 9.3 billion, Sri Lanka's US$ 4.1 billion, and Bangladesh's US$ 3.3 billion. Others failed to reach the billion mark.

Southeast Asia accounted for 24 percent of Asia's share of world trade, far better than South Asia (Figure 4). Tiny Singapore was the economic Goliath of the subregion. Singapore, unquestionably the most competitive, led the others in world trade with exports valued at US$ 125 billion compared to Malaysia's US$ 78.4 billion, Thailand's US$ 53.7 billion, Indonesia's US$ 49.8 billion, the Philippines' US$ 20.4 billion, and Vietnam's US$ 7.1 billion. The ASEAN countries altogether exported merchandise valued at US$ 335 billion.

East Asia is the most competitive subregion of Asia. It accounted for 72 percent of Asia's share of the world trade that translated into US$ 990.5 billion in 1996 (Figure 4). Japan led the way with exports of merchandise valued at US$ 411 billion. Hong Kong came second with exports of US$ 181 billion, China third with US$ 151 billion, South Korea fourth with US$ 130 billion, Taiwan fifth with US$ 116 billion, and Macau sixth with US$ 2 billion.

The competitive superiority of the four "Tigers" becomes apparent from their share of Asia's total world merchandise exports. That share is 40 percent compared to Japan's 30 percent (Figure 5).

The World Economic Forum (1997–99) ranked Singapore (first) and Hong Kong (second) at the top of the global competitiveness sweepstakes both in 1997 and 1998 (though it ranked Hong Kong third in 1999). It used an analytical framework of eight factors to determine the ranks of 53 countries that produced more than 95 percent of world output, trade, and investment flows: openness, government, finance, technology, infrastructure, management, labor, and institutions. Within that framework, five other Asian economies earned positive scores in 1998: Taiwan (6th), Japan (12th), Malaysia (17th), South Korea (19th), and Thailand (21st), while five economies—China (28th), Indonesia (31st), Philippines (33rd), Vietnam (39th), and India (50th) earned negative scores.

Two other organizations, Heritage Foundation and Fraser Institute, ranked Singapore quite high (Freedom House, 1997). The Heritage Foundation rated Singapore as the second freest nation (for investment) among the 140 it surveyed in 1995. Singapore's low tax rate, the small share of gross domestic product consumed by government, and its foreign investment laws explained these high ratings.

However, Freedom House (1998) rated Singapore as "partly free" in its annual evaluation of political rights and civil liberties worldwide. (This is different from its "not free" assessment of Singapore vis-à-vis press freedom.) Singapore fared poorly on three factors: the ruling party's *de facto* control of the trade unions, the difficulties private firms faced in competing against government-linked companies in several areas, and the Singaporean authorities' tendency to treat earning a living or operating a business as a privilege rather than a right.

Six Asian economies—China, Singapore, Indonesia, Hong Kong, the Philippines, and Malaysia—topped the ranks in WEF's 1998 Growth Index with scores ranging from 4.69 points to 5.87 points. Five other Asian economies showed positive but slower growth—Thailand (4.67), Taiwan (4.24), India (3.61), South Korea (3.34), and Japan (2.60). WEF's 1998 Market Growth Index ranked Japan second. It was outdone by only the United States. China occupied the third rank followed by India (9th), Taiwan (13th), Hong Kong (15th), South Korea (16th), Indonesia (17th), Singapore (20th), Thailand (21st), Malaysia (29th), and the Philippines (32nd).

In terms of political rights and civil liberties, Freedom House (1998) ranked Japan, South Korea, Taiwan, Mongolia, and the Philippines as "free" in Asia. It ranked Bangladesh, India, Thailand, Nepal, Sri Lanka, Malaysia, pre-Musharraf Pakistan, and Singapore as "partly free." It gave the "not free" rank to Brunei, Indonesia,[11] Maldives, Cambodia, Laos, Bhutan, Myanmar, China, North Korea, and Vietnam.

6. A STRUCTURAL VIEW

One can apply the elements of the dependency/world-system theory to analyze the center–periphery structure emerging in Asia based on world merchandise exports. Barnett et al. (1996) used this theoretical framework to examine and evaluate the structure of the global telecommunication network. Their findings supported the basic premise of the theory that the "position in the world telecommunication system affects a country's economic and social development" (p. 40).

---

[11] The post-Suharto changes have shifted Indonesia from this category.

The early dependency models (for example, Frank, 1969; Galtung, 1971) attributed a country's internal class structure to external domination, but the subsequent modifications of the model (like Cardoso & Faletto, 1979) recognized the potential for internal class struggle and reform in the periphery without a radical break with the center. The world system theory (for example, Frank and Gills, 1993; Wallerstein, 1979) explained the long-term cycles associated with shifts in the international system. This theory, which used the world system as the basic unit of analysis, incorporated the core–periphery concepts of the dependency model and added another level of development, the semi-periphery, that allowed "for the possibility of upward and downward mobility in the world system" (Barnett et al., 1996, p. 22). Both theories, which focus on distribution and exchange rather than production, share a basic premise: that a country's position in the world system affects its development and well-being.

The structure of the countries in Asia in the world system, as well as within the region, emerges when we assign the countries to the three levels conceptualized in the dependency world-system theory on the basis of their ability to compete in the global economy. If exports of commercial merchandise and services are a reasonable measure of competitiveness, the following picture emerges:

- In terms of subregions, East Asia is the center; Southeast Asia, the semi-periphery; and South Asia, the periphery.
- Within East Asia, Japan is the center. The semi-periphery is Hong Kong. South Korea, China, and Taiwan. The periphery is Macau, Mongolia, and North Korea.
- Within Southeast Asia, Singapore is the center. The semi-periphery comprises Malaysia, Thailand, Indonesia, and the Philippines. The periphery is Vietnam, Brunei, Myanmar, Cambodia, and Laos.
- South Asia has no center as such. India may, however, fit into that position by default. All other countries—Pakistan, Sri Lanka, Bangladesh, Nepal, Maldives, and Bhutan—occupy the periphery.

Japan is the overall center of Asia (as evident from its 29 percent share of Asia's world exports in goods and services in 1996). The overall semi-periphery is Hong Kong (14 percent), China (10 percent), South Korea (10 percent), Singapore (9 percent), and Taiwan (8 percent). A second tier semi-periphery comprises Malaysia (5 percent), Thailand (4 percent), Indonesia (3 percent), India (2 percent), and Philippines (2 percent), The periphery is the rest of Asia (see Table 6).

The 1997 data of the WTO documented that in 1996 Asia accounted for 25.6 percent of the world merchandise exports, next to Western Europe's 44.6 percent. The same pattern held true for world exports of commercial services: Asia's share was 22.7 percent, next to Western Europe's 48 percent.

Although Asia, as defined for this volume, represents 55 percent of the world's 6 billion people (Table 5), its share of the world trade falls far behind its potential in human resources. Asia's competitiveness in the world material economy should more than double in the next millennium to overtake Western Europe, which has established itself on the foundation of a long colonial history. The trade data show that the large majority of Asian economies have little to do with Asia's success in the global economy. That success reflects the enterprise of Japan and the semi-periphery economies.

A less satisfactory way to look at the center–periphery structure is to arrange the world economies on the basis of per capita GNP. We may confer the status of the *center* on those that the World Bank has categorized as *high-income* economies. These economies are Japan, Singapore, Hong Kong, Brunei Darussalam, Macau, Taiwan, and South Korea. Japan is the supreme leader in this center group.

The *semi-periphery* will then consist of what the World Bank calls *upper middle-income* economies. Malaysia is the only economy in Asia that falls into this category. Then come the *second tier semi-periphery* economies—Thailand, Philippines, Indonesia, Maldives, and North Korea. The *low-income* economies comprise the *periphery*. The world's two Goliaths—China and India—and all other Asian economies fall into this category. This analysis is less satisfactory because it fails to take into account the ability to compete in the global economy. Moreover, the range of income within each category is relatively arbitrary.

The less satisfactory method of determining the center–periphery structure places 82 percent of Asia's population in the *periphery*. It places 11 percent in the *second tier semi-periphery* and a mere 7 percent in the *center* and the *first tier semi-periphery*. It is this last category that is responsible for more than three-fourths of the 26 percent share of Asia's world merchandise exports, and for more than three-fourths of the 20 percent share of world exports of services. The periphery lags way behind in world exports of merchandise and services. It contributes slightly more than one-sixth to Asia's share of merchandise exports, and a mere one-ninth to Asia's share of exports of services.

As Roach (1998) puts it: "Asian countries other than Japan account for just 7 percent of global trade—or just 1.5 percent of the world's gross domestic product. Even if Asia collapsed completely, it would hardly bring the global economy to [its] knees" (p. A21). This structural analysis based on trade and economic data indicates that economic progress in Asia is tremendously lopsided, with 93 percent of the population yet to learn how to compete successfully in the world material economy.

The center–periphery structure of Asia based on trade flow is important because information flow among countries tends to follow the trade flow. Mowlana (1997) says: "Interestingly, the nature, pattern, and direction of the world economy are more or less parallel and depict the directionality of world information flow. In almost all kinds of information flow, whether it is news or data, educational, scientific, or human flow, the pattern is the same" (p. 218). Global-information-flow analysts who construct hypotheses within the structural framework, however, should recognize the potential of generating spurious results if they analyze only the elite media. The periphery's "bridgeheads" or elites have interests similar to those in the center (see Galtung, 1971). Because the Internet is largely the preserve of the elites in the developing countries, the on-line media in the center and the periphery may show more similarities than differences. Gunaratne (2000) has examined the prospects and limitations of the world-system theory for media analysis.

7. ABOUT THIS VOLUME

This volume provides a fresh look at the media in Asia to complement the work of the Euromedia Research Group (1997) on the media in Western Europe. It also supplements and updates, wherever possible, other publications on the media in Asia or its subregions (for example, AMIC, 1994; Goonasekera & Holaday, 1998; Vanden Heuvel & Dennis, 1993; Lent, 1971, 1978, 1982; Mehra, 1989). Moreover, unlike the Western interpretations of Third World mass media (see Hachten, 1999; Merrill, 1995), this volume provides a predominantly Asian interpretation of the Asian media. However, an Asian interpretation does not necessarily imply disharmony with Western interpretation(s).

The country profiles draw our attention to some significant trends in the development of media in Asian countries at the beginning of the millennium.

● The main proponents of the "Asian values" thesis—Singapore, Malaysia, and Indonesia—are conceding greater media freedom because of the power of the Information Superhighway. In this volume Kuo and Ang point out that Singapore, which aims to become Asia's information hub, will have to gradually yield to the cyberspatial forces that are making a mockery of domestic censorship. Safar, Sarji, and Gunaratne point out that despite its all-encompassing *Rukunegara* philosophy, Malaysia has agreed to let cyberspace operate freely in the interest of making its Multimedia Super Corridor a success. Idris and Gunaratne point out that Indonesia, which is in the process of building its vast Nusantara information highway, is delinking itself from the all-encompassing *Pancasila* philosophy of the Suharto era.

● The communist or former communist countries in Asia are making concessions to media freedom in varying degrees. North Korea, as Gunaratne and Kim point out, is sticking to the Leninist model of the press with a touch of Kim II Sung's "anti-Japanese guerilla method." The media propagate Kim's *Jucheism* (self-help) as a national philosophy. On the other hand, as Lowe and Gunaratne show, the former communist Mongolia has taken giant strides to establish media freedom. Yan points out that China is in the process of redefining the role of the media. She says that as more journalists enjoy more freedom with the commercialized media in China, they will require a legally guaranteed freedom. In Vietnam, Panol and Do assert, "although newspapers are still either government-owned or affiliated and hence not dependent on advertising income, they are now aggressively competing for advertisers and readers," In Laos, Morgan and Loo point out, central censorship is no longer imposed on the press. Nevertheless, they say, "ambiguity and caution prevail, and individual journalists generally censor their own stories according to their perceptions of the government's sensitivities."

• The press in Asia's authoritarian countries also show varying characteristics ranging from post-democratic ambivalence in Musharraf-led Pakistan to dictatorial determination in Myanmar. In Cambodia, Clarke says, even though government and party ownership of the press has declined rapidly, politics and violence have caused the erosion of press freedom. In Bhutan, Conlon says, the government has consistently considered the media as tools for promoting development; and dissent and the reporting of dissent are difficult. In the Maldives, as Karan and Viswanath point out, the conventional wisdom among journalists and the governing elite is that any discussion on press freedom and press regulation should take into account the fragile and "homogeneous" structure of the Maldivian society. In Brunei, Safar and Yussof assert, the press operates within the framework of the Malay Islamic Monarchy concept: The government controls "the media not primarily to keep them from harming the ruling elite, but to channel the power of the media into what the state sees as constructive educational, developmental and political goals." In Myanmar, Chadha and Kavoori say, strict censorship rules are the norm: "Editors and publishers tend to avoid potentially objectionable writing and select only such materials that are likely to please the Press Scrutiny Board."

• The majority of the subcontinental bloc of countries in the SAARC group is straddling the middle of the press freedom quandary. Despite being no better off than Sub-Saharan Africa economically, these countries are making more concessions to accommodate a freer press. Nepal (Rao and Koirala), Pakistan (Ali and Gunaratne), and Bangladesh (Bhuiyan and Gunaratne) reverted from authoritarianism to democracy. (Pakistan, however, returned to military rule late in 1999 when Gen. Pervez Musharraf deposed Prime Minister Nawaz Sharif, declared a state of emergency, and appointed himself the country's chief executive. Thus, Pakistan has moved back to the authoritarian category.) Sri Lanka (Wattegama and Gunaratne), however, has taken little action to dismantle the government ownership of the country's largest newspaper group despite the ruling party's 1994 election pledge to do so, whereas Bangladesh and Pakistan have dissolved the government-owned press. India (Karan and Viswanath) carries the honors for steadily following a press freedom policy marred only briefly during Indira Gandhi's 1975–77 Emergency. Hong Kong, which also straddles the middle, is continuing to enjoy a high degree of press freedom as a SAR under China, despite widely held predictions to the contrary, according to So, Chan, and Lee. However, the media have lowered their standards under market-driven journalism, leading to ethical concerns.

• Japan—along with Taiwan, South Korea, Philippines, and Thailand—has a freer press than in the rest of Asia. As Saito points out, Japan is concerned with issues such as the resale price maintenance system of the newspapers and digitization of broadcasting rather than censorship issues that plague most of Asia. Writing on Taiwan, Wang and Lo point out: "The media critics' major concern now is no longer the lack of press freedom but the lack of respect for it and increasingly confused ethical principles." Heo, Uhm, and Chang draw attention to the intense competition among the media in South Korea, where the democratization process set off in 1987 has enabled the media to be freer than ever to criticize the government and to cover issues. The Philippines, Maslog says, has a constitutional guarantee that is very similar to the US First Amendment. However, ethics has become a major concern with the deteriorating standards of media content and the active intrusion of politicians, including the president, into journalistic roles. In Thailand, Ekachai points out, the 1997 Constitution has brought a breath of fresh air to create an environment conducive to greater media freedom.

The work on this volume started in late 1997 with an international search for contributors. The editor completed the manuscript with the regional introductions in May 1999 after the Thailand chapter arrived from a new contributor. Coordinating the work of 36 contributors was a challenge despite the technological facilities that enabled rapid exchange of lengthy manuscripts through cyberspace. The editor wishes to thank the contributors and the publisher for their cooperation throughout the project.

However, one monumental problem the editor faced was getting the latest reliable data on the traditional media—newspapers, radio, and television—for each of the 25 economies that are in varying stages of social, economic, and political development. Latest data on the new electronic media are more readily available because of the current emphasis on achieving faster development through telecommunications. Most Asian countries do not have independently audited newspaper circulation data. UNESCO takes about two years to release its data on newspapers, radio, and television, based mostly on government sources. UNESCO's statistical surveys fail to adhere to a uniform standard because some countries use different definitions, classifications, and methods of enumeration. Even though newspaper circulation data should refer to the number of copies distributed, in some cases the figures actually reported are the number of copies printed (World Bank, 1999). Moreover, radio owners fail to report ownership in those countries that impose radio license fees to help pay for public broadcasting. Thus the estimates of newspaper and radio penetration vary widely in reliability.

Both UNESCO and ITU often present divergent data on television penetration for the same country. For instance, UNESCO's and ITU's 1996 estimates on TV receivers in Indonesia are 13.5 million and 25 million respectively. ITU obtains data on TV sets and cable TV subscribers through annual questionnaires sent to national broadcasting authorities and industry associations in countries that require registration of TV sets. UNESCO data on radio penetration also differs often from the data in the *World radio TV handbook*. For instance, UNESCO's 1996 estimate of the number of radio receivers in the Philippines is 11.5 million in comparison to *World radio TV handbook*'s current estimate of 8.3 million. The *Editor & publisher international yearbook* continues to list defunct newspapers, such as *Sinar Harapan* of Indonesia and *Dawasa* of Sri Lanka, and also to publish old circulation data with no warning.

Thus readers should use caution in interpreting the data on the penetration of newspapers, radio, and television. Readers who detect inconsistencies in the tabulated data should check the source.

8. STATISTICS

Table 1
South Asia: Human Development Index

	Life expectancy at birth 1997	Adult literacy rate (%) 1997	Combined 1st, 2nd, & 3rd level gross enrollment ratio (%) 1997	Real GDP per capita (PPP$) 1997	HDI value 1997	HDI rank
Sri Lanka	73.1	90.7	66	2,490	0.721	90
Maldives	64.5	95.7	74	3,690	0.716	93
India	62.6	53.5	55	1,670	0.545	132
Pakistan	64.0	40.9	43	1,560	0.508	138
Nepal	57.3	38.1	59	1,090	0.463	144
Bhutan	60.7	44.2	12	1,467	0.459	145
Bangladesh	58.1	38.9	35	1,050	0.440	150
South Asia	**62.7**	**52.2**	**52**	**1,803**	**0.544**	–

Source: UNDP, 1999.
Note: UNDP, 1999, includes Iran in the aggregate data for South Asia.

Table 2
Southeast Asia: Human Development Index

	Life expectancy at birth 1997	Adult literacy rate (%) 1997	Combined 1st, 2nd, & 3rd level gross enrollment ratio (%) 1997	Real GDP per capita (PPP$) 1997	HDI value 1997	HDI rank
Singapore	77.1	91.4	73	28,460	0.888	22
Brunei	75.5	90.1	72	29,773	0.878	25
Malaysia	72.0	85.7	65	8,140	0.768	56
Thailand	68.8	94.7	59	6,690	0.753	67
Philippines	68.3	94.6	82	3,520	0.740	77
Indonesia	65.1	85.0	64	3,490	0.681	105
Vietnam	67.4	91.9	62	1,630	0.664	110
Myanmar	60.1	83.6	55	1,199	0.580	128
Cambodia	53.4	66.0	61	1,290	0.514	137
Laos	53.2	58.6	55	1,300	0.491	140

Source: UNDP, 1999.
Note: UNDP, 1999, does not provide a regional aggregate for the ASEAN 10. It combines Southeast Asia with five Pacific island nations.

Table 3
East Asia: Human Development Index

	Life expectancy at birth 1997	Adult literacy rate (%) 1997	Combined 1st, 2nd, & 3rd level gross enrollment ratio (%) 1997	Real GDP per capita (PPP$) 1997	HDI value 1997	HDI rank
Japan	80.0	99.0	85	24,070	0.924	4
Hong Kong	78.5	92.4	65	24,350	0.880	24
Korea (S)	72.4	97.2	90	13,590	0.852	30
Korea (N)	71.6	95.0	75	4,058	0.766	75
China	69.8	82.9	69	3,130	0.701	98
Mongolia	65.8	84.0	55	1,310	0.618	119
East Asia	**70.0**	**83.4**	**69**	**3,601**	**0.712**	**–**

Source: UNDP, 1998, 1999.
Note: UNDP, 1999, does not provide the data for Macau, Taiwan, and North Korea. The data for North Korea in this table are for 1995 (UNDP, 1998).

Table 4
Asia's Commitment to International Human Rights Instruments

	A	B	C	D	E	F	G	H
South Asia								
Bangladesh	•		•	•	•	•	•	
Bhutan			*		•	•		
India	•	•	•	•	•	•	*	
Maldives			•	•	•	•		
Nepal	•	•	•	•	•	•	•	
Pakistan			•	•	•	•		
Sri Lanka	•		•	•	•	•	•	
Southeast Asia								
Brunei				•				
Cambodia	•		•	•	•	•		
Indonesia				•		•		
Laos			•	•	•	•		
Malaysia				•		•		
Myanmar			•	•	•	•		
Philippines	•	•	•	•	•	•	•	
Singapore				•	•	•		
Thailand		•		•				
Vietnam	•	•	•	•	•	•		
East Asia								
China	*	*	•	•	•	•		
Japan	•	•	•	•	•	•		
Korea (N)	•	•		•	•			
Korea (S)	•	•	•	•	•	•		
Mongolia	•	•	•	•	•	•		

Source: UNDP, 1998, 1999.

Table 4 contd

Note: A = International covenant on economic, social, and cultural rights, 1966
B = International covenant on civil and political rights, 1966
C = International convention on the elimination of all forms of racial discrimination, 1969
D = Convention on the prevention and punishment of the crime of genocide, 1948
E = Convention on the rights of the child, 1989
F = Convention on the elimination of all forms of discrimination against women, 1979
G = Convention against torture and other cruel, inhuman or degrading treatment or punishment, 1984
H = Convention relating to the status of refugees, 1951
• = Ratification, accession, approval, notification of succession, acceptance, or definitive signature
* = Signature not yet followed by ratification as of February 1, 1999.

Table 5
Asia: Demographic and Media Indicators

Country	Demographic indicators					Media indicators per 100 people				
	GNP per capita in US$[1]	Popu-lation[1] (in millions)	Adult literacy rate[1]	Urban popu-lation %	Tertiary Enroll-ment as % of age group	Daily news-paper circu-lation[2]	Radio[2] receiv-ers	TV[3] receiv-ers	Main tele-phone lines[3]	Internet hosts[4] per 10,000 January
	1998	1998	1998	1998	1995	1996	1996	1997	1998	1999
South Asia										
Maldives	1,167	0.3	92.6	32		1.8	12.2	3.9	6.58	4.00
Sri Lanka	827	19.0	89.3	23	5.1	2.9	21.0	9.2	2.84	0.29
Pakistan	492	136.8	37.8	35	3.4	2.1	9.2	2.2	1.85	0.22
Bhutan	450	0.8	42.2	7	0.2		1.9	1.9	1.04	0.58
India	436	989.2	52.1	28	6.4	3.1	10.5	6.9	1.85	0.78
Bangladesh	289	130.0	38.1	20	6.1	0.9	5.0	0.7	0.26	0.00
Nepal	225	23.4	27.5	14	4.8	1.1	3.7	0.4	0.77	0.07
Southeast Asia										
Singapore	21,828	3.2	93.1	100	33.7	32.4	73.9	29.2	54.29	259.84
Brunei	20,400	0.3	89.2	67	6.6	6.9	30.0	41.7	24.68	38.98
Malaysia	3,092	22.7	93.7	56	11.0	16.3	43.2	16.6	19.49	30.21
Thailand	1,850	62.1	93.8	36	20.1	6.5	20.4	23.4	8.02	7.25
Philippines	907	74.7	94.0	57	27.9	8.2	15.9	10.6	2.87	3.00
Indonesia	460	207.7	84.4	38	11.3	2.3	15.5	9.7	2.70	1.97
Myanmar	765	48.8	82.0	27	5.7	1.0	8.9	0.7	0.48	0.00
Laos	258	5.3	56.6	22	1.6	0.4	13.9	0.4	0.55	0.00
Cambodia	270	10.9	37.8	22	1.6	0.1	12.7	12.3	0.18	0.06
Vietnam	310	79.4	91.9	21	4.1	0.4	10.6	18.0	2.07	0.00
East Asia										
Japan	33,340	126.5	100.00	79	41.4	58.0	95.7	70.6	47.86	133.64
Hong Kong	24,716	6.8	92.2	95	25.7	80.0	69.5	41.2	56.08	356.67
Macau	16,054	0.4	74.8	94	27.8	44.8	35.2	28.9	40.91	3.41
Taiwan	12,040	22.0	93.2	58	46.0		40.1	32.7	49.96	142.75
Korea (S)	6,810	46.9	97.4	84	52.0	39.4	103.7	34.2	44.40	60.47
Korea (N)*	900	22.8	N/A	61		20.0	14.7	11.5	4.82	0.00
China	783	1,268.7	81.5	33	5.7	4.2	19.5	27.0	5.62	0.84
Mongolia	396	2.5	95.0	62	17.0	2.7	13.9	5.9	3.66	0.08
World	**5,180**	**5,820**	**78.0**	**46**						

Source: [1] *Asiaweek* (The Bottom Line), December 17, 1999 <http://www.pathfinder.com/asiaweek/99/1217/bottom.html>
[2] UNESCO, 1999, *Statistical yearbook*; World Development Indicators, 1999 <www.worldbank.org>
[3] ITU Telecommunication Indicators <http://www.itu.int/ti/industryoverview/index.htm>; *World media handbook*, 1995
[4] Network Wizards <http://www.nw.com/zone/WWW/dist-bynum.html>; ITU, 1999.
* *APT yearbook*, 1998, 1999.

Table 6
Structural View of Asia

	Share of Asia's portion of world trade 1996 (%)	Per capita GNP (US$) 1996	Press restriction score 1998
Center			
Japan	29.3	40,940	19
Semi-periphery 1			
Hong Kong	13.5	24,290	N/A
China	10.4	750	81
Korea (S)	9.5	10,610	28
Singapore	9.5	30,550	66
Taiwan	8.1	[12,240]	25
Semi-periphery 2			
Malaysia	5.5	4,370	66
Thailand	4.3	2,960	30
Indonesia	3.4	1,080	53
India	2.4	380	37
Philippines	1.8	1,160	30
Periphery			
Pakistan	0.7	480	60
Vietnam	0.4	290	71
Sri Lanka	0.3	740	58
Bangladesh	0.2	260	59
Brunei	0.2	[17,556]	74
Macau	0.1	[17,542]	N/A
Nepal	0.1	210	59
Myanmar	0.0	[765]	97
Mongolia	0.0	590	30
Cambodia	0.0	300	62
Laos	0.0	400	66
Maldives	0.0	1,080	66
Bhutan	0.0	390	80
Korea (N)	[0.0]	[900]	100
	100		

Sources: WTO, 1997; World Bank, 1998; Sussman, 1999.

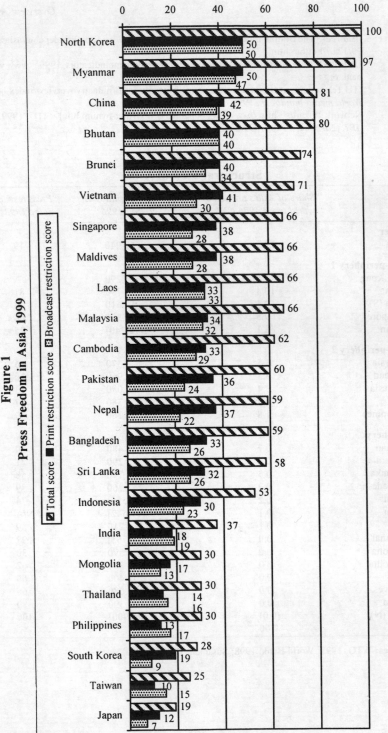

Figure 1
Press Freedom in Asia, 1999

Total score ▨ Print restriction score ■ Broadcast restriction score ▥

Country	Total score	Print restriction score	Broadcast restriction score
North Korea	100	50	50
Myanmar	97	50	47
China	81	42	39
Bhutan	80	40	40
Brunei	74	40	34
Vietnam	71	41	30
Singapore	66	38	28
Maldives	66	38	28
Laos	66	33	33
Malaysia	66	34	32
Cambodia	62	33	29
Pakistan	60	36	24
Nepal	59	37	22
Bangladesh	59	33	26
Sri Lanka	58	32	26
Indonesia	53	30	23
India	37	18	19
Mongolia	30	17	13
Thailand	30	14	16
Philippines	30	17	13
South Korea	28	19	9
Taiwan	25	10	15
Japan	19	12	7

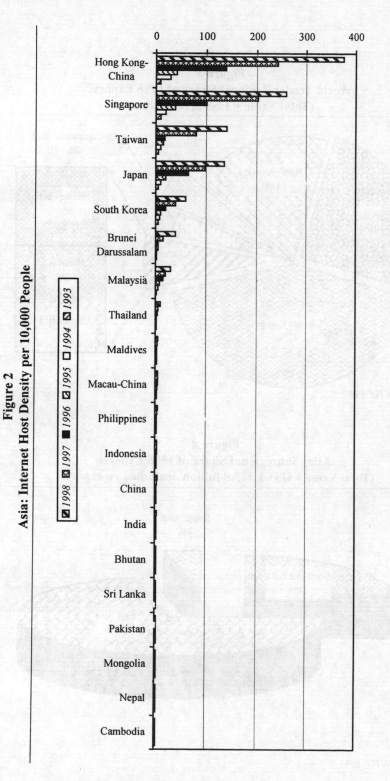

Figure 2
Asia: Internet Host Density per 10,000 People

1998 1997 1996 1995 1994 1993

0   100   200   300   400

Hong Kong-China
Singapore
Taiwan
Japan
South Korea
Brunei Darussalam
Malaysia
Thailand
Maldives
Macau-China
Philippines
Indonesia
China
India
Bhutan
Sri Lanka
Pakistan
Mongolia
Nepal
Cambodia

Source: Network Wizards.
Note: Bangladesh, North Korea, Laos, Myanmar, and Vietnam had zero density up to 1998.

Figure 3
World Trade: Regional Share of 1996 Exports
(Total Value = US$ 5,115 billion)

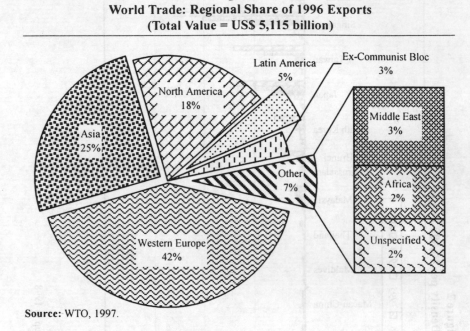

Latin America
5%

Ex-Communist Bloc
3%

North America
18%

Asia
25%

Other
7%

Western Europe
42%

Middle East
3%

Africa
2%

Unspecified
2%

Source: WTO, 1997.

Figure 4
Asia: Subregional Share of 1996 Exports
(Total Value = US$ 1,375.8 billion, including re-exports)

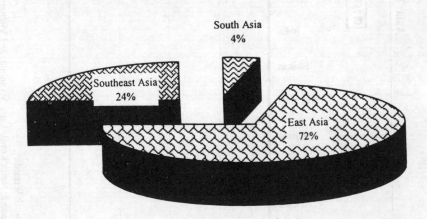

South Asia
4%

Southeast Asia
24%

East Asia
72%

Source: WTO, 1997.

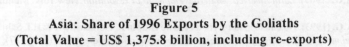

Figure 5
Asia: Share of 1996 Exports by the Goliaths
(Total Value = US$ 1,375.8 billion, including re-exports)

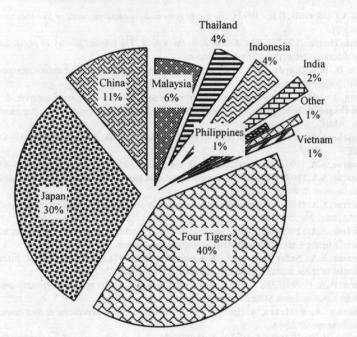

Source: WTO, 1997.

9. REFERENCES

AMIC (Asian Mass Communication Research and Information Center). (1994). *Press systems in SAARC.* Singapore: AMIC.

AMIC (Asian Mass Communication Research and Information Center). (1997). *Communication ethics: A South Asian perspective.* Singapore: AMIC.

Ang, P.H., & Yeo, T.M. (Comps.). (1998). *Mass media laws and regulations in Singapore.* Singapore: AMIC.

APT (Asia-Pacific Telecommunity). (1998, 1999). *The APT yearbook.* Bangkok and Sutton, Surrey: APT & Icom Publications.

Barnett, G.A., Jacobson, T., Young, C., & Sun-Miller, S. (1996). An examination of the international telecommunication network. *The Journal of International Communication, 3* (2), 19–43.

Bauer, J.R., & Bell, D.A. (Eds.). (1999). *The East Asian challenge for human rights.* New York: Cambridge University Press.

Cardoso, F.H., & Faletto, E. (1979). *Dependency and development in Latin America.* Berkeley: University of California Press.

Euromedia Research Group. (1997). *The media in Western Europe: The Euromedia handbook.* London: Sage Publications.

Faruqui, S.S., & Ramanathan, S. (Comps.). (1998). *Mass media laws and regulations in Malaysia.* Singapore: AMIC.

Frank, A.G. (1969). *Latin America: Underdevelopment or revolution.* New York: Monthly Review Press.

Frank, A.G. (1993). No end to history! History to no end? In K. Nordenstreng & H.I. Schiller (Eds.), *Beyond national sovereignty: International communication in the 1990s* (pp. 3–27). Norwood, NJ: Ablex.

Frank, A.G., & Gills, B.K. (1993). *The world system: Five hundred years or five thousand?* London: Routledge.

Freedom House. (1997, 1998). *Freedom in the world: The annual survey of political rights and civil liberties.* New York: Freedom House.

French, D., & Richards, M. (Eds.). (1996). *Contemporary television: Eastern perspectives.* New Delhi: Sage Publications.

Galtung, J. (1971). A structural theory of imperialism. *Journal of Peace Research, 8,* 81–118.

Gaziul Hoque, A.N.M. (Comp.). (1992). *Mass media laws and regulations in Bangladesh.* Singapore: AMIC.

Goonasekera, A., & Holaday, D. (Eds.). (1998). *Asian communication handbook 1998.* Singapore: AMIC.

Gunaratne, S.A. (1976, summer). An Asian contagion. *Index on Censorship, 5,* 62–63.

Gunaratne, S.A. (1978). Media subservience and developmental journalism. *Communications and Development Review, 2* (2), 3–7.

Gunaratne, S.A. (1993). Roundtable: News organizations are slow to fess up to their own mistakes. *Media Asia, 20,* 151, 180.

Gunaratne, S.A. (2000). Prospects and limitations of world system theory for media analysis: The case of Middle East and North Africa. Unpublished paper.

Gunaratne, S.A., Safar Hasim, M., & Kasenally, R. (1997). Small is beautiful: Informatization potential of three Indian Ocean rim countries. *Media Asia, 24,* 188–205.

Hachten, W.A. (1999). *The world news prism: Changing media of international communication* (5th ed.). Ames: Iowa State University Press.

Hamelink, C.J., & Mehra, A. (Eds.). (1990). *Communication development and human rights in Asia.* Singapore: AMIC.

Hartmann, P., Patil, B.R., & Dighe, A. (1989). *The mass media and village life: An Indian study.* New Delhi: Sage Publications.

Hsiung, J.C. (Ed.). (1985). *Human rights in Asia: A cultural perspective.* New York: Paragon House Publishers.

ITU (International Telecommunication Union). (1999). *Challenges to the network: Internet for development.* Geneva: ITU.

Jabbar, J., & Isa, Q.F. (Comps.). (1997). *Mass media laws and regulations in Pakistan—and a commentary from a historical perspective.* Singapore: AMIC.

Latif, A. (Ed.). (1998). *Walking the tightrope: Press freedom and professional standards in Asia.* Singapore: AMIC.

Lent, J.A. (Ed.). (1971). *The Asian newspapers' reluctant revolution.* Ames, IA: Iowa State University Press.

Lent, J.A. (Ed.). (1978). *Broadcasting in Asia and the Pacific: A continental survey of radio and television.* Philadelphia: Temple University Press.

Lent, J.A. (Ed.). (1982). *Newspapers in Asia: Contemporary trends and problems.* Hong Kong: Heinemann Asia.

Lerner, D. (1958). *The passing of traditional society: Modernizing the Middle East.* New York: The Free Press.

Locke, E.A. (1998, July 3). Celebrate core values of the West. *The* (Fargo, ND) *Forum,* p. A4.

Mahathir M., & Ishihara, S. (1995). *The voice of Asia: Two leaders discuss the coming century.* Tokyo: Kodansha International Ltd.

Masterton, M. (Comp.). (1996). *Asian values in journalism.* Singapore: AMIC.

Mehra, A. (1986). *Free flow of information: A new paradigm.* Westport, CT: Greenwood Press.

Mehra, A. (Ed.). (1989). *Press systems in ASEAN states.* Singapore: AMIC.

Merrill. J.C. (Ed.). (1995). *Global journalism: Survey of international communication* (3rd ed.). White Plains, NY: Longman Publishers USA.

Mowlana, H. (1997). *Global information and world communication* (2nd ed.). London: Sage Publications.

Muntarbhorn, V. (Comp.). (1998). *Mass media laws and regulations in Thailand.* Singapore: AMIC.

Naisbitt, J. (1996). *Megatrends Asia: Eight Asian megatrends that are reshaping our world.* New York: Simon & Schuster.

Pokhrel, G.P., & Koirala, B.D. (Comps.). (1995). *Mass media laws and regulations in Nepal.* Kathmandu and Singapore: Nepal Press Institute and AMIC.

Roach, S.S. (1998, February 24). Asia may pinch us yet. *The New York Times,* p. A21.

Schramm, W. (1964). *Mass media and national development.* Stanford, CA: Stanford University Press.

Seow, F.T. (1998). *The media enthralled: Singapore revisited.* Boulder, CO: Lynne Rienner Publishers.

Selvakumaran, N., & Edrisinha, R. (Comps.). (1995). *Mass media laws and regulations in Sri Lanka.* Singapore: AMIC.

Sussman, L.R. (1998). *Press freedom 1998: Global warning—press controls fuel the Asian debacle.* Washington, DC: Freedom House.

Sussman, L.R. (1999). *Press freedom 1999: News of the century.* Washington, DC: Freedom House.

Teodoro, L.V., & Kabatay, R.V. (Comps.). (1998). *Mass media-laws and regulations in the Philippines.* Singapore: AMIC.

Traber, M., & Nordenstreng, K. (Eds.). (1992). *Few voices, many worlds: Towards a media reform movement.* London: World Association for Christian Communication.

UNDP (United Nations Development Program). (1998, 1999). *Human development report.* New York: Oxford University Press.

US Census Bureau, International Data Base. (1998, December 28). *IDB: Countries ranked by population* [On-line]. Available: (http://www.census.gov/cgi-bin/ipc/idbrank.pl).

Vanden Heuvel, J.V., & Dennis, E.E. (1993). *The unfolding lotus: East Asia's changing media.* New York: The Freedom Forum Media Studies Center.

Venkateswaran, K.S. (Comp.). (1993). *Mass media laws and regulations in India.* Singapore: AMIC.

Venkateswaran, K.S. (1996). *Media monitors in Asia.* Singapore: AMIC.

Wallerstein, I. (1979). *The capitalist world-economy: Essays.* New York: Cambridge University Press.

WEF (World Economic Forum). (1997–99). *The global competitiveness report.* Geneva: WEF.

World Bank. (1998, 1999). World Development Indicators [On-line]. Available: (http://www.worldbank.org/data/wdi).

WTO (World Trade Organization). (1997). *Annual report 1997,* Vols. 1 & 2. Geneva: WTO.

Xu, X. (1998). Asian values revisited in the context of intercultural news communication. *Media Asia, 25,* 37–41.

◆

South Asia

INTRODUCTION

Shelton A. Gunaratne

1. MULTIMEDIA ACCESS

The International Telecommunication Union (ITU, 1999) says that the "Internet is the equivalent of a telephone, fax, computer, radio and television all rolled into one service". From just 213 hosts and several thousand users in August 1981, the Internet has grown to 56 million hosts spread among 200 million users as of July 1999. Traditional media, the focus of this volume, will have to adjust themselves to the "Digital Age" characterized by multimedia access—a powerful mechanism to accelerate development through electronic commerce, telemedicine, distance learning, and the like. The seven country-wise chapters in this section briefly analyze the state of the Internet and the telecommunication infrastructure in the poorest of the three regions in Asia. Table 1 summarizes where each country stands in the new millennium. None of the countries is even close to reaching the world average in the three categories encompassing multimedia access. In mid-1999, only Maldives had an Internet host density of 7.2 per 10,000 people. The density in all other counties ranged from zero to one.

2. STATE OF THE PRESS AND OF BROADCASTING

In January 1999, the Freedom House ranked the media in India, Sri Lanka, Bangladesh, Nepal, and Pakistan as "party free" and those in Maldives and Bhutan as "not free" (see Table 2). All South Asian countries scored high on "political pressures and controls on media content" of broadcast operations. All, except India, scored high on the same criterion in relation to the press as well. This introduction uses the press freedom rankings by Freedom House to list the countries for the discussion of highlights.

2.1 India

Freedom House researcher Sussman (1999) points out India as "an example of the continued limitation on the press despite improvement in the country's political and civil rights" (p. 1). The latest Freedom House survey of political and civil liberties has raised India from the status of "partly free" to "free," even though the country *remains* in the "partly-free-press" category. This reflects the reach of the state-run Doordarshan TV network, which delivers news and views to 80 percent of India's population, in addition to the state-run All India Radio, which controls almost all radio stations. At the same time, some 35 million Indians already have access to independent satellite television, while increasing numbers have also joined the cable television audience. Moreover, Indians make wide use of video and audio cassettes. Despite these positive developments, as well as the country's "robust print press in many languages," Sussman says that "the bulk of news reaching the public favors government interests" (p. 1) either by omission of negative information or by emphasis on officials or their policies. Because the government has a monopoly on broadcasting news programs, information about matter such as fighting in Kashmir is either not reported or is reported with bias. Politics has stalled the promised legislation to privatize the electronic media. Journalists covering controversial stories also face possible violence. Viswanath and Karan point out in this section that autonomy for public broadcasting and the right to information have become major issues in India. An additional concern is the inadequacy of the telecommunication infrastructure.

2.2 Sri Lanka

Press freedom suffered a heavy blow when the government reimposed censorship in mid-1998 to prevent independent reporting of the war between the government forces and Tamil insurgents. Freedom House observed: "In addition to restricting sources of military and related information, government officers invaded homes and offices of leading journalists and arrested several. Criminal investigators entered the offices of two major newspapers and demanded to know the source of their information" (Sussman, 1999, p. 30). Sri Lanka's press restriction score went up by eight points over the previous year in the 1999 freedom survey. In this section, Gunaratne and Wattegama have analyzed the development of the media in Sri Lanka and pointed out the significance of the 1998 Colombo Declaration on Media Freedom and Social Responsibility. The country's minister for media has expressed concern that "the implementation of the contents of this declaration has been left in abeyance" (*Daily News*, May 3, 1999). A Parliamentary Select Committee is studying the changes required in laws governing the media. The minister has expressed the government's commitment to freedom of expression.

2.3 Bangladesh

The media in Bangladesh face some 23 restrictive laws, dating from 1861 to the present. Freedom House states that the government can influence the print media by adjusting sales quotas on newsprint and by providing government advertising to "friendly" media. In this section, Bhuiyan and Gunaratne have drawn attention to the current government's endeavor to refrain from such practice. Radio remains a state monopoly, while the granting of a license to set up a private TV station in 1999 broke the state monopoly in television. Although people can receive BBC and CNN telecasts, the authorities sometimes censor the content. Critics often attack cable television as "un-Islamic." Sussman (1999) says: "Nine major newspapers, owned by prominent families or the Awami League, provide mostly bland support for their owners' positions and little editorialization" (p. 9). In 1998, an editor, whose newspaper regularly exposed gang activity, political corruption, and human rights abuses, was assassinated. Assaults on and arrests of journalists, as well as the ransacking of a newspaper office, further eroded the freedom of the press. The country's press restriction score notched up two points in the 1999 survey.

2.4 Nepal

Nepal's Constitution restricts news coverage that subverts national security and public order, and disrespects the monarchy. The law requires the licensing of journalists. In this section, Rao and Koirala point out that despite the popular demand for privatization of the official media, the government continues to own and operate the only national radio and television stations and two of the largest daily newspapers. None of these provide adequate coverage to opposition views. In 1998, according to Freedom House, the government confiscated six newspapers for reporting the misconduct of security officers; and jailed or charged at least three journalists for reporting on corruption or Maoist activities. On the positive side, people have access to broadcasts from China, India, and Bangladesh. Unrestricted access to satellite television is possible for those who can afford it. Private newspapers and magazines vigorously criticize government policies.

2.5 Pakistan

In Pakistan, laws and constitutional provisions restrict freedom of expression over broad subjects, including the army and Islam. Many repressive laws remain, such as the Official Secrets Act, the Security of Pakistan Act, and the Maintenance of Public Order Ordinance, all of which can be used by the government to punish news organizations and journalists. Freedom House observes that since radio and television are owned and operated mainly by the state, hence broadcast reporting generally favors the ruling party. In 1998, monitors recorded some 22 cases of serious violations of freedom. Among these were the murder of a journalist, physical attacks on eight other journalists, the arrest of 21 journalists in 10 separate incidents, the suspension of eight newspapers, and the raiding and ransacking of five newspaper offices. On the positive side, newspapers provide a greater diversity of opinion. The English-language press, which has come under strong government attacks, is among the most outspoken in South Asia. In this section, Ali and Gunaratne assert that "the past few years have seen a definite trend toward greater press freedom, and the government remains under pressure to free the electronic media from government control." The press, however, still faces the challenge of working with nascent democratic institutions that have not yet developed the fundamental democratic tenet of tolerance for opposing viewpoints. (Pakistan returned to military rule in October 1999. The state of emergency allows the country's chief executive to curtail media freedom.)

2.6 Maldives

The Maldivian Constitution guarantees freedom of speech and expression of thought, orally and in writing, as long as the specific provisions of the *Shariat* and the law are not contravened. "Incitement" of the population is prohibited, but truth can be a defense against libel. In this section, Karan and Viswanath point out that the conventional wisdom is that any discussion on press freedom and press regulation should take into account the fragile and "homogeneous" structure of Maldivian society. The government can shut down newspapers and sanction journalists for stories allegedly containing unfounded criticism. Thus journalists practice self-censorship. However, even though the government owns and controls the country's only radio and television stations, they carry some pluralistic views. The mainly private press carries some criticism of the government, but not of Islam.

2.7 Bhutan

In this section, Conlon says that although no explicit legal or regulatory framework exists for the media in Bhutan, the government has consistently considered the media as tools for promoting development and has adopted a policy of "cautious modernization," and of weighing the balance between tradition and modernity. Freedom of speech is restricted, and criticism of the king is not permitted, except indirectly during the discussions of the National Assembly. Freedom House observes that the state-owned weekly *Kuensel*, Bhutan's only regular publication, offers mainly pro-regime propaganda. Government ministries regularly review editorial material and equally regularly suppress or change content. The government has banned all private television reception, as well as satellite dishes. All television antennas and satellite receiving dishes have, since 1989, been dismantled under government order. Bhutan's press restriction score rose 15 notches to 80 in the January 1999 survey.

3. PROBLEMS AND PROSPECTS

With the exception of the Maldives and Sri Lanka, illiteracy stands out as the major problem in the majority of SAARC countries. Until the governments solve this problem, computer literacy and multimedia access—prerequisites for world competitiveness in the Information Age—are unlikely to spread in South Asia in the face of projected population increase. Population projections show India overtaking China by 2025 when each of the two countries would have 1.4 billion people.

South Asia would then have a population of 1.88 billion, which is 23.8 percent of the world population of 7.89 billion (see Table 3) or 44.2 percent of Asia's population of 4.24 billion. (Currently, South Asia accounts for 39.2 percent of Asia's population.) Although South Asia can be proud of its "partly free" press at the turn of the century, one might wonder whether it could move on to the "free" press category if economic progress and literacy were to fall behind the increasing population rate.

4. STATISTICS

Table 1
Multimedia Access in South Asia

Overall world rank	Country	Main telephone lines per 100 people		TV sets per 100 people		Internet hosts per 10,000 people	
		1997	Rank	1997	Rank	1997	Rank
138	Maldives	6.6	124	3.9	156	1.91	93
149	Sri Lanka	1.7	159	9.2	130	0.37	124
158	India	1.9	155	6.9	142	0.08	144
165	Pakistan	1.8	157	2.1	164	0.09	142
174	Bhutan	1.0	164	1.9	170	0.03	155
181	Nepal	0.8	173	0.4	191	0.07	145
199	Bangladesh	0.3	194	0.7	180	0.00	176
World Average		**18.9**		**24.1**		**52.79**	

Source: ITU, 1999.

Table 2
Press Freedom in Asia–January 1999
(Freedom House Ratings)

South Asia		A	B	C	D	Total	Rating on political rights ❶ and civil liberties ❷
India	Broadcast	2	12	3	2	37	
	Print	2	5	8	3	PF	F 2, 3
Sri Lanka	Broadcast	9	12	5	0	58	
	Print	9	11	7	5	PF	PF 3, 4
Bangladesh	Broadcast	5	13	8	0	59	
	Print	5	12	12	4	PF	PF 3, 4
Nepal	Broadcast	12	10	0	0	59	
	Print	14	10	8	5	PF	PF 3, 4
Pakistan	Broadcast	6	13	0	5	60*	
	Print	9	13	9	5	PF	PF 7, 5
Maldives	Broadcast	15	13	0	0	66	
	Print	15	14	8	1	NF	NF 6,5
Bhutan	Broadcast	15	15	10	0	80	
	Print	14	14	8	4	NF	NF 7, 6

Table 2 contd

Source: http://freedomhouse.org/pfs99

Note: Press freedom criteria:
A = Laws and regulations that influence media content; scale: broadcast, 0–15; print, 0–15
B = Political pressures and controls on media content; scale: broadcast, 0–15; print, 0–15
C = Economic influences over media content; scale: broadcast, 0–15; print, 0–15
D = Repressive actions (killing journalists, physical violence, censorship, self-censorship, arrests, etc.); scale: broadcast, 0–5; print, 0–5
RATING: free: 0–30; partly free: 31–60; not free: 61–100; * pre-military coup rating

GOVERNANCE:
❶ First number in column = rating on political rights
❷ Second number in column = rating on civil liberties
RATING: 1 = most free; 7 = least free

Table 3
South Asia: Estimated Population in 2025

World rank	Country	Population
1	India	1,415,273,665
5	Pakistan	211,675,333
8	Bangladesh	179,129,264
38	Nepal	42,576,135
56	Sri Lanka	24,087,501
140	Bhutan	3,340,681
168	Maldives	623,150
	Total	**1,876,705,729**

Source: US Census Bureau, 1998.

5. REFERENCES

ITU (International Telecommunication Union). (1999). *Challenges to the network: Internet for development.* Geneva: ITU.
Sussman, L.R. (1999). *Press freedom 1999: News of the century.* New York: Freedom House.
US Census Bureau, International Data Base. (1998, December 28). *IDB: Countries ranked by population* [On-line]. Available: (http://www.census.gov/cgi-bin/ipc/idbrank.pl).

◆

BANGLADESH

Serajul I. Bhuiyan & Shelton A. Gunaratne

1. NATIONAL PROFILE

1.1 Geography

Bangladesh, with a land area of 144,000 sq km (slightly smaller than Wisconsin) lies to the east of the South Asian subcontinent. It faces the Bay of Bengal to the south, while it is bordered by India on all other directions for 4,053 km except for a 193-km border with Myanmar to the southeast. Separated from Bangladesh by short stretches of Indian territory are Bhutan, China, and Nepal. The Ganges (Padma) and the Brahmaputra (Jamuna) rivers merge in Bangladesh before flowing into the Bay of Bengal. The country's terrain is mostly flat alluvial plain except for the hilly southeast. It has a tropical climate: cool, dry winters (October to March); hot, humid summers (March to June); and cool, rainy monsoons (June to October). Although 73 percent of the land is arable, the country faces the hazards of droughts, cyclones, and floods (*World factbook*, 1999).

1.2 People

Bangladesh is the world's eighth most populous, as well as the world's most densely populated, country with an estimated 127.2 million people (*Asiaweek*, June 4, 1999). Bengalis constitute 98 percent of the people, with fewer than one million tribals and 250,000 Biharis. In religious terms Muslims make up 88.3 percent, Hindus 10.5 percent, and others 1.2 percent (*World factbook*, 1999). The country's adult literacy rate is 38.9 percent and life expectancy is 58 years.

Bangladesh is the beneficiary of Arabic, Dravidian, European, Indo-Aryan, Mongol–Mughal, Persian, and Turkic cultures. About A.D. 1200, Sufi Muslim invaders supplanted the Hindu and Buddhist dynasties, and converted most people to Islam. In the 16th century, the Mughal Empire absorbed Bengal. Portuguese traders and missionaries reached Bengal in the late 15th century, followed by the Dutch, the French, and the British. After defeating the French in 1757, the British extended their commercial contacts and administrative control. In 1859, the British Crown replaced the East India Company. During the independence movement, mounting tension between Hindus and Muslims led to a series of bitter inter-communal conflicts.

In June 1947, Britain declared that it would grant full dominion status to two successor states—India and Pakistan, the latter comprising the Muslim-majority districts of western British India and parts of Bengal. Thus, Pakistan, created on August 14, 1947, became a bifurcated Muslim nation separated from India by more than 1,600 kilometers. Friction between West and East Pakistan culminated in the 1971 army crackdown against Sheikh Mujibur Rahman's dissident movement in East Pakistan. Combined Indian-Bengali forces soon overwhelmed Pakistan's army contingent.

1.3 Government and Politics

After the bloody war, what was East Pakistan became independent Bangladesh on March 26, 1971 (though it took Pakistan until December 16 to acknowledge the independence of Bangladesh). Mujibur's government adopted the 1972 Constitution—later suspended from 1982 (March 24), after the coup, until 1986 (November 10), and also amended many times—that created a strong prime ministership, an independent judiciary, and a unicameral legislature called the National Assembly (*Jatiya Sangsad*), which now has 330 members—300 elected for a five-year term in single-seat constituencies and 30 women elected by the parliamentarians. More importantly, it enunciated as state policy the Awami League's four basic principles—nationalism, secularism, socialism, and democracy.

Having failed to solve the endemic economic problems, Mujibur proclaimed a state of emergency in 1974 and amended the constitution to limit the powers of the legislative and judicial branches, establish an executive presidency, and institute a one-party system. Mujibur, who assumed the presidency to lead the "Second Revolution," dissolved all political parties except the Bangladesh Krishak Sramik Awami League (BAKSAL). Mid-level army officers assassinated Mujibur in August 1975.

Successive military coups culminated in the emergence of Gen. Ziaur Rahman (Zia) as strongman. Martial law followed. Zia, who was elected president in 1978, removed the restrictions on political parties. His Bangladesh Nationalist Party (BNP) won the February 1979 elections. Military dissidents assassinated Zia in 1981. Following a period of emergency rule, Lt Gen. H.M. Ershad assumed power in a bloodless coup in March 1982. He dissolved the parliament and once again, declared martial law. In December 1983, he assumed the presidency, and on January 1, 1986, he restored full political rights. Ershad, who established the Jatiya Party as his political vehicle, was elected president in October 1986. He declared a state of emergency in November 1987, dissolved parliament in December, and scheduled new parliamentary elections for March 1988. The new parliament passed a controversial constitutional amendment making Islam the state religion. Ershad resigned in December 1990.

On February 27, 1991, an interim government oversaw the most free and fair elections in the nation's history. The center-right Bangladesh Nationalist Party won a large number of votes and formed a coalition government with the Islamic fundamentalist party Jamaat-e-Islami (JI). Prime Minister Begum Khaleda Zia, the widow of the assassinated former president, implemented changes to the constitution in September 1991, creating a parliamentary system and returning the governing power to the office of the prime minister. Following a period of political turmoil, the country held fresh elections on June 23, 1996, with the Awami League garnering the highest number of seats. Prime Minister Sheikh Hasina Wazed has re-established democracy in Bangladesh.

1.4 Economy

Asiaweek (June 4, 1999) reported that Bangladesh's gross domestic product (GDP) at purchasing power parity stood at US$ 124 billion; its per capita GDP (PPP) at US$ 1,000; and its nominal per capita GNP at US$ 283. Bangladesh exported US$ 5.1 billion worth of merchandise over the last 12 months for which data were available, while its reserves, excluding gold, stood at US$ 1.6 billion (*Asiaweek*, June 4, 1999). Its main exports were garments, jute and jute goods, leather, frozen fish, and seafood.

Bangladesh has an agricultural peasant economy with 75 percent of the population engaged in agriculture. It has limited natural resources and virtually no industrial base. Recently, however, the rate of direct foreign investment and joint venture efforts has increased in the industrial sector. The country's principal resources are its rivers, its fertile deltaic land, and its untapped reserves of huge natural gas.

2. DEVELOPMENT OF PRESS AND BROADCASTING

2.1 Brief Early History

The press had its beginnings during the British period (1780–1947). Christian missionaries brought the printing press to India in the 16th century to publish evangelical literature. The British East India Company set up printing presses in Bombay (Mumbai), Madras (Chennai) and Calcutta in 1674, 1772, and 1779 respectively (Raghavan, 1994). In 1780, J.A. Hicky printed the first newspaper on the subcontinent, *Bengal Gazette* or *Calcutta General Advertiser*. A Bengali monthly magazine for youth, *Dig-Darshan*, came out in 1818, followed by the weekly *Samachar Darpan* and the monthly *Friend of India* in 1819 (Wolseley, 1971). Being a hub of commerce and industry, the capital of the central government of British India, and a center of socio-cultural activities, Calcutta became the heartland of newspaper publication from 1780 to 1846 (Bangladesh, Press Council, 1984; Salam, 1997).

Rangpur Barta, which was published in 1847, survived until 1857. The *Amrita Bazar Patrika*, an outstanding newspaper, came out of Jessore in 1868. The English biweekly *Bengal Times* started in Dhaka in 1871. Other weeklies and monthlies like, for example, *Rangpur Dikprakash, Kabita Kushumabali* (Dhaka), and *Dhaka Prakash*, emerged in East Bengal between 1860 and 1861. By 1873, Dhaka also published newspapers like *Mahapap, Bangabandhu*, and *Balyabibah*, while Barishal published *Gram Dut, Balaranjika, Hitasandhani*, and *Barishal Barta*; and Rajshahi published *Hindu Ranjika* (Bangladesh, Press Council, 1984; Salam, 1997).

Salam (1997) writes that from 1900 to 1947, in the period of national awakening and political consciousness against the British, what later became East Pakistan and then Bangladesh, published more than 65 newspapers. Most were opinion journals devoted to literary and socio-cultural problems while some focused on religion and socio-cultural reform.

Radio broadcasting arrived in Bangladesh territory in 1939, when the British government set up the first radio station in Dacca (now Dhaka) as a complement to the Calcutta station. The listening range of the 5kW station was 64km, and it covered about 8 percent of the area in East Pakistan (Al-Mujahid, 1978).

2.2 Developments since 1945

2.2.1 Print

In 1947, the year of Partition, two dailies—the *Daily Purbo Pakistan* and the *Paigam*—and a weekly, *Zindegi*, started publication in East Pakistan (now Bangladesh). In 1948, the *Daily Azad* (1936) and the *Morning News* (1942) moved from Calcutta to Dhaka. Three dailies—the *Pakistan Observer* (English), the *Sangbad*, and the *Ittefaq* came out in 1948, 1950, and 1955 respectively (Lent, 1982). Today the *Ittefaq* and the *Sangbad* are two of the leading national dailies in Bangladesh.

The 1952 State Language Movement gave rise to the demand for provincial autonomy. In 1958, Pakistan declared martial law to silence the agitation. When the war between India and Pakistan broke out, Pakistan's military rulers adopted the Defense of Pakistan Ordinance of 1965 and the Defense of Pakistan Rules to suppress newspapers such as the *Ittefaq* and the *New Nation*. In 1972, the year after the establishment of independent Bangladesh, the Mujibur government took over the ownership of four daily newspapers and a periodical, which it found abandoned, under the Presidential Order 16 of 1972 (Hoque, 1992, p. 24). The Bangladesh Press (Administration) Order of 1972 gave the legal basis for the administration of those papers (Huda, 1994, p. 21).[1]

Subsequently, the government enacted the Special Powers Act No. 14 of 1974 to "provide for special measures for the prevention of certain prejudicial activities" and allow for the "speedy trial and effective punishment of certain grave offences"

---

[1] Moraseda, 1983, has documented the extent of press censorship during the 1971 war of liberation. Tabi, 1992, has analyzed the role of *Dainik Sangram*, a Bengali daily, in communal news reporting during the struggle for independence from Pakistan.

(Hoque, 1992, p. 32). Sections 16 (prohibition of prejudicial acts, etc.), 17 (pro-scription of certain documents) and 18 (regulation of publication of certain matters) of the Act enabled the government to harass journalists and close down newspapers, thereby curtailing severely the liberty of the press. The application of these provisions in peaceful times violated the constitutionally guaranteed fundamental rights. The Act also empowered the government to detain without trial, to pre-censor or prohibit publications, and to jail editors or publishers for prejudicial reports, whether true or false. Such "offences" were also non-bailable.

Commenting on the state of the Bangladesh press in 1974, Lent (1982) cate-gorized the following as government-administered newspapers: *Morning News, Azad, Observer, Dainik Bangla* (1964), and *Purbodesh* (1969). He identified *The People* (1969), *Banglar Buni* (1971), and *Sangbad* (1950) as pro-government. Opposition or independent newspapers were the *Ganakantha* (1971), *Ittefaq,* and *Janapad* (1973). Lent did not categorize *Bangabarta* (1973), *Evening Post* (1959), *Nabajat* (1962), and *Samaj* (1972). He also listed the following Chittagong-based newspapers that were circulating in 1974: *Andolon* (1973), the pro-government *Azadi* (1959), *Dainik Michiil* (1972), *Dainik Swadhinata* (1972), *The Eastern Examiner* (1952), and *People's View* (1970). The *Dainik Bangladesh* (1972) was published out of Bogra.

The legislature passed the 1974 Press Council Act, which created a quasi-judicial body, presumably to "safeguard freedom of the press and protect individual citizens and institutions from media harassment and exploitation," as well as to maintain and improve the standard of newspapers and news agencies in Bangladesh (Bangla-desh, Official Home Page, 1998; Hoque, 1992). However, The Newspaper (Annul-ment of Declaration) Act passed in June 1975 annulled all the newspapers in Bangladesh but four. The Government Owned Newspaper (Management) Act of 1975 created a management board to run those four papers. After August 1975, the new government repealed the two laws and restored some degree of press freedom. Until 1997, however, government-created trusts continued to run two dailies, *Dainik Bangla* and *Bangladesh Times*; a weekly, *Bichitra,*[2] and a fortnightly, *Ananda Bichitra* (Hoque, 1992, p. 24). Several dailies commenced publishing in the second half of the 1970s, including *Dainik Kishan* of Dhaka; *Daily Life* and *Dainik Naya Bangla* of Chittagong; *Dainik Probha, Daily Janabarta,* and *Tribune* of Khulna; and *Thinkara* and *Sphulinga* of Jessore.

The 1984 Press Commission made 102 recommendations, which some critics described as "too simplistic and in some cases contradictory" (Anwar, 1994, p. 25). The commission recommended the abolition of public-sector dailies and government-managed news agencies, the "diffusion of ownership and control of larger newspapers," the guaranteeing of freedom of the press "in practice," the appointment of a commission to review the press laws, and the enactment of the freedom of information legislation. Recommendations 43 through 46, which per-tained to the Press Council, suggested the amendment of the 1974 Press Council

---

[2] More recently, a private-sector weekly bearing the same title *Bichitra* commenced publication.

Act to empower the council, inter alia, to suspend "accreditation of journalists, and public sector advertisements, postal concession," and the like to offending publications. It also recommended the practice of "development-oriented communication" and the "better utilization of the press as a change agent," while not reducing the press to the level of a public relations outfit of the government. Moreover, the commission accepted "reasonable restrictions" in the form of laws to ensure the growth of "a responsible press" (Anwar, 1994; Hassan, 1996). Professional representatives on the commission, however, added supplementary notes to the report stating that press freedom must precede the concern with journalistic responsibility. The Ershad government, however, failed to take action on the commission's recommendations.

The 1980s saw the emergence of more dailies in Dhaka; these included *New Nation* (1981), *Daily Shakti* (1982), *Dainik Janata* (1984), *Dainik Khabar* (1985), *Daily Inqilab* (1986), *Dainik Patrika* (1986), and *Dainik Dinkal* (1987). Chittagong also claimed one more daily, *Daily Burbokone* (1986). Each major political party in the late 1980s had one or more newspapers that supported it, and each used its own newspapers to publish its official views. Repression of the media varied from the banning of some publications for extended periods to officially pressurizing publishers to regulate the content of news articles. For example, the English-language *Bangladesh Observer* was banned for three months in 1987, and the weekly *Banglar Bani* (Bengal's Message) was banned through much of 1987 and 1988. The weekly *Joyjatra* (Victory March) was banned in February 1988 for publishing "objectionable comments" referring to the possibility of Ershad's resignation. In 1988, the government closed the *Dainik Khabor* (Daily News) for 10 weeks under the Special Powers Act of 1974 because the newspaper had released an article with a map in which Bangladesh seemed to look like a part of India, thus inflicting "injury to the independence and sovereignty of the country." In addition to this, the operations of the British Broadcasting Corporation (BBC) were banned under the Special Powers Act from December 14, 1987, to May 2, 1988, and one of its correspondents was jailed for having allegedly manufactured "continuing hostile and tendentious propaganda" (Heitzman & Worden, 1988).[3]

The February 1991 general elections re-established parliamentary democracy in Bangladesh under the BNP Prime Minister Khaleda Zia. The pro-democracy movement, which toppled Gen. Ershad and brought the BNP to power, forced the Zia government in 1991 to drop sections 16, 17, and 18 of the Special Powers Act that fettered the freedom of the press and the freedom of speech. Simultaneously, however, the government amended sections 99A, 99B, and 99D as well as Schedule II of the Code of Criminal Procedure (see Section 3.1) that virtually restored the sections omitted from the Special Powers Act (Hoque, 1992, p. 245). Many new newspapers commenced publishing in the democratic environment that

---

[3] Ullah, 1991, has documented the press censorship and the consequent political developments in Bangladesh during the 1980s while Alama, 1992; and Kibriya, 1985, have focused on the freedom of the press and mass media issues.

followed the fall of Ershad, starting with the daily *Ajkere Kagog* on February 21, 1991—a newspaper that produced a new dimension in journalism. Among the dailies that followed were Dhaka's Bengali-language *Janakantha* (1991) and the Bengali tabloid *Daily Manavzamin* (1998).[4] The English-language *Morning Sun* (1990) had already been in circulation. A good number of young and energetic people turned to journalism in the early 1990s.

2.2.2 Radio

The Dhaka radio station occupied a small rented building and had extremely meager resources until 1948. Until 1947, it failed to have even a teleprinter. Because the Pakistan government gave high priority to building communication links between its two widely separated wings, it installed the country's first 100kW and 1,000kW medium wave and shortwave transmitters in Dhaka between 1959 and 1963. The government set up relaying stations in Chittagong, Rajshahi, Sylhet, Rangpur, and Khulna between 1954 and 1971. Except for national broadcasts and commentaries from Karachi, the East Pakistan radio network functioned independently of its West Pakistan counterpart. The 1971 war of liberation caused the destruction of numerous broadcasting installations, including the transmitters and the studios in Khulna (Al-Mujahid, 1978).

From the outset, broadcasting in Bangladesh was a government monopoly. Bangla Betar—or Radio Bangladesh—along with its eight regional stations, has been the nation's sole broadcaster. In 1965, Bangla Betar's primary domestic service covered 95 percent of the country's land area and population. In June 1975, Bangladesh opened its first earth satellite station at Betbunia, 140 miles southeast of Dhaka, with US$ 8 million assistance from the Canadian International Development Agency.

2.2.3 Television

Television broadcasting commenced in 1964 when Bangladesh was still East Pakistan. President Ayub Khan's government brought Pakistan into the television era even before India entered it. The first TV station in Dhaka started as a three-month pilot project in late 1964 with a 3kW transmitter. Nippon Electric Co. of Japan had partial ownership of the pilot TV project, which operated initially for three hours daily, six days a week. A satellite station was set up in Chittagong in the late 1960s, followed by two relay stations in Khulna and Rajshahi. These stations covered more than half the country's population. Weekly telecasts in the early 1970s totaled about 35 hours, the bulk of which was in Bengali. However, it was only those who could afford to buy the expensive TV receivers who actually

---

[4] The tabloid-format *Daily Manavzamin* is "the first of this kind in Bangladesh," says news editor Ahmed Faruque Hassan. The paper claims a circulation of 100,000. The editor-in-chief is Matiur Rahman Chaudhary (Personal communication, April 9, 1999).

benefited (Al-Mujahid, 1978). Nothing came out of a proposal to set up a broad-casting corporation outside government ownership.

After the creation of Bangladesh, the Mujibur government nationalized the TV network in December 1971. The Bangladesh Television Corporation operated the TV network, with the government as the controlling shareholder, and NEC as the other major shareholder. In 1974, the government announced its plan to shift the Dhaka TV station to the Rampura quarter of Dhaka with new equipment, multiple studios and a large auditorium. The plan called for one of the largest TV stations in South Asia.

2.2.4 News Agencies

Bangladesh has five news agencies: Bangladesh Sangbad Sangstha (BSS), Eastern News Agency (ENA), United News of Bangladesh (UNB), South Asian News Agency (SANA), and Bangladesh News Agency (BNA). BSS is a government-run news agency while ENA, UNB, SANA, and BNA are privately owned.

BSS (then known as the Associated Press of Bangladesh) became the national news agency under a government order in January 1972. The Bangladesh Sangbad Sangstha Ordinance No. 20 of 1979 provided for its legal establishment "as a national news agency for undertaking and promoting news agency service in Bangladesh, obtaining international news agency service, mobilization of national news, and for matters connected therewith or incidental thereto" (Hoque, 1992, p. 68). It began with the APB's skeleton staff and almost no equipment. It soon set up links for direct reception of news from PTI in India and subsequently, from global wire services (Reuters, AFP, and UPI). Over the years, it has concluded exchange agreements with several other regional and national news agencies.

The first privately owned news agency of Bangladesh, ENA, was established in Dhaka in March 1970. It developed into a full-fledged news agency before the war of independence. UNB started in January 1988 as an independent agency with the Associated Press as its principal anchor. It was the first news agency in Bangladesh to introduce computers in its operations. UNB also introduced a modern photo service. It has an agreement to distribute AFP pictures and features in Bangla-desh. BNA, a bilingual news service, began in March 1993 as a limited liability company. SANA emerged in December 1995 with the broader objective of covering news from the South Asian Association of Regional Cooperation (SAARC) group of countries. It has bureaus in India, Sri Lanka, Maldives, Nepal, and Bhutan.

3. THE PRESS

3.1 Policy and Legal Framework

Hoque (1992), Anwar (1996), and Huda (1994), among others, have described the policy and legal framework affecting the Bangladesh press. This framework has its roots in the British colonial rule in the subcontinent (1799–1947). Press laws did not change for the better with the birth of Pakistan on August 14, 1947, or with the birth of Bangladesh on March 26, 1971.

Bangladesh's Constitution guarantees freedom of expression. Article 39 (1) guarantees the freedom of thought and conscience. However, Article 39 (2) states that this right shall be "subject to any reasonable restrictions imposed by law in the interests of the security of the state, friendly relations with foreign states, public order, decency or morality, or in relation to contempt of court, defamation or incitement to an offence" (Hoque, 1992, pp. 25, 45).

Apart from the constitutional provisions, Hoque (1992, p. 43) lists 23 laws and codes applicable to the mass media: the Printing Presses and Publications (Declaration and Registration) Act 1973; the Press Council Act, 1974; the Bangladesh Sangbad Sangstha Ordinance, 1979; the Special Powers Act, 1974; the Code of Criminal Procedure, 1898; the Penal Code, 1860; the Dramatic Performance Act, 1876; the Indecent Advertisement Prohibition Act, 1963; the Children Act, 1974; the Telegraph Act, 1885; the Post Office Act, 1869; the Wireless Telegraphy Act, 1933; the Official Secrets Act, 1923; the Foreign Relations Act, 1932; the Censorship of Film Act, 1963; the Cinematograph Act, 1918; the Amusement Tax Act, 1922; the Contempt of Courts Act, 1926; the Copyright Ordinance, 1962; the Newspaper Employees (Conditions of Service) Act, 1974; the Industrial Relations Ordinance, 1982; and the Employment of Labor (Standing Orders) Act, 1965.

The arbitrary application of the Special Powers Act of 1974 had been a threat to the fundamental rights of the citizens. Sections 16, 17, and 18 of the Act were clear restraints on the freedom of the press (see Section 2.2.1). Although these sections were amended in 1991,[5] the government introduced a new clause in Section 99A of the Code of Criminal Procedure that practically made the law relating to the press more stringent. This is so because, as Hoque (1992) explains, "the voice of the press may be gagged by the government at any time by resorting to the provisions of Clause (b) of Section 99 A (1) of the Code on the plea that the printed matter is defamatory of the president of Bangladesh or the prime minister of the government" (p. 245). In addition, Hoque (1992) points out that "the punishment prescribed for the offence has been made severe by enhancing the sentence of two years to seven years, by amending Section 505 of, and by introducing Section 505A, in the Penal Code" (p. 245). The amendments to the Code of Criminal Procedure and the Penal Code[6] also placed definite restrictions on the freedom of the press, speech, and association. The only difference is the removal of the restriction on granting bail under Section 32 of the Special Powers Act.

Furthermore, the government also amended the Printing Presses and Publications (Declaration and Registration) Act of 1973 and established a Press Appellate Board.

[5] The Special Powers (Second Amendment) Ordinance 1991.
[6] The Code of Criminal Procedure (Third Amendment) Ordinance of 1991 amended Sections 99B and 99D of the 1898 Code by changing the words "any treasonable or seditious or other matter of such a nature" to "any such matter, word sign or visible representation." The Penal Code (Amendment) Ordinance of 1991 amended the provisions of the Penal Code of 1860 applicable to the mass media.

Through this amendment, the government transferred some of its powers to the Press Appellate Board, "whose decision shall be final in matters of authentication and cancellation of authentication of publication" (Hoque, 1992, p. 246). However, Hoque argues that the amendments to the Criminal Code and the Penal Code might have negated the degree of press freedom envisaged in the transfer of power to the appellate board.

Section 11 (2) of the Press Council Act entrusts the council with preserving the freedom of the press, helping newspapers to maintain their independence and professional standards, and also building a code of conduct for the journalists to maintain a high professional standard. The Act empowers the council to fulfill the unwritten requirement of the constitution to protect the fundamental rights of the citizen against an unscrupulous or irresponsible newspaper, news agency, or journalist. The Press Council Act upholds the right of journalists to protect the confidentiality of news sources. The Act though, has *no* provisions empowering the council to take action against the government for alleged encroachment into the constitutionally guaranteed freedom of the press. Nor does the Act require the government to have recourse to the council before taking any action against the press.

Hoque (1992) has observed that the mass media laws in Bangladesh have an overall tendency to curtail the liberty of the press in general. This is particularly so in reference to the application of the Special Powers Act. The practical deviations made in respect of the authentication of the declaration under the Printing Presses and Publications (Declaration and Registration) Act of 1973, also shows the government's tendency to limit the publication of newspapers and periodicals (Hoque, 1992, pp. 37–39).

3.2 Financial Aspects: Circulation, Advertising, Marketing Strategies

The government (Bangladesh, Official Home Page, 1998) reported in 1998 that "no less than 216 dailies and 180 weeklies" are published in the country while Dhaka alone has 73 dailies and 92 weeklies. Most are in Bengali. The circulation of Bengali dailies was 2.05 million while that of the English ones was 182,312 (Moslem, 1998). However, UNESCO (1999) data show a much lower circulation (see Table 1).

In contemporary newspaper operations, circulation activities range from market planning among top executives through distribution and collection to collaboration with advertising agencies on a targeted delivery of special sections. In Bangladesh, the scope of such activity is different from one newspaper to another reflecting the differences in circulation, frequency of publication, labor conditions, and management philosophies.

Although circulation is the basis of almost all print media revenue in Bangladesh, the publishers have not used a standard definition of newspaper sales. Inflated circulation figures have been used to appeal to advertisers. Independent newspaper-space sales agents also used inflated circulation figures to justify higher space rates and their commissions. Circulation wars too encouraged such exaggeration.

The government established the Bangladesh Audit Bureau of Circulation to standardize circulation figures and make them reliable and comparable. Today, ABC sets the standards for newspaper sales and audits 70 percent of all the daily newspaper circulation. ABC has established net paid circulation as the standard figure for comparison, and (see Bangladesh, Audit Bureau, 1996) it calculates the net paid circulation on a daily basis (net paid daily) and averages the data over a five-day period to derive the average weekly net paid circulation.

The press in Bangladesh functions within a competitive structure just like other private businesses. However, Bangladesh has a history of government intervention in the newspaper business: the annulment of all newspapers but four in June 1975; and the use of newsprint and advertising subsidies to influence editorial content. Government-sponsored advertising and allocations of newsprint imported at a favorable tariff rate are central to the financial viability of many newspapers. Although the publishers receive additional income from other related business activities, the bulk of their finance comes from the sale of copies and of advertising space. The government buys some 41,000 column inches on an average per month from daily and weekly newspapers (Salam, 1997).

Seiden (1974) argues that newspapers have two powerful and potentially conflicting obligations: to play a decisive informational role in their community and to attract enough readers and adequate advertising to achieve financial stability. These two activities can lead to a split personality when the newspaper succeeds admirably in one role but fails in the other. Each publisher chooses a balance between the business and the social institutional roles of the newspaper by establishing a series of policies, defining in the process, the notion of circulation, as well as of editorial and advertising success. Bangladesh newspapers have made uncomfortable compromises based on the knowledge that profitability is the only sure means to pursue editorial autonomy.

Since the return of democratic rule in 1991, the government has discontinued the practice of press advice and other devices of media control. However, the government has continued to use its clout as the largest advertiser to influence newspaper reporting and editorial policy. Moslem (1998) writes: "They cannot penalize the media any more, but they can reward them profusely. This is one lever the government uses very cunningly to mould the media according to their wishes" (p. 6). However, a monitoring group exists to oversee the government's centralized policy of advertising distribution. Salam (1997) points out that, in 1982, the government's advertising distribution policy prescribed a fixed 60:40 ratio between Dhaka newspapers and non-Dhaka newspapers. Of the quota earmarked for Dhaka, the ratio between dailies and weeklies was fixed at 85:15. The government, however, still appears to use advertising to influence the media. For example, from 1991 to 1996, the low-circulation *Dainik Bangla*, a government-owned daily, received the largest chunk of government advertising revenue, Taka 780 million. In contrast, the highest-circulated *Ittefaq* received only Taka 215 million (Moslem, 1998). The present Awami League government claims it has ended the "evil practice" of distributing advertising based on political considerations in favor of distribution based on circulation (Bangladesh, Official Home Page, 1998).

Referring to the Bangladesh media in the 1970s, Nyrop (1975) observed that five fundamental factors affected the newspaper industry despite the best efforts of editors and circulation managers—factors that are still valid:

- economic pressures caused by technological changes in publishing;
- increased competition for circulation and advertising revenue;
- standardization of newspaper content, which produced a loss of individuality and reader appeal;
- a lack of social and economic need for several newspapers in some markets; and
- inept and uncreative newspaper management.

Describing Bangladesh's journalistic constraints in the late 1990s, the US Department of State (1999) asserted that almost all print journalists practiced self-censorship to some degree. They were reluctant to criticize the politically influential personalities in both the government and the opposition, or write sensitive stories because they feared possible harassment, retaliation, or physical harm.

3.3 Structure and Organization

In 1997, the Awami League government discontinued the public or government-controlled newspapers (for example, the *Bangladesh Times* and *Dainik Bangla*) run by government-created trusts as pledged during the 1995 election. Controversy existed with regard to public ownership because the newspapers so owned showed ineffective management and suffered long-term financial difficulties, whatever the quality of the newspapers. Now, the Bangladesh press is almost entirely privately owned, mostly by limited liability companies.

Two types of newspaper ownership exist—private and chain or group. Private owners are editors-publishers who control and maintain full financial secrecy, formulate policy and run the press according to a unique personal vision. A chain or group newspaper is one of several owned by the same person, family or company, like the Ittefaq Group, the Inqilab Group, the *Bangladesh Observer* and the *Sangbad/Daily Independent*. The Ittefaq Group publishes two newspapers—the daily *Ittefaq* in Bengali and the daily *New Nation* in English, besides the weekly *Robbar*. Income from several newspapers allows the chain or group not only to balance profits and losses better but also to use resources for internal management training and the development of young talent.

Nyrop (1975) has traced three stages in the development of newspapers in Bangladesh: the pioneering, the institutional, and the corporate. In the pioneering stage, newspapers owed their emergence mostly to the social, political, literary, or cultural passions of some individuals. These were enterprising and selfless idealists coming generally from not too affluent middle-class backgrounds who demonstrated extraordinary courage and imagination in bringing out publications under almost impossible circumstances. The ownership pattern was highly individualistic and non-institutional. In the institutional stage, a few newspapers with high circulation grew into institutions, with their founders still at the helm of affairs. In the corporate stage, the institutional newspapers plunged into new and varied publications. The corporate or group publications lent a newspaper organization more resilience, greater weight and influence, and a higher scope for developing in both quality and content.

After the emergence of Bangladesh, the publication of daily newspapers drew a large number of investors. Over the years, the combined circulation of newspapers and periodicals has increased steadily with the growth of the press and overall economic and socio-cultural development (Bangladesh, Government of, 1983).

3.4 Quality and Popular Press

Anam (1998) is of the view that of the mainstream press in Bangladesh, "six dailies in English and about a dozen in Bangla constitute the quality print media" (p. 90). Rahman (1999) identified the "nine leading daily newspapers" (p. 50) in Bangladesh as the Bengali-language *Ittefaq, Bhorer Kagoj, Janakantha, Sangbad, Inqilab*, and *Dainik Bangla*; and the English-language *Observer, Star*, and *Independent*.

In general, much of the press practices advocacy journalism, thereby mixing reporting and opinion. The few exceptions to this practice include the *Ittefaq*, the *Star*, and the *Observer*. The general quality of journalism is poor both in terms of physical appearance as well as writing, scope of coverage, and orientation to the readers' needs. Bangladeshi journalists seem to be producing the same kind of newspapers as they did in the recent past.

As Curran, Gurevitch, and Woollacott (1982) maintain, it is the internal logic of media organizations, rather than objective reality, which determines much of their news reporting because "media organizations exist in a symbolic relationship with their [social, economic and political] environment, drawing on it not only for their economic sustenance but also for the 'raw materials' of which their contents are made" (p. 20). There is evidence to demonstrate that the internal logic of media organizations and external power actors determine much more of news reporting in Bangladesh than does objective reality (Anwar 1994). Referring to the quality of the press, Anwar (1994) writes: "Looking into the newspapers' contents, there is evidence of divergent news treatment depending on who is sitting at the desk. This subjective tilt is yet another reason why the press often falters in portraying the realities at the popular level" (p. 24). More obviously, inadequate education and professional training, political leanings, and a dearth of economic and technical resources have substantially contributed to the low quality of journalism. Political leanings strongly characterize the press in Bangladesh.

The *Ittefaq* has the reputation of being a neutral and objective newspaper even though its owner-cum-editor has been a minister in two regimes. Despite limited space, it covers rural news from every corner of the country through its network of correspondents. The *Sangbad*, popularly known as a socialist newspaper, supports the cause of left-of-center political parties, including the Awami League. The editorial and op-ed pages of both papers command high regard.[7]

The *Star* maintains a unique standard of professionalism in the footsteps of its late founder and editor S.M. Ali. The *Observer* also ranks well in terms of professionalism because of its experienced journalists and editors. The daily *Inqilab* has the characteristic of a right-wing leaning religious newspaper. Its founder, the president of a religious professional association, created a group of readers through compulsory institutional subscription to the paper.

The Dhaka-based Bengali dailies with a mass circulation are *Ittefaq, Inqilab, Banglar Bani, Sangbad, Janakantha, Bhorer Kagoj*, and the *Banglabazar Patrika* (see Table 2). A newcomer is the tabloid *Daily Manavzamin*. The *Observer* has the largest circulation among the English dailies followed by the *Star*, the *Independent*, and *New Nation*.

The leading Bengali weeklies include *Jaiy Jaiy Din*, the *Robbar, Bartaman Dinkal, Purniam, Sanglad, Sandwip*, and *Agami*. The major English weeklies are *Holiday, Dialogue, Dhaka Courier*, and *Friday*. These weeklies, which originated in Dhaka, circulate nationwide. The districts also publish their own newspapers which concentrate on local issues.

Maslog (1985) has drawn attention to another type of successful newspaper exemplified by *Jugabheri*, a weekly newspaper published from Sylhet since 1930. "The paper has tried its best to help in the development of the community and has succeeded in lobbying for bridges, roads, airport facilities and a college" (p. 25). Maslog also found *Amod*, a weekly paper published from Comilla since 1955, to have "contributed to the town's development by prodding local government to build or repair roads, canals, drainage, public markets and other public works" (p. 8).

3.5 Distribution and Technology

Mainly local distributors handle the distribution of print media. The Ittefaq Group maintains a very strong circulation network that covers every corner of the country. In general, it takes five to six hours for newspapers printed in Dhaka to reach subscribers in remote areas by train, bus, steamer, and boat. The government, however, asserts that "all the newspapers have gained in circulation and have, [because] improved surface communication, penetrated deep into the villages where literacy has been rising and income level improving" (Bangladesh, Official Home Page, 1998).

The newspaper industry in Bangladesh is undergoing rapid modernization with the adoption of advanced printing technology. Although technological improvements have lowered the production cost of newspapers with a high circulation, the increased cost of printing equipment has required major capital

---

[7] Ahmed, 1998, who analyzed the contents of *Ittefaq, Sangbad, Bangladesh Times*, and *Dainik Bangla*, found that the latter two newspapers owned by the government carried less development news than the other two.

investment. Almost every newspaper published from Dhaka uses color printing technology to attract readers with front-page color photographs. The big newspaper groups have been enthusiastic about using new media technology. The *Ittefaq,* the *Daily Star*, and the *Daily Independent* and some weeklies are already reaching a global audience through their on-line editions. Some major newspapers are printed simultaneously from several regional cities (Bangladesh, Official Home Page, 1998). The *Janakantha* publishes its daily edition from Dhaka, Chittagong, Bogra, and Sylhet using new communications technology. The Ittefaq Group has attempted to use new technology for several years but has met with vigorous resistance from its labor union. The newspapers, which no longer depend entirely on the supply of newsprint from the Khulna mill, are using high quality imported newsprint.

4. BROADCASTING

4.1 Policy and Legal Framework

Unlike in the case of the press, discussions on the deregulation of broadcasting have not yet generated significant democratic changes except for the government's decision in March 1999 to license the country's first private TV station named Ekushey TV. The government maintains complete control over radio. Anwar (1996) says that both Bangladesh Television (BTV) and Bangladesh Betar still have to observe the 27 official guidelines that the defunct National Broadcasting Authority promulgated in January 1986. The Ministry of Information issues directives to the broadcasters and monitors their execution through an informal mechanism. Additionally, the functionaries of BTV and Bangladesh Betar themselves exercise a high degree of self-regulation. A censorship committee headed by the director of programs formally screens all foreign movies prior to their broadcast. The two broadcasting organizations are also answerable to the parliamentary standing committee on information (Anwar, 1996).

The government-owned radio and television did not provide balanced coverage of the news. The activities of the prime minister occupied the bulk of prime time radio and TV news bulletins, followed by the activities of the ministers. Opposition party news got little coverage (US Department of State, 1999). Before the parliamentary elections of February 1991 and June 1996, the two main political parties—the Bangladesh National Party and the Awami League—called for a free and democratic national broadcasting system under an independent authority. The Awami League leader Sheik Hasina Wazed wanted "our fundamental right [to] be respected to express our views and opinions in our newspapers and in independent radio and television broadcasts" (*Ittefaq*, July 24, 1996). On September 9, 1996, the Awami League government set up an independent 16-member body, the Asafuddowlla Committee, to recommend measures for authorizing private radio and television broadcasts. The committee submitted a report to the government in 1997, but the report has not been released to the public, and no changes in the existing framework have been announced. The minister of information termed some of the committee's recommendations "unrealistic" (US Department of State, 1999).[8] The government acknowledged that the committee had "almost finalized its report" (Bangladesh, Official Home Page, 1998). The State Information Minister Abu Sayeed has said the ETV license was not intended as "an alternative to our commitment for autonomy to BTV to ensure [a] free flow of information" (*Daily Star*, March 10, 1999). Among the factors that account for the delay in broadcasting deregulation are: technological backwardness; nationalist policies of the political parties in power; financial problems of the media resulting mainly from a dearth of advertising; and shortage of indigenous private capital.

4.2 Structure and Organization

4.2.1 Radio

Radio Bangladesh functioned as an independent government department under the sponsorship of the Ministry of Information until 1984, when the martial law administration merged it with Bangladesh Television under the new National Broadcasting Authority. The NBA, under the Ministry of Information and Broadcasting, had the responsibility of developing a policy that would shape and balance the broadcasting service, establish patterns and priorities and determine guidelines for its better functioning (Salam, 1997).

However, radio broadcasting continues to be a state activity. A director-general heads Radio Bangladesh (Bangla Betar) with the assistance of a deputy director-general (in charge of programming), 10 directors and a chief engineer. Radio Bangladesh has a workforce of 2,638. The main domestic programs originate from Bangla Betar's eight medium wave stations in Dhaka (1,000kW, 100kW and 10kW), Rajshahi (10kW), Chittagong (10kW), Sylhet (20kW), Rangpur (20kW), Khulna (100kW), Thakurgaon (10kW), and Rangmati (10kW). The recent power boost in Shavar (100kW, 100kW), and Comilla (10kW) stations has brought the entire country within broadcasting range. Bangla Betar uses its short wave transmitters in Shavar principally for its overseas service (Nyrop, 1975; Salam, 1997; Moslem, 1998). These stations operate on medium wave frequencies: 558; 630; 693; 846; 873; 963; 999; 1,053; 1,080; 1,161; and 1,170 kHz.

The FM service operates on 100MHz in Dhaka, 101MHz in Sylhet, 102.5MHz in Chittagong, 103MHz in Rajshahi, 105.5MHz in Rangpur, and 106.5MHz in Khulna. The shortwave service operates on 4,880kHz and 15,520kHz in Shavar.

4.2.2 Television

A director-general heads Bangladesh Television with the assistance of a deputy director-general (for programming), a general manager, seven directors and two

---

[8] In 1984, Gen. Ershard had appointed a press commission, whose report contained some 102 recommendations (see Section 2.2.1), which the government also shelved.

chief engineers. BTV, which employs, 1,520 people, has a network of 11 stations—Rangpur (360kW), Mymensingh (390kW), Noakhali (390kW), Satkhira (250kW), Sylhet (136kW), Khulna (91kW), Natore (90kW), Dhaka (60kW), Rangamati (55kW), Chittagong (15kW), and Cox's Bazar (7kW).

BTV has commissioned relay stations in Jhenaidah, Thakurgaon, and Brahmanbaria, in addition to a relay center in Patuakhali. The BTV station in Dhaka has a radius of about 96 km. The relay and satellite stations have enabled the expansion of coverage to 95 percent of the population. BTV's second TV station in Chittagong, CTV, is now in operation. CTV originates and transmits 30 minutes of programs daily. CTV also transmits programs on the national network. BTV broadcasts a single channel terrestrially, throughout the country. It uses the PAL B/G TV used in India and Germany. In Dhaka, terrestrial transmissions are on Channel 9; and in Chittagong on Channel 5.

In March 1999, the government gave the go-ahead "in principle" for the country's first private channel, Ekushey Television, to go on air by the end of the year. ETV will be a Bengali-language terrestrial and satellite channel, which will broadcast news and current events, drama, entertainment, documentaries, and educational programs for up to 12 hours a day under a 15-year license. With an investment of Taka 950 million (US$ 1.2 million), ETV will broadcast its programs nationwide on very high frequency (VHF). Its programs will be accessible in West Bengal, South and Southeast Asia, the Middle East, Europe, and North America. ETV has agreed to follow the existing censorship laws and guidelines. The government will monitor the ETV programs every month to review the possibilities for giving permission to more private TV channels (*Daily Star*, March 10, 1999).[9]

Cable TV, which began operations in Bangladesh in the early 1990s, has become a popular medium for the dissemination of entertainment programming. The country has more than one million cable and satellite homes with about 2,000 cable operators offering their services. An average cable operator in the country has 200 to 250 subscribers. Dhaka and Chittagong have the largest cable penetration. Rajshahi, Khulna, and Bogra also have a significant number of cable homes (Montu, 1999).

Despite the country's low per capita income, cable subscribers in Bangladesh pay an average monthly CATV charge of Taka 150 (US$ 3) to Taka 200 (US$ 4.10). While the lowest charge is around Taka 100 (US$ 2), subscriptions run as high as Taka 500 (US$ 10.25) per month (Taka1 = 2 US cents). Particularly in metropolitan cities, smaller networks are joining hands to form larger networks that can afford and install better quality equipment and provide a larger number of channels to their subscribers. Cable operators in Bangladesh require a license from the government. BTV issues this license on behalf of the government. The operators pay an annual fee of Taka 25,000 (US$ 514) for service in the four metropolitan cities of Dhaka, Chittagong, Rajshahi, and Khulna. For the rest of

---

[9] Ekushey TV may go on air by the end of the year, *Daily Star*, March 10, 1999 [On-line]. Available: (http://www.dailystarnews.com/199903/10/index.htm).

Bangladesh, the license fee is Taka 10,000 (US$ 205) per year per cable network (Montu, 1999).

However, television in Bangladesh remains, largely, a medium for the elite. The number of licensed sets in the country was estimated to be 1.5 million (Moslem, 1998) even though UNESCO and ITU estimates are much lower (see Table 1). Although locally assembled TV sets are available, most are imported from Singapore, Hong Kong, and Japan. The majority cannot afford TV receivers. Community viewing has not yet become widespread because the government has not distributed that many TV sets free of cost.

4.3 Program Policies

4.3.1 Radio

Altogether, Bangladesh Betar broadcasts for approximately 3,285 hours per month including external services. Programming generally consists of news (3 percent); entertainment (65 percent); educational (5 percent); cultural/religious (9 percent); and others, 18 percent (Moslem, 1998). Both radio and television "broadcast parliament proceedings in an undistorted form" (Bangladesh, Official Home Page, 1998).

Bangladesh Betar's external service uses the shortwave transmitters in Khabirpur to broadcast in Arabic (30 minutes), Bengali (one hour), English (1.15 hours), Hindi (30 minutes), Nepali (30 minutes), and Urdu (30 minutes) and, on occasions, in other languages. These broadcasts are then beamed to South Asia, the Middle East, and Europe for communicating Bengali culture, heritage, thoughts and ideas, and progress and development. The external service also broadcasts its Voice of Islam (30 minutes) to Europe (*World radio TV handbook*, 1999).

Al-Mujahid (1978) observed two decades ago that Bangladesh Betar appeared to be constrained by staff limitations and pressure to present programming slanted by the government's viewpoint. This situation still applies to a large degree. Frequently, the president or the prime minister addresses the nation by radio. Using celebrities or popular speakers to propagate the government viewpoint is not uncommon, especially at the time of national or governmental crises.

4.3.2 Television

All programs, which must adhere to the 1986 official guidelines, are transmitted terrestrially by BTV through the network of 15 transmitters. These programs, produced in Dhaka, are fed in to the regional relay stations in the national network. The average transmission time is about nine hours daily except on Fridays and Saturdays. On Fridays, BTV's transmission time is about 14 hours and on Saturdays it is 11 hours. About 79 percent of the programs are produced locally while 21 percent are imported. Programming is generally slotted thus: entertainment (55.3 percent); news (14.7 percent); cultural/religious (6.8 percent); educational

(9.5 percent); commercial (9.1 percent), and others (4.6 percent). More than 77 percent of broadcasts are in Bengali (Moslem, 1998).

Bangladesh Television takes 40 minutes of news coverage daily via satellites from EVN-1 and Asia Vision under the auspices of the ABU in Kuala Lumpur. BTV also broadcasts BBC and CNN programs for six hours daily. Open University programs also have a regular slot. BTV also shows TV films from the United Kingdom, the United States, Canada, Germany, Australia, Singapore, Italy, EU, Iran, India, Japan, Indonesia, and China.

An average Cable TV network in the country provides 20 channels to its subscribers. Satellite channels that cover India comprehensively with their foot-prints automatically include Bangladesh. Hence, popular pay channels in Bangladesh include Zee TV, Home TV, CNN, BBC, MTV, Music Asia, DW TV, MCM, CNBC, Sony, and PTV. All cable networks operate below 300 MHz. No UHF channels are thus transmitted (Montu, 1999).

The new private channel, Ekushey TV, will provide a domestic alternative to BTV. The agreement stipulates that ETV will allocate 41.6 percent of transmission time for entertainment, 37.5 percent for news and current affairs, and 20.9 percent for educational and informative features. ETV will also broadcast one BTV news bulletin daily (*Daily Star*, March 10, 1999).

4.4 Ownership and Financing

Radio and television, which are under strict government control, depend for survival on receiver license fees, advertising, and a government allotment. Although the government underwrites all expenses for radio broadcasting, the radio licensing system requires every owner of a radio receiver to pay an annual fee.

In 1996, BTV's annual recurrent revenue was US$ 20.4 million. Government grants made up 35.2 percent; advertising, 45.5 percent; licenses, 19.2 percent; and others, 0.1 percent (Moslem, 1998). BTV also received a capital outlay grant of US$ 448,062 from the government. The annual recurrent revenue budget of Bangladesh Betar comprised a government grant of US$ 72,594 (Moslem, 1998).

The private channel ETV expects to fund itself entirely from advertising, which shall not exceed more than five minutes per hour. ETV has agreed to pay Taka 2.5 million (US$ 51,546) annually as a license fee and deposit a non-refundable Taka 10 million (US$ 206,185) as security. It will not receive any government subsidy or fees from viewers (*Daily Star*, March 10, 1999).

As was the case during the British and the Pakistani eras, the Bangladesh government uses the public service media concept as a cover for paternalistic or authoritarian broadcasting. Since independence, it has legitimized state responsibility for broadcast media on the grounds of political, educational, and cultural importance of the media for national development. Government restrictions and controls—justified in terms of technical standardization, scarcity of frequencies, and special national priorities and interests—have severely limited broadcasting. Dutta (1980) concluded that the growth of the mass media in Bangladesh was unrelated to the country's national development. He found no significant relationship between growth in radio receivers and developmental indicators. Moreover, government control of broadcast media had not caused them to disseminate more developmental messages than the print media. Dutta observed that the mass media alone were not enough to enhance national development.

5. NEW ELECTRONIC MEDIA

5.1 Internet and On-line Media

Bangladesh has eight Internet service providers who use the 42 VSAT terminals that the Bangladesh Telegraph and Telephone Board (BTTB) has established to facilitate high speed data communication services. BTTB has also established a packet-switched data network for low speed data communication. Internet access is available through the Information Service Network, which is linked to the Internet backbone by a VSAT link to Hong Kong. BTTB has planned to set up its own Internet gateway (APT, 1998). The current ISPs are Agni Systems, BRAC BDMail Network, Global Information Network, Grameen Cybernet, Information Services Network, PraDeshta, Bangladesh Online Internet Services, and Pimedia. With Internet host density well below 1 per 10,000 people, and TV-set and telephone density also not reaching 1 per 100 people, Bangladesh ranked 199th out of 206 economies in multimedia access (ITU, 1999).

However, several Bangladesh publications are now accessible on the Web. These include *Daily Star* (http://www.dailystarnews.com), *Economic Observer* (http://www.economic-observer.com), *Independent* (http://independent-bangladesh.com), *Ittefaq* (http://www.daily-ittefaq.com), *Muktakantha* (http://www.muktakantha.com), *New Nation* (http://www.nation-online.com), *Weekly Dhaka Courier* (http://www.dhakacourier.com), *Weekly Holiday* (http://www.bagla.net/holiday), and *Weekly Jai Jai Din* (http://www.jaijaidin.com). BanglaRadio.Com (http://Bangla radio.com/News.htm) provides news from Bangladesh Betar News, BBC Bengali Service, Voice of America Bangla Newscast, BBC News, DW Bangla Program, and CFMB Radio Montreal–Bengali program.

5.2 Telecommunications Infrastructure

With 482,534 main telephone lines, Bangladesh had a telephone density of 0.4 per 100 people in 1998 (APT, 1999)—one of the lowest among developing nations (see Table 3). Urban mainlines stood at 91 percent, compared to 9 percent rural (ITU, 1998). More than 40 percent of the telephones are in Dhaka, 21 percent are in Chittagong, 9.7 percent are in Khulna, and 6.8 percent are in Rajshahi. The number of cellular subscribers increased from 52,900 in 1997 to 75,000 in 1998 (APT, 1999; ITU, 1999). Pacific Bangladesh Telecom Ltd introduced the country's first cellular telephone service in 1993. The government has issued licenses to three more private operators to provide cellular communications—Grameen Phone,

Sheba Telecom, and TMIB (APT, 1999). The government-run BTTB is responsible for the operation, maintenance, and development of basic telecommunication services in the eight telephone zones of the country.

Bangladesh set up its first satellite earth station in 1975 at Betbunia. It set up a second earth station in 1982 at Talibabad, which now provides direct links to 13 countries. A third station that came up in 1994 in Dhaka is now working with 20 carriers. A fourth station commissioned at Sylhet in 1995 works with an Intelsat satellite (APT, 1998).

6. POLICY TRENDS FOR PRESS AND BROADCASTING

The policies and laws relating to the mass media in Bangladesh do tend to curtail the liberty of the press. The enactment of the 1974 Special Powers Act in particular and its continued application reflect this tendency. In practice, the government has been prone to deviate in respect of authentication of declaration under the Printing Presses and Publications (Declaration and Registration) Act of 1973. That tendency has had a limiting effect on the publication of newspapers and periodicals (Hoque, 1992, p. 39). The negative actions of the government that affected press freedom in 1998 included:

- Filing of sedition charges (in February) against the editors and the publisher of a newspaper, which published a story alleging that the government was attempting to make the country's defense system complementary to India's.
- Using the Official Secrets Act of 1980 to charge three journalists (on April 20) for allegedly leaking questions from school exams.

However, the prospects of the mass media striving to promote democratic rule are not necessarily dim. Bangladesh's Constitution guarantees the freedom of the press, speech, and expression. The superior courts have the responsibility to protect the fundamental rights of the citizens. Under Article 102 of the Bangladesh Constitution, the High Court Division of the Supreme Court of Bangladesh, upon an application by an aggrieved person, can declare unlawful any arbitrary act or oppressive order of any authority entrusted with the affairs of the republic (Hoque, 1992, p. 39).

Democratic reforms in Bangladesh have enabled the restitution of parliamentary political democracy and party pluralism to some degree. With the country lacking a democratic political culture, political institutions in Bangladesh are extremely fragile. Intolerance of criticism and the absence of any consensual model of democracy reflect this fragility. The democratic revolutions in Bangladesh have not resulted in major breakthroughs in media de-regulation, quality programming, or new forms of media organization and management. Although limited economic, technical, and staff resources have certainly hindered post-independence Bangladesh from media restructuring, political impediments have not been a less significant factor. The debate on the future of the media is divided along party political lines and is related to the division of power among political agents. In this context, the granting of a license to a private TV channel, coupled with the State Minister Abu Sayeed's reassertion of the government's "commitment for autonomy to BTV," gives some hope for the de-regulation of broadcasting in Bangladesh.

As in many other countries, Bangladesh has paid attention to new media technologies, even though not much has materialized so far. It is far from clear what channels and services Bangladesh viewers and Bangladesh households would prefer and could afford. The business climate of the mass media industry is changing as a result of the new technologies. Profit-motivated information services are likely to replace the present ethos of publishing. Technological development resulting from the integration of telecommunications and broadcasting will affect the distribution of technology as well. Digital radio and TV are the technologies of the near future.

7. MAIN ISSUES

● Press freedom

Freedom House (Sussman, 1999) rated Bangladesh as "partly free" with a restriction score of 59 out of 100 compared to India's 37 and Pakistan's 60. Bangladesh fared poorly on the criterion of political pressures and controls on media content, with a score of 13 out of 15 for broadcast and 12 out of 15 for print. It fared equally poorly on the issue of economic influences over media content, with a score of 8 out of 15 for broadcast and 12 out of 15 for print. It fared relatively better on the criterion of laws and regulations that influence media content, with 5 for broadcast and 5 for print out of 15 each. The fourth criterion regarding repressive actions revealed a mixed bag: zero for broadcast and 4 for print out of 5 each. Thus issues related to the political and economic pressures on the media are likely to get international and national attention in the immediate future. Anam (1998) points out that democracy and press freedom are "organically linked" (p. 91). Anwar (1994) asserts that about 25 restrictions that curtail freedom of the press in Bangladesh are "not considered reasonable" (p. 25).

● Literacy

An adult literacy rate of 38.9 percent in a country with 127.2 million people is unacceptable as the world enters the Information Age. The expansion of the traditional mass media or the new electronic media are unlikely to occur unless the government accords the highest priority to attacking illiteracy. The only other countries in Asia with a lower literacy rate are Afghanistan (31.6 percent) and Nepal (38.1 percent).

● Human rights

Ullah (1990) points out that human rights violations are quite frequent and diverse in Bangladesh, which has many restrictive laws. "The government is equipped with many legal weapons and other means to suppress news concerning human rights issues" that may range from press freedom to voting rights. Ullah says: "Often the media are themselves partners in an unholy alliance with the state" (p. 17). Numerous attacks on and threats to journalists—including the gunning down of editor Saiful Alam Mukul of the *Daily Runner* on August 30, 1998; the death threats of the Chattra League, the ruling party youth-wing, against two Dhaka journalists on August 10, 1998; and the ransacking of *Daily Manavzamin* premises on May 26, 1998, by Jatiya Party backers—have also impinged on human rights. This issue too, will continue to be a matter of significant debate.

8. STATISTICS

General Profile

Exchange rate	US$ 1 = 49.35 Taka (September 1999)*
Population (mid-1999)	127.2 million
Geographical size	147,570 sq km
Population density (1998)	935 per sq km

Source: *OANDA Historical Currency Table [On-line]. Available: (http://www.oanda.com/converter/cc=table?lang=en).

Table 1
Estimated Mass Media Penetration

	Radio receivers		TV receivers		Daily newspapers		
	Number ('000)	*Per 100 people*	*Number ('000)*	*Per 100 people*	*Number*	*Circ'n ('000)*	*Per 100 people*
1980	1,500	1.7	80	0.09	44	274	0.3
1985	4,000	4.0	261	0.26	60	591	0.6
1990	4,855	4.4	525	0.49	52	700	0.6
1995	5,600	4.7	700	0.59	51	950	0.8
1996	6,000	5.0	750	0.62	37	1,117	0.9
1997	6,150	5.0	770	0.63			
1998			850*	0.70*			

Source: UNESCO, 1999; *ITU, 1999.
Note: Moslem, 1998, however, provides the following data:
    Daily newspaper circulation (1996): 2,237,960 or 2 copies per 100 people
    Non-dailies circulation (1996): 987,810 or 0.9 copies per 100 people

Table 2
Daily Newspaper Data

	Frequency	Established	Language	Circulation
Published in Dhaka				
Ittefaq	Daily a.m.	1955	Bengali	215,900
Dainik Inqilab	Daily	1986	Bengali	180,140
Janakantha	Daily	1991	Bengali	150,000
Daily Manavzamin	Daily	1998	Bengali	100,000*
Sangbad	Daily a.m.	1950	Bengali	73,005
Bhorer Kagoj	Daily	1992	Bengali	70,000*
Dainik Sangram	Daily	1970	Bengali	50,980
Bangladesh Observer	Daily a.m.	1948	English	42,830
Dainik Dinkal	Daily	1987	Bengali	40,300
Daily Star	Daily	1991	English	30,010
Dainik Khabar	Daily	1985	Bengali	24,535
Dainik Janata	Daily	1984	Bengali	20,090
Banglar Bani	Daily	1971	Bengali	20,000
Ajker Kagog	Daily	1991	Bengali	20,000*
Morning Sun	Daily	1990	English	18,125
Daily Shakti	Daily	1982	Bengali	16,510
Banglabazar Patrika	Daily	1992	Bengali	15,000*
Daily Independent	Daily	1994	English	15,000*
New Nation	Daily	1981	English	10,920
Dainik Patrika	Daily	1986	Bengali	6,260
Dainik Kishan	Daily	1976	Bengali	6,030
Published in Chittagong				
Daily Burbokone	Daily	1986	Bengali	28,875
Zamana	Daily a.m.	1955	Bengali	17,000
Daily Life	Daily a.m.	1977	English	16,065
Azadi	Daily a.m.	1959	Bengali	13,000
Dainik Naya Bangla	Daily	1978	Bengali	12,000
People's View	Daily	1970	English	4,018
Purba Tara	Daily	1970	Bengali	4,003
Published in Khulna				
Daily Purbanchal	Daily	...	Bengali	42,000
Dainik Probha	Daily	1977	Bengali	10,505
Tribune	Daily a.m.	1978	English	8,060
Jana Barta	Daily	1974	Bengali	5,000
Daily Janabarta	Daily	1976	Bengali	3,175
Purbachal	Daily	1974	Bengali	3,000
Published in Rajshahi				
Dainik Barta	Daily a.m.	1976	Bengali	3,000
Rajshahi Barta	Daily	1961	Bengali	1,120
Published in Jessore				
Runner	Daily	1980	Bengali	3,150
Thinkana	Daily	1976	Bengali	3,150
Sphulinga	Daily	1976	Bengali	3,050
Published in Dinajpur				
Dainik Uttara	Daily	1974	Bengali	6,705

Source: *Editor & publisher international yearbook*, 1999; Lent, 1982; *Personal communication.

Table 3
New Electronic Media

	Mainline telephones		Cellular telephones		Computers		Internet	
	Number ('000)	Per 100 people	Number ('000)	Per 100 people	Number ('000)	Per 100 people	Number of hosts	Number of users
1990	241.8	0.22	...	0.00	...	...	0	...
1996	316.1	0.26	2.5	0.00	...	...	0	...
1997	...	...	52.9	0.04	...	...	0	...
1998	482.5	0.40	75.0	0.06	...	...	0	...

Source: ITU, 1998, 1999; APT, 1999.
Note: The top Internet providers are: Grameen Cybernet; Information Network Services; and Pradeshta.

Broadcasting Data (1996)

Radio
Bangladesh Betar (Radio Bangladesh) Stations   9
Program by type:
  News   90 h/m
  Entertainment   2,120
  Educational   175
  Cultural/Religious   300
  Other   600

Television
BTV (government owned)   2 stations
                                                     12 relay stations

Program by type:
  News   123.30 h/quarter
  Entertainment   463.00
  Educational   79.19
  Cultural/Religious   56.57
  Commercial   76.18
  Others   38.36

Ekushey TV (Privately owned: to start end of 1999)

Advertising Data

Locally owned advertising agencies   245
Accredited:
  25 with television
  60 with radio
  60 with newspapers
Top 10 Billing:
  Adcomm   Taka 200 million
  Asiatic   120
  Bitopi   110
  Unitrend   100
  Popular   90
  Madonna   80
  Interspeed   70
  Rubicom   70
  Expressions   67
  Mattra   65

9. USEFUL ADDRESSES

New Nation Printing Press (*Ittefaq, New Nation*)
1 Ramakrishna Mission Road
Dhaka 1203
Telephone: (880-2) 256 075 & 252 037
Fax: (880-2) 865 776 & 245 536

Bangladesh Publications Ltd (*Dainik Sangram*)
423 Elephant Road
Dhaka 1217
Telephone: (880-2) 405 279
Fax: (880-2) 414 450

Inqilab Enterprise (*Dainik Inqilab*)
2/1 Ramakrishna Mission Road
Dhaka 1203
Telephone: (880-2) 240 147 & 868 440
Fax: (880-2) 833 122 & 232 881

Sangbad
36 Purana Paltan
Dhaka 1000
Telephone: (880-2) 238 147/8
Fax: (880-2) 865 159

Bangladesh Observer
33 Toyenbi Circular Road
Motijheel, Dhaka 1000
Telephone: (880-2) 235 105
Fax: (880-2) 833 565

Daily Manavzamin
21-Kazi Nazrul Islam Ave.
Dhaka 1000
Email: mzamin@bol-online.com

Bangladesh Radio
121 Kazi Nazrul Islam Ave.
Dhaka 1000
Telephone: (880-2) 865 294
Fax: (880-2) 862 021
Email: dgradio@drik.bdg.toolnet.org

Bangladesh Television
TV Bhaban
Rampura, Dhaka 1219
Telephone: (880-2) 330 131/9
Fax: (880-2) 832 927

10. REFERENCES

Ahmed. Q.Z. (1998). *Development news in the newspapers of Bangladesh*. Unpublished doctoral dissertation, Howard University, Washington, DC.

Alama, M.K. (1992). *Samadapatrera svadhinata* (in Bengali). Dhaka: Subarna.

Al-Mujahid, S. (1971). After decline in Ayub era, Pakistan's press thrives, improves. *Journalism Quarterly, 48*, 526–535.

Al-Mujahid, S. (1978). Bangladesh. In J.A. Lent (Ed.), *Broadcasting in Asia and the Pacific: A continental survey of radio and television* (pp. 227–235). Philadelphia: Temple University Press.

Anam, M. (1998). Bangladesh. In A. Latif (Ed.), *Walking the tightrope: Press freedom and professional standards in Asia* (pp. 85–93). Singapore: AMIC.

Anwar, M.T. (1994). Bangladesh: Fewer 'black laws'. In *Press systems in SAARC* (pp. 23–27). Singapore: AMIC.

Anwar, M.T. (1996). Media monitors in Bangladesh. In K.S. Venkateswaran (Comp.), *Media monitors in Asia* (pp. 12–16). Singapore: AMIC.

APT (Asia-Pacific Telecommunity). (1998, 1999). *APT yearbook*. Bangkok: APT.

Bangladesh, Government of. (1983). *Gazette extraordinary*. Dhaka: Bangladesh Government.

Bangladesh, Press Council. (1984). *Decisions of the press council*. Dhaka: Bangladesh Government.

Bangladesh, Audit Bureau. (1996). *Annual report of the Audit Bureau of Bangladesh*. Dhaka: Bangladesh Government.

Bangladesh, Official Home Page. (1998). *The mass media* [On-line]. Available: (http://www.bangla deshonline.com/gob/bang_in9.htm).

Curran, J. Gurevitch, M., & Woollacott, J. (1982). The study of the media: Theoretical approaches. In M. Gurevitch, T. Bennett, J. Curran, & J. Woollacott (Eds.), *Culture society and the media* (pp. 11–29). London: Methuen.

Dutta, J.P. (1980). Mass media and national development: A case study of Bangladesh. *Dissertation Abstracts International, 42* (2), 435A. (University Microfilms No. AAG91-17420).

Editor & publisher international yearbook. (1999) New York: E&P.

Freedom House Survey Team. (1998). *Freedom in the world: The annual survey of political rights and civil liberties, 1997–1998*. New York: Freedom House.

Hassan, A.F. (1996). *Bamladeseara ganamadhyama* (Bangladesh mass media). Dhaka: Agami Prakasani.

Heitzman, J., & Worden, R. (Eds.). (1988) *Bangladesh: A country study*. Washington, DC: Federal Research Division, Library of Congress [On-line]. Available: http://lcweb2.loc.gov/frd/cs/bdtoc.html#bd0126

Hoque, A.N.M.G. (Comp.). (1992). *Mass media laws and regulations in Bangladesh*. Singapore: AMIC.

Huda, N. (1994). Bangladesh: Changes amid growth. In *Press systems in SAARC* (pp. 19–22). Singapore: AMIC.

ITU (International Telecommunication Union). (1998, 1999). *World telecommunication development report*. Geneva: ITU.

Khan, N.A. (1991). *Press and government relations in India, Pakistan and Bangladesh: A historical-critical analysis*. Unpublished doctoral dissertation, University of Southern Mississippi.

Kibriya, G. (1985). *The press in Bangladesh and issues of mass media*. Dhaka: Sunday Publications.

Lent, J.A. (1982). Bangladesh. In J.A. Lent (Ed.), *Newspapers in Asia: Contemporary trends and problems* (pp. 428–441). Hong Kong: Heinemann Asia.

Maslog, C.C. (1985). *Five successful Asian community newspapers*. Singapore: AMIC.

Montu, A.T. (1999, May). CATV in Bangladesh. *Satellite & Cable TV, 7* (3) [On-line]. Available: http://www.web-maniacs.com/scat/bancatv.html

Moraseda, H.H. (1983). *Abaruddha samadapatra '71, ebam svadhinata yuddha Bamladesa sasastra bahinira rananiti o ranakausala* (in Bengali). Dhaka: Nasasa.

Moslem, S. (1998). Bangladesh. In A. Goonasekera & D. Holaday (Eds.), *Asian communication handbook* (pp. 5–15). Singapore: AMIC.

Nyrop, R. (1975). *Area handbook for Bangladesh*. Washington, DC: US Government Printing Office.

Raghavan, G.N.S. (1994). *The press in India: A new history*. New Delhi. Gyan Publishing House.

Rahman, M.G. (1999). Communicating drug issues: Lessons from newspaper coverage in Bangladesh. *Media Asia, 26*, 48–54, 56.

Salam, S.A. (1997). *Mass media in Bangladesh: Newspapers, radio and television*. Dhaka: South Asian News Agency.

Seiden, M.H. (1974). *Who controls the mass media? Popular myths and economic realities*. New York: Basic Books Inc.

Sussman, L.R. (1999). *Press freedom 1999: News of the century*. New York: Freedom House.

Tabi, A.A. (1992). *Muktiyudda Dainika Sangramera bhukima* (in Bengali) Dhaka: Halimullaha Khaddara.

Ullah, M. (1990). Bangladesh. In C.E. Hamelink & A. Mehra (Eds.), *Communication development and human rights in Asia* (pp. 1–18). Singapore: AMIC.

Ullah, M. (1991). *Press ayadabhaisa* (in Bengali). Dhaka: Anindya Prakasana.

UNESCO (United Nations Educational, Scientific and Cultural Organization). (1998). *Statistical Yearbook*. Paris: UNESCO.

US Department of State. (1999, February 26). *Bangladesh: Country report on human rights practices for 1998* [On-line]. Available: (http://www.state.gov/www/global/human_rights/ 1998_hrp_report/banglade.html).

Wolseley, R.E. (1971). India: History and development. In J.A. Lent (Ed.), *The Asian newspapers' reluctant revolution*. Ames: The Iowa State University Press.

World factbook. (1999). Bangladesh [On-line]. Available: (http://www.odci.gov/cia/publications/ factbook/bg.html).

World radio TV handbook. (1999). Amsterdam: Billboard Publications.

◆

2

BHUTAN

C.J. Conlon

1. NATIONAL PROFILE

1.1 Geography

Bhutan (the "Land of the Thunder Dragon"), with a land area of 47,000 sq km, is a country landlocked between India and China. The Great Himalayan Range separates it from China, with which it shares a 470-km border to the north and west. It shares a 605-km border with India to the south and east. It chiefly has a mountainous terrain with some fertile valleys and savanna. Its altitude ranges from the 97-meter Drangme Chhu to the 7,553-meter Kula Kangri I. Deep valleys and high passes characterize its landscape, which is noted for its diversity of vegetation. Only 2 percent of the land is arable. The variations in temperature are correspondingly extreme. The southern plains are hot and humid, the central valleys have cool winters and hot summers, and the Himalayas have severe winters and cool summers. The capital, Thimphu, with a population of 40,000 lies in the central west (*World factbook*, 1999).

1.2 People

The World Bank (1999) estimated the population of Bhutan in 1998 at 759,000. However, other estimates vary between 600,000 and 1.9 million (*World factbook*, 1999).[1] The country has three distinct ethnic groups—Bhote (50 percent), ethnic Nepalese (35 percent), and indigenous or migrant tribes (15 percent) who use three main languages—Dzongkha, Nepalese, and Sharchop, as well as English. Dzongkha is the official language. About 75 percent of the people are Buddhists

Acknowledgments: The author is grateful to Siok Sian Pek, Choy Arnaldo, Renald Lafond, Penny O'Donnell, and Tanja Dreher for their assistance.

[1] The US Census Bureau's International Data Base estimated Bhutan's mid-1999 population at 1.9 million.

and the rest are Hindus. Life expectancy at birth is 60.7 years. The adult literacy rate is 44.2 percent though women's literacy is only 30.1 percent (UNDP, 1999). UNESCO (1999) estimated the literacy rate at 47.3 percent in 2000. The urban population is a mere 7 percent (*Asiaweek*, September 3, 1999).

Buddhism came to Bhutan from Tibet in the 8th century but little is known of the country before the arrival of Shabdrung Ngawang Namgyal, a Tibetan monk of the Drukpa Kagyu sect, in 1616. The Shabdrung ("At whose feet one submits") unified the country over the next 30 years and established the foundations for national government and the Bhutanese identity. Thus, the country's historical, religious, and cultural ties with Tibet are strong. Immigration to Bhutan occurred in two waves in recent history. The most recent occurred after 1959 when China established authority in Tibet (Xizang). Bhutan granted asylum to more than 6,000 Tibetan refugees, many of whom chose to adopt Bhutanese citizenship.

Nepali Bhutanese (Lotshampas), who migrated to the southern lowlands in the late 19th century, became a challenge to the Drukpa (Bhote) identity in recent times. In 1985, the Bhutanese government enacted a citizenship law that retroactively stripped citizenship from Nepalese immigrants who could not document their presence prior to 1958. Nepali Bhutanese initiated the Lotshampas movement in 1990 to retaliate against the Buddhist Drukpa domination of the government, and some 91,000 of them left Bhutan to live in refugee camps run by UNHCR in Nepal (Hutt, 1997). In 1994, the Sharchop, Bhutan's third main ethnic group from the eastern region, also formed a multiethnic Druk National Congress in exile to press for democratic reform (Freedom House, 1999; Hutt, 1996).

Dzongkha, based on the classical Tibetan script, is the language of the power-holding Druks in western Bhutan. It has been a written language for only three decades. The Lotshampas in southern Bhutan speak Nepali dialects, while Sharchop is spoken in the eastern districts. English is the medium of instruction in schools. Dzongkha is a compulsory subject.

1.3 Government and Politics

Bhutan is an absolute monarchy and has maintained sovereignty throughout its history. Until the early 20th century, the country adopted the Tibetan model of government with *Je Khenpo* (chief abbot) as the theocratic head and *Desi* as the temporal leader. With Britain's guidance, Bhutan became a hereditary monarchy on December 17, 1907, a date still celebrated as National Day. King Ugyen Wangchuk, who ascended the throne in 1907, ruled until 1926. The present king is Western-educated Jigme Singye Wangchuk, who ascended the throne in 1972 (Bray, 1993, p. 214).

Bhutan's policy of isolationism ended in 1959 when China established authority over Tibet, thereby creating fears of Chinese imperialism. King Jigme Dorji paved the way for the country's modernization by launching the First Five-Year Plan (1961–66) and establishing long-term friendly relations with India. India helped build Bhutan's first road link from Thimphu to the Indian border in 1962.

Bhutan has no written constitution. The king is the chief of the state and the head of government. In 1953, King Jigme Wangchuk (1952–72) established the unicameral National Assembly (*Tshogdu*), which now has 150 members: 105 elected by village constituencies, 10 by religious bodies, and 35 designated by the king to represent government and other secular interests. Members serve three-years terms (*World factbook*, 1999; Pommaret, 1991). At the executive level, the Council of Ministers (*Lhengye Shungtsog*), first set up in 1968, and the Royal Advisory Council (*Lodoi Tsokde*), first set up in 1965, assist the king. The 10-person advisory council, which is always in session, is the key policy-making forum (*World factbook*, 1999; Sinha, 1994, 1995).

In June 1998, the king conceded two important rights to the National Assembly: First, a two-third majority of the Assembly could force the king to abdicate in favor of the crown prince. Second, the Assembly could elect the majority of the Council of Ministers (BBC World Service, July 2, 1998). However, political parties and trade union activity are still illegal. The Supreme Court of Appeal is the king, who also appoints the High Court judges.

1.4 Economy

Bhutan's economy is one of the world's smallest and least developed. In 1998, its estimated gross domestic product at purchasing power parity was US$ 1.9 billion (*World factbook*, 1999). The per capita GDP at purchasing power parity is US$ 1,570 while the nominal per capita GNP is US$ 450 (*Asiaweek*, December 10, 1999). Bhutan is well off by the standards of other low-income countries because it has zero unemployment, its people are well fed and housed, and 98 percent of its farmers own their land (Pommaret, 1991). Since the early 1980s, a small, foreign-educated elite has taken an increasingly significant role in Bhutan's development process.

Although more than 80 percent of the people are farmers, agriculture, forestry and fishing represent only 46 percent of the GDP—largely the result of hydropower development since 1986. Bhutan's non-agricultural economy centers on government investment and a few large companies. The bulk of Bhutan's external trade is with India (Hutt, 1996). Bhutan's exports in 1998 totaled US$ 0.1 billion, and its reserves stood at US$ 0.3 billion (*Asiaweek*, December 10, 1999).

The First Five-Year Plan (1961–66) marked the beginning of Bhutan's cautious transition from a medieval country to a modern Asian state. Indian aid almost entirely funded the first four plans from 1961–81 (http://www.indiagov.org/foreign/bhutan.htm#plan). The plans prioritized the development of basic infrastructure and, subsequently, they implemented programs in forestry, agriculture, public health, electricity, mines, and education. India is the largest single aid donor, and Indian aid remains predominantly in the form of grants rather than loans (Shah, 1989). In the Eighth Five-Year Plan (1997–2002), 30 percent of the budget comes from bilateral Indian aid and 35 percent from other international agencies (http://www.kuensel.com/archives/archive/eco/280697.html).

2. DEVELOPMENT OF PRESS AND BROADCASTING

2.1 Brief Early History

The mass media in Bhutan did not take root until the second half of the 20th century. The country's isolationism and the high illiteracy level of its small population were not conducive to the growth of mass media. Until the 1950s, the only formal education available in Bhutan was through Buddhist monasteries, where monks continue to use ancient woodblock printing methods to reproduce classical texts.

2.2 Developments since 1945

Bhutan's national newspaper, *Kuensel* (Clarity), began as an official government gazette in 1965 (Dorji, 1994a). Its growth paralleled the modernization program that started with the First Five-Year Plan in 1961. *Kuensel* began first as a bimonthly and then as a weekly publication. "It expanded with the establishment and growth of the Bhutanese civil service as Bhutan launched itself into the process of socio-economic development" (http://www.kuensel.com). In 1986, the information wing of the Bhutanese government converted the bulletin to a serious newspaper with the assistance of the UN Development Program. Produced on an Apple Macintosh-based system, it was established as a 12-page Saturday weekly tabloid in three languages: Dzongkha, English, and Nepali.

The Fifth Five-Year Plan (1981–86) augured well for the development of mass media in the country because it recognized the important role that media could play in national development, self-reliance and, the achievement of economic goals (Servaes, 1994a, 1994b). In addition to *Kuensel*, the government set up the Bhutan Broadcasting Service (BBS), as well as the Development Support Communication Division (DSCD), later renamed the Development Communication Corporation—all under the Ministry of Communications.

In 1993, the Human Rights Organization of Bhutan established the monthly *Bhutan Review* with the backing of the Bhutanese Appeal Movement Coordinating Council. Both are Nepal-based political opposition groups.

2.2.1 Radio

Radio in Bhutan started in 1972 as an amateur one-hour weekly program of the National Youth Association of Bhutan. The association, which used a 40-watt transmitter to broadcast only to the capital, requested the government to manage the station when it was no longer able to maintain its operation on a voluntary basis. The Ministry of Communications took over the station in 1979 to establish the Bhutan Broadcasting Service, the country's sole broadcaster.

Until 1986, the Development Support Communication Division, an audiovisual unit, also engaged in broadcasting. Both BBS and DSCD came under the Ministry of Communications and Tourism where they remained until October 1992, when they became corporatized under the same royal edict that corporatized *Kuensel*.

In 1986, UNESCO gave BBS a 10kW shortwave transmitter that enabled broadcasting to the whole country for the first time (Tshong, 1993). BBS relocated itself in a new India-sponsored studio complex in March 1991, supported by a 50kW shortwave transmitter. It started broadcasting daily for 30 hours per week in four languages: Dzongkha, English, Nepali (Lotsamkha), and Sharchop. A daily FM program in English began broadcasting, in 1987, to Thimphu only, using a 10-watt FM transmitter supplied by UNESCO.

In response to a request for assistance by the government, UNESCO and the Danish International Development Association (DANIDA) implemented a major project between 1989 and 1992 to develop BBS and ensure the continuity of standardized broadcasting practices. With a budget of US$ 1.14 million, the project supplied production and transmission facilities to complement BBS's new studio complex, developed technical operations, field recording, news organization and production, and identified and provided technical and production training (Arnaldo & Krogh, 1991).

The Fifth Five-Year Plan (1981–86) placed particular emphasis on the role of the media in the development process, particularly radio, because of the high level of illiteracy in rural areas, where the BBS audience is strongest. In 1989, fewer than 25 percent of all households had radio receivers (Arnaldo & Krogh, 1991). In 1998, a media survey conducted jointly by Kuensel Corporation and the BBS found that more than 60 percent of the population owned radio receivers (Pek, 1998).

2.2.2 Television

Bhutan had no domestic television service until June 2, 1999. In 1989, the king banned private satellite dishes and ordered the dismantling of the then 28 privately owned dishes. Bhutan received broadcast signals from Bangladesh and India in the lowland areas in the south. UNESCO (1999) estimated that Bhutan had 11,000 TV receivers in use in 1997. The high mountains had provided a natural barrier to trans-border signals but the development of satellite broadcasting has challenged this (Pek, 1998). Geographically, Bhutan is centrally located under STAR Television's AsiaSat 1 and 2 footprints, which cover most of Asia (http://www.STAR TV.com/india/set19/info/history.html).

However, the government saw locally produced audiovisual media both as a means of carrying development messages to the rural population and as a counter move against the rising popularity of foreign films. Audiovisual production began in 1981 with the setting up of the DSCD, which became the DCC in 1992. The DSCD/DCC compiled a library of dramatized development-oriented programs for local consumption and documented cultural, religious, and political events. It also produced training materials mostly for government departmental units and assisted in the formulation of development communication strategies. However, financial concerns and the inadequacy of community viewing centers, resulted in the DCC's demise in 1996. Its small video unit was transferred to BBS (Pek, 1998).

3. THE PRESS

3.1 Policy and Legal Framework

No explicit legal or regulatory framework exists for the media in Bhutan. Until corporatization in 1992, the director of information of the Ministry of Communications administered the media organizations. The government has consistently considered the media as tools for promoting development and has adopted a policy of "cautious modernization," and of weighing the balance between tradition and modernity. Pek (1998) suggests the control of international satellite broadcasts via a "mother" receiver in Bhutan to enable the selection and repackaging of appropriate programs for domestic transmission.

Early five-year plans gave priority to the development of the basic infrastructure and an administrative framework, while the Fifth Five-Year Plan (1981–86) represented a turning point in government policy and emphasized economic growth and self-reliance through decentralization (Pommaret, 1991).

The Sixth Five-Year Plan (1987–92) aimed to foster better communication between government and the people; to disseminate information about government policies and programs; to provide public fora for discussion on issues of interest, and to enable greater understanding of the cultural, social, and economic issues affecting the country. In short, the media were to be at the service of the country, the king and the people (*Tsa Wa Sum*) (Servaes, 1994a). The plan placed supreme importance on national values, including the development of the Tibetan-derived national language Dzongkha, which acquired a written form in the 1960s.

The Seventh Five-Year Plan (1992–97) was the forerunner to the corporatization of the media. Emphasizing private sector development, decentralization, and the participation of people from all regions of the country, it required the information services to help foster individual and community endeavors geared toward national development by implementing the following objectives (Servaes, 1994b, p. 32):

- Dissemination of government policies, strategies, and programs to bring about better communication between the government and the people;
- Provision of a public forum for discussion on issues of interest;
- Promotion of greater understanding of cultural, social, and economic issues throughout the country.

The royal edict of September 18, 1992, which de-linked the media organizations from the government, stated that its purpose was to "facilitate and encourage the professional growth of the Bhutanese media, which must play an important and responsible role in all areas of development. Such a role is especially relevant to the national policy of decentralization, which aims to involve all sections of the

Bhutanese society in the socio-economic and political development of the kingdom" (Dorji, 1994b, p. 3).

The editor-in-chief determines editorial policy at *Kuensel*. Dorji (1994b) says that editorial freedom is determined more by what readers will accept than by the state itself. The introduction of public debates and criticism through the opinion and editorial pages is a very sensitive one for journalists and editors alike, who "are forced to play a responsible role in a society, which is particularly sensitive to this new development" (Dorji, 1994b).

3.2 Financial Aspects: Circulation, Advertising, Marketing Strategies

In 1997, *Kuensel* had a combined circulation of 11,000: English, 8,100; Dzongkha, 2,700; and Nepali, 330 (*The Europa world yearbook*, 1998). A 1998 media survey conducted by *Kuensel* and BBS showed that *Kuensel* had a weekly readership of 120,000 (Pek, 1998), or 46 percent of the literate population. The 1999 circulation was estimated at 15,000 (David, 1999).

Prior to corporatization in 1992, *Kuensel* was funded entirely by the government. Kuensel Corporation negotiated printing equipment and a license with the government; and in its first year as an independent paper, it generated more than 50 percent of its revenue. In 1997, *Kuensel* received 18 percent funding support from the government.[2]

Kuensel earned 40 percent of its 1998 revenue from advertising and 30 percent from color printing services (Interview with Rigden, February 25, 1999). Advertisers are mostly from Bhutan's largest trading partner, India. Sales of newspapers and international advertising are promoted through *Kuensel's* website. Because Bhutan constitutes a small consumer market, economic survival for the Kuensel Corporation is a challenge despite increased literacy and economic growth rates. *Kuensel* benefits from advertising revenue but is challenged by disproportionately high production costs and limited revenue earning potential. All the materials required for print, including paper, ink, offset printers, and computers are imported (Dorji, 1994b).

3.3 Structure and Organization

Kuensel Corporation, an autonomous corporation registered under the Companies Act, is the publisher of *Kuensel*. It is a national paper published weekly in three languages: English, Nepali, and Dzongkha. As an autonomous corporation, *Kuensel* is responsible to a seven-member National Editorial Board formed in October 1992. The board comprises senior representatives from religious, business, educational, and media organizations. The secretary to the Ministry of Finance, the only civil servant on the board, is the chairman.

---

[2] Tenzin Rigden, news editor of *Kuensel*, says that the newspaper has been wholly independent of the government as of 1999 (Interview, February 25, 1999).

Kuensel has an editor-in-chief, three separate language editors, a news editor, and seven reporters, one of whom is at Trashigang in the east and another in Phuentsoling in the south.

No alternative newspapers are published within Bhutan. HUROB publishes the *Bhutan Review*, an anti-government monthly paper that supports the Nepali Bhutanese, from Kathmandu.

3.4 Quality and Popular Press

Although Bhutan has no quality or popular press of its own, high-quality foreign publications are available predominantly in the urban centers. *Kuensel* contains national news, official announcements, and some international news, usually from Reuters, Inter Press Service, and, to a lesser extent, Gemini. It accords the highest priority to the activities of the king. More recently, it introduced an editorial and opinion page, which has encouraged debate and served as a means of providing feedback to the government on important national issues. Consistent with the government's objectives for the media as "a most vital aspect of development," part of *Kuensel's* responsibility is to educate the public on matters of national interest (Dorji, 1994b, p. 34).

Since ethnic conflict erupted with the Nepali Bhutanese along the southern border in the early 1990s, the Bhutanese press has been confronted, for the first time, with the task of reporting dissent. Critics argue that the reporting of the national newspaper has been less than objective because it mirrors the perceptions and values of the indigenous and dominant Drukpa in the capital. Hutt (1997) observed that up to mid-November in 1996, *Kuensel* carried about a dozen stories on armed robberies and assaults in southern Bhutan, branding the culprits as "terrorists" and "illegal immigrants" of Nepalese ethnicity. They included references to an "anti-national camp" in the Jalpaiguri district and arrests of people carrying "explosives and anti-national leaflets" (p. 158).

Kuensel reporters go through three months of basic training with the *Straits Times* in Singapore. Two of the present staff members have had international postgraduate education in journalism. *Kuensel* shares a news pool with the national broadcaster, BBS.

3.5 Distribution and Technology

Dorji (1994a) says: "*Kuensel* is distributed around the country on the public transportation system—a network of buses. In the more remote places, it is carried by messengers and travelers. While the newspaper reaches most towns and valleys on the publication day, it sometimes takes about four days to reach some parts of the country because of the rugged terrain" (p. 33). About one-third of the country's 20 district centers (*dzongkhag*) receive *Kuensel* the same day.

At the commencement of the development process in the early 1960s, Bhutan's facilities for communications and transportation were fairly minimal. The government has given priority to infrastructure development but Bhutan's mountainous terrain has made the building of transport routes extremely costly. Villages are scattered throughout remote regions and about 80 percent of the population has no electricity (Pek, 1998).

Kuensel has received assistance from bilateral donors, particularly Denmark and India. Late in 1996, the Kuensel Corporation began a project to upgrade its printing facilities and to establish a quality color printing system fully functional by 1998. This project, assisted by DANIDA through the Bhutanese government, was a comprehensive configuration of the modern printing press, from the latest color separation technology to quality post-production equipment. In July, 1999, *Kuensel* published its first color edition—"a hefty 100 pages crammed with ads" (David, 1999, p. 46).

4. BROADCASTING

4.1 Policy and Legal Framework

The provisions contained in the more recent five-year plans, outlined in the policy and legal framework for the press (Section 3.1), also pertain to the broadcast media. BBS is also responsible to the seven-member National Editorial Board. Freedom House (Sussman, 1999) rated the Bhutan media "not free" giving them a restriction score of 80 out of 100. On the criterion of laws and regulations that influence media content, broadcasting scored the maximum, 15 (compared to print's 14); on political pressures and controls on media content, again broadcasting scored the maximum, 15 (compared to print's 14); on economic influences over media content, broadcasting scored 10 out of 15 (compared to print's 8); and on repressive actions, broadcasting scored zero out of 5 (compared to print's 4).

The South Asian Media Association sources indicate that the BBS is in the process of developing or revising its editorial policy and a code of ethics. According to SAMA, the objectives of broadcasting as outlined in the Seventh Five-Year Plan policy document may no longer be binding (Anonymous, 1995).

4.2 Structure and Organization

4.2.1 Radio

BBS, the only broadcaster in Bhutan, transmits 30 hours of programs per week nationally by shortwave (on 5030/6030/9615kHz) in four languages: Dzongkha, English, Nepali (Lotsamkha), and Sharchop. A daily FM program in English broadcasts to the capital Thimphu on 96/98MHz.

A chairman heads BBS. An executive director is responsible for all operations of BBS, followed by directors of technical operations, programming, and news.

For administrative communications, 52 radio outlets were in use in 1994. Of these, 34 were for internal communications (to which the public had access), and three were external stations serving Bhutan House at Kalimpong and the Bhutanese diplomatic missions in India and Bangladesh. A further 11 stations are for hydrological and meteorological purposes (*The Europa world yearbook*, 1998, p. 631).

4.2.2 Television

Bhutan's first domestic TV station began transmission on June 2, 1999. In April 1998, the king announced at the presentation of satellite dishes to three tertiary institutions that the government would introduce television when the country was ready to produce its own programs. In June 1998, the king, himself a soccer fan, permitted the installation of a large screen at the sports ground in Thimphu for fans to watch the World Cup via Indian television. However, in 1989, a royal decree banned satellite dishes in the interest of "cultural sustainability."

In the absence of television, urban Bhutanese who owned videocassette recorders and monitors watched rented foreign movies. Video shops trading in foreign films flourish and have been very popular since the 1980s. Concern exists that the popularity of foreign films may undermine traditional Bhutanese values and culture. Pirated videos are imported from Thailand and India. Hindi movies from India and Kung Fu movies from Hong Kong are in great demand, particularly among Indian workers in Bhutan. Pornography is banned but available. Pek (1998) estimated that 10 percent of Bhutan's urban population watches video every day.

4.3 Program Policies

4.3.1 Radio

Guidelines for BBS radio programs and news approved in May 1992 (Servaes, 1994a, p. 118) state that no program shall:

- denigrate any religious faith;
- disregard the feelings of listeners;
- contain material amounting to contempt of court;
- include criticism of friendly countries;
- contain obscene or defamatory material;
- incite any person to violence;
- simulate news or events in such a way as to mislead or alarm listeners;
- present as desirable the use of intoxicating liquor, smoking, and narcotics, except under medical direction;
- include the use of horror for its own sake; and
- contain material amounting to the denigration of *Tsa Wa Sum* (country, king, and people).

BBS programs mainly comprise news and current affairs, cultural programs, and government-agency sponsored programs relating to specific areas such as education, health, and environment, which serve to broadcast development messages to rural areas. A scarcity of trained journalists throughout the country is partially overcome by close cooperation with *Kuensel*. BBS has a network of stringers in the districts, but their contributions are few and contain mainly official news (Pek, 1998). International news is mainly monitored from BBC World service, All India Radio, and Radio Nepal (Servaes, 1994b).

4.4 Ownership and Financing

Bhutan Broadcasting Service, which became an autonomous corporation in 1992, is registered under the Companies Act (Tshong, 1993). Even after corporatization, BBS continues to rely wholly on government subsidy for its operation (Pek, interview, October 26, 1998). Bhutan has not imposed license fees on receivers. The government closed the DCC, the audiovisual unit, in 1992 because of financial problems.

Unlike *Kuensel*, which benefits from advertising revenue and the introduction of ancillary commercial printing to top up its income, BBS has continuing difficulty in creating revenue and receives no more than 3 percent of its revenue from advertising (Dasho Yeshe Zimba, interview, November 8, 1998). Private-sector advertising on BBS is virtually non-existent. The financial stresses experienced by BBS since corporatization have contributed to an already difficult set of challenges for a young national broadcaster seeking to produce programs for a national audience in four languages.

5. NEW ELECTRONIC MEDIA

5.1 Internet and On-line Media

DrukNet, the first Internet service provider in Bhutan, began operating on June 2, 1999, simultaneously with the beginning of domestic television. It expects to pick up 500 subscribers within a year, mostly from among the 5,000 Thimphu residents who have telephone connections (David, 1999). The July 1999 Internet Software Consortium survey showed 68 Internet hosts in Bhutan. The Division of Telecom of the Ministry of Communication started DrukNet, which also serves as Bhutan's Network Information Center (BTNIC), with the assistance of Canada's International Development Research Center. However, Bhutanese publications were using the Web well before DrukNet. With more than a decade of news publishing expertise, international education, and a proactive strategy for financial survival following corporatization, Kuensel Corporation began publishing an on-line edition of its newspaper in 1997 through Cyberville Technologies in Singapore. In 1999, the website was hosted from Bhutan (http://www.kuensel.com.bt). By June 1998, the site was getting 55,000 hits per month, according to *Kuensel* journalist Thuji Lhamu (Interview, October 11, 1998).

By 1998, Bhutan had approximately 4,000 personal computers, about 80 percent of which were located in Thimphu (Pan Asia Networking, 1998). Until late 1998,

Bhutan did not have direct Internet access. However, the UNDP had provided some e-mail assistance to the media organizations through its own network.

In 1998, the Division of Telecommunications, with IDRC assistance, built a national Intranet infrastructure to provide international e-mail access (Pan Asia Networking, 1998). The project provided a national Intranet comprising a central server and gateway point in the capital, Thimphu, as well as local dial-up access in Phuentsholing in the south and Trashigang in eastern Bhutan. Phuentsholing was selected as a "point of presence" because of the large business community, and Trashigang because it is the furthest point of telecommunications in the east that would also benefit Sherubtse College in Kanglung.

At the domestic level, Intranet services include e-mail, conferencing, and document handling based on World Wide Web technology. The international e-mail gateway is accessible to users of the national Intranet service. It is likely that community access centers to the networking facilities will be established, similar to the public communications offices, which already offer public access to STD, ISD, and fax services (Pan Asia Netwroking, 1998).

5.2 Telecommunications Infrastructure

The number of mainline telephones in Bhutan increased at a compound annual growth rate of more than 19 percent from 1,871 in 1990 to 6,430 in 1997—a telephone density of 1.04 per 100 people or 2.4 per 100 households. In 1998, ITU estimated the number of mainline telephones at 10,400, a density of 1.64 per 100 people. More than 58 percent of the telephones were in Thimphu, which had a teledensity of 17.68. Almost 79 percent of the telephones were digital (ITU, 1999).

The Division of Telecommunications, under the Ministry of Communications, operates and maintains all telecommunication services in Bhutan. Although discussions have taken place on making the division a public corporation, procedures for its implementation are unlikely to be ready for a couple of years.

Until recently, it was impossible to communicate from one region of Bhutan to another because the telecommunication network had three independent networks for the western, central, and eastern regions. A digital telecommunication network linking all urban centers with the 20 districts (*dzongkhag*) serves Bhutan, enabling reliable modem connections at 28,800bps.

The upgrading and modernization of telecommunication services began in 1989–90 with the installation of a satellite earth station and an international gateway switch in Thimphu. Japan provided the impetus to modernize the national network. In 1990, ITU and UNDP helped Bhutan prepare a telecommunication master plan and a comprehensive strategy for the development of a unified telecommunication network. The backbone network, completed in 1998, consists of 34 Mbs/s digital microwave radio transmission links and digital switching centers (Pan Asia Networking, 1998).

The Division of Telecommunications has direct links and traffic transit arrangements with Singapore Telecommunications, British Telecommunications, and

KDD (Japan) through the Intelsat satellite network. In addition, the Division of Telecommunications also has direct voice grade circuits to India through an analog microwave transmission link (Pan Asia Networking, 1998).

No restrictions exist on the use of fax machines, modems, and other standard telephone equipment.

6. POLICY TRENDS FOR PRESS AND BROADCASTING

Emphasis on private sector development in the Seventh Five-Year Plan (1992–97) paved the way for the privatization of the media organization by a royal edict dated September 18, 1992. The edict states:

> [It] is the aim of the government to facilitate and encourage the professional growth of the media in all areas of national development, in line with the national decentralization policy, ...which aims to involve all sections of the Bhutanese society in the socio-economic and political development of the kingdom." (Cited in Tshong, 1993)

Consistent with world trends in public broadcasting, as well as the government's stated aims of achieving economic growth, the move to corporatize the media sector also relieved the government of the financial burden of maintaining organizations which, at the time of the edict, were not producing revenue. The Eighth Five-Year Plan (1997–2002) refines the objectives of the seventh plan (above) with the addition of "the preservation and promotion of cultural and traditional values, self reliance, national security, balanced development, institutional strengthening, and human resource development, privatization, and private sector development" (RGOB Planning Commission 1996, cited in Pek, 1998).

Hutt (1996, p. 208) notes the intensifying of an ethnic nationalism emerging in the policy making of the 1980s, when it became apparent that Bhutan could no longer afford to consist of a northern and a southern sector whose populations lived in separate cultural spheres. The implementation of government policies derived from traditions of the north has tended to fuel the conflict in the south. Exposure to growing international criticism of the refugee problem places increasing pressure on the media in Bhutan to objectively report and analyze the conflict.

The king's approach to the ethnic issue has been conciliatory. Nevertheless, dissent and the reporting of dissent are difficult in a country such as Bhutan, where deference to authority, viewed from a Western perspective, can be seen as endemic. From the perspective of a very traditional society in a mountain kingdom, respect for royalty and the authority associated with it is paramount. Hutt (1993) suggests that the absence of an information culture or a tradition of literary dissent in Bhutan is a contributing factor.

The government of Bhutan showed little commitment in 1998 to starting a domestic television service. Creating, regulating, and delivering TV content suitable for local consumption appears to be a daunting task. The king has said, "We don't want our youth to confuse Westernization with modernization" (Cited in Pek, 1998, p. 61). In 1998, about 80 percent of the people did not have electricity, and the average farmer could not afford a television set.

Having whetted the appetite of the urban Bhutanese for global media transmissions, it will be difficult to contain the rising demand for foreign media, particularly from western-educated urban elites. Satellite restrictions are becoming more difficult to enforce. Phuentsholing, on the southwestern border with India, receives trans-border broadcasts. Also, the installation of dish antennas in neighboring Jaigoan, the supply route for all imports from India, has had an influence on the Bhutanese along the border. Pek (1998) says the explosion of international satellite broadcasting in recent years has led Bhutan to accept the inevitability of such an "invasion" (p. 56), and she predicts that television will become available, even in remote areas, in the next few years.

The Government of India continues its support for BBS through in-government training in broadcast journalism with All India Radio. DANIDA also helped with further training of journalists, radio technicians, and management. Pek (1998) says BBS's biggest challenge is to expand its shortwave broadcast time to exceed 30 hours per week—a challenge hampered by long delays in technical troubleshooting resulting from a shortage of local technical expertise and the need to import all replacement parts, usually from Europe.

The physical difficulties facing the development of a communications infrastructure in Bhutan are the mountainous terrain, poor roads, and a population which is scattered and remote. Shortwave signals and electricity supply are frequently disrupted in poor weather. In addition, the provision of aid and technical specifications originating from more than one donor country has added to the complexity of the development and maintenance of the technologically dependent radio broadcasting in Bhutan. The task of negotiating, assessing, and overcoming local conditions confronts the Bhutanese and aid agencies alike.

The government is committed to linking the 196 village blocks (geog) to the telecommunications network within the current five-year plan (Pek, 1998).

7. MAIN ISSUES

● A media strategy to accommodate ethnic differences

The emergence of pro-democracy campaigns in the east, and most notably the south, present the need for the development of a media strategy that accommodates and values difference within an ethnically diverse population. The impact that broad-based data services will have on the expression of public opinion, discussion, and debate of national issue is yet to be seen, but it's likely that the steady increase of one-to-one and one-to-many communications throughout the country will serve to strengthen Bhutan's inter-regional communications.

● Satellite broadcasting

Once buffered between two giants, India and China, a third now looms in the form of STAR Television's AsiaSat 1 and 2 footprints. Western-educated urban Bhutanese yearn for foreign media broadcasts and the government recognizes the benefits that the country could derive from satellite broadcasting, particularly for education. Despite government policies of balanced development, there continues to be a marked discrepancy between modern services available in rural and urban Bhutan. Bhutan's primary challenge is to develop and implement a broadcasting policy framework that will allow it to access the benefits of satellite technology, and also allow for the production and consumption of appropriate programming that supports Bhutan's identity, not as a feudal kingdom but as a distinctly Bhutanese, modern Asian state.

8. STATISTICS

Table 1
General Profile

Exchange rate (September 1999)	US$ 1 = 43.52 Ngultrum (on par with Indian Rupee)*
Population (1999)	Estimates vary from 618,000 to 1.9 million
Population density	Estimates vary from 13.3 to 31 per sq km
Nominal GNP per capita	US$ 435
Adult literacy	44.2 percent
HDI rank	145 out of 174
Urban population	7 percent
Geographical size	46,500 sq km

Source: *Asiaweek*, September 3, 1999; *World factbook*, 1999; UNDP, 1999; * OANDA Historical Currency Table [On-line]. Available: (http://www.oanda.com/converter/cc_table?lang=en).

Table 2
Estimated Mass Media Penetration

	Radio receivers		TV receivers		Daily newspapers		
	Number ('000)	Per 100 people	Number ('000)	Per 100 people	Number	Circ'n	Per 100 people
1980	7	0.50	–	–	–	–	–
1985	18	1.20	–	–	–	–	–
1990	24	1.50	–	–	–	–	–
1995	30	1.60	10	0.54	–	–	–
1996	35	1.80	10	0.55	–	–	–
1997	37	1.90	11	0.55	–	–	–
1998			12*	1.90*			

Source: UNESCO, 1999; * ITU, 1999.

9. USEFUL ADDRESSES

Ministry of Communications
Deputy Minister: Dasho Leki Dorji
Tashichhodzong, POB 278
Thimphu, Bhutan.
Telephone: +975.2.22567
Fax: +975.2.22184

Division of Telecommunications
Director: Sangey Tenzin
PAN-Bhutan Project Leader: Thinley Dorji
Telephone: +975.2.22346
Fax: +975.2.24312/22098

Kuensel
Editor-in-chief: Kinley Dorji
Editors: R.N. Mishra (Nepali); Tenzin Rigden (English); Mindu Dorji (Dzongkha)
PO Box 204, Thimphu, Bhutan
Telephone: +975.2.24688/22483
Fax: +975.2.22975
E-mail: kuensel@nono.undp.org
URL: http://www.kuensel.com

Bhutan Broadcasting Service
Chairman: Dasho Yeshe Zimba
Executive Director: Sonam Tshong
PO Box 101, Thimphu, Bhutan.
Telephone: +975.2.23071
Fax: +975.2.23073

The Bhutan Review
PO Box 172, Patan Dhoka,
Lalitpur, Kathmandu, Nepal.
Fax: +977.1.523819

10. REFERENCES

Anonymous. (1995, December 27). Continuing evolution of the broadcasting media in Bhutan: The case of Bhutan Broadcasting Service. *SAMA Journal, 1*, 40–45.

Arnaldo, C., & Krogh, T. (1991). *Mid-term tripartite review of development of Bhutan Broadcasting Service*. Paris: UNESCO.

Bray, J. (1993, November). Bhutan: The dilemmas of a small state. *World Today*, pp. 213–216.

David, A. (1999, September 3). Shangri-La wake-up call. *Asiaweek, 25* (35), pp. 44–47.

Dorji, K. (1994a). Bhutan: Media's unique role. In *Press systems in SAARC* (pp. 31–34). Singapore: AMIC.

Dorji, K. (1994b, March) *Bhutan*. Paper presented at AMIC seminar on media and pluralism in South Asia, Kathmandu, Nepal.

Europa world yearbook, The. (1998). London: Europa Publications.

Freedom House Survey Team. (1999). *Freedom in the world: The annual survey of political rights and civil liberties, 1998–1999*. New York: Freedom House.

Hutt, M. (1993). Refugees from Shangrila. *Index on Censorship, 22* (4), 9–14.

Hutt, M. (1996). Bhutan in 1995: Weathering the storm. *Asian Survey, 36* (2), 204–208.

Hutt, M. (1997). Bhutan in 1996: Continuing stress. *Asian Survey, 37* (2), 155–159.

ITU (International Telecommunication Union). (1999). *World telecommunication development report*. Geneva: ITU.

Pan Asia Networking. (1998). *PAN-Bhutan proposal* [On-line]. Available: (http://www.PanAsia. org.sg/nserv/bt/netbt1.htm).

Pek, S.S. (1998). *The establishment of television in a developing nation: Lessons for Bhutan.* Unpublished master's thesis, Macquarie University, Sydney.

Pommaret, F. (1991). *Introduction to Bhutan.* Hong Kong: The Guidebook Co.

Servaes, J. (1994a). Broadcasting in Bhutan: Between tradition and modernization. *Asian Journal of Communication, 4* (1), 111–133.

Servaes, J. (1994b). Bhutan: The dragon awakes to 'modern' broadcasting. *Media Development, 41* (3), 31–34.

Shah, S. (1989), Developing Bhutan's economy. *Asian Survey, 29* (8), 816–831.

Sinha, A.C. (1994). Bhutan in 1993: Continuing ethnic stalemate. *Asian Survey, 34* (2), 181–184.

Sinha, A.C. (1995). Bhutan in 1994: Will the ethnic conflict be resolved? *Asian Survey, 35* (2), 166–170.

Sussman, L.R. (1999). *Press freedom 1999: News of the century.* New York: Freedom House.

Tshong, S. (1993, October). *Bhutan.* Paper presented at AMIC Seminar on Legal and Regulatory Aspects of Satellite Broadcasting, New Delhi, India.

UNDP (United Nations Development Program). (1999). *Human development report.* New York: Oxford University Press.

UNESCO (United Nations Educational, Scientific and Cultural Organization). (1999). *Statistical yearbook.* Paris: UNESCO.

World Bank (1999). *Bhutan at a glance* [On-line]. Available: (http://www.worldbank.org/).

World factbook. (1999). Washington, DC: CIA [On-line]. Available: (http://www.odci.gov/cia/ publications/factbook/bt.html).

◆

3

INDIA

K. Viswanath & Kavita Karan

1. NATIONAL PROFILE

1.1 Geography

The seventh largest country in the world, constituting an area of 3.3 million sq km, India is well marked off from the rest of Asia by mountains and the sea. Bounded by the great Himalayas in the north, it stretches southwards and tapers off into the Indian Ocean at the Tropic of Cancer with the Bay of Bengal on the east and the Arabian Sea on the west. Countries that have a common border with India are Pakistan to the northwest; China, Bhutan, and Nepal to the north; and Myanmar and Bangladesh to the east. Sri Lanka is at the southern tip, separated from India by the narrow Palk Strait. India, which dominates the South Asian subcontinent, has a tropical monsoon-type climate. The climatic conditions from north to south, however, can vary widely. It has a rich and varied vegetation, and flora and fauna, which only a few countries of comparable size possess.

1.2 People

The United States Census Bureau's International Data Base estimated India's mid-1999 population at 1,000.8 million.[1] Of this total, 74 percent is rural. India has about 16 percent of the world's population, though it covers only 2.4 percent of the world's landmass. Thus, it has a very high population density: 337 people per sq km. At least 10 districts have a density of more than 2,000 people per sq km.

Acknowledgments: The authors are grateful to Professor Shelton A. Gunaratne and Bob Johnson for their help in writing this paper.

[1] *Asiaweek* (December 17, 1999) has placed India's current population at 989.2 million. The demographic summary data in the US Census Bureau's International Data Base is available: (http://www.census.gov/cgi-bin/ipc/idbsum).

Twelve cities have a population of more than a million people.[2] The country's overall literacy rate is 53.5 percent though the rate varies with variables such as gender and region. For example, men (67 percent) are more literate than women (39 percent), except in the southwestern state of Kerala, which has the highest literacy rate in the country (see Table 1). The urban population is more literate than the rural. Life expectancy at birth is 62.9 years.

Although Article 343 of India's 1950 Constitution specifies Hindi (in Devanagari script) as the "official language of the Union," it also allows for the continued use of English "for all official purposes of the Union" under parliamentary law. English is the principal language of commerce. The Eighth Schedule of the Constitution recognizes 14 other major languages: Assamese, Bengali, Gujarati, Kannada, Kashmiri, Malayalam, Marathi, Oriya, Punjabi, Sanskrit, Sindhi, Tamil, Telugu, and Urdu. These, along with Hindustani, constitute India's 17 major languages. People also speak 844 dialects.[3] At least six major religions have substantial followings. Hindus constitute 82 percent of the population. Muslims make up about 12 percent, which means that India has the third largest Muslim population in the world, next only to Indonesia and Bangladesh. Other religions include Christianity (2.4 percent), Sikhism (2 percent), Buddhism (0.7 percent), Jainism (0.4 percent), and others (0.4 percent), including Zoroastrianism (*World factbook*, 1999).

Indians often boast of a civilization dating back to the great pre-Christian civilizations of Harappa and Mohenjodaro (Basham, 1959). For several reasons, the South Asian subcontinent has attracted foreign friends and foes. Its strategic location between west Asia and east Asia, its well-developed natural seaports, its rich natural resources, and its highly evolved culture attracted traders and invaders from the West. Successive generations of visitors and invaders have both contributed to and been absorbed into the resilient Hindu culture. They have left behind an admixture of Eastern and Western cultures that give India the diversity that characterizes it today.

1.3 Government and Politics

India attained independence on August 15, 1947. It chose to become a republic on January 26, 1950. The country is officially a "sovereign socialist secular democratic republic"—a union of 26 states and six union territories—with a parliamentary system of government. Though the president is the titular head of the state, the real power lies with the prime minister and the council of ministers who are members

---

[2] The data in this chapter with no specific citation are from *India 1998*, an annual reference published by the Ministry of Information and Broadcasting, Government of India. Literacy data are from UNDP, 1999.

[3] India: country profile (http://www.meadev.gov.in/info/profile/intro.htm). No consensus exists on the number of major languages and dialects. The *India Book 1994–95* lists 325 recognized Indian languages (http://www.sanyal.com/india/indlang.html). The *World factbook*, 1999, mentions 24 major languages, each spoken by more than a million people.

of parliament. The states have a parallel system with a governor as the titular head, and a chief minister and his cabinet exercising actual power.

The national legislature is bicameral. It consists of the *Rajya Sabha* (Council of States) and the *Lok Sabha* (House of People). The *Rajya Sabha* has 245 members of whom 233 are elected by the legislative bodies of the states, and 12 are nominated by the president from among distinguished citizens. One-third of its membership retires every two years. The 545-seat *Lok Sabha*, except for two nominated seats, has its members directly elected on the basis of adult suffrage. Elections are held every five years, unless parliament is dissolved earlier.

1.4 Economy

India's gross domestic product (GDP) at purchasing power parity currently stands at US$ 1,710 billion, with the corresponding per capita GDP at US$ 1,760. However, the nominal per capita gross national product (GNP) stands at US$ 436 (*Asiaweek*, December 17, 1999). India once had a "mixed economy," which meant state involvement and investment in major economic enterprises. From the early 1990s onwards, the placement of the public sector at the "commanding heights" of the economy has come into question. A resurgence of private-sector initiatives has taken place in almost all sectors of the economy, including mass communications. Another feature of India's economy is that even though two-thirds of the country's workforce is employed in the agricultural sector, agriculture generates only one-third of the country's income. Thus India is more complex and diverse than many other nations. It is the 10th most industrialised country in the world and the sixth country in the world to have ventured into outer space. It has also attained self-sufficiency in agricultural production.

The complex social changes in India are reflected in a variety of developmental stages, ranging from highly industrialized and technologically advanced conditions to highly traditional and barely developed communities where even the "minimum" amenities of the 20th century are hardly present. Thus, Indian society is a "palimpsest" (Bell, 1976) where 20th century developments are overlaid on "traditional" systems and cultures.

2. DEVELOPMENT OF PRESS AND BROADCASTING

2.1 Brief Early History

2.1.1 Print Media

The British were the last set of invaders whose colonization left a mark on India's polity, culture, and industry. British rule, starting in the 18th century, had two significant influences germane to the development of the country's mass media.

First, they introduced India to the English language, which became the primary language of commerce; second, a British citizen, James Augustus Hicky, started the early press; and it was the British again who started the system of broadcasting.

A struggle between two groups with competing ideologies and goals marks the history of the press in India (Raman, 1995): one group engaged in a continuing struggle against authority, whether British or Indian, to gain and maintain independence; and the other was characterized by loyalty to the regime in power. Barring a few exceptions, Englishmen started newspapers to support the British Empire, while crusading Indians started their own newspapers to promote social, religious, educational, and political reforms.

Christian missionaries brought the first printing presses to India in the 15th and 16th centuries to publish religious literature. Hicky, a Briton, published the first newspaper, the *Bengal Gazette*, on January 29, 1780, amidst much controversy. Some called it a scandal sheet even as it professed its independence. Other papers followed, but none survived long for either economic or political reasons (Kumar, 1981).

Four stages distinguish the development of the press in India (Ram, 1989). The first stage, 1818–67, marked the efforts of social reformer Raja Ram Mohun Roy, and the struggle against censorship, harassment, deportation, and persecution. Roy, a literate and urban intellectual, used his publications—*Sambad Kaumudi, Mirut ul Akhbar, Brahminical Magazine*, and others—to reform Hindu society. He attacked social practices such as *Sati*, which he rightly considered evil. Roy inspired Gangadhar Bhattacharjee to found the short-lived *Bengal Gazette*, the first Indian-owned English-language daily, in 1816 (Parthasarathy, 1989).

Calcutta (Bengal) and Mumbai (Maharashtra) were the active centers of the Indian press. The Indian-language press was slower to emerge in other parts of India. Indians owned a few newspapers during this stage. Robert Knight founded *The Times of India* in 1861 through a merger of three papers.[4] The nationalist *Indu Prakash* also appeared in 1861. The largely British-owned press was often critical of the Indians. During the 1857 Indian Mutiny, often called the "first war of Indian independence," the British-owned press attacked the Indian establishment in almost "racial" overtones (Parthasarathy, 1989). The bias of the British-owned press set the scene for the next stage.

The second stage, 1867–1918, marked the emergence of a press deeply involved in the nationalist struggle against the British Raj, despite competition from those supporting the colonial regime. Well-known Indian nationalists like Bal Gangadhar Tilak, Mahadev Govind Ranade, Dadabhai Naoroji, and others, used the press as a pulpit to advocate reforms and protest against colonial injustices. Among the prominent newspapers that took up cudgels were *Indu Prakash, Kesari* (circa 1878), and *Mahratta*. The other major developments included the laying of the

---

[4] The precursor to the *Times, The Bombay Times and Journal of Commerce*, first appeared in 1838.

telegraph lines and the emergence of prominent Indian newspapers like Calcutta's *Amrita Bazar Patrika* in 1868; Calcutta's *Statesman*, which Robert Knight founded in 1875; and Chennai's *The Hindu*, which was founded by G. Subramania Aiyer in 1878. Rudyard Kipling, born in Bombay, acquired his journalistic skills at the *Civil and Military Gazette*, founded in Lahore (now in Pakistan) in 1872, and subsequently, at the *Pioneer* in Allahabad. During this stage, reform-minded writers used the press to attack Hindu practices such as child marriage; they also advocated reforms such as widow remarriage and abolition of caste.

The government enacted the 1878 Vernacular Press Act to prevent the Indian-language press from being critical of the British rule, thereby engendering widespread opposition both in India and Britain. The nationalist press forged ahead to sow the seeds of the struggle for independence. The Indian National Congress, founded in 1885, was led by nationalists like Surendranath Banarjee, Bipin Chandra Pal, G. Subramania Aiyer, Motilal Gosh, Narendranath Sen, Bal Gangadhar Tilak, and Dadabhai Naoroji, many of whom were also active in journalism. The colonial government's repression of the press became frequent and vehement.

The third stage, 1919–36, marked the Indian newspapers' close alignment with the struggle for independence. Prominent leaders of the independence movement, including Mahatma Gandhi, owned or edited newspapers to advance their ideas. Gandhi was involved with *Young India* (1919), *Harijan* (1932), and the Gujarati weekly *Navjivan* (circa 1920). As a journalist, Gandhi advocated free expression of ideas and mobilized the people to articulate their sentiments. In Madras, T. Prakasam started the *Swarajya* in 1922 to support the nationalist struggle for independence. During its decade of existence, *Swarajya* became the training ground for many writers such as Khasa Subba Rao who went on to become a prominent figure in journalism. The New Delhi-based *The Hindustan Times*, an English newspaper, was founded in 1923 with the support of prominent Congress leaders, including Jawaharlal Nehru and his father, Motilal Nehru. It too drew the ire of the colonial government because it supported the nationalist movement.

The fourth stage, 1937–47, was the pre-independence decade when the press became increasingly professional and assertive. The press was concerned not only with the freedom struggle but also with practical matters like newsprint availability and the modernizing of printing machinery. The onset of World War II and the intensification of the freedom movement made this period quite turbulent. Nationalist leaders were divided on whether to support Britain unconditionally during the war, or to make a conditional offer of support. This debate was played out in both the nationalist and the "moderate press." The government's endeavor to place restrictions on the press was one reason for the formation of the All India Newspaper Editors Conference in 1940. Several newspapers closed their operations in 1942 in support of Gandhi's "Quit India" movement.

Jawaharlal Nehru, the first prime minister of independent India, founded the *National Herald* (1938) to advance the nationalist cause. With the start of World War II in 1939, newspapers such as the *Herald* came under increasing scrutiny by the imperial government, which repeatedly censored the content of the newspaper, and imposed fines and jail sentences on journalists, including Nehru. The *Herald* ceased publication in 1942 at the beginning of the Quit India Movement, but reappeared in 1945. Throughout this stage, the Indian press worked closely with the nationalist movement until the attainment of independence. (For other historical details, see Eapen, 1971, 1982; Natarajan, 1962; and Wolseley, 1971.)

2.1.2 Broadcasting

Radio broadcasting in India started during British colonial rule. The authorities allowed the establishment of an amateur radio club in 1924 in Madras. In 1927, the Indian Broadcasting Co., a private operator, started radio in Bombay and Calcutta. Even after the beginning of the regular broadcasting service, amateur clubs continued for a while. The entrepreneurship of amateur clubs in radio broadcasting foreshadowed what was to happen in the private TV arena today. Just as amateur radio clubs forced the government to build the broadcasting system, almost seven decades later, private cable operators forced the government to partially privatize Indian television (see Section 4.2.4).

The colonial government took over radio broadcasting in 1930 and named it the Indian State Broadcasting Service (ISBS). In 1936, the name changed to All India Radio (AIR) or *Akashvani* (Awasthy, 1978; Luthra, 1986). Radio stations began sprouting in both colonial India and in the princely states of Hyderabad, Travancore, Baroda, Mysore (which contributed the name *Akashvani*), Trivandrum, and Aurangabad. The pre- and post-Independence governments took action to control these stations, which often supported anti-government positions. The early history of ISBS was not smooth as it faced extinction several times because of financial difficulties. It, however, acquired firm government support in 1934, with the appointment of P.G. Edmunds as the first controller of broadcasting (Awasthy, 1978). By the time India attained Independence (1947), almost all major cities—including Delhi, Mumbai, Calcutta, Chennai, Lucknow, Peshawar (now in Pakistan), and Dhaka (now in Bangladesh)—had at least a semblance of a broadcasting service.

As some scholars (for example, Lee, 1980; Katz & Wedell, 1973) have pointed out, in many colonies radio served as an extended arm of the colonial government to enable social and state control. This was not dissimilar to the Indian experience, especially during World War II. Radio became an important tool for dissemination of information, as well as for propaganda. In fact, from the very beginning, the colonial government insisted that programs should be "non-political" in nature (Luthra, 1986, p. 23). The government was sensitive to the potential of radio in the nationalist struggle and gave itself the power to censor the transmission of information. The issue of control—through licensing or institutional mechanisms such as censorship, advisory boards, or departmental supervision—became an enduring feature that plagued the medium for decades until *Akashvani* eventually became a part of an autonomous organization in 1997 (see Section 4.1).

2.2 Developments since 1947

2.2.1 Print Media

The post-Independence press was originally sympathetic to the government. It offered cautious support to the government's efforts at building the nation. The government appointed the 1952 and the 1977 press commissions (see Section 3.1.3.1) to inquire into the press laws and other developments affecting the press and its operations. The Press Council was established in 1965 (see Section 3.1.3.2).

The country, as well as the press, faced a traumatic development in June 1975 when Prime Minister Indira Gandhi declared a political emergency, suspended civil rights, and imposed restrictions on free speech and the press. During the 19-month long Emergency, her government, among other acts, detained 253 journalists, expelled seven foreign correspondents, muzzled the press, and dissolved the Press Council (Lent, 1982, p. 400). This period also witnessed an ineffective yet spirited struggle by some in the press.

After the Emergency, the press evolved into a highly professional, market-oriented business. It introduced new technologies, designs, and magazines, and a new style of journalism. For example, newspapers and magazines use the latest technology in printing and production. They use computerized typesetting equipment (Aggarwal, 1988) and print facsimile editions. Many also have websites. Sensing changes in the market, several leading Indian newspapers and media companies have diversified along three broad trajectories. A newspaper like *The Indian Express* is an exemplar of geographical diversification. It publishes 19 different editions with common national news, but tailors the local news to each particular region. A second type of diversification is reflected in the offer of specialized content, focusing on readers with different topical interests. *The Hindu*, for example, publishes supplements throughout the week on different subjects: science, technology and engineering, education, sports, gardening, entertainment, and so on. A consequence of segmentation, of course, is that it also attracts advertising interested in that target audience. A third type of diversification occurs when media companies enjoy cross-media ownership. Thus, companies such as Ushodaya Publications, publishers of the Telugu daily *Eenadu*, also entered the business of cable television by starting *Eenadu TV* (see Section 4.2.3).

The mood of specialization characteristic of the post-emergency era also affected the booming magazine industry. Major Indian magazines in different languages targeted different kinds of audiences and specialized in topics such as women, children, finance, health, films, and business (see Section 3.4).

2.2.2 Broadcasting

Soon after the country's independence in 1947, AIR became an important communication vehicle to promote government-directed policies and to serve what the ruling regimes considered vital developmental goals of the nation. Along with

Doordarshan (the Indian TV), it focused, for example, on producing programs for the country's rural audience with content that was expected to be of interest to them, like agriculture, adult literacy, and folk music, among other things. Further, priority health issues such as family planning programs received prominent coverage and production time (see Viswanath, 1982).[5]

Doordarshan started as an experiment in 1959 in New Delhi, primarily for educational purposes, with All India Radio providing its programming. Regular broadcasting on a very small scale started in 1965 in New Delhi and spread to fewer than a dozen other cities in the next decade.

The growth of the medium was stalled, in stark contrast to radio, until 1982. A major reason behind the limited expansion lay in a view widely held by the government that television was to be used for guided social change. Two forces had a major impact on the expansion of the medium. One came in 1975–76, when the Indian Space Research Organization (ISRO) borrowed a satellite from the US National Aeronautics and Space Administration (NASA) to televise programs to about 2,400 villages in different parts of India. "Community television sets" placed in public settings allowed rural audiences to gather, watch, and even discuss the programs. This effort by the Satellite Instructional Television Experiment, popularly called SITE, to use the medium in promoting guided social change might have had an impact on subsequent policy-making (Agrawal, 1978).[6] The experiment demonstrated the viability of TV production in multiple languages and the viewers' receptiveness to television.

The second source of influence was the 1982 Asian Games in New Delhi. Color television was introduced during the games. The expansion of the medium started from that point on as evident from the 2,600 percent increase in transmitters to 519 by 1990 (*India 1998*). The number of *Doordarshan* transmitters increased to some 900 by 1997 (see Section 4.2.2).

Today, All India Radio and *Doordarshan* are parts of an autonomous body, the Prasar Bharati (Broadcasting Corporation of India) set up in late 1997. The idea behind Prasar Bharati is the creation of a critical public service broadcaster in the country even while it is expected to be immune to any interference by the state or the party in power (see Section 4.1).

3. THE PRESS

The Indian press is experiencing a fundamental transformation because of changes occurring in the larger polity and the economy. Liberalization, globalization, and competition from the electronic media are forcing the print media to adopt new

[5] For a critical review and overview of the development of the electronic media in India, see Awasthy, 1978; Chatterjee, 1987; Kumar, 1981, 1996; Luthra, 1986; Masani, 1985, Reddi, 1996; Sinha, 1996; Vilanilam, 1996; the "Verghese Committee" report (*India 1978*), and Viswanath, 1982.
[6] Several scholars have extensively evaluated the SITE program, e.g., Agrawal, 1978, 1981; Block et al., 1979; Eapen, 1979; Mody, 1979; and Shukla, 1979.

technologies, become more professional, and be more sensitive to the market structure (see Sections 2.2.1, 3.4, 4.2.3, and 4.2.4). Today, India's print media structure offers a product line that is dizzying in its diverse array of languages, ownership structures, and topics.

3.1 Policy and Legal Framework

The Indian press is vigorous, activist, and pluralistic even though it operates under various constraints, which include laws governing the operations of the press, demands of advertising, labor conditions, government control and regulation of newsprint, activist role of the owners, and institutionalized regulations through such bodies as the Press Council and the press commissions.

3.1.1 The Legal Framework

Article 19 (1) (a) of the Indian Constitution guarantees the freedom of expression. Singapore's Constitution modeled its guarantee of freedom of expression on this article of the Indian Constitution (see the chapter on Singapore in the South East Asia Section of this volume). The Supreme Court of India has explicitly stated that even though it is not explicitly indicated in the Constitution, yet 19 (1) (a) also covers freedom of the press. (Basu, 1996; pp. 9–28).[7] Clauses (2) and (6) of Article 19, however, impose some limitations on this guarantee. Clause (2) permits restrictions in matters relating to public order, friendly relations with foreign states, and incitement to offence. Clause (6) specifies the limits of the right to practice a profession, occupation, trade, or business. These restrictions, however, are well within the purview of the Constitution, and therefore subject to judicial review. Through liberal interpretations, the Supreme Court of India has moved towards a free press interpretation closer to the United States than the United Kingdon (Basu, 1996, p. 21).

Several salient points about the rights of free expression stand out:

- The Supreme Court could dismiss restrictions on the press that it deems as not "reasonable."
- Restrictions should be closely connected to Clauses (2) and (6) of Article 19.
- The court could invalidate restrictions unrelated to these two clauses if such restrictions were likely to have a "direct" impact on the practice of journalism or if they were to restrict the freedom of expression.
- The court would strike down restrictions that may directly affect the circulation, subscriptions, and size of the newspapers.
- The rights are extended to individuals, not institutions. In the Indian system then, the journalists do not have a "preferred position" different from any other citizen of India.

[7] Basu, 1996, documents in detail the philosophical and legal factors affecting press freedom in India.

- The rights do not extend to non-citizens.
- However, although non-citizens are not covered, thereby indirectly opening up the possibility of restrictions on foreign-owned media entities, Indian citizens, as individuals and shareholders, can challenge any restrictions imposed on foreign media corporations.

Limitations on the press can be of two kinds: regulatory and penal. Regulatory laws are those that are applicable to content before publication—prior restraint, including censorship, whereas penal laws are those that are applicable as retaliation after publication (Basu, 1996, p. 31).[8] The major laws that potentially affect the operations of the press include:

- Criminal laws, particularly those in § 144 of the Indian Penal Code, intended to maintain public order. Penal Code provisions on sedition (§ 124A), promotion of class hatred (§ 153A), obscenity (§ 292), defamation (§ 499), and "public mischief" (§ 505) also apply to the press.
- The 1962 Customs Act (§ 11), which prohibits the import or export of goods that "undermine the security of India, maintenance of public order or standards of morality or decency."
- The 1971 Contempt of Courts Act, which deals with any publication that can "lower the authority of the court," interfere with judicial proceedings or in the obstruction of justice.
- Provisions pertaining to the press and the legislature, including rules that empower the Speaker to regulate the entry of non-legislators to legislative proceedings and privileges relating to the publication of those proceedings.
- The 1923 Indian Official Secrets Act, which proscribes the gathering and publication of any sketch, plan, or note that an enemy of the state could use.
- The 1954 Drugs and Magic Remedies (Objectionable Advertisements) Act, which deals with injurious advertising.
- General laws on taxation in so far as they do not "single out" the press and place any unfair burdens to limit circulation of the press.
- The 1867 Press and Registration of Books Act, which mandates that every copy of a paper or book printed in the country must contain the name of the owner, editor, publisher, place of printing, date, and price of publication.
- The 1898 Indian Post Office Act, which regulates the transmission of "indecent or obscene" material and seditious matter, and allows for interception in the interest of public safety.
- Laws that regulate industrial relations, as well as those relating to operations of business, also apply to press. These include the 1948 Factories Act, the 1933 Children (Pledging of Labor) Act, the 1953 Collections of Statistics Act, and the 1970 Contract Labor (Regulation & Abolition) Act.

---

[8] Several such laws exist that could potentially limit the functioning of the press, a detailed discussion of which is beyond the purview of this chapter. Basu, 1996, provides a compilation of the laws and regulations relating to India's mass media.

- The 1936 Payment of Wages Act and the 1955 Working Journalists (Conditions of Service) and Miscellaneous Provisions Act—both of which deal specifically with the working conditions of journalists.
- The 1957 Copyright Act, which protects intellectual property under certain conditions.

3.1.2 Constraints from Ownership

Owners, particularly those who head large media empires, have also been a source of suppression if not outright repression, as has been the case in many parts of the world. It is not unusual to hear of cases where many Indian journalists and editors have been forced to leave because of issues related to editorial freedom and control.[9]

3.1.3 Institutional Regulation

Soon after independence, the government institutionalized regulation of the press through several bodies: the press commissions, the Press Council, and the office of the Registrar of Newspapers.

3.1.3.1 The press commissions: The first press commission (1952–54) inquired into several areas affecting the functions of the press: the working conditions of the journalists, freedom of the press, newsprint supply, censorship and journalistic conduct. It also dwelt on a code of conduct for journalists, reviewed the constraints on the supply of information, and touched on improving the methods of recruitment, education, and training of professionals, as well as on publishing reports on the performance of the press. The second press commission (1977) went deeper into the role of the press in a developing and democratic society, ownership patterns, government–press relations, all aspects of the Official Secrets Act, Contempt of Court, and the economics of newspaper industry.

3.1.3.2 Press Council: Press councils are controversial mechanisms that have often helped to protect the press, as well as to make them accountable.[10] The Press Council Act of 1965 established the first Press Council of India in 1966. It was dissolved in 1975 during the Emergency, but was re-established under the Press Council Act of 1978. The council comprises 28 members and a chair, who has

---

[9] B.G. Verghese, a former editor of *The Hindustan Times*, was reportedly dismissed by the owner of the newspaper. Other examples include the dismissals of Khushwant Singh, another prominent journalist; and of Arun Shourie, who quit *The Indian Express* after leading an anti-government campaign. The government still controls the distribution of newsprint, thus potentially limiting the autonomy of the press.

[10] The United States, for example, has only one functioning press council in Minnesota, while the efforts to re-establish a national press council have failed. On the other hand, several Northern European nations have full-fledged functioning press councils. Press councils provide an alternative mechanism to resolve disputes arising from news coverage.

traditionally been a retired judge of the Supreme Court. The chair is nominated by a committee of three: the heads of the two Houses of Parliament and an elected member from the council itself (*India 1998*). The council has the power to initiate, hear, and adjudicate complaints against the press, as well as against the authorities. It also occasionally acts as a forum to organize symposia on press-related issues.

3.1.3.3 Registrar of Newspapers: The Registration of Books Act (1867) was amended in 1956 to establish the office of the Press Registrar of India. The law requires all newspapers, magazines, journals, and news agencies to register. The Registrar of Newspapers is the statutory authority with responsibility for the collection of statistics on the press.

3.2 Financial Aspects: Circulation, Advertising, Marketing Strategies

The country's periodicals appear in many different languages. Among the top circulating newspapers are *The Times of India*, an English daily (1,296,000); the Malayali daily *Malayala Manorama* (1,014,000) and the weekly *Malayala Manorama* (1,140,475); *Gujarat Samachar* (842,000) in Gujarati; a Punjabi newspaper, *Punjab Kesari* (780,000); *Mathrubhumi* (719,000) in Tamil; *Eenadu* (708,000) in Telugu; *The Hindu* (695,000) in English; *Dainik Jagran* (635,000) in Hindi; *Sandesh* (607,000) in Gujarati; *Aj* (569,000) in Hindi; *The Hindustan Times* (552,000) in English; and the Bengali daily, *Ananda Bazar Patrika* (501,577). The *Manorama* is published in Kerala, the state that has the highest literacy rate in the country (WAN, 1999; *India 1998*). The number of newspapers (daily, weekly, fortnightly, monthly, and other periodicals) is increasing at the rate of 5.6 percent per year. No data are available on the number that goes out of business every year.

By the end of 1996, the last year for which official data were available, India had about 39,000 publications, including dailies, weeklies, and monthlies. This is an increase of almost 59 percent from 1987 when India had 24,629 publications (*India 1998, 1989*). Of the 4,453 daily newspapers, about 320 were in English and 2,004 in Hindi.[11] Even though the circulation of all kinds of newspapers and magazines is evident, the biggest story in the last two decades is the success of the regional press, primarily in languages other than English and Hindi. Regional newspapers such as *Malayala Manorama, Amrita Bazar Patrika, Eenadu, Navbharat Times*, and *Punjab Kesari*, among others, have adopted sophisticated marketing strategies. These include the introduction of innovative editorial features, regional or zonal editions, and language use. Success has enabled them to diversify into television and compete with national and international channels.

The display advertising revenue share of the newspapers and magazines in 1998 was 57 percent compared to television's 36 percent, the outdoor's 5 percent, and

---

[11] The *1999 UNESCO statistical yearbook*, does not provide data on India's dailies. The *World press trends* (WAN, 1999) however, refers to 402 dailies beyond 1985 in India with a circulation of 26.5 million for 1998, viz., 2.8 copies per 100 people.

radio's 2 percent. In 1994, the share of newspapers and magazines was 61 percent. The total advertising expenditure in 1998 was Rupees 56.25 billion (US$ 1.32 billion) compared to Rupees 32.92 billion (US$ 1.05 billion) in 1994 (WAN, 1999)[12]

3.3 Structure and Organization

Even before the emergence of the debate on globalization and its impact on the Indian media, both public and private groups have discussed the issue of ownership and control. Although the ownership structure shows a wide range—from individual to corporate—a few major national chains dominate the system (see Table 2). The chain publications deal with a variety of topical areas; general interest, women's magazines, children's magazines, business periodicals, science journals, and even comics.

The major chain is the Bennett Coleman & Co. Ltd (The Times of India group). It is India's largest publishing house with 15 news-interest publications commanding a circulation of 1.72 million—the highest in the country. Its closest competitor is the Indian Express Newspapers with 33 news-interest publications, which have a circulation of 1.47 million copies. The main groups publish multiple editions of their daily newspapers: *The Times of India* (7), *The Indian Express* (19), and *The Hindu* (7), to enable penetration into different areas of the country. Kasturi & Sons Ltd publishes *The Hindu*. Regional chains include the Ananda Bazar Patrika Ltd, the Hindustan Times Ltd, the regional Malayala Manorama Co. Ltd in Kerala, and the Ushodaya Enterprise (Pvt) Ltd (*Eenadu*) in Andhra Pradesh.

With the expansion of television, some of the major print media companies that publish such dailies as *The Times of India, The Hindustan Times, Malayala Manorama*, and *Eenadu* are becoming larger media empires by moving into television production and channel ownership. Whether the conglomeration of India's media system will actually limit the diversity of information and increase control over information is yet to be seen. It is a subject of considerabel debate in the United States where some evidence suggests that conglomeration can lead to a reduction in diversity in the information environment, while other studies show no such evidence (Demers, 1996).

3.4 Quality and Popular Press

Wolseley (1971) observed that India had "newspapers of wide varieties of appearance, quality, and purpose." He found them to be "an amalgam of British and U.S. publications" (p. 273). Eapen (1982) wrote that India's press was "diverse and irregular in quality" (p. 457). Kaushal (1997) asserted that a few English-language

---

[12] The rupee-to-dollar conversions in this chapter are based on exchange rates related to specific years.

newspapers tended to "influence the thinking of the ruling elite" (p. 71): *The Times of India, The Hindu, The Indian Express, The Hindustan Times, The Economic Times*, and *The Statesman*. These newspapers, which stand out as India's quality press, have a wide appeal, particularly among the educated and the young. One publisher has noted that 35 percent of the newspaper readers are in the age group 14–24 (Goenka, 1996).

In general, newspapers concentrate on political news, particularly political actors, though they also include other features such as investigative stories, science features, and medical and technological news.[13] The diversity of magazines reflects the diversity in the taste and information needs of the readers. The quality press includes general newsmagazines with a high circulation such as *India Today, The Week, Frontline, Outlook*, and *Malayala Manorama* catering to an elite audience.[14]

The economic reforms in 1991 led to an emphasis on more market-oriented policies, one consequence of which has been the growth of capital markets. Interest in the performance of markets and the corporate sector, in general, has led to an increasing interest in business and economic journalism as evident in topic-specific dailies and periodicals such as *The Economic Times, The Financial Express, Business Standard, Business India*, and *Business World*. Goenka (1996) reported that the number of financial dailies had grown by 192 percent between 1991 and 1995 compared to a growth rate of 15 percent in English-language general-interest dailies.

Magazines on movies exist in almost every major Indian language, attesting to the popularity of movies in India. Some of the prominent ones are *Stardust, Filmfare, Cine Blitz, Movie*, and *Showtime* among others. Sports magazines and extensive coverage of sports in the leading English and regional newspapers reinforce the popularity of sports. More magazines on fashion, interior design, health and beauty, and travel have sprung up in the last decade.

3.5 Distribution and Technology

The newspapers of the major publishing groups have a national circulation. The multi-editions of *The Times of India* and *The Indian Express* circulate throughout the country. Most newspapers have switched to computer technology for page makeup and layout. The use of satellite technology has made it easier to transfer information and advertisements to print multi-editions of newspapers from various centers.

India has four major national news agencies and several smaller regional agencies. The Press Trust of India (PTI), the United News of India (UNI), Hindustan Samachar, and Samachar Bharati are the major national news agencies. The Press Information Bureau (PIB) serves as a major source of information for the print and electronic media on government initiatives and achievements. It uses English, Hindi, Urdu, and 13 regional Indian languages. The Non-Aligned News Agencies

---

[13] In this context, see the "world of news" study conducted by Sreberny-Mohammedi, 1984.
[14] However, some of these magazines also publish editions in regional Indian languages.

Pool (NANAP), established in 1976, disseminates and receives news and information from the member countries and contributes Indian news in exchange.

The PTI, founded in 1905, is a non-profit, member-owned cooperative, which supplies news to newspapers, commercial services, and central and state governments. UNI (1961) was formed after the United Press of India (established in 1933) closed down. The operations of UNI are controlled and directed from Delhi. It provides commercial, financial, and background information to various sectors, including the media, government, and the banking and corporate sectors. Hindustan Samachar, the first multilingual news agency, started operations in 1948 as a private limited company; and, in 1957, turned into a workers' cooperative with more than 150 subscribers. It supplies news in different languages using Hindi as the link language. Similarly, Samachar Bharati, the multilingual news agency set up in 1965, meets the needs of regional language newspapers and promotes the cause of small- and medium-sized language newspapers. The agency supplies news mainly in Hindi, and provides translated versions to newspapers published in other languages.

4. BROADCASTING

Broadcasting media are fast emerging as extremely popular. Television, in particular, is fast becoming the medium of choice for news and entertainment, particularly in light of the "neo-liberal" policies adopted by the state in the realms of both economics and communication (McDowell, 1997). The original intention for the establishment of broadcasting media, however, was completely different.

Television commenced in 1959 as an educational experiment involving television clubs in New Delhi where some 21 community TV sets received the programs. Regular broadcasting was introduced in New Delhi in 1965. The expansion of the medium was tentative with about a dozen cities receiving TV signals by 1975. From such a modest beginning, starting in 1982, the TV system has expanded into one of the largest networks in the world. Indian television is modeled on the European model representing a strong network dedicated to public service and a number of private satellite channels primarily offering entertainment programs. This "mixed" model offers a challenge to regulators.

4.1 Policy and Legal Framework

The government's control over broadcasting rests in Article 246 of the Indian Constitution and in several other laws, including the Indian Telegraph Act (1885) and the Indian Wireless Act (1933). The Indian Parliament has the power to enact legislation on communication-related areas such as post and telegraph, telephone, wireless, broadcasting, and other forms of communication. The current broadcasting policy is based on Article 19 (2) of the Indian Constitution and the AIR code of 1970. These provisions mandate that broadcasts should not indulge in the criticism of friendly countries, attack religion or communities, air obscene or defamatory material, incite violence, and the like.[15]

The control of government over television and radio has been a subject of an extensive and long-standing debate and study in India for several decades, most of which have determined that the electronic media should be free of government control.[16] After several tentative steps by different administrations, the government control over public radio and television is in the process of change following the establishment of an autonomous corporation, the Prasar Bharati (Broadcasting Corporation of India), at the end of 1997. On October 29, 1997, Prime Minister I.K. Gujral's United Front government promulgated by ordinance a modified version of the 1990 Prasar Bharati Act, which had been "mothballed" for seven years. The 1990 Act envisaged the setting up of a 22-member parliamentary committee to oversee the corporation, as well as a Broadcasting Council to hear complaints—both of which were excluded from the ordinance. (Earlier, in May 1997, the UF government had introduced the country's first Broadcasting Bill in Parliament proposing the setting up of an autonomous body for regulating all broadcasting services in the country.) Prime Minister A.B. Vajpayee's BJP government, which did not agree with the modifications in the ordinance, allowed it to lapse the next year. Aware of its inadequate strength in the *Rajya Sabha* (Upper House) to get through new legislation, the BJP government took the route of promulgating the Prasar Bharati Amendment Ordinance to reintroduce some provisions of the original Act. The intention behind the law establishing the corporation was to insulate the public broadcasting system from state control. A panel of distinguished citizens, assisted by a chief executive officer, was to run the corporation. Despite these moves, considerable scepticism remains over the future of the organization on the expiry of the current ordinance. Whether the corporation is accountable to the Ministry of Information and Broadcasting or to the Parliament is still unclear.[17]

The boom in the development of cable television led to the enactment of the 1994 Cable Television Networks (Regulation) Act, which mandates the registration of cable networks before starting operations, specifies the use of standard equipment, requires a program code, and prohibits the transmission of certain programs. The regulation legalizes the seizure and confiscation of equipment and the imposition of penalties for non-compliance.

---

[15] Venkateswaran, 1993, provides the legal framework in detail while Xavier & Eashwer, 1998, cover the more recent developments.

[16] For an extensive discussion and historical background, see *India 1978*; and Viswanath, 1982.

[17] For example, in June 1999, the government of India appointed a high-ranked civil servant as an interim CEO of the organization raising questions about the autonomy of the organization (*All India News*, June 11, 1999 [http://www.allindianews.com/display.asp?nid=199906112200255110]).

4.2 Structure and Organization

India has no syndicated, commercial audience measurement system at the national level though some private-sector market research organizations have initiated efforts toward a systematic measurement of TV exposure in larger cities. Based on audience studies by the government and commercial agencies, it is estimated that India has about 60 million TV hoseholds drawing about 296 million people, about 42 percent of whom are in the rural areas. TV viewing in India is communal in some neighborhoods, that is, members of non-TV households may also participate in watching a given household set. This phenomenon increase the number of TV viewers to about 448 million people out of the estimated 1 billion (*India 1997*).

4.2.1 Radio

From a network of six stations at the time of independence, All India Radio had grown, by 1997, into a major network of almost 200 radio stations and 389 transmitters covering about 90 percent of the area of the country and 97 percent of the population.[18] The *1999 UNESCO statistical yearbook* estimated that India had 116 million radio receivers in 1997—a density of 12 sets per 100 people.

4.2.2 Public Television

The public TV broadcasting network, *Doordarshan*, has 19 channels with programs produced from about 40 different centers. Its more than 900 transmitters of varying power cover about 70 percent of the geographical area and about 87 percent of the population—an expansion of more than 230 percent in 15 years. It produces programs in about a dozen languages. Its main channel, DD-1 claims to attract an audience of almost 300 million—more than the entire population of the United States. It uses a combination of at least three different satellites and 900 terrestrial transmitters to reach the people (*India 1997*). The 1999 ITU *Yearbook of statistics* gives the following data on India for 1997: 66 million TV receivers, 63 million TV households, and 18 million cable-TV subscribers. UNESCO's *Statistical yearbook* for 1999 says that India had 63 million TV receivers in 1997, a density of 6.5 per 100 people.

4.2.3 Private Television

Over the last 10 to 15 years, the TV landscape has changed radically in India. Global and local forces have combined to create an environment conducive to private TV channels. Both cable and satellite channels emerged in the mid-1980s, and these have become an essential part of the landscape (see Tables 3 and 4).

---

[18] *India 1997*, and the Ninth Five-Year Plan (1997): (http://www.nic.in/ninthplan/vol2/chap7-4&5.doc).

Murdoch's Satellite Television Asia Region (STAR TV) network, CNN, BBC, Discovery, TNT/Cartoon, and MTV, among others, have entered the nation on their own or with the help of local partners (McDowell, 1997; Xavier & Eashwer, 1998).

Twenty-four hour broadcasting of news, sports, business, music, movies, and cartoons is no longer the exception. Programs of Zee TV (1993), and Indian-owned news and entertainment channel, are among the top 10 in India. The other channels include ABNi, Asianet, ATN, Cable, CNBC, Channel V, Eenadu TV, ESPN, Gemini TV, Home TV, Music Asia, National Geographic, Punjabi World, Raj TV, Sony TV, Star Movies, Star Plus, Star Sports, Star News, Surya TV, Sun TV, TVI, Udaya TV, and Vijay TV. (*Via Media*, 1999, http://www.mudra.com/wnew_con.htm).

Competition, particularly in southern India, has lately emerged from such channels as Sun TV, Raj TV, and Vijay TV, which televise in Tamil; Eenadu and Gemini TV in Telugu; Udaya in Kannada; and Asianet in Malayalam. National and international media companies also collaborate to produce programming in India (Sharma, 1998).

The government's latest telecom policy allows media companies (with at least 80 percent of Indian equity) direct satellite uplink of their programs instead of making them go through the current government monopoly, Videsh Sanchar Nigam Ltd (VSNL).

4.2.4 Cable Television

Cable television in India has been the result of sheer entrepreneurial genius in the absence of a cohesive communication policy. It is an exemplar of entrepreneurial initiative leading and outrunning government policy.[19] Cable television entered as a closed circuit television in skyscraper apartments in the middle- and lower middle-class localities, which were wired to central control rooms. Videoplayers transmitted Indian and foreign films and programs taped abroad. From these modest beginnings, cable networks expanded from 0.41 million in January 1992 to 9.2 million in 1996. National surveys show that the number of households with cable and satellite TV expanded from zero households in 1990 (before the introduction of Cable TV) to almost 31 percent of the TV households by 1997 (Balasubramanian, 1999) (see Table 3). Most large villages have cable connections.

Given the popularity and growth of local and satellite TV channels, major media conglomerates have diversified into program production, supplying programs to both public and private channels. The more prominent producers include Times Television (TTV), Hindustan Television from the Hindustan Times group, Televison Bazar from the Ananda Bazar group, Eenadu Television (ETV) from the Ushodaya group, Plus Channel, Durga Khote Productions, United Television (UTV), and Cinevista Communications.

[19] Also see Reddi, 1996.

4.3 Program Policies

4.3.1 Radio

AIR broadcasts in all the major Indian languages (Hindi, English) plus in dozens of other Indian languages and dialects. Program variety ranges from popular music (usually music from the movies), classical music, as well as programs on health, agriculture, and other topics targeting special audiences as expected of a public broadcasting system (*India 1998*).

AIR provides an active news program backed by about 90 journalists reporting from different centers in India and abroad. The government also perceives AIR as an "electronic ambassador" broadcasting programs and news in 24 languages to audiences abroad. Two of AIR's primary objectives are to reach the Indian diaspora settled abroad and to communicate the Indian point of view on international issues, thereby also serving a counter-propaganda function. It also has an office that monitors major foreign broadcast networks, and issues reports and abstracts to the government.

4.3.2 Public Television

Doordarshan, the public TV broadcasting system, has explicit policies to guide its programming. Its objectives are very similar to the objectives and values that have been traditionally expected of public broadcasting systems all over the world:

- Promotion of national integration;
- promotion of guided social change;
- programming for specialized audiences, such as women and children;
- preservation and promotion of cultural heritage;
- education and propagation of family planning, agriculture, and the like.

These, however, have become "vulnerable" with the onset of commercialized, privatized broadcast systems (Blumler, 1992).

Several scholars have identified barriers that hinder public television from achieving its programming objectives. Such barriers include lack of a coherent ideology, conflicting interests, lack of autonomy, and limited resources (Kumar, 1996; Sinha, 1996; Reddi, 1996; Vilanilam, 1996). Vilanilam (1996), for example, doubts the ability of the public television to compete with private television under the present configuration. Reddi (1996) points out the widespread dissatisfaction with the national TV structure and the program services it provides and doubts whether any one type of medium or arrangement can hold the loyalty of the Indian viewer. On education, Kumar (1996), based on an analysis of international news on television, concludes that international news, to some extent, is influenced by the availability of footage from trans-national news agencies. What is covered as international news is thus determined only partly in India and mostly by the suppliers of the news, though he also refers to the role of local gatekeeping. Vilanilam

(1996) argues that cultural problems have become widespread in India as the new communication opportunities that television offers bring together the subcontinent's religious cultures and the political movements associated with them, and often take advantage of them.

Sinha (1996) succinctly summarizes these dilemmas between market logic and public service broadcasting:

> On one side are the market forces pumping more and more money to increase consumption. On the other side is the changing hi-tech scene demanding more resources while constraining program policy. On another side are the Indian masses expecting television to help them escape from their present plight; and on still another side is the resource constraint, a State helplessly watching the dilemma and not in a position to empower the medium to take up its development role wholeheartedly. (p. 319)

4.4 Ownership and Financing

Two significant developments are worth nothing. Although AIR used to rely on internal resources for programming, lately, it has also been buying programs from private producers—a significant departure from its previous practice. It also buys programs from the major networks of other countries. Second, it has increasingly come to rely on a mixed model of operation. Earlier, the sources or revenue to run the network were either the license fee or parliamentary appropriations. Lately, It has placed greater reliance on revenue collected from advertising. The total commercial revenue for 1996–97 exceeded Rupees 796.3 million (US$ 22.47 million). Thus it has moved from an exclusively state-sponsored and state-supported medium to a mixed model with some of its revenue coming from the private sector.

The public TV network is parallel to the radio network in terms of its revenue model. It receives substantial funding from the government for program production and expansion. Yet, it also attracts considerable advertising revenue. In 1997, for example, *Doordarshan* earned about Rupees 5,727 million (US$ 145.7 million) from advertising—this represents an increase in earnings that is greater than the previous four years combined, suggesting the revenue potential of the public broadcasting system in India (*India, 1997*). The display advertising revenue share of television increased from 21 percent in 1993 to 26 percent in 1997. The share of radio was 2 percent in 1997 (WAN, 1998).

The Euromedia Research Group has documented that public broadcasting systems all over the world have come under increasing pressure from more commercialized private TV channels to attract the audience (Siune et al., 1992). India has been no exception. To meet the threat from external competitors and to attract revenue, the public broadcasting network "went commercial" in 1976 though it was not a major factor until in 1984 when the public broadcasting system introduced "DD-2," a channel focused on the young urban audience that the private television channels had increasingly siphoned away. The decision to go commercial made "financial" sense to the extent that it has increased its commercial revenue by almost 90 percent, from Rupees 3.01 billion (US$ 116.14 million) in 1991–92 to Rupees 5.73 billion (US$ 160.5 million) in 1996–97.

5. NEW ELECTRONIC MEDIA

India's telecommunications infrastructure is changing rapidly. The government is under tremendous pressure to adapt to the rapid pace in the development of new communication technologies, market forces, and the demand for telecommunication services.

5.1 Internet and On-line Media

Internet services exemplify the contrasts in India's communications services. India is one of the largest software producers in the world. The demand for Internet services has grown rapidly. Inadequate telecommunication services and the government's Internet monopoly had, however, until late 1998, hampered the growth of the Internet.

From August 1995 to November 1998, Videsh Sanchar Nigam Ltd (VSNL), an incorporated company formed in 1986 under the Ministry of Communications, had been the country's main Internet service provider. Two other government agencies—the National Informatics Centre and the Educational and Research Network of the Department of Electronics—operated NICnet and ERNET respectively, to provide Internet services to specific, closed user groups (APT, 1999). VSNL operated through the country's four international telecommunication gateways—Calcutta, Chennai, Mumbai, and New Delhi. In December 1998, the Department of Telecommunications (DoT) privatized the sector by issuing ISP licenses to 20 private operators, as well as the state-owned Mahanagar Telephone Nigam Ltd (MTNL). By mid-1999, 116 ISPs had received licenses (*IndiaExpress.Net*, June 11, 1999 http://www.indiaexpress.net/news/technology/19990611-0.html). Cable companies are also likely to compete in the Internet market.

When VSNL reduced the access fee from Rupees 15,000 (US$ 353) to Rupees 10,000 (US$ 235.29) for 500 hours of usage, the number of subscribers reportedly increased 25 percent. The license fee has also been reduced or waived up to five years to boost Internet use. Internet parlors or cyber cafes have emerged in metropolitan areas. The Integrated Services Digital Network has been operational in 12 major cities.

India had an estimated 2.7 million personal computers in 1998 (ITU, 1999) and an estimated 2.3 million computer users (Nayar, 1998a). The July 1999 survey of the Internet Software Consortium (www.isg.org) showed an estimated 114,062 Internet hosts in India—indicating an annual compound growth rate of more than 98.5 percent since 1994. ITU (1999) estimated that in 1997, India had 300,000 Internet users. Reporting the results of a survey, the National Association of Software and Services Companies placed the number of Internet subscribers at 250,000—a figure that may increase to 1.5 million by 2000 (*IndiaExpress.Net*, April 14, 1999 http://www.indiaexpress.net/news/technology/19990414-0.html).[20]

---

[20] Estimates given by different organizations vary. India's Ninth Five-Year Plan projects 1.6 million Internet subscribers by 2002, whereas the NASSCOM survey predicts 8 million subscribers by then (APT, 1998).

The results of another survey showed that e-mail accounted for 90 percent of Internet usage in India; research and information seeking, 30–70 percent; and e-commerce, 20 percent (*IndiaExpress.Net*, March 17, 1999 http://www.indiaexpress.net/news/technology/19990317-0.html).

The federal and the state governments have set up software technolgoy parks to attract multinational IT giants for research and development. Government Intranets and public service websites are also in operation. ERNET has taken steps to develop Indian-language websites for business, education and entertainment. The National Task Force on Information Technology and Software Development, which studied the provision of IT services, has been influential on Internet policy making. It recommended major investments in the development of the information infrastructure by allowing private and public sectors to build fiber-optic networks.

Banks and other consumer-service companies are entering the market to capitalize on e-commerce, estimated to increase from US$ 2.8 million in 1997 to US$ 160 million by 2001 (Nayar, 1998b). Several retailers—banks, restaurants, and textile- and furniture-outlets, among others—are already using e-commerce (Pande, 1998). One survey estimated that 32 percent of businesses that had PCs also had access to the 'Net. The same survey reported that about 500,000 businesses owned PCs (*IndiaExpress.Net*, March 17, 1999 http://www.indiaexpress.net/news/technology/19990317-0.html).[21]

Many Indian newspapers have gone on-line. Indians living abroad are their main audience. These newspapers put out special daily or weekly IT supplements to popularize and familiarize the use of the Internet for educational, research, business, and employment purposes. Efforts are also afoot to use the Internet for distance learning (Gonsalves, 1998). Some organizations are using the Internet for political communication as well. The Indian Army website gives its version of the event in Jammu & Kashmir (*India Abroad*, 1998). The Bharatiya Janata Party set up India's first party website during the 1998 elections. Other political parties have followed suit. Advertising agencies are also using the Internet to sell their products and services.

5.2 Telecommunications Infrastructure

The Indian telephone system was notorious for its inadequacies, including long waits for connections, poor service, and limited access. In mid-1980s, India embarked on an ambitious program to modernize its telecommunciation system by promoting indigenous technology and expanding private-sector participation. Several government departments are directly or indirectly involved in telephone operations: Department of Telecommunication (DoT), Center for Development of Technology (C-DOT), Telecom Research Center (TRC), and Indian Telephone Institute (ITI). The government announced a national telecommunications policy

---

[21] These data refer only to the top eight urban cities in India: Delhi, Mumbai, Calcutta, Chennai, Bangalore, Hyderabad, Ahmedabad, and Pune.

in mid-1994 and established the Telecom Regulatory Authority of India (TRAI) in March 1997 to regulate telephones in India.

As of March 1998, India had a network of 23,406 telephone exchanges with 21.3 million lines and 17.8 million telephone connections—2.3 telephones for 100 people.[22] It also had about 1,195,400 cellular subscribers (ITU, 1999).[23] The Ninth Five-Year Plan (1997–2002) expects the demand for telephones in the country to be 38.1 million. The plan envisages the private sector to provide 5.2 million telephones. In 1997, about 3.47 million subscribers were still waiting for telephone connections (Ninth Five-Year Plan, Infrastructure-Telecom Sector, 1998). DoT has initiated policies to accelerate the provision of telecommunication services to all the villages, the figure estimated to settle at 683,000. About 216,332 villages already have public phones. Another 75,000 were expected to have them by the end of 1998.

India's long-distance transmission network comprises microwave, UHF, coaxial and optical fiber connections, and 170 fixed satellite earth stations. Digitization of the network has reached 56 percent. India's indigenously designed INSAT-II satellite systems provide 4,662 two-way speech circuits through 235 earth stations across the country. Most recently, India launched the last of its second generation of multipurpose satellites, INSAT-2E in April 1999 (*IndiaExpress.Net*, April 10, 1999 http://www.indiaexpress.net/news/technology/19990410-0.html). VSNL operates seven satellite earth stations—at Arvi, Dehradun, Mumbai, New Delhi, Calcutta, Chennai, and Bangalore—and three submarine telephone cables—Chennai to Penang; Mumbai to Fujairah, UAE; and SEA-ME-WE-2. VSNL will outlay US$ 1.5 billion to expand these facilities, which will include participation in the FLAG and SEA-ME-WE-3 submarine fiber-optic cables (APT, 1998).

6. POLICY TRENDS FOR PRESS AND BROADCASTING

India provides opportunities to examine the developments related to communications and their implications for social change on a scale matched by only a few countries. The government's new telecommunication policy:

- favors the Indian national television system, the *Doordarshan*;
- widens the application of current laws regulating advertising to private TV channels; and
- proposes to privatize telephones at some future point (*IndiaExpress Network*, March 26, 1999 http://www.indiaexpress.net/news/technology/19990326-0.html).

---

[22] The estimated telephone density in rural areas is about 0.25 lines per 100 people. APT, 1999, and the Ninth Five-Year Plan estimate India's telephone density at 1.72 percent. The ITU, 1999, estimate for 1998 is 2.20 percent. Also see (http://www.nic.in:80/India-Image/PIB/Foc2406981.html).

[23] See (http://www.nic.in:80/India-Image/PIB/Foc2406981.html).

6.1 Autonomy for the Public Broadcasting System

For more than two decades, the country has witnessed a vigorous debate on the extent to which the state-owned radio and television should be granted autonomy (*India 1978*). The Prasar Bharati Bill granting autonomy to state radio and television received presidential assent in 1990. Seven years later, effective September 15, 1997, the government set up an autonomous corporation for the electronic media to function freely. The corporation, managed democratically, is accountable to the Broadcasting Council and the relevant parliamentary committee with various powers reserved for the government. The board has a chair, a chief executive officer, several part-time members and representatives of officials and employees of AIR and *Doordarshan*. The president of India appoints the chair on the advice of a committee comprising the chair of the Council of States, the chair of the Press Council of India and a nominee of the president of India. The organization itself is in the formative stages, struggling to find a foothold in the new information environment. It remains to be seen how the future will shape the organization, and its programming policies, and what role it will play in leading or influencing the TV landscape in the country.

6.2 The Right to Information

To promote transparency in governmental operations, legislation to allow greater access to information is now under consideration. Despite the controversy accompanying it, two states in India—Rajasthan and Tamil Nadu—have already passed such a law. The consequences of openness, as well as how it is practised, are empirical questions worthy of investigation in the future.

6.3 Policy on Internet

The demand for Internet services is booming among private citizens and corporate entities. The appeal is particularly noticeable among the young, urban, educated citizenry and the wealthy. This may portend yet another instance of the influence of middle- and affluent-classes on the government's telecommunication policy. How the government reacts to this pressure and attempts to balance concerns for equity and social justice with market demands will be a matter for future research. The government ended its monopoly on Internet services when it issued licenses to more than 100 ISPs, thereby increasing competition over price and services (*IndiaExpress.Net*, April 22, 1999 http://www.indiaexpress.net/news/technology/19990422-0.html).

7. MAIN ISSUES

To recapitulate, India is undergoing massive changes in its social structure. The struggle between seemingly inexorable forces of globalization and liberalization, on the one hand, and forces—for ideological and not so noble reasons—that want to maintain a strong state presence, on the other, is being played out in several public arenas, including the media. That the media are implicated in this struggle and that media and communication policies are an important component of these changes should not surprise anyone. Several issues in this regard will continue to be a subject for the attention of scholars, elites, and the public.

- Autonomy for the public broadcasting system

How the public broadcasting system will fare in the new media landscape vis-à-vis the private sector will be debated for a few more years. This will continue to be a potential and fruitful topic for scholarly attention for years to come.

- The spreading movement over the right to information

This could potentially become controversial. The state may face increasing problems over the control of information given the new communication technologies and the demand for governmental transparency from organized pressure groups.

- Telecommunications infrastructure

For a nation that seeks to nurture and develop its informatics industry, particularly in the area of software development and exports, India's telecommunication infrastructure, though extensive, is woefully inadequate. Pressure will continue to mount on the government to be active in policy-making and in satisfying demands.

- Working conditions of journalists

The journalist movement in India has been active in promoting issues such as protection, compensation, and the working conditions of journalists. The Working Journalists Act of 1955 recognized journalists as industrial workers. The Act guided successive efforts to set minimum wages for journalists. Two organizations are broadly representative of journalists: the Indian Federation of Working Journalists (IFWJ) and the National Union of Journalists (NUJ). What shape will the labor movement take in the future era of liberalization is an empirical question.

- Globalization

The globalization of the Indian economy and media systems is having a profound influence on the formats, institutional practices, and media content, a subject that warrants a more thorough, systematic and extensive empirical examination in the future (Balasubramanian, 1999; Griffin et al., 1994).

- Media use and reliance

Given the changing media landscape described above, future research may examine issues of access, as well as media usage. For example, a recent survey of media use—the Indian National Readership Survey conducted jointly by the Media Research Users Council and ORG-MARG—showed that television enjoyed the largest reach among the media: 44.5 percent of the people surveyed reported that they had access to television compared to 33.3 percent for print media. Access and usage, however, varies in relation to the complexity of the community. In urban India, 75.4 percent watch television, 58.1 percent read newspapers and magazines, and 21.1 percent listen to the radio. This is in contrast to the rural areas where 32.8 percent watch television, 24 percent depend on print media, and 19.2 percent have access to radio (*The Hindu*, October 19, 1998). The urban–rural gap in access and usage, as well as the implications of the "knowledge" and access gaps, are worthy of investigation (Viswanath & Finnegan, 1996).

8. STATISTICS

Table 1
General Profile

Exchange rate (September 1999)	US$ 1 = 43.51*
Population mid-1999	1008.8 million**
Sex Ratio (No. of females for 1000 males)	935.72**
Percentage of literacy (1997)	53.5
Percentage of literacy (males)	66.7
Percentage of literacy (females)	39.4
Percentage of working population	41.7
Density per sq km (1999)	336.6 persons**
Total number of newspapers and periodicals as on 31 December 1996	39,149
Population covered by radio	97% (1997)
Population covered by television	87% (1997)

Source: The data are estimates culled from various sources including *India 1998*; the Ninth Five-Year Plan, 1997–2002; UNDP, 1999; * OANDA Historical Currency Table [On-line]. Available: (http://www.oanda.com/converter/cc_table?lang=en); ** US Census Bureau's International Data Base Estimates [On-line]. Available: (http://www.census.gov/cgi-bin/ipc/idbsum).

Table 2
Newspaper Ownership Patterns

Form of ownership	Number for which circulation available	Circ'n ('000)	Percentage share in total circulation
Individual	4,646	22,397	36.6
Joint stock companies	515	22,266	36.4
Firms/partnerships	407	6,351	10.4
Societies/associations	1,347	4,495	7.6
Trusts	275	3,306	5.4
Government	213	1,347	2.1
Others	219	985	1.5
Total	**7,622**	**61,147**	**100.0**

Table 3
Estimate of Penetration of Cable & Satellite Television, 1992–97

June 1992	1.28 million
February 1993	3.30 million
October 1993	7.28 million
June 1995	9.30 million
June 1997	14.9 million

Source: Various: National Readership surveys, 1995 & 1997; Ministry of Information and Broadcasting, 1997; Balasubramanian, 1999.

Note: The numbers refer only to urban areas.

Table 4
Satellite Channels

Satellite	Location	Channels
Asiasat-1	100.5 E	STAR Plus, STAR Sports, Channel V, ZEE, Zee Cinema, ELTV
Asiasat-2	105.5 E	STAR Movies, NBC, CNBC, PTV-2
PAS-4	68.5 E	Sony, Home, ATN, BBC World, ABNI, TNT, Cartoon Network, Discovery, CNN, MTV
Intelsat-703	57 E	Sun, Sun Music, Sun Movie, NEPC, TV India, Gemini
Intelsat-704	66 E	Eenadu, Vijay
Gorizont-42	142.5 E	Music Asia, Raj

Table 5
Penetration of Telecommunications

	1986	1990	2000
Telephone connections	3.16 million	4.5 million	19 million
Subscribers awaiting telephones	1 million	1.5 million	Nil
Telex connections	32,000	43,000	200,000
Villages with public phones or exchanges	32,000	43,000	600,000
Public call offices in cities/towns	20,000	35,000	1 million
Voice/data in business/industry	negligible	10,000	800,000

Source: Department of Telecommunications, 1987.

Note: 25% of the urban population has 90% of all telephones; less than 6% of the villages have public phones; of 3,000 cities, 400 have international STD facilities; there are 33 earth stations providing 4000 trunk circuits

9. USEFUL ADDRESSES

All India Radio
Akashvani Bhavan
Parliament Street
New Delhi, 110 001
India
Telephone: 91-11-3714061, 91-11-3710300
Fax: 91-11-3714967, 91-11-3711956
URL: http://www.allindiaradio.net

Business Standard Ltd
5, Pratap Bhavan
Bahadur Shah Zafar Marg
New Delhi, 110 002
India
Telephone: 91-11-3720202 / 3739840
Fax: 91-11-3720201
URL: http://www.business-standard.com

Dainik Jagran
2, Sarvodaya Nagar
Kanpur, 208005 UP.
India
Telephone: 91-512-216161
Fax: 91-512-216972
URL: http://www.jagran.com

Deccan Chronicle
36, Sarojini Devi Road
Secunderabad, 500 003
India
E-mail: deccan@hdl.vsnl.net.in
URL: http://www.deccan.com

Deccan Herald
75, Mahatma Gandhi Road
Post Box No 5331
Bangalore, 560 001
India
Telephone: 91-80-5588999
Fax: 91-80-5587675
URL: http://www.deccanherald.com

Directorate of Advertising and Visual Publicity
3rd Floor, Press Trust of India Building
Parliament Street
New Delhi, 110 001
India
Telephone: 91-11-3717923
Fax: 91-11-3739083
URL: http://www.nic.in/davp

Directorate of Film Festivals
Lok Nayak Bhavan, 4th Floor
Khan Market
New Delhi, 110 003
India
Telephone: 91-11-4694920
Fax: 91-11-6493089

Doordarshan
Doordarshan Bhavan
Copernicus Marg
New Delhi, 110 001
India

Telephone: 91-11-3387786
Fax: 91-11-3388707
URL: http://www.ddindia.com

The Economic Times
Times House, 7 Bahadurshah Zafar Marg
New Delhi, 110 002
India
Telephone: 91-11-3312277
Fax: 91-11-3715832
URL: http://www.economictimes.com

Film Division
24-IN, C. Deshmukh Marg
Mumbai
India
Telephone: 91-22-3861421
Fax: 91-22-3860308

Femina
Bennett, Coleman & Co. Ltd
The Times of India Building
Dr D.N. Road
Mumbai, 400 001
India
Fax: 91-22-2620290
URL: http://www.feminaindia.com/index1.html

Frontline
859-860 Anna Salai
Chennai, 600 002
India
Telephone: 91-44-8413344
Fax: 91-44-8535325
E-mail: frontline@indiaserver.com
URL: http://www.the-hindu.com/fline

The Hindu
Anna Salai
Chennai, 600 002
India
Telephone: 91-44-8413344
Fax: 91-44-8535325
E-mail: thehindu@indiaserver.com
URL: http://www.hinduonline.com

The Hindustan Times
18-20 Kasturba Gandhi Marg
New Delhi, 110 002
India
Telephone: 91-11-3704590
Fax: 91-11-3704551

E-mail: htedo@nda.vsnl.net.in.
URL: http://www.hindustantimes.com

India Today
Living Media India Ltd
F-14/15 Connaught Place
New Delhi
India
Telephone: 91-11-3315801
Fax: 91-11-3316180
URL: http://www.india-today.com

The Indian Express
Bahadurshah Zafar Marg
New Delhi, 110 002
India
Telephone: 91-11-3318528
Fax: 91-11-3716037
URL: http://www.indian-express.com

Indian Institute of Mass Communication
Aruna Asif Ali Marg
New Delhi, 110 067
India
Telephone: 91-11-6856532
Fax: 91-11-6856532

Manushi
C/174, Lajpat Nagar 1
New Delhi, 110 024
India
Fax: 91-11-6839158
URL: http://www.freespeech.org/manushi

Press Council of India
Faridkot House
Copernicus Road
New Delhi, 110 001
India
Telephone: 91-11-3381681

Press Information Bureau
"A" Wing, Shastri Bhavan
New Delhi, 110 001
India
Telephone: 91-11-3383643
Fax: 91-11-3383169
URL: http://www.nic.in/India-Image/PIB

Press Trust of India
4, Parliament Street
New Delhi, 110 001
India

Telephone: 91-11-3719597
Fax: 91-11-3718714

Publications Division
Government of India
Patiala House
New Delhi, 110 001
India
Telephone: 91-11-3386879

Outlook
AB-10 Safdarjung Enclave
New Delhi, 110 029
India
Fax: 91-11-6191420
URL: http://www.outlookindia.com

Registrar of Newspapers for India
West Block No. 8, Wing No. 2
R.K. Puram
New Delhi, 110 066
India
Telephone: 91-11-6108788
Fax: 91-11-6108432

STAR TV
NEWS TELEVISION (I) PVT LTD
SM Center, 2nd Floor, Andheri Kurla Road
Marol Naka, Andheri (East)
Mumbai, 400 059
India
Telephone: 91-22-8513433
Fax: 91-22-8514409
URL: http://www.startv.com/india/set18/index.html

The Statesman
Statesman House
4 Chowringhee Square
Calcutta, 700 001
India
Telephone: 91-33-2257070
Fax: 91-33-2250018

The Telegraph
6 Prafulla Sarkar St
Calcatta, 700 001
India
Telephone: 91-33-274880, 91-33-278000
Fax: 91-33-2253240, 91-33-2253241
URL: http://www.telegraphindia.com

The Times of India
Times House, 7 Bahadurshah Zafar Marg

New Delhi, 110 002
India
Telephone: 91-11-3312277
Fax: 91-11-3715832
E-mail: editor@timesofindia.com
URL: http://www.timesofindia.com

United News of India
9, Rafi Marg
New Delhi, 110 001
India
Telephone: 91-11-3711700
Fax: 91-11-3716211

Videsh Sanchar Nigam Ltd (VSNL)
Videsh Sanchar Bhavan
M.G. Road, Fort
Mumbai, 400 001
India
Telephone: 91-22-2623608
Fax: 91-22-2624000
URL: http://www.vsnl.net.in

Zee Telefilms Ltd
Continental Bldg.
135, Dr A.B. Road, Worli
Mumbai, 400 018
India
Telephone: 91-22-4965609
URL: http://www.zeetelevision.com

10. REFERENCES

Aggarwal, S.K. (1988). *Press at the crossroads in India*. New Delhi: Udh Publishing House.
Agrawal, B.C. (1978). *Satellite instructional television experiment: Television comes to village. An evaluation of SITE*. East Lansing, MI: National Center for Research on Teacher Learning (ERIC Document Reproduction Service Ed 201 301).
Agrawal, B.C. (1981). *SITE social evaluation: Results, experiences and implications*, Ahmedabad, India: Space Applications Center.
APT (Asia-Pacific Telecommunity). (1998, 1999). *The APT yearbook*. Bangkok: APT.
Awasthy, G.C. (1978). India. In J.A. Lent (Ed.), *Broadcasting in Asia and the Pacific: A continental survey of radio and television* (pp. 197–211). Philadelphia: Temple University Press.
Balasubramanian, K. (1999). *The impact of globalization of media on media images: A study of Indian media images between 1987–1997*. Unpublished master's thesis, Ohio State University, Columbus.
Basham, A.L. (1959). *The wonder that was India*. New York: Grove Press.
Basu, D.D. (1996). *Law of the press*. New Delhi: Prentice Hall.
Bell, D. (1976). *The coming of post-industrial society*. New York: Basic Books.
Block, C., Foote, D.R., & Mayo, J.K. (1979). SITE unseen: Implications for programming & policy. *Journal of Communication, 29*, 4, 114–124.
Blumler, J.G. (1992). *Television and the public interest*, London: Sage Publications.
Chatterjee, P.C. (1987). *Broadcasting in India*. New Delhi: Sage Publications.

Demers, D.P. (1996). *The menace of the corporate newspaper: Fact or fiction*, Ames, IA: Iowa State University Press.

Department of Telecommunications. (1987). *Telecom Mission draft report*. New Delhi: Government of India.

Eapen, K.E. (1971). India: An overview. In J.A. Lent (Ed.), *The Asian newspapers' reluctant revolution* (pp. 282–297). Ames: Iowa State University Press.

Eapen, K.E. (1979). The cultural component of SITE: *Journal of Communication, 29,* 4, 106–113.

Eapen, K.E. (1982). India. In J.A. Lent (Ed.), *Newspapers in Asia: Contemporary trends and problems* (pp. 442–459). Hong Kong: Heinemann Asia.

Goenka, V. (1996, June 22). Journalism in India: A changing perspective. *Editor & Publisher, 129* (68), 56–57.

Gonsalves, M. (1998, October 9). University on the 'Net to begin courses'. *India Abroad*, p. 26.

Griffin, M., Viswanath, K., & Schwartz, D. (1994). Gender advertising in the U.S. and India: Exporting cultural stereotypes. *Media, Culture and Society, 16,* 487–507.

ITU (International Telecommunication Union). (1998, 1999). *World telecommunication development report*. Geneva: ITU.

Karan, K. (1994). *Political communication in the 1991 general election in India with special reference to Andhra Pradesh*. Unpublished doctoral dissertation, London School of Economics, UK.

Katz, E., Wedell, G., Pilsworth, M., & Shinar, D. (1977). *Broadcasting in the Third World: Promise and performance*. Cambridge: Harvard University Press.

Kaushal, N. (1997). Press and democracy in India. In G.H. Peiris (Ed.), *Studies on the press in Sri Lanka and South Asia* (pp. 53–79). Kandy, Sri Lanka: International Center for Ethnic Studies.

Kumar, K.J. (1981). *Mass communication in India*. Bombay: Jaico Publishing House.

Kumar, K.J. (1996). International news on Indian television: A critical analysis of the World This Week. In D. French & M. Richards (Eds.), *Contemporary television: Eastern perspectives* (pp. 282–301). New Delhi: Sage Publications.

Lee, C.C. (1980). *Media imperialism reconsidered*. Beverly Hills: Sage Publications.

Lent, J.A. (1982). Freedom of the press in South Asia. In J.A. Lent (Ed.), *Newspapers in Asia: Contemporary trends and problems* (pp. 396–427). Hong Kong: Heinemann Asia.

Luthra, H.R. (1986). *Indian broadcasting*. New Delhi: Publications Division of Government of India.

Masani, M. (1985). *Broadcasting and the people*. New Delhi: National Broadcast Trust.

Ministry of Information & Broadcasting. (1978). *Akash Bharati* (National Broadcast Trust): Report of the Working Group on Autonomy for Akashwani & Doordarshan. New Delhi: Government of India.

Ministry of Information & Broadcasting. (1980). *Report of the Working Group on National Film Policy*. New Delhi: Government of India.

Ministry of Information & Broadcasting. (1985). *An Indian personality for television*, Volumes I & II (Report of the Working Group on Software). New Delhi: Government of India.

Ministry of Information & Broadcasting. (1989). *Press in India 1989*. New Delhi: Government of India.

Ministry of Information & Broadcasting. (1994–95). *Mass media in India*. New Delhi: Publications Division, Government of India.

Ministry of Information & Broadcasting. (various years). *India*. New Delhi: Government of India.

Mody, B. (1979). Programming for SITE. *Journal of Communication, 29,* 4, 90–98.

McDowell, S.D. (1997). Globalization and policy choice: Television and audiovisual services policies in India. *Media, Culture & Society, 19,* 151–172.

Natarajan, S. (1962). *A history of the press in India*. Bombay: Asia Publishing House.

Nayar, K.S. (1998a, October 9). Graduating from information sidewalk to highway. *India Abroad*, p. 24.

Nayar, K.S. (1998b, October 9). Industry eagerly awaits new loans on e-commerce. *India Abroad*, p. 26.

Pande, T. (1998, October 9). Of Web surfers, cybershopping, takeaways & being cool. *India Abroad*, p. 26.

Parthasarathy, R. (1989). *Journalism in India: From the earliest times to the present day*. New Delhi: Sterling Publishers.

Planning Commission. (1997). *Ninth five-year plan, 1997–2002*, Vols. I & II. New Delhi: Government of India [On-line]. Available: (http://www.nic.in/ninthplan/).

Ram, N. (1989). Foreword (v–xx). In R. Parthasarathy. *Journalism in India: From the earliest times to the present day*. New Delhi: Sterling Publishers

Raman, A.S. (1995). The press in India. *Contemporary Review, 267*, 70–74.

Reddi, U.V. (1996). Rip van Winkle: A story of Indian television. In D. French & M. Richards (Eds.), *Contemporary television: Eastern perspectives* (pp. 231–245). New Delhi: Sage Publications.

Sharma, A. (1998). India. In A. Albarran & S.M. Chan-Olmstead (Eds.), *Global media economics: Commercialization, concentration and integration of world media markets* (pp. 255–265). Ames, IA: Iowa State University Press.

Sharma, S.P. (1996). *The press: Socio-political awakening*. New Delhi: Mohit Publications.

Shukla, S. (1979). The impact of SITE on primary school children. *Journal of Communication, 29*, 4, 99–105.

Sinha, A. (1996). Development dilemmas for Indian television. In D. French & M. Richards (Eds.), *Contemporary television: Eastern perspectives* (pp. 302–320). New Delhi: Sage Publications.

Sinha, B. (1994). *Press and the National Movement in India (1911–1947)*. New Delhi: Manak Publications Pvt Ltd.

Siune, K., Truetzschler, W., & The Euromedia Research Group. (1992). *Dynamics of media politics*. London: Sage Publications.

Sreberny-Mohammedi, A. (1984). The "world of news." *Journal of Communication, 34*, 1, 121–134.

UNDP (United Nations Development Program). (1999). *Human development report*. New York: UNDP & Oxford University Press.

UNESCO (United Nations Educational, Scientific and Cultural Organization). (1999). *Statistical yearbook*. Paris/Lanham; MD: UNESCO & Berman Press.

Venkateswaran, K.S. (Comp.). (1993). *Mass media laws and regulations in India*. Singapore: AMIC.

Vilanilam, J.V. (1996). The socio-cultural dynamics of Indian television: From SITE to insight to privatization. In D. French & M. Richards (Eds.), *Contemporary television: Eastern perspectives* (pp. 61–90). New Delhi: Sage Publications.

Viswanath, K. (1982). *A communication policy for All India Radio*. Unpublished master's thesis, Osmania University, Hyderabad, India.

Viswanath, K., & Finnegan, J.R. (1996). The knowledge gap hypothesis: Twenty five years later. In B.R. Burleson (Ed.), *Communication Yearbook 19* (pp. 187–227). Thousand Oaks: Sage Publications.

Wolseley, R.E. (1971). India: History and development. In J.A. Lent (Ed.), *The Asian newspapers' reluctant revolution* (pp. 268–281). Ames: Iowa State University Press.

WAN (World Association of Newspapers). (1999). *World press trends*. Paris: WAN.

World factbook. (1999). Washington, DC: CIA [On-line]. Available: http://www.odci.gov/cia/publications/factbook/country-frame.html.

Xavier, F.S., & Eashwer, L. (1998). India. In A. Goonasekera & D. Holaday (Eds.), *Asian communication handbook* (pp. 49–65). Singapore: AMIC & NTU.

◆

4

MALDIVES

Kavita Karan & K. Viswanath

1. NATIONAL PROFILE

1.1 Geography

Maldives is an archipelago nation of some 1,190 coral islands grouped into 26 atolls that lie in the heart of the Indian Ocean, 800 km to the south-southwest of India and Sri Lanka. Lying astride the Arabian Sea and the Laccadive Sea, it has only about 200 inhabited islands. The islands, which cover an area of 300 sq km, have a hot and humid tropical climate with two seasons determined by the dry northeast monsoon (November to March) and the rainy southwest monsoon (June to August). The archipelago runs a north–south distance of almost 885 km (*World factbook*, 1999).

1.2 People

The estimated population of the Maldives in mid-1999 was 0.3 million. It has thus, one of the higher population densities in the world—1,000.7 people per sq km (US Census Bureau's International Data Base).[1] Almost all are Sunni Muslims, though in its early history, people are believed to have widely practiced Buddhism. The official language is Divehi, which, it is believed, has both Arabic and Sinhala influences. The adult literacy rate at 95.7 percent is the highest in South Asia (UNDP, 1999; *World factbook*, 1999; Reynolds, 1993). Maldivians use English as their international language.

People from India and Sri Lanka are believed to have been settled on the islands since 500 B.C. These countries have continued to provide immigrants to the

Acknowledgments: Professor Shelton A. Gunaratne, Bob Johnson, and Ben Lewis also contributed to this chapter.

[1] This figure should be understood in context as several of Maldivian islands are uninhabited and people live on about 200 islands.

archipelago. Others believe that the earliest inhabitants had settled on the islands as early as 1500 B.C. The first contact with the Arab world occurred about A.D. 947, when Islam started replacing early Buddhist practices—a process that reached completion by about 1153. Given this history, Maldivians have an ethnic mixture of South Indians, Sinhalese, and Arabs, though a great deal of assimilation has also taken place.

Sultans and sultanas from Maley Hilaly and Utheem dynasties, among others, ruled the Maldives for several centuries. The Portuguese attempted to colonize Maldives in the 16th century. From 1887 to 1965 Maldives was a British protectorate. The country began governing on the basis of a written constitution from December 22, 1932, following which Sultan Shamsuddeen III was forced to abdicate on October 2, 1934. Although Sultan Hassan Nooraddeen II succeeded him, he too was forced to abdicate on April 8, 1943. The Huraage dynasty ruled the country until January 1, 1953, when Mohamed Amin proclaimed a republic and assumed the duties of president. The country experienced some turmoil with power changing hands from a republic to a sultanate and back to a republic. Ibrahim Mohamed Didi, the vice president, and senior government officials plotted the downfall of Amin's eight-month rule, and reinstalled the monarchy on March 7, 1954, with Mohamed Fareed I as the sultan.

Maldives gained independence on July 26, 1965 (Adeney & Carr, 1975). Prime Minister Ibrahim Nasir reinstalled a republic and became president in 1968.[2] Two protests against Nasir took place in 1974 and 1975, fuelled by the rising prices of food. Nasir resigned voluntarily to pave the way for the election of the then Transport Minister Maumoon Abdul Gayoom as president on November 11, 1978. Since then, Gayoom has continued as president (Adeney & Carr, 1975; Freedom House, 1999).

1.3 Government and Politics

Maldives is a presidential republic of which Male is the capital. The legal system is a mixture of Islamic and English common law, which evolved over time (Phadnis & Luithui, 1985). The official religion is Islam, and the law is based on the Islamic *Shariat* (Hecker, 1986).

The head of the government is the president, elected for a five-year term by members of the parliament, the *Majlis*. The electorate then ratifies the decision through a referendum. The president must be a *Sunni* Muslim (Hecker, 1986). A cabinet of ministers, who may or may not be members of parliament, assist the president.

The unicameral legislature, the citizens' *Majlis*, comprises 50 members: 42 elected by popular vote and eight appointed by the president. The members are

---

[2] For a more elaborate account of the Maldives, see Phadnis & Luithui, 1985; Heyerdahl, 1986; and Reynolds, 1993.

elected for five-year terms, two from Male and two each from 20 atolls.[3] Any constitutional amendment must be enacted by a specially constituted parliament convened for that purpose. A newly amended constitution that came into effect on January 1, 1998, provided more rights and freedoms for the people. Although political parties are not banned, none exists. This highlights the lack of political pluralism in the country. Federally appointed officials administer atolls with the assistance of local officials. A chief justice heads the highest court. Several lower courts exist at the regional and atoll levels.

Phadnis and Luithui (1985) say that despite the separation of powers, the contemporary history of the Maldives is replete with incidents where power has been centralized in the presidency. The history of the islands, its geography, social structure, and culture have all been conducive to an open, but often consensual, political culture. With its rather small elite base, all programs and policies in Maldives are individualized. Personality and charisma have continued to be crucial factors in influencing political choice (Phadnis & Luithui, 1985).

1.4 Economy

Given its location and geographical structure, Maldives has made tourism a major source of revenue, constituting 18 percent of its gross domestic product, estimated at US$ 0.9 billion (purchasing power parity). Fishing is another source of foreign exchange for the country. Other small-scale industries do exist, but they are of limited consequence in the overall economy. Industry, which consisted mainly of garment production, boat building, and handicrafts, accounted for about 15 percent of the GDP. The country's real growth rate stood at 5.8 percent (*World factbook*, 1999; *Asiaweek*, December 17, 1999). Its per capita GDP at purchasing power parity is US$ 3,395 while its nominal per capita GNP is US$ 1,167.[4]

Owing to its high population growth rate and limited arable land, Maldives imports much of its food, including its staple, rice. It exported merchandise to the tune of US$ 0.1 billion over the last 12 months, with its reserves—excluding gold—standing at US$ 0.1 billion (*Asiaweek*, December 17, 1999).

2. DEVELOPMENT OF PRESS AND BROADCASTING

2.1 Brief Early History

Saleem (1994) states that the Maldivian press has a history of some 56 years with "some form of organized press" dating back to as early as 1943 (p. 60). The first

---

[3] The most recent special *Majlis*, which was dissolved in 1998, has produced yet another revised constitution for liberalizing the country's political system, leading potentially to a decentralization of power.

[4] See: (http://visitmaldives.com/rg).

newspaper is reported to be *Al Islah*. Other early newspapers included *Sarukaaruge Khabaru* and *Viyaafari Miyadhu*. Among the early magazines published in the country were *Munnaru, Male Times*, and *Moonlight* (The story of Haveeru, 1991).

The country's politics underwent intermittent periods of turmoil that often tempted governments to clamp down on dissent, seemingly in the interest of maintaining consensual politics. Although the early history is unclear, much of it appears to be a struggle to maintain a semblance of independence from the government by expressing dissent.[5] In early 1990, Gayoom initiated democratic reforms with particular attention on the freedom of the press. He dropped the idea because it was not uniformly well received. At that time, the emergence of several "outspoken" magazines and journals, including *Sangu* and *Hukuru*, made the government and the elite skittish about a "free press." By June, the government reversed its policy of liberalization and banned publications that it had not permitted. Writers and journalists were arrested (*The Europa world yearbook*, 1998; Freedom House, 1998). The conditions for press freedom remain a source of tension between journalists and the government.

2.2 Developments since 1945

Previous research suggests that Maldives had two weeklies, *Hafta* in Divehi and *Outlook* in English, as well as three monthlies—*Aabaaru, Amaaz*, and *Faiythoora*, all in Divehi (Kurian, 1982). The Haveeru News Service published *Spectrum*, another magazine in English (Saleem, 1994). Government-owned or -sponsored publications included *Dheenuge Mage* (Path of Religion) published by the president's office; *Faiythoora*, published by the National Council for Linguistic and Historical Research; *Furadhaana*, by the Ministry of Information, Arts, and Culture; and *Jamaathuge Khabaru* (Community News), by the Non-Formal Education Center. A decade-old report suggests that Maldives had two dailies, two weeklies, two monthlies, two fortnightlies, and 38 different magazines. The country's two dailies—*Haveeru* and *Aafathis*—were established in 1978 and 1979 respectively.

The radio system, Voice of Maldives, was founded in 1962, and Television Maldives, in 1978. Both are government operations.

3. THE PRESS

3.1 Policy and Legal Framework

Among journalists and the governing elite of the country, the conventional wisdom is that any discussion on press freedom and press regulation should take into account the fragile and "homogeneous" structure of the Maldivian society. Moreover, the

---

[5] See: ⟨http://lcweb2.loc.gov/cgi-bin/query/r?frd/cstdy:@field[docid+mv0033]⟩.

operation and regulation of the press should also be considered in the light of the Islamic nature of the society (Mohamed, 1995; Saleem, 1991). Foreign ownership of media, therefore, is restricted (Mohamed, 1995).

Article 13 of the Maldivian Constitution guarantees the freedom of "speech and expression of thought, orally and in writing" (Hecker, 1986, p. 9). The caveat is that the right is guaranteed "as long as the specific provisions of the *Shariat* and the law are not contravened" (Hecker, 1986, p. 9). Other related rights include the freedom to acquire and "impart" knowledge, and the freedom from government intrusion on private correspondence and telecommunication messages. All these are, however, subjected to limitations of *Shariat* and the law. Another germane provision is Article 35, which gives the president and the government the right to enact temporary orders in the event of emergencies. While press freedom is guaranteed and extended under Articles 13 and 14, more or less 30 other clauses and laws place limits on such freedom (Mohamed, 1995).

Law No. 47/78 requires the registration of newspapers and magazines with the Department of Information and Broadcasting. Article 5 of Law No. 3/68 gives the publishers and journalists the right to express their views, provided as outlined in Article 8 of Law No. 4/68, they do not touch on three things the law specifies as unconstitutional (Freedom House, 1996; Saleem, 1991, 1994):

- anything that contravenes the principles of Islam;
- anything that may cause damage to the stability and integrity of the society; and
- anything that may damage or defame the dignity of an individual.

Within this legal framework, press censorship, while not extensive, is prevalent in the Maldives. One source reported that in 1990, amidst debate on free speech in the parliament, the government closed down those publications that were critical and did not have its "sanction." The authorities arrested several writers and publishers.[6] Two organizations, the Committee for the Protection of Journalists (CPJ) and Amnesty International, reported the case of journalist Mohamed Nasheed, whom the authorities arrested for writing a critical article on Maldivian elections. Nasheed's magazine *Sangu*, which he co-founded in 1989, was banned in 1990. Other journalists and writers have been detained for exercising their freedom of expression and their magazines have been closed down.[7] Another publication, *Hukuru*, was also closed down (Freedom House, 1996). Occasional monitoring of personal communications is also suspected (Freedom House, 1996).

Freedom House (1999) points out the following:

- The Penal Code bans speech or actions that could "arouse people against the government" (p. 304) although a 1990 amendment decriminalized factual newspaper reports about government errors.

---

[6] See: ⟨http://lcweb2.loc.gov/cgi-bin/query/r?frd/cstdy:@field[DOCID+mv0033]⟩.
[7] See: ⟨http://www.amnesty.se/aixweb97/2ebe.htm⟩. Also see: ⟨http://farm.el.net/cgi-bin/Tango3.acgi$/cpj/cpj.taf?function=detail&ID=4697⟩.

- A 1968 law prohibits any speech that is considered inimical to be a Islam, a threat to national security, or libelous.
- The strict 1990 Prevention of Terrorism Act can be applied retroactively and was used to imprison several journalists arrested in 1990.
- The government can shut newspapers and sanction journalists for articles allegedly containing unfounded criticism. Regulations make editors responsible for the content of published material.

Some structural constraints also make controversial reporting difficult. Saleem (1991, 1994) reports that the "smallness of the community"—the fact that people know each other—makes reporting difficult (see also Mohamed, 1995). This phenomenon of constraints on journalists operating in a homogeneous community environment has extensive documentation in US research (Tichenor et al., 1980; Viswanath & Demers, 1999). In 1993, the government set up a National Press Council for reviewing, monitoring, and developing journalism (*The Europa world yearbook*, 1998).

3.2 Financial Aspects: Circulation, Advertising, Marketing Strategies

The afternoon daily *Haveeru* has a circulation of 4,500 while the morning *Aafathis* has a circulation of 300 (*Editor & publisher international yearbook*, 1999).[8] The small population of the country dispersed in 20 atolls cannot support a multiplicity of media backed by advertising. The government subsidizes the press through minimal taxation on the media revenues and lowered registration fees (Mohamed, 1995).

3.3 Structure and Organization

The Maldives' print media system is small because of the population size. UNESCO (1999) lists two daily newspapers (Table 2).[9] One is *Haveer* or *Haveeru*, founded in 1978 (Kurian, 1982),[10] and the other is *Aafathis*, established in 1979. Both newspapers appear in Divehi and English, and both have on-line editions. A third daily, *Miadhu*, also has an on-line edition. A predominant characteristic of the Maldivian media system is that almost all of the print media are published and circulated in the nation's capital of Male with the rural population being served intermittently (Nafiz, 1986).

---

[8] This is at variance with the numbers reported in another source, which says that *Haveeru* has a circulation of 2,500 and *Aafathis* has about 300.
[9] The UNESCO yearbook, 1999, on the other hand, puts the combined circulation of both daily newspapers at 5,000, though it does not report the breakdown.
[10] Also see: (www.maldives-info.com/at-maldi.htm, and http://lcweb2.loc.gov/cgi-bin/query/r?frd/cstdy:@field[DOCID+mv0033]).

3.4 Quality and Popular Press

The distinction between quality and popular press is hard to make in a market that has only two principal dailies with a small circulation. Newsgathering is less organized here than in some other countries. Press conferences and briefings were not routine until recently, when efforts were made to arrange regular meetings between journalists and officials (Saleem, 1991).

3.5 Distribution and Technology

The fact that there are about 200 inhabited islands with only water taxis as a means of communication poses a challenge for distribution. Newspapers do not often make it beyond the nation's capital, Male, and even when they do, they are often outdated by the time they arrive (Nafiz, 1986). The geographical spread also imposes a financial burden in importing technology and newsprint (Saleem, 1994). Yet another barrier in the distribution of newspapers was the absence of technology to print *Thaana*, the written language of Maldives. Successful experiments with assistance from agencies such as UNESCO, allowed for the development of software that is likely to facilitate distribution of the newspapers electronically across atolls (Arnaldo, 1988).

Maldives has three listed news agencies—Haveeru News Services (HNS), founded in 1979; the Hiyama News Agency; and the Maldives News Bureau (MNB), a department of the Maldives Ministry of Information, Arts, and Culture (*The Europa world yearbook*, 1998).

4. BROADCASTING

4.1 Policy and Legal Framework

Since both radio and television are owned and operated by the government, the degree of autonomy, if any, enjoyed by the broadcasting system is unclear. Freedom House (1998) reported that the "government-owned" radio and the "state-run television service carry some pluralistic views" (p. 304). However, journalists practice self-censorship.

4.2 Structure and Organization

Maldives has three radio stations—two AM and one FM (Reddy, 1994). It has about 34,000 radio receivers, which roughly correspond to about 12.9 receivers per 100 people (UNESCO, 1999). One study reports that about 90–95 percent of the population listen to the radio (*Maldives: Radio is prime medium*, 1992). Voice of Maldives (VoM) operates for about 16 hours a day. Broadcasts are in both

Divehi and English.[11] Radio is believed to have the greatest reach among the island's population (Mayer, 1993). The citizens also can theoretically receive broadcasts from foreign media, such as the BBC, Radio Australia, and Radio Beijing.[12]

The lone television station, Television Maldives, broadcasts for about six to seven hours on weekdays and more on weekends. Maldives has about 10,000 TV receivers—about 3.9 receivers per 100 people (see Table 2). The Indian television network, *Doordarshan*, as well as CNN, CFI, and Arab broadcasters, have provided technical assistance in satellite transmission and reception (Ahmad, 1993).

Given the inadequate infrastructural development in cinema, private entrepreneurs operate "video-cinemas." With the aid of video players, television monitors, and power generators, Hindi- and English-language movies are shown to small groups of people in temporarily erected structures, an ingenious way to exhibit movies at a low cost in different islands.

4.3 Program Policies

Nafiz (1986) reported that almost 37 percent of the programming on VoM comprised "general information," followed by 32 percent for entertainment, 16 percent for education, and almost 15 percent for religion. Given the primarily urban characteristic of the print media in Maldives, radio has become the more important medium for nationwide communication. The rural population, people on atolls away from the capital, depend primarily on radio for news and information (Nafiz, 1986). VoM uses radio extensively, for distance education in collaboration with the ministries of health, agriculture, and fisheries, among others. It creates and distributes supplementary material to follow up on educational broadcasts. One example is a series of self-learning modules called "Holhu Ashi" (*Maldives: Radio is prime medium*, 1992). VoM also spawned an experimental "wall magazine." This involved copying and displaying slowly read VoM news bulletins in public spaces in rural islands for public consumption (Nafiz, 1986).

With regard to TV programming, although Maldivians are sensitive to the issue of cultural integrity, India appears to have considerable influence on their production values (Mayer, 1993). One report suggests that only 20 percent of TV programming requirements are met from local production and the rest is filled either with imports or with repeats (*Maldives: Radio is the prime medium*, 1992). Yet, according to another estimate, 60 percent of the programs are foreign in origin, the highest figure in South Asia (IIMC, n.d.). According to a report in the World Broadcast News (1990), 47 percent of the program time is taken up by entertainment, followed by news (29 percent), religion (18 percent), and education (6 percent).

Apart from providing entertainment and news, television is also being used to provide "distance education" through the Educational Media Services Unit with assistance from the Commonwealth of Learning. As of 1994, 12 atolls received

[11] See *The Europa world yearbook*, 1998; and *World radio TV handbook*, 1998.
[12] See: (http://lcweb2.loc.gov/cgi-bin/query/r?frd/cstdy:@field[DOCID+mv0033]).

instruction on the English language (Khan & Walker, 1994). Yet another important objective of television is to promote "national unity," a sense of common identity given the spread of population over several islands (Maldive islands united by TV, 1990).

4.4 Ownership and Financing

The Voice of Maldives (radio) and Television Maldives (Channel 7) are both government-operated and -funded.

5. NEW ELECTRONIC MEDIA

5.1 Internet and On-line Media

The Internet service in Maldives started in 1996. The country has more than 3,000 computers—a density of 1.23 percent. The Internet Software Consortium's July 1999 survey estimated that Maldives had 217 Internet hosts—a density of 7.2 per 10,000 people. All three daily newspapers of the country—*Haveeru, Aafathis*, and *Miadhu*—are available on-line. Internet dial-up service is available throughout the archipelago, where there is telephone access (APT, 1999).

5.2 Telecommunications Infrastructure

Maldives has the highest telephone density in South Asia—7.5 mainlines per 100 people overall (see Table 3) and a rural density of 1.56 percent. Male has a telephone density of 23 percent. A cellular mobile telephone service that was started in January 1997 provided 1,606 telephones by the following year. All 20 administrative atolls have telecommunication services, with telephones in 172 out of the 198 inhabited islands. Telecommunication services to the far southern atolls of Seenu, Gaafu Alifu, Gaafu Dhaalu, and Gnaviyani are provided via satellite. Earth stations are located in Villingili on Male atoll and Hithadoo on Seenu atoll (APT, 1999).

The first telegraph to Sri Lanka was established in 1943. The system has, since then, expanded steadily though slowly. Maldives embarked on privatization in 1988, with the establishment of Dhiraagu, a joint venture company of the Maldivian government (55 percent of shares) and Britain's Cable and Wireless, to provide national and international telecommunication services. Dhiraagu has provided telephone access to 93 percent of the country's population and 80 percent of the geographical area (APT, 1999).

6. POLICY TRENDS FOR PRESS AND BROADCASTING

Three policy trends are worth watching:

- The extent to which the 1998 constitutional amendments will embolden the journalists and other activists to express dissent openly despite the homogenous power structure.
- Whether efforts to improve communications among the atolls will take effect in the realm of broadcast and print media.
- The extent to which the ambitions of the telecommunication company to rapidly introduce new media technologies, including telephones and the Internet, will be realized over the next several years.

7. MAIN ISSUES

- Cultural autonomy

Given its small size and proximity to India and Sri Lanka, Maldives does come under the influence of India in terms of media reach. Movies, magazines, and newspapers from India find a hospitable audience in Maldives. This certainly raises a concern about cultural autonomy, though it has not been an issue so far.

- Censorship

Because of censorship issues, some have argued that the press is likely to play a limited role in nurturing Maldives' democracy. The question is what would happen in the future when the inevitable clash occurs between the forces of change and the advocates of the status quo. This would be all the more significant when the country is slowly adopting contemporary and more Westernized political structures.[13]

- Press freedom

Freedom House (Sussman, 1999) gave Maldives a "not free" score of 66 out of 100 on press freedom. Maldives scored the maximum, 15 out of 15 each, for broadcasting and print on the criterion of laws and regulations that influence media content; 13 out of 15 for broadcast; 14 out of 15 for print on the criterion of political pressures and controls; eight out of 15 for print and zero for broadcasting on the criterion of economic influences; and one out of five for print and zero for broadcast on the criterion of repressive action. These criteria are founded on Article 19 of the Universal Declaration of Human Rights. Therefore, activists are bound to press the Maldivian government to relax its grip on the media. Tensions between the

---

[13] See: (http://lcweb2.loc.gov/cgi-bin/query/r?frd/cstdy:@field[DOCID+mv0033]).

perception of the governing elite that the fragile nature of the "homogeneous" Maldivian society should be protected on one hand, and the pressures from social change internally and internationally on the other hand, are only likely to increase and influence future development (Mohamed, 1995).

● Journalistic training

There is no mechanism for formal training in journalism. The occupation of journalism still remains a craft, a "hobby," because of the limited potential for earnings. Given the increasing importance and steady expansion of media in the country, development of journalistic skills and training are important issues that have to be addressed in the future.

8. STATISTICS

Table 1
General Profile

Exchange rate (September 1999)	US$ 1 = Rufiyaa 11.29*
Gross Domestic Product (Purchasing Power Parity)	US$ 0.9 billion
Per capita GDP (PPP)	US$ 3,395
Per capita GNP (nominal)	US$ 1,167
Population (estimate) 1999	0.3 million**
Number of females to 1,000 males	952**
Percentage of literacy	95.7
Density per sq km	1,000.7 (varies by island)

Source: UNDP, 1999; *Asiaweek*, December 17, 1999; * OANDA Historical Currency Table [On-line]. Available: (http://www.oanda.com/converter/cc_table?lang=en); ** US Census Bureau's International Data Base [On-line]. Available: (http://www.census.gov/cgi-bin/ipc/idbrank.pl).

Table 2
Estimated Mass Media Penetration

	Radio receivers		TV receivers		Daily newspapers		
	Number ('000)	Per 100 people	Number ('000)	Per 100 people	Number	Circ'n	Per 100 people
1980	13	8.2	1	0.7	2	1,000	0.6
1985	19	10.3	3	1.7	2	2,000	0.8
1990	25	11.6	5	2.4	2	3,000	1.2
1995	31	12.4	7	2.6	2	3,000	1.2
1996	33	12.9	7	2.7	2	5,000	1.9
1997	34	12.9	7	2.8			
1998			10*	3.9*			

Source: UNESCO, 1999; * ITU, 1999.

Table 3
Estimated Telephone and Computer Density

	Mainline telephones		Cellular telephones		Personal computers		Internet	
	Number	Per 100	Number	Per 100	Number	Per 100	Hosts	Users
1990	6,240	2.94	...	...	...	...	...	...
1996	15,286	5.81	20	0.01	3,000	1.23	33	575
1997	17,967	6.58	1,290	0.47	...	...	52	906
1998*	19,985	7.50	1,606	0.60	...	...	109	1,899
1999	...	...	...	...	...	...	217	3,780

Source: ITU 1999; * APT, 1999

9. USEFUL ADDRESSES

Ministry of Information, Arts and Culture
Buruzu Magu
Male 20-04
Telephone: (960) 323836
Fax: (960) 326211
E-mail: informat@dhivhinet.net.mv

Ministry of Transport and Communications
Huravee Building
Ameer Ahmed Magu
Male 20-05
Telephone: (960) 323991
Fax: (960) 323994

Voice of Maldives (VoM)
"Moonlight Higun"
Male 20-06
Telephone: (960) 325577/313456
Fax: (960) 325 371/8357
MW: 1458kHz, 5kW; FM: 104.2 MHz, 20W; SW: 7350 kHz; 1kW.

Television Maldives [Channel 7; 1kW]
Buruzu Magu
Male 20-04
Telephone: (960) 322106
Fax: (960) 325083

***Aafathis* (a.m.) [Divehi/English; Established 1979; Circulation 300]**
Silver Star 4
Maafannu
Haveeree Hingun
Male
Republic of Maldives
Telephone: (960) 318630, (960) 328730
Fax: (960) 32906
E-mail: aafathis@dhivhinet.net.mv

Haveeru Daily (p.m.) |Divehi/English; Estd. 1978; Circ'n 4,500|
G. Olympus (North Side)
P.O. Box 20103
Telephone: (960) 325671
Fax: (960) 323103
E-mail: haveeru@dhivhinet.net.mv
URL: http://www.haveeru.com

Miadhu Daily
Telephone: (960) 320700
Fax: (960) 320500
E-mail: http://www.miadhu.com

Haveeru News Service (HNS)
Husnuheena Magu
P.O. Box 20103
Male 20-04
Telephone: (960) 323685
Fax: (960) 323103

Maldives News Bureau
Ministry of Information, Arts, Culture
Buruzu Magu
Male 20-04
Telephone: (960) 323836
Fax: (960) 326211

10. REFERENCES

Adeney, M., & Carr, W.K. (1975). The Maldives Republic. In J.M. Ostheimer (Ed.), *The politics of western Indian Ocean islands* (pp. 139–160). New York: Praeger.

Ahmad, M. (1993, October 21–23). *Television Maldives*. Paper presented at the AMIC Seminar on Legal and Regulatory Aspects of Satellite Broadcasting, New Delhi.

APT (Asia-Pacific Telecommunity). (1999). *The APT yearbook*. Bangkok: APT.

Arnaldo, C. (1988). Writing electronically or how to bypass Gutenberg. *Media Asia, 15*, 194–195.

Editor & publisher international yearbook. (1998). New York: E & P.

Europa world yearbook, The. (1999). Bedford Square, UK: Europa Publications.

Freedom House Survey Team. (1996). *Freedom in the world: The annual survey of political rights and civil liberties, 1995–1996*. New York: Freedom House.

Freedom House Survey Team. (1999). *Freedom in the world: The annual survey of political rights and civil liberties, 1998–1999*. New York: Freedom House.

Hecker, H. (1986). The Maldives. In A.P. Blaustein & G.H. Flanz (Eds.), *Constitutions of the world* (pp. 1–27). New York: Oceania Publications.

Heyerdahl, T. (1986). *The Maldive mystery*. London: George Allen & Unwin.

IIMC (Indian Institute of Mass Communication). (n.d.). *Media in South Asia*. Draft report prepared for UNESCO's *World communication report*, Indian Institute of Mass Communication, New Delhi.

ITU (International Telecommunication Union). (1999). *Yearbook of statistics: Telecommunication services 1988–1997*. Geneva: ITU.

Khan, A.W., & Walker, D. (1994). Appropriate media for small-scale distance education systems. *Media Asia, 21*, 142–149.

Kurian, G. (1982). *World press encyclopedia*. New York, NY: Facts on File.

Maldive islands united by TV. (1990, October). *World Broadcast News.*

Maldives: Radio is prime medium. (1992). South and South East Asia media assembly for people-to-people understanding. Singapore: AMIC.

Mayer, D. (1993). Teaching audio-visual production in Africa and Asia: A personal account. *Media Development, 40* (1), 35–38.

Mohamed, S.I. (1995, December 27–28). *National communication policies and legal frameworks in affecting pluralism in Maldives.* Paper presented to the South Asian Regional Roundtable on "Making peace out of pieces: The role of media in conflict resolution in South Asia," Lahore, Pakistan.

Nafiz, A.Z. (1986, November 12–14). *Rural press in Maldives.* Paper presented to the Workshop on Rural Press Development in Asia, Singapore.

Phadnis, U., & Luithui, E.D. (1985). *Maldives: Winds of change in atoll state.* New Delhi: South Asian Publishers.

Reddy, M.A. (Ed.). (1994). *Statistical abstract of the world.* Detroit, MI: Gale Research Inc.

Reynolds, C.H.B. (1993). *Maldives.* Oxford: Clio Press.

Saleem, M. (1991, April 2–5). *Press system in Maldives.* Paper presented at the conference on AMIC Consultation on Press Systems in SAARC, Kathmandu, Nepal.

Saleem, M. (1994). Maldives. In *Press systems in SAARC* (pp. 59–62), Singapore: AMIC.

Sussman, L.R. (1999). *Press freedom 1999: News of the century.* New York: Freedom House.

The story of Haveeru. (1991). Male: *Haveeru Daily.*

Tichenor, P.J., Donohue, G.A., & Olien, C.N. (1980). *Community, conflict & the press.* Beverly Hills, CA: Sage Publications.

UNDP (United Nations Development Program). (1999). Human development report, 1999. New York: UNDP & Oxford University Press.

UNESCO (United Nations Educational, Scientific and Cultural Organization). (1999). *Statistical yearbook.* Lanham, NJ: Bernan Press, & Paris: UNESCO.

Viswanath, K., & Demers, D. (1999). Mass media from a macrosocial perspective. In D. Demers & K. Viswanath (Eds.), *Mass media, social control & social change*, Ames, IA: Iowa State University Press.

World factbook. (1999). Maldives [On-line]. Available: (http://www.odci.gov/cia/publications/factbook/mv.html).

World radio TV handbook. (1998). Maldives (pp. 220, 416). New York: Billboard publications.

◆

5

NEPAL

Sandhya Rao & Bharat Koirala

1. NATIONAL PROFILE

1.1 Geography

Nepal, a landlocked mountain kingdom nestled in the Himalayas, is surrounded by India in the east, south, and west, and by Tibet in the north. It covers an area of 140,800 sq km—slightly larger than Arkansas (*World factbook*, 1999). The country is known for its geographical diversity, with its terrain rising from almost sea level to the highest point on earth—Mount Everest at 8,848 meters. It contains eight of the world's 10 highest peaks. The temperature ranges from below freezing point in the mountains to humid sub-tropical warm temperatures in the Kathmandu Valley in summer.

1.2 People

The nation's capital Kathmandu is home to about half a million of Nepal's estimated population (1999) of 24.3 million people (US Census Bureau, International Data Base). The official language is Nepali, which is spoken by more than 50 percent of the population. The 20 other languages include Maithili and Bhojpuri, spoken in the southern plains of the Terai. More than 86 percent of the population is Hindu, almost 8 percent Buddhist, and more than 3 percent Muslim. The remaining 3 percent include followers of traditional religions and other major world religions. (Census, 1991). Nepal's ethnic composition—Newars, Indians, Tibetans, Gurungs, Magars, Tamangs, Bhotias, Rais, Limbus, and Sherpas—is as diverse as its terrain. According to the Nepal government's Ninth Five-Year Plan, the adult literacy rate is 40 percent.[1] More than 86 percent of the people live in rural areas.

---

[1] UNDP, 1999, has estimated Nepal's 1997 adult literacy rate at 38.1 percent—males, 55.7 percent; females, 20.7 percent.

1.3 Government and Politics

Nepal is a constitutional monarchy with executive power vested in the king and the council of ministers, which is answerable to the House of Representatives. The constitution provides for a bicameral parliament. The House of Representatives (*Pratinidhi Sabha*) has 205 members elected by popular vote to serve five-year terms. The National Council (*Rastriya Sabha*) has 60 members (35 appointed by the House of Representatives, 10 by the king, and 15 elected by an electoral college), with one-third of the members elected every two years to serve six-year terms.

Nepal was unified as one country after King Prithvi Narayan Shah of Gorkha in Central Nepal conquered the kingdoms of Kathmandu Valley and other principalities in the late 1760s. At the height of Nepal's expansion, the country stretched from Sikkim in the east right up to the borders of Punjab in the west. It lost much of this territory to the British in the Anglo-Nepal Wars of 1814–16. The Ranas, a family of court officials, seized power in the 1840s and established themselves as hereditary prime ministers, reducing the king to a figurehead. They ruled the country for more than 100 years until 1951, when the Nepal Congress Party (NCP) restored King Tribhuvan to power and established a limited constitutional monarchy. With Tribhuvan's death in 1955, his son Mahendra took over and promulgated Nepal's first constitution in 1958. Multi-party general elections brought the NCP to power with B.P. Koirala as the first popularly elected prime minister. However, differences between the king and the prime minister brought democracy to an end in December 1960. The king assumed absolute power and established a government based on the village council (*panchayat*) system, with the prime minister appointed by the king. With Mahendra's death in 1972, his son Birendra came to power. King Birendra is the 10th monarch in the present dynasty. By 1979, amid national unrest, demand for a multi-party democracy emerged. In May 1980, the king held a referendum which endorsed, by a slight majority, the *panchayat* system over a full-fledged multi-party system. The king amended the constitution on the advice of a Constitutional Reforms Commission. Legislative elections on a non-party basis took place in May 1981. When successive government reshuffles failed to stamp out official corruption and economic mismanagement, the NCP began a campaign demanding a return to a multi-party political system and parliamentary rule under a constitutional monarchy.

A movement for restoration of democracy led by the NCP and the United Left Front boiled over into violent street protests in 1990. King Birendra was forced to appoint an interim government to pave the way for free elections and a constitutional monarchy. The current constitution was promulgated on November 9, 1990. Twenty political parties participated in the 1991 general elections. The NCP contested alone and won the majority of parliamentary seats, followed by the Communist Party of Nepal/United Marxist-Leninist (CPN/UML) combination. The instability of the NCP government forced a mid-term general election in 1994 in which the CPN/UML won the majority of seats and formed the next government under M.M. Adhikari. A coalition of the NCP, the National Democratic Party, and the Nepali

Sadhbavana Party replaced the CPN/UML government in September 1995, when the latter failed a parliamentary vote of confidence. The new government under NCP leader Sher Bahadur Deuba also failed a parliamentary vote of confidence in March 1997. A coalition of the NDP, the CPN/UML, and the NSP formed the new government with NDP leader L.B. Chand as prime minister (*The Europa world yearbook*, 1997). Chand soon gave way to NDP's S.B. Thapa. In April 1998, NCP leader G.P. Koirala returned as prime minister (New premier, 1998). Nepal held elections once again in May 1999, and the NCP led by Koirala emerged victorious. Koirala however, stepped aside to make way for NCP's Krishna Prasad Bhattarai to become prime minister (Bearak, 1999).

1.4 Economy

Since the early 1950s, Nepal has been following five year plans for national development. Agriculture accounts for 41 percent of Nepal's gross domestic product. The service sector accounts for 37 percent of the GDP, and industry for 22 percent—with most of the earnings coming from the traditional cottage industries. Tourism has emerged as a major source of foreign exchange in recent years. The main source of imports is India, and the main market for exports is Western Europe, with other major trading partners being Japan, Singapore, Thailand, and the United States. Nepal's isolated location, rugged terrain, and a general lack of natural resources make the country one of the least developed in the world (*The Europa world yearbook*, 1997). The country's political instability has obstructed economic restructuring and slowed down the growth rates ever since the introduction of parliamentary democracy in 1990 (Deveney, 1997). Nepal's per capita GDP at purchasing power parity is US$ 1,100. Its nominal per capita GNP is US$ 225 (*Asiaweek*, December 17, 1999).

2. DEVELOPMENT OF PRESS AND BROADCASTING

2.1 Developments since 1945

2.1.1 Print Media

The first newspaper in Nepal, *The Gorkhapatra*, was established in 1901 as a mouthpiece for the Rana family, which ruled the country for more than a century until 1951. *The Gorkhapatra* began as a literary weekly, became a biweekly in 1943, and a daily in 1966 (Rana, 1982; Verma, 1988). The introduction of democracy in 1951 led to a proliferation of newspapers, including vernacular weeklies which espoused different political views and ideologies. Both the government and the private sector published newspapers (Koirala, 1998). However, Prime Minister K.I. Singh imposed repressive pressures on the press in 1957. Despite this, the government accepted a long-standing demand of the journalists for a press commission to examine their problems. The king, however, dismissed the Singh government even before the commission could submit a report (Joshi & Rose, 1966).

The growth in the number of private newspapers came to a halt in 1960 when King Mahendra dissolved the elected parliament and assumed power. Repression of the freedom of expression and severe restrictions on media in the private sector became hallmarks of the *panchayat* system of government introduced in 1962. However, *The Gorkhapatra* and *The Rising Nepal*, the government-controlled dailies established in 1965, continued to receive financial support (Koirala, 1998). Under the *panchayat* system, suppressed political parties published clandestine newspapers to express their opinions. The government jailed some editors and censored or banned their newspapers. Burghart (1993) says: "The journalists, however, were often courageous and enterprising. It happened not infrequently that editors were arrested because of critical reports and that the same editors, after they had been released, published their paper under a different name, which they had already registered before their arrest as a precautionary measure" (p. 11). The general public relied on private newspapers to get the real news because the government press merely disseminated propaganda.

Changes in press laws in 1981 fostered the development of small, weekly tabloids, which multiplied more than four-fold from about 90 to 400, in just two years. The private-sector press criticized the authoritarian political system (Koirala, 1998). In the 1980s, this press exposed the increasing corruption in the government and brought attention to the discontent caused by this among liberal supporters of the *panchayat* system. But these newspapers were unable to criticize the king (Burghart, 1993). The pressure on the press increased particularly between February 15 and March 26, 1990, when the authorities confiscated the printruns of privately-owned newspapers on at least 18 occasions and detained about 45 journalists (Hutt, 1993). The re-establishment of a multi-party democracy and constitutional monarchy in April 1990 ended nearly three decades of repression of the media and triggered the growth of newspapers in urban centers. Newspaper circulation received a boost from government subsidies to larger newspapers, the increase in literacy rate, growing political awareness, and the improved standards of newspapers (Koirala, 1998).

In 1962, the government established Nepal's news agency, the Rastriya Samachar Samiti (RSS), with correspondents in all the districts. The agency has exchange arrangements with foreign wire services, such as the Associated Press (United States), Agence France Presse, and Xinhua (Chaudhary & Chen, 1995). However, there is a growing demand for a private national news agency, considering that the government-run RSS is prone to ignore events and stories critical of the government. It operates with a government subsidy, and its main clients are the official media. The bulk of the country's newspapers do not subscribe to the RSS service.

2.1.2 Broadcast Media

2.1.2.1 Radio: Broadcasting began in Nepal with the establishment of the government-owned and -operated Radio Nepal in 1951. Before 1951, the Rana regime did not allow people to own radio receivers. King Mahendra favored Nepali as the official language, and the 1962 Education Act made Nepali the medium of instruction in schools. In 1965, Radio Nepal stopped news broadcasts in Hindi and Newari (Burghart, 1993). Radio made considerable progress only after the government approved a National Communications Plan in 1971. Technical assistance from the United States, Great Britain, Japan, and Australia has enabled Radio Nepal to use modern equipment. As a low-cost medium, the government has used radio for educational purposes and for rural upliftment. Next to wrist-watches, radio is popular in Nepal as a symbol of modernity (Sheffield & Lent, 1978). Radio news is broadcast in Nepali, English, and several other languages.

Five years after the 1991 communication task force made its recommendations, the government granted a license to the Nepal Forum of Environmental Journalists to operate the first privately owned FM radio station in the Kathmandu Valley. Funded by UNESCO, this small community radio station serves as a model for similar stations to be set up elsewhere in Nepal. The government-owned Radio Nepal, however, set up an FM station without having to go through the lengthy process involved in obtaining a license. Radio Nepal's FM station airs 18 hours of entertainment programs produced by private companies, but the government appears reluctant to grant licenses for new private radio stations. Radio Sagarmatha received a license with enough restrictions to make it very difficult to operate smoothly (Koirala, 1998). However, with a new coalition taking over the reins of government in 1997, several companies and the Kathmandu Municipality have begun to operate commercial FM stations in Kathmandu. The biggest is Kantipur FM owned by the Kantipur Group, the publisher of *Kantipur*, the Nepali newspaper with the highest circulation. Among those to receive a license was the village of Madan Pokhara in the western district of Palpa. Radio Sagarmatha and the Madan Pokhara radio stand out as the only non-commercial, public service stations in Nepal. Both, however, have an extremely limited reach: Radio Sagarmatha FM because its transmission capacity is restricted to 100 watts, and Madan Pokhara because it is restricted to a remote village with a small population.

2.1.2.2 Television: Whether Nepal should have television or not was debated hotly in and outside parliament in the early 1980s. Initially, some people questioned the relevance of television to Nepal's economy (Karp, 1995). With the media supporting the establishment of television, the government set up a Television Project to look into the prospect of establishing television in the country. With several concrete steps taken in this direction, the government converted the project into Nepal Television Corporation (NTV). It started broadcasting in the Kathmandu Valley with a low power transmitter in December 1985. But the popularity of NTV's locally produced programs, including its news and current affairs programs, compelled the government to invest more money to make NTV signals available to people outside the capital. Nepal Television registered an unexpectedly high growth. Satellite television entered Nepal in October 1994, when a private entrepreneur started the Space-time Network (Karp, 1995), following the government's decision to give licenses to private cable operators who could use the existing transmission facilities. Shangrila Channel is the other main provider of cable services in the Kathmandu Valley. Image Channel and Young Nepal Television started broadcasting their own programs at times when NTV's programs were not broadcast (Koirala, 1998). However, Young Nepal Television closed down recently because of financial problems.

3. THE PRESS

3.1 Policy and Legal Framework

Pokhrel and Koirala (1995) describe in detail the mass media laws and regulations in Nepal. Article 12(a) of the Constitution of Nepal, promulgated on November 9, 1991, guarantees freedom of expression and thought in general, and Article 13 deals more specifically with the press and publication rights of citizens. Article 16 states that every person shall have the right to demand and receive information on any matter of public importance. The press, by promoting a freer government and protesting against the restrictions, was partly responsible for the changes that have taken place after three decades of repression (Koirala, 1998).

In the century-old history of the Nepalese press, the aim of almost all the press-related laws and regulations was to restrict press freedom. The most restrictive measure was the Rastriya Samachar Samiti Act of 1962 that empowered the government to dissolve Nepal's two independent news agencies and to replace them with the government-run Rastriya Samachar Samiti or National News Agency. Several newspapers lost their licenses for being critical of the government. The Press and Publications Act of 1975 placed further restrictions on the press.

Faced with growing public unrest against these severe restrictions, King Birendra announced in 1979 that he would grant freedom of expression to the Nepali press (Belbase & Murphy, 1983). Government–press relations became an issue of national concern during this period. Responding to a call by the Nepal Journalists' Association, the government set up a Royal Press Commission, which not only made a number of recommendations but also introduced the Press and Publication Act of 1982 and the Press and Publication Regulation of 1983 that would control the media in other ways. However, even though the regulation was amended twice, it failed to improve government–press relations (Rai, 1987). Rai wrote:

Not infrequently, truth, freedom and democratic ideals enshrined in the Constitution become broad public issues vis-à-vis the system of media control, the concept of responsibility, and the codes of ethics devised within the post-1980 national communications policy framework. Such issues become all the more sensitive and intractable as they rebound upon the Panchayat polity. (p. 153)

In 1991, following the promulgation of the constitution, the government appointed a task force to bring about improvements in the communication sector. However, many of its recommendations failed to materialize because of frequent changes in government (Koirala, 1998).

A national communications policy began to emerge after the overthrow of the autocratic Rana regime in 1951. In the decade that followed, professional organizations such as the Nepal Journalists' Association, private news agencies, the Nepal Sambad Samiti, and the Sagarmatha Sambad Samiti emerged, and the government appointed the first Press Commission. The *panchayat* form of government recognized the need for using communication strategies to achieve national development goals. Thus, it set up a ministry of information and broadcasting. In 1971–73, the government came up with a National Communications Plan (NCP) to improve communication in the government and corporate sectors. The NCP became a part of the nation's five-year plan and served to strengthen the country's communication infrastructure. In the 1980s, the government extended the national communications policy to achieve cooperation in the South Asian region. As a member of the South Asian Association for Regional Cooperation (SAARC), Nepal began to explore joint ventures with South Asian private media agencies (Rai, 1987). Nepal's national communication policy furthered private ownership of the media but did not encourage single individuals to control the media (Bahadur, 1994).

3.2 Financial Aspects: Circulation, Advertising, Marketing Strategies

In 1990, Nepal had 26 daily newspapers with an estimated circulation of 173,000. In 1998, it had 29 dailies with an estimated circulation of 260,000—or 1.3 copies per 100 people (see Table 2). Nepali-language newspapers account for more than 82 percent of the circulation. English-language newspapers follow with more than 16 percent of the circulation (Koirala, 1988). The Goenka Prakashan (Pvt) Ltd (later known as Kantipur Publications after a change of ownership)—the publisher of *Kantipur*, a Nepali daily, and *The Kathmandu Post*, an English daily—is the only company doing well with an annual turnover exceeding Rupees 230 million. (Koirala, 1998). Two vernacular dailies, *Ajako Samacharpatra* and *Himalaya Times*, are beginning to assert an influential role in the media market. At least three daily newspapers—the *Everest Herald, Lokpatra*, and *Sri Sagarmatha*—folded up in the last two years because of economic hardship.

The government, the largest advertiser, siphons off a large share of its advertising to the government-owned media (see Table 3). Moreover, having invested in the corporate publishing sector, the government uses its influence to get official information published, sometimes bypassing the editors (Chaudhary & Chen, 1995).

Throughout the 30 years of *panchayat* rule, the government followed the policy of giving a fixed subsidy to those newspapers that supported the political system. The Department of Information openly handed out the subsidy every month to daily and weekly publications at predetermined rates—a practice that not only created a sense of dependency among newspaper publishers, but also prevented entrepreneurship and creativity. Those that did not support the government did not receive the subsidy and also suffered harassment. The government used the subsidy as a weapon to suppress dissident journalists. With the restoration of democracy in 1990, the practice of doling out subsidies ended. The government promised to find a better way of helping newspapers to survive the new atmosphere of competition in the limited media market. It announced in 1990 that only newspapers with a large circulation would receive advertising subsidies to purchase newsprint. Although several new broadsheet dailies emerged, they could not all survive in a relatively small market. Journalists continue to demand the right to publish government advertisements, still monopolized by the government media. The government has continued to subsidize the price of newsprint supplied to newspapers by the National Trading Corporation.

3.3 Structure and Organization

In 1901, the government published Nepal's first newspaper, the *Gorkhapatra*. It was a weekly with a small establishment comprising an editor, a manager, and a few technicians to manage the press. It functioned as a wing of the government's publicity department and was a mouthpiece of the government. In 1960, the *Gorkhapatra* became a daily newspaper under the management of the Gorkhapatra Corporation created by the government under the Gorkhapatra Corporation Act. The creation of a public-sector corporation to run the newspaper, gave some vestige of autonomy to the newspaper, but the government ran it directly. In 1965, it started publishing another daily, *The Rising Nepal*, which became the first broadsheet English daily in Nepal. Now, the Gorkhapatra group publishes the weekly *Sunday Dispatch* and a number of other magazines.

The Gorkhapatra Corporation has the typical management structure of a modern newspaper establishment with separate independent news departments headed by editors and a general manager to oversee the production, distribution, and financial aspects of the paper. The government, however, appoints the members of the governing board. Although the management claims no censorship, government interference clearly exists (Sharma, 1995).

Since the overthrow of the Rana regime and the establishment of democracy in 1951, a systematic growth in the private-sector press has occurred. Although in the initial period (1951–60) the country had only a handful of newspapers, mostly weeklies, a quantitative growth took place under both the *panchayat* system (1960–90) and the multi-party system (1990 to the present). Until recently, private-sector newspapers have been single-person operations. The newspaper editor combined the roles of the publisher and editorial staff. Often, newspapers were published for social status rather than profit. These are mainly party-oriented weekly newspapers, mostly of a sensational nature, without a regular newsroom operation.

Many prominent editors in Nepal have been publishing their newspapers as small family enterprises, making profit from printing, and invariably subsidizing the newspapers (Sharma, 1995). One reason for the slow growth of the press in the private sector since 1951 was that successive governments pampered the government press, thus paying inadequate attention to the resource-starved private press. The situation continued even after the restoration of democracy and the promulgation of a constitution that guaranteed freedom of expression and protected the press from persecution. Fear of confiscation and jail sentences was a major reason for the lack of investment in the private-sector media. None could criticize the monarchy, the system of government, or the country's nonaligned foreign policy. The imbalance in investment in the government and the private press resulted in the government press introducing modern offset machines and computerized phototypesetters, while private newspapers continued to use obsolete letterpress machines. The gap between the private press and the government press grew not only in technology but also in the quality of journalism, especially as most training opportunities overseas went to journalists working for government papers.

Institutionalization of private-sector newspapers began in the mid-1990s when, feeling secure and confident because of reassuring clauses in the new constitution, several individuals and businesses established newspaper companies to publish broadsheet dailies. Substantial investment went into printing plants and editorial operations. Between 1994 and 1997, as many as seven new daily newspapers (two in English) appeared. Not all were able to survive the stiff competition. The Kantipur Publications, which had a lead of two years over the rest, is the only daily newspaper group in the private sector making a profit. The *Samacharpatra* is said to be at the point of breaking even, while the *Himalaya Times* is still losing money. Some of the weekly newspapers with a relatively larger circulation but without much advertising, are said to be making some profit from sales. The importance, as well as the circulation, of the government-sector press is slowly diminishing because it continues to remain the mouthpiece of the parties and governments in power. The promise of each successive government to take steps to privatize the government press has not materialized. Because it has been the oldest newspaper, and for about 50 years the only one in the country, *The Gorkhapatra* continues to enjoy a fairly large circulation though its share is diminishing. For many years, the official press enjoyed a monopoly over advertising, both government and private, because of its large circulation and size. But the new broadsheet dailies have already eaten into this advertising pie and will continue to do so in the context of the existing uncertainties in the official press. All journalists are required to obtain a work permit from the Ministry of Communication, and all newspapers have to register themselves (Chaudhary and Chen, 1995).

3.4 Quality and Popular Press

The quality press is better written, better edited, and better printed. It caters to a more serious clientele. The major broadsheet dailies—*The Gorkhapatra, The Rising Nepal, Kantipur, Kathmandu Post, Himalaya Times,* and *Ajako Sama-charpatra*—belong to this category. The latest entrant is *Himal Khabarpatrika*—a full-color fortnightly printed in glossy newsprint and published by Himalmedia Pvt Ltd—which aspires to be a worldclass newsweekly for the Nepali market. Himalmedia also brings out a South Asian magazine, *Himal*. Nepal's elite reads the English-language dailies—*Kathmandu Post* and *The Rising Nepal*—and the weeklies, *Spotlight* and *Independent*. These are also the newspapers preferred by Kathmandu's large expatriate population employed in embassies, UN agencies and NGOs. The circulation of the English press is much lower than that of the vernacular press. Some smaller dailies that have existed for more than 40 years, such as The *Commoner* and *The Motherland*, have failed to attract readers.

The popular press mainly comprises weekly newspapers, of which there are hundreds in Nepal. As mentioned in Section 3.3, these are mostly tabloids with highly sensational news and a low circulation. They are not economically viable, although some of the larger ones are known to be doing well. Individuals publish them as public relations tools to promote parties or causes. These publishers/editors are accorded a status in society that is difficult for others to get. During the *panchayat* days, the weekly newspapers played either an adversarial or a supportive role vis-à-vis the government. The former suffered persecution while the latter enjoyed government largesse. After 1990, it became fashionable for the weeklies to enter partisan politics to gain favors and receive support from political parties (Adhikary, 1996). Fully independent newspapers are rare in Nepal.

3.5 Distribution and Technology

The distribution of newspapers is a Herculean task in a country like Nepal, two-thirds of which is mountainous (UNESCO, 1995). Large sections of the country are cut off for lack of roads, rail, or air services. The postal service is slow and unreliable. In short, much of the country does not get any newspapers. The distribution is also limited by the extremely low rate of literacy among the rural population (see footnote 1). Besides, massive poverty prevents people from buying newspapers on a regular basis.[2]

For these reasons, some media institutions are promoting a community approach to newspaper publishing. Several small towns now have their own newspapers published with the help of modern computers and printing presses. Support for the initial establishment has come from donors promoting mass media development.

---

[2] UNDP, 1999, estimated Nepal's 1997 urban population at 10.9 percent while *Asiaweek* (December 17, 1999) estimated the current urban population at 14 percent. Nepal ranked 144th in UNDP's 1997 Human Development Index. The population below income poverty line was 53.1 percent.

Efforts to encourage the rural population to publish wall newspapers have also surfaced. As they are written in very large, bold Nepali typeface, neo-literates in the villages could read such papers pasted on the walls of public buildings. Critics, however, opine that these donor-driven projects are of limited value because they are unsustainable.

Newspapers are switching over from obsolete letterpress technology to offset printing and computerized typesetting. Most corporate media, which now own or have ordered imagesetters, regularly use color-scanning facilities and have upgraded printing to four-color web units. The owners of private newspapers have sought the government's financial support to make heavy investments in new technologies. The government has been promising the private press all the facilities available to industries. This, however, has not yet materialized. However, it has provided some concessions in import duty and taxes to encourage newspapers to import modern equipment (Bahadur, 1992).

A Media Development Fund under the Press Council—with initial capital from the Danish aid agency DANIDA—has been set up to assist those newspapers in districts that are still using old technology. The fund lends money to newspapers to purchase capital equipment. The government has also provided some funds as a matching contribution. Many small-time newspaper publishers in different parts of the country have already modernized their operations with the help of the funds and its loan operation, handled by the Himalayan Bank. Many newspapers now look better in terms of layout and design and enjoy a much better circulation in their area.

4. BROADCASTING

4.1 Policy and Legal Framework

4.1.1 Radio

The government owned and operated the broadcast media—one radio station and one TV station—until 1997. Radio Nepal, which the government established as a department under the Ministry of Information and Broadcasting, never had a legal framework. In the 1980s, the government turned Radio Nepal into a semi-autonomous body called the Broadcasting Development Service in an attempt to give it credibility. Even so, no official charter regulated broadcasting.

Widespread demand for a media communication policy to accommodate the changed political environment following the restoration of democracy led to the appointment of a task force in 1992, headed by parliamentarian Narahari Acharya. The task force formulated a communication policy, which the government officially adopted. The involvement of the private sector in broadcasting was among the proposed changes. This included the granting of licenses to operate radio stations on the FM band if the government deemed an individual or company capable of doing so. This paved the way for Nepal's first National Broadcasting Act, which allowed the private sector to operate radio stations (Boafo & Arnaldo, 1995). However, the government took another year-and-a-half before it formulated the National Broadcasting Regulations, which specified license fees and other conditions for private broadcasters. Still fearing that the liberalization of broadcasting would lead to chaos on the airwaves (and, perhaps, loss of political control as well), the government allowed Radio Nepal to operate the first FM radio in Kathmandu. The government made an attempt to imply that the station qualified to be part of the private sector because it sold airtime to the private sector. It took a year of intense campaigning for Radio Sagarmatha,[3] a station proposed by a consortium of four media-related agencies—Nepal Forum of Environmental Journalists, Nepal Press Institute, Himal Association, and Worldview Nepal—to receive a license for which it had applied four years before. The license was issued in the name of Nepal Forum of Environmental Journalists (UNESCO, 1995). It also became South Asia's first privately-owned and -operated public radio station.

4.2 Structure and Organization

4.2.1 Radio

Radio Nepal operates as a semi-autonomous broadcasting authority with its own board of directors and its own sources of income. It has the authority to broadcast both commercial and public service programs. However, it is the government which appoints its director and the members of the governing board. The board chairman is the secretary to the Ministry of Information and Communication. Regarded as an information and propaganda organ of the government, Radio Nepal broadcasts 18 hours a day on shortwave and medium wave. Its medium wave broadcasts reach about 60 per cent of the population, and its policy is to expand the medium wave service to cover the entire population. Radio Nepal's main studio and transmitters are in Kathmandu. It is making a systematic attempt to establish relay stations and studios in other parts of the country. Six such stations are already in place. Radio Nepal's FM station in Kathmandu sells airtime to six different companies, which broadcast mainly music programs for about 18 hours a day. This is one of the principal sources of income for Radio Nepal.

Recently, the government granted licenses to six other groups to operate FM stations. With the exception of the Madan Pokhara community radio and the Kathmandu Municipality radio, all the rest are commercial stations. One of the six to receive a license, the Kantipur 96.1 FM, is already test transmitting for 12 hours a day. Radio Nepal broadcasts mainly in the Nepali language with news broadcast in several other languages, including English and Hindi. But the FM stations broadcast musical programs in several languages for the benefit of Nepal's diverse ethnic fabric.

---

[3] Sagarmatha ("the head in the heavens") is the Nepali word for Mount Everest.

Radio Nepal has medium wave stations in Bardibas, Dhankuta, Dipayal, Kathmandu, Pokhara, and Surkhet. Its shortwave transmitter is in Khumaltar, which is also the location of FM100. The private Radio Sagarmatha broadcasts on FM102.4 (*World radio TV handbook*, 1999).

4.2.2 Television

A board of directors and a a general manager appointed by the government run Nepal Television (NTV), as in the case of Radio Nepal. The chairman is a political appointee representing the ruling party. Nepal Television broadcasts for about four hours every evening and for a few hours on Saturday afternoons. It also broadcasts for a few hours in the morning. Although some say that Nepal Television has become bolder in reporting the government's shortcomings or any misuse by it, it still functions as the mouthpiece of the government and the parties in power. The government has given permission to private companies to establish networks or to buy airtime from Nepal Television. Currently, Image Channel, a private company, broadcasts one-and-a-half hours in the morning. Two cable companies are also in operation—Space-time Network, which uses cables to serve a network of several thousand customers in Kathmandu and several other towns; and Shangri-la Channel, which uses a broadcast network to supply satellite channels to its clients in the Kathmandu Valley. Nepal Television claims to reach about 40 percent of the population in the capital, the main cities and the southern plains of the Terai. It covers an estimated 28 percent of the geographical area. Nepal being a mountainous country, the reach of television is very limited. In recent months, the government has been considering the use of communication satellites to make Nepal Television accessible to the entire population. However, considering the high level of poverty, only very few can afford a TV receiver. Another obstacle is that only 15 percent of the population has electricity.

4.3 Program Policies

The Broadcasting Act of 1992 broadly specifies what can and cannot be broadcast both by radio and television stations. It stipulates that any program that is in bad taste, casts aspersions on individuals or institutions, incites crimes or uprisings against the state, causes offense to religious beliefs, or creates disunity and hatred, would be punishable. The Broadcasting Regulation specifies punitive measures for such offenses. Although broadcasting organizations and communication specialists are talking about the need for a code of conduct, the formulation of such a code, acceptable both to government and to private stations, has not made much headway.

The Broadcasting Act broadly divides broadcasting stations into three categories:

- National broadcasting: At present only Radio Nepal, owned and operated by the government, can broadcast on AM and shortwave to reach the entire country.

- Commercial broadcasting: Most of the FM stations have received licenses for commercial broadcasting, currently confined to Kathmandu.
- Public service or community broadcasting: The three groups that have received licenses for community broadcasting are Radio Sagarmatha, the Kathmandu Municipality, and Madan Pokhara.

The Broadcasting Regulation specifies license fees for each of the categories, with lower fees for community broadcasting because of its public service nature. In the case of television too, the private broadcasters who use the transmitting facilities of Nepal Television have to pay for airtime and studio facilities, in addition to their license fee. Image Channel continues to do so, but the Young Nepal Television had to close down because production costs, as well as the cost of airtime, placed a heavy burden in a market where advertising is scarce. The Shangri-la Channel and Space-time Network too pay a fee to the government for their operation.

4.4 Ownership and Financing

The government funds and operates Radio Nepal and Nepal Television even though their charters identify them as autonomous corporations. In addition to advertising revenue, which they earn as the only national broadcasting stations in the country, they also receive government subsidies. Both corporations enjoy a monopoly on advertising targeted at a national audience. They also earn money by selling airtime. Radio Nepal sells airtime to six different companies on its FM100 station while Nepal Television earns fees from the use of its transmitters by Image Channel, Young Asia Television, and other groups that broadcast on NTV.

The six private companies that broadcast programs on Radio Nepal's FM station do enjoy some revenue from advertising but they also pay for airtime. No study has assessed the incomes of these companies. Being a community radio station, Radio Sagarmatha cannot accept advertising.

5. NEW ELECTRONIC MEDIA

5.1 Internet and On-line Media

The July 1999 survey of the Internet Software Consortium estimated that Nepal had 160 Internet hosts compared to 60 in January 1997, when the country had an estimated 500 Internet users. As these indicators show, the use of the new electronic media is still new and not widespread.

The government requires the registration of as well as a payment fee for all dish antennas, e-mail services, and cordless telephones. However, not many agencies or individuals have complied with that requirement on the grounds that the government should not charge fees for services that it did not render (Koirala, 1998). No clear-cut policy exists regarding the role of the private sector in the growth of the electronic media. This has resulted in a haphazard growth (Koirala, 1998): The top three Internet providers are the Mercantile Office System, Computer Land, and Worldlink.

Three Nepal dailies—*The Kathmandu Post* (http://www.south-asia.com/news-ktm.htm), *The Rising Nepal* (http://www.south-asia.com/news-trn.htm), and *Kantipur* (http://www.south-asia.com/news-knt.htm)—have set up Internet editions primarily for the benefit of the Nepalese living abroad. Seven weeklies—*Deshantar, Independent, Janmabhoomi Saptahik, People's Weekly, Sunday Post, Telegraph*, and *Weekly Chronicle*—also have websites, in addition to the fortnightly *Cyber Post* and the monthly *Sarbottam* and *Himal Magazine*. Radio Nepal (http://www.catmando.com/news/radio-nepal/radionp.htm) and Kantipur FM 100 (http://www.south-asia.com/hitsfm/) have also gone on-line.

5.2 Telecommunications Infrastructure

The number of main telephone lines increased from 57,320 in 1990 (0.32 per 100 people) to 233,784 in 1998 (1 per 100 people). The number of mainline telephones per 100 households in 1996 was 3.3 (ITU, 1999). The rural telephone density was a mere 0.06 percent. Nepal also had 10,000 cellular subscribers in 1998 (APT, 1999).

The Nepal Telecommunications Corporation has fully digitized the country's telecommunications network. It has connected all 75 districts in the country with broadband and narrowband digital microwave radio links. Four districts are equipped with VSAT technology. Optical fibers connect the exchanges in the Kathmandu Valley and beyond. Satellite and terrestrial links connect Nepal directly to 131 countries. However, terrestrial links are working only with India (APT, 1998).

The Telecommunications Act of 1962 gave the government the exclusive rights to establish, maintain and operate all telecommunication networks and services. The Communication Corporation Act of 1972 transferred those rights to the NTC. The Ministry of Information and Communication, which set the nation's telecommunications policy, has recognized the need to be responsive to global developments. The Telecommunications Act of 1997 allowed for opening up the telecommunications sector and provided for an autonomous telecommunications authority to regulate the sector. The government has instituted the National Telecommunication Authority as the apex policy-making body to recommend new measures to modernize the country's telecommunications.

6. POLICY TRENDS FOR PRESS AND BROADCASTING

Communication practitioners and specialists have called on the government for a comprehensive communication policy that will provide a clear vision for the 21st century. Media organizations, including the Nepal Press Institute, are debating the nature of such a policy document that should take into account not only the traditional mass media—newspapers, films, radio, and television—but also the new electronic media. This entails going well beyond Nepal's 1992 national communication policy, the main objectives of which were to safeguard and promote freedom of expression and the right to information so as to ensure the development of democracy (Nepal, 1994, p. 7). Its main proposals included the freeing of the national news agency and the Gorkhapatra Corporation from government ownership, giving autonomy to broadcasting organizations, and privatizing telecommunications.

New technologies such as the Internet, cellular telephones, computers, and satellite communication, have opened up new possibilities for communication to play a positive role in development.

In recent years, some positive developments have occurred in journalism education. This began in 1976 with a small department at Tribhuvan University's Ratna Rajya Laxmi campus. The Nepal Press Institute, established in 1984, offered practical training to meet the needs of the mass media industry (Maslog, 1990). Following the reintroduction of democracy and the speedy growth of the print and broadcast media, other institutes offering courses in journalism have mushroomed. These include courses offered by two women's groups, Sancharika Samuha and Asmita Publications, to train women journalists. More recently, the Nepal Press Institute has established two regional media resource centers in two key cities, Biratnagar in the east and Nepalgunj in the west, to offer journalism courses to newspapers based in the districts. This has helped to improve substantially the quality of journalism in different parts of the country and has led to the establishment of a community media in rural Nepal. Trainees of the Nepal Press Institute have established small village newspapers, wall newspapers, audio towers, and FM radio stations. Friedrich Ebert Stiftung and Panos Institute, which have set up regional offices in Kathmandu, are funding skill-building programs in journalism. DANIDA is also funding a large training program through the Nepal Press Institute.

In spite of the positive trends, journalism training in Nepal still has a long way to go. Many journalists get their advanced training in India, the United States, Britain, or Germany. Tribhuvan University has to contend with inadequate funding and a lack of trained staff. Comprehensive training facilities are necessary for meeting the needs of the print and broadcast media. The policy of involving the private sector in broadcasting could trigger the growth of media research and training. Until recently, research has been carried out occasionally, and on a small scale. The growth of professional institutions in the private sector has enabled both the government and private agencies to carry out more research, which would help make projections for the future growth of the media industry. The new trends are definitely toward greater involvement by the private sector in the development of both press and broadcasting.

7. MAIN ISSUES

● Despite the popular demand for privatization of the official media, the government continues to own and operate the only national radio and television stations, and two of the largest daily newspapers. Even though the government had promised to privatize newspapers and to involve the private sector in the electronic media, it has not taken any concrete steps to achieve this. Some argue that privatization is not necessarily a good thing because the state-owned media can function without government control.

● Because newspapers in the private sector are not independent of partisan politics or business interests, they too lack credibility. A majority of the newspapers support the Congress Party or one of the divided wings of the Communist Party. Currently, no newspaper can be considered independent.

● Very little investment has taken place in the print or electronic media. Many newspapers, especially in the districts, continue to use obsolete equipment and command very limited circulation. Even those in the capital lack modern equipment.

● The government continues to subsidize newsprint to help newspapers. However, the newspapers do not seem to benefit much from such a scheme because they have very small circulations and use little newsprint.

● The majority of the weekly newspapers, which tend to reflect the country's political and economic conditions, thrive on sensationalism. Accuracy and ethical standards are missing. No concerted action has taken place to sensitize journalists to sound journalistic values. Newspapers and other media organizations still do not have a code of conduct.

● No debate has taken place on how to cope with the international satellite TV programs that are now invading the country. Because of the availability of satellite channels, fewer people are watching Nepal Television. The government has not come up with a policy statement on satellite TV channels.

● Because the urban-based mainstream media target the elites, there is deep concern about the need to promote a community press comprising small newspapers and printing presses that rural communities can own and operate. Of late, a media development fund has issued loans to eight rural-based publishers resulting in the publication of 53 newspapers using modern technology. To enable the media to serve as development tools, such assistance is necessary.

● The government has started issuing licenses to private radio stations on the FM band. The rural communities interested in establishing local stations need technical know-how and start-up capital. Radio being a suitable medium for a country like

Nepal which is geographically difficult and where the bulk of the population is illiterate, the focus should be on establishing more radio stations (Press Council, Nepal, 1998).

8. STATISTICS

Table 1
General profile

Exchange rate (September-1999)	US$ 1 = Nepali Rs. 65*
Number of inhabitants (mid-1999)	24.3 million
Population density (1998)	160 per sq km
GNP per capita (nominal)	US$ 225
GDP per capita (PPP)	US$ 1,100
Adult literacy (1997)	38.1
Life expectancy	57.9 years
Urban population	14%
Geographical size	140,800 sq km

Source: UNDP, 1999; *Asiaweek* (December 17, 1999); *Nepal Government's Ninth Five-Year Plan Document*; * OANDA Historical Currency Table [On-line]. Available: (http://www.oanda.com/converter/cctable?lang=en); Nepal Ministry of Finance Economic Survey 1997–98.

Table 2
Number and Circulation of Daily Newspapers

	1980	1985	1990	1995	1996	1997	1998
No. of dailies	23	34	26	30	–	30	29
	(28)	(28)	(28)	(28)	(29)		
Total circulation	149,000	182,000	173,000	189,000	–	260,000	260,000
	(120,000)	(130,000)	(150,000)	(160,000)	(250,000)		
Circulation per	0.99	1.09	0.93	0.95	–	1.3	1.3
100 inhabitants	(0.8)	(0.8)	(0.8)	(0.7)	(1.1)		

Source: Nepal Press Institute Survey, 1999 (UNESCO, 1999 estimates are in parentheses).

Table 3
Percentage of Advertising Share of the Newspaper Groups

	1995	1996	1997	1998
Gorkhapatra Corporation	70	55	50	35.0
Kantipur Publications	20	32	35	45.0
Samacharpatra	5	6	8	12.5
Himalaya Times	3	4	5	6.0
Others	2	3	2	1.6

Source: Nepal Press Institute Survey, 1999.

Table 4
Number and Penetration of Radio Receivers

	1980	1985	1990	1995	1996	1997	1998
No. of receivers ('000s)	1,500	1,772	2,000	2,200	1,800*	1,822	1,888
	(300)	(450)	(650)	(780)	(810)	(840)	
Receivers per 100	9.98	10.66	10.85	11.11	8.51	8.49	8.23
inhabitants	(2.1)	(2.7)	(3.5)	(3.7)	(3.7)	(3.8)	

Source: Nepal Press Institute Survey, 1999 (UNESCO, 1999 estimates are in parentheses).
Note: Since 1996, there has been a declining trend.

Table 5
Number and Penetration of TV Receivers

	1980	1985	1990	1995	1996	1997	1998
No. of receivers ('000s)	No TV	No TV	100	400	800	900	1,000
	–	(20)	(35)	(110)	(120)	(130)	
Receivers per 100	–	–	0.54	2.02	3.78	4.19	4.51
inhabitants		(0.12)	(0.19)	(0.52)	(0.55)	(0.58)	

Source: Nepal Press Institute Survey, 1999 (UNESCO, 1999 estimates are in parentheses).

Table 6
Telecommunications Facts

	1996	1997	1998	1999
Number of mainline				
telephones	112,645	160,244	194,000	
per 100 inhabitants	(0.53)	(0.77)	(0.85)	.
Number of cellular telephones	–	–	–	–
per 100 inhabitants		–	–	–
Number of fax machines ('000)	0.6	–	–	–
Number of PCs per 100				
inhabitants	–	–	–	–
Number of Internet hosts	60	139	154	160
per 10,000 inhabitants	0.03	0.07	0.07	0.07

Source: ITU (1998, 1999); Network Wizards (http://www.nw.com).

Table 7
Circulation Data for Daily Newspapers

Name of newspaper	Language	Location	Circulation
Aparanha	Nepali	Kathmandu	2,000
Aajako Samacharpatra	Nepali	Kathmandu	20,000
Aadarsha Samaj	Nepali	Pokhara	1,500
Blast Times	Nepali	Dharan	2,850
Bhiswabhumi	Newari	Kathmandu	8,324
Bibechana	Nepali	Jhapa	1,000
Chautari	Nepali	Butwal	1,000
City Times	Nepali	Kathmandu	2,000
Daily News	Nepali	Kathmandu	500
Gorkhapatra	Nepali	Kathmandu	25,000
Hijo Aaja	Nepali	Jhapa	500
Himalaya Times	Nepali	Kathmandu	22,000
Jana Patra	Nepali	Biratnagar	500
Janamat	Nepali	Pokhara	500
Jana Sangharsha	Nepali	Butwal	5,000
Kantipur	Nepali	Kathmandu	30,000
Koseli	Nepali	Biratnagar	500
Kamandar	Nepali	Kathmandu	2,000
Lumbini	Nepali	Butwal	4,000
Mahanagar	Nepali	Kathmandu	5,000
Nepali	Hindi	Kathmandu	500
Nhugu Bhiswabhumi	Newari	Kathmandu	2,000
Prateek	Nepali	Birgunj	2,610
Purbanchal	Nepali	Jhapa	2,000
Sandhya Times	Newari	Kathmandu	3,000
Sandhyakalin	Nepali	Kathmandu	19,000
The Rising Nepal	English	Kathmandu	10,000
The Kathmandu Post	English	Kathmandu	10,000
The Commoner	English	Kathmandu	3,000
Valley News	Nepali	Kathmandu	8,500

Source: Press Council, Nepal, 1999.

9. USEFUL ADDRESSES*

Ministry of Information and Communication
Singha Durbar, Kathmandu.
Telephone: 220150
Fax: 221729

Department of Information
Naya Baneshwor,
Kathmandu
Telephone: 222317 and 222152
Fax: 977-1-223418

* **Source:** *National mass media directory*, 1998.

9.1 Press Associations

Nepal Press Institute
P.O. Box 4128, Kathmandu
Telephone: 264154 and 264155
Fax: 228943
E-mail: npiktm@wlink.com.np

Federation of Nepalese Journalists
Ramshahpath, P.O. Box 285, Kathmandu
Telephone: 225226
Fax: 225226

Press Council, Nepal
RSS Bldg., Prithvi Path
P.O. Box 3077, Kathmandu
Telephone: 262829 and 262894
Fax: 262894

Nepal Forum of Environmental Journalists
Thapathali, P.O. Box 5143, Kathmandu
Telephone: 261991 and 260248
Fax: 261191
E-mail: nefej@gn.apc.org

Sancharika Samuha (Association of Women Communicators)
Anamnagar, Kathmandu.
Telephone: 242970

Himal Association
Patan Dhoka, P.O. Box 42, Lalitpur
Telephone: 523845
Fax: 521013
E-mail: himal@himpc.oms.com.np

9.2 News Agencies

Rastriya Samachar Samiti
Prithvi Path, P.O. Box 220
Kathmandu
Telephone: 227912 and 231728
Telex: 2234
Fax: 227698

9.3 Electronic Media Organizations

Radio Broadcasting Service (Radio Nepal)
Singha Durbar, P.O. Box 634, Kathmandu
Telephone: 223910
Telex: 2590
Fax: 221952

Nepal Television Corporation
Singha Durbar, P.O. Box 3826
Kathmandu
Telephone: 228447

Telex: 2458
Fax: 228312

Worldview Nepal
Kupondol, Lalitpur, P.O. Box 2912
Kathmandu
Telephone: 525031
Fax: 536856

9.4 Media Training Institutions

Department of Journalism and Mass Communication
Ratna Rajya Laxmi Campus, Exhibition Road, Kathmandu
Telephone: 225819

Media Point
Anamnagar, Kathmandu
Telephone: 278707

Media Services International
Tripureswar, P.O. Box 3887
Kathmandu
Telephone: 260989

Nepal Institute of Mass Communication
Anamnagar, Kathmandu
Telephone: 242970

9.5 Principal Publishing Houses

Kamana Publications (Pvt) Ltd
P.O. Box 2045, Kathmandu
Telephone: 261179
Fax: 227488

Gorkhapatra Corporation
Dharmapath, Kathmandu.
Telephone: 248634
Fax: 245015

Kantipur Publications (Pvt) Ltd
P.O. Box 8559, Kathmandu
Telephone: 480100
Fax: 470178

Himalaya Times
New Baneshwor, Buddhanagar
P.O. Box 11672, Kathmandu
Telephone: 483044
Fax: 480554

10. REFERENCES

Adhikary, D.H. (1996). Media monitors in Nepal. In K.S. Venkateswaran (Comp.) *Media monitors in Asia* (pp. 47–50). Singapore: AMIC.
APT (Asia-Pacific Telecommunity). (1998, 1999). *The APT yearbook.* Bangkok: APT.

Bahadur K.C.S. (1992). The press in Nepal: Past and present. *Media Asia, 19* (3), 169–173.
Bahadur, K.C.S. (1994). Nepal: Starting afresh. In *Press systems in SAARC* (pp. 65–72). Singapore: AMIC.
Bearak, B. (1999, June 6). Democracy is taking root in thin soil in Nepal. *New York Times*, p. Y3.
Belbase, S., & Murphy, J.E. (1983). Press performance in Nepal during two political climates. *Journalism Quarterly, 60*, 61–66.
Boafo, S.T.K., & Arnaldo, C.A. (1995). The UNESCO communication program: Building capacity and protecting press freedom. *Media Development, 42* (1), 3–7.
Burghart, R. (1993). The political culture of panchayat democracy. In M. Hutt (Ed.) *Nepal in the 'nineties* (pp. 1–13) Oxford: Oxford University Press.
Chaudhary, A.G., & Chen, A.C. (1995). Asia and the Pacific. In J.C. Merrill (Ed.), *Global journalism: Survey of international communication* (pp. 269–328). White Plains, NY: Longman Publishers.
Deveney, P.J. (Comp.). (1997, December 18). Nepal offers economic outlook. *The Wall Street Journal*, p. A16 (w).
Europa world yearbook, The (Vol. II). (1997). London: Europa Publications.
Hutt, M. (1993). The Nepali literature of the democracy movement and its aftermath. In M. Hutt (Ed.), *Nepal in the 'nineties* (pp. 82–97). Oxford: Oxford University Press.
ITU (International Telecommunications Union). (1998). *World telecommunication development report.* (1998). Geneva: ITU.
ITU (International Telecommunication Union). (1999). *Yearbook of statistics: Telecommunication services 1998–1999.* Geneva: ITU
Joshi, B.L., & Rose, L.E. (1966). *Democratic innovations in Nepal.* Berkeley and Los Angeles: University of California Press.
Karp, J. (1995, January 26). Ready for prime time. *Far Eastern Economic Review, 158* (4), p. 56.
Koirala, B. (1998). Communication scene: Nepal. In A. Goonasekera & D. Holaday (Eds.), *Asian communication handbook* (pp. 109–122). Singapore: AMIC & NTU.
Maslog, C.C. (Ed.). (1990). *Communication education in Asia: Status and trends in India, Indonesia, Malaysia, Nepal, Philippines and Thailand.* Manila: Press Foundation of Asia.
National mass media directory. (1998). Kathmandu: Press Council Nepal, Worldview Nepal and Nepal Press Institute.
Nepal, Ministry of Communication. (1994). Nepal restructures media (experts from National Communication Policy, 1992). In *Press systems in SAARC* (pp. 7–8). Singapore: AMIC.
New premier follows in family footsteps. (1998, April 13). *Los Angeles Times*, p. A8.
Pokhrel, G.P., & Koirala, B.D. (Comps.). (1995). *Mass media laws and regulations in Nepal.* Singapore & Kathmandu: AMIC & Nepal Press Institute.
Press Council, Nepal. (1998). *Journalism and its challenges.* Kathmandu: Press Council Nepal.
Rai, D.L. (1987). Nepal's communication policy then and now. *Media Asia, 14* (3), 149, 152–153.
Rana, B.B. (1982). Nepal. In J.A. Lent (Ed.), *Newspapers in Asia: Contemporary trends and problems* (pp. 462–577). Hong Kong: Heinemann Asia.
Sharma, S. (1995, June). *The state of the Nepali Press.* Paper presented at the Newspaper Management Seminar sponsored by Nihon Shinbun Kyokai, Tokyo.
Sheffield, M., & Lent, J.A. (1978). Nepal. In J.A. Lent (Ed.), *Broadcasting in Asia and the Pacific: A contemporary survey of radio and television* (pp. 252–260). Philadelphia: Temple University Press.
UNDP (United Nations Development Program). (1999). *Human development report 1999.* New York: UNDP.
UNESCO (United Nations Educational, Scientific and Cultural Organization). (1995). Nepal's Radio Sagarmatha empowers the people. *Media Development, 42* (1), 7.
UNESCO (United Nations Educational, Scientific and Cultural Organization). (1999) *Statistical yearbook.* Paris: UNESCO.
Verma, Y.P. (1988). *The press in Nepal: An appraisal.* Kathmandu: Pratibha Publications.
World factbook. (1999). Washington, DC: Central Intelligence Agency [On-line]. Available: (http://www.odci.gov/cia/publications/factbook/country-frame.html).
World radio TV handbook (1999). Oxford: Windsor Books International.

♦

6

PAKISTAN

Owais Aslam Ali & Shelton A. Gunaratne

1. NATIONAL PROFILE

1.1 Geography

Pakistan shares a 2,912 km border with India to the east, a 523 km border with China to the north, and a 909 km and 2,430 km border with Iran and Afghanistan respectively to the west. It faces the Arabian Sea to the south. The country has an area of 803,940 sq km—slightly less than twice the size of California. Islamabad is the capital of Pakistan.

It has a varied climate: mostly hot in the dry desert, temperate in the northwest, and arctic in the north. The flat Indus plain is in the east, with mountains to the north and northwest, and the Balochistan plateau to the west. The highest point is the 8,611-meter Mount Godwin-Austen. Pakistan controls the Khyber Pass and the Bolan Pass, the traditional invasion routes between Central Asia and the South Asian subcontinent (*World factbook*, 1999).

1.2 People

The country's estimated mid-1999 population of 138.1 million showed an annual growth rate of 2.6 percent. More than 95 percent of the people are Muslims (of whom 77 percent are Sunni and the rest Shi'a). Christianity, Hinduism and other religions account for the balance. Although Urdu, the national language, is the mother tongue of only 8 percent of the population, it is widely spoken and understood throughout the country and serves as the link language. Other major languages which are spoken in different provinces, include Punjabi, the mother tongue of 48 percent of the people; Sindhi (12 percent); Seraiki (10 percent); Pashtu (8 percent); Baluchi (3 percent); Hindko (2 percent); Brahui (1 percent); Burushaski and others (8 percent). English, the legacy of colonial rule, is the official language (*World factbook*, 1999).

Pakistan's adult literacy rate is 40.9 percent for the country as a whole. It is substantially lower in the rural areas. The urban population constitutes a mere 35 percent. Life expectancy is estimated to be 63 years (*Asiaweek*, December 17, 1999).

1.3 Government and Politics

Pakistan came into being on August 14, 1947, when Britain agreed to carve out, from British India, a separate country for the Muslims to allay their fears of Hindu domination. Until 1971, the country comprised two wings—East and West—separated by 1,600 kilometers of Indian territory. That year, East Pakistan broke away after a bloody civil war and formed independent Bangladesh.

Pakistan is a federal republic with four provinces: Punjab, Sindh, Balochistan, and the Northwest Frontier Province (NWFP). Administratively, the four provinces are divided into *divisions*, which are further broken into *districts* and still smaller *tehsils* and *sub-tehsils*. The area of Azad Kashmir enjoys a special status.

Pakistan, which had been ruled by military and civilian dictators for long periods, reverted to parliamentary democracy from 1988 to late 1999.[1] Under the constitution, the president is elected by Parliament (*Majlis-e-Shoora*) for a five-year term as the head of state. The prime minister, assisted by a cabinet of ministers, heads the government. The parliament comprises the Senate and the National Assembly. The provincial assemblies indirectly elect the 87 members of the Senate to serve six-year terms with one-third of the members coming up for election every two years. The National Assembly has 217 members elected by popular vote to serve five-year terms, with 10 members representing non-Muslims. A federally appointed governor heads each province; and a chief minister elected by each provincial assembly governs each province (*World factbook*, 1999).

1.4 Economy

Pakistan is an agricultural country, whose main crops are wheat, cotton, rice, sugarcane, and tobacco. Textile is the main industry. Other important industries are fertilizer, steel products, chemicals, food processing, oil and gas products, and cement. The main exports are raw cotton, rice, cotton yarn, textiles, and fruits and vegetables. The main imports are crude oil, cooking oil, fertilizers, and machinery. Pakistan exported merchandise valued at US$ 8.3 billion during the preceding 12 months. It has a negative current account balance of US$ 1.8 billion and reserves of US$ 1.5 billion. Pakistan's gross domestic product at purchasing power parity

[1] Gen. Pervez Musharraf deposed Prime Minister Nawaz Sharif and took over as the country's chief executive on October 12, 1999, after declaring a state of emergency. Readers should be alert to this development when they read this chapter written months before the coup. An editorial in the October 17, 1999, edition of *Dawn* said: "Prolonged deviations from the democratic path have invariably led to more problems than have been solved. Ayub Khan's rule was a long deviation from democracy. Yahya Khan's was shorter but far more destructive. Zia's rule was also justified on the grounds of accountability and Islamization. All these stretches of military rule proved disastrous for Pakistan. The present military rulers must guard against the dangers of moving in the same direction. Although there has been a conscious attempt to put a cosmetic facade over the imposition of military rule—which is the reason why we have a chief executive and not a chief martial law administrator—everyone understands what has been put in place" (http://www.dawn.com/daily/19991017/ed.htm).

stood at US$ 219 billion. The per capita GDP at purchasing power parity was US$ 1,570 while the nominal per capita GNP was US$ 492 (*Asiaweek*, December 17, 1999).

2. DEVELOPMENT OF PRESS AND BROADCASTING

2.1 Brief Early History

The origin of the Pakistani press, Al Mujahid (1982) points out, was "enmeshed in subcontinental journalism" (p. 481) that began in 1780 when James Augustus Hicky published the *Bengal Gazette*. Al Mujahid identified three principal strands of the press in colonial India—the Anglo-Indian press, the nationalist press, and the Muslim press. The press and persecution went hand in hand during British rule. Thus, Niazi (1986) traces the genesis of Pakistan's intolerance of the press to the colonial period.[2]

The Anglo-Indian papers adopted a pattern similar to that of British newspapers and developed into the most professional, financially stable, and influential segment of the Indian press. Their influence continued until the independence of India and Pakistan. The harsh attitude of the British East India Company towards the first newspaper, the *Bengal Gazette*, set the example for the future. When the newspaper attacked officials of the Company, including the governor-general and his wife, the authorities retaliated, first by denying postal services to the paper and, later, by imprisoning Hicky and seizing his paper (Ali, 1969; Shamsuddin, 1986).

The nationalist press, mostly Hindu-owned, emerged in the 1820s in several vernacular languages. The first vernacular paper, started in 1822, was the Persian-Urdu *Jaam-e-Jahan Numan* published under the supervision of the East India Company by editor Lala Suda Sukh and printer William Hope King (Shamsuddin, 1986). In the early 20th century, the Hindu-owned press became closely aligned with the Indian National Congress and came to be called the "nationalist" press, which stood for independence from British rule and for a united India.

The subcontinent's Muslim press, which marks the origin of the Pakistani press, emerged in 1836, with the publication of Maulvi Muhammed Baqar's *Urdu Akhbar*. It began as a literary paper in Delhi, but as relations between the local population and the British deteriorated, it became political and highly critical of British rule. The number of Muslim-owned papers grew rapidly until the uprising of 1857,[3] when the Muslim press came out openly against the British occupation of India.

[2] For more details on the development of the Pakistan mass media, see Al Mujahid, 1978, 1982, 1991, and 1994; and Khurshid, 1971.
[3] Indian soldiers of the British Indian Army, drawn mostly from Muslim units from Bengal, mutinied at the Meerut cantonment, near Delhi, starting a year-long insurrection against the British. The mutineers then marched to Delhi and offered their services to the Mughal emperor. The insurrection was a reaction by the indigenous population to the rapid changes in the social order that were engineered by the British over the preceding century. Imperial historians called this the Indian or Sepoy Mutiny.

The British authorities closed all but two Muslim-owned publications, hanged Baqar, and treated the other editors harshly (Haider, 1990). After the uprising, Sir Syed Ahmed Khan tried to promote a reconciliation between Muslims and the British rulers. In 1866, he founded the *Scientific Society Magazine*, a bilingual publication in Urdu and English. In 1870, he started the Urdu *Tehzibul Akhlaq* on the pattern of the *The Tatler* and *The Spectator*. These publications set a new standard of independent and critical thinking among Muslims.

The turning point for Indian Muslims was the creation of the All India Muslim League in 1906 for the promotion of Muslim interests. This awakening was also reflected in a number of Muslim papers started during the first quarter of the 20th century. By 1925, the Muslim press comprised 220 papers in nine languages, including Urdu (120), English (18), and Bengali (14) (Kurian, 1982). Most of these papers had a precarious existence because of poor circulation and meager revenues, but a few became influential among Muslims. These included Maulana Hasrat Mohani's *Urdu-e-Moalla*; Maulana Abul Kalam Azad's *Al-Hilal* and *Al-Balagh*; Maulana Mohammed Ali's *Comrade* in English and *Hamdard* in Urdu; and Maulana Zafar Ali Khan's *Zamindar*. Leading political figures edited them and they served as a means of communicating with the people and the government. They faced many hardships, including imprisonment and heavy fines, because they fearlessly criticized British policies inimical to Muslim interests.

When the Muslims began their struggle for a separate homeland, they faced the hostility of both the Hindu-owned nationalist press and the British-owned press. Therefore, in the late 1930s and the 1940s, Mohammad Ali Jinnah, then president of the Muslim League, and later the first governor-general of Pakistan, encouraged the establishment of newspapers to project the aspirations of Indian Muslims.

Jinnah helped establish the English weekly *Dawn* in the 1930s. It became a daily in 1942. By the mid-1940s, Muslim papers appeared in every province of India. The most influential Muslim papers included *Azad, The Star of India*, and *Morning News* of Calcutta; *Manshoor* and *Anjam* of Delhi; *Nawa-e-Waqt, The Pakistan Times*, and *Eastern Times* of Lahore; *The Weekly Observer* of Allahabad; *Sind Times* of Karachi; *New Life* of Patna; and *Khyber Mail* of Peshawar. Many provincial governments controlled by nationalists opposed the demand for Pakistan and confiscated a number of Muslim newspapers, including the *Star, New Life*, and *Zamindar* (Kurian, 1982).

Peshawar was the first city in areas now comprising Pakistan to have a radio station. Sardar Abdul Qayyum Khan, who had gone to London to participate in the round table negotiations among the Muslims, Hindus, and the British, made the request for a radio station to Marconi, inventor of the radio. Marconi, who also sent 30 receiving sets to Sardar Qayyum, personally designed the transmitter. In 1936, Peshawar became the second city in India, after Delhi, to have a radio station. In 1942, the Peshawar radio station shifted to a new building with a 10kW transmitter (Ali, 1997).

Two years after the Peshawar station went on air, on December 26, 1938, a 5kW station started operating from the YMCA building in Lahore. The colonial government used radio as a propaganda organ with little emphasis on entertainment. With the start of World War II, the propaganda role of radio was magnified, as there was great interest in news about the war. Gradually, however, drama, music, and literary programs began to be broadcast.

2.2 Developments since 1945

2.2.1 Press

The press was weak in those areas of India that became Pakistan. Not a single daily was published in East Pakistan (Khurshid, 1971) or Balochistan at the time of independence.[4] The NWFP had two daily papers, but they were financially unstable. Lahore was the most prominent newspaper center of Pakistan, followed by Karachi. However, even in these cities, a majority of journalists and publishers were Hindus or Sikhs who had migrated to India after the creation of Pakistan (Shamsuddin, 1986).

Those Muslim newspapers that moved from India to Pakistan filled the void only partially. *Dawn* shifted to Karachi after its Delhi offices were burnt in August 1947. *Jang* and *Anjam*, the leading Urdu papers of Delhi, also relocated to Karachi. The Bengali daily *Azad* and the English *Morning News* transferred their operations from Calcutta to Dhaka in East Pakistan. In 1953, *Morning News* also started publishing from Karachi. Many newspapers that moved to Pakistan, including *Anjam*, could not survive the drastic change in the political, economic and competitive environment. However, some papers including *Dawn, Jang*, and *Nawa-e-Waqt* have not only survived but have developed into the country's major media groups (Ali, 1992).

2.2.1.1 The post-independence period (1947–58): The newly independent Pakistan inherited a number of laws for controlling and regulating the press. Some of the more important laws relating to the press (Al Mujahid, 1991; Pakistan, 1959) in force at the time of independence included:

- The Press and Registration of Books Act, 1867
- The Press (Emergency Powers) Act, 1931
- The States (Protection Against Disaffection) Act, 1922
- The Foreign Relations Act, 1932
- The Criminal Law (Amendment) Act, 1932
- The States (Protection) Act, 1934
- The Post Office Act, 1898
- The Official Secrets Act, 1923
- The Telegraph Act, 1885, and
- The Sea Customs Act, 1885.

[4] However, two dailies—the *Daily Purbo Pakistan* and the *Paigam*—began publication in East Pakistan in 1947 (see the chapter on Bangladesh).

Because of the hostility between Pakistan and India, which led to a war in Kashmir in 1949, the early governments believed that a completely free press could threaten the country's security. The authorities in Pakistan, therefore, not only retained the colonial laws, but also added further constraints on the press. In 1949, they reimposed the Public Safety Act, which the British had enacted during World War II, for one year and renamed it Public Safety Ordinance. The other restrictive law, enacted in 1952, was the Security of Pakistan Act. This law curtailed the right of professional secrecy and opened the possibility of press censorship (Al Mujahid, 1991). During the first seven years of Pakistan's existence, the government banned 33 newspapers in Punjab alone: 15 for one year, 9 for six months, and the rest for lesser periods. Another 15 had to furnish heavy security deposits (Napoli, 1991).

In spite of restrictions on press freedom, rapid growth occurred in both the number and the circulation of newspapers and magazines. Between 1947 and 1958, the number of periodicals nearly doubled from 556 to 1,106; and the number of dailies increased threefold from 34 to 103. The increase in circulation was even more dramatic. During the seven years beginning 1947, the circulation of daily papers increased from 125,000 to 716,000 (Shamsuddin, 1986). With the exception of the period just after the first imposition of martial law in 1958, and more recently in the mid-1990s, the growth of the Pakistani press has continued.

2.2.1.2 The authoritarian period (1958–85): The strongest, most sustained and most damaging attacks on press freedom occurred during the rule of Field Marshal Ayub Khan, who came to power in 1958. The Ayub regime set the pattern of press censorship and imposed the system of legally binding "press advice," which gave government officials the power to dictate what could or could not be published. Gunaratne (1970) points out that Ayub was "not the man responsible for initiating obnoxious press laws.... He started out as a dictator amply taking advantage of the precedents established by the so-called democratic governments that preceded him" (p. 41). The restrictive press environment of this period caused the number of dailies to decline from 102 in 1959 to 74 in 1960, and that of weeklies and bi-weeklies from 379 in 1958 to 260 in 1969 (Khurshid, 1971).

In 1959, the government took over Lahore's Progressive Papers Ltd, publishers of the leading English newspaper *Pakistan Times* and the Urdu daily *Imroze*. The government then took over (in 1961), the Associated Press of Pakistan, one of the two news agencies in the country. In 1964, the government created the National Press Trust which took over the PPL papers and acquired *Morning News*, as well as several other newspapers.

The Ayub government was also responsible for the imposition of the infamous Press and Publication (Amendment) Ordinance of 1963. The PPO, which Niazi (1986) describes as "the blackest of the black laws" (p. 98), gave the government absolute powers to grant or deny permission for new publications and to prohibit reporting on a wide range of subjects. The second war with India, in 1965, led to the declaration of a state of emergency and the imposition of the draconian Defense of Pakistan Rules (DPR). The emergency and the DPR remained in force for 20 years, and successive governments used them to ban papers, seize printing presses, and jail journalists.

In 1969, when Ayub was forced to resign because of countrywide civil unrest, he handed over power to the Army Chief Gen. Yahya Khan, who also imposed martial law and became president. Yahya Khan imposed press censorship during the civil war in East Pakistan, keeping the people of the western wing ignorant of the scale of atrocities being committed there.

After the secession of East Pakistan in December 1971, Zulfikar Ali Bhutto assumed power as the president and chief martial law administrator. Despite his liberal rhetoric, Bhutto, who subsequently assumed the position of prime minister, continued the repressive policies against the press, including censorship, "press advice," banning of papers and use of threats, physical assaults, and arrests of journalists. He brought the NPT papers under his direct control; and his regime also engaged in extra-legal actions against journalists and media organizations, including the forcible transfer of Pakistan Press International, the country's independent news agency, to a member of the ruling Pakistan People's Party. Bhutto initiated large scale nationalization of heavy industries, banking, and insurance, which gave the government control over a large proportion of the country's advertising expenditures. The Bhutto government routinely used the allocation of advertising and newsprint quotas as tools to punish uncooperative newspapers and magazines and to reward the compliant ones.

Gen. Mohammad Zia-ul-Haq removed Bhutto from power in July 1977 following widespread civil unrest over the rigging of the elections. However, Zia-ul-Haq continued past practices against the press and went a step further when, in 1978, four journalists were whipped for their opposition to the government.

2.2.1.3 The post-martial law period (1985–present): The transformation towards a freer political environment began at the end of 1985 with the withdrawal of martial law and the state of emergency. The Defense of Pakistan Rules lapsed automatically. Following the death of Zia-ul-Haq, the caretaker government repealed the PPO in 1988. This was another positive development. Earlier, in April 1984, the Shariat Court had ruled in *Tamseel Javed vs. the Federation of Pakistan* that some sections of the PPO were repugnant to Islam. The court asserted that Islam laid "great emphasis on freedom of expression and human dignity" and not only gave "people the right of dissent but [also made] it obligatory on them to protest against tyranny, injustice and oppression" (Jabbar & Isa, 1997, p. 780). The court recommended changes in the procedures for issuing declarations, fixing a time limit for pending applications and ruled that appeals be allowed against refusal. The Zia-ul-Haq government appealed against the judgement (Bhatti, 1993). However, the caretaker government, instead of pursuing the appeal, decided to repeal the PPO and introduce a milder Registration of Printing Presses and Publications Ordinance (RPPPO) in 1988. The RPPPO continued to be promulgated as an ordinance until it lapsed in 1997 (see Section 3.1). Both the PPO and the RPPPO had their legal effect through promulgation and not through the legislative process.

In 1990, the government of Benazir Bhutto ended its monopoly over the import and distribution of newsprint. A sustained struggle by journalists and pressure from national and international media organizations have paved the way for a gradual return to democracy and a freer press in Pakistan.

2.2.2 Radio

At the time of partition in 1947, India and Pakistan divided the assets of All India Radio, and Pakistan inherited three low-powered radio stations at Lahore, Dhaka, and Peshawar. A year later, Karachi, the then federal capital, acquired a medium wave transmitter station, which added two 50kW transmitters soon afterwards (Al Mujahid, 1978; Siddiqui, 1991). In August 1949, Radio Pakistan formally inaugurated five external services from Karachi. Rawalpindi came on the air in 1950. Within a decade, Hyderabad and Quetta also had radio stations. In 1974, Pakistan set up its first earth satellite station at Deh Mandro, north of Karachi (Al Mujahid, 1978).

Until recently, the government had a monopoly over radio broadcasting—the only true mass medium in Pakistan because of the country's low literacy rate. In 1995, however, the Bhutto government allowed the introduction of private sector FM broadcasting in Karachi, Lahore and Islamabad. The private FM service, identified as FM100, broadcasts popular music and listener call-in programs (Akif & Siddiqui, 1998). Gilani (1998) says that the private FM channel has an audience of roughly four million adults. Allegations exist that the exclusive permits to establish these stations were awarded to a close friend of the Bhutto family (Jabbar & Isa, 1997, p. 124).

2.2.3 Television

In October 1963, the government took the decision to establish a general-purpose television service with the participation of private capital under the general supervision of the government. Subsequently, the government signed an agreement with Japan's Nippon Electronic Co., allowing it to operate two pilot stations in Pakistan. The first of these stations went on air in Lahore on November 26, 1964. In 1965, after the experimental phase, the government set up a private limited company named Television Promoters Co., which later became a fully government-owned public limited company called Pakistan Television Corporation Ltd in 1997 (Akif & Siddiqui, 1998).

Pakistan TV established television centers in Karachi and Rawalpindi/Islamabad in 1967, and in Peshawar and Quetta in 1974. It began satellite transmission in December 1972, and started using the national microwave link in 1975. PTV transmission switched over from black and white to color in December 1976. In

November 1992, with a grant from Japan, PTV established an additional channel, PTV-2, mainly to televise educational programs. In January 1994, it began beaming its programs through AsiaSat, the first pan-Asian commercial satellite system, to 38 countries, and started another satellite channel called PTV World in 1998, to enable overseas Pakistanis in Asia to see its news and entertainment programs. It also started Prime TV to transmit PTV programs for Pakistanis living in Europe (*The News International*, November 3, 1998, p. 8). In February 1999, PTV launched the Mid-East Channel for the large number of Pakistanis living in the Middle East (*The Nation*, February 26, 1999, p. 12).

In 1989, the first Benazir Bhutto government authorized Shalimar Recording Co. Ltd, in which the government held 54 percent shares, to establish the country's second TV channel under the name People's Television Network—later changed to Shalimar Television Network (STN). The new channel had sought to establish transmitting stations in 22 cities (Tahir, 1996). STN started its transmission in 10 cities: Islamabad, Karachi, Lahore, Faisalabad, Peshawar, Quetta, Larkana, Bahawalpur, Multan, and Hyderabad. The "monopolistic contract" requires STN to transmit the PTV news bulletins (Jabbar & Isa, 1997, p. 121). In 1996, the second Bhutto government granted a license to Shaheen Pay TV, a private company with 50 percent foreign equity, to establish the country's first pay-TV channel using the "wireless" MMDS technology. Allegations have surfaced that this permit also belonged to the same party that received the exclusive permit to run the FM stations though under a different corporate identity (Jabbar & Isa, 1997, p. 124).

3. THE PRESS

3.1 Policy and Legal Framework

Chapter 1 of the Constitution of Pakistan guarantees 20 fundamental rights, including the freedom of movement, assembly, association, speech, and religion. Article 19, which provides for the freedom of speech and freedom of the press subject to a number of restrictions, reads as follows:

> Every citizen shall have the right to freedom of speech and expression, and there shall be freedom of the press, subject to any reasonable restrictions imposed by law in the interest of the glory of Islam, or the integrity. security or defense of Pakistan or any part thereof, friendly relations with foreign states, public order, decency or morality, or in relation to contempt of court, defamation or incitement to an offence. (Jabbar & Isa, 1997, p. 176)[5]

The constitution prohibits the ridicule of Islam, of the armed forces, or of the judiciary. The state can prosecute for treason anyone who damages the constitution by any act, including the publication of statements that are against the spirit of the

[5] See also Mahmood and Shaukat, 1993 (p. 141); Sajid, 1996 (p. 53); and Rizvi, 1990 (p. 76).

constitution. The Penal Code mandates the death sentence for anyone defiling the name of the Prophet Mohammed, life imprisonment for desecrating the Koran, and up to 10 years in prison for insulting another's religious beliefs (US Department of State, 1999).[6] The restrictions sanctioned by the Constitution allowed the retention of laws inherited from colonial India, as well as the laws enacted by the military and authoritarian regimes. Thus, many repressive laws remain on the statute book, such as the Official Secrets Act, the Security of Pakistan Act, and the Maintenance of Public Order Ordinance, all of which the government can use to punish news organizations and journalists.[7]

However, the fundamental rights specified in the constitution remained suspended under the emergency rule, which the government lifted only in 1985. Since then, a gradual assertion of fundamental rights, including freedom of the press, has taken place. Currently, no law governs the registration of publications. Until 1997, the Registration of Printing Presses and Publications Ordinance (RPPPO) was the basic law that governed publications. The government, which never presented the RPPPO to parliament for enactment, routinely re-promulgated the Ordinance every four months as required by the constitution. However, when President Farooq Leghari re-promulgated the Ordinance on March 12, 1997, the newly elected government of Prime Minister Nawaz Sharif claimed that the president had acted on his own without the authority of the government. During this controversy, the media put forth the view that the time had come to allow the press a greater degree of freedom than that envisioned in the RPPPO.

The basic elements of the RPPPO prohibited the publication of any periodical without a declaration authenticated by a district magistrate. The district magistrate could refuse to authenticate a declaration on two grounds: the existence of another newspaper bearing the same title in the same province, or evidence that the applicant publisher or printer had been convicted of any moral offence during the previous five years (Jabbar & Isa, 1997, p. 232). If the district magistrate took no action within four months, the declaration would be deemed authenticated (p. 233). The RPPPO forbade newspapers from publishing material that could incite people to commit violence or to use material based on "false rumors calculated to cause public alarm" or obstruct public officials in "the discharge of their public duties." It also forbade the publication of material that could bring the government into "hatred or contempt," provoke defiance of its authority, or "create or excite feelings of enmity, ill-will or hatred" among sections of the population (pp. 236–237). The law, however, makes it clear that criticism of the government and attempts to bring about lawful change would not be considered significant enough in bringing

---

[6] On January 19, 1998, the editor and several other journalists of the Urdu daily *Pakistan* were arrested and held briefly for publishing a routine passage from a serialization of a popular account of the life of the Prophet Mohammed.

[7] In 1995, Zafaryab Ahmad, a Lahore-based free lance journalist was arrested and charged with sedition after he reported on child labor. He was accused of working with Indian Intelligence to damage Pakistan's carpet-industry exports through false reporting (US Department of State, 1999).

the government into hatred, nor would furtherance of the legitimate interest of a section of the population be seen as creating ill will (p. 237). The RPPPO restricted foreign ownership of periodicals to no more than 25 percent and that only with "the previous approval of the government" (p. 235).

A number of other laws also affect the press. For example, Section 6 (a) of the West Pakistan Maintenance of Public Order Ordinance (MPO) (Ordinance 31 of 1960 as amended in 1963 and 1964), gives provincial governments sweeping powers to control publications if the authorities are "satisfied that such action is necessary for the purpose of preventing or combating any activity prejudicial to the maintenance of public order" (Jabbar & Isa, 1997). The Ordinance allows the government to "prohibit the printing or publication in any document," including a newspaper or periodical, "any matter relating to a particular subject or class of subjects" (p. 616). It also gives the authorities the power to censor or to suspend the publication of newspapers or magazines for up to six months.

The power of the MPO Ordinance became apparent on June 29, 1995, when the Sindh provincial government banned six Urdu dailies with a mass circulation in Karachi for 60 days—*Qaumi Akhbar, Public, Evening Special, Aghaz, Parcham*, and *Awam*. This action effectively eliminated the vernacular evening press of Karachi. Later, the government cancelled the publishing licenses of 122 newspapers to ensure that the banned publications did not reappear under new names. However, a nationwide newspaper strike forced the government to withdraw the ban (Ali, 1996).

The Newspaper Employees (Conditions of Service) Act (Act 58 of 1973 as amended in 1975) determines the terms and conditions of all newspaper personnel. It sets down the rules for appointment, termination of employment, provident fund benefits, hours of work, leave, medical care, and other matters related to newspaper employees (Jabbar & Isa, 1997, pp. 274–277). It mandates the setting up of wage boards, reconstituted every five years, to determine the employees' wages, allowances, fringe benefits, increments, and pensions. Wage board awards are legally binding on newspapers, news agencies, and periodicals, except in the case of very small operations. Conflicting viewpoints exist on the effect of this law on press freedom. Journalists and their unions say that the law strengthens press freedom. Editors and publishers, however, say that wage boards violate free market operations thereby obstructing the industry's growth and expansion. In September 1997, the management of the Dawn Group closed down two dailies, *Dawn Gujarati* and *Vatan*, citing the determination of salaries by wage board awards as a reason (*Dawn*, September 30, 1997, p. 5).

Jabbar and Isa (1997) point out that the "three most profound changes in the laws of Pakistan relating to mass media" took place during the tenure of two un-elected caretaker governments (p. 61). The first was the repeal of the black press law of 1963 and its replacement with the more reasonable press law of 1988 under Caretaker President Ghulam Ishaq Khan. The second and the third were the promulgation of the Freedom of Information Ordinance[8] on January 29, 1997, and of the Electronic Media Regulatory Authority Ordinance[9] on February 14, 1997—both under the caretaker government of President Leghari and Prime Minister Malik Meraj Khalid. The last two Ordinances lapsed in May–June 1997 under the Nawaz Sharif government, which had assumed power following the February 1997 general election (Zeitlin, 1999).

3.2 Financial Aspects: Circulation, Advertising, Marketing Strategies

3.2.1 Circulation

The All Pakistan Newspaper Society claimed that the newspaper industry showed "amazing growth" in 1988 (WAN, 1999, p. 147) after the government relaxed the policy on the declaration of new publications. The number of newspapers and magazines stood at 1,223 in 1997, but "fell" to 736 in 1998, when the government removed irregular publications from its published list. The APNS estimated that in 1997, the total circulation of daily newspapers and other periodicals was 3.5 million (WAN, 1998). It said that in 1998 the number of dailies increased to 303 while the number of non-dailies fell to 247 from the previous year's 681 (WAN, 1999). The daily circulation of newspapers has ranged from one to two copies per 100 people over the last two decades (see Table 1). The main reasons for the low circulation are the low literacy rate, the urban orientation of the press, and the comparatively high price of newspapers in relation to the average income. Because of the absence of a regional or rural press that could highlight the concerns and problems of rural areas, the potential readership outside the cities is largely untapped.

Jang is the country's top daily with a circulation of 850,000 followed by *Nawa-e-Waqt*, 500,000; *Pakistan*, 279,000; *Khabrain*, 232,000; *The News*, 120,000; *Dawn*, 109,000; *The Nation*, 27,000; and *Business Recorder*, 22,000; (WAN, 1998, 1999). Urdu newspapers and magazines command the largest circulation followed by the English and the Sindhi press (Sajid 1996). Although the English newspapers appeal primarily to a small, and better educated elite, they have a prestige and influence far greater than their share of circulation. Sindhi is the only regional language with a well developed press.

Except for a few major groups, Pakistani media organizations face chronic financial problems because of factors like low circulation base; low level of advertising expenditure; high cost of imported newsprint, printing machinery, and supplies; and the government's regulation of the salaries of newspaper employees at a level higher than what the market forces would allow.

---

[8] Ordinance No. 15 of 1997 appears in Jabbar & Isa, 1997 (pp. 472–475).
[9] Ordinance No. 25 of 1997 appears in Jabbar & Isa, 1997 (pp. 424–431).

3.2.2 Advertising

Display advertising revenue for all media stood at Rupees 6.62 billion (US$ 120 million) in 1998. Television had the largest share of advertising revenue with 49 percent; followed by newspapers, 32 percent; magazines, 10 percent; outdoor, 6 percent; and radio, 3 percent (WAN, 1999). The largest advertiser is the government, which accounted for about 30 percent of all advertising in national newspapers—an estimated Rupees 650 million in 1997. Smaller newspapers, particularly those published in small towns, are highly dependent on government advertising support (Akif & Siddiqui, 1998). The Press Information Department (PID) of the federal Ministry of Information and Media Development is responsible for channeling government advertising. All government organizations, autonomous and semi-autonomous, send their advertisements to the PID for distribution to the media. APNS observed that multinational advertising agencies had created a "rapidly rising passion for creativity and excellence in advertising" (WAN, 1999, p. 147).

3.2.3 Marketing Strategy

Newspapers prefer to publish from the two major cities—Karachi and Lahore—and from Islamabad, the national capital. This enables them to get higher rates for government advertising. Karachi continues to be the biggest and most lucrative market for newspapers because most of the major business houses are based there. Even publications that are not based in Karachi have a strong marketing presence in the city. In recent years, newspapers with a strong regional focus have become very popular, especially in Karachi and Lahore. However, as these publications matured, they could not resist the temptation to start editions in other cities. Thus, papers such as *Din, Khabrain*, and *Pakistan*, which have a strong presence in Lahore, have begun publishing a number of editions.

3.3 Structure and Organization

Since the repeal of the PPO in 1988, scores of newspapers have appeared in Pakistan's larger cities headed by Karachi (population 5.2 million) and Lahore (population 2.9 million). A few new entrants have been quite successful. Newspapers are also published from Faisalabad (population 1.9 million), the twin cities of Rawalpindi (population 920,000) and Islamabad (population 150,000), Hyderabad (population 795,000), Multan (population 742,000), Peshawar (population 555,000), Quetta (population 285,000), and several other smaller cities.

With the privatization of newspapers belonging to the National Press Trust by the government of Benazir Bhutto in 1995–96, the government no longer owns or controls newspapers, although it owns and operates one of the two major news agencies, the Associated Press of Pakistan. The three main media groups in Pakistan are the Jang Group, the Herald Group, and the Nawa-e-Waqt Group.

Jang Publications is the largest media group. Its flagship is the Urdu daily *Jang*, published from Karachi, Lahore, Rawalpindi, and Quetta, as well as from London. *Jang* enjoys a virtual monopoly of Urdu readership in Sindh and Rawalpindi–Islamabad federal territory; it also has a major share of the market in Lahore and Quetta. The group also publishes *Akhbar-e-Jehan*, the largest circulating weekly magazine in Urdu, and two evening papers—*Daily News* (English) and *Awam* (Urdu). In 1991, the Jang Group started an English morning paper, *The News*, from Karachi, Lahore, Rawalpindi, and London. *The News* was the first newspaper in Pakistan to use computers in all stages of production.

Pakistan Herald Publications Ltd publishes *Dawn*, which, until *The News* started publication, had a near monopoly over English-language readership in Karachi. Even today, despite competition from *The News* and other newspapers sent to Karachi from Lahore and Islamabad, *Dawn* has maintained its dominant position in Karachi. *Dawn* recently started publishing a Lahore edition. The Herald Group also publishes the *Star* (circulation 38,000), an English evening paper; and *The Herald*, an influential English monthly. In January 1999, the group started publishing the monthly *Spider* that focuses on the Internet. The publications of the Herald Group, targeted at the better educated and more affluent section of Pakistani society, follow a liberal editorial policy.

The Nawa-e-Waqt Group publishes *Nawa-e-Waqt* from Lahore, Rawalpindi, Multan, and Karachi. The group started the English daily *The Nation* from Lahore in the mid-1980s; and, encouraged by its success, began an Islamabad edition in 1990. The group also publishes the Urdu weekly *Family*.

In addition to these large groups, a number of other significant groups and independent publications also exist. The more important daily newspaper chains that started in recent years include *Khabrain, Pakistan, Ausaf,* and *Din*. Other important dailies are *The Frontier Post*, published from Peshawar, and the *Business Recorder* and *Amn* from Karachi.

Political parties own two major newspapers. The conservative Jammat-e-Islami controls the Urdu daily *Jasarat* (50,000), published from Karachi, while the Pakistan People's Party controls the Urdu daily *Mussawat*, published from Lahore. A number of publications in Karachi strongly support the Muttahada Qaumi Movement (MQM), the dominant political party in the urban areas of Sindh, of which Karachi is the capital.

Pakistan has two main news agencies. The Associated Press of Pakistan (APP) is part of the Ministry of Information and Media Development. Pakistan Press International (PPI) is the independent news agency in the private sector. In recent years, several more news agencies, some of which are funded by political parties and groups, have emerged.

3.4 Quality and the Popular Press

The most influential English-language dailies are *The News* and *Dawn*, while *The Nation* and *Frontier Post* are lagging behind in circulation. Among the Urdu-language dailies, *Jang* remains the unquestionable leader, followed by *Nawa-e-Waqt, Pakistan*, and *Khabrain*.[10]

The emergence of the popular press is a relatively recent phenomenon related to the political turmoil following the country's return to democracy in 1988. Since then, a number of evening newspapers that cover political events in a sensational and highly partisan manner have come into the market. This trend has been especially strong in Karachi, which has been in turmoil since 1998. Sensational evening newspapers in Urdu have become an established part of the media environment. Even the Jang Group, the country's largest and most well-established newspaper group, has come out with a popular evening daily, *Awam*. The increase in the price of established papers has led to the emergence of lower-priced six-to eight-page morning newspapers. These papers have not only captured a substantial part of newspaper readership but have also forced the established papers, especially in Lahore, to reduce their cover prices.

3.5 Distribution and Technology

Most newspapers and magazines aim for a national readership. A well organized and independent network of newspaper hawkers distributes the publications. In smaller towns, hawkers also act as stringers for newspapers. A number of major dailies such as *Dawn, The News, Jang, Nawa-e-Waqt, The Nation, Khabrain*, and *Pakistan* are published simultaneously from a number of cities. The newspapers also publish multiple editions to facilitate their delivery to different parts of the country. Where schedules allow, the newspapers are even airfreighted to different cities. They also use buses for distribution in nearby towns.

4. BROADCASTING

4.1 Policy and Legal Framework

4.1.1 Radio

Article 10 of the Pakistan Broadcasting Corporation Act (Act 32 of 1973) requires PBC to, among other functions, "carry out instructions of the Federal Government with regard to general pattern or policies in respect of programs, announcements and news to be put on the air from time to time" (Jabbar & Isa, 1997, p. 314). Chapter 3 of the Act sets forth the corporation's management structure, while Chapter 6 specifies matters pertaining to its finance.

---

[10] *Dawn* and *Jang* have maintained their pre-eminence for a long stretch. Khurshid, 1971, described *Dawn* as the "best English language daily" and *Jang* as "the most widely circulated daily" in Pakistan (p. 307).

4.1.2 Television

The memorandum of association of Pakistan Television Corporation Ltd, drawn up in accordance with the Companies Ordinance, as well as its articles of association, cover all aspects of PTV (Jabbar & Isa, 1997, pp. 346–402). The memorandum of association of Shalimar Recording Co. Ltd (pp. 402–415) and the Television Receiving Apparatus (Possession and Licensing) Rules of 1970 (pp. 415–423) also affect the policy and legal framework of Pakistani television.

4.2 Structure and Organization

4.2.1 Radio

Pakistan Broadcasting Corporation Act converted Radio Pakistan into a statutory corporation in 1973. A board of directors consisting of a chairman, a director-general, and six directors appointed by the government manages PBC. The secretary of the Ministry of Information and Media Development is the chairman of the organization.

The headquarters of PBC are in Islamabad. It has 22 other stations in Abbottabad, Azad Kashmir, Bahawalpur, Chitral, Dera Ismail Khan, Faisalabad, Gilgit, Hyderabad, Karachi, Khairpur, Khuzdar, Lahore, Larkana, Loralai, Multan, Muzaffarabad, Peshawar, Quetta, Rawalpindi, Sibi, Skardu, and Turbat (Akif & Siddiqui, 1998). PBC has 16 shortwave and 26 medium-wave transmitters with a total transmitting capacity of 3,762kW. Radio reaches almost 100 percent of the population.

In September 1998, PBC established an FM broadcasting service in Karachi, Lahore and Islamabad (*Dawn*, October 1, 1998, p. 8). A private FM service already exists in these three cities.

4.2.2 Television

The Pakistan Television Corporation Ltd is a public limited company, in which the government holds all the shares. PTV has 10 divisions, each headed by a full-time director: news, current affairs, programs, sports, international relations, engineering, finance, administration and personnel, PTV academy, and educational television (ETV). PTV also has six television centers, each headed by a general manager in Lahore, Karachi, Islamabad, Peshawar, Quetta and the ETV center in Islamabad (PTV-2). It relays the majority of programs on Pakistan Telecommunication Corporation's terrestrial microwave network, which links PTV's centers and the 32 high-powered re-broadcast stations throughout the country. Television reaches 86 percent of the population and 37.5 percent of the country's territory.

4.3 Program Policies

The Pakistan Broadcasting Corporation (PBC) broadcasts its home-service programs in 20 languages. It broadcasts 18 national news bulletins in Urdu and English, as well as 24 in regional languages and dialects. In addition, each radio station broadcasts local news bulletins featuring news and announcements of local interest. PBC's analysis of its programs showed the following breakdown: 48 percent related to music; 12.5 percent to religion; 11 percent to news and current affairs; 10 percent to rural and farm topics; 5 percent to women, children, and workers; 3 percent to youth and students; 2.5 percent to sports; 2 percent to the armed forces; 2 percent to drama/features; 2 percent to publicity campaigns; and 2 percent to science, technology, and health; (http://www.radio.gov.pk/general.html). PBC's FM service features music, entertainment and call-in programs.

Pakistan Broadcasting's external services broadcast to 70 countries in 15 languages: Urdu, English, Arabic, Bengali, Burmese, Persian, Dari (the Afghan dialect of Persian), French, Gujarati, Hindi, Indonesian, Sylheti, Swahili, Tamil, and Turkish. It broadcasts 25 bulletins in the External Services and the World Service for foreign and Pakistani listeners abroad. It also broadcasts three general overseas slow speed bulletins for Pakistan's missions abroad.

Pakistan Television Corporation's national news bureau in Islamabad produces PTV news with news units in the provincial capitals and six regional centers. PTV televises news in Urdu, English, and all the major regional languages, as well as in Arabic. An analysis of PTV-1 and PTV-2 programs in 1996 revealed that 56 percent related to entertainment, 16 percent to news and current affairs, 10 percent to education, 8 percent to culture and religion, 4 percent to advertising, and the balance to other categories (Gilani, 1998). Almost 54 percent of PTV-1 programming was in Urdu. PTV subscribes to satellite feeds of international television news agencies and is a member of Asiavision. The news bulletins of PBC and PTV faithfully follow the official policies. There is hardly any discussion or coverage of opposing viewpoints. These bulletins either downplay or altogether ignore the realities that would portray the government in a bad light.

In the private sector, the main programs of Shalimar Television Network (STN) include news bulletins of CNN and the BBC. Occasionally, the station has been closed because of financial difficulties and disputes with Ministry of Information. No private station is permitted to produce news and public affairs programming. STN routinely censors foreign segments considered socially or sexually offensive. The government monitors advertising on all broadcast media, editing or removing commercials that are deemed morally objectionable. SPTV mainly re-televises international channels to viewers in Pakistan. It is obliged to carry specified state-owned PTV programs and to abide by the government's guidelines relating to news and current affairs. For national news, all TV networks have to use the news bulletins produced by PTV.

4.4 Ownership and Financing

Pakistan Television Corporation (PTV) and Pakistan Broadcasting Corporation (PBC) run the state-owned TV and radio broadcasting services. In addition, two privately owned TV channels and an FM radio network are in operation.

PTV no longer receives an annual government subsidy that used to make up about a fifth of its total revenue. A breakdown of PTV's revenue budget of Rupees 1.3 billion showed that 63–67 percent of the funding came from advertising, 22 percent from license fees, and 11 to 15 percent from the sale of programs and other sources (Gilani, 1998). PTV's educational channel attracts no advertising. Moreover, the extension of PTV services to some remote areas has increased the corporation's expenses without bringing in revenue. Since 1998, PTV has started a number of projects such as PTV World and Mid-East Channel, which have proved to be commercially successful and have substantially improved the financial position of the organization.

A breakdown of PBC's 1995–96 revenue budget of Rupees 668.2 million showed that 85 percent of its funding came from government grants, 11 percent from advertising, and 2.3 percent from license fees (Gilani, 1998). PBC faced more financial problems than PTV because of declining advertising revenue and dependence on government grants in the face of rising costs.

In the private sector, STN is partly owned by Shalimar Recording, in which the government has a majority share. Shaheen Pay TV (SPTV) is 50 percent foreign owned. Its local equity is equally divided between PAY-TV and the Shaheen Foundation, the welfare organization of retired air force personnel. Although it is independent, SPTV has to operate under the rules and regulations of the Ministry of Information and Media Development. The company had earlier been granted permission to operate a nationwide cable TV network and three FM radio stations, one each in Karachi, Lahore, and Islamabad.

5. NEW ELECTRONIC MEDIA

5.1 Internet and On-line Media

Internet became accessible to computer users in Karachi in July 1995 via Digicom, a private e-mail provider. Pakistan Telecommunication Corporation Limited (PTCL) made its packet data network available for nationwide local-call access to the Internet in April 1996. PTCL set up PakNet to provide Internet access through shell accounts. In 1996, Fascom started an Internet service in Karachi (APT, 1999). ITU (1999) has estimated that Pakistan had 600,000 computers and 511 Internet hosts in 1996, with an estimated 4,000 Internet users. The January 1999 Network Wizards' survey showed that the number of Internet hosts in Pakistan has increased more than six-fold to 3,102—a density of 0.22 per 10,000 people. The number of Internet subscribers was 60,000 (APT, 1999).

Despite the small number of Internet users in relation to the country's population, several newspapers have established Internet editions for overseas Pakistanis. All leading Pakistani newspapers—Including, *Jang, Nawa-e-Waqt, Dawn, The Nation, The News International*, and *Business Recorder*—are available on-line. Other newspapers on the Web include *Din, Daily Hot News* (in English, from Islamabad), *Jasarat, Friday Times* (weekly in English), *The Frontier Post, Hi Pakistan, Information Times, Millat Online, News Network International, Pakistan Link, Pakistan News Service*, and *Pakistan Press International* (PPI). Radio Pakistan news is available on PBC's website. PTV has also established a website.

5.2 Telecommunications Infrastructure

Pakistan had an overall telephone density of 2.2. percent in mid-1998, with the number of main telephone lines in service standing at 2.83 million. The rural telephone density was a mere 0.14 percent (APT, 1999). ITU estimated that in 1998 the country had 202,000 cellular subscribers—a density of 0.14 per 100 people—who received service from three joint-venture operators—Paktel, Pakcom and Pakistan Mobile Communications Ltd (PMCL). The number of mainline telephones has increased at a compound annual growth rate of 16 percent since 1990, when the telephone density was 0.75 percent. The number of mainline telephones per 100 households stood at 7.2 in 1996 (ITU, 1998).

The Pakistan Telecommunication (Reorganization) Act 1996[11] replaced the Pakistan Telecommunication Corporation with four new entities—Pakistan Tele-communication Corporation Ltd (PTCL), Pakistan Telecommunication Authority (PTA), the National Telecommunication Corporation (NTC), and the Frequency Allocation Board (FAO)—and created a new body, the Pakistan Telecommunication Employees Trust (PTET). The PTA regulates the telecommunications sector while the NTC handles government and defense telephony. PTCL provides domestic and international telephone, telex and Internet services, as well as a number of value-added services. It has invested in the SEA-ME-WE3 submarine cable and the Trans Asia-Europe fiber-optic cable. It has also joined the ICO Global Com-munications and established an earth station and an international gateway exchange in the middle of Pakistan (APT, 1999).

6. POLICY TRENDS FOR PRESS AND BROADCASTING

6.1 Press

The framework of government–media relations in Pakistan is undergoing significant changes. The past few years have seen a definite trend toward greater press freedom and the government remains under pressure to free the electronic media from

---

[11] Act No. 17 of 1996 (Jabbar & Isa. 1997. pp. 432–472).

government control. The higher courts have also delivered landmark decisions in favor of the media in cases involving contempt, as well as defamation. Given the global trend toward democracy, the Pakistani press expects to enjoy an increasing degree of freedom. Pressure from national and international organizations has had a positive impact on the freedom of press during the last decade. This is especially true in cases of attacks on rural journalists by local officials and landlords who act without the approval or knowledge of the higher authorities.

Freedom House (1999) asserted that despite the restrictive laws and institutional provisions, "Pakistan's press is among the most outspoken in South Asia" (p. 356). It has placed the Pakistani press in the "partly free" category. Freedom House gave Pakistan the maximum score on the criterion of repressive actions on the press and also placed it high on the criterion of political pressures and controls on media content—13 out of 15 for both broadcast and print media (Sussman, 1999).

Because the RPPPO, the press law of 1988, had repealed the PPO, the black press law of 1963, the repeal in 1997 of the RPPPO itself has created some doubts about the existence of any law governing the registration of publications.[12] The absence of a legal framework for the registration of publications is probably temporary. It is most likely that the government will introduce some elements of the RPPPO, including the requirement for registration of publications, in a new law such as the proposed legislation for a press council.

The liberalization of foreign exchange in 1990 brought about a liberalization of newsprint allocation as well. Newspapers and periodicals can import newsprint at a reduced duty rate. The quota is issued according to circulation figures certified by the Audit Bureau of Circulation, a department of the Ministry of Information and Media Development. These figures are also the basis for setting rates for government advertising. However, the ABC figures lack credibility. Allegations exist that, at times, publications with limited circulation are able to obtain certificates based on inflated numbers and re-sell the excess newsprint in the open market. Over the years, media organizations have urged the entrusting of auditing to some independent organization. The practice of reduction or withdrawal of the subsidized newsprint quota for newspapers that are critical of the government has occurred in the past.

The government, as the largest newspaper advertiser, plays a major role in shaping the financial viability of the press. The nationalization of large industries in the early 1970s brought 60 percent of Pakistan's total advertising expenditure under government control. Although the share of government advertising has been declining since 1990, because of the privatization of major industries and banks, it still constitutes an important source of revenue for newspapers.

---

[12] Currently, no legal requirement exists for registration, but the government too has said nothing about it. Hence the confusion. Many unregistered publications appear in the market. However, the post office requires a registration number for concessional postal rates.

6.2 Broadcasting

In broadcasting, perhaps the greatest impact on the media environment has been the popularity of satellite dishes, which have provided people access to entertainment and news channels such as STAR TV, BBC, and CNN. Satellite dishes, which are readily available, are popular not only in cities but in rural areas as well. The authorities have made no attempts to control their sale. South Asian satellite channels (usually India-based) have become very important sources of news and information, as well as popular entertainment.

6.3 New Electronic Media

The Pakistan Telecommunication Authority (PTA), the licensing authority for electronic services, has imposed a number of restrictions on Internet use. The license agreement prohibits the use of any sort of data encryption. Users also have to agree to the monitoring of their electronic communications by government agencies. The license prohibits voice transmission via the Internet, and the violation of this clause can lead to prosecution and termination of service without notice. Internet service providers (ISPs) also have to agree to use only the authorized means of communications provided by the government-owned Pakistan Telecommunication Corporation (PTC) for all data communication. The purpose of these clauses is to protect the commercial interests of PTC. ISPs are also responsible for ensuring that the programs and information provided through electronic services do not "come into direct clash with accepted standards of morality and social values in Pakistan" (Ali, 1997).

7. MAIN ISSUES

● Press independence

Although press freedom has improved considerably since 1985, the press still faces the challenge of working with nascent democratic institutions that have not yet developed the fundamental democratic tenet of tolerance for opposing viewpoints. Political groups continue to intimidate the press and journalists. Rural journalists, in particular, have to face unchecked abuses of power by local authorities, feudal lords and political groups, all of whom have the means and the will to deliver brutal private punishment (Ali, 1997, p. 37). In early 1999, even the Jang Group, the country's largest and most powerful newspaper group, had to face government harassment and heavy-handed tactics, which included raiding offices in Rawalpindi on December 14, 1998, presumably for being too critical of the government and the alleged financial misdealing relating to the prime minister's business interests. The government also retaliated by suing the group for sedition.[13]

---

[13] US Department of State, 1999, reported that violence against and intimidation of journalists is a nationwide problem. Examples: In January 1998, the federal police ransacked the home of Raja

However, as in all previous cases, the government had to withdraw actions against the newspaper; and in mid-February 1999, the government released the newsprint that it had seized and the impounded bank accounts, and removed Federal Investigation Agency personnel from the Jang office premises. The May 1999 arrest of editor Nijam Sethi for "treason" (that is, "anti-Pakistan conduct and ridiculing the very foundation and ideology of the country") is another example of the government's continued effort to discourage the press from investigating high-level corruption (Dasgupta, 1999). Following this episode, a panel of journalists described Pakistan as a country plagued by crises of politics and economics, with its press a pawn in the hands of a powerful, landholding elite (Arora, 1999).

● Press Council

Representatives of the government, editors, and newspaper owners were unable to reach an agreement in August 1997 on the establishment of a press council and the adoption of a code of ethics. In February 1998, the government produced and sought comments on a draft law for establishing a 15-member press council. Major organizations of journalists, including the Pakistan Federal Union of Journalists, have rejected the draft, which has drawn considerable criticism. Skepticism exists that the government may use the concept of the press council to restrict some of the freedom that the press has won after decades of hard struggle. The Council of Pakistan Newspaper Editors (CPNE) has also put up conditions for the establishment of a press council. Mehmudul Aziz, acting president of the CPNE, has said that the organization would consider the press council proposal only after the parliament passed the Freedom of Information Act and the CPNE's proposed amendments to the RPPPO. The CPNE has taken the stand that any code of ethics for the press must also apply to the official media, including the electronic media (Ali, 1998).

● Freedom of Information Ordinance

Journalists have urged the reintroduction of the Freedom of Information Ordinance promulgated by the caretaker government in January 1997. The ordinance allowed access to public records and obligated the government to provide the citizens with details of decisions taken by ministries and government departments. The law also covered the superior courts, the armed forces, financial institutions, and the

---

Tariq, a crime reporter for *Jang*. On June 21, police officers beat journalist M. Ismail Jatoi in Shikarpur for photographing a policeman, allegedly in the act of taking a bribe. A bomb exploded in the offices of *Dawn* on July 9. On July 19, police in Hyderabad beat two journalists. On August 16, PML youth wing activists attacked the editor-in-chief of a local weekly newspaper in Chukwal, Punjab, for publishing what they considered an anti-PML story. On September 15, Pervaiz ul Hassan was arrested for reporting on local police corruption.

intelligence agencies. Before coming to power, the Pakistan Muslim League welcomed the ordinance as a positive step forward in making the country a more open and democratic society. The then PML spokesman Mushahid Hussain, who became minister of information and media development, had said that his party believed that the citizens of any democratic society should have the fundamental right of access to information from government departments. He had given the assurance that the PML, if elected, would make the ordinance more meaningful and effective. However, after the PML swept into power in February 1997, it did not move the ordinance in parliament but instead allowed it to lapse in May.

● Loosening government control of broadcast media

Considerable support also exists for the Electronic Media Regulatory Authority Ordinance, which would have ended private monopolies and exclusive rights over the electronic media. The caretaker government promulgated the Ordinance in February 1997. During the election campaign, the PML had committed itself to ending monopolies in the electronic media to open the field for private-sector participation. However, after coming into power, the PML government allowed the EMRA to lapse. The Citizens Media Commission, headed by Javed Jabbar, a member of the caretaker cabinet that passed the EMRA Ordinance, has launched a campaign for the passage of the Ordinance as an act of parliament (Zeitlin, 1999).

8. STATISTICS

General Profile

Exchange rate (September 1999)	US$ 1 = Rupees 51.76*
Per capita GDP (PPP)	US$ 1,570
Per capita GNP (nominal)	US$ 492
Literacy	40.9 percent
Population (mid-1999 estimate)	138.1 million
Households (1997)	21.5 million
No. of daily newspapers (1998)	303
Main telephone lines in use (mid-1998)	2.83 million
Telephone density (mid-1998)	2.2 percent
Internet hosts (January, 1999)	3,102
Internet subscribers (mid-1998)	60,000

Source: *Asiaweek*, December 17, 1999; APT, 1999; ITU, 1999; * OANDA Historical Currency Table [On-line]. Available: (http://www.oanda.com/converter/cc-table?lang=en).

Table 1
Estimated Mass Media Penetration

	Radio receivers		TV receivers		Daily newspapers		
	Number ('000s)	Per 100 people	Number ('000s)	Per 100 people	Number	Circula'n ('000s)	Per 100 people
1980	5,500	6.4	938	1.1	106	1,032	1.2
1985	8,500	8.4	1,304	1.3	118	1,149	1.1
1990	10,650	8.9	1,989 (2,900)*	1.7 (2.6)*	398	1,826	1.5
1995	12,500	9.2	2,680 (6,500)*	2.0 (5.0)*	223	2,800	2.1
1996	12,900	9.2	3,000 (7,600)*	2.1 (5.7)*	264	–	–
1997	13,500	9.4	3,100 (9,000)*	2.2 (6.5)*	271**	1,499**	1.1**
1998	–	–	(12,500)*	(8.8)*	303**	–	–

Source: UNESCO, 1999; * ITU, 1998; ** WAN, 1998, 1999.

9. USEFUL ADDRESSES

9.1 Newspaper Groups

The Jang Group
PO Box 52
I.I. Chundrigar Road
Karachi
Telephone: (92-21) 263-7111 10 lines
Fax: (92-21) 263-6066, 263-4395
E-mail: jang@jang-group.com
URL: www.jang-group.com

The Dawn Group
Haroon House
Dr. Ziauddin Ahmed Road
Karachi
Telephone: (92-21) 111 444 777, 520080
Fax: (92-21) 568-3801, 568-3188
E-mail: editor@dawn.xiber.com
URL: http://dawn.com

The Nawa-e-Waqt Group
Nipco House
4 Shahra-e-Fatima Jinnah
Lahore
Telephone: (92-42) 636-7551 4 lines
Fax: (92-42) 636-7583
E-mail: editor@nation.com.pk
URL: http://www.nation.com.pk

9.2 Media Associations

The All Pakistan Newspaper Society
3rd Floor, 32 Farid Chambers
Abdullah Haroon Road
Karachi 3
Telephone: (92-21) 567-1314, 567-1256
Fax: (92-21) 567-1310

The Council of Pakistan Newspaper Editors
1 Victoria Chambers
Abdullah Haroon Road
Karachi
Telephone: (92-21) 512697
Fax: (92-21) 735726
Telex: 23035

The Pakistan Federal Union of Journalists
Karachi Press Club
Sarwar Shaheed Road
Karachi
Telephone: (92-21) 568-6910

9.3 News Agencies

Pakistan Press International (PPI)
Press Centre
Shahrah Kamal Ataturk
Karachi
Telephone: (92-21) 263-1123
Fax: (92-21) 263-1125
E-mail: pakpres4@khi.comsats.net.pk
URL: www.pakistan-news.com

Associated Press of Pakistan (APP)
18-Mauve Area, G-7/1
Islamabad
Telephone: (92-51) 819980-93
Fax: (92-21) 919986-87
URL: http://www.pak.gov.pk/govt/app.htm

9.4 Press Foundations

The Pakistan Press Foundation
Press Centre
Shahrah Kamal Ataturk
Karachi
Telephone: (92-21) 263-0562, 263-0563
Fax: (92-21) 263-7754
E-mail: owais.ali@ibm.net
URL: www.oneworld.org/ppf

9.5 Broadcasting

Pakistan Broadcasting Corporation
National Broadcasting House
Constitution Avenue
Islamabad
Telephone: (92-51) 829021
Telex: 5861
E-mail: cnoradio@isb.comsats.net.pk
URL: http://www.radio.gov.pk

Pakistan Television Corporation
Federal TV Complex
Constitution Avenue
1221 F-5/1 Islamabad
Telephone: (92-51) 828651
Fax: (92-51) 823406
Telex: 5833
URL: http://www.ptv.com.pk

The Ministry of Information and Media Development
Block M, Pakistan Secretariat
Islamabad
Telephone: (92-51) 920-2891, 920-7066
Fax: (92-21) 920-7008, 920-8940
Telex: 5782
E-mail: fakhar@ptv.com.pk
Internet: http://www.pak.gov.pk/govt/index1.htm

10. REFERENCES

Akif, S.A.A., & Siddiqui, A.A. (Comp.). (1998). *Pakistan advertising scene 1997.* Karachi: Orient McCann-Erickson.

Ali, K. (1997, April 10–16). Radio Station Peshawar. *Dawn Review,* p. 19

Ali, O.A. (1992). *Pakistan's national news agencies: Their evolution and operations.* Unpublished master's thesis, University of Wales College of Cardiff.

Ali, O.A. (1996, January). Trial by fire and firearm. *CPU News,* p. 4.

Ali, O.A. (1997). *Report on attacks on the media in 1996.* Karachi: Pakistan Press Foundation.

Ali, O.A. (1998). *Pakistan press freedom report 1997.* Karachi: Pakistan Press Foundation.

Ali, S.M. (1969). *Early phases of journalism in Indo-Pakistan.* Dacca: Society for Pakistan Studies.

Al Mujahid, S. (1978). Pakistan. In J.A. Lent (Ed.), *Broadcasting in Asia and the Pacific: A continental survey of radio and television* (pp. 211–227). Philadelphia: Temple University Press.

Al Mujahid, S. (1982). Pakistan. In J.A. Lent (Ed.), *Newspapers in Asia: Contemporary trends and problems* (pp. 480–502). Hong Kong: Heinemann Asia.

Al Mujahid, S. (1991). Press system in Pakistan. *Media Asia, 18,* 123–131.

Al Mujahid, S. (1994). Pakistan: A crippling legacy. In *Press systems in SAARC* (pp. 75–92). Singapore: AMIC.

APT (Asia-Pacific Telecommunity). (1999). *The APT yearbook.* Bangkok: APT.

Arora, A. (1999, May 27). Pakistani press: A pawn amid politics, economy, journalists say. *The Freedom Forum* [On-line]. Available: (http://www.freedomforum.org/international/1999/5/27pakistanpress.asp).

Bhatti, R. (1993 November 9–11). *The influence of policies and government on communication ethics.* Paper presented at AMIC seminar on Communication Ethics from a South Asian Perspective, Colombo.

Dasgupta, P. (1999, May 29). New test for Pakistan democracy: Sharif out to bend press. *Deccan Herald* [On-line]. Available: (http://www.deccanherald.com/deccanherald/may29/top.htm).

Freedom House Survey Team. (1999). *Freedom in the world: The annual survey of political rights and civil liberties, 1998–1999.* New York: Freedom House.

Gilani, I. (1998). Pakistan. In A. Goonasekera and D. Holaday (Eds.), *Asian communication handbook* (pp. 123–134). Singapore: AMIC & NTU.

Gunaratne, S.A. (1970). Press in Pakistan under President Ayub Khan. *Gazette, 16* (1), 39–53.

Haider, N. (1990, June 5). The role of the press in Pakistan. *The Muslim* [11th Anniversary Supplement], p. 6.

ITU (International Telecommunication Union). (1998, 1999). *World telecommunication development report.* Geneva: ITU.

Jabbar, J., & Isa, Q.F. (Comps.). (1997). *Mass media laws and regulations in Pakistan—And a commentary from a historical perspective.* Singapore: AMIC.

Kurian, G.T. (1982). Pakistan. In G.T. Kurian (Ed.), *World press encyclopaedia* (pp. 707–714). London: Mansell Publishing.

Khurshid, A.S. (1971). Pakistan. In J.A. Lent (Ed.) *The Asian newspapers' reluctant revolution* (pp. 298–316). Ames: The Iowa State University Press.

Mahmood, S., & Shaukat, N. (1993). *The constitution of the Islamic Republic of Pakistan:* Lahore: Legal Research Centre.

Napoli, J. (1991). Benazir Bhutto and the issues of press freedom in Pakistan. *Journal of South Asian and Middle Eastern Studies, 14* (3), pp. 57–76.

Niazi, Z. (1986). *Press in chains.* Karachi: Karachi Press Club.

Pakistan, Government of. (1959). *Report of the press commission.* Karachi: Government of Pakistan.

Rizvi, S. (1990). Pakistan. In C.J. Hamelink and A. Mehra (Eds.) *Communication development and human rights in Asia* (pp. 69–86). Singapore: AMIC.

Sajid, Z. (1996). Media monitors in Pakistan. In K.S. Venkateswaran (Comp.). *Media monitors in Asia* (pp. 51–54), Singapore: AMIC.

Shamsuddin, M. (1986). *British press coverage and the role of Pakistani press from independence to the emergence of Bangladesh.* Unpublished doctoral dissertation, The City University, London.

Siddiqui, I. (1991). *Radio journalism in Pakistan.* Lahore: Ferozsons (Pvt) Ltd.

Sussman, L.R. (1999). *Press freedom 1999: News of the century.* New York: Freedom House.

Tahir, S.N. (1996). Television in Pakistan: An overview. In D. French and M. Richards (Eds.), *Contemporary television: Eastern perspectives* (pp. 113–131). New Delhi: Sage Publications.

UNESCO (United Nations Educational, Scientific and Cultural Organization). (1999). *Statistical yearbook.* Paris: UNESCO.

US Department of State. (1999, February 26): *Pakistan: Country report on human rights practices for 1998* [On-line]. Available: (http://www.state.gov/www/global/human_rights/1998_hrp_report/pakistan.html).

WAN (World Association of Newspapers). (1988, 1999). *World press trends.* Paris: WAN.

World factbook. (1999). Pakistan [On-line]. Washington, DC: Central Intelligence Agency. Available: (http://www.odci.gov/cia/publications/factbook/pk.html).

Zeitlin, A. (1999, February 23). Movement afoot to ease government control of broadcast media in Pakistan [On-line]. *The Freedom Forum.* Available: (http://www.freedomforum.org/international/1999/2/23pakistan.asp).

◆

7

SRI LANKA

Shelton A. Gunaratne & Chanuka Lalinda Wattegama

1. NATIONAL PROFILE

1.1 Geography

Sri Lanka (Ceylon) is located 7 degrees north of the equator, off the southern tip of India. It has an area of 65,610 sq km, making it slightly larger than West Virginia. Forests and woodland cover 32 percent of the land area. The highest point is the 2,524-meter Mount Pidurutalagala.

1.2 People

Sri Lanka has a population of 19.1 million (US Census Bureau, International Data Base), 23 percent of whom live in urban areas. The ethnic composition is Sinhalese, 74 percent; Sri Lankan Tamils, 12 percent; Indian Tamils, 6 percent; Moors, 7 percent; and Burghers, Malays, and Veddahs, 1 percent. The religious composition is Buddhists, 69 percent; Hindus, 15 percent; Christians, 8 percent; and Muslims, 8 percent. Both Sinhala and Tamil are national languages. English, spoken by about 10 percent of the people, is widely used in government. The Indian Tamil population, whom the British brought in the 18th century to work in tea plantations, lives in the central highlands.

The country's adult literacy rate exceeds 90 percent. Almost 4.3 million students attended the country's 10,906 schools in 1996. An estimated 33,948 students—2 percent of the relevant age group—attended the country's 12 universities the same year (Central Bank of Sri Lanka, 1997).

Since 307 B.C., when the king of Anuradhapura embraced Buddhism, the majority Sinhalese—descendants of an Indo-Aryan group led by Prince Vijaya who migrated to the island around 500 B.C.—have continued to be adherents of Buddhism. Invasions by Dravidians in South India forced the Sinhalese to shift their capital to Polonnaruwa in the 11th century and further south thereafter. The minority Tamils, Hindu descendants of these Dravidians, settled in the northern and eastern parts of the island. Thus the Sinhalese–Tamil ethnic conflict, which has killed more than 60,000 people since the rise of the Liberation Tigers of Tamil Eelam (LTTE) in the early 1980s, has deep historical roots.

The Portuguese captured the southern coastal belt in 1505 and ruled it until the Dutch ousted them in 1658. The British replaced the Dutch in 1796, captured the last independent Sinhalese kingdom in Kandy in 1815, and unified the country's administration in 1833. They also established a Legislative Council of appointed members in 1833 with the British governor as the presiding officer. Since 1931, people have periodically elected their leaders through universal franchise. The country's legal system is a highly complex mixture of English common law, Roman–Dutch, Muslim, and Sinhalese law(s), and customary law.

1.3 Government and Politics

Sri Lanka gained independence from Britain on February 4, 1948, and it became a republic on May 22, 1972. On August 16, 1978, the country adopted its current constitution, under which the executive power shifted from the prime minister to a president who was elected directly by the people. Since independence, Sri Lanka has practiced parliamentary democracy, with power shifting periodically between the two major political parties—the United National Party (UNP) and the Sri Lanka Freedom Party (SLFP)—and their allies. The UNP held power from independence to 1956, from 1965 to 1970, and from 1977 to 1994, while the SLFP-dominated left-wing coalitions held power at other times.

Two Sinhalese youth insurrections—the Maoist Janata Vimukthi Peramuna uprisings of 1971 and 1987–89—and the continuing LTTE insurgency have marred the country's recent history.

1.4 Economy

With the exception of the Maldives, Sri Lanka is ahead of other South Asian countries with regard to its Gross National Product per capita at market prices (US$ 827) and literacy (90 percent). The Gross Domestic Product at purchasing power parity was estimated at US$ 46 billion, and the corresponding per capita GDP at US$ 2,625 (*Asiaweek*, December 17, 1999).

In 1977, Sri Lanka shifted its economic strategy from an import-substitution trade policy to a market-oriented export policy. The country's most dynamic industries today are food processing, textiles and apparel, food and beverages, telecommunications, and insurance and banking. By 1996, plantation crops made up only 20 percent of exports, while textiles and garments accounted for 63 percent (US$ 4 billion). Economic growth accelerated in the first half of the 1990s with the GDP growing at an annual average rate of 5.5 percent until a drought and a deteriorating security situation lowered growth to 3.8 percent in 1996. The economy rebounded in the second half of 1996 and recorded a 6.4 percent growth in 1997.

The government's counter-insurgency efforts have caused defense expenditures to overshoot budget targets (*World factbook*, 1999). The central bank has recorded a growth rate of 5.3 percent for 1998. The country is now in the World Bank's lower-middle income classification.

2. DEVELOPMENT OF PRESS AND BROADCASTING

2.1 Brief Early History

The Dutch set up the first printing press on the island in 1737. The British produced the first regular publication—the weekly *Government Gazette* in 1802, the year when the country became a crown colony. Perera (1994) points out that the country's press was largely unregulated from its beginnings in 1802 until 1973. The patronage of the colonial government and the commercial interests of the British colonists ensured a high degree of government–press harmony in the early history of the press. Governor R.W. Horton sponsored the first English newspaper, the short-lived biweekly *Colombo Journal*, in 1832. In 1834, a group of English merchants started another biweekly, the *Observer and Commercial Advertiser*, the country's oldest newspaper today. Several English newspapers came out thereafter, for example, the *Ceylon Chronicle* (1837), the *Ceylon Herald* (1837), the *Ceylon Times* (1846–1978), the *Ceylon Independent* (1888), the *Jaffna Freeman* (1862–70), the *Galle Telegraph* (1870–71), the *Kandy Herald* (1868–69), the *Morning Leader* (1907–32), and the *Ceylon Daily News* (1918 onwards). Until the middle of the 19th century, Englishmen published the island's press in English mainly for fellow Englishmen. Hulugalle (1960) and Gunaratne (1970, 1975, 1982) provide more details on the history of the English press.

The Sinhala press began in the provincial city of Galle with the publication of *Lankaloka* in 1860. However, *Lakmini Pahana*, which commenced on September 11, 1862, was the first Sinhala newspaper registered under the Newspaper Ordinance of 1839. Other Sinhala newspapers followed: *Lakrivikirana* (1863–1902), *Gnanartha Pradipaya* (1866 onwards), *Sarasavi Sandaresa* (1880–1951), *Dinapatha Pravurthi* (1895–1908), *Sinhala Jathiya* (1903–51), *Sinhala Bauddhaya* (1906–79), *Dinamina* (1909 onwards), *Lakmina* (1912–56), and Sunday *Silumina* (1931 onwards). In contrast to the pro-Western and pro-Christian bias of the English press, the Sinhala press "exuded a remarkable pro-nationalistic and pro-Buddhist bias" (Gunaratne, 1975, p. 3). The Sinhala daily press started with the short-lived *Dinapatha Pravurthi* (Daily News). *Lakrivikirana*, which started as a weekly in July 1863, turned itself into the second Sinhala daily in 1896. The demise of these two dailies paved the way for H.S. Perera to start the longest surviving Sinhala daily, *Dinamina*, on December 17, 1909. Three years later, on September 3, 1912, Alexander Welivita started the fourth Sinhala daily, *Lakmina*, which continued publication for 43 years. Pannasekera (1965–71) has examined the history of Sinhala newspapers and magazines in nine volumes.

Muthulingam (1997) and Thillainathan (1997) have outlined the development of the Tamil press in Sri Lanka. The early Tamil publications were religious and ethno-nationalist in orientation. *Udaya Tharakai* (1841) served a Jaffna clientele for more than 130 years. The news periodical *Udayadithan* served Colombo Tamils while the short-lived Roman Catholic publication *Usaithalu* (1845) targeted Jaffna as well. Other early publications included *Paliya Narsan* (1865), *Elangai Pathukaralan* (1868), and *Alamat Lankapuri* (1869). Hindu revivalism was the aim of publications such as *Illangai Nasen* (1877) and *Sivabhimani* (1884). The Tamil-speaking Muslim traders started *Muslim Nasen* (1882), *Islam Mithiran* (1905–40), and other newspapers. The national Tamil press emerged with Jaffna-based *Eelakesari* (1930–58), and Colombo-based *Virakesari* (1930 onwards) and *Thinakaran* (1932 onwards). The last two are the country's longest surviving Tamil dailies.

2.2 Developments since 1948

At the beginning of the post-independence era, broadcasting was a state monopoly and the press was a private duopoly. Over the last half century, the country's media scene has changed considerably, with the government asserting a dominant role in press operations, while conceding the private sector a role in broadcasting operations. Television did not arrive in the country until 1979.

2.2.1 Print Media

At independence, two private newspaper groups—the Associated Newspapers of Ceylon Ltd (ANCL), and the Times of Ceylon Ltd—dominated the country's press. ANCL, also known as Lake House because of its location by the Beira Lake in Colombo, was the more dominant. It published the country's morning dailies with the largest circulation in all three languages: *Dinamina* (Sinhala), *Daily News* (English), and *Thinakaran* (Tamil). It also published the afternoon daily *Observer* (English) and, since 1953, the afternoon daily *Janatha* (Sinhala). Its weekend papers—*Silumina* (Sinhala), published since 1930; *Sunday Observer* (English), published since 1923; and Sunday *Thinakaran* (Tamil), published since 1948—were also circulation leaders.

The afternoon daily *Times of Ceylon* (English), which started as *Ceylon Times* in 1846, was the flag bearer of the second group. The Times group also published the morning daily *Lankadipa* (Sinhala), an innovative newspaper started by journalist D.B. Dhanapala in October 1947, and commenced publishing another English daily, *Morning Times* in 1954. The latter folded four years later, but resurfaced in 1961 as the *Ceylon Daily Mirror*, a morning tabloid that continued until 1979. The Times group also tried out a short-lived Tamil daily, *Eelamani*, in 1972. The group's weekend publications were the *Sri Lankadipa* (Sinhala), which started in 1951, and the *Sunday Times* (English), which began in 1923.

A third newspaper group specialized in the Tamil press. Its flag bearer was the Tamil morning daily *Virakesari* started in 1930. The group started an afternoon Tamil daily *Mithran* in 1966, but it has ceased publication recently. Now known as the Express Newspapers Ltd, this group ventured into publishing the English weekly *Weekend Express* in 1995.

The Swadeshi Newspapers Ltd made an unsuccessful attempt in the 1950s to capture a share of the daily newspaper market. The company was the publisher of the nationalist weekly *Sinhala Jathiya*, which began in 1903 and became popular under the editorship of novelist Piyadasa Sirisena. In 1954, it started two dailies—*Jathiya* (Sinhala) and *Guardian* (English)—and the Sunday *Pictorial* (English), all of which incurred heavy losses and folded.

A more successful challenge to the press duopoly took place when the country's largest book publisher, M.D. Gunasena & Co. Ltd, formed the Independent Newspapers Ltd. Dhanapala left the Times Group in 1961 to edit the new group's flag bearer, the Sinhala daily *Dawasa*, and its weekend counterpart *Rividina* (later *Riviresa*). It also tried out an afternoon Sinhala daily, *Sawasa*. The group started newspapers in English and Tamil as well—the *Sun* (1964) and its weekly *Weekend*, (1965) in English; and the morning *Thinapathi* (1966), the afternoon *Thanthi* (1967), and the weekend *Chintamani* (1966) in Tamil. This group, which had the blessings of the SLFP-led socialist coalition, soon surpassed the Times group as ANCL's closest competitor.

The country's newspaper scene changed when the SLFP-led left-wing coalition passed the Associated Newspapers of Ceylon Ltd (Special Provisions) Law and took over Lake House on July 20, 1973. The law required "broadbasing" the ownership of Lake House, which had been the bastion of support for the right-wing UNP under the ownership of the family of its founder, D.R. Wijewardene. The first attempt by the SLFP-led coalition to take over Lake House failed in late 1964, when the issue led to parliamentary crossovers and the dissolution of parliament. The coalition lost the March 1965 general elections, thereby prolonging the Wijewardene hold on Lake House for seven more years. Now, more than a quarter of a century after the takeover, Lake House remains the faithful "mouthpiece" of the party in power, and no government has taken action to redistribute the shares of the company.

The venerable Times of Ceylon Ltd closed down on January 31, 1985, after a colorful 139 years in operation (Liyanage, 1993, p. 116). Financial and employee problems, political conflicts and changes in ownership were the main reasons for its demise. Internal conflicts among its directors had enabled the then SLFP stalwart Anura Bandaranaike, son of Prime Minister Sirimavo Bandaranaike, and his cohort Harris Hulugalle to take control of the company in August 1975. Nine days after the UNP won the July 1977 general elections, the Colombo municipal commissioner issued a notice to auction the Times group to recover the taxes that the company had not paid. J.R. Jayewardene, the new prime minister (and the soon-to-be executive president) of the UNP government, immediately appointed a competent authority to administer and restore the company. However, despite the government subsidies, the company's newspapers failed to achieve profitable circulation levels.

The Independent Newspapers Ltd closed down on December 26, 1990, after a lifespan of almost three decades (Liyanage, 1993, p. 138). It supported the SLFP at the 1970 general elections because of differences with the UNP government on school textbook publication, a matter of intense interest to Gunasena & Co. However, the group also fell out with the new SLFP-led coalition government over the group's lockout of trade union employees (Liyanage, 1993). Taking advantage of the emergency regulations, which had gone into force on March 16, 1971 to counter the JVP insurrection, the government sealed the group's printing press and reintroduced press censorship on April 20, 1974. Prime Minister Sirimavo Bandaranaike claimed that the press was sealed for supporting the opposition's civil disobedience campaign and for the "flouting of emergency regulations preventing the transport of rice" (Gunaratne, 1975, p. 31). The group resumed publication following the expiry of emergency regulations on February 16, 1977. Its newspapers adopted an anti-government stance in the period leading to the general elections of July 1977 in contrast to the government-controlled ANCL and the Times groups. However, internal problems, as well as the inability to compete with two newspaper groups that emerged in the 1980s with modern printing machinery, led to its demise less than 14 years later.

At the end of the century, three newspaper groups dominate the island's newspaper scene: the ANCL, which has been under government control since 1973; the Upali Newspapers Ltd, under private ownership, with close family connections to both the UNP and the SLFP leadership; and the Wijeya Newspapers Ltd, also a family concern, with close family connections to the UNP leadership, and started by the previous ANCL owner Ranjit Wijewardene (Wijetunga, 1996, p. 107).

Upali Wijewardene, a successful businessman and cousin of the country's first executive President J.R. Jayewardene, established the Upali Newspapers Ltd, and on October 4, 1981, commenced publishing two Sunday newspapers—the *Divaina Irida Sangrahaya* (Sinhala) and the *Sunday Island* (English). Their daily counterparts, *Divaina* and the *Island*, began on February 4, 1982. Upali Wijewardene was known to have political ambitions of succeeding his cousin as the country's president, which caused him to antagonize two UNP stalwarts, Prime Minister R. Premadasa and Finance Minister Ronnie de Mel. The new publisher disappeared in a mysterious plane crash in February 1983, and the control of the company passed on to his widow, Lakmini. The actual control, however, passed on to her father, Sivali Ratwatte, the brother of SLFP leader Sirimavo Bandaranaike. Wijetunga (1996) wrote that although this group's reporting on the party platforms during the 1994 general elections "appeared to be less biased," the bias against the People's Alliance (PA) "was more apparent in the content." The group showed "undisguised prejudice and hostility" toward the PA leader, the current President Chandrika Kumaratunge, although it supported her mother, Sirimavo (p. 109).

Ranjit Wijewardene, who lost the ownership of ANCL in 1973, re-entered the newspaper business with the establishment of the Wijeya Newspapers Ltd. He had bought the newspaper titles of the defunct Times group and re-launched them beginning with the weekend *Irida Lankadipa*, on February 23, 1986. The *Sunday Times* followed on June 7, 1987; the daily *Lankadipa* on September 10, 1991; and in 1995, the *Midweek Mirror.* (The group revived the *Daily Mirror* (1961–79) in mid-1999.)

Wijetunga (1996) reported that the Wijeya group, which was closer to the UNP than the Upali group, "adopted even a more circumspect attitude in its reporting" of the 1994 elections, "perhaps because it was also eager to establish itself as the market leader in the media business" (p. 110).

2.2.2 Broadcasting

The broadcasting of the British governor's speech on July 27, 1924, marked the first official demonstration of the new medium. The Telegraph Department set up a Government Broadcasting Station in December, 1925. Broadcasting was only in English until 1931, when Sinhala and Tamil services also began operations. Experiments in shortwave broadcasting began in 1934. Originally, broadcasting came under the authority of the postmaster general and director of telegraphs (and later, of telecommunications). Like elsewhere in the former British colonies, broadcasting in Sri Lanka was a government monopoly until the mid-1980s. A committee headed by Kanthiah Vaithianathan, appointed in 1940 to report on broadcasting, made several recommendations to the then State Council, but preoccupation with the war delayed their implementation.

Broadcasting improved in 1945, when Britain handed over to Sri Lanka the powerful shortwave transmitters of the South East Asia Command. In 1949, the year after independence, the government merged the Government Broadcasting Station and Radio SEAC to form the Department of Broadcasting, which came to be known as Radio Ceylon. A commercial service, in addition to the original national service, began in September 1950. Simultaneous broadcasting in all three languages of the country—Sinhala, Tamil, and English—began in the same year. An educational service began in September 1951. Improvements in transmission occurred in 1955 with the installation of a 10kW shortwave transmitter in Ekala. Experimental stereo transmission started in 1981.

Broadcasting went through the scrutiny of three commissions after independence—N.E. Weerasoria Commission of 1953, H.A.J. Hulugalle Commission of 1965, and V.C. Jayasuriya Commission of 1970 (Gunaratne, 1978). The UNP government, which implemented the main recommendation of the Hulugalle Commission, passed the Broadcasting Act of 1966 and converted Radio Ceylon into the Ceylon (now, Sri Lanka) Broadcasting Corporation in 1967 on the lines of the New Zealand Broadcasting Corporation.

Today, the SLBC's home services reach the population through medium-wave, shortwave, and FM transmissions. The corporation has 23 medium-wave transmitters, island-wide. It also has eight FM stations in various parts of the country. The Sinhala Commercial Service, which attracts 84 percent of the Sinhala audience, is SLBC's most popular service. Its Sinhala National Service attracts 23 percent of the Sinhala audience, while the Tamil service attracts 15 percent of the Tamil audience (Central Bank of Sri Lanka, 1998).

Television commenced in Sri Lanka on April 15, 1979, when two private entrepreneurs, Anil Wijewardene and Shan Wickremasinghe, established the Independent Television Network with the blessings of the UNP government. However, less than two months later, on June 5, the government took over the network over a dispute with the two investors. The network's location shifted to Wickramasinghapura in 1982.

Meanwhile, the Sri Lanka Rupavahini Corporation Act of 1982 created the SLRC as the apex of the country's television structure. With headquarters built with Japanese assistance and located next to the SLBC, the new corporation commenced its services on February 15, 1982. Television remained a state monopoly for another decade, until 1992, when the government allowed private investors to enter the field under the control and supervision of the SLRC. (Six private channels were in operation in 1998.)

With a transmitting station on Mount Pidurutalagala and two sub-transmitting stations at Kandy and Kokavil (the latter destroyed by the LTTE in July 1990), SLRC was able to provide its services to 84 percent of the population. It added Namunukula and Sooriyakanda transmission stations in February 1986 to expand its reach. The corporation commenced educational telecasting in 1983, and it set up a TV training institute in October 1984. An agreement with CNN World gave it access to "voiced TV reports." A dubbing studio came into operation in February 1989 (Central Bank of Sri Lanka, 1998).

3. THE PRESS

3.1 Policy and Legal Framework

Chapter III of the 1978 Constitution contains a justiciable Bill of Rights. Article 10 guarantees the freedom of thought, conscience, and religion. Article 14 (1) (a) guarantees the freedom of speech and expression, including publication. However, Article 15 (2) states that this right "shall be subject to such restrictions as may be presented by law in the interest of racial and religious harmony or in relation to Parliamentary Privilege, contempt of court, defamation or incitement to an offence." Article 15 (7) goes on to declare that the fundamental rights—right to equality; freedom from arbitrary arrest; freedom from arbitrary detention; and freedom of speech, assembly, association, occupation, and movement—shall be subject to restrictions as may be presented by law, including the pertinent *regulations*, in the interests of national security, public order, and the protection of public health or morality ... or of meeting the just requirements of the general welfare of a democratic society. Udagama (1986) says, "The scope of the restrictions are so broad as to render the guarantee virtually nugatory" (p. 27).

The country enjoyed considerable press freedom for the first quarter of a century after independence. Thereafter, for almost 20 years beginning 1973, the state usurped much of that freedom with laws aimed at taming the press (Gunaratne, 1975; Liyanage, 1993). Udagama (1986) wrote that in the mid-1980s, the press was "almost totally under governmental control" (p. 75). Two controversial pieces of legislation that "had profound consequences for the freedom of the press" were the Sri Lanka Press Council Law of 1973 and the Associated Newspapers of Ceylon Ltd (Special Provisions) Law of 1973 (Selvakumaran & Edrisinha, 1995, p. 11).

The Press Council Law set up a seven-member council to regulate the press—six appointed by the government with the director of information as the *ex officio* seventh member. The council has quasi-judicial powers to inquire into complaints against the press. Udagama (1986) asserts that this law "severely curtails the freedom of publication of specific types of information without prior permission of government officials," which amounts to prior censorship" (p. 4). She contends that the prohibition of publishing matters relating to government policy-making, such as cabinet meetings and fiscal policy, "keeps people in the dark as to the policies that may govern them and also prevents the free discussion of issues that affect the general public" (p. 39). The Press Council Law also "somewhat super-fluously makes criminal defamation as defined by S. 479 of the Penal Code an offence" (p. 40).

The ANCL Law called for the vesting of 75 percent of Lake House shares in the public trustee on behalf of the government. The former shareholders could retain the balance 25 percent, while in the process of broadbasing, no single shareholder could hold more than 2 percent of the shares. The law empowers the public trustee to appoint a new board of directors.

Udagama (1986) points out that although the "purported intention of the government in enacting these two laws was the establishment of a free and responsible press," what actually happened was "the creation of a press tightly controlled by the government which denied freedom of expression to the press and the public and also freedom of information to the public" (p. 5). Except for the requirement of registration of printing presses and newspapers, Sri Lanka had no form of government control of the press until 1973. Another exception, however, was censorship during the operation of emergency regulations under the Public Security Ordinance No. 25 of 1947. Civil and ethnic unrest in 1953, 1958, 1959, 1968, and 1971 caused the government, irrespective of the party in power, to implement media censorship under emergency regulations.

The emergency declared in 1971 to suppress the first JVP insurrection, continued until 1977. Following the emergencies in 1982 and 1983, rule by emergency powers has itself become the rule rather than the exception. The continuing LTTE-led ethnic war and the second JVP insurrection of 1987–89 provided justification for the government to rule under states of emergency, with built-in media censorship. The government sealed the printing press of the Independent Newspapers Ltd in 1974 and of *Aththa* in 1982.

Among the other statues whose provisions impinge on the freedom of publication are the Parliamentary (Powers and Privileges) Act of 1953 as amended in 1978, 1980, 1984, and 1987; the Official Secrets Act of 1955; and the Prevention of Terrorism (Temporary Provisions) Act of 1979 (Coomaraswamy, 1981; Udagama, 1986).

Selvakumaran and Edrisinha (1995) provide an overview of the statutory enactments and constitutional provisions pertaining to the media (pp. 3–8), as well as a summary critique of the regulatory framework on freedom of expression. The provisions of the Penal Code on defamation (Section 479), offences against the state (Sections 118 and 120) and offences affecting public decency or morals or religious harmony (Sections 285–287 and 291A&B) are relevant to the media. Other enactments affecting the media include the Newspapers Ordinance of 1839, Printers and Publishers Ordinance of 1885, Printing Presses Ordinance of 1902, Obscene Publications Ordinance of 1927, Profane Publications Act of 1958, and Code of Intellectual Property Act of 1979.

3.2 Financial Aspects: Circulation, Advertising, Marketing Strategies

Audited newspaper circulation data for Sri Lanka are not available. Peiris (1997) points out "a glaring mismatch" between the circulation data produced by newspaper producers and the estimates for newspaper purchasers derived from surveys of household expenditure (p. 83). Data recorded by the Central Bank of Sri Lanka show a dip in the annual Sinhala daily newspaper circulation in the mid-1990s: 89.3 million in 1989; 97.7 million in 1992; 102.3 million in 1993; 142.7 million in 1994; and 116 million in 1995. On this basis, the average Sinhala daily circulation has been between 370,000 and 450,000 in the mid-1990s.

The newspaper groups keep the true circulation data a top secret in the hope of attracting advertisers, who have had to increasingly rely on market research for media selection. Estimated circulation data and Lanka Market Research Bureau's readership data (reported in WAN, 1999) show the daily with the top circulation to be the *Lankadipa* (circulation, 134,000; readership, 670,000). The other eight dailies in descending order are: *Divaina* (circulation, 130,000; readership, 650,000), *Daily News* (circulation 75,000; readership, 375,000), *Dinamina* (circulation, 55,000; readership, 275,000), *The Island* (circulation, 47,000; readership, 235,000), *Virakesari* (circulation, 30,000; readership, 150,000), *Thinakaran* (circulation, 29,000; readership, 145,000), *Observer* (circulation, 19,000; readership, 57,000), and *Janatha* (circulation, 5,000; readership, 15,000). These figures add up to an aggregate daily circulation of 524,000 (2.8 copies per 100 people) and a daily readership of 2.6 million (13.7 readers of dailies per 100 people, which equals 19 percent of the population above the age of 15). The Sinhala dailies account for 62 percent of the total circulation; the English dailies, 27 percent; and the Tamil dailies, 11 percent.

Peiris (1997) draws attention to several factors that could explain the country's slow or negative growth in newspaper circulation: the increasing popularity of the electronic media; the "nationalization" of the country's dominant newspaper group in 1973; the sharp increase in the price of newspapers since early 1980s; and the ongoing ethnic war in the north and the east (p. 84). At Rupees 6–12 a copy—the equivalent of 9–19 cents in US currency, the readers find the price of a Sinhala daily relatively high in relation to a per capita GNP of US$ 814. The price of Sunday newspapers varies from Rupees 16–18—the equivalent of 23–26 US cents.

Reporting on a national sample survey, Samarasinghe (1997) confirms the rank of *Lankadipa* (Wijeya) as the "most preferred" Sinhala daily, followed by *Divaina* (Upali) and the government-run *Dinamina* (ANCL); the rank of *Daily News* (ANCL) as the "most preferred" English daily; and the rank of *Virakesari* (Express) as the "most preferred" Tamil daily; followed by *Thinakaran* (ANCL) and *Thinamarasu*. The "most preferred" Sinhala Sunday is the *Irida Lankadipa* (Wijeya), followed by *Silumina* (ANCL), *Divaina Irida Sangrahaya* (Upali), and the new *Lakbima* (Sumathi). Among the English newspapers, *Sunday Observer* (ANCL) is at the top, followed by *Sunday Times* (Wijeya), *The Leader* (Leader), and *Sunday Island* (Upali). *Virakesari Vara Veliyeedu* (Express) tops the Tamil Sundays, followed by *Thinakaran Varamanjari* (ANCL) and *Eelanadu*.

The estimated circulation of the 12 Sunday newspapers in 1998 was 1.28 million (WAN, 1999) which works out to seven copies per 100 people. The Samarasinghe (1997) survey, however, reported 35.7 percent of the adults claiming to have read the daily newspapers regularly, and 35 percent claiming to have read the Sundays regularly (p. 271). The estimated Sunday circulation data, therefore, cannot bear credence, and the popular belief that more people read the Sundays than the dailies in Sri Lanka needs further investigation. The estimated circulation of the 31 non-dailies was 1.32 million.

The advertising industry spent Rupees 1.3 billion (US$ 24.2 million) in 1995, Rupees 1.5 billion (US$ 26.6 million) in 1996 and Rupees 2.1 billion (US$ 34 million) in 1997 on the major media in the country. Of that money, the share of the press declined from 40.5 percent in 1995 to 33.8 percent in 1996 and to 30.7 percent in 1997. The share of television, on the other hand, increased over the same period: 43 percent, 44 percent, and 47 percent respectively. The share of radio also showed improvement: 15.5 percent, 22.2 percent, and 22.3 percent respectively (Phoenix Advertising, 1998). In 1998, the newspaper advertising revenue was Rupees 1.14 billion (US$ 16.7 million). The media shared national advertising expenditure as follows: newspapers and magazines, 25.4 percent; television, 35.6 percent; radio, 16.6 percent; and others, 22.4 percent (WAN, 1999).

The government-owned ANCL received almost half of the advertising pie allocated to the press. The top advertising sectors were banking and finance, consumer goods, real estate, employment, motor vehicles, alcohol and tobacco, and entertainment. Display advertising accounted for 85 percent and classifieds for 15 percent of advertising revenue.

3.3 Structure and Organization

In 1998, Sri Lanka had nine dailies, 12 Sundays, and 31 non-dailies. The dailies sold 161.4 million copies during the year while the Sundays sold 66.5 million and the non-dailies 68 million. The newspapers employed 1,014 journalists and 2,690 other staff (WAN, 1999).

Three major newspaper groups dominate Sri Lanka's newspaper industry—the Associated Newspapers of Ceylon Ltd (Lake House), Wijeye Newspapers Ltd, and Upali Newspapers Ltd. A fourth player is the Express Newspapers Ltd. ANCL is the only group that publishes newspapers in all the three languages—Sinhala, Tamil, and English. Upali and Wijeya groups publish dailies in Sinhala and English. The Express group has specialized in Tamil newspapers and has recently ventured into publishing an English weekly.

A new player is Sumathi Publishers, which publishes the Sinhala Sunday *Lakbima*. It started publication in October 1994. Yet another new player is the English Sunday *Leader*, which made its debut on June 3, 1994. Multi-Packs (Ceylon) Ltd and Lal Wickrematunge own the Leader Publications (Pvt) Ltd. The *Peramuna* became the latest Sunday newspaper in 1998.

Colombo is the center of newspaper publication in Sri Lanka. However, Jaffna was the headquarters of the Tamil daily *Eelanadu* (established in 1959), which ceased publication in the 1970s in the face of LTTE threats. Other Jaffna-based newspapers—*Uthayan, Murasoli, Eelanatham*, and *Eelamurasu* (established in 1984)—emerged to promote sectarian interests. *Tamil Murasu* based in Vavuniya and *Ceithi* based in Kandy were two other Tamil regional newspapers. The LTTE assassinated the *Eelamurasu* owner, M. Amirthalingam, after taking over his newspaper. The escalation of ethnic turbulence caused these publications to either disappear completely in the mid-1980s or to be published only intermittently. As a result, the Colombo-based *Virakesari* has established itself as the major Tamil daily. A new Tamil daily, *Thinakkural*, began publication in April 1997 on the initiative of a section of Jaffna Tamil journalists who had worked for *Virakesari* earlier.

A significant feature of the country's newspaper scene is the politically oriented alternative press (*vikalpa puvathpath*). The two famous examples are the weekly *Ravaya* (Echo), edited by Victor Ivan alias "Podi Athula," a rebel leader of the 1971 JVP insurrection (Chandraprema, 1991, p. 1), and *Yukthiya* (Justice), edited by Sunanda Deshapriya, another rebel leader in the 1971 JVP insurrection (Chandraprema, 1991, p. 1). The popular belief about their influence seems to be misplaced in the light of the Samarasinghe (1997) survey, which showed only 3.1 percent claiming to read such politically oriented periodicals regularly.

The country's press has another feature: specialized Sinhala tabloids that the major newspaper groups put out for various interest groups. They target women (*Tharunee* [ANCL], *Navaliya* [Upali], and *Sirikatha* [Wijeya]); children (*Mihira* [ANCL], *Wijeya* [Wijeya], and *Bindu* [Upali]); sports enthusiasts (*Kreeda* [ANCL], and *Visura* [Ravaya]); and movie fans (*Sarasaviya* [ANCL]). Educational papers, like *Vidusara, Samatha, Sadhana,* and *Sathara,* are popular among students preparing for the General Certificate of Education (ordinary and advanced level) examinations.

Several political parties also publish their official organs in Sinhala: the SLFP weekly *Podujana* (People); UNP weekly *Siyarata* (My Country); and Nava Sama Samaja Party weekly *Haraya* (Substance). The Communist Party weekly *Aththa* (Truth), which was reputedly the most popular political newspaper, has ceased publication. Other Sinhala periodicals include *Vathmana, Sivdesa, Manahara, Vivarana,* and *Mathota.* Pornographic tabloids like *Sondura,* and *Navasarana,* also circulate in the country.

Eelam People's Democratic Party backs the Tamil weekly *Thinamarasu,* which supports the LTTE on some issues. Another Tamil weekly, *Navamani,* targets the Tamil-speaking Muslim community. Several Tamil Nadu publications are also registered as newspapers in Sri Lanka.

The English press also includes *Lanka Woman* (Wijeya), *Guardian* (an independent monthly), *Pravda* (a political journal), *Business Today* (a monthly), and *Lanka Monthly Digest.*

3.4 Quality and Popular Press

Sri Lanka does not have an upmarket or quality press as in the United States or Britain. The English-language press caters to a more elite group of readers, but the newspapers themselves fail to meet Merrill and Fisher's (1980) standards of an elite press.

Although all three Sinhala morning dailies are broadsheets, both in content and layout they are closer to the popular press. Politically, the *Lankadipa* (Wijeya) leans toward the pro-UNP sympathies of its owner. However, it is the most independent of the four Sinhala dailies. Most of the *Lankadipa* journalists came from the now defunct *Dawasa* group. They have continued to concentrate heavily on the rural readers as they did at *Dawasa. Lankadipa* is noted for highlighting crime, especially sex-related crime. *Lankadipa* also puts out seven provincial editions, all of them printed in Colombo. Provincial news pages differ in these editions. *Dinamina* (ANCL), once the country's leading daily, lost its standing after the government takeover of Lake House. Its circulation has dipped well below its two competitors. Yet, it is much superior to ANCL's afternoon tabloid *Janatha,* which targets primarily the clerical workers in Colombo and the vicinity. *Divaina* (Upali), which takes a clear anti-government and Sinhala nationalist stand, is popular among the ultra-nationalists and the Buddhist clergy. *Divaina* vehemently opposes the PA government's political package for the nation's Tamils.

The *Daily News* (ANCL), despite its ownership by government, continues to be the country's leading English daily. Advertising is heavier in the English newspapers than in the Sinhala press (Karunanayake, 1996). Despite its low credibility, business circles and the more affluent elites prefer the *Daily News* because it carries much of the public-sector advertising. Its only competitor, *The Island* (Upali), caters more to a minority of anti-PA intellectuals than to the wider needs of the affluent English educated. The ANCL's afternoon daily *Observer* circulates mainly in Colombo and its vicinity, just like its Sinhala counterpart.

The Tamil dailies target three minority communities—the indigenous Tamils, the upcountry Indian Tamils, and the Muslims. Most Tamil papers take a Tamil-Hindu stand on issues, and this is particularly so with *Virakesari* (Express). The pro-government *Thinakaran* (ANCL) is more popular with the Muslims in the Eastern Province.

Among the Sinhala Sundays, *Irida Lankadipa* (Wijeya) stands at the top because of its relatively independent political views and the large space it devotes to political news, interviews with politicians, and political reviews. *Divaina Irida Sangrahaya* (Upali) follows its sister daily as an anti-PA Sinhala nationalist newspaper. *Silumina* (ANCL), the country's leading Sinhala Sunday before the government takeover, has lost its credibility. However, it is rich in advertising. A 16-page tabloid named *Rasanduna*, which concentrates on literary issues, accompanies the paper. *Lakbima* (Sumathi) has the potential of a quality Sunday.

The English Sundays, with the exception of the pro-government *Sunday Observer* (ANCL), favor the UNP-led opposition. However, the *Sunday Times* (Wijeya) often attempts to maintain a degree of political independence. The Sunday *Island* (Upali) follows the group's pro-UNP line. The *Sunday Leader* is noted for its investigative attacks on the PA government. It also popularized political gossip columns, which are now a regular feature of all the Sunday newspapers.

3.5 Distribution and Technology

The newspapers of the four publishing groups have a national circulation. *Lanka-dipa* has an extremely wide circulation network that covers every part of the island except some areas of the Northern Province. It is the only newspaper available in some rural areas.

Sinhala Sunday papers are available in the market either on the preceding Friday or on Saturday morning. Thus spontaneous news that may develop on Friday or Saturday cannot get into the Sunday edition. Distributors say that even a delay of two hours in early delivery may cost the newspaper about half of its sales. Thus, when a suicide bomber strapped in explosives assassinated President Premadasa on a Saturday afternoon at a May Day political rally in 1993, the next day's Sinhala Sundays were already out without that story.

The cost of distribution represents about 10 percent of a newspaper's cover price, which varies from Rupees 6 to Rupees 12. Single copy sales account for 68 percent of newspaper distribution while home delivery constitutes 26 percent and postal deliveries 6 percent. All nine dailies have four-color printing capability (WAN, 1999).

Four of the Sinhala Sundays issue tabloids for "light reading." The most popular is *Ridhma* that comes with *Lakbima*. The tabloid *Rasanduna* comes with *Silumina,*

Irida Lankadipa issues the 16-page tabloid *Sandella*, and *Divaina Irida Sangrahaya* provides a tabloid called *Meevitha*.

The English Sundays also issue tabloids: *Mirror* comes with the *Sunday Times*, *Islet* with *The Island*, *Now* with the *Sunday Leader*, and the *Magazine* with the *Sunday Observer*.

4. BROADCASTING

4.1 Policy and Legal Framework

The constitutional and penal code provisions outlined in the policy and legal framework for the press (Section 3.1) also pertain to the broadcast media as do the other statutory enactments except the Press Council Law and the ANCL Law. The policy and legal framework for the broadcast media are set forth in the Sri Lanka Broadcasting Corporation (SLBC) Act No. 37 of 1966 and the Sri Lanka Rupavahini Corporation (SLRC) Act No. 6 of 1982. Additionally, three 1981 acts—Parliamentary Elections Act, Refer-endum Act, and Presidential Election Act—define the rights of political parties and candidates to use radio and television.

4.2 Structure and Organization

4.2.1 Radio

The government-run SLBC dominates radio broadcasting in the country. It offers services in all three languages—Sinhala, Tamil, and English. At present, it offers seven home services, three regional services, six community services, and seven overseas services.

The Sinhala National Service is the main home service. The others are the Sinhala Commercial Service, the Tamil Commercial Service, the English Commercial Service, the Regional Service(s), and the Education and Sports Service(s). SLBC, with ITN coöperation, launched *Lakhanda*, a 24-hour Sinhala service, in January 1997 (Central Bank of Sri Lanka, 1998). This new service uses the successful techniques that MBC Networks' *Sirasa* FM has adopted, for example, audience interaction and the use of simpler language.

The three regional services are the *Rajarata Sevaya* (centered in Anuradhapura since April 1979) for the North Central Province, the *Ruhunu Sevaya* (centered in Matara since 1980) for the Southern Province, and the *Kandurata Sevaya* (centered in Kandy since 1983) for the Central Province (*World radio TV handbook*, 1999).

The six community services are located in Aralaganwila, Girandurukotte, Kotmale, Maha Illuppallama, Jaffna and Vavuniya. These services commenced with the setting up of the Mahaweli community radio in 1981 and its expansion into the Girandurukotte community radio in 1986 (David, 1993). The Jaffna community service commenced in January 1997, the Vanni service (Vavuniya) in August 1997, and *Pulathisi Ravaya* (in Aralaganwila in the Polonnaruwa District) in April 1998.

The latter is a new multiethnic community service on FM 100.7 (*Sunday Observer*, April 12, 1998).

The SLBC uses English, Sinhala, Japanese, Nepali, and several Indian languages—Hindi, Kannada, Malayalam, Telugu, and Tamil—to broadcast its external services: World Service, Southeast Asia, Asia Hindi, Asia Tamil, Asia English, and Middle East. Hindi accounts for almost 60 percent of the external transmission followed by Tamil (16 percent).

Eleven private-sector radio-broadcasting services have emerged since the government relaxed its monopoly in 1984. They offer five English services: Capital Radio, TNL 90/101.7FM, Yes FM, Sun FM99.9, and Gold FM89.8; four Sinhala services: *Sirasa, Savana, Hiru* FM107.9, and *Tharu* FM96.7; and two Tamil services: FM99 and *Suriyan* FM103.2.

4.2.2 Television

The government-run SLRC and ITN dominate television broadcasting in the country. Six ministerial appointees constitute the SLRC, including one representing the SLBC and another representing the National Film Corporation. SLRC started a second channel in mid-1999 to tap into the TV advertising market.

The government relaxed its television monopoly in 1992. Since then four private companies have introduced six television channels—MTV and MTV Newsvision, Swarnavahini, ETV, TNL and Dynavision, the country's first stereo TV broadcast station. (Sirasa TV, which replaced the MTV channel in June 1998, became the first nationwide private sector TV channel. It planned to televise 18 hours a day. MTV itself replaced the MTV Newsvision channel to concentrate primarily on greater Colombo and Kandy.) In 1999, the Sri Lanka Telecommunications Authority allowed two other private TV services: Comet Cable TV run by Ruhuna 2001 Multivision, a subsidiary of Vancouver-based Rystar; and Channel 9, the country's first direct-to-home pay TV service, operated by TV and Radio (Pvt) Ltd, a joint Sri Lanka–Australia venture. In late 1999, it planned to introduce digital television linked to satellite communication for the benefit of expatriate Sri Lankans (*Sunday Observer*, August 8, 1999).

4.3 Program Policies

The SLBC Act of 1966 requires that the programs broadcast by the corporation take precautions to maintain good taste and decency, to not cause incitement to crime or disorder, or cause offence to religious beliefs or public feelings. The Act also requires that programs maintain a proper balance in their subject matter and a high standard of quality. Moreover, it requires that news programs adhere to accuracy and impartiality. However, the Act contradicts the last requirement when it also mandates the corporation to comply with the government's broadcasting policy and implement the general and specific directions of the minister-in-charge. The corporation, through regulations issued by the minister, can control and supervise the programs of the private broadcasting services as well (Selvakumaran & Edrisinha, 1995).

The SLRC Act of 1982 has similar provisions to those of the SLBC Act with regard to programming. The Act requires the corporation to maintain a proper local, regional, and international balance in its programs. The corporation can refuse to televise advertisements that are not in the public interest. Those who wish to produce and market TV program material have to register with the corporation, which can refuse such registration. The Act authorizes the corporation to exercise supervision and control over foreign and other TV crews producing programs for export, as well as over the use of videocassettes and the production of programs on such cassettes for export. As in the case of the SLBC, the corporation must comply with the general or specific directions issued by the minister (Selvakumaran & Edrisinha, 1995). Mahendra (1996) says that the TV programs show "monotony and biases" because of state propaganda; and that severe censorship has restricted creative standards (p. 225).

In 1982, about 52 percent of the SLRC fare comprised imported English programs, compared to 39 percent Sinhala and 9 percent Tamil. By 1996, the share of the Sinhala programs had increased to 53 percent and Tamil programs to 16 percent while English programs dipped to 31 percent. The SLRC's annual telecasting time in 1996 was 3,825 hours—an increase of 79 percent from 1982. The telecasting time of local programs increased from 59 percent in 1983 to 69 percent in 1996 (Central Bank of Sri Lanka, 1998). Rupavahini relays Discovery Channel on digital stereo in addition to its local programs in three languages. ITN relays Deutschewelle in addition to other programs, which are carried on Lakhanda radio as well.

Most private TV stations also have re-broadcast arrangements with international TV services: *Sirasa* TV relays Sun TV India in addition to local programs, which are simulcast on *Sirasa* FM radio; MTV relays BBC World; TNL relays Music Television in addition to local programs, which are simulcast on FM 89 MHz; Swarnavahini relays Raj TV and ATN India in addition to local programs; ETV relays Sky News, CNBC Asia, CBS News, and ABC News; Dynavision relays CNN and Cartoon Network; and Channel 9 relays Star TV, ESPN Sports, films, news, and special programs in several languages. Channel 9 has proposed to keep Sri Lanka in world news daily with a 10-minute news bulletin for international viewers with at least two minutes of internationally important news from Sri Lanka (*Sunday Observer*, August 8, 1999).

4.4 Ownership and Financing

The SLBC (radio) and the SLRC (television), which make up the apex of the broadcasting structure in Sri Lanka, are public corporations. The SLRC budget shows that its funding comes primarily from license fees (25 percent) and advertising (67 percent). SLRC claimed a record income of Rupees 669.7 million (US$ 9.8 million) and a pre-tax profit of Rupees 142.5 million (US$ 2.1 million) for 1998 (*Observer*, April 25, 1999). The ITN operates as a government-owned business undertaking. *Lakhanda*, the new Sinhala radio broadcasting service, has become an ITN responsibility. ITN claimed a profit of Rupees 41 million (US$ 600,029) for the 1997–98 financial year (*Daily News*, June 7, 1999).

The 11 private-sector radio broadcasting services operate on commercial lines. MBC Networks (Pvt) Ltd, a joint venture of the giant Maharaja Organization Ltd, and Singapore Telecom International, runs two 24-hour FM services—Yes FM in English (on 89.5 and 101 MHz) and *Sirasa* FM in Sinhala (on 88.9, 105.9, 106.1, and 106.5 MHz). As data on advertising expenditure indicate, these two appear to be extremely popular commercial stations. Colombo Communications (Pvt) Ltd, owned by Livy Wijemanne, also runs two FM services—Capital Radio in English (on 100.4 MHz) and *Savana* in Sinhala (on 99 MHz), which also functions as FM99 in Tamil. Shan Wickremesinghe is the owner of TNL 90/101.7FM (English), which has been broadcasting for an international audience on the Internet since November 1996. *Sirasa* FM has followed TNL into cyberspace. Asia Broadcasting Corporation, a "contemporary hit radio" station, started two 24-hour radio services—Sun FM99.9 (English) and *Hiru* FM107.9 (Sinhala)—in July 1998. A US$ 9 million joint UK–Sri Lanka venture, ABC added three more services in September—Gold FM (English), *Tharu* FM (Sinhala), and *Suriyan* FM (Tamil).

Trans World Radio, a religious station based in Cary, North Carolina, has a transmitting station, which broadcasts on 882 kHz from Sri Lanka to South Asia in Bengali, Gujarati, Kannada, Malayalam, Marathi, Oriya, Tamil, Telegu, and a handful of other languages. Deutsche Welle, Radio Japan, and Voice of America have relay stations on the island (*World radio TV handbook*, 1999).

The six private sector television channels also operate on commercial lines. MTV Channel (Pvt) Ltd another joint venture of Maharaja and STI, operates two channels—MTV (renamed *Sirasa* TV), and MTV Newsvision (renamed MTV). EAP Network (Pvt) Ltd owned by E.A.P. Edirisinghe Film & Theatre Ltd, also operates two channels—*Swarnavahini* and ETV, originally called ETV1 and ETV2 (standing for extra-terrestrial television). The original investor, Nihal Wijesuriya, sold the two channels to the Edirisinghes in April 1996 for Rupees 200 million (about US$ 36.6 million). Telshan Network (Pvt) Ltd, controlled by Shan Wickremasinghe, operates TNL TV (affiliated with TNL Radio). Dynavision Broadcasting Co. (Pvt) Ltd, a subsidiary of I.W. Senanayake's IWS Holdings, operates the Dynavision channel. Survey Research Lanka data show, that in 1996, Rupavahini had an audience share of 45 percent; ITN, 34 percent; MTV, 12 percent; TNL, 7 percent, and others 1 percent or below (Rajapakse, 1997).

5. NEW ELECTRONIC MEDIA

5.1 Internet and On-line Media

Several researchers have drawn attention to the need for a highly literate country like Sri Lanka to join the Global Information Infrastructure (GII) to compete in the global economy (Gunaratne, 1997; Gunaratne et al., 1997; Induruwa, 1996; Wattegama & Sreekanth, 1988). Three dailies and six non-dailies have taken advantage of the GII to go on-line. The first newspaper to go on-line was ANCL's *Daily News* (September 4, 1995) and the first weekly to go on-line was ANCL's *Sunday Observer* (September 10, 1995). Wijeya group's *Sunday Times* went on-line next (February 18, 1996). The group's *Lankadipa* was the first Sinhala daily to start a weekly Internet edition (April 11, 1997) and *Midweek Mirror* followed. Upali group's *Island* and *Sunday Island* also have an interactive Internet edition. The Express group has set up the first Sri Lankan Tamil newspaper on-line—the *Virakesari Illustrated Weekly* (September, 1997). The independent *Sunday Leader* launched its inaugural Internet edition on December 15, 1996. Two of the country's radio stations have also entered cyberspace. TNL 90FM broke new grounds in November 1996 when it turned into a cyberspace station. MBC's *Sirasa* FM has gone into cyberspace as well.

In 1994, an Internet server in the United States served as the host for Sri Lanka's first website at the University of Moratuwa. However, the country did not have direct commercial Internet access until April 26, 1995. In 1989, University of Moratuwa asked the Sri Lanka government to help set up the Lankan Experimental Academic and Research Network (LEARN), which became a reality in 1994. Using 64 kbps leased lines based on Internet protocol, LEARN became the country's first wide-area network to provide end-to-end IP connectivity. Moratuwa connected its network server to the IP routers at the University of Colombo and the Open University. The National Science Foundation (formerly NARESA) joined the network in July 1996. LEARN, which established a direct Internet connection in 1996, also provides dial-up Internet access to more than 15 academic and research institutes. It is not registered as a commercial ISP.

Lanka Internet Services Ltd was the first ISP to install a local gateway in Sri Lanka. Sri Lanka now has eight gateways, run by eight ISPs—Lanka Internet Services Ltd, Sri Lanka Telecom, Eureka Online Pvt Ltd, CEYCOM Global Communications, ITMIN Ltd, Pan Lanka Networking Ltd, Electrotecks Ltd, and Lanka Communication Services (Pvt) Ltd. The government has no control over the gateways, and the ISPs are free to decide the tariff structures and the communication channels. The vast majority of the country's Internet users in Sri Lanka are in Colombo and the suburbs.

The International Telecommunication Union (ITU, 1997) reported that in 1995, Sri Lanka had seven Internet host computers, which increased to 350 in 1996. Network Wizards' January 1999 survey (http://www.nw.com/zone/WWW/dist-bynum.html) reported 542 host computers in Sri Lanka—0.29 hosts per 10,000 people—while the Internet Software Consortium's July 1999 survey indicated that Sri Lanka has 983 Internet hosts—0.51 hosts per 10,000 people. The number of e-mail and Internet subscribers in 1997 was 9,045 (http://www.lanka.net/trcsl/stats.html).

5.2 Telecommunications Infrastructure

An advanced telecommunications structure and a reliable and adequate power supply are essential prerequisites for informatization (Gunaratne, 1997; Samarajiva, 1997). Sri Lanka had paid inadequate attention to this aspect until the late 1980s.

New realities faced the Department of Posts and Telecommunications, which had relied heavily on telex to transmit messages internationally.

The postmaster general operated and regulated the country's telecommunications monopoly for a long time. The first step to restructure the telecommunication sector took place in 1980 when the government separated postal services from the telecommunication services. The department faced competition when Datanet (Lanka Communication Services), which had an X75 node in Sri Lanka connected to the global packet-switched system via Singapore, introduced X25 packet switching services in the late 1980s. The department, as well as Electroteks Network, also had to provide similar services because businesses, such as banks and shipping agencies, demanded them.

The second step was the passage of the Telecommunication Act of 1991, which converted the telecommunication department into Sri Lanka Telecom, a government-owned autonomous corporation, and created the Sri Lanka Telecommunications Authority as the regulatory body (APT, 1998, 1999; Gunasekera, 1994; Ranasinghe, 1996). A third step was the conversion of SLT into a government-owned limited liability company in September 1996 (Central Bank of Sri Lanka, 1997); Nippon Telegraph and Telephone Corporation, the Japanese telecom giant, bought 35 percent of the SLT shares for US\$ 225 million in August 1997.

These moves have stimulated the growth of the country's telecommunication system. SLT-provided connections exceeded 350,000 just before the buyout. Moreover, SLT has taken steps to upgrade the obsolete telecommunication equipment in many of its telephone exchanges, mainly in outstations. Hideki Kamitsuma, SLT's new CEO, has taken steps for SLT to provide ISDN facilities in the country.

Two companies, Suntel and Lanka Bell, have introduced another facet of telecommunication: Wireless Local Loop technology. By March 1998, the two companies, which hold a duopoly in WLL until 2000, had provided 30,800 telephone connections covering many parts of the island. Suntel's connections enable access to the Internet at a speed of 14.4 kbps and Lanka Bell's at 28.8 kbps. Lanka Bell also provides 64 kbps leased lines to corporate customers. Of the four cellular operators in Sri Lanka, only Dialog GSM is based on digital transmission, which enable Internet connections. Sri Lanka is also about to enter the VSAT era. Ceycom Global Communications Ltd has a license from SLT to provide VSAT.

In 1998, Sri Lanka had 523,529 main telephone lines—a density of 2.84 per 100 people. This represents an annual compound growth rate of 20 percent since 1990 when the country had 121,388 main telephone lines—a mere 0.71 lines per 100 people. In 1998, Sri Lanka also had 174,200 cellular mobile subscribers—a density of 0.94 per 100 people (ITU, 1999).

6. POLICY TRENDS FOR PRESS AND BROADCASTING

The People's Alliance, which defeated the UNP government in August 1994, pledged to ensure the freedom of the media in its election manifesto, which stated:

The PA ... attaches the greatest importance to strengthening the media and providing a framework within which the media can function independently and without inhibition. This entails significant changes with regard to structures on ownership, policy objectives, the legislative instruments applicable, administrative policy in respect of such matters as facilities and the attitude of the government, which are indispensable for a sound media policy. Major constraints arising from provisions contained in the Constitution, the Public Security Ordinance, the Press Council Law, the Official Secrets Act and the Parliamentary (Powers and Privileges), Act, will be removed by amendment of this legislation. Committees of parliament will no longer punish journalists. Action will be taken to broad base the ownership of the Associated Newspapers of Ceylon Ltd., in keeping with the intentions of parliament, as set out in the original legislation. (Quoted in Mudliyar, 1998)

Press freedom had suffered badly toward the late 1980s. Wijetunga (1998) asserted that from 1988 to 1993 journalists were under threat from both the state and the insurgents. Although the latter threat had receded after 1990, "the former continued with even greater intensity against the independent media." Intimidation and violence had become commonplace, together with occasional violent deaths of journalists. The situation in the LTTE-controlled North was much worse, "with no respect for any fundamental rights" (p. 171). President D.B. Wijetunge, who succeeded the assassinated President Premadasa in mid-1993, brought in hope for greater media freedom. The victory of the People's Alliance, which pledged to restore press freedom, gave greater hope.

The PA government appointed an official committee, the R.K.W. Goonesekara Committee,[1] to report on laws affecting media freedom and freedom of expression. The committee recommended, *inter alia*, the enactment of a Freedom of Information Act, the setting up of an independent broadcasting authority, and the replacement of the Press Council Law with a Media Council Act. It also called for the repeal of the Official Secrets Act, the outdated criminal defamation law, and the Parliament (Powers and Privileges) Act of 1953 as amended in 1978, 1980, 1984, and 1987. These amendments had empowered parliament to sit "on judgement on journalists and impose penalties on them" (*Daily News*, September 10, 1997).

However, after five years in power, the government has not gone beyond repealing (on September 11, 1997) the 1978 Parliamentary Privileges Special Provision Act, which had given parliament the right to fine and imprison journalists. Instead of repealing the criminal defamation law, the government has, since mid-1995, caused the attorney general to use that law to indict the editors of five newspapers—the *Sunday Times*, the *Sunday Leader*, the *Island*, *Lakbima*, and *Ravaya*, Although one judge sentenced the Times editor to a suspended seven-year prison term for allegedly defaming the president, another judge acquitted the *Lakbima* editor on a similar indictment. On the positive side, the Supreme Court, in late May 1997, rejected as unconstitutional the Sri Lanka Broadcasting Bill, which would have

---

[1] The committee comprised Goonasekara (chairman), Shirani Bandaranayake, Rohan Edrisinha, Victor Gunawardena, Lucien Rajakarunanayke, Jayampathi Wickremaratne, and Suriya Wickremasinghe.

placed the annual licensing of privately owned audiovisual media under the political control of a government-led authority. The opposition UNP, like all previous parties in the opposition, has continued its agitation against the government's attempts to muzzle the media. UNP leader Ranil Wickremasinghe has pledged to implement a policy to decontrol all state-owned media.

The harassment of journalists has not ceased. Udagama (1996) has described, in detail, several cases of harassment. The government continues to use emergency regulations to censor the media. The police searched the home of the *Sunday Leader* editor in September 1995. Even though the PA government had given all electronic media the right to gather and broadcast news independently, it temporarily withdrew the news broadcasting license of *Sirasa* FM in April 1996, because the station aired an incorrect report on military action. Police detained a director of TNL in January 1997 under the Prevention of Terrorism Act—an action that led to a massive demonstration by 1,000 journalists. On February 12, 1998, five gunmen, suspected to be connected to the security forces, forcibly entered the home of the defense reporter of the *Sunday Times* and attempted to abduct him. On June 5, 1998, the government clamped down a total censorship on security-related matters and, for the first time, appointed a military censor. The database of the Committee to Protect Journalists shows 68 cases of threats, attacks, expulsion harassment, censorship, and legal action against journalists and media in Sri Lanka from February 1993 to March 1998.

In order to curb these negative trends, three media organizations—the Free Media Movement, the Editors' Guild, and the Newspaper (Publishers) Society—issued the Colombo Declaration on Media Freedom and Social Responsibility on April 29, 1998 (*Sunday Times*, May 3, 1998). The Working Journalists Association was also expected to endorse it. The document, hammered out with "the encouragement of allies within the government and opposition parliamentarians" (Neumann, 1998, p. 60), sets forth the issues that media pressure groups would ask future governments to deal with (see Section 7).

Udagama (1986) wrote that "the blatant abuse of emergency powers by the government of Sri Lanka, especially in relation to media censorship for its own advantage, is utterly reprehensible and is clearly in violation of its international obligations" (p. 74). As the more recent examples show, such abuses will continue to occur irrespective of the political party in power unless well organized pressure groups take action to force the rulers to keep their pledges on media freedom. The Colombo Declaration provides a useful policy framework for press and broadcasting. That framework will be pertinent to the emerging cyberspace-based new media as well.

The PA government has drafted a new constitution, Article 16 (1) of which says: "Every person is entitled to freedom of speech and expression, including publication; and this right shall include the freedom to hold and express opinions and to seek, receive and impart information and ideas either orally, in writing, in print, in the form of art or through any other medium." Such a right to information is unlikely to make a difference if other laws and regulations take precedence over it.

Meanwhile, the island's broadcasting scene is going through rapid change to attract larger audiences. Broadcasters are following the trailblazing techniques that *Sirasa* FM has adopted to become the most popular service: interactivity with the audience, use of colloquial and simpler language, downmarket orientation, greater attention to sports and music—in short, unabashed commercialization. *Lakhanda*, which broadcasts islandwide on FM band, also represents the new genre of radio offering. An official associated with it says:

> Its programs cater to listeners on a novel concept in that a two-way radio communication process is introduced. Listeners can air their views, their problems, their needs and their complaints at the same time. In addition to a public service broadcasting set up, it is also a commercial service both linked together in one channel. Lakhanda has deviated from the age-old broadcasting pattern by embarking on this two-way process between the listeners and communicators. (M.J.M. Ashroff, *Daily News*, November 14, 1998)

7. MAIN ISSUES

The Colombo Declaration (April 29, 1998) draws attention to the main issues that Sri Lanka should deal with as it enters the new millennium. The Declaration calls for:

- Adopting a better constitutional definition of freedom of expression, opinion and information, conforming to the language used in the International Covenant on Civil and Political Rights or the South African Constitution.
- Avoiding the derogation of fundamental rights under emergency regulations.
- Adopting a Freedom of Information Act with appropriate exceptions.
- Adopting a new Press Council Act within the ICCPR framework.
- Broadbasing Lake House as set forth in the ANCL Act of 1973.
- Repealing the criminal defamation provision both in the Press Council Law and the Penal Code.
- Repealing the Sixth Amendment provisions that impinge on freedom of expression for the peaceful advocacy of secession.
- Bringing censorship under emergency regulations within the ICCPR framework.
- Lowering the exorbitant duties on newsprint that make publications costly.
- Creating a genuinely independent broadcasting authority for licensing private and public broadcasting and community radio services, and for ensuring fair pre-sentation of alternative points of view on broadcasting services.
- Adopting legislation to ensure protection of source confidentiality.
- Introducing a voluntary code of ethics that includes, *inter alia*, a right of reply; fair, balanced and accurate reporting of news; and divulging conflicts of interest.

An all-party motion calling on the government to present legislation for vital media law reforms was listed for debate in Parliament on October 8, 1999. The motion called for legislation to implement proposals for the repeal of criminal defamation laws; the replacement of the press council with a media council with a majority of non-government members; the codification of laws related to *subjudice* and contempt of court; and the introduction of a freedom of information act (*Sunday Times*, August 8, 1999). However, the intervention of an early presidential election in late 1999 delayed parliamentary action. Kumaratunge was re-elected to a second presidential term on December 21, 1999, with 51.1 percent of the vote.

8. STATISTICS

General Profile

Exchange rate (September 1999)	US$ 1 = 71.75*
Population (mid-1999)	19.1 million
Population density (1997)	290 per sq km
GNP per capita (1997)	US$ 814
Human Development Index ranking	90 (out of 174)
Adult literacy	90.2%
Urban population	23%
Geographical size	65,610 km

Source: Central Bank of Sri Lanka, 1997; ITU, 1998; * OANDA Historical Currency Table [Online]. Available: (http://www.oanda.com/converter/cc_table?lang=en).

Table 1
Number and Circulation of Daily Newspapers

	1980	1985	1990	1995	1996	1998
No. of dailies	21	17	18	9	9	9
Total circulation	450,000	390,000	550,000	515,000	530,000	524,000
Circulation per 100 inhabitants	3.0	2.4	3.2	2.9	2.9	2.8

Source: UNESCO, 1998; WAN, 1999.

Table 2
Advertising Share of the Newspaper Groups

	1995 (US$ 9.8 million) percent	1996 (US$ 9 million) percent	1997 (US$ 10.4 million) percent
ANCL	50	48	45
Wijeya	20	23	24
Upali	21	20	19
Express	5	5	7
Sumathi	2	2	3
Leader	2	3	2

Source: Phoenix Advertising, 1998; Rajapakse, 1997.

Table 3
Number and Penetration of Radio Receivers

	1980	1985	1990	1995	1996	1997
No. of receivers ('000s)	1,000	2,551	3,400	3,700	3,800	3,850
Receivers per 100 inhabitants	10.1	15.9	19.9	20.6	21.0	21.1

Source: UNESCO, 1999.

Table 4
Number and Penetration of TV Receivers

	1980	1985	1990	1995	1996	1997	1998
Est. no. of TV receivers ('000s)	35	450	750	1,480	1,550	1,530	1,700*
Receivers per 100 inhabitants	0.2	2.8	4.4	8.3	8.6	8.4	9.2*

Source: UNESCO, 1999; * ITU, 1999.

Table 5
Advertising Share of Radio Broadcasters

	1995 (US$ 4 million) percent	1996 (US$ 6 million) percent	1997 (US$ 7.6 million) percent
MBC (Maharaja)	58	59	51
SLBC	34	24	17
FM99/CCL	3	10	23
TNL	5	7	4
Lakhanda	–	–	5

Source: Phoenix Advertising, 1998; Rajapakse, 1997.

Table 6
Advertising Share of TV Stations

	1995 (US$ 10.4 million) percent	1996 (US$ 11.7 million) percent	1997 (US$ 16 million) percent
SLRC	42	44	34
ITN	24	21	17
MTV	18	21	23
TNL	7	7	6
ETV1/Swarnavahini	5	4	14
ETV	4	4	3
Dynavision	–	–	–

Source: Phoenix Advertising, 1998; Rajapakse, 1997.

Table 7
Circulation Data by Newspaper Group

Newspapers published in Colombo (population 1.2 million)						
Group	Title	Established	Frequency	Language	Circulation (E&P)	Circulation (WPT)
ANCL	Dinamina	1909	Daily a.m.	Sinhala	140,000	55,000
	Janata	1953	Daily p.m.	Sinhala	15,000	5,000
	Silumina	1930	Sunday	Sinhala	254,000	285,000*
	Thinakaran	1932	Daily a.m.	Tamil	18,500	29,000
	Thinakaran Varamanjari	1948	Sunday	Tamil	22,430	45,024*
	Daily News	1918	Daily a.m.	English	85,000	75,000
	Observer	1834	Daily p.m.	English	14,000	19,000
	Sunday Observer	1923	Sunday	English	120,000	118,000*
Wijeya	Lankadipa Irida	1947/1991	Daily a.m.	Sinhala	–	134,000
	Lankadipa Midweek	1951/1986	Sunday	Sinhala	259,172	275,500*
	Mirror	1961/1995	Wednesday	English	–	N/A
	Sunday Times	1926/1987	Sunday	English	–	125,000*
Upali	Divaina	1982	Daily a.m.	Sinhala	100,000	130,000
	Divaina·Irida Sangrahaya	1981	Sunday	Sinhala	–	252,144*
	The Island	1982	Daily a.m.	English	33,000	47,000
	Sunday Island	1981	Sunday	English	87,000	79,443*
Express	Virakesari	1930	Daily a.m.	Tamil	48,000	30,000
	Virakesari Vara Veliyeedu	1930	Sunday	Tamil	–	84,500*
	Weekend Express	1995	Saturday	English	–	N/A
Independent	Sunday Leader	1994	Sunday	English	–	75,000*
	Lakbima	1994	Sunday	Sinhala	–	136,000*
	Thinakkural	1997	Daily a.m.	Tamil	–	N/A
	Peramuna	1998	Sunday	Sinhala	–	N/A

Source: *Editor & publisher international yearbook*, 1999; WAN, 1999; * Peiris, 1997.

Table 8
Radio Broadcasting

Group	Service	Language	Hours/Month	Percent
Government/Public Sector				
SLBC		Sinhala	2,599	65.3
		Tamil	743	18.7
		English	637	16.0
SLBC/ITN	Lakhanda	Sinhala	730	100.0
Private sector				
MBC Network	Yes FM	English	1,400	67.6
	Sirasa	Sinhala	672	32.4
CCL	Capital Radio	English	1,470	68.6
	Savana	Sinhala	588	27.5
	FM99	Tamil	84	3.9
TNL Radio	TNL 90FM	English	2,190	100.0
ABC	Gold FM89.8	English		
	Sun FM99.9	English	730	
	Tharu FM96.7	Sinhala		
	Hiru FM107.9	Sinhala	730	
	Suriyan FM103.2	Tamil		

Source: Wijetunga, 1998.

Table 9
Television

Channel	Hours/Week				Hours/Month
	Sinhala	Tamil	English	Hindi	
Government/Public Sector					
Rupavahini					
(national)	40.5	10	16	–	285.0
ITN					
(national)	33.5	5.25	17	5.25	261.4
Private Sector					
Sirasa TV					
(national)	25.5	31	54.5	3.5	490.7
MTV					
(Colombo & Kandy)	2.5	2.5	79.5	–	362.1
Swarnavahini	26	30.2	41.5	7.8	452.1
ETV	–	–	77	–	330.0
TNL	17	2.7	38.8	3	263.5
Dynavision	–	–	143	–	612.9

Source: *Sunday Times*, May 24, 1998.

Table 10
Telecommunications Facts

Number of mainline telephones per 100 people (1998)	2.84
Number of cellular telephones per 100 people (1998)	0.94
Number of fax machines per 1,000 people (1996)	0.6
Number of Internet host computers (July 1999)*	983*
Electric power capacity (hydro/thermal) (1997)	1,515 megawatts
[Central Bank, 1997]	

Sources: ITU (1997, 1998, 1999); * Internet Software Consortium, 1999.

Table 11
Advertising Earnings of Press, Radio, and TV

Year	Ad earnings (rupees)	Ad earnings (US$)
1995	1,319,187,350	24,167,512
1996	1,508,808,313	26,585,202
1997	2,095,998,544	33,976,136

Source: Phoenix Advertising, 1998.

9. USEFUL ADDRESSES

9.1 Newspaper Organizations

Associated Newspapers of Ceylon Ltd
P.O. Box 248, Lake House
35 D.R. Wijewardena Mawatha
Colombo 10
Telephone: (94-1) 545433
Fax: (94-1) 449069
E-mail: edcdn@sri.lanka.net
URL: http://www.lanka.net/lakehouse

Express Newspapers Ltd
P.O. Box 160
185 Grandpass Road
Colombo 14
Telephone: (94-1) 320881
E-mail: virakesari@lanka.ccom.lk
URL: http://www.ccom.lk/virakesari

Upali Newspapers Ltd
P.O. Box 1942
223 Bloemendahl Road
Colombo 13
Telephone: (94-1) 24001
E-mail: island@lanka.ccom.lk
URL: http://www.upali.lk/island

Wijeya Newspapers Ltd
10 Hunupitiya Cross Road
Colombo 2
Telephone: (94-1) 4308037 / 326247 / 331275
Fax: (94-1) 449504 / 423258 / 423922
E-mail: editor@suntimes.is.lk
URL: http://www.lacnet..org/suntimes
    http://www.ccom.lk/midweekmirror
    http://www.ccom.lk/lankadeepa

Leader Publications (Pvt) Ltd
101, 2nd Floor, Collette's Building
D.S. Senanayake Mawatha
Colombo 8
Telephone: (94-1) 686047
Fax: (94-1) 699968
E-mail: leader@sri.lanka.net
URL: http://www.lanka.net/sundayleader

9.2 Electronic Media Organizations

9.2.1 Television: Public

Independent Television Network (ITN)
Wickramasinghepura
Battaramulla
Telephone: (94-1) 864591
Fax: (94-1) 864591

Sri Lanka Rupavahini Corp. (SLRC)
P.O. Box 2204, Independence Square
Colombo 7
Telephone: (94-1) 580136
Fax: (94-1) 580929 / 696806
E-mail: ruvahini@slt.lk

9.2.2 Television: Private

Dynavision Broadcasting Co. (Pvt) Ltd
451/A Kandy Road
Kelaniya
Telephone: (94-1) 913550-1
Fax: (94-1) 910469

EAP Network (Pvt) Ltd (Swarnavahini & ETV)
676 Galle Road
Colombo 3
Telephone: (94-1) 503819
Fax: (94-1) 503788
E-mail: eapnet@slt.lk

MTV Channel (Pvt) Ltd (Sirasa TV & MTV)
109 Collets Building
D.S. Senanayake Mawatha
Colombo 8
Telephone: (94-1) 689324-6
Fax: (94-1) 689328

Telshan Network (Pvt) Ltd (TNL)
Innagale Estate
Dampe-Piliyandala
Telephone: (94-1) 575436
Fax: (94-1) 574962

Ravaya Publishers Ltd
83 Piliyandala Road
Maharagama
Telephone: (94-1) 851672-3; 851814

Sumathi Newspapers (Pvt) Ltd
445/1 Sirimavo Bandaranaike Mawatha
Colombo 14
Fax: (94-1) 449593

Eelamurasu
140 Navalar Road
Jaffna
Telephone: (94-21) 22389

Eelanadu
P.O. Box 44
165 Sivan Kovil West Road
Jaffna
Telephone: (94-21) 22329

9.2.3 Radio: Public

Sri Lanka Broadcasting Corporation
P.O. Box 574, Independence Square
Colombo 7
Telephone: (94-1) 696329
Fax: (94-1) 695488
E-mail: slbcweb@sri.lanka.net

9.2.4 Radio: Private

Colombo Communications (Pvt) Ltd
250 R.A. de Mel Mawatha
Colombo 3

MBC Network (Pvt) Ltd
Araliya Uyana, Depanama
Pannipitiya
URL: http://www.mega.lk/sirasafm

TNL Radio
25 Station Road
Colombo 4
URL: http://www.lanka.net/tnl

10. REFERENCES

APT (Asia-Pacific Telecommunity). (1998, 1999). *The APT yearbook.* Bangkok and Surrey: APT & ICOM.

Central Bank of Sri Lanka. (1997). *Annual report 1997.* Colombo: CBSL.

Central Bank of Sri Lanka. (1998). Infrastructure and services—communication and mass media. In *Economic progress of independent Sri Lanka 1948–1998* (pp. 138–147). Colombo: CBSL.

Chandraprema, C.A. (1991). *Sri Lanka: The years of terror—the JVP insurrection 1987–1989.* Colombo: Lake House Bookshop.

Coomaraswamy. R. (1981). Regulatory framework for the press in Sri Lanka. *Marga Quarterly Journal, 6* (2), 66–96.

David, M.J.R. (1993). *Mahaweli community radio: A field producer's notebook.* Laguna: Institute of Development Communication, University of the Philippines, Los Banos.

Editor & publisher international yearbook (1999). New York: Editor & Publisher.

Gunaratne, S.A. (1970). Government–press conflict in Ceylon: Freedom versus responsibility. *Journalism Quarterly, 47,* 530–543; 552.

Gunaratne, S.A. (1975, May). The taming of the press in Sri Lanka. *Journalism Monographs, 39.*

Gunaratne, S.A. (1978). Sri Lanka (Ceylon). In J.A. Lent (Ed.), *Broadcasting in Asia and the Pacific: A continental survey of radio and television* (pp. 260–272). Philadelphia: Temple University Press.

Gunaratne, S.A. (1982). Sri Lanka. In J.A. Lent (Ed.), *Newspapers in Asia: Contemporary trends and problems* (pp. 506–535). Hong Kong: Heinemann Asia.

Gunaratne, S.A. (1997). Sri Lanka and the third communication revolution. *Media Asia, 24,* 83–89.

Gunaratne, S.A., Hasim, M.S., & Kasenally, R. (1997). Small is beautiful: Informatization potential of three Indian Ocean rim countries. *Media Asia, 24,* 188–205.

Gunasekara, A. (1994). Sri Lanka forges a new framework. *Asian Communications, 8* (8), 38–43.

Hulugalle, H.A.J. (1960). *The life and times of D.R. Wijewardene.* Colombo: The Associated Newspapers of Ceylon Ltd.

Induruwa, A. (1996). *High performance computing: The next wave of IT development in Sri Lanka* [On-line]. Available: www.http://www.cs.ukc.ac.uk/people/staff/asil/cssl/papers/paper.htm

ITU (International Telecommunication Union). (1997). *Challenges to the network: Telecoms and the Internet.* Geneva: ITU.

ITU (International Telecommunication Union). (1998). *World telecommunication development report 1998: Universal access.* Geneva: ITU.

ITU (International Telecommunication Union). (1999). *Yearbook of statistics: Telecommunication services 1988–1997.* Geneva: ITU.

Karunanayake, N. (1996). *The press in Sri Lanka: Towards a sound policy framework.* Colombo: Media publishers.

Liyanage, G. (1993). *Lankaawe puwathpath mellakireema* (The taming of newspapers in Sri Lanka). Colombo: S. Godage & Bros.

Mahendra, S. (1996). A note on television in Sri Lanka. In D. French & M. Richards (Eds.), *Contemporary television: Eastern perspectives* (pp. 221–227). New Delhi: Sage Publications.

Merrill, J.C., & Fisher, H.A. (1980). *The world's great dailies: Profiles of 50 newspapers.* New York: Hastings House.

Mudliyar. (1998, May 17). Government makes criminal defamation civil defamation. *The Sunday Times* [On-line]. Available: (www.http://www.is.lk/times/980517/mudli.html).

Muthulingam, P. (1997). Evolution of the Tamil press of Sri Lanka. In G.H. Peiris (Ed.), *Studies on the press in Sri Lanka and South Asia* (pp. 181–192). Kandy: International Center for Ethnic Studies.

Network Wizards. (1999, January). Internet host survey [On-line]. Available: (http://www.nw.com/www/dist-bynum.htm).

Neumann, A.L. (1998, July/August). Sri Lanka: Reform's key moment—journalists' face off with the military. *Columbia Journalism Review, 37,* 59–60.

Pannasekera, K. (1965–71). *Sinhala puvathpath sangara ithihasaya* (History of Sinhala newspapers and magazines). (Vols. 1–9). Colombo: M.D. Gunasena & Co. Ltd.

Peiris, G.H. (1997). Media in Sri Lanka: Recent trends of change. In G.H. Peiris (Ed.) *Studies on the press in Sri Lanka and South Asia* (pp. 81–105). Kandy: International Center for Ethnic Studies.

Perera, J. (1994). An intolerant climate. In *Press systems in SAARC* (pp. 95–103). Singapore: AMIC.

Phoenix Advertising. (1998). Personal communication from Phoenix Advertising, Colombo.

Rajapakse, A. (1997, March). Evaluating ad spending '96. *Business Today, 1* (11), 25–27.

Ranasinghe, N.E. (1996, April). Radio spectrum management in Sri Lanka. *APT Journal, 8* (2), 20–22.

Samarajiva, R. (1997). Institutional reform of Sri Lankan telecommunications: The introduction of competition and regulation. In E.M. Noam (Ed.), *Telecommunications in Western Asia and the Middle East* (pp. 38–61). New York: Oxford University Press.

Samarasinghe, S.W.R. de A. (1997). Reading, listening and watching: A national sample survey of the Sri Lankan news media. In G.H. Peiris (Ed.), *Studies on the press in Sri Lanka and South Asia* (pp. 265–297). Kandy: International Center for Ethnic Studies.

Selvakumaran, N., & Edrisinha, R. (Comps.). (1995). *Mass media laws and regulations in Sri Lanka.* Singapore: AMIC.

Thillainathan, S. (1997). Contemporary Tamil media scene in Sri Lanka. In G.H. Peiris (Ed.), *Studies on the press in Sri Lanka and South Asia* (pp. 193–204). Kandy: International Center for Ethnic Studies.

Udagama, N.D. (1986). *Freedom of the press in Sri Lanka.* Unpublished Master of Law dissertation, University of California, Berkeley.

Udagama, N.D. (1996). Freedom of expression and media freedom. In E. Nissan, (Ed.), *Sri Lanka: State of Human Rights 1995.* Colombo: Law & Society Trust.

UNESCO (United Nations Educational, Scientific and Cultural Organization). (1999). *Statistical yearbook.* Paris: UNESCO.

WAN (World Association of Newspapers). (1999). *World press trends.* Paris: World Association of Newspapers.

Wattegama, C., & Sreekanth, K.M. (1998, June). *Proliferation of Internet in Sri Lanka and India: A comparative study.* Paper presented to the 17th annual session of the Computer Society of Sri Lanka.

Wijetunga, W.M.K. (1996). Mass media, elective politics and multi-party democracy in Sri Lanka. *Asian Journal of Communication, 6* (2), 92–118.

Wijetunga, W.M.K. (1998). Sri Lanka. In A. Goonasekera & D. Holaday (Eds.), *Asian communication handbook 1998* (pp. 171–173). Singapore: AMIC & NTU.

World factbook. (1999). Washington, DC: US Central Intelligence Agency [On-line]. Available: (http://www.odci.gov/cia/publications/factbook).

World radio TV handbook. (1999). Amsterdam: Billboard Publications.

◆

Southeast Asia

INTRODUCTION

Shelton A. Gunaratne

1. MULTIMEDIA ACCESS

The 10 chapters in this section analyze the state of the telecommunication infrastructure and of the Internet in Southeast Asia. Multimedia access is unlikely to proliferate in most of the countries in the near future. In 1997, only Singapore, Brunei Darussalam, and Malaysia had exceeded the world average in telephone density, that is, main telephone lines per 100 people (Table 1). Singapore and Brunei had also surpassed the world average in TV sets per 100 people with Thailand trailing just below the world average. However, in Internet host density per 10,000 people, Singapore was way above the world average while all other countries in Southeast Asia were well below. (By the end of 1998, the world average of Internet host density had risen to 74.1 while Singapore's density had reached 259.88, Brunei's 38.98, Malaysia's 30.21, and Thailand's 7.25.)

2. STATE OF THE PRESS AND OF BROADCASTING

The Philippines and Thailand are the leading exponents of a free press in Southeast Asia. Vietnam, Brunei, and Myanmar are at the "not free" end. Indonesia made dramatic gains in press freedom while Cambodia too made gains following the mid-1998 elections. Laws and regulations that influence media content are high in all countries but three (Table 2). The same is true in regard to political pressures and controls on media content. Economic influences over media content are high for the print media in Indonesia, Laos, Singapore, Vietnam, Brunei, and Myanmar, where broadcast media also feel the brunt. Repressive actions have reached the highest point affecting the print media in Cambodia and Myanmar. This introduction uses Freedom House's press freedom rankings to list the countries for the discussion of highlights.

2.1 Philippines

Freedom House describes the Philippines' print press as "lively ... vigorous and diversified and often sensational" (Sussman, 1999, p. 27). The country has no licensing requirement to publish a newspaper, but radio and TV stations need licenses. The January 1999 Freedom House survey ranked the Philippines and Thailand as the only countries with a free press in Southeast Asia. Maslog, in this section, says that the country's press freedom is one that borders on license. Maslog also points out that the Philippines is perhaps the only country whose constitution "recognizes the vital role of communication and information in nation-building." Despite a resurgence of fatal violence against two broadcasters, the press remained in the "free" column. Freedom House says that journalists, particularly broadcasters, face hazards in reporting on gambling, illegal logging, government corruption, and the drug trade. Corporate influences on editorial policies have hampered the private press. One radio broadcaster was shot to death in his studio, another en route to a news conference. In April 1999, editors at *The Manila Times* resigned over an apology by its owners to President Joseph Estrada for a report that prompted him to file a 101 million peso (US$ 2.6 million) libel suit over a story that said he was an "unwitting godfather" for an allegedly improper government contract.

2.2 Thailand

The print media in Thailand have adopted a new openness, which the broadcast media, still mostly operated by the government or the military, have been less apt to follow. Ekachai, in this section, says that the new national information act promotes transparency within the government. Freedom House observed:

> Because the Asian media had failed to warn of the crisis, the press, particularly in Thailand, was regarded as a necessary element in improving the country's financial position. Lively political and economic news has become routine fare in many newspapers and magazines whose content had traditionally been entertainment news and fiction. The papers have also been investigating the social implications of the economic crisis.

On the negative side, 1998 started badly with one journalist shot to death after refusing a bribe.

2.3 Indonesia

Idris and Gunaratne, in this section, examine Indonesia's new era of *reformasi* that began in mid-1998, offering the Indonesian media the opportunity to test press freedom against the restrictive *Pancasila* press system imposed under the 1945 Constitution. Former President Habibie acted on pledges to promote greater freedom and respect for human rights by granting some 742 new publishing licenses from June 1998 onwards. Indonesia moved from having one of the most restricted to one of the freer press systems in Asia. Freedom House placed the country in the "partly free" category with a press restriction score of 53 compared with the previous years's "not free" score of 77. On the negative side, violence accompanied demonstrations for economic reforms. Arrests and attacks on journalists resumed as the police repulsed demonstrators. A reporter received a death threat from a regional military commander, a Canadian journalist was expelled, and security forces attacked four print journalists covering street clashes. Because of violence, the press has resorted to self-censorship. Press freedom is likely to gain momentum under President Abdurrahman Wahid, who has already abolished the Ministry of Information.

2.4 Cambodia

Clarke, in this section, examines the vicissitudes of press freedom in Cambodia from Khmer Rouge rule to transitional democracy. She says that the 1995 Law on the Press gives the right to maintain confidentiality of sources, the right to publish information from public meetings, the right to access government records, and the right to form journalists' associations. It also outlaws pre-censorship. However, Articles 11 and 12 prohibit publication of "anything that may affect public order by directly inciting one or more persons to commit violence" and "any information that may affect national security and political stability." Freedom House reported that the government threatened to shut down two local newspapers and expel foreign reporters because of their "flawed" reporting of the 1998 elections. One journalist close to the local Communist Party was shot.

2.5 Malaysia

Freedom House notched up Malaysia's press restriction score by 5 points to 66 in the January 1999 survey. The score on repressive action on broadcast media shot up from zero to 3 (out of a maximum of 5) while political pressures and controls on print media content went up from 13 to the maximum of 15. The reason for this change was the financial crisis that caused domestic disturbances. The government blamed and censored foreign journalists and increased pressure on the domestic media, although Freedom House attributed the financial crisis partly to the lack of transparency. An official threatened to jail local journalists without trial if he believed they were undermining the country's leadership. In this section, Safar, Sarji, and Gunaratne draw attention to the Printing Presses and Publication Act 1984, as amended in 1987, that requires anyone who wants to print, import, publish, sell, or distribute a newspaper to obtain a permit from the minister of home affairs, who can revoke or suspend the permit, which is valid for one year only. This is among the 42 odd pieces of legislation and ordinances that regulate the media. On the positive side, the Multimedia Super Corridor's Bill of Guarantee stipulates that Malaysia will not censor the Internet. This stipulation is radical in the context of laws governing the traditional mass media. The Communication and Multimedia Act 1998, which came into force on April 1, 1999, contains the "no censorship" clause (Section 3[3]).

2.6 Laos

Morgan and Loo, in this section, observe that impartiality and fairness are conspicuously absent from the Laotian media code. They say:

> The emphasis, instead, is on the media as *khuangmu an lemkhom* [sharp instrument] and *phasana* [vehicle] for the party. The notion of *ve thi* [forum] refers to *sai nyai* [linking the people to the party]. The media are not included in the liberal policies applied to economic production and trade. They remain instruments for the delivery of party policy to the masses and the provision of *suksa op-hom* [education and training] in political ideology.

In Laos, the government controls all radio and television as a matter of policy. However, news from abroad has greater freedom than in the past to enter the country. Satellite dishes are legal upon payment of a fee to the government. Cross-border satellite programming from Thailand is imminent. Freedom House adds that the government controls newspapers and reacts harshly to expressions of political dissent. Moreover, the penal code forbids slandering the state, distorting state or party policies, or spreading false rumors that lead to violence. "The pressure of avoiding violations of the generalized code, even in staterun media, greatly limits the diversity of content in the mass media" (Sussman, 1999, p. 21).

2.7 Singapore

Kuo and Ang, in this section, explain: "Singapore press operates within a strict legal framework.... It deems the libertarian concept unworkable in Singapore because of racial, religious and cultural differences." Freedom House clarifies that although the broadcast and print media are free in principle, they are subject to stringent government controls. A government-backed commercial company owns all major newspapers and 20 percent of the cable television network. The editorial policies of these media routinely favor the ruling party. A government-owned corporation runs all four free TV channels and 10 of 15 radio stations. (On March 1, 1999, this corporation launched Channel News Asia, an 18-hour all-news station.) Of the other five, only the BBC is free of government control. The authorities also officially censor videos and the Internet, which users can access only through a government server. Freedom House adds, "The government does not tolerate reports of government corruption, nepotism, or a politically compliant judiciary. Unauthorized release to the media of government data is prohibited" (Sussman, 1999, p. 29). Singapore leader Lee Kuan Yew's most recent statement that "information technology is rapidly undermining whatever monopoly control of the media governments might have known" has created hopes for greater media liberalization in the near future.

2.8 Vietnam

Panol and Do, in this section, say that Vietnam's dual system—a Communist government and a quasi-market economy—poses unique problems to the press. Although newspapers are still either government-owned or -affiliated and hence not dependent on advertising income, they are now competing aggressively for advertisers and re .ders. Low-quality tabloids, reporting mainly on sex and crime to increase circulation, have invaded the market. Also, the government's ambivalence about the degree of control to be exercised over the press and advertising has resulted in the sporadic changing of regulations and enforcement procedures. Freedom House, however, observes that the government exerts tight control over the flow of information. The state operates television and radio, which the regime sees as the most important media. Laws permit charging journalists with treason if they reveal "sensitive information." Strict laws restrict individuals from acquiring access to foreign satellite television. "The government also restricts individual access to the Internet. Another law limits the number of foreign journalists. The minister of culture must approve news reports and press conferences" (Sussman, 1999, p. 34). In 1998, a gang attacked a print journalist and government agents attacked another for their reporting. A journalist is on trial for "damaging the interests of the state, social organizations and citizens" after reporting on corruption.

2.9 Brunei Darussalam

Safar and Yussof, in this section, argue that the media system of this hereditary sultanate fits Lowenstein's social-centralist theory best in the context of the Malay Islamic Monarchy concept. Freedom House asserts the sultanate lacks the democratic means to change the government or provide free access to information or a free flow of news. Freedom House adds, "The sole privately owned newspaper practices self-censorship on political and religious issues. The state-owned radio and television operate the only local broadcast media, and their services are uncritical of the government. A cable network offers international programming" (Sussman, 1999, p. 11).

2.10 Myanmar

The State Peace and Development Council (SPDC), according to Freedom House, continues to exercise absolute control over domestic media. In 1998, the SPDC expanded its control, expelling or detaining six foreign reporters who were critical or who interviewed opposition leader Aung San Suu Kyi. In this section, Chadha and Kavoori say the media in Myanmar "are among the most repressed in the world. Heavy-handed control and censorship constitute the linchpins of the military government's media policy." The only non-government controlled news sources for the country are the broadcasts of foreign radio services such as the BBC, the VoA, and Radio Free Asia.

3. PROBLEMS AND PROSPECTS

By 2025, Southeast Asia would have a population of 721.1 million—9.1 percent of the world population (Table 3) or 17 percent of Asia's population. Currently, Southeast Asia accounts for 15.6 percent of Asia's population. Indonesia, the population Goliath of the region, would have 83 million more people than its current size; Philippines, 46.6 million more; Vietnam, 24.5 million more; Myanmar, 18.3 million more; Malaysia, 11.8 million more; Cambodia, 10.5 million more; Thailand, 8.6 million more; Laos, 4.8 million more; and Singapore, 1 million more. Such increases will pose problems for countries with low literacy rates, such as Cambodia (66 percent) and Laos (58.6 percent), as well as for countries at the lower end of the infrastructure needed for multimedia access. The high literacy rates in the Philippines, Thailand, and Indonesia augur well for the maintenance and further promotion of media freedom despite the population increases.

4. STATISTICS

Table 1
Multimedia Access in South Asia

Overall world rank	Country	Main telephone lines per 100 people		TV sets per 100 people		Internet hosts per 10,000 people	
		1997	Rank	1997	Rank	1997	Rank
35	Singapore	44.8	32	29.2	56	205.66	17
50	Brunei	25.8	54	41.0	39	11.06	50
80	Malaysia	19.5	76	16.6	110	20.13	51
97	Thailand	7.9	113	23.4	83	4.86	77
131	Philippines	2.8	146	10.6	127	1.71	95
139	Indonesia	2.5	149	9.7	128	1.25	99
157	Vietnam	2.1	152	18.0	104	0.00	176
170	Cambodia	0.1	204	12.3	123	0.05	149
196	Myanmar	0.5	183	0.7	181	0.00	176
198	Laos	0.5	182	0.4	188	0.00	176
World Average		18.9		24.1		52.79	

Source: ITU, 1999.

Table 2
Press Freedom in Asia–January 1999
(Freedom House Ratings)

Southeast Asia		A	B	C	D	Total	Rating on political rights ❶ and civil liberties ❷
Philippines	Broadcast	5	7	3	2	30	
	Print	5	3	5	0	F	F 2, 3
Thailand	Broadcast	7	7	2	0	30	
	Print	5	3	5	1	F	F 2, 3
Indonesia	Broadcast	12	5	3	3	53	
	Print	10	5	12	3	PF	PF 4, 4
Cambodia	Broadcast	7	15	5	2	62	
	Print	8	15	5	5	NF	NF 6, 6
Malaysia	Broadcast	10	14	5	3	66	
	Print	11	15	7	1	NF	PF 5, 5
Laos	Broadcast	13	10	10	0	66	
	Print	13	10	10	0	NF	NF 7, 6
Singapore	Broadcast	13	8	7	0	66	
	Print	13	10	15	0	NF	PF 5, 5
Vietnam	Broadcast	15	15	0	0	71	
	Print	15	15	10	1	NF	NF 7, 7
Brunei	Broadcast	14	15	5	0	74	
	Print	14	15	11	0	NF	NF 7, 5
Myanmar	Broadcast	15	15	15	2	97	
	Print	15	15	15	5	NF	NF 7, 7

Source: http://freedomhouse.org/pfs99

Note: Press freedom criteria:
A = Laws and regulations that influence media content; scale: broadcast, 0–15; print, 0–15
B = Political pressures and controls on media content; scale: broadcast, 0–15; print, 0–15
C = Economic influences over media content; scale: broadcast, 0–15; print, 0–15
D = Repressive actions (killing journalists, physical violence, censorship, self-censorship, arrests, etc.); scale: broadcast, 0–5; print, 0–5
RATING: free: 0–30; partly free: 31–60; not free: 61–100

GOVERNANCE:
❶ First number in column = rating on political rights
❷ Second number in column = rating on civil liberties
RATING: 1 = most free; 7 = least free

Table 3
Southeast Asia: Estimated Population in 2025

World rank	Country	Population
4	Indonesia	287,985,072
11	Philippines	120,519, 345
14	Vietnam	103,908,883
20	Thailand	70,315,728
21	Myanmar	68,106,967
46	Malaysia	34,248,134
62	Cambodia	21,434,433
91	Laos	9,804,562
128	Singapore	4,230,872
170	Brunei	529,595
	Total	**721,083,591**

Source: US Census Bureau, 1998.

5. REFERENCES

ITU (International Telecommunication Union). (1999). *Challenges to the network: Internet for development.* Geneva: ITU.

Sussman, L.R. (1999). *Press freedom 1999: News of the century.* New York: Freedom House.

US Census Bureau, International Data Base. (1998, December 28). *IDB: Countries ranked by population* [On-line]. Available: (http://www.census.gov/cgi-bin/ipc/idbrank.pl).

◆

8

BRUNEI DARUSSALAM

H.M. Safar & Yussof Ladi

1. NATIONAL PROFILE

1.1 Geography

Brunei Darussalam (Brunei, abode of peace) is located in the northwest corner of Borneo. It has a 381-km land border with the East Malaysian state of Sarawak, which physically cuts the sultanate into two parts at the Brunei Bay. It has a 161-km coastline along the South China Sea. Covering an area of 5,765 sq km, it is slightly smaller than the US state of Delaware. It comprises four districts: Brunei Muara, Tutong, Belait, and Temburong. The capital, Bandar Seri Begawan, is in the Brunei Muara district, the main center of population and administration. Rain forests and woodlands cover about 85 percent of the land (*World factbook*, 1999).

Because of its equatorial climate, the country has a uniformly high temperature, heavy rainfall, and high humidity, with only minor seasonal variations. At 1,850 meters, Bukit Pagon is the country's highest point.

1.2 People

Brunei's population was estimated at 322,982 in mid-1999. It has a literacy rate of 90.1 percent (UNDP, 1999). Malays (66.9 percent) comprise the largest ethnic group, followed by Chinese (15.2 percent). Other indigenous peoples (5.9 percent) constitute most of the rest. The religious composition is: Muslim (63 percent), Buddhist (14 percent), Christian (8 percent), and indigenous beliefs and others (15 percent). Brunei Muara district has the largest population of 65.9 percent, Belait has 20.3 percent, Tutong has 11 percent, and Temburong has 2.9 percent (*World factbook*, 1999; Brunei, 1995b).

Documented evidence from the 5th century indicated that Brunei was a Hindu–Buddhist city-state in A.D. 414. Muhammad Shah, the first sultan, became a Muslim in the mid-14th century. During the 15th and the first half of the 16th century, the sultanate had sovereignty over all of Borneo and several islands of the Philippines.

European intervention—Spanish in the Philippines and British in Borneo—from 1571 until the third quarter of the 19th century put an end to Brunei's hold on its territories. In 1888, Brunei became a British protectorate.

In 1906, Brunei became part of the British residential system. The British government nominated a resident representative to advise the sultan on all matters except Malay customs and traditions, and Islam. In fact, the British began running the country under the pretext of "advising" the sultan, a situation similar to that of the sultanates in Malaya.

1.3 Government and Politics

Brunei Darussalam is a Malay Islamic monarchy, which adheres to traditional Islamic values. Its first written constitution, established with British agreement on September 29, 1959, gave Brunei internal self-government. Some provisions of the constitution were suspended under a state of emergency declared in December 1962, while the other provisions were suspended after Brunei became independent of Britain on January 1, 1984 (*World factbook*, 1999). Sultan (Sir) Ali Saifuddin declared a state of emergency after the Parti Rakyat Brunei (People's Party), which won the state's legislative elections in August 1962, started a revolt on December 8, 1962, following his refusal to convene the assembly (Amnesty International, 1983). The declared purpose of the revolt was to drive the British out of Brunei (Leake, 1990). The British crushed the revolt several days later. Parti Rakyat leader A.M. Azahari was against Brunei joining Malaysia. He wanted the British to give independence to the three Borneo states (including Sabah and Sarawak) as a united entity. Independent candidates won the Legislative Council elections held in 1965 (Brunei, 1980). The only organized political party at that time, Parti Perikatan Ra'ayat Brunei received only 8.5 percent of the total 14,068 votes cast. The only political party currently in existence is the Parti Perpaduan Kebangsaan Brunei (Brunei National Solidarity Party) established under the Societies Act. Other political parties—Pertubuhan Kebangsaan Brunei (PKB), Pergerakan Bersatuan Brunei (PBB), Parti Perikatan Ra'ayat Brunei (PPRB), Barisan Kemerdekaan Rakyat (People's Independence Front), and Parti Perpaduan Kebangsaan Rakyat (Brunei People's National United Party)—have disappeared or have not been active.

The sultan is both the chief of state and head of government. As both sultan and prime minister, he presides over the council of cabinet ministers, which deals with executive matters. A religious council advises the sultan on religious matters, a privy council deals with constitutional matters, and a council of succession determines the succession to the throne if the need arises. The sultan appoints the members of all the councils.

Brunei has a unicameral Legislative Council (*Majlis Mesyuarat Negeri*) that serves only in a consultative capacity. A decree of the sultan made the council an appointive body in 1970. Although an elected legislative council is under consideration, elections are unlikely to take place in the immediate future. Political parties are banned, deregistered, or inactive. Islamic law forms the basis of the legal system (*World factbook*, 1999).

1.4 Economy

Brunei's nominal per capita Gross National Product (GNP) stands at US$ 20,400. Its purchasing power parity per capita Gross Domestic Product (GDP) is US$ 20,100. The latest GDP was US$ 5.9 billion (*Asiaweek*, December 17, 1999). Bruneians do not pay income tax.

Oil and liquefied natural gas dominate the Brunei economy. The three main exports are crude oil, petroleum products, and liquefied natural gas. Japan, the United States, and the ASEAN countries are Brunei's principal markets. The latest annual exports stood at US$ 2.3 billion (*Asiaweek*, December 17, 1999). Construction is the second most important economic activity. Development and infrastructure projects in the five-year national development plans are the reasons for this boom in construction.

The sultanate has entered a new phase of development—a shift from an oil and a liquefied natural gas-based economy to a non-oil and gas-based economy. The diversification began in 1975 with the implementation of the Investment Incentive Act. The formation of the Ministry of Industry and Primary Resources in 1989 added to the momentum. Brunei's external reserves, excluding gold, stood at US$ 20 billion (*Asiaweek*, December 17, 1999). It has significant investment in other countries, especially in Britain, the United States, and Singapore.

2. DEVELOPMENT OF PRESS AND BROADCASTING

2.1 Development of the Press since 1945

In 1948, the British Resident introduced an official newsletter for the members of his staff. Tinggal (1989) says this was the "first form of reading material" published in Brunei (p. 16).

In 1952, the British Petroleum Co. published *Salam* (Peace), the sultanate's first newspaper (Brunei, 1952). Published in English and Malay, all the company employees as well as schools and government departments received it free. The publication continued as a major private newspaper even after the company changed its name to Brunei Shell Petroleum Co. *The Borneo Bulletin* was the country's second newspaper. Published by the Brunei Press Sdn. Bhd., it came out on November 7, 1953 (Brunei, 1953). It began as an English-language newspaper for a community of expatriate workers in a petroleum company in Kuala Belait, and became a daily on September 3, 1990. It is the only English daily newspaper in Brunei, and is now available on-line as well (http://web3.asia1.com.sg/borneo). *Pelita Brunei* (Torch of Brunei), the third newspaper, started as a weekly in 1956. Published by the Department of Information, its content is mainly in Malay (Brunei, 1956). The government distributes the newspaper free to all government employees and the public (Brunei, 1996/1997 [http://www.brunet.bn/news/pelita]). *Suara Raayat* (People's Voice), a Malay-language newspaper in Roman script, appeared briefly from January to June 1957 in Kuala Belait (Lim, 1992). *Berita Brunei* (Brunei News), which later became *Berita Borneo*, began as a weekly Malay newspaper in March 1957 but ceased publication in 1958. Another short-lived newspaper was *Malaysia*, published in 1958 (Brunei, 1958). After bringing out several issues in the market, it ceased publication the same year. *Suara Bakti* (Voice of Service), a weekly Friday newspaper, first appeared in October 1961 but ceased publication on December 22, 1961. A new management under A.A. Hafiz took over publication in the following week, but after a few issues, the attempt failed. *Bintang Harian* (Daily Star) came out on March 27, 1966, in English and Malay (Brunei, 1966). Its Sunday edition, with four pages each in Malay and English, circulated beyond Brunei in neighboring Sabah and Sarawak and in Peninsular Malaysia as well. The paper contained local and foreign news, news features, and writings in Malay literature. Its first edition had a pressrun of 10,100 copies (Brunei, 1976). It folded in 1971 even though it had increased its pressrun to 15,000 copies that year.

Three short-lived Chinese newspapers also appeared as supplements inserted in three main newspapers published in Kuala Belait. *Pelita Brunei* carried *Pai li ta Pao/Bai li da Pao*, *Salam* carried *Sha La YuPao/Sha LanYou Bao*, and the *Daily Star* carried *Hsing kuang Jih Pao/Xing Guang Ri Bao* (Lim 1992). The Chinese readership in Brunei depended on Chinese newspapers published in the neighbouring Sarawak town of Miri.

Brunei Darussalam Newsletter, a major government newspaper, started as an English-language monthly in October 1985. Published by the Department of Information, its initial run of 6,000 copies went gratis to local and foreign readers overseas. Its printrun increased to 10,000 in 1986 and 16,000 in 1991 (Brunei, 1984/1985). In 1992, the paper became a bimonthly with a printrun of 12,000.

Writing in the late 1980s, Tinggal (1989) observed that between 5,000 to 6,000 copies of foreign newspapers and magazines were also available in the Brunei market, and that the youth were "beginning to look beyond the South China Sea" (p. 16). He claimed that the "lack of proper gatekeepers" had affected the development of the local press (p. 16). The country's population was too small "for competitive advertising to sustain newspaper publishing in the country" (p. 16). Brunei had fewer than 30 reporters, and its social structure did "not allow for much development of the media," which had "to survive between censorship and self-control" (p. 17).

Another government newsletter, the English-language *Brunei Darussalam Daily Digest*, started in 1990 with 500 mimeographed copies a day. The newsletter provided important government news to all ministries, government departments, and diplomatic missions in Brunei and overseas. BruNet has made this paper accessible on the Internet since 1996.

Media Permata (Jewel of the Media) is a more recent newspaper published in Malay by Brunei Press Sdn. Bhd. It began as a weekly in January 1994. Generally, the newspaper carries current local and international news, creative writing, and news on social and economic development. In August 1998, *Media Permata* became the country's second daily newspaper. It is also available on-line linked to the *Borneo Bulletin*. Brunei's newest daily is the tabloid *News Express*, which Prince Sufri, the titular head of the Southeast Asian Games committee, launched in mid-1999 as the "official newspaper" for the events (*Asiaweek*, August 13, 1999).

2.2 Development of Broadcasting since 1945

The groundwork for a broadcasting service in Brunei began in 1956, when the Brunei Legislative Council approved the formation of a small local radio station with the objective of establishing rapport between the government and the people by conveying information and entertainment (Brunei, 1956). The broadcasting service, Radio Brunei, officially commenced on May 2, 1957 (Brunei, 1957). Its initial broadcasting, both in Malay and English, was limited to only two-and-a-half hours everyday, starting from 7.30 p.m. daily. It also aired Chinese and Ghurkali broadcasts (Lent, 1978). Among the programs aired were music, religious talks, radio drama, discussion, and local and international news. Administered by the Broadcasting Department, it was the only broadcasting service in the country. With the introduction of television in 1975, the Broadcasting Department became the Department of Radio Television Brunei.

In 1996, after nearly four decades of operation, the department restructured its radio section into four separate networks: National Network, Pelangi Network, Harmony Network, and Optional Network. In 1997, it added a Nur Islam Network (Brunei, 1996/1997).

Television broadcasting in Brunei began on March 1, 1975 (Brunei, 1975). Lent (1978) says that Brunei "started color-television transmissions, using the most modern equipment in the area and doing it quite rapidly—the whole operation was designed and built in less than seven months" (p. 93). The introduction of television was part of Brunei's five-year plan for economic development (Solley, 1975).

The TV transmission was beamed from Subok Hill, near Bandar Seri Begawan. It operated on 3 Band VHF using the PAL color system. Channel 5 transmits from Subok Hill, while Channel 8 transmits from Andulau Hill (*World radio TV handbook*, 1998).

3. THE PRESS

The Brunei government plays an active role in the press, along with the private sector. Government newspapers are free, largely because the government can afford it. Brunei's major petroleum company publishes its own free newspaper. The country cannot afford many commercially run newspapers because of its small population. This affects the development of the advertising industry as well. *Borneo*

Bulletin and *Media Permata* have representatives in Kuala Lumpur and Singapore to handle advertising for the two newspapers.

Seven newspapers circulate in Brunei. Four are daily newspapers: *Borneo Bulletin* (English), *Media Permata* (Malay), *News Express* (English), and *Brunei Darussalam Daily Digest* (English), with the latter accessible only through the Internet (BruNet). Two are weeklies: *Pelita Brunei* (Malay) and *Brunei Darussalam Newsletter* (English). *Salam* (Malay/English) is a bimonthly.

3.1 Policy and Legal Framework

At least six laws affect the press in Brunei: Local Newspapers Act, Undesirable Publications Act, Sedition Act, Societies Act, Internal Security Act, and the Penal Code (Tinggal, 1989).

The Local Newspapers Act of 1958, as amended in 1984, provides the primary legal framework. Its 15 sections cover licensing of the press and penalties for contravention. Section 3(1) requires the registration of every local newspaper in accordance with regulations made under Section 15. The penalty for contravening this provision is a year's imprisonment and a fine of Brunei dollar (B$) 10,000. A bond of B$ 50,000, which may accrue interest, is required to apply for an effective registration. A magistrate may suspend the registration of a local newspaper for up to six months (on application by the public prosecutor) if the newspaper is found to have published any matter intended to persuade or induce anyone to commit an offence or support any unlawful society as defined in the Societies Act (s4[1][a]). Suspension of registration is also possible under Section 4(1)(b) if the printer, publisher, or editor were convicted of committing an offence, in respect to anything published in that newspaper, under Chapter VI of the Penal Code, or Section 4 of the Sedition Act, or Section 4 of the Undesirable Publications Act. Conviction for an offence prejudicial to the security of Brunei or the maintenance within Brunei of peace or public order may also lead to such suspension.

Publication of false news likely to alarm the public or disturb public order is an offence punishable with imprisonment for one year and a fine of B$ 10,000 (s7[1]). However, prosecution under this section requires the consent of the public prosecutor. This section allows a defense: proving that the publication took reasonable measures to verify the truth of the news (s7[3]). Section 15 empowers the executive to make regulations for implementing the Act. Such regulations may encompass the registration of news agencies and the licensing of newspaper distributors, among others.

3.2 Financial Aspects: Circulation, Advertising, Marketing Strategies

In 1996, the circulation of daily newspapers per 100 people in Brunei stood at 6.9 (Table 1). The *Borneo Bulletin* has an estimated weekday circulation of 20,000 and a weekend circulation of 25,000. *Pelita Brunei* has a weekly circulation of 45,000.

The government provides the money for the production of its newspapers and pays the salaries of the editorial and printing staff. The Brunei Shell finances the publication of *Salam*, a free paper.

The Brunei Press, which publishes *Borneo Bulletin* and *Media Permata*, carries on other publishing and printing activities. The majority of advertisements in the local media in Brunei are from distributors of famous products in neighbouring countries. However, the trend is changing as more business organizations are being set up in the country. The combined advertising revenue of the Brunei media was B$ 8.4 million in 1998 (Radio: B$ 300,000; Television: 2,100,000; Brunei Press: 6,000,000). In the print media, Brunei Press leads in terms of publications and profits through advertisements published in *Borneo Bulletin* and *Media Permata*, which reach about 25,000 consumers. Print advertising was introduced in *Borneo Bulletin* in 1965. On the other hand, advertising through the electronic media has just started and is slowly gaining popularity. Outdoor and billboard advertisments are also quite common. A simple classified 10-word advertisement in *Borneo Bulletin* costs less than B$ 10. On the other hand, a full-page advertisement in a *ConTech Directory* costs about B$ 4,000 but has a longer lifespan. A 90-second film advertisement during the English news time-slot costs about B$ 2,700. Radio advertisements are much cheaper and the rate varies from B$ 60 to B$ 280 depending on the duration, time, and day of the week.

Because Brunei is a small country, the marketing strategy of the private sector involves expanding the circulation base to neighboring Malaysia. The *Borneo Bulletin*, for instance, circulates widely in Brunei and spills over to the Malaysian states of Sabah and Sarawak. Its cover price is 80 Brunei cents for the weekday editions and B$ 1 for the weekend edition.

3.3 Structure and Organization

The Brunei government owns: *Pelita Brunei, Brunei Darussalam Newsletter* and *The Brunei Darussalam Daily Digest*. These newspapers disseminate information and news on current government and national affairs.

The Brunei Press Sdn. Bhd., the country's major private newspaper group—an arm of Foreign Minister Mohamad Bolkiab's QAF Group—owns and publishes *The Borneo Bulletin* and *Media Permata*. The Brunei Shell Co., which is primarily in oil and gas industry operations, publishes *Salam*, which places emphasis on news relating to the operation and organization of Brunei Shell.

3.4 Quality and Popular Press

Brunei does not have a locally produced quality press in the Western sense. Tinggal (1989) maintains: "Because of the nature of Bruneian society, until recently, newspaper reading was not a habit except for the economically conscious minority" (p. 16). However, judging from the circulation of *Borneo Bulletin* and the recently launched *Media Permata* and *News Express*, people are catching up on newspaper reading.

3.5 Distribution and Technology

From an initial figure of 3,500 copies in 1952, *Salam* increased its printrun to 9,200 in 1997. Brunei Shell distributes it free to all the company and government employees in Brunei.

The two dailies of the Brunei Press, *The Borneo Bulletin* and *Media Permata*, circulate in Brunei and beyond. The *Bulletin*, which started with a weekly printrun of 3,500 copies in 1953, reached a high of 30,000 in the 1980s. However, when it became a daily in 1990, its circulation dropped to about 10,000, a figure that has remained steady up to the present. Its daily edition sells for 80 cents (less than 50 US cents) while its weekend edition sells for B$ 1 (60 US cents). It is distributed in Sabah, Sarawak, Peninsular Malaysia, and Singapore as well. The newest daily, *Media Permata*, also sells for 50 US cents, with its circulation spilling over to Sabah and Sarawak.

The Department of Information distributes the government newspaper *Pelita Brunei* through various outlets. It distributes the newspaper free through the department's head office in Bandar Seri Begawan and its branch offices in Belait, Tutong, and Temburong districts. It is also distributed through mosques, hospitals, airports, and village headmen throughout the nation. From a monthly stenciled printrun of 1,000 in 1956, it expanded its printrun to a weekly 45,000 in 1997 (Brunei 1996/ 1997). The government-owned *Brunei Darussalam Newsletter*, which initially started with 6,000 copies a month, has doubled its circulation. All ministries and government departments, educational institutions, as well as embassies and high commissions within and outside Brunei, receive the newsletter free. From 1990 to 1995, the government also distributed the *Brunei Darussalam Daily Digest* free to all ministries, government departments, and diplomatic missions, within and outside Brunei. In 1996, the digest went on-line. It is accessible through BruNet.

4. BROADCASTING

4.1 Policy and Legal Framework

The Emergency (Broadcasting) Order 1997, gazetted on April 16, 1999, provides the primary legal framework for broadcasting in Brunei. It has provisions for the licensing of broadcasting services, as well as of broadcasting apparatus. It also deals with foreign broadcasting services and with the ownership and control of broadcasting services.

Chapter 3 (2) of the Order empowers the minister to undertake the licensing and regulatory functions of broadcasting services and broadcasting apparatuses, to act internationally as Brunei's representative on broadcasting matters, to encourage the development of broadcasting and related services, to assign frequencies to broadcasting licensees, and to regulate the public service broadcasting obligations of the licensees. A broadcasting license is required to operate a broadcasting service in Brunei. The minister of broadcasting, with the approval of the sultan, grants licenses on specific terms and conditions, enumerated in Chapter 11 of the Order. The minister may require the licensee to pay a fee for the license, and also has the right to modify the conditions of the license during the period to which it relates. These conditions, *inter alia*, may require the broadcasting of programs in specific languages.

Chapter 32 (1) deals with foreign broadcasting services. The minister may make an order proscribing a foreign broadcasting service if he considers the quality or content of that service unacceptable. Chapter 33 (2) provides that any resident committing the following acts is guilty of an offence:

- supplying any equipment or other goods for use in connection with the operation of day-to-day running of a proscribed service;
- supplying, or offering to supply, programs to be included in any broadcasting service transmitted as part of a proscribed service;
- arranging for, or inviting, any other person to supply programs to be so included;
- advertising, by means of programs transmitted as part of a proscribed service, goods supplied by him or services provided by him;
- publishing the times or other details of any programs to be transmitted as part of a proscribed service or publishing advertising matter calculated to promote a proscribed service;
- supplying, or offering to supply, any decoding equipment designed or adapted to be used primarily to enable the reception of programs transmitted as part of a proscribed service; and
- promoting financially or otherwise, a proscribed service.

Conviction on a broadcasting licensing offence may result in imprisonment up to three years or a fine not exceeding B$ 200,000, or both (Chapter 40). Conviction on a broadcasting-apparatus licensing offence may result in imprisonment for up to three years, or a fine not exceeding B$ 40,000 or both; and the government can forfeit any broadcasting apparatus installed or found in the possession of any person so convicted (Chapter 41).

4.2 Structure and Organization

The radio section of Radio Television Brunei (RTB) operates five networks:

- The **National Network** includes radio magazine, current affairs, forum, religious packages, discussions, development quizzes, contemporary and current music entertainment, and educational programs. It broadcasts for 20 hours each day.
- The **Pelangi Network** targets the younger generation. It carries musical programs, interactive discussion with listeners, student notes, current quizzes, discussions on developmental topics, religion, educational programs, and general knowledge. It broadcasts for 18 hours a day starting at 6 a.m.

- The **Harmony Network** carries family-oriented programs related to religion and sports, as well as family forums, family packages, family quizzes, and music and entertainment from the 1960s, 1970s, and 1980s. It also broadcasts for 18 hours a day starting at 6 a.m.
- The **Optional Network** provides information and entertainment in English and Chinese for local listeners who do not understand the Malay language.
- The **Nur Islam Network** carries broader Islamic religious programs for all segments of the audience in the country. It operates for 18 hours a day from 6 a.m. onwards.

Two television services are operated by RTB: one using terrestrial transmission on VHF Band 3 for national coverage, and the other using Transponder 11V on Palapa C2 at 113 degrees east for regional coverage. It televises a wide range of programs, produced locally and overseas, for about 18 hours daily. It owns and operates Subok earth station capable of receiving and transmitting access to Palapa and any linear polarized satellites above the region. The four districts of Brunei Darussalam can be linked simultaneously via digital microwave and fiber-optic cable to the RTB studios. Brunei has an estimated 125,000 radio receivers—40 per 100 people—and an estimated 95,000 TV receivers—30 per 100 people (CBA, 1998).

The television section of the department uses both Malay and English to televise its local and imported programs. It has arrangements with regional and international broadcasting organizations for the acquisition and exchange of broadcasting news and programs, while increasing the use of locally produced programs. It is the only TV network operating in the country.

Bruneians also receive broadcasts from Malaysian channels such as TV1, TV2, and TV3. STAR television channels are also accessible in the country via decoders that people can purchase locally.

4.3 Program Policies

Radio Television Brunei has the legal obligation to broadcast such programs as the minister may require at a specific time or period. The minister may also prohibit or restrict the broadcasting of specified advertising.

Radio Television Brunei is facing stiff competition from foreign TV stations in Malaysia—TV1, TV2, and TV3—as well as from STAR TV with its 10 channels. However, RTB is holding its own with news, information, and local entertainment. It has continued to improve the quality of local programming to win the audience (Yussof, 1998). STAR TV, which used to be free, is now available only on subscription from DST Network's KRISTAL, a company that began operations in January 1999. Its smartcard comes in two packages: B$ 190 for six months and B$ 340 for 12 months, while a renewal costs B$ 150 for six months and B$ 300 for 12 months. Subscribers have to use a decoder to access the STAR TV channels. The decoder also allow parents to control their children's viewing habits. With this new arrangement, Brunei has declared ASTRO channels from Malaysia to be illegal. However, in early 2000, cooperation between KRISTAL (Brunei) and ASTRO (Malaysia) has made ASTRO channels available again in Brunei Sky TV at affordable rates.

4.4 Ownership and Financing

Previously, both radio and television were government monopolies. Since 1999, a private radio station, KRISTAL FM has come into operation. However, the country has no private TV broadcasting service, although the Emergency (Broadcasting) Order, 1997 enables the setting up of such services.

Bruneians do not pay a license fee to operate a radio or television receiver. This is because the government finances the broadcasting services, which also air commercials. The revenue earned from advertising is not known. However, television carries much more advertising than radio.

5. NEW ELECTRONIC MEDIA

5.1 Internet and On-line Media

Gearing itself to interconnect with the Global Information Infrastructure (GII), Brunei has launched the Rangkaian Global Aliran Multimedia 21 (RAGAM 21) initiative, which will introduce an optical transport and access network infrastructure to enable full multimedia capability (APT, 1999). Under Brunei's latest five-year plan, which commenced in 1996, the Jabatan Telecom Brunei (Telecom Department) will build the Brunei information infrastructure while the private sector will develop its contents and applications. The BII's RAGAM 21 will interconnect with the GII. The plan envisages a host of new services and products: intelligent network services, broadband-ISDN for high speed transmission of multimedia services, ATM services through a fiber-optic access network, and the like (APT, 1998). International video conference services are readily available. Subscribers have ready access to Data Plus (Data Packet Link Usage Service) and other services.

In October 1995, the JTB set up BruNet, the country's on-line system that connects to the Internet. Since April 1998, BruNet has provided access to 60 countries through Global Reach Internet Connectivity (APT, 1999). Brunei has a computer density of 2.9 per 100 people. The Network Wizards' January 1999 survey showed Brunei had 1,197 Internet hosts—a density of 39 per 10,000 people. This compares favorably with the 1996 figure of 206 hosts with 3,391 users (ITU, 1998). The *Borneo Bulletin*, published in Kuala Belait, has an on-line edition (http://www.brunet.bn/news/bb/), and at the Asia 1 site mentioned above, RTB also has a website (http://www.brunet.bn/rtb/).

5.2 Telecommunications Infrastructure

The country has two operators providing telecommunications services—Jabatan Telecom Brunei (JBT) and DST Communications Sdn. Bhd (DST). The JBT is a government department under the Ministry of Communications. DST is a private company and began the country's cellular service in April 1995 (APT, 1998). The number of main telephone lines stood at 77,700 or 24.7 per 100 people in 1998—the second highest density in ASEAN. The number of cellular subscribers stood at 49,129 or 15.6 per 100 people in 1998 (ITU, 1999). Brunei's first public video-phone service started on January 27, 1998. The telecommunications network has achieved full digitization. An overlay of fiber-optic cables supplements the digital microwave system.

The country has two fiber-optic cable connections: one with Singapore and the other with Malaysia and the Philippines. In 1999, it became a landing point of SEA-ME-WE-3 fiber-optic submarine cable. It has two satellite earth stations—one pointing to Intelsat's Indian Ocean region and the other to the Pacific Ocean region (APT, 1998, 1999).

6. POLICY TRENDS FOR PRESS AND BROADCASTING

Tinggal (1989) broadly described the Brunei press system as one that "fits some-where between Libertarian and Authoritarian patterns" (p. 17). Based largely on the country's laws and regulations, as well as political pressures and controls affecting the media content, Freedom House (Sussman, 1999) designated the Brunei press system as "not free." The Freedom House Survey Team (1999) reported that, "The sole privately owned newspaper practices self censorship on political and religious issues" (p. 64). The *Borneo Bulletin*, however, claimed that it maintained an independent editorial policy, while adhering to objective, fair, and factual coverage (http://web3.asia1.com.sg/borneo/bbonline/wed/wed.htm).

Yussof (1998, p. 244) points out that Ralph Lowenstein's social-centralist theory best fits the Brunei press system in the context of the Malay Islamic Monarchy concept. Under the social-centralist theory, as Merrill (1974) explains, "government ownership and/or government regulation of the media system ... would control the media not primarily to keep them from harming the ruling elite, but to channel the power of the media into what the state sees as constructive educational, developmental and political goals" (p. 37).

The situation in Brunei today is a far cry from what Tinggal (1989) wrote a decade ago as "very much inward looking" (p. 16). The Bruneians have become more outward looking with their exposure to satellite TV and broadcasts from Malaysia (TV1, TV2, and TV3). *Borneo Bulletin* and *Media Permata* carry the programs of the 24-hour STAR TV—STAR World, STAR Movies, STAR Sports, CNN International, ESPN, HBO, Discovery Channel, and Channel V. RTB too is available through satellite. Brunei is also playing an active role as a member of the

Association of Southeast Asian Nations and of the Asia–Pacific Economic Cooperation (APEC). It will be the host of the next APEC summit in 2000.

The sultan is the benefactor of the Malay Islamic Monarchy (MIM) philosophy. Under the present system, the people enjoy tax-free personal income, free education, free healthcare treatment, and subsidized housing. Political opposition or even discontent remain virtually impossible to detect, according to the Institute of South East Asian Studies (*Regional outlook 1998–1999*). The occasional anonymous letter to the *Borneo Bulletin* and a minor leaflet campaign represented the sum total of opposition in 1997 (*Regional outlook 1998–1999*). Tinggal (1989) claims the 1962 uprising "strengthened the people's belief in the [MIM] system, and its preservation has now become the public interest" (p. 15).

Mitton (1997) found Bruneians willing to talk openly about politics and official accountability. Official talk about adopting limited democracy has brought about a "distinct thaw" though not a full-fledged *perestroika* (*Asiaweek*, September 12, 1997). Mitton noted that critical letters appeared in the "feistier" *Borneo Bulletin* probably because the paper is owned by Prince Mohamed, the sultan's younger brother, and because "it acts as an escape valve that lets authorities know where the national pressure points are." *The News Express* has planned to offer a daily "dissent" page of letters (*Asiaweek*, August 13, 1999).

When *Borneo Bulletin* reported that an issue of *Asia Times* (a supplement in the widely sold Singapore *Straits Times*) had been banned, the Home Affairs Ministry chastised the *Bulletin* for revealing the ban. When the Internal Security Department visited the *Bulletin's* offices to demand the addresses of readers who had written letters complaining about government services and public utilities, the newspaper did not comply. This may be another sign that Brunei is opening up (*Asiaweek*, September 12, 1997).

Various village or *mukim* consultative councils, as well as the appointed Legislative Council at the higher level, have affected the contact between the government and the people. Newspapers can provide a hotline between the people and the government through more open reporting and feisty readers' pages.

Brunei is likely to continue with the present system, particularly because of its strong economy. The MIM concept remains entrenched with the sultan elevating his son as the heir to the throne in 1998. Market size will continue to determine the viability of competitive newspapers and is likely to be the major reason for the lack of participation by the private sector in the media.

7. MAIN ISSUES

● Freedom House (Sussman, 1999) has placed Brunei in the world's "not free" category in relation to press freedom. Freedom House gave Brunei a press restriction score of 74 out of 100 based on four criteria: laws and regulations that influence media content (14 out of 15 for print and broadcast media each), political pressures and controls on media content (15 out of 15 for print and broadcast media each), economic influences over media content (5 out of 15 for print and 11 for broadcast), and repressive actions (nil out of five for both media). Freedom of the press will remain a sore issue until Brunei allows multi-party democracy and amends the various laws affecting the emergence of a multiplicity of media.

● Tinggal (1989) was disappointed a decade ago that journalism in Brunei had not developed into a profession. Professionalism in mass communications is likely to develop only if the government encourages the development of free private media that will attract more young Bruneians to study journalism and related fields as a stepping stone.

8. STATISTICS

General Profile

Location	Northwest of the Island of Borneo
Capital	Bandar Seri Begawan
Population	322,982 (July 1999)
Population growth rate	3.1 percent (1996)
Language	Malay
Religion (official)	Islam
Government type	Constitutional monarchy
Gross domestic product	US$ 5.9 billion (1999)
Real GDP growth rate	3.5 percent (1999)
Exchange rate (1999 average)	US$ 1 = 1.70 Brunei dollars*
Major industries	Oil and gas industry, textiles, food and beverages, building materials
Major exports	Oil and gas, ready-made garments
Major imports	Machinery and transport equipment, manufactured goods, food and chemicals

Source: *Asiaweek*, December 17, 1999; ASEAN, 1998; * OANDA Historical Currency Table [Online]. Available: (http://www.oanda.com/converter/cc_table?lang=en).

Table 1
Estimated Mass Media Penetration

Year	Radio receiver		Television receiver		Daily newspapers		
	Number ('000)	Per 100 people	Number ('000)	Per 100 people	Number	Circ'n	Per 100 people
1980	41	21.2	26	13.5	1	4,000	2.1
1985	55	24.7	45	20.2	1	5,000	2.7
1990	68	26.5	60	23.3	1	10,000	3.9
1995	80	27.2	70	23.8	1	20,000	6.8
1996	90	29.9	75	24.9	1	21,000	6.9
1997	93	30.2	77	25.0			
	(125)*	(39.5)*	(95)*	(30.1)*			
1998			(196)**	(63.8)**			

Source: UNESCO, 1999; * *World radio TV handbook*, 1998; ** ITU, 1999.

Table 2
Population: 1993–99

Year	Population
1993	276,300
1994	284,500
1995	296,000
1996	305,100
1997	310,000
1998	320,000
1999	322,982

Source: Brunei, 1996/1997; *Economic report*, 1998/1999.

Table 3
Newspapers: 1952–98

Newspaper	Year published	Period of circulation
Salam	1952–	1952–
Brunei Bulletin	1953	1953–
Pelita Brunei	1956	1956–
Berita Brunei/Berita Borneo	1957	1957–58
Malaysia	1958	1958–58
Suara Bakti	1961	1961–61
Daily Star/Bintang Harian	1966	1966–71
Brunei Darussalam Newsletter	1985	1985–
Brunei Darusslam Daily Digest	1990	1990–
Media Permata	1994	1994–

Source: Brunei, 1952, 1953, 1956, 1957, 1958, 1975/1976, 1979/1980, 1995a, 1996/1997.

Table 4
Local Radio and Television Services: 1957–98

Network	Year of operation	Network ownership
Radio Brunei (radio service)	1957 until 1996 (restructured)	The Department of Broadcasting Brunei
Television Brunei (television service)	1975–	The Department of Radio Television Brunei
National Network (radio service)	1996–	The Department of Radio Television Brunei
Pelangi Network (radio service)	1996–	The Department of Radio Television Brunei
Harmony Network (radio service)	1996–	The Department of Radio Television Brunei
Optional Network (radio service)	1996–	The Department of Radio Television Brunei
Nur Islam Network (radio service)	1997–	The Department of Radio Television Brunci

Source: Brunei, 1975/1976, 1984/1985, 1996/1997.

Table 5
Telecommunications Data: 1990–96

Year	Number of direct exchange lines	Teledensity	International telephone traffic	Traffic to Sabah & Sarawak	Pager	BruNet
	('000)	*(per 100 lines)*	*(Million Minutes)*		*Subscriptions*	
1990	33.01	13	7.6	5.72	–	–
1991	39.09	15	9.9	6.93	5,171	–
1992	44.66	16.9	13.28	8.55	7,819	–
1993	55.23	20	14.28	9.15	8,777	–
1994	61.62	21	16.27	9.66	9,980	–
1995	68.13	23	30.7	13.63	9,218	819
1996	78.79	26	35.16	14.45	10,075	3,335
1997*	86.06	25	32.29	–	–	–
1998*	79.80	25	29.30	–	16,874	9,996

Source: Brunei, 1996/1997; * Telecommunication Department, Ministry of Communications (relevant years).

9. USEFUL ADDRESSES

The Department of Information
Prime Ministers' Office
Lapangan Terbang Lama Breaches
Bandar Seri Begawan
Brunei Darussalam
Telephone: 02-383-400

The Department of Radio Television Brunei
Prime Ministers' Office
Bandar Seri Begawan
Brunei Darussalam
Telephone: 02-383-400

The Brunei Press Sdn. Berhad
Lot 8 & 11, Perindustrian Beribi II,
Gadong, Brunei Darussalam
Telephone: 02-451468

10. REFERENCES

Amnesty International. (1983). *Amnesty international report.* London: Amnesty International Publications.
APT (Asia-Pacific Telecommunity). (1998, 1999). *The APT yearbook.* Bangkok: APT.
ASEAN. (1998). *Asean macroeconomic outlook 1997/1998.* Jakarta: Asean Secretariat.
Brunei. (1952). *The state of Brunei annual report.* Kuching: British Resident Office.
Brunei. (1953). *The state of Brunei annual report.* Kuching: British Resident Office.
Brunei. (1956). *The state of Brunei annual report.* Kuching: British Resident Office.
Brunei. (1957). *The state of Brunei annual report.* Kuching: British Resident Office.

Brunei. (1958). *The state of Brunei annual report.* Kuching: British Resident Office.
Brunei. (1962). *State of Brunei annual report.* Bandar Seri Begawan: Chief Minister's Office.
Brunei. (1966). *State of Brunei annual report.* Bandar Seri Begawan: Chief Minister's Office.
Brunei. (1975). *State of Brunei annual report.* Bandar Seri Begawan: The Department of Information.
Brunei. (1975/1976). *Brunei statistical yearbook.* Bandar Seri Begawan: Statistics Division, Economic Planning Unit, Ministry of Finance.
Brunei. (1976). *Brunei statistical yearbook.* Bandar Seri Begawan: Statistics Division, Economic Planning Unit, Ministry of Finance.
Brunei. (1979/1980). *Brunei statistical yearbook.* Bandar Seri Begawan: Statistics Division, Economic Planning Unit. Ministry of Finance.
Brunei. (1980). *Far East and Australia.* London: Europa Publications.
Brunei. (1984/1985). *Brunei statistical yearbook.* Bandar Seri Begawan: Statistics Division, Economic Planning Unit, Ministry of Finance.
Brunei. (1986). *Brunei statistical yearbook.* Bandar Seri Begawan: Statistics Division, Economic Planning Unit, Ministry of Finance.
Brunei. (1995a). *Brunei Darussalam in brief.* Bandar Seri Begawan: Information Department, The Prime Minister's Office.
Brunei. (1995b). *Brunei statistical yearbook.* Bandar Seri Begawan: Statistics Division, Economic Planning Unit, Ministry of Finance.
Brunei. (1996/1997). *Brunei statistical yearbook.* Bandar Seri Begawan: Statistics Division, Economic Planning Unit, Ministry of Finance.
CBA (Commonwealth Broadcasting Association). (1998). *Directory 1998* [On-line]. Available: (http://www.oneworld.org/cba/whoswho/a-cd98.htm#_Toc411430711).
Freedom House Survey Team. (1999). *Freedom in the world 1998–1999: The annual survey of political rights and civil liberties.* New York: Freedom House.
ITU (International Telecommunication Union). (1998, 1999). *World telecommunication development report.* Geneva: ITU.
Leake, D., Jr. (1990). *Brunei: The modern Southeast-Asian Islamic sultanate.* Kuala Lumpur: Forum.
Lent. J.A. (Ed.). (1978). *Broadcasting in Asia and the Pacific: A continental survey of radio and television.* Philadelphia: Temple University Press.
Lim, P.H. (1992). *Singapore, Malaysia and Brunei: An international union list.* Singapore: Institute of South East Asian Studies.
Merrill, J.C. (1974). *The imperative of freedom: A philosophy of journalistic autonomy.* New York. Communication Arts Books, Hastings House.
Mitton, R. (1997, September 12). Fun Brunei? *Asiaweek,* pp. 30–34.
Regional outlook: Southeast Asia 1998–1999. Singapore: Institute of Southeast Asian Studies.
Solley, A. (1975, February 7). Communication: Brunei on the air in record time. *Far Eastern Economic Review,* p. 46.
Sussman, L.R. (1999). *Press freedom '99: Global warning—press controls fuel the Asian debacle.* New York: Freedom House.
Tinggal, Z. (1989). Brunei Darussalam. In Á. Mehra (Ed.) *Press systems in Asean states* (pp. 15–25). Singapore: AMIC.
UNDP (United Nations Development Program). (1999). *Human development report.* New York: Oxford University Press & UNDP.
UNESCO (United Nations Educational, Scientific and Cultural Organisation). (1999). *Statistical yearbook.* Paris: UNESCO.
World factbook. (1999). Washington, DC: CIA [On-line]. Available: (http://www.odci.gov/cia/publications/factbook).
World radio TV handbook. (1998). New York: BPI Communications.
Yussof, Ladi. (1998). *Media system in Brunei Darussalam: Development, roles, ownership and control from 1950 to 1997.* Unpublished master's thesis, Universiti Kebangsaan Malaysia, Bangi, Malaysia.

◆

9

CAMBODIA

Judith Clarke

1. NATIONAL PROFILE

1.1 Geography

Cambodia lies in Southeast Asia, abutting Thailand to the west and northwest, Laos to the north, and Vietnam to the east and southeast. Its southwestern boundary is the coastline of the Gulf of Thailand. It has a tropical climate, with a monsoon season from May to November and a dry season from December to April. Its terrain chiefly comprises plains covered in forest and woodland. Low mountain ranges lie to the north and the southwest. The Mekong flows into Cambodia from Laos and out to Vietnam, and at Phnom Penh meets the Bassac-Tonle Sap river. The Tonle Sap, or Great Lake, expands every year when water is forced up from the confluence into the central plain.

1.2 People

Cambodia's population, estimated at 11.63 million in mid-1999 (US Census Bureau, International Data Base) has suffered through a long period of internal strife. The country's adult literacy rate was 66 percent in 1997 (UNDP, 1999). The estimated literacy rate was 35 percent—males, 48 percent; and females, 22 percent (*World factbook*, 1999). Average life expectancy at birth was 53.4 years in 1997 (UNDP, 1999).

Cambodia's prehistoric people mainly ate fish, and lived in raised dwellings that were reached by ladders. Their circular fortified villages date back to about 1000 B.C. No agreement exists on when the forebears of today's inhabitants arrived, and from where—China, India, or the islands of Southeast Asia. Experts believe that people speaking Khmer-related languages lived in the area at least from the beginning of the Christian era, when *Indianization* (the absorption of an Indian way of life, including Hinduism and Buddhism) occurred as a peaceful process through trade and settlement (Chandler, 1993). Almost 95 percent of the people are Therevada Buddhists (*World factbook*, 1999).

The Khmers constitute 90 percent of Cambodia's population. The other ethnic groups include Vietnamese (5 percent), Chinese (1 percent), and a number of minorities (4 percent) (*World factbook*, 1999). Over the centuries, the Vietnamese and Chinese have settled in the area: the former are predominantly fisher-folk and the latter are mostly merchants. The Muslim Chams and the hill tribes of the rural north and northwest form the minorities (Kiernan, 1996).

1.3 Government and Politics

Up to the 8th century, a number of small kingdoms existed within Cambodia's boundaries. Then the great realm of Angkor rose under Jayavarman II in the early 9th century and held sway for more than 600 years. Its influence spread far to the west and the east into what is today Thailand and southern Vietnam respectively. The fabulous temple complex of Angkor in northwestern Cambodia, built in the 12th century, is the national symbol of Cambodia. The decline of Cambodia was followed by wars with Thailand, and Cambodia became increasingly subject to Thai influence. By the 19th century, Vietnamese influence was pressing in as well, and both large neighbors attacked Cambodia. Its survival as a national unit was assured by the imposition of a French protectorate in 1863. The French maintained Cambodia's political and social institutions, including the monarchy, but instituted a stringent tax system and an administration staffed largely by Vietnamese (Chandler, 1993).

Colonial rule ended in 1953 under King Norodom Sihanouk, who marginalized the democratic movement and the left wing to emerge as the champion of independence. He abdicated in 1955 but remained head of state and led his own movement, the *Sangkum Reastr Niyum* (People's Socialist Community). As the turmoil of the Vietnam War grew, he maintained a careful balance between the left and right at home, while trying to stay neutral internationally. In 1969, the United States started bombing Cambodian routes used by Vietnamese and Khmer communists. The next year, Prime Minister Lon Nol overthrew Sihanouk and set up the right wing Khmer Republic. The prince stationed himself in Beijing and joined the communists (known as the Khmer Rouge) in a guerrilla war. Despite continued US bombing until 1973 in support of the Khmer Republic, the Khmer Rouge were victorious in 1975. Led by Pol Pot and calling themselves Democratic Kampuchea, they emptied the cities, killed people associated with the former governments, and set the population to work on rural projects. Estimates of the number of deaths from execution and negligence vary between several hundred thousand and 3 million.

The Khmer Rouge instigated border clashes with the Vietnamese, who, in late 1978, invaded and ousted Pol Pot. Hanoi put in power a group of Khmers who formed the People's Republic of Kampuchea (PRK) in early 1979. The Khmer Rouge retreated to the Thai border, where they received support from Thailand and China as well as recognition from the international community as Cambodia's government. In 1982, they formed the Coalition Government of Democratic Kampuchea (CGDK) with Sihanouk's followers—the National United Front for an

Independent, Neutral and Cooperative Cambodia, known by its French acronym FUNCINPEC—and another group called the Khmer People's National Liberation Front (KPNLF) formed mainly by Lon Nol era officials. The CGDK gained the recognition of the United Nations as Cambodia's government. Guerrilla war continued until the Paris peace accords of 1991, which provided for a ceasefire, disarmament, and UN-supervised elections. A Supreme National Council (SNC) comprising all four groups took over sovereignty, and UN personnel oversaw the May 1993 poll. FUNCINPEC, led by Sihanouk's son Prince Norodom Ranariddh, won the elections for the first Royal Government of Cambodia (RGC), but formed a coalition with the runner-up Cambodian People's Party (CPP), the party of the former PRK administration (which had changed its name to the State of Cambodia, SoC, in 1989, and ruled almost intact until the election). Prince Ranariddh and Hun Sen, the former SoC prime minister, became first and second prime minister respectively. The Buddhist Liberal Democratic Party (BLDC), formed after a split in the KPNLF, and led by the former KPNLF leader Son Sann, won a small number of seats.

The National Assembly adopted a constitution in September 1993, making the country a kingdom and restored Sihanouk to the monarchy. In 1994, it outlawed the Khmer Rouge, which returned to resistance on the Thai border. However, the group was riven by disputes, leading many cadres to switch allegiance to the RGC. Pol Pot himself died in 1998. In mid-1997, forces belonging to Ranariddh and Hun Sen clashed in Phnom Penh. Ranariddh was ousted and left the country; many FUNCINPEC officials were killed or imprisoned. Others fled Cambodia and renewed the resistance struggle from Thailand. Former FUNCINPEC member Ung Huot, who set up a separate party, became the first prime minster. The Sam Rainsy Party (SRP), formed by the ex-FUNCINPEC finance minister Sam Rainsy, along with FUNCINPEC, returned from exile and campaigned for the general elections on July 26, 1998. The CPP won 41 percent of the vote and 64 seats in the 122-seat National Assembly. FUNCINPEC won 32 percent of the vote and 43 seats. These two parties reached a compromise to share government posts with Hun Sen as prime minister and Ranariddh as chairman of the National Assembly. The SRP, which won 14 seats, remained in opposition. The coalition agreed in November 1998 to create a bicameral legislature with a senate (*World factbook*, 1999).

1.4 Economy

According to the latest data, Cambodia's nominal per capita Gross National Product was US$ 270. Its per capita Gross Domestic Product at purchasing power parity was US$ 1,350. Cambodia's exports in 1999 totaled US$ 0.8 billion (*Asiaweek*, December 17, 1999).

Cambodia's economy is predominantly agricultural. Since French colonial days, it has been dependent largely on rubber, rice, and other primary products. Industry stated to develop in the 1960s but was held back by the Vietnam War and the subsequent civil war. The back-to-the-soil policies of the Khmer Rouge put peasants in charge of large infrastructure projects, thus ruining agriculture. They generally ignored the industrial sector. From 1979, reconstruction took place with the help of Vietnam and the Soviet Union, as well as with aid provided to the Thai border by Western countries, but it was hampered severely by the isolation of the PRK from the non-Soviet world. In the late 1980s, when Soviet aid dried up, the PRK began to replace the communist-style system with a free market one, boosting the economy. After the peace accords, foreign investment flowed in, particularly from Southeast Asia. The 1993 Constitution instituted a market economy. Overseas funds helped set up factories and businesses mainly in and around Phnom Penh. However, the 1997 clash precipitated economic stagnation and led to the abandonment of many foreign ventures.

There have been allegations that drug trafficking is rife in Cambodia (Thayer, 1995) and that officials, including prime ministers, have ignored the illegal logging of the forests that once covered most of the country (Global Witness, 1997).

2. DEVELOPMENT OF PRESS AND BROADCASTING

2.1 Brief Early History

French- and Vietnamese-language publications existed well before any in the local language, though most, perhaps all, were published in Vietnam. The first Khmer-language newspaper was *Nagaravatta* (The Land of Pagodas), published in 1936 by the nationalists Pach Chhoeun and Sim Var, joined later by Son Ngoc Thanh. It came out twice weekly and became very popular among the small Cambodian elite, who, for the first time, were able to read about the world in their own language. By 1937 it had a circulation of 5,000 and an even higher readership. It encouraged Khmers to take a more active role in the economy and advocated equal treatment for them. When the Japanese arrived in the early 1940s, they allowed the French to remain in power, and *Nagaravatta* became anti-French (and pro-Japanese). In 1942 the authorities suppressed the newspaper and arrested Pach Chhoeum for leading demonstrations in Phnom Penh. Thanh fled to the countryside and later to Japan. The only other Khmer-language periodical of this time was *Kampuchea Soria* (Cambodian Sun), a monthly publication of the French-funded Buddhist Institute. However, it carried only literary and religious material until the 1950s, when it added news to its repertoire (Chandler, 1993; Kiernan, 1985; Mehta, 1997a).

2.2 Developments since 1945

2.2.1 Press

After World War II, with the establishment of an elected National Assembly, the new political parties started their own newspapers. The Democratic Party, which grew out of *Nagaravatta* supporters, produced *Pracheathippathai* (Democracy), while the Renovation Khmer party of Lon Nol and Sihanouk's ally Nhek Tioulong started *Khemara* in 1947. Son Ngoc Thanh started *Khmer Krok* (Cambodians

Awake) in 1952, when he returned briefly from exile before fleeing to the Thai border (Chandler, 1993). The government set up the national news agency Agence Khmère de Presse (AKP) in 1951 to provide news for other outlets. A law passed that year allowed anyone who gave notice to the Ministry of Information to publish in Khmer, but in practice the government could suppress publications by withdrawing their licenses. Newspapers had a very narrow market. The biggest in 1952 was the biweekly *Pracheathippathai* with a circulation of 9,000. The best-selling daily at the time was the Chinese-language *Cong Thuong Pao*, with fewer than 2,000 subscribers (Steinberg et al., 1957, 1959).

Newspapers flourished immediately after independence. However, in the six months before the 1955 elections, Sihanouk suppressed right- and left-wing publications. He banned four pro-Thanh newspapers and jailed one editor. *Pracheachon* (People), the left inclined organ of the communist group of the same name, was shut down and its editor arrested. In the same year, two other newspapers and their editors shared the same fate (Kiernan, 1985).

After Sihanouk was declared the winner of the elections, he freed the press again. In 1956, Cambodia had 16 newspapers (including three dailies) in French, Khmer, and Chinese. Many had connections with political parties or politicians (Steinberg et al., 1957, 1959). There were also Vietnamese papers. Sihanouk himself had started *Réalités Cambodgiennes*, a weekly, and in the mid-1950s opened *La Dépêche* (The Dispatch), the semi-official daily newspaper of his Sangkum. Both were in French (Noel, 1967). *Pracheachon* returned, as did other left-wing papers, though they were shut down frequently. In 1959 *Pracheachon's* editor, Nop Bophann, was shot dead in Phnom Penh. In 1960, Khieu Samphan, editor of the French-language *L'Observateur*, was stripped in the street and later beaten by the chief of the security services. Following this, the authorities banned the four left-wing papers (Kiernan, 1985).

However, the communists reorganized their newspapers using different titles. More than half the French- and Khmer-language press in the early to mid-1960s was left wing. *Pracheachon* was again closed in 1962, but the leftist Chau Seng was now running *La Dépêche* (Kiernan, 1985). During the 1960s, Prince Sihanouk himself established two weekly semi-official magazines, *Sangkum* and *Kambuja*. Both were run, like *Réalités*, by Frenchmen (Osborne, 1994). In 1966, he created the *Counter-Government (CG) Bulletin* to criticize the new center-right government. A daily mimeographed publication, it produced some investigative journalism (Noel, 1967). However, that year, Sihanouk's relations with the left deteriorated, and he stamped out two successors to *Pracheachon* (Noel, 1967).

In 1967, Cambodia had 13 daily newspapers in Khmer, French, Chinese, and Vietnamese, with a combined circulation of 70,000. The handful of Khmer-language publications, whose readership now overtook that of the Chinese papers, reportedly had "a penchant for crime news, gory and gossipy" (Noel, 1967, p. 18), and they did briefly do some muckraking in response to the example set by the *CG Bulletin*, as well as Sihanouk's two weekly magazines and three monthlies (Noel, 1967).

Later that year, Sihanouk closed all newspapers after Chau Seng's pro-Beijing *La Nouvelle Dépêche* published a telegram that was hostile to the prince. The Chinese side of the Sino-Khmer Friendship Association had sent the telegram to the local branch (Mehta, 1997a; Soth & Sin, 1982). This ended the overt left-wing press. The right-wing, French-language *Phnom Penh Presse* of Sim Var also disappeared, but his Khmer-language *Khmer Ekareach* (Khmer Independent), whose offices had been attacked and damaged by a demonstration, reopened. Also, a number of new publications appeared, including *Koh Santhepheap* (Island of Peace) and *Ariyathor* (Civilization). Sim Var's paper took a very anti-Sihanouk stand and was suspended on several occasions. The very similar anti-government *Nokor Thom* (Great Country) appeared in 1969. As opposition to Sihanouk grew, it became very successful (Soth & Sin, 1982).

Despite initial censorship in the Khmer Republic, newspapers flourished. In 1970, the total circulation was estimated between 55,000 and 60,000 (Whitaker et al., 1973). *Nokor Thom, Khmer Ekareach, Koh Santhepheap*, and *Ariyathor* all continued to be published. The new administration took over *Réalités* and AKP, the latter continuing to publish official government reports and foreign news from the international agencies. Private newspapers were still controlled dominantly by individuals, chiefly political players, but they also assumed a watchdog role, criticizing mismanagement by and the corruption of the new government. The new regime lifted censorship in August but reimposed it in December, and immediately suspended *Nokor Thom* for criticizing the regulations. A month later, the government agreed to stop pre-censoring newspapers in return for an end to subversive and obscene articles (Whitaker et al., 1973; Soth & Sin, 1982).

The press, however, continued to attack individuals. A man criticized in the papers was blamed for the bombing of the car of the director of *Nokor Thom* and an attack on a director of *Khmer Ekareach* in early 1972. A press law passed in June that year permitted criticism of the government as long as it was not injurious to it and did not impede government action, but it forbade the press to cast slurs on the honor of an individual or on national security and morality. This vagueness meant that even criticism of officials might contravene the law. At this point, some 20 to 30 daily newspapers in French, Khmer, and Chinese were still in circulation, but the authorities closed four for "disseminating false news, disrupting public order, damaging the unity of the Khmer people, and insulting the government" (Whitaker et al., 1973, p. 166).

In 1973, the government imposed emergency measures that included the suspension of all private papers. Some opened again in May 1974. *Nokor Thom* and *Khmer Ekareach* were, however, suppressed, even though the former produced a highly successful farewell edition in July 1974 blaming the government for the assassination of two of its officials. The editor left for Paris and the printing press was confiscated. In early 1975, three Khmer papers were suspended for covering an interview with Sihanouk (Soth & Sin, 1982).

In the Khmer Republic, French-language publications thrived on official advertising while the Chinese press attracted advertising from the local business community. The former, however, was much poorer. With its small readership and large number of publications, advertising was low and thinly spread. Most Khmer newspapers comprised a single broadsheet folded in two to produce four pages, often with soft features or fiction on the inside (Soth & Sin, 1982).

The Khmer Rouge takeover ended the "press," as it was known in previous administrations. Journalists either fled the country or were drafted into the rural labor program. Many died or were killed. Only a handful of party publications were put out (Mehta, 1997a).

The PRK set up a communist-style media system, with all organs being owned and run by the party and government. While the PRK was still in Vietnam, it revived the official news agency in late-1978 under the name of Sapordamean Khmer (SPK). It also started a national weekly newspaper, *Kampuchea*, in January 1979 under Khieu Kanharith. Newspapers were also set up for the army—*Kangtoap Padevoat* (Revolutionary Army)—in 1979, and for Phnom Penh in 1981. In October 1985, a party newspaper using the old name *Pracheachon* appeared. All the media came under the control of the Commission for Propaganda and Education of the Central Committee of the Kampuchean People's Revolutionary Party, the forerunner of the CPP. Before the Paris peace accords of 1991, Cambodia had only five newspapers, but no daily (*Asiaweek*, March 30, 1986; Ross, 1987; Hodson & Kimsong, 1998). The resistance had its own limited press during the 1980s. Sihanouk continued to put out a newsletter, as did branches of FUNCINPEC and the KPNLF (SPK-AJA, 1991; Marston, 1996).

In April 1992, the SoC National Assembly adopted new regulations allowing a free-market media system, but still giving the administration some control (UNTAC, 1992). This angered the other groups in the SNC because they felt they should have been brought into the process. UNTAC, charged with instilling professional standards of journalism, prepared its own media guidelines (UNTAC, n.d.) and oversaw a tremendous growth in publications, though it failed to produce a planned official charter. A reporter for *Cambodia Daily* wrote that UNTAC "brought changes to the Cambodian media and the way we saw ourselves.... It had an enormous effect on our sense of national identity" (Chea, 1997, p. 10).

The BLDP started publishing an anti-CPP weekly bulletin in January 1992, but the CPP hampered its distribution, and its editor was shot at and wounded in March. A former *Kampuchea* journalist published *Santhepheap* (Peace), a weekly. Two English-language newspapers started in mid-year: an American couple who had worked on the Thai border launched *Phnom Penh Post*, and a Malaysian company with business interests in Cambodia produced *Cambodia Times*, the latter also adding a Khmer-language edition (Marston, 1996). In 1993, a slew of newspapers opened in the months before the election. Thong Uy Pang, who had been chief editor of the pre-1975 *Koh Santhepheap*, started a newspaper bearing the same title. A Thai company set up another Khmer-language paper called *Rasmei Kampuchea* (Light of Cambodia). By May, when the elections took place, there was a score of new newspapers alongside the SoC ones. All the new Khmer-language newspapers were supportive of one party or the other, in some cases blatantly so (Marston, 1996; Clarke, 1995).

The 1993 Constitution guaranteed freedom of the press, and by mid-1994, the number of newspapers had increased to 36 (Clarke, 1995). In 1998, about 80 of them were registered with the Ministry of Information, though many were irregular or non-functional. According to the research conducted by Raoul Jennar, in May 1998 there were 43 Khmer-language newspapers actually in operation. One-third of them were anti-CPP, a decrease from 19 in July 1997. In August 1998, the Cambodia Communications Institute (CCI), a body set up with overseas aid under the auspices of the Ministry of Information (to monitor the press and to train journalists) recorded 81 Khmer-language papers, though 35 were said to be infrequent or defunct (CCI, 1998; author's interviews, 1998). Fifteen of the total, including *Samleng Yuvachon Khmer* (Voice of Khmer Youth) and *Udom Katek Khmer* (Khmer Ideal), were opposed to the CPP, though five of these were not being published at that time.

A survey by Radio Free Asia (RFA) of 841 people in eight provinces and in Phnom Penh in December 1998 found that 66 percent did not read newspapers at all. Of those who did, more than half read *Rasmei Kampuchea* and nearly one-fifth read *Koh Santhepheap*, both pro-CPP papers, but nearly half reported reading anti-CPP newspapers (RFA, 1999). No official estimates of readership exist but a 1994 survey reckoned that the total circulation was between 62,000 and 70,000 a day (Clarke, 1995).

2.2.2 Broadcasting

Radio Cambodge started under the French in 1946 using leftover Japanese equipment. In 1951, a new and more powerful American transmitter came into use. France bequeathed the radio operation to Cambodia at the time of its independence. In 1955, there were four stations in Phnom Penh under the Department of Information, two of 1 kW each and two of 10 kW each. By 1958, however, only Khmer National Radio, a 10-kW station, was still broadcasting. China donated a 20-kW station in 1959. In 1951, Cambodia had only 3,500 radio receivers, and even in 1958 the number was restricted to 7,000. Information broadcast on the radio, however, quickly passed around by word of mouth (Steinberg et al., 1957, 1959).

In Sihanouk's time, the government station became "literally, the dominant voice in the country" (Noel, 1967, p. 2). In the mid-1960s, it had three services: a domestic service, and two international shortwave services, one in English and French, and the other in local languages directed at nearby Asian nations. The domestic service concentrated on the doings of Sihanouk and the government, and programs were often interrupted to broadcast his speeches (Noel, 1967). Radio continued to expand, and in 1974 the country had an estimated 100,000 receivers (Lichty & Hoffer, 1978).

Television remained much more underdeveloped. The government station, TVRK, started in 1966, when there were only about 300 television sets (Lichty & Hoffer, 1978). By 1968, broadcasting ran for six hours a day (PFA, 1968), but it had little influence because the country had so few sets (So, 1970). Television was used little in Democratic Kampuchea, but the government took over the state radio station. It broadcast for six hours a day, both for domestic and foreign audiences. These broadcasts provided virtually the only link with the outside world (Mehta, 1997a; Lichty & Hoffer, 1978).

In late 1978, the future PRK set up Radio Television Kampuchea and began the Voice of the Kampuchean People (VoKP) radio station. Television began limited landline broadcasting in 1979, and the Phnom Penh radio station also began operation early in the PRK years. Using transmitters in Phnom Penh with the assistance of the Vietnamese and the Soviet bloc, the TV station—Television Kampuchea or TVK—began broadcasting regularly from December 1984. Color transmission began in July 1986 (Ross, 1987; SPK-AJA, 1991; author's interviews, 1994). Radio and television came under the direction of the Kampuchean Radio and Television Commission, created in 1983. In 1986, Cambodia had about 200,000 radio receivers, and 4,000 television sets. The VoKP broadcast programs in Khmer, Vietnamese, French, English, Lao, and Thai for two-and-a-half hours a day. By 1986, TVK operated for two hours every evening, four days a week only in the Phnom Penh area. Cambodian viewers began to receive Soviet TV programs after March 1987, through a satellite ground station that the Soviet Union had built in Phnom Penh (*Asiaweek*, March 30, 1986; Ross, 1987).

In 1979–92, all three resistance groups operated radio stations. The Khmer Rouge beamed from southern China and Thailand, while FUNCINPEC and KPNLF, based on the Thai border, operated mobile stations with funds received from the United States via Thailand and other ASEAN countries. A transmitter in Chiang Mai was also available to the latter two (Marston, 1996). Voice of America (VoA) also maintained a Khmer-language service throughout this period.

The UN Transitional Authority in Cambodia also did its own radio broadcasts, at first using SoC and VoA facilities. In October 1992, it set up its own station, which played an important role in encouraging voters to turn out for the election (Zhou, 1994). VoA continued its Khmer-language service, and the US-government-funded RFA started its own in 1997. Now, both the French international radio station, RFI, which is relayed by the French Cultural Center in Phnom Penh on 92 MHz, and the BBC World Service have services there.

Table 1 provides data on the penetration of radio and television. An RFA survey conducted in late 1998 found that 65 percent of respondents owned a television, while 79 percent owned a radio. Amongst TV viewers, 30 percent watched the military channel, 16 percent watched TVK, 14 percent watched Channel 3, 9 percent watched Apsara, and 8 percent watched Channel 9. Nearly one-fifth did not watch television at all. Of those who listened to the radio, about one-fifth each listened to NRC, COA, and RFA (RFA, 1999).

3. THE PRESS

3.1 Policy and Legal Framework

Article 41 of the 1993 RGC Constitution guarantees freedom of expression, both of the press and of publication. The article states: "Khmer citizens shall have free-dom of expression, press, publication and assembly. No one shall exercise this right to infringe upon the rights of others, to affect the good traditions of the society, to violate public law and order and national security. The regime of the media shall be determined by law." However, in the absence of a specific RGC law, SoC law and UNTAC guidelines were used rather inconsistently as sources for reference in instances when the government took action against publications and journalists. Conflicting views of the component parties of the government hampered negotiations over a new law, and the National Assembly passed the Law on the Press only in July 1995 (CLRDC, 1998). This law gives the right to maintain confidentiality of sources, the right to publish information from public meetings of the government, the legislature, and of court proceedings, the right to access government records, and the right to form journalists' associations. It also outlaws pre-censorship. However, Articles 11 and 12 prohibit publication of "any-thing that may affect public order by directly inciting one or more persons to commit violence" and "any information that may affect national security and poli-tical stability." The ambiguity in these terms allows enormous scope for inter-pretation. Given the return to the rambunctious press style of the pre-1975 era and the sensitivity of a government made up of two rival parties, the press has viewed these as instruments used by the government for political reasons and ends.

In 1993, Ieng Mouly of the BLDP was appointed to head the Ministry of Infor-mation, which oversees the media and maintains the register of newspapers and broadcasters, while Khieu Kanharith of the CCP became second in command. This structure reflected the problematic nature of the government and "sometimes in effect paralyzed the everyday operations of the ministry" (Marston, 1996, p. 229). However, Mouly led a section of the BLDP away from Son Sann in 1994 and moved closer to the CPP. When he failed to be re-elected in 1998, his position went to Lu Lay Sreng, a FUNCINPEC stalwart. Kanharith, however, remained in place. The new combination promised further tensions.

The Khmer Journalists Association (KJA) was set up in 1993 with the support of foreign aid. It elected as its leader Pin Samkhon, a newspaper proprietor who had stood for election on behalf of the small Democrat Party but lost. The associ-ation produced a code of ethics in 1994 (KJA, 1994). In mid-1995, pro-CPP journal-ists formed the League of Journalists in opposition to the KJA. After the 1997 clashes, Samkhon left the country, and the KJA is now almost defunct. The League continued to operate and claimed 63 members in 1998 (author's interviews, 1998).

In the early years of the RGC, a number of outspoken newspapers received official warnings and were shut down briefly for printing articles and cartoons seen to be insulting to the government, especially to those associated with Sam Rainsy and FUNCINPEC. These included *Samleng Yuvachon Khmer, Udon Katek,* and *Sereipheap Thmei* (New Liberty News). Nguon Nonn of *Domnoeng Pel Proeut* (Morning News) was arrested in July 1994 for coverage of the apparent coup attempt early that month and was jailed, without any sentence, for five weeks. The same happened later in the year. Chan Rotana of *Samleng Yuvachon Khmer* and Hen Vipheak of *Sereipheap Thmei* were both fined and jailed in 1995, though the king pardoned them in 1996. Thun Bunly of *Udom Katek* was fined twice in 1995. There were also attacks on newspaper offices and on journalists themselves. Six more journalists, including Bunly, were murdered or else died in suspicious circum-stances between 1994 and 1998 and two others were injured in attacks, one of them being Uy Pang of *Koh Santhepheap*. Another journalist was among the 19 killed in a grenade attack on a rally led by Sam Rainsy in March 1997. Two dozen more journalists were reported hurt.

After the clash of July 1997, 44 journalists reportedly fled to Thailand and many papers closed down. However, journalists soon started to trickle back in, and the re-emergence of the opposition press was clear by the end of September. *Proyuth* (Fighter) was shut down for 30 days for allegedly inflating casualty figures among CPP troops in the fighting against FUNCINPEC on the Thai border, and 10 other newspapers received similar complaints but avoided punishment by apologizing. Late in 1997, Ung Huot, the first prime minister, was criticizing news-papers for a lack of professionalism. In early January, six anti-CPP newspapers were suspended, but on the orders of Hun Sen, they were again allowed to operate a week later.

Media regulations of the National Election Commission (NEC) prohibited the publication of biased items in the 30 days before the election of July 1998. Despite journalists' complaints at the restriction, there were no reported transgressions. In September, *Moneaksekar Khmer* (Khmer Conscience) was threatened with closure for insulting the king. Several weeks later, amidst CPP anger at the adoption by the US Congress of a resolution condemning Hun Sen, Khieu Kanharith stated that the two major English-language papers, *Cambodia Daily* and *Phnom Penh Post*, as well as the German news agency, might be shut down for their reporting on an apparent assassination attempt on Hun Sen. However, no action followed.

3.2 Financial Aspects: Circulation, Advertising, Marketing Strategies

Newspapers that started before the elections made easy profits, initially from sales, because of the pent-up demand for news and the need for information about the parties and candidtaes. However, the pace has slowed owing to the huge increase in the number of publications. Circulations rarely run beyond a few thousand and many go to press with little or no advertising. The need for funds has encouraged political patronage, either voluntary or forced, by threats of exposure.

Koh Santhepheap, which gets about 40 percent of all advertising in Phnom Penh's Khmer-language press (Hodson & Kimsong, 1998), has remained successful. *Rasmei Kampuchea* is doing well, displaying advertisements on the front page in full color. The *Phnom Penh Post* and *Cambodia Daily* find it ever harder to make ends meet (Dodd, 1998; Marston, 1996; Clarke, 1995; author's interviews, 1998).

3.3 Structure and Organization

The SoC government newspapers were bequeathed to the RGC, but official funding petered out. The *Phnom Penh* weekly folded in 1993 after its talented editor left and joined *Rasmei Kampuchea*. The police newspaper, opened not long before, and briefly popular for its gory details of crime and accidents, disappeared, as did the army newspaper. *Kampuchea* and SPK soldiered on as RGC media, the latter reverting to the old name AKP and publishing daily bulletins like its predecessors had done. Neither news organization had much more than prestige, and their journalists often moonlighted elsewhere or left to start their own newspapers (Clarke, 1995).

Party ownership continued. The CPP daily *Pracheachon* was profitable, partly because it owned a sizeable printing press, which many other newspapers used. The publication itself took on a more commercial style and officially became a private paper, but many still regarded it as the organ of the CPP. Its future is not optimistic, however, with more printing presses being imported. The only other openly party-owned newspaper was that of the small Khmer Neutral Party.

The private papers, which form the majority, are owned by their editors, directors, or other senior staff. Even though they include among them the widely circulated *Koh Santhepheap*, yet most are tiny operations. Many support and are supported by political parties, although they do not acknowledge this. Some non-Khmer papers have foreign owners: *Phnom Penh Post, Cambodia Daily* (and *Cambodia Times*, which folded in 1997), several publications in French, and some others in Chinese. Some Khmer-language newspapers also had foreign ownership, most notably *Rasmei Kampuchea*, but it has shed its Thai connections and is owned solely by the local tycoon Teng Bunma, while others have folded (Clarke, 1995; author's interviews, 1998).

3.4 Quality and Popular Press

The newspapers that adherents of all sides cite as the most professional are *Rasmei Kampuchea, Phnom Penh Post*, and *Cambodia Daily*. The latter two are generally regarded as independent, though CPP officials tend to see them as pro-opposition. A case in point is the reaction to their coverage of the assassination attempt on Hun Sen. *Rasmei Kampuchea* is a 12-page broadsheet daily featuring a range of news items and a full-color front page. *Phnom Penh Post*, a fortnightly, prints all

16 tabloid-size pages in full color. Its own reporters produce its stories. *Cambodia Daily* comes out six days a week in folded A3 format with its own local news and the foreign news from the wire services. It has sections in Khmer and Japanese and also produces a weekly review.

Many other newspapers are considered to be politically tainted or unprofessional, or both. With a few exceptions, comprising chiefly the foreign-language press, they are fairly similar to the Khmer papers of old. They consist of a single folded broadsheet of badly printed black-and-white newsprint, folded to make four pages. Front pages have poor-quality pictures of leading politicians, and the more racy, including *Koh Santhepheap*, display gory pictures of corpses. Some have outspoken political cartoons, for which the Cambodian press is famed. The inside pages often contain fictional stories illustrated by violent or sexy drawings.

Hodson & Kimsong (1998) say that because of the Khmer-language newspapers' volatile articles and venomous verbal assaults on political leaders, media watchers have summed up Cambodia's six years of press freedom since 1992 as "free but foul-mouthed" (p. 8). In 1994, an editorial in *The Nation*, a Thai daily, called most Cambodian newspapers "crude publications, filled with graphic pictures of multilated corpses or pornographic scenes" (p. 8).

3.5 Distribution and Technology

Many of the new newspapers published after the 1991 peace accords were printed on presses bought by the *Pracheachon* in the 1980s (Mayon, 1995). Thong Uy Pang renovated some pre-1975 presses when he set up *Koh Santhepheap* (author's interview, 1994). Of the two other working presses, only one could print in color. (Mayon, 1995). *Rasmei Kampuchea* and several other newspapers used to be printed chiefly in Thailand, while some were printed in Malaysia. However, *Rasmei Kampuchea* now has its own printing press with four-color capacity (author's interview, 1998). Many newspapers distribute copies up-country, especially in other urban areas such as Siem Reap and Sihanoukville, but the majority are sold at newsstands in Phnom Penh.

4. BROADCASTING

4.1 Policy and Legal Framework

No specific counterpart to the 1995 press legislation exists for the broadcasting sector. The government requires radio and TV stations to obtain a license before they begin operating, but no laws or regulations actually cover the process. The Ministry of Information, according to a UN report, "has relied solely on administrative fiat to deny or approve licenses and allocate frequencies" (United Nations, 1998, n.p.). Neither official oversight nor regulations concerning content exist.

4.2 Structure and Organization

4.2.1 Radio

The former SoC radio stations have remained under the government but are still run mainly by the old staff. National Radio of Cambodia broadcasts a home service on the medium wave from Battambang, Phnom Penh, Sihanoukville, and Stung Treng, and also an overseas service—Voice of Cambodia Radio International—with 15 minutes each in English, French, Thai, Laotian, and Vietnamese (*World radio TV handbook*, 1998). Phnom Penh radio has been leased to a private company though it is still said to be controlled by the CPP. The FUNCINPEC radio station moved to Phnom Penh in February 1993, and broadcasts as FM90. Its modern format has made it highly popular. The BLDP made many representations to the government for a broadcasting license. After the party split, the Son Sann faction received the green signal, and despite CPP opposition, it started the Voice of Peace in March 1997. Requests for a license for the KNP, later SRP, were refused (United Nations, 1998).

During the July 1997 clashes, government troops occupied FM90, which was subsequently dismantled. The government handed over the station in early 1998 to the former deputy director who had shifted his allegiance to Prime Minister Ung Huot. FUNCINPEC obtained permission to start a new station in June 1998 but was unable to do so. FM90 reportedly stopped broadcasting after Ung Huot failed to be re-elected in 1998 and left the country. Following the plunder of all its equipment during the 1997 clashes, BLDP radio also went off air. The Son Sann Party received a new license for the old wavelength in May 1998, but had neither the time nor the money to resume broadcasts (United Nations, 1998).

Several pro-CPP groups obtained licenses. The Ieng Mouly faction of the BLDP, now aligned with the CPP, started broadcasting on FM88. Ung Huot's group set up a station called Bayon on FM95. A Thai company and the armed forces began broadcasting on FM98. Another station called Apsara, on FM97, is said to be a quasi-official CPP operation. Yet another station was started on FM99 under a pro-CPP individual. Only one anti-CPP station, Beehive, remained in 1998. Operated by the leader of a small party, it broadcasts on FM105 (United Nations, 1998). The government closed it down in September 1998, thus ensuring that all the remaining local radio stations were pro-CPP.

Khmer Rouge radio continued to broadcast, moving to new headquarters in Anlong Veng in 1994 after the group was outlawed in Phnom Penh. As the group split, some broadcasters followed the section that settled legally in Pailin and opened Radio Pailin FM (Grainger, 1998).

4.2.2 Television

The main SoC television station, renamed Television of Kampuchea (TVK), has taken a central role in broadcasting. Like the radio, it has remained dominated by the CPP. Another CPP-controlled TV station, Channel 3, opened more recently in

Phnom Penh. FUNCINPEC, which started operating a TV station on the Thai border in 1991, shifted the station to Phnom Penh calling it Channel 9, in early 1993. IBC TV Cambodia, a Thai-owned company, opened in April that year. Both stations provided for a wider variety of programming than TVK and were very popular. However, both had to refer to TVK for guidance on their news coverage (Clarke, 1995; author's interviews, 1994). IBC increasingly became subject to official complaints on the "foreignness" of its content. In late 1995, its ownership shifted to another Thai company, which supplied funding for a newly licensed army station, the Royal Armed Forces Television, on Channel 12. The government issued two more licenses that year to the CPP's Apsara Television and a private station, Bayon, which is reported to belong to Hun Sen.

During the July 1997 clashes, the FUNCINPEC TV station was emptied of its staff, and all its equipment, save the transmitters. The staff returned later and broadcasts began again. However, the station had to use TVK news and support the government. This meant that all six TV stations were either part of the CPP or controlled by it. A UN survey of TV coverage in May, before the official election campaign began, found that the CPP appeared 448 times and Ung Huot's party 91 times, while FUNCINPEC was on screen only nine times, and the SRP and other smaller parties featured even fewer times (United Nations, 1998). However, NEC rules allowed equal airtime to all parties in the 30 days before the July poll, and a media monitoring unit, set up with European Union help, reported no transgressions.

Cambodians with satellite dishes can view STAR TV, the French international station CFI, and other stations available in the region.

4.3 Program Policies and Financing

Finding enough programs to fill all the radio and television stations has been difficult, and the government cites this as the main reason for not issuing more licenses. However, financing has also posed problems. All stations take advertising, but reports at the beginning of 1999 indicated that advertising revenues at TVK had dropped drastically since the 1997 clash. It seems likely that new stations would either find it difficult to stay afloat or would deprive existing broadcasters of their income. Although local stations make some programs, there has been a preponderance of films from Thailand, Hong Kong, and Hollywood; and in early 1999 Lu Lay Sreng asked executives to show at least three hours of Khmer movies a week (Watson & Khieu, 1999).

TV 3, which broadcasts from 5 p.m. to 11.30 p.m. on weekdays and from 11 a.m. onwards on weekends, has its daily schedule on its website. The typical Friday schedule looks as follows:

17.00–17.05:	TV 3 Signing On
17.05–17.30:	Daily Programs Announcement
17.30–17.40:	No Trail, No Acknowledge

17.40–17.55:	Cambodia Women Center
17.55–18.00:	Cartoon
18.00–19.00:	Live Broadcasting of "Hello Ozone" Program
19.00–19.25:	News
19.25–19.30:	Cartoon
19.30–20.20:	Thai Serial Movies
20.20–20.30:	News
20.30–21.20:	Thai Serial Movies
21.20–21.30:	News
21.30–23.30:	USA Feature Movies

4.4 Ownership

Sections 4.2.1 and 4.2.2 make it clear that despite UN intentions to allow all parties access to the broadcasting sector, all six Cambodian-language TV stations, as well as the 11 radio stations are now under the direct or indirect control of the CPP (Dodd, 1998). The CPP-backed TV 3 states on its website that, along with Radio FM 103MHz, it is a joint venture of KCS Cambodia Co. Ltd and the Phnom Penh Municipality. Associated with these two are Radio FM 97.5MHz, as well as Radio FM 100.5MHz in Kampong Cham Province.

5. NEW ELECTRONIC MEDIA

5.1 Internet and On-line Media

Widespread poverty severely limits hardware purchases while electricity supplies are erratic even in Phnom Penh and simply do not reach many rural areas. CamNet, the first Internet provider in Cambodia, began service in May 1997. It is a cooperative effort between the Ministry of Posts and Telecommunications of Cambodia (MPTC) and the International Development Research Center of Canada. The Australian company Telstra, in conjunction with the MPTC, established the Big Pond Cambodia Internet service in June 1997. It provides e-mail services and access to the World Wide Web, though costs are high—a US$ 60 joining fee and a minimum deposit of US$ 100. Monthly charges start at US$ 30, including three hours' access. Each extra hour costs US$ 8.

The country had an estimated 9,000 personal computers in 1997. The Internet Software Consortium (http://www.isc.org), in its July 1999 survey, estimated that Cambodia had 144 Internet host computers, far below one host per 10,000 people. In 1998, the *Phnom Penh Post*, in conjunction with Big Pond, became the first Cambodian newspaper to go on-line. It is available free of charge within Cambodia, but others pay an annual subscription of US$ 50. The *Cambodia Daily* also has a weekly Internet edition, developed by the Khmer Internet Development Service (KIDS) (a student-run service), in association with CamNet. The Voice of Cambodia international broadcasting service, as well as TV 3, has a website.

5.2 Telecommunications Infrastructure

The number of main telephone lines in Cambodia increased from 3,115 in 1990—0.04 per 100 people—to 8,054 in 1996—0.08 per 100 people. This number leaped to 24,300 in 1998—a density of 0.23 percent. Phnom Penh had 81.6 percent of the country's telephones. Because of the poor fixed line services, mobile telephones have become the norm for urban dwellers. The number of cellular subscribers was 23,000 in 1996, far more than fixedline subscribers in the same year. This number increased to 61,300 in 1998—a penetration of 0.57 percent (ITU, 1999).

6. POLICY TRENDS FOR PRESS AND BROADCASTING

The CPP, now the dominant force in politics, as well as in the media, will again have to face the question of the extent to which it should allow other parties the freedom to put out publications and set up broadcast outlets. Anti-CPP newspapers have been the subject of official complaint and physical attacks, but they are also often rightly accused of poor professional standards: Better training is certainly a government priority, but funds are lacking. However, in early 1999, the prospects for a revival of opposition broadcast stations were very low.

Price (1997), a media consultant, wrote that regional radio and television in Cambodia were "in their infancy, whether in supplying the networks in Phnom Penh or in offering broadcasting services on a regional or local level" (p. 150). The cost of fuel was the biggest problem for regional stations. Price suggested that the first priority of Cambodia's public broadcasting should be the development of an information programming policy that the audience could trust. He said the second priority should be the education of a whole nation. The third priority should be the development of a balanced program schedule that should embrace information, education, and entertainment. The creation of an independent broadcasting commission, Price argued, "could provide, in one stroke, both a political and economic solution to the structural problems facing the media" in Cambodia (p. 151).

7. MAIN ISSUES

The issues in Cambodia's media are related to the politics of a country emerging from a long struggle that had created an overarching unity during the last decade or so of the Cold War. Although the changing international situation has resolved the global conflicts of that period and removed the supporters from the opposing sides in Cambodia's war, the underlying domestic divide remains. Moreover, many aspects of social and political life remain undeveloped. As Mehta (1997b) states: "Cambodia would be deserving of democracy and an attendant free press provided it first puts in place both a system of laws to protect a fledgling democracy, and an independent judiciary to protect free speech, on the one hand, and safeguard the rights of citizens, on the other" (p. 74). As for the news media, the lack of professionalism is a source of concern to Cambodians of all parties, and efforts to train journalists are under way. The problem of financing the news remains an obstacle to professional development.

The imposition of a liberal media system by the 1991 peace accords may have allowed far greater freedom of expression than ever before in Cambodia's history, but the many voices unleashed in the press have contributed to the chaos. The backlash of government control has caused Freedom House (Sussman, 1998, 1999) to rate Cambodia's press as "not free." (The score of 62 out of 100 is a slight improvement from the previous year's 65.) The country's broadcast and print media scored 15 out of 15 for being bound by political pressures and by other controls that influence media content. Out of a maximum of 5 on repressive actions, the Cambodian media scored 5 for print and 2 for broadcast. It also scored 5 out of 15 each on vulnerability to economic influences, as well as 7 for broadcast and 8 for print out of a maximum of 15 each on laws and regulations that influence media content. However, while neighboring countries quietly control their news media to varying extents, Cambodia is more vulnerable to criticism because of its openness and the international publicity given to the attacks on journalists. Such incidents are to be condemned severely, but in the context of the overall level of violence in the country and the political nature of the press, they are not unusual.

8. STATISTICS

General Profile

Exchange rate (1999 average)	US$ 1 = 3,970 Riel*
Population (mid-1999)	11.6 million
Geographical area	181,035 sq km
Population density	65.9 per sq km
Life expectancy at birth (1998)	53.4 years
GDP (PPP)	US$ 14 billion
Per capita GDP (PPP)	US$ 1,350
Per capita GNP (nominal)	US$ 270
Literacy (1997)	66 percent**
Urban population	22 percent
People per television	115.5
People per telephone	435
Internet hosts (July 1999)	144

Source: *Asiaweek*, January 14, 2000; ITU, 1998; *World factbook*, 1999; US Census Bureau 1999; * OANDA Historical Currency Table [On-line]. Available: (http://www.oanda.com/converter/cc_table?lang=en); ** UNDP, 1999.

Table 1
Estimated Mass Media Penetration

	Radio receivers		Television receivers		Newspapers		
	Number ('000)	Per 100 people	Number ('000)	Per 100 people	Number	Circ'n ('000)	Per 100 people
1980	600	9.2	35	0.54	–	–	–
1985	800	10.8	52	0.70	–	–	–
1990	942	10.9	68	0.79	–	–	–
1995	1,120	11.2	85	0.85	–	–	–
1996	1,300	12.7	90	0.88	2	17	0.17
1997	1,340	12.8	94	0.9	–	–	–

Source: UNESCO, 1999.

9. USEFUL ADDRESSES

Ministry of Information
62 Monivong Blvd.
Phnom Penh

Cambodia Communication Institute
Ministry of Information Compound
62 Monivong Blvd.
Phnom Penh
Telephone: 23 368322
Fax: 23 426163
E-mail: CCI.PNP@bigpond.com.kh

TVK
19 942 St.
Phnom Penh

National Radio of Cambodia
106 Monivong Blvd.
Phnom Penh.

Rasmei Kampuchea
476 Monivong Blvd.
Phnom Penh.
Circulation: 10,000–15,000 daily
Chief Editor: Pen Samitthy
Telephone: 23 362472, 3622881
Fax: 23 362472

Phnom Penh Post
10a, Street 264
Phnom Penh.
Circulation: 5,000 per fortnight
Publisher and editor-in-chief: Michael Hayes

Managing director:	Kathleen Hayes
Telephone:	23 426568, 210309
E-mail:	editor.pppost@worldmail.com.kh
URL:	http://www.newspapers.com.kh/PhnomPenhPost

Cambodia Daily
50B, Street 240
Phnom Penh.

Circulation:	3,500 daily (six days a week)
Editor-in-chief:	Chris Decherd
Telephone:	23 426602/490
Fax:	23 426573
E-mail:	cambodia.daily@bigpond.com.kh

10. REFERENCES

CCI (Cambodia Communication Institute). (1998). *List of newspapers in Cambodia.* Phnom Penh: CCI.

Chandler, D.P. (1993). *A history of Cambodia* (2nd ed.). St Leonards: Allen & Unwin (originally published by Westview Press in 1992).

Chea, S. (1997). Journalists play an important role in strengthening Cambodia. *Media Development, 44* (2), 10–11.

Clarke, J. (1995). Phoenix from the ashes: The influence of the past on Cambodia's resurgent free media. *Gazette, 55,* 93–111.

CLRDC (Cambodian Legal Resources Development Center). (1998). *Laws of Cambodia.* Phnom Penh: CLRDC.

Dodd, M. (1998, December 24). Muzzled: Cambodia's independent media are under threat. *Far Eastern Economic Review,* pp. 26–27.

Global Witness. (1997). *Just desserts for Cambodia: Deforestation & the co-prime ministers' legacy to the country.* London: Global Witness.

Grainger, M. (1998, April 24–May 7). The voice of Pol Pot now sings a softer tune. *Phnom Penh Post* (Internet edition), pp. 7, 8.

Hodson, J., & Kimsong, K. (1998, August 20). Progress of the press: Cambodian newspapers take slow road to respectability. *The Cambodia Daily* (Fifth Anniversary Supplement) [On-line]. Available: (http://www.camnet.com.kh/cambodia.daily/Fifth_Anniversary/page_8.htm).

ITU (International Telecommunication Union). (1998). *World telecommunication development report.* Geneva: ITU.

ITU (International Telecommunication Union). (1999). *Yearbook of statistics: Telecommunication services 1988–1997.* Geneva: ITU.

Kiernan, B. (1985). *How Pol Pot came to power.* London: Verso.

Kiernan, B. (1996). *The Pol Pot regime.* New Haven: Yale University Press.

KJA (Khmer Journalists Association). (1994). *The 1994 media guide.* Phnom Penh: KJA.

Lichty, L.W., & Hoffer, T.W. (1978). Khmer Republic. In J.A. Lent (Ed.), *Broadcasting in Asia and the Pacific: A continental survey of radio and television* (pp. 118–120). Philadelphia: Temple University Press.

Marston, J. (1996). Cambodian media in the UNTAC period and after. In S. Heder & J. Ledgerwood (Eds.), *Propaganda, politics, and violence in Cambodia* (pp. 208–242). Armonk: M.E. Sharpe.

Mayon, M. (1995, April 11–14). *Newspaper printing technology in Cambodia: A country survey.* Paper delivered at the Asia-Pacific Regional Seminar on Information Technology for Newspaper Publishing, Madras.

Mehta, H.C. (1997a). *Cambodia silenced: The press under six regimes.* Bangkok: White Lotus.

Mehta, H.C. (1997b). The chilling fields: Cambodia's press under six regimes. *Media Asia, 24*, 72–78.

Noel, D., Jr. (1967). *Cambodia: The mass media*. New York: The Alicia Patterson Fund.

Osborne, M. (1994). *Sihanouk: Prince of light, prince of darkness*. Chiang Mai: Silkworm Books.

PFA (Press Foundation of Asia). (1968). *Asian press 1968: Preliminary survey*. Seoul: PFA.

Price, G. (1997). Cambodia: Broadcasting and the hurdle of poverty. In D. Atkinson and M. Raboy (Eds.), *Public service broadcasting: The challenges of the 21st century* (pp. 149–151). Paris: UNESCO.

RFA (Radio Free Asia). (1999). *Summary of the media survey in Cambodia*. Washington, DC: RFA.

Ross, R.R. (Ed.). (1987). *Combodia: A country study*. Washington, DC: Federal Research Division, Library of Congress.

SPK-AJA (Sapordarmean Kampuchea-Australian Journalists Association). (1991). *A guide to the news media in Phnom Penh*. Phnom Penh: SPK-AJA Media Course.

So, W. (1970). Kingdom of Cambodia. In *Asian press 1970* (pp. 15–17). Seoul: Readership Research Center.

Soth, P., & Sin, K. (1982). Kampuchea. In J.A. Lent (Ed.), *Newspapers in Asia: Contemporary trends and problems* (pp. 219–237). Hong Kong: Heinemann Asia.

Steinberg, D.J., Bain, C.A., Burlingham, L., Duff, R.G., Fall, B.B., Greenhouse, R., Kramer, L. & McLellan, R.S. (1957, 1959). *Cambodia: Its people, its society, its culture*. New Haven: HRAF Press.

Sussman, L.R. (1999). *Press freedom 1999: News of the century*. New York: Freedom House.

Thayer, N. (1995, November 23). Medellin on the Mekong. *Far Eastern Economic Review*, pp. 24–47, 30, 31.

United Nations. (1998), *The special representative of the United Nations' secretary-general for human rights in Cambodia appeals for a new review of the media situation*. New York: UN.

UNDP (United Nations Development Program). (1999). *Human development report 1999*. New York: Oxford University Press & UNDP.

UNTAC (UN Transitional Authority in Cambodia). (n.d.). *Guide a l'usage des medias du Cambodge*. Phnom Penh: UNTAC.

UNTAC (UN Transitional Authority in Cambodia). (1991). *The public information media situation in Cambodia*. Phnom Penh: UNTAC.

UNTAC (UN Transitional Authority in Cambodia). (1992). *Press law*. Phnom Penh: State of Cambodia (unofficial UNTAC translation).

US Census Bureau. (1998). *International data base* [On-line]. Available: (http://www.census.gov/cgi-bin/ipc/idbsum).

UNESCO (United Nations Educational, Scientific and Cultural Organisation). (1999). *Statistical yearbook*. Paris: UNESCO.

Watson, R., & Khieu, K. (1999, January 6), TV chiefs urged to help save film jobs. *South China Morning Post*, p. 10.

Whitaker, D.P., Heimann, J.M., MacDonald, J.E., Martindale, K.W., Shinn, R.S., Townsend, C. (1973). *Area handbook for the Khmer Republic (Cambodia)*. Washington, DC: US Government Printing Office.

World factbook.(1999). Cambodia. Washington, DC: CIA [On-line]. Available: (http://www.odci.gov/cia/publications/factbook).

World radio TV handbook. (1998). Cambodia. (pp. 181, 410, 544). Oxford: Windsor Books International.

Zhou, M. (1994). *Radio UNTAC of Cambodia: Winning ears, hearts and minds*. Bangkok: White Lotus.

◆

10

INDONESIA

Naswil Idris & Shelton A. Gunaratne

1. NATIONAL PROFILE

1.1 Geography

Indonesia, which under colonial rule was known as the Dutch East Indies, is the world's largest archipelago. It comprises 17,508 islands and islets, of which about 6,000 are inhabited. It is situated along the equator, between the Asian mainland and Australia, and it shares land boundaries with Malaysia and Papua New Guinea. Indonesia's territory extends more than 5,000 km from east to west and 1,750 km from north to south. The total land area is 1.9 million sq km, almost three times the size of Texas. Puncak Jaya at 5,030 meters is its highest point. About 10 percent of the land is arable (*World factbook*, 1999; Indonesia: DPPLN, 1996).

1.2 People

After China, India, and the United States, Indonesia is the world's fourth most populous country, with an estimated population of 207.7 million (*Asiaweek*, January 14, 2000).[1] More than 100 ethnic groups inhabit Indonesia. The Javanese, comprising 45 percent of the population, are the largest group; the Sundanese make up 14 percent, the Madurese 7.5 percent, and the coastal Malays 7.5 percent (*World factbook*, 1999). Approximately 585 languages and dialects exist in the archipelago. The national language is Bahasa Indonesia. Almost 87 percent of the population is Islamic. Christians (9 percent), Hindus (2 percent), and Buddhists (1 percent) make up the rest. The great diversity is symbolized in the state motto: *Bhinneka Tunggal Ika* (Unity in Diversity). The adult literacy rate is 85 percent, and life expectancy at birth is 65.

---

[1] The international database demographic summary of the US Census Bureau estimates Indonesia's mid-1999 population at 216.1 million (http://www.census.gov/cgi-bin/ipc/idbsum).

1.3 Government and Politics

Administratively, Indonesia is divided into 27 provinces, which are in turn divided into 246 districts and 56 municipalities, 3,639 sub-districts, and 62,061 urban and rural villages (Indonesia: DPPLN, 1996).

Indonesia proclaimed independence from the Netherlands on August 17, 1945 (*World factbook*, 1999), and "provisionally" adopted a unitary constitution, with *Pancasila* as the ideological and philosophical basis of the new republic. In Sanskrit *Pancasila* means five (panca) principles (sila). This state philosophy comprises the following inseparable and interrelated principles: belief in the one and only God; espousal of a just and civilized humanity; the unity of Indonesia; democracy guided by the inner wisdom arising from the unanimity based on deliberations among representatives; and social justice for all the people of Indonesia. The constitution was not fully implemented when the transfer of sovereignty from the Netherlands went into effect on December 27, 1949. The 1949 agreement called for the establishment of the federal Republic of the United States of Indonesia (RUSI). Subsequently, a provisional constitution adopted in February 1950 provided for the election of a constituent assembly to write a permanent constitution. On August 14, a new constitution (technically an amendment to the RUSI Constitution) was ratified, and was to remain in force until an elected constituent assembly completed its work. The new interim constitution provided for a cabinet system of government, with the cabinet and prime minister being responsible to a unicameral legislature. On July 5, 1959, President Sukarno decreed the dissolution of the constituent assembly, and ordered a return to the 1945 Constitution. Martial law had already been proclaimed on March 14, 1957, and Sukarno claimed that under martial law his legal authority stemmed from his position as the supreme commander of the armed forces.

The 1945 Constitution provided for six organs of the state: the People's Consultative Assembly (*Majelis Permusyawaratan Rakyat* [MPR]); the presidency; the House of Representatives (*Dewan Perwakilan Rakyat* [DPR]); the Supreme Advisory Council (*Dewan Pertimbangan Agung* [DPA]); the State Audit Board (*Badang Pemeriksa Keuangan* [BPK]; and the Supreme Court (*Mahkamah Agung* [MA]) (Indonesia: DPPLN, 1996).

The People's Consultative Assembly (MPR) is the highest political institution in the state, and is responsible for sanctioning Indonesia's Constitution, determining the guidelines of state policy, and electing the president and the vice president. In the past, the assembly has met in a general session at least once in every five years. On January 28, 1999, the MPR passed three new laws governing elections, political parties, and the structure of legislative bodies. The "Legislatures Law" specifies a 700-member MPR, comprising the 462 elected members of the DPR, as well as the DPR's 38 appointed military (*Angkatan Bersenjata Republic Indonesia* or ABRI) representatives, 200 additional appointed members of whom 135 are chosen by the provincial assemblies (five from each of the country's 27 provinces), and 65 representatives of functional groups.[2] The existence of functional seats in the MPR gives some, as yet unidentified, elite-based groups, substantial say in the choice of the president (NDI, 1999).

Under the 1999 Legislature Law, the House of Representatives (DPR) continues to have 500 members: 462 elected proportionally by province, and 38 appointed by the military (Article 11). However, the law specifies that a party's winning candidates should be chosen on the basis of district results. The military also appoints its representatives to 10 percent (compared to 20 percent under the 1995 law) of the seats in the provincial and district legislatures (Articles 18 and 25). The law also requires the holding of simultaneous elections for the provincial assemblies (*Dewan Perwakilan Rakyat Daerah I* or DPRD I) and the district assemblies (*Dewan Perwakilan Rakyat Daerah II* or DPRD II).

The new legislative framework owes much to *Tim Tujuh* (Team Seven), which hammered out the rules for the 1999 general and presidential elections. The team, among other things, aimed to foster a multi-party system, shift more power to the DPR, reduce the number of seats reserved for the military (ABRI), and prepare the way for regional autonomy. A multi-party system emerged when interest groups formed more than 70 parties (McBeth, 1998), although only 48 parties were deemed eligible to compete in the general election on June 7, 1999. The number of seats reserved for ABRI in the national legislature decreased from 75 to 38, and in the provincial and local assemblies from 20 percent to 10 percent (NDI, 1999).

1.4 Economy

Indonesia has had a successful record of economic growth and diversification over the last two decades (Indonesia: DPPLN, 1996). Its nominal per capita gross national product is US$ 460, and its purchasing power parity per capita gross domestic product is US$ 2,940. Thus, Indonesia has fallen into the low-income category. The country's estimated gross domestic product (GDP) is US$ 601 billion. Following the Asian economic crisis of 1997, Indonesia's GDP growth rate had slowed down to 0.5 percent. In late 1999, the rate of inflation stood at 2 percent (*Asiaweek*, January 14, 2000).

Until the 1997 crisis, foreign investment had boosted Indonesia's manufacturing output and exports. Continuing expansion of non-oil exports drove the country's economic growth. Plantation crops (rubber and palm oil), textiles, and plywood are being encouraged both for export and for job generation. Industrial output is based on diverse natural resources, including crude oil, natural gas, timber, metals, and coals. Japan remains Indonesia's most important customer and supplier of aid (*World factbook*, 1999). Indonesia exported merchandise valued at US$ 48.2 billion in 1999 (*Asiaweek*, January 14, 2000).

[2] Under Law No. 5 of 1995, MPR was a 1,000-member body comprising the 500 members of the DPR; 253 representatives of political parties, the functional groups, and the armed forces; 147 delegates from the first-level regions or provinces; and 100 representatives of professional groups.

2. DEVELOPMENT OF PRESS AND BROADCASTING

2.1 Brief Early History

The Dutch press preceded the indigenous press in Indonesia. A bulletin for the employees of the Dutch East India Company, *Memorie des Nouvelles*, appeared in 1615. The first newspaper of general interest, *Bataviaise Nouvelle en Politique Raisonnementen*, appeared in 1744. Following this short-lived newspaper, other Dutch newspapers appeared in Batavia (Jakarta since 1950) through the last part of the 18th century (Crawford, 1971). They carried hardly any local news because their clients were dominantly Dutch people who yearned for news from home. Strict censorship limited the range of comment in these newspapers, which began to appear in Surabaya and other expanding towns (Van der Kroef, 1954).

The Dutch also published the first Indonesian-language newspapers, including *Bromartini* (1855) in Surakarta, *Soerat Kabar Bahasa Malajoe* (1856) in Surabaya, *Slompret Melajoe* (1860) in Semarang, and others. However, the true beginning of the Indonesian press had to wait until after 1908, when the Indonesian nationalist movement began. *Pewarta Deli* (1910) of Medan was one of the first nationalist newspapers (Crawford, 1971). Chinese-language newspapers also appeared to serve the more prosperous Chinese community. Backed by the Dutch government, D.W. Bretty set up Indonesia's first news agency, ANETA, in 1917. In 1937, Indonesian editors founded Antara, a news agency aiming to serve the Indonesian-language press. During their occupation of the country (1942–45), the Japanese took over the entire press and reconstituted it as the official Japanese propaganda apparatus. They forbade the use of Dutch (Crawford, 1971).

Sinaga (1989) wrote that "among the heroes of independence were dedicated journalists who suffered persecution from the colonial authorities.... Even during the harsh Japanese military rule, the freedom fighters continued to fight for Indonesia's freedom through subtle messages and articles in the military-controlled press" (pp. 28–29).

Radio development began when the Dutch government inaugurated "radiotelegraphy" in Sabang on September 8, 1911. During the next two years, the government opened radio facilities in Situbondo, Kupang, and Ambon. Meanwhile, the Dutch navy operated its own radio station in Weltevreden (Jakarta). *Bataviasche Radio Vereniging* (BRV) came into operation in Weltevreden on June 16, 1925. It broadcast its first program in Dutch from a room at the Hotel des Indies, and also established itself in Tanjung Priok. In 1934 BRV became *Netherlands Indische Radio Omroep Maatschappij* (NIROM) (Zakaria et al., 1995).

In 1926, Vereniging van Radio Amateurs set up a radio facility called PMY in Bandung. In 1930, a station named *Meyers Omroep Voor Allen* (MOVA) opened in Medan. Another station called *Algemene Radio Vereniging Oost Java* (ARVO) opened in Surabaya on July 12, 1934. On December 26, 1935, ARVO and PMY established the *Federatie van Radio Omroep Vereniging in Netherlands Indie* (FRONE), and in 1938 Zeipkust Radio Amateurs set up *Radio Omroep Padang* (AROF) (Zakaria et al., 1995).

In April 1933, Sultan Pangeran Mangkunegara VII sponsored the first Indonesian-language broadcasts from Surakarta through *Solosche Radio Vereniging* (SRV). This tried to promote Javanese music, arts, and shadow play (*wayang*) (Eapen & Lent, 1978). Other such stations followed: *Veriniging voor Oosterch Radio Omroep* (VORO) in Jakarta (1934); *Siaran Radio Indonesia* (SRI) in Solo (1934); and CIRVO in Surabaya (1936).

With the surrender of the Dutch in March 1942, the Japanese reorganized the country's broadcasting structure under a radio service in Jakarta by the name of *Hoso Kanri Kyoku* (HKK). During the Japanese occupation, HKK established branches in all major towns. The Indonesians used radio "for propagation of nationalism" during this period (Eapen & Lent, 1978, p. 164).

2.2 Developments since 1945

2.2.1 Press

The Indonesians declared themselves independent at the conclusion of Japanese occupation and the return of the Dutch. When the Dutch refused to accept the Indonesian declaration, the newspapers in the Republican areas drummed up support for the nationalists and expanded their circulation at the expense of Dutch papers. However, divisions within the independence movement culminated in a communist uprising in Madiun in east Java late in 1948. A crackdown by the Dutch resulted in the disappearance of one-third of the Indonesian-language press. When world opinion turned against the Dutch, they conceded independence in December 1949 enabling Sukarno to become Indonesia's first president (Crawford, 1971).

A congress held in Solo set up the Indonesian Journalists Association (*Persatuan Wartawan Indonesia* [PWI]) in February 1946, while Indonesian publishers met in Yogyakarta to form the Association of Newspaper Publishers (*Serikat Penerbit Surat-kabar* [SPS]) on June 8, 1946. Sinaga (1989) says: "The press played a vital role by publishing news, views, anti-colonial slogans and editorials that supported the independence struggle" (p. 29).

Indonesia banned all Dutch newspapers in late 1957. The first English-language daily had appeared in 1952, and, by 1957 there were three English dailies with a circulation of 25,000. By 1957, the 17 Chinese-language dailies had expanded their circulation to 129,500, while Jakarta's leading communist daily, *Harian Rakyat* (People's Daily), had reached a circulation of 60,000. The press enjoyed freedom during what Sinaga (1989) calls the "Western liberal democracy era" (1945–59). Even though the trend was toward party-related newspapers, Mochtar Lubis' *Indonesia Raya* (Glorious Indonesia) became renowned for courageous journalism. Lubis had also founded the first English-language newspaper, *Times of Indonesia*, in 1952. Following a rebellion in Sumatra, the army arrested Lubis in 1956 and, despite his acquittal in 1957, held him under house arrest for almost a decade (Crawford, 1971). Sinaga (1989) however, complains that: "The press did not contribute much toward the needed stability in the country. Instead, it became an instrument of the various political parties and political groups" (p. 30).

"Guided Democracy" came into full operation in 1959 when, under chaotic political conditions, Sukarno dissolved the constituent assembly and replaced the amended constitution of 1950 with the original constitution of 1945. To obtain publication permits, editors and publishers had to sign a 19-point agreement tying them to the government. The government also banned the opposition press for alleged violations. It took over the Antara news agency and merged it with PIA (formerly ANETA). During 1964, the Jakarta press, led by *Harian Rakyat* and the independent *Merdeka* (Freedom), conducted "wild debates" between the communists and their opponents (Crawford, 1971, p. 168). When the communists attempted to seize power in October 1965, the army stepped in to restore order. All communist papers, as well as several leftist papers, were banned. Sinaga (1989) says that during the "Guided Democracy" era (1959–65), the dominant political parties used the press as their propaganda organs. The press "continued to be compartmentalized more or less along ideological lines in accordance with the political situation that prevailed during this period" (p. 31).

Gen. Suharto replaced Sukarno on March 11, 1966. Sinaga (1989) calls this the beginning of the "New Order" period signifying the adoption of the *Pancasila* press system. Suharto banned the Communist Party, as well as all the existing Chinese-language newspapers, which were replaced by one official Chinese daily named *Harian Indonesia* (Indonesia Daily). Thus, despite the long history of the press in Indonesia, the country failed in having newspapers with a substantial history. Most newspapers appeared and disappeared except for a few established newspapers like *Merdeka* (1945), *Jawa Pos* (1949) of Surabaya, *Suara Merdeka* (1950) of Semarang, *Surabaya Post* (1953), and *Pikiran Rakyat* (1956) of Bandung. *Sinar Harapan* of Parkindo, the Protestant party, began in 1961, and *Kompas*, a Roman Catholic daily, began in 1965. In the same year, the armed forces also established two newspapers—*Berita Yudha* (Military News) and *Angkatan Bersendjata* (Armed Forces). Maslog (1985) wrote that *Pikiran Rakyat*, owned and managed collectively by the staff, was "one of the most successful provincial (community) newspapers in Indonesia" (p. 55) with its three editions published from Bandung, Ciamis, and Cirebon.

Anderson (1982) reported that in 1972, Indonesia had about 130 dailies with a circulation of about 1.4 million. However, figures for 1975 listed only 65 dailies. *Suara Karya* (Work Voice), emerged in 1971 as the organ of Golkar, the government political organization. Other newspapers established in the 1970s included the *Pos Kota* (1970); *Sinar Pagi* (1971); *Harian Terbit* (1972), an afternoon daily; *Indonesia Times* (1974), which replaced the banned *Jakarta Times*; and *Pelita* (1974), the pro-Golkar Islamic daily.

According to Anderson (1982), *Kompas* was "the country's largest and most respected newspaper" (p. 199). *KAMI*, of the "Generation of '66," suspended in 1974, was "an intellectual, cosmopolitan publication" (p. 200). *Merdeka* was the flagship of publisher-politician M.B. Diah's publishing empire, which also published the *Topik* newsmagazine. Anderson observed: "Newspaper mortality rate is very high, and few editors can afford to operate truly independent newspapers" (p. 201).

Hill (1994) wrote that the circulation successes in 1970 were *Merdeka* (80,000), *Kompas* (75,000), *Berita Yudha* (75,000), and *Sinar Harapan* (65,000). Twelve publications, including *Indonesia Raya* and *Jakarta Times*, lost their publishing permits after the eruption of public demonstrations in January 1974. Further unrest in January 1978 resulted in the banning of seven Jakarta dailies and seven student newspapers. In the 1980s, two more dailies fell victim to the law. *Sinar Harapan* lost its publishing license in October 1986, and *Prioritas* lost its in June 1987. *Suara Pembaruan* (Renewal Voice) replaced the former in February 1987 (see Section 3.3). The 1980s also saw the establishment of *Jakarta Post* (1983), *Bisnis Indonesia* (1985), the Army-related *Jayakarta* (1985), and *Surya* (1986). *Republika*, the pro-government Muslim paper associated with Habibie, started in 1993.

2.2.2 Radio

Just 25 days after the proclamation of independence on August 17, 1945, *Radio Republik Indonesia* (RRI) came into operation. Eight months later, the information ministry recognized RRI as a government body, and broadcasting became an important tool to promote the "revolution" against the Dutch. With the Dutch reoccupation of Java, the RRI stations went underground, until the Dutch transferred *de jure* powers to the national leadership in December 1949. A Broadcasting Advisory Council, appointed in 1954, attempted to improve program quality. In the late 1960s, RRI was broadcasting in Java on three stations—National, *Ibu Kota* (Capital City), and *Chusus*, the last targeting programs for the military and the police (Eapen & Lent, 1978).

In the early 1970s, Indonesia had about 100 *Radio Daerah* (regional government) stations, in addition to about 50 RRI stations. Set up by the provincial administrations, Radio Daerah stations began broadcasting their own programs, although they usually relayed RRI news. Meanwhile, the Voice of Indonesia, RRI's overseas service, broadcast daily for 10 hours in Dutch, English, French, Chinese, Arabic, Hindi, and Urdu. Owing to colonial ties, Indonesia depended heavily on Radio Netherlands to produce attractive material in Indonesian. The number of radio receivers in the country increased from 960,502 in 1963 to 13.8 million in 1975 (Eapen & Lent, 1978), to 31.5 million in 1997 (UNESCO, 1999).

In 1972, Indonesia had some 324 licensed amateur and commercial transmitters—several were in Indonesian universities and about half were owned by Christians. Sukarno's overthrow in the mid-1960s generated an atmosphere of a new freedom that unshackled these stations until 1968, when Suharto's military regime raided the Student Action Front's station for being too critical of the government and imposed high registration fees on amateur operations. Two types of commercial stations served different audiences: *Elshinta* targeting older people, and *Nanggala* the young. The air force operated a commercial station as well (Eapen & Lent, 1978).

Beginning in July 1969, Indonesia implemented the radio farm forum technique, while rural broadcasting program contests were initiated in 1974. In 1993–94, the country was reported to have had about 89,000 groups of rural radio listeners, newspaper readers, and TV viewers (*Kelompencapir*) (Zakaria et al., 1995). School broadcasting started earlier in 1966. Educational broadcasting experiments took place in Jogjakarta, Semarang, and Irian Jaya. Christian religious broadcasting facilities, operating within the *Pancasila* national philosophy, contributed sophisticated radio programs. The Catholics' Sanggar Prathivi production unit became known for independently produced quality programming (Eapen & Lent, 1978).

2.2.3 Television

The state-owned *Televisi Republik Indonesia* (TVRI) came into operation in Jakarta in 1962 as a showcase for the Asian Games held that year. As an arm of the government, TVRI became an instrument for communicating government policies and programs to the public under President Sukarno's "Guided Democracy" of the early 1960s (Agassi, 1969). Thereafter, as Sumadi (1971) points out, the government used television to help build "a modern, just and prosperous society where the people enjoy a degree of well-being, in a physical–material sense, as well as in a mental–spiritual way" (p. 2).

Color television arrived in the mid-1970s, when Indonesia signed a US$ 40 million agreement with German and British companies for color-TV studios and equipment. The TVRI network relayed most of the programs from Jakarta to other stations on microwave repeaters and translators or on videotape. Eapen and Lent (1978) reported that about 30 percent of TVRI's programs were foreign in origin.

At the beginning of the First Five-Year Plan (Repelita I) in 1969, TVRI had only two stations and seven transmitters with a total power of 48kW with a radius of 18,200 sq km. By 1983, TVRI had nine stations and 190 transmitters, and by 1994, it had 12 stations and 328 transmitters with a radius of 806,116 sq km. Repelita II (1974–79) produced a US$ 153 million national communication satellite system.

At the end of Repelita IV, the government had allowed several private TV stations to go on air. In 1995, five private TV stations were in operation: *Rajawali Citra Televisi Indonesia* (RCTI), *Surya Citra Televisi* (SCTV), *Cipta Televisi Pendidikan Indonesi* (TPI), *Cakrawala Andalas Televisi* (ANteve or ANTV), and *Indosiar Visual Mandiri* (IVM). RCTI, which received a license in 1987, was the pioneering Indonesian commercial TV station. SCTV, the second commercial station, received its license in 1989, but was attached to the government until August 1993. TPI, the educational commercial station, received its license in August 1990. ANteve, the fourth commercial station, which had a smaller reach, received its license in January 1993. IVM, the fifth commercial station, received its license in 1991 but did not go on air until January 1995 (D'Haenens et al., 1999). Lau and Ang (1998) point out that these five commercial networks have the backing of "influential conglomerates" (p. 321). The Bismantara Group, controlled by Suharto's son Bambang Trihatmodjo, owned both RCTI and SCTV. However, the *Far Eastern Economic Review* (May 13, 1999) reported that by mid-1999, the Bismantara Group was falling apart, with many of its pieces "likely to be seized by creditors or sold." Salim Group, Indonesia's largest privately owned company, owned IVM while the Bakrie Group owned ANteve.

3. THE PRESS

3.1 Policy and Legal Framework

The new era of *reformasi* that began in mid-1998 offered the Indonesian media the opportunity to test the freedom of the press against the restrictive *Pancasila* press system imposed under the 1945 Constitution. President Habibie acted on pledges to promote greater freedom and respect for human rights by granting some 742 new publishing licenses from June 1998 onwards (Cohen, 1999).

On November 13, 1998, and extraordinary session of the People's Consultative Assembly (MPR) revoked its 1978 decree (Decision No. 2/MPR/1978) on the propagation and implementation of *Pancasila* rules. It endorsed a decree on human rights (Decision No. 17/MPR/1998) requiring that all state institutions respect and enforce all the UN conventions on human rights[3] (Jakarta Press, 1998). The 10 chapters in the Human Rights Decree, comprising 44 clauses, specifies the rights to life, reproduction, self-development, justice, independence, freedom of information, security and safety, happiness, obligation, and protection.[4] The clause on the rights to freedom and freedom of information, reproduced below, should guide Indonesia's policies on communication:

- Everyone has the right to communicate and to provide information for his or her personal and social environmental development.
- Everyone has the right to seek, receive, possess, store, process, and impart information by using any available channel.
- The state will guarantee and protect the right of citizens to communicate and to provide information.
- Everyone has the right to express his or her thoughts and attitudes in consonance with his or her heart.
- Everyone has the freedom to choose his or her education and learning.

[3] Ch. Himawan, a member of the National Human Rights Commission, had urged the MPR to promulgate such a decree in an article published in the *Jakarta Post* (October 16, 1997). Said, 1990, credited the press for regularly reporting on human rights cases and issues, and he asserted, "Media coverage of violations and denials of these rights has had a positive impact on efforts to enhance national life" (p. 45).
[4] The National Commission on Human Rights, 1999, has called on the government to swiftly bring into effect Decision No. 17/MPR/1998 in order to ratify international human rights instruments and to incorporate them as a source of national law.

- Everyone has the freedom to choose his or her profession.
- Everyone has the freedom to choose his or her citizenship.
- Everyone has the freedom to live anywhere in the country, to leave the country, and to return to his or her country.
- Everyone has the freedom to join an organization and to gather and express his or her point of view.

Sukarno's "Guided Democracy" forced the Indonesian press to follow the principles of the *Pancasila* press system, which, as Sinaga (1989) points out, emphasized the "importance of freedom and responsibility" (p. 35). During the Suharto presidency (1966–98), the *Pancasila* system continued. Sinaga explains that the government regarded the press as "a very important element in the process of nation-building," and that it constantly reminded the press "to avoid writing tendentiously or sensationally" about issues related to *Suku* (group or clan), *Agama* (religion), *Ras* (ethnicity or race), and *Antar-golongan* (inter-group affairs), popularly abbreviated as SARA (p. 34). Sinaga says that the "conscience of the press, of society and of the government" determines the "balance between freedom of the media and responsibility from the media" (p. 35).

Indonesia's press had to observe the basic principles embodied in Press Act No. 21 of 1982. This act amended the Press Act No. 11 of 1966 as amended by Act No. 4 of 1967. In addition to these basic principles, the press had to heed the 1984 ministerial decrees, and the SARA rules, as well as the Anti-Subversion Law (Presidential Decree No. 11/PPNS/1963), and Articles 134, 154–157 and 160 of the Criminal Code known as KUHP (Razak & Tobing, 1996). Ministerial Decision No. 22 B of 1972 determined the regulation of the foreign press and of foreign journalists in Indonesia.

Article 28 of the Indonesian Constitution states that "freedom of association and assembly, freedom of expression and thoughts in writing and the like shall be prescribed by statute" (Razak & Tobing, 1996, p. 25). Thereby it empowered the relevant minister to draft legislation and issue regulations relating to the media. Although the basic press law—the 1966 Press Act as amended in 1982—states that "no censorship or bans shall be applied to the national press," ministerial regulations have had "the effect of negating that general guarantee" (p. 25). The basic press law spelled out the duties and the procedural framework of the press. It required all publications to obtain a Press Publication Business License, better known as a SIUPP (*Surat Izin Usaha Penerbitan Pers*) and limited their ownership and management to Indonesians. It empowered the minister to revoke a license after consultation with the Press Council (created by the Press Act of 1966), and allowed the government to screen the key staff of any press establishment. SIUPP had replaced the previous requirement in the 1966 Press Act stipulating that all publications must obtain a permit, *Surat Ijin Terbit* (SIT), and the SIUPP law was more all inclusive than the SIT because it applied to press corporations as well.

The 1984 ministerial decisions—No. 1 on SIUPP and No. 214A on the procedures and requirements for SIUPP applications—generated considerable controversy.

Vanden Heuvel and Dennis (1993) asserted that SIUPP enabled the government to control the number of newspapers and to "block a strong newspaper group from expanding" (p. 115). Information Minister Harmoko had set up a practice whereby he could "revoke a publication's SIUPP after three warnings" (p. 115). *Sinar Harapan* and *Prioritas* were closed in 1986 and 1987 respectively, although they resumed publication under new management and with new names, *Suara Pembaruan* (Voice of Renewal) and *Media Indonesia* respectively. In 1990, the tabloid *Monitor* lost its license, and its editor was jailed. Three newsmagazines—*Tempo, DeTIK* (Moment) and *Editor*—lost their licenses in June 1994. The latest victim was the weekly tabloid *ParOn*, which was closed on June 9, 1998, apparently for investigating Suharto's hidden wealth.

The SIUPP law was changed following the resignation of Suharto on May 21, 1998, and the inauguration of President Habibie. On June 5, 1998, Information Minister Yunus Yosfiah issued ministerial decree No. 132/SK/MENPEN/1998, which streamlined the SIUPP law by reducing the number of requirements for a publication license from 16 to three. The change enabled editor Indrus Indas to receive a license for which he had applied in 1985 (Antara, June 26, 1998). The minister also issued Regulation No. 133/PER/MENPEN/1998 repealing a 1975 regulation that made the Indonesian Journalists Association (PWI) the sole representative for the country's journalists. That move effectively legalized the Alliance of Independent Journalists, the body that had promoted a free and pluralistic press under Suharto (Luwarso, 1998).

Commenting on the new regulations covering the press and radio broadcasting, as part of what the information minister called "reformation in the information sector," Astraatmadja (1998) says that they fell well short of the young journalists' expectations. Under these regulations, the information minister could no longer revoke the licenses of publications, although publishers who violated the terms of their licenses could be brought to trial. However, the minister retained the power to suspend, for an unspecified period, the licenses of publications that violated the terms of their permits. The new regulations also allow journalists to establish organizations besides the 50-year-old PWI, because the requirement that journalists become members of a professional organization may violate the rights of those journalists who do not want to join a group. As for the sought-after revisions of the country's press law, the minister said that these would take time because parliament had to ratify any such changes. The new regulations obviously failed to fulfill the demands of the young journalists for "total reform," a phrase that has become popular among university students, intellectuals, and other advocates of political reform across the country.

The Anti-Subversion Law (Presidential Decree No. 11 of 1963) enabled the government to take action against inciting or disseminating feelings of hostility, thereby causing "social splits, conflicts, chaos, disturbances, or anxiety" (Razak & Tobing, 1996). Moreover, Article 134 of the Criminal Code made it an offence to make public statements "deliberately intended to disparage the president or the vice president" (p. 26). Articles 154–157 made it an offence to publish material likely to "incite feelings of hostility, hatred or insult" against the government or against any ethnic or religious group (p. 26). Article 160 prohibited statements that "counsel disobedience to the public authority" (p. 26). The Criminal Code also contained provisions against violation of privacy, defamation, sedition, and the like. The SARA rules continued to apply.

The Press Council, as a policy-making body on matters relating to the print media, has influenced the country's press since its formation in 1967. Presidential Decision No. 1 of 1984, which defined the role of the council, gave it the authority to oversee how the press personnel observed the six-point PWI Code of Ethics. (A nine-member Council of Ethics under the PWI umbrella also had a mandate to monitor and police violations of the code.) The Press Council had the obligation to promote positive interaction between the government, the press, and society. It has 25 members: five government officials, eight representatives of the Indonesian Journalists Association, six from the Publishers Association, one each from the associations of graphics and printing and of media advertising agencies, and four scholars and educational experts representing the society.

The policy and legal framework of the Indonesian press will undergo further changes with the impending passage of a unified Mass Media Act that will supercede the current basic press and broadcasting laws. Because of differences among competing groups, the new mass media legislation proposed by the Ministry of Information had already gone through 10 drafts in 11 months since May 1998 (Zeitlin, 1999).

3.2 Financial Aspects: Circulation, Advertising, Marketing Strategies

The 1998 figures show that Indonesia's 79 dailies had a circulation of 5.02 million. The 20 national dailies had a circulation of 2.73 million while the 59 regional dailies had a circulation of 2.29 million. This is the equivalent of 2.3 copies per 100 people (WAN, 1999). In 1997, Indonesia also had 88 non-dailies with a circulation of 5.07 million. Of these, 23 were national in scope (with a circulation of 3.16 million), and 65 were regional (with a circulation of 1.92 million). SGV Oetomo audits the circulation of Indonesian newspapers while Survey Research Indonesia measures the readership (WAN, 1999).

The revenue share of newspapers from display advertising in 1998 was 5 percent lower than in 1993, despite the increase in the absolute amount. In 1998, the Asian financial debacle cut in half the advertising revenue of newspapers from that in 1997. Display advertising generated 70 percent while classified advertising generated only 30 percent of the advertising revenues procured by newspapers. However, the advertising revenues of Indonesian dailies increased progressively from Rupiah 484.1 billion in 1993 to Rupiah 1,344.3 billion in 1997. The advertising revenues of the non-dailies increased from Rupiah 4.8 billion to Rupiah 24.2 billion during the same time span. In descending order, the top advertising sectors in the daily press were vehicles, property, media, banking and insurance, education, travel and tourism, drinks, photocopiers and computers, and cosmetics (WAN, 1998a).

Although "newspaper management and marketing techniques were practically unknown" in Indonesia three decades ago (R. Toruan quoted in Vanden Heuvel & Dennis, 1993, p. 113), newspapers such as *Kompas* and *Media Indonesia* (see Section 3.3) have used successful marketing strategies to expand their circulation. *Kompas* became the country's foremost newspaper by subjecting itself to independent circulation audits and "selling" its credibility. Oetama (1989), the chief editor of *Kompas*, explained that the development of a commercial aspect was natural and inevitable as the ideals of good journalism need to be financially supported by sound business management.

The Surabaya-based Jawa Pos Group, which posted profits of US$ 2.8 million in 1998 by capitalizing on the new freedoms provided under the *reformasi*, is engaged in stiff competition with the Jakarta-based Kompas-Gramedia Group. The Jawa Pos Group controls an empire spanning 49 publications, of which 17 were introduced in the post-Suharto period. This group's market strategy is to place emphasis on provincial newspapers. In Surabaya's morning-dailies market, *Jawa Pos*, with a claimed circulation of 352,000, outsmarted the *Surya* (backed by Kompas-Gramedia) which claimed a circulation of 140,000 (Cohen, 1999).

In East Timor, the pro-Indonesian daily *Novas* (circulation 2,500), started in 1998 by a businessman, Gil Aves da Costa, folded in early 1999 because of financial problems. The former Portuguese territory with a population of 800,000 now has only one daily, the pro-independence *Suara Timor Timur*, which has boosted its circulation to about 7,000 (Associated Press, 1999).

3.3 Structure and Organization

Indonesia's press structure shows a hierarchical organization. It has a national press and a regional press. Both dailies and non-dailies fall into these two categories. Obviously, Jakarta is the center of the national press even though there are exceptions to the rule such as the Jawa Pos Group of Surabaya. Indonesia also has an identifiable and successful rural press exemplified by *Pikiran Rakyat* (1956). The Indonesian-language newspapers dominate the press hierarchy. Only one Chinese daily, *Harian Indonesia* (1966), exists through government decree. Unlike the influential English dailies in the British Commonwealth countries in Asia, the three English-language dailies in Indonesia—the *Jakarta Post* (1983), the *Indonesia Times* (1974), and the *Indonesia Observer* (1966)—have little influence.

The press in Indonesia is a subsystem of the national system. Thus the pre-Habibie press conformed to the national system and the national interest as dictated by the *Pancasila* ideology. The Indonesian Journalists Association (PWI) and the Indonesian Publishers Association (SPS) were integral parts of the press subsystem. Until mid-1998, PWI membership was a prerequisite to practice journalism. The PWI-sanctioned code of ethics promises not to publish anything that may be destructive and prejudicial to the nation and state, anything that may create social chaos, or anything that may offend the common standards of decency, religion, faith, or belief of a person or a group protected by the law. SPS membership and recommendation were prerequisites to purchase newsprint.

Indonesia's media are privately owned. Hill (1994) identified four major press enterprises: the Kompas-Gramedia Group, the Sinar Kasih Group, the Tempo-Grafiti/Jawa Pos Group,[5] and the Media Indonesia/Surya Persindo Group. In the early 1990s, the government was concerned with the trend towards forming conglomerates, and it blocked the attempt by *Kompas* to buy rural newspaper licenses. These big conglomerates, allegedly linked to the "New Order" regime, largely controlled Indonesia's media. In the mid-1990s, critics alleged that a large sector of the print media was owned by Suharto's family or his close allies like Hasan, and by former Information Minister Harmoko.

Kompas (http://Kompas.com) is the flagship of the Kompas-Gramedia Group, which pursued a strategy of diversification and reinvestment in the 1980s. By the early 1990s, the group had diversified itself through 38 subsidiaries dealing with radio, book publishing, travel, banking, insurance, advertising, hotels, shrimp farming, and the like. (Vanden Heuvel & Dennis, 1993). From 1989 onwards, the group also began investing in regional newspapers in Banda Aceh, Bandung, Palembang, Surabaya, and Yogyakarta. It produced a number of targeted specialist publications, including the remarkably successful *Monitor*. Hill (1994) asserted that this group "has demonstrated most explicitly its preparedness to operate within the constraints imposed by the New Order Government" (p. 86).

Suara Pembaruan (http://www.suarapembaruan.com), the reincarnation of *Sinar Harapan* (Ray of Hope) banned in 1986, is the flagship of the Sinar Kasih Group. It began its diversification in 1971 with the establishment of the Sinar Agape press; and it invested in companies dealing with book publishing, advertising, broadcasting, travel, transportation, and the like. The group published the popular magazine *Mutiara* (Pearl) and co-published several weekly magazines (*Tribun*, for example) and specialized monthlies (TIM and *Higina*). It also ventured, rather unsuccessfully into collaborative agreements with smaller regional papers (Hill, 1994).

Tempo (http://www.tempo.co.id), the PT Grafiti Pers magazine banned from mid-1994 until its post-Suharto revival in October 1998, and the daily *Jawa Pos* (http://www.jawapos.com) were the flagships of the third conglomerate (see footnote 5). Grafiti established *Tempo* in 1971, moved into book publishing, and established a string of related magazines, including *Matra, Humor, Medika*, and *Kalam*. Grafiti gained control of *Jawa Pos* of Surabaya in 1982 and placed it under entrepreneur Dahlan Iskan, who has built a newspaper empire spanning 49 publications, including provincial papers, weekly tabloids, and party newspapers

---

[5] The corporate relationship between *Tempo* and *Jawa Pos* changed after *Tempo* was banned in 1994. Today, 40 percent of the Jawa Pos company is owned by *Tempo*'s former publisher, Grafiti Pers, with 20 percent held by Jawa Pos employees and smaller stakes by several individuals. Among these are former *Tempo* director Lukman Setiawan and *Tempo* chief editor Goenawan Mohamad, who is president-commissioner (Cohen, 1999).

(Cohen, 1999). Its provincial papers include *Fajar* (Dawn) in Ujung Pandang in South Sulawesi (circulation 35,000) and *Riau Pos* in Pekanbaru, Riau (circulation 40,000). Among its weekly tabloids are *Oposisi* (Opposition) with a circulation of 400,000 and *Gugat* (Accuse) with a circulation of 250,000. The group also printed and distributed four party newspapers: *Amanat* (Mandate) of the National Mandate Party, *Demokrat* of the Indonesian Democratic Party, *Duta* (Ambassador) of the National Awakening Party, and *Abadi* (Eternal) of the Crescent Moon and Star Party.

Surya Paloh, a Sumatran who had no prior experience in journalism, set up PT Surya Persindo, the fourth conglomerate, in 1985. He started off with the controversial daily *Prioritas*, which the government revoked in June 1987 for violating SIUPP provisions. When the government denied his application for a new SIUPP to start another daily, he initiated the co-publication of *Vista*, an entertainment magazine that he later renamed *Vista TV*. In early 1989, he circumvented the denial of a publishing permit by becoming co-publisher of *Media Indonesia*, a daily started by Teuku Yousali Syah in 1969 (Hill, 1994). Paloh injected fresh life into *Media Indonesia* (http://www.mediaindo.co.id) thereby increasing its circulation more than threefold. By the beginning of the 1990s, the company had diversified into regional publishing in Banda Aceh, Medan, Padang, Pelambang, Lampung, Bandung, Yogyakarta, Pontianak, Manado, and Denpasar. Paloh's aggressive marketing strategies antagonized the established publishers; and the economic difficulties of the 1990s hit his company the hardest, forcing him to sell several of the regional publications. However, in late 1992, the company successfully revamped *DeTIK*, a Jakarta newsweekly established in 1977. Although the Suharto regime closed *DeTIK* in June 1994 (and it remained closed till Suharto's fall in mid-1998), the company fleetingly replaced it with *Simponi* (Symphony), a weekly dating to 1972.

At the level of the rural press, the government-backed "Newspapers for the Village" (SKUD) project started in 1977. Originally confined to five provinces with a daily newspaper circulation of 36,000, it expanded to 27 provinces in 1985–86 with three daily newspapers—*Suara Karya, Berita Buana*, and *Angkatan Bersenjata*—circulating 99,976 copies. Nine years later, two more publications—*Pelita* and *Neraca*—joined the project expanding the circulation to 2.18 million. In 1996–97, *Terbit* and *Berita Yudha*, also joined the project, further expanding the circulation to 2.35 million copies. These newspapers and magazines disseminated development-related information.

"Newspapers Develop the Village" (KMD) was another project begun by the government in 1979, and including 34 publishers in 13 provinces. By 1996–97, KMD had expanded to 61 publishers with a circulation of 136,581 copies.

3.4 Quality and Popular Press

Crawford (1971) observed that the Indonesian press was not a "mass" medium because, except in minor ways, it did not cater to the "popular" tastes of the masses.

He surmised that on the whole it was "a rather sophisticated press" (p. 173). He also concluded that the English-language dailies, published primarily for the foreign community, had no political influence.

Anderson (1982) concurred that an important characteristic of the Indonesian press was "that it addressed itself primarily to elite, urban Indonesians rather than to the masses" (p. 198). The most successful papers were the "independents" with the government-linked newspapers coming a distant second. Anderson rated *Kompas* as the country's "most respected newspaper" (p. 199), *Sinar Harapan* as one of the "better papers," *Indonesia Raya* (Glorious Indonesia) as one of the country's prestigious older dailies, *KAMI* as "journalistically, one of the best papers," and *Pos Kota* (City Post) as "extremely popular with the average newspaper buyer" (pp. 200–201).

In the contemporary scene, *Pos Kota* remains the most popular "mass" newspaper with a readership of 2.93 million. *Kompas* maintains its "most respected" identity with the second highest readership of 2.21 million. Shah and Gayatri (1994) also identified *Kompas* as an elite newspaper and *Pos Kota* as a non-elite newspaper whose "readership is less educated and of lower socio-economic status than the readers of *Kompas*" (p. 412).

Jawa Pos of Surabaya, a relatively old newspaper dating back to 1949, maintains a high readership of 799,000 despite its high cover price of 38 US cents, compared to *Pos Kota*, which costs 17 cents, and *Kompas*, which costs 30 cents. *Suara Pembaruan* (replacement of the suspended *Sinar Harapan*), with a readership of 793,000, is still among the "better papers" selling at 30 US cents a copy. *Pikiran Rakyat* of Bandung stands in a class of its own. Though its circulation, with a cover price of 26 US cents, stands at 180,000, it commands a readership of 754,000. *Surya* also has a high readership figure of 668,000, though its circulation, at a cover price of 32 US cents, is only 139,000. *Media Indonesia* (replacement of the suspended *Prioritas*), with a readership of 445,000, and *Suara Merdeka* (Free Voice), with a readership of 418,000, sell for 30 and 34 US cents respectively. *Suara Karya* (Work Voice), with a readership of 293,000, and *Berita Buana* (World News), with a readership of 206,000, make up the lower end of Indonesia's top 10 newspapers, all of which are broadsheets. These two are "rural development" newspapers, which sell for 26 and 21 US cents respectively (WAN, 1998a).

3.5 Distribution and Technology

The distribution cost of the average Indonesian newspaper is estimated at 40 percent of the cover price (WAN, 1998a). Razak (1995) points out that big papers use the latest printing technologies and computerized newsrooms to survive the fierce competition. The Jawa Pos Group has made major investments in seven hi-tech printing presses and a large new paper mill in Surabaya. Half of the 100 tons of newsprint that the mill produces daily is exported to India, Malaysia, and Taiwan (Cohen, 1999). Other newspapers have looked for new strategies of survival, with smaller papers merging with bigger media enterprises on a joint management

scheme. The press faces hard competition from the five private TV stations. Afternoon papers have to rush against time to compete with the prime time news broadcast on television.

4. BROADCASTING

In Indonesia, "central broadcasting" means government broadcasts that all national
broadcasting systems throughout the country are obliged to transmit. "National
broadcasting" includes all broadcasts whose transmissions cover all, or a part of,
the country.

4.1 Policy and Legal Framework

The Broadcasting Act No. 24 of 1997, the first such act in Indonesia, gave the
government sweeping powers to regulate the industry, including advertising and
the new communication technologies. Although the act formally ends the government monopoly on news broadcasting, it allows for a licensing mechanism similar
to that of the press, with the minister exercising the power to revoke licenses
(Idris, 1998). Ministerial decrees regulated the industry until the passage of this
act. The framework that guided broadcasting in Indonesia comprised the 1945
Constitution, the Broad Guidelines of State Policy (GBHN), and the *Pancasila*
national ideology, including the associated SARA framework. The November 1998
special MPR session revoked the March 1998 GBHN decree and replaced it with
"a scaled-down document" to cover the period up to mid-1999 (Jakarta Press,
1998). The post-Suharto *reformasi* period brought several policies into consideration in consonance with Decision No. 17/MPR/1998 (see Section 3.1):

● A unified Mass Media Act (encompassing broadcasting, press, and film) is expected to replace the new Broadcasting Act No. 24/1997. Information Minister Yunus
Yosfiah has indicated that the revised legislation will allow each broadcasting
station to manage its internal affairs with less interference by the government. It
will enable private broadcasting stations to relay fewer hours of government news,
while it will also allow government broadcasting stations to broadcast the pros
and cons of the government's development programs.
● Ministerial Decree No. 134/SK/MENPEN/1998 has already decreased the obligation of private radio broadcasters to relay government news from 13 to thrice a
day (at 6 a.m., 1 p.m., and 7 p.m.), and to relay local news only once. This decree
thus modified the old Ministerial Decree No. 226/KEP/MENPEN/1984, which
regulated the relaying of news, the use of foreign material, and the use of languages
other than Bahasa Indonesia.
● A new ministerial decree will change the organization of private radio broadcasting as outlined in Ministerial Decree Nos 242/KEP/MENPEN/1997 and 245/
B/KEP/MENPEN/1985. The Federation of Indonesian National Commercial

Broadcasters (PRSSNI)[6] will no longer have the monopoly of representing private broadcasters.

● The Directorate General of Radio, Television, and Film has simplified the licensing procedure for private radio broadcasting by amending the complicated procedures outlined in the four previous RTF decrees: No. 1050/RTF/RSS/K/87, No. 175/RTF/K/II/89, No. 100/RTF/K/I/92, and No. 1351/RTF/K/VIII/93.

● The government will discuss the termination of the regulation requiring a monthly tax on TV ownership.

● The Ministry of Information will facilitate the establishment of additional private TV stations by deleting Clause 27.2a of the Ministry Decree No. 04A/1993.

● TVRI will not have permission to carry advertising because it already receives 12.5 percent of the advertising revenue of private TV stations.

Under the Broadcasting Act 24/1997, which currently determines the legal framework of the industry, only an Indonesian citizen or a corporate body that a court of law has never declared guilty of activities against *Pancasila*, can set up a private broadcasting station. Such stations are prohibited from broadcasting programs promoting certain political ideas, ideologies, religions, and sects. All capital shares of such stations must belong to Indonesian citizens or corporate bodies. After obtaining government approval, private broadcasters are eligible to seek supplementary capital through a stock exchange under the relevant statutory regulations. They cannot receive financial assistance from foreign sources.

The law prohibits the setting up of any foreign broadcasting station in Indonesia. Government permission is a prerequisite for any foreign broadcaster to engage in temporary broadcasting or journalistic activity in the country. With government permission, such temporary broadcasters can bring broadcasting transmitter(s) for satellite uplink. Those broadcasters who rent transmitting facilities provided by Indonesia's satellites for international broadcasting can, with government permission, transmit their broadcasts from Indonesia.

4.2 Structure and Organization

The government's broadcasting institutions consist of Radio Republik Indonesia, Televisi Republik Indonesia, the Indonesian International Radio Broadcasting Services, and the Indonesian International Broadcasting Television Services.

4.2.1 Radio

Widarto (1998) documents 973 radio broadcasting stations in Indonesia under the following categories:

● 52 RRI broadcasting stations (one national broadcasting center in Jakarta; five regional Nusantara stations in Medan, Yogyakarta, Banjarmasin, Ujung

---

[6] Persatuan Radio Siaran Swasta Nasional Indonesia.

Pandang, and Jayapura; 26 Regional I stations in the provincial capitals; and 20 Regional II stations in important cities);

- 780 commercial stations (with a permitted power of 0.5kW);
- 133 stations managed by local administrations (provincial governments, districts, and municipalities);
- four non-commercial stations; and
- four stations under the auspices of different departments.

Zakaria et al. (1995) reported that RRI had 49 broadcasting stations. RRI increased the number of transmitters from 252 (with a power 2,550kW) in 1978–79 to 414 (with power of 3,106.6kW) in 1993–94.

Broadcasting is under the authority of the state. The Directorate General of Radio, TV, and Film is responsible for its development and supervision. Radio comes within the direct purview of the Directorate of Radio. The PRSSNI represents the commercial broadcasters. Government broadcasting institutions are accountable to the responsible minister, and they have to give priority to provide broadcasting services equitably to all layers of society. They are obliged to provide a channel featuring educational programs.

4.2.2 Television

Since Repelita IV, the government has allowed five private television stations[7] to go on air:

- Rajawali Citra Televisi Indonesia (RCTI) in Jakarta,
- Surya Citra Televisi (SCTV) in Jakarta and Surabaya,
- Televisi Pendidikan Indonesia (TPI) in Jakarta,
- Andalas Televisi (ANteve or ANTV) in Jakarta and Lampung, and
- Indosiar Visual Mandiri (IVM) in Jakarta

TVRI Channel 2 commenced in 1991, in anticipation of the impact of commercial television, whose programs chiefly target urban and metropolitan audiences. This channel, initially confined to Jakarta and Surabaya, will soon expand to Yogyakarta, Bandung, Denpasar, and Medan.

In 1996–97, TVRI had 14 television stations and nine mobile production units (SPK), 369 transmitter stations with a total power of 350.2kW and a radius of 828,601 sq km, serving 164 million viewers. The government built four new transmitters in Batu Licin (south Kalimantan), Kisaran (north Sumatra), Waigeo (Irian Jaya), and Linge (Aceh, Sumatra).

Private TV stations provide the audience with more choice. Following the post-Suharto liberalization of the media, eight new TV stations are likely to supplement the original five (Fight for TV Slot Frequency, *Tempo*, March 8, 1999):

---

[7] Freedom House, 1998, alleged that all five stations "are owned by Suharto supporters and accept restrictions on news coverage" (p. 284). D'Haenens et al., 1999, provide the details of ownership.

- PT Media Televisi Indonesia (Group Surya Persindo/Surya Paloh),
- PT Televisi Transformasi Indonesia (Group Para/Chairul Tanjung),
- PT Pasaraya Mediakarya (Alatief Corp./Abdul Latief),
- PT Telesindo Prima Lestari,
- PT Cakrawala Tiara Kencana,
- PT Tifar Admanco,
- PT Pupuk Kaltim, and
- IIFTIHAR

4.3 Program Policies

Broadcasting Act No. 24 of 1997 states that broadcasting in Indonesia aims to:

- Increase the quality of human resources;
- channel constructive public opinion in social, national, and state life, as well as enhance the active role of society in development;
- enhance the resilience of the national culture;
- improve the nation's economic capabilities to provide equitable distribution of economic resources, and to reinforce the competitive edge of the economy;
- enhance legal awareness and national discipline; and
- strengthen a viable and dynamic national stabilization (a peaceful and ordered society).

Broadcasting generally operates within the SARA framework (see Section 3.1). As a medium for information, education, and entertainment, it aims to strengthen the ideological, political, economic, social, and cultural framework of Indonesia, as well as to secure its defense needs.

RRI's central station in Jakarta directs its home services, which comprises two national programs (*Programa Nasional*) and two metropolitan programs (*Programa Ibukota*). Table 3 shows the varied nature of programs aired on RRI, the public radio, in 1998. If we collapse similar categories, the broader categories that emerge are: news (20 percent), information (10 percent), education (7 percent), entertainment and culture (50.5 percent), religion (5 percent), and others (7.5 percent).

All RRI regional stations have to broadcast a number of national programs, including news. Non-RRI radio stations, in line with existing regulations, are also obliged to relay RRI news, current affairs, and other important programs. The overseas service, Voice of Indonesia, broadcasts for 12 hours per day: two hours in Indonesian, three hours in English, and between half an hour to one hour every day in eight other languages—Arabic, Chinese, French, German, Japanese, Malay, Spanish, and Thai (*World radio TV handbook*, 1999).

Table 4 analyzes the mix of program aired on TVRI and on three private commercial stations. Compared with TVRI, private TV stations depend heavily on foreign programs, which comprise roughly 60 percent of the content of TPI, 55 percent of the content of SCTV, and 34 percent of the content of RCTI.

4.4 Ownership and Financing

The financial sources for government broadcasting are: the state budget; revenue from dues, contributions, and permit costs of broadcasting organizations; advertising revenue of RRI; and revenue from legal business. TVRI carries no advertising because it receives 12.5 percent of the advertising revenue of private TV stations. TVRI relies dominantly on license fees and the state budget allocations of Rupiah 135 billion (US$ 60 million) a year. To implement its mission as a public broadcasting facility, TVRI spends US$ 300,000 a year to subscribe to news broadcasts from international news suppliers and another US$ 150,000 on international agencies. Lau and Ang (1998) reported that only RCTI was "turning a profit," while the other commercial networks were "trying to find the right programming mix to attract ratings and advertising" (p. 322). Three foreign investment banks filed a bankruptcy claim against ANteve on January 14, 1999, charging the station with failing to pay its debts. As the country's economic slump has slashed TV advertising, other commercial stations have called for a revision of the 1997 Broadcast Law to draw in foreign investment and thus tide over the current crisis.

The law limits private ownership of broadcasting stations to Indonesian citizens or corporate bodies. It forbids them from receiving financial assistance from foreign parties, and, except in the case of cable broadcasters, from collecting compulsory subscription fees.

Television reaches more than 60 percent of Indonesia's 26 million people, while radio reaches about 90 percent. Table 2 shows that in 1998 the biggest slice of advertising revenue went to television. Of the five commercial TV stations, RCTI was the most preferred channel to advertise on (See Table 5).

5. NEW ELECTRONIC MEDIA

5.1 Internet and On-line Media

Revised data (ITU, 1999) based on the January 1999 Network Wizards' survey showed that Indonesia had 39,649 Internet hosts—a density of 1.97 per 10,000 people, reflecting a compound annual growth rate of 20.8 percent since 1994. The APT (1999) estimated that Indonesia had 67,500 Internet subscribers in 1998, while ITU (1999) estimated 250,000 Internet users in 1997. Idris (1998) reported 200,000 registered Internet users at the end of 1996—a number now estimated to have reached 300,000. Indonesia also had an estimated 1.6 million personal computers in 1997—a density 0.76 per 100 people (ITU, 1999).

The market for modems in Indonesia had been growing at an estimated 20 to 30 percent (APT, 1998, 1999) until the mid-1990s, when the growth rate skyrocketed to an estimated 100 percent per year. The first Internet service provider, IndoInternet, started commercial operations in September 1994, and was followed by three others—IGN, Radnet, and IdOLA—in 1995. Telekom and Indosat are supporting these Internet service providers (ISPs). The country now has about 45 ISP license holders. The more established electronic bulletin board networks also draw extensively from the Internet.

The Internet has more freedom than any other mass medium in Indonesia (Basuki, 1998). *Tempo*, banned in 1994, established a website in 1996 without encountering any objections from the government, which has established its own websites to compete with opposing views. The military had suggested the need for some sort of "toll gate" to "black out" news that could potentially damage culture or affect security. It had also suggested registering uses and users (Sorenson, 1996). Pudjomartono (1998) wrote that the government intended to regulate the Internet, though the mechanism it would use remained unclear. The Department of Tourism, Posts, and Telecommunication issues ISP licenses in conformity with the 1997 Ministerial Decision No. KM.114/PT.102/MPPT/97. ISP licenses are subject to review every five years.

On-line publications in Indonesia include the *Bali Post, Bisnis Indonesia, Gatra, Indonesia Observer* (Jakarta), *Jawa Pos* (Surabaya), *Kompas, Manado Post, Media Indonesia, Pikiran Rakyat* (Bandung), *Republika, Riau Pos* (Pekanbaru), *Solo Pos* (Solo), *Suara Merdeka, Suara Pembaruan, Surabaya Post, Mahasiswa Boulevard, Tempo*, and *Waspada Daily* (Medan).

Popular websites in Indonesia are those specializing in pornography, exchange rates, and political information. Although Indonesia does not allow the circulation of *Playboy* and *Penthouse* magazines, it has not blocked the magazines' websites, which are very popular. Another popular website is Indopubs.com, a clearinghouse for rumors on Indonesian politics, especially with those dissatisfied with the news coverage of the local media. It had a high rate of usage during Suharto's last days in office.

Indonesia is in the midst of implementing its Nusantara-21 vision project, aiming to prepare all parts of the archipelago to join the Global Information Infrastructure by the first year of the 21st century. That vision has the help of the Palapa domestic satellite system, which Indonesia launched in August 1976. Nusantara-21 envisages that by 2001, all the major islands will be linked by wideband fiber-optic systems, while all the major cities will be served by terrestrial and submarine cable systems or multimedia broadband satellite systems. By that time, 11 multimedia cities are expected to be fully wired so that Indonesia's National Information Infrastructure (NII) will be well placed to connect to the regional Asia Pacific Information Infrastructure (APII), as well as with the global information infrastructure. Action plans are ready for the development of various applications, such as government online, electronic commerce, health care, education, tourism, telecommuting, banking, and financial services (Parapak, 1998a).

Nusantara-21 will also use global mobile personal communication by satellite (GMPCS), the new technology with the potential to close the gap not only between the developing and developed countries but also between urban and rural areas within a country. Indonesia will develop regional mobile communication through Asia Cellular Satellite (AceS), a type of GMPCS developed for regional use. The satellite was ready to be launched in 1999 to serve several countries in the region.

Another Indonesian initiative is the M2A satellite system, which will provide fixed multimedia satellite services throughout Asia and the Pacific. It is a cost competitive, satellite-based, two-way direct-to-subscriber, telecommunications platform (Parapak, 1998b). Another venture, Satellite Telecom 1, will offer voice and data services (APT, 1998).

Nusantara-21 will also get the benefit of SEA-ME-WE-3, an undersea cable network, which has the longest and largest capacity network in the world enabling wavelength division multiplexing technology. An additional 2,200 km of fiber-optic cable will link Java, Kalimantan, and Sulawesi islands (APT, 1998).

5.2 Telecommunications Infrastructure

In 1998, Indonesia had 5.57 million main telephone lines—a density of 2.7 per 100 people reflecting a compound annual growth rate of 21 percent from 0.59 per 100 people in 1990 (ITU, 1999; APT, 1999). The residential mainlines per 100 households stood at 8.6 in 1997 (ITU, 1999). The new cellular network, Excelcomindo, has increased the number of cellular subscribers as well. In 1998, Indonesia had 1.07 million cellular subscribers—a density of 0.52 per 100 people (ITU, 1999).

Currently, PT Telekom (mostly state-owned) and PT Ratelindo operate the domestic telecommunication services in the country, while PT Indosat (mostly state-owned) and PT Satelindo operate the international services. The Directorate General of Posts and Telecommunications (within the Ministry of Communications) is the body that formulates policy and regulates the industry. New legislation designed to de-regulate telecommunications will replace the Telecommunication Act No. 3 of 1989.

The trans-Sumatra digital microwave system connects almost all the big cities on Sumatra. A synchronous digital hierarchy network will link Jakarta (Java) with Denpasar (Bali). The "Northern Route" will run the whole length of Java, using 15,000 km of landline and undersea fiber-optic cable. The state-run Indosat operates four international gateway exchanges in Jakarta, Medan, and Surabaya (APT, 1999). Idris (1998) provides a detailed account of the telecommunication development in Indonesia.

6. POLICY TRENDS FOR PRESS AND BROADCASTING

Beginning with the second half of 1998, a freer policy environment for the media was taking shape in Indonesia, despite some uncertainties and setbacks. MPR Decision No. 17/MPR/1998 could lead the way towards greater press freedom. *Kompas* has called on the government to revise all the old acts and regulations relating to the press, broadcasting, films, advertising, VCRs, and the like, to conform to this landmark decision. In an article titled "*UU penyiaran tak lindungi kebebasan pers*" (December 16, 1998), *Kompas* pointed out the need to repeal the Suharto regime's 1997 Broadcasting Act No. 24, which placed the development and supervision of broadcasting under the authority of the state, giving almost no voice to the broadcasters. On National Press Day 1999, President Habibie said that the government had created polices to make press freedom a reality. "The government will no longer control the press...no longer telephone news editors about news they wish to publish," he said. He added, however, that the new freedoms would require the media to bear greater responsibility toward the public (Associated Press, February 9, 1999).

Freedom House (Sussman, 1999) has placed Indonesia in the "partly free" category with a press restrictive score of 53 out of 100, based on four criteria related to Article 19 of the Universal Declaration of Human Rights. On laws and regulations that influence media content, Indonesia got 10 out of 15 on the print media, and 12 out of 15 on the broadcast media. On political pressures and controls that influence media content, it got 5 out of 15 each for the print and broadcast media. On economic influences on media content, it got 12 out of 15 for print and 3 out of 15 for broadcast media. On repressive actions, it got 3 out of 5 each for the print and broadcast media.

Although the philosophical foundation of the *Pancasila* press system (Sinaga, 1989) had merit, its actual operation caused much dissatisfaction, both domestically and internationally. Pudjomartono (1998), the chief editor of *Jakarta Post*, wrote, "Press freedom is curtailed.... All the media exercise self-censorship" (p. 102). Romano's (1998) research showed that the *Pancasila* press philosophy was inconsistent with the conceptualization of grassroot practitioners about "their role and their relationship as mediators between the people and the state" (p. 81). The post-Suharto *reformasi* period unleashed press freedom to a degree comparable to that of the early 1950s, with the Habibie government relaxing the licensing requirements and appointing a team of seven people headed by rector Ryaas Rasyid to recommend constitutional reforms. The multi-party political system that relegated the ruling Golkar behind Megawati Sukarnoputri's Indonesian Democratic Party for Struggle (PDI-P) in the June 1999 parliamentary elections may augur well for a freer press within a less authoritarian political framework. However, following the elections, the Jakarta police summoned three editors[8] in connection with the defamation charges filed by suspended Attorney General Lt Gen. Andi Muhammad Ghalib. The Alliance of Independent Journalists interpreted the summons as police intimidation or pressure on the press (*Kompas*, June 25, 1999).

When the Habibie government removed the "license regulation for press publishing" from the basic press law, it automatically paved the way for the re-emergence of the de-licensed publications. In July 1998, the 24-page *DeTak* (Pulse) tabloid, known as *DeTIK* when the Suharto regime banned it in 1994, along with the weeklies *Tempo* and *Editor*, which had been banned for critical reporting, was back in print. In October 1998, Goenawan Mohamad's *Tempo*, the feisty news-

---

[8] Those summoned were August Parengkuan, deputy chief editor of *Kompas*; Djafar Assegaf of *Media Indonesia*; and chief editor Jasofi Bachtiar of *Merdeka*.

magazine, suppressed for reporting an internal government split over the purchase of 39 former East German warships ordered by Habibie, was also back in print. *Tempo*'s reporting "on the Suharto family, economic corruption, and human rights abuses in East Timor were an embarrassment to the regime" (Neumann, 1998a). Its first reincarnated issue covered the rape of Chinese women during the May riots that overthrew Suharto. Neumann (1998a) reported that Information Minister Yunus Yosfiah had become "a born-again believer in a free press," by more than doubling the number of permits issued for publications.

Many of Indonesia's new titles, according to Richardson (1998), "are tabloids with bold front-page headlines and photographs that promise readers an exposé of the latest political and sex scandals. Others offer weightier criticism of a government that is struggling to gain credibility for its reformist credentials" (p. 6).

However, by the end of 1998, Habibie's patience with the unshackled press took a sour turn because of commercial station SCTV's aggressive coverage of "Black Friday." In a sudden about-face on recent debt-restructuring agreements, the government opened the way to acquire 52.5 percent of the station's shares by getting the state-owned Bank Bumi Daya to call in SCTV's loan. The company, the media arm of the so-called Suharto Inc., labeled the plan "an authoritarian move to control the national media." Mitra Sari Persada, a company co-owned by Suharto's cousin Sudwikatmono, was SCTV's majority shareholder with Datakom Asia, run by SCTV board member Peter Gontha, holding the balance. Timsco, a company run by the president's brother Timmy Habibie, reportedly negotiated to acquire the SCTV shares. Timsco was also negotiating to buy 40 percent of IVM, another TV station owned mainly by the pro-Suharto Salim Group (*Asiaweek*, December 18, 1998). These moves came to a halt with the end of the Habibie government on October 20, 1999, when the MPR elected Abdurrahman Wahid of the National Awakening Party as the country's president. The next day, the MPR elected Megawati Sukarnoputri of PDI-P as vice president.

Widarto (1998) says Indonesia's TV industry is undergoing profound changes. Direct satellite broadcasting, pay television, commercial television, and interactive communication coming via the Information "Superhighway" have broadened audience choices both in terms of programming content and delivery channels.

The new Broadcasting Law 24/97 was signed officially on September 27, 1997, but became effective two years later (September 27, 1999). However, a unified Mass Media Act was expected to replace both broadcasting laws, as well as the basic press laws. Meanwhile, preparations were also afoot to amend the 1989 Telecommunications Act No. 3. The intent of the new legislation was to break the telephone monopoly, emphasizing universal service and customer protection; and to clearly separate the functions of policy, regulation and operation. The government envisaged withdrawing gradually from regulation and operation.

On September 23, 1999, the MPR introduced a new Press Law. This forbids censorship, and prohibition of the right to publish or broadcast, and guarantees the right of the press to look for, acquire, and disseminate ideas and information. Those convicted of trying to obstruct media freedom face a maximum sentence of two years and a fine of US$ 60,000 or more. The law permits foreigners to invest up to 49 percent of the shares in news media.

7. MAIN ISSUES

• Press freedom versus publishing economics

Although the government has relaxed the licensing system for publications, the quadrupling of the price of newsprint during 1998 has become an obstacle to the growth of the press. Leo Batubara, the head of the Indonesian Publishers Association, has predicted that 70 percent of the 230 periodicals in circulation (in mid-1998) might have to shut down. Newspapers have slashed the number of pages, or have converted to tabloid size to cut costs. Economic woes have also hurt the numerous "alternative media" (Eng, 1998). Richardson (1998) reported: "Across Asia, media organizations are cutting costs—and in some cases journalistic standards—to survive as recession eats into their advertising revenue and subscriber bases, while the sharp fall in the value of local currencies makes newsprint and other imported materials more expensive" (p. 1).

• Licensing journalists

President Habibie's a statement that all working journalists should have "licenses" to practice their profession has caused international concern. Bengt Braun, president of the World Association of Newspapers, has pointed out that any licensing system is open to abuse and will "almost inevitably lead to censorship or self-censorship," thereby contravening Article 19 of the Universal Declaration of Human Rights (WAN, 1998b). Much more important is the democratization of communication as eloquently set forth in the MacBride Report (UNESCO, 1980). In this regard, the decision of the Habibie regime to rescind the 1975 press regulation, which required a journalist to belong to the Indonesian Journalists Association (PWI), was a welcome move. This meant that the Alliance of Independent Journalists (AJI) was recognized as an alternative to the government union. However, another issue had arisen because of the requirement that a journalist still had to be a member of a journalists' group: Astraatmadja (1998) has pointed out that this might violate the rights of journalists who may not want to join a group. The Wahid regime was most likely to make this issue irrelevant.

• Public broadcasting versus commercial broadcasting

A very serious threat to public television has arisen owing to the influx of numerous international satellite programming channels, as well as local commercial channels. Public broadcasting has to determine the type of programming that suits the new environment of competition. National public television will have to review its programming policy as it enters the new millennium.

8. STATISTICS

General Profile

Exchange rate in May 1999	US$ 1 = 7,758 rupiahs
Population mid-1999	216.1 million
Population density	118.3 per sq km
Per capita GDP (PPP)	US$ 2,940
Per capita GNP (nominal)	US$ 460
Literacy	85%

Table 1
Estimated Mass Media Penetration

	Radio receivers		Television receivers		Daily newspapers		
	Number (million)	Per 100 people	Number (million)	Per 100 people	Number	Circ'n (million)	Per 100 people
1980	18.0	11.9	3.0	2.0	84	2.28	1.5
1985	21.5	12.8	6.4	3.8	97	3.01	1.8
1990	26.5	14.5	10.5	5.7	64	5.14	2.8
1995	29.5	14.9	13.0	6.6	74	4.70	2.4
1996	31.0	15.5	13.5	6.7	69	4.66	2.3
1997	31.5	15.5	13.7	6.8	74•	4.67•	2.3•
			(27)*	(9.7)*			
1998					79	5.02	2.4

Source: UNESCO, 1999; • WAN, 1998a, 1999; * ITU, 1999.

Table 2
Advertising Share by Media Category

Media	*1993		1996		1997		1998	
	Billion Rp	%	Billion Rp	%	Billion Rp	%	Billion Rp	%
Radio	113	8	189	4.6	206	4.0	113	4.3
Newspapers	484	35	1,202	29.0	1,540	30.2	775	29.8
Magazines	108	8	270	6.5	311	6.1	126	4.8
Cinema	10	1	10	0.2	9	0.2	4	0.2
Outdoor	53	4	266	6.4	350	6.9	175	6.7
Television	613	44	2,203	53.2	2,678	52.6	1,406	54.1
Total	1,381	100	4,140	100	5,094	100	2,599	100

Source: *WAN, 1998a; PPPI, 1998.

Table 3
Program Mix of Public Radio (Radio Republik Indonesia)

Program category	Total minutes per week	Percent
Pop music	4,032	40.0
Classical music	154	1.5
Drama	308	3.0
Light entertainment	98	1.0
Children's programs	196	2.0
News	2,016	20.0
Information	1,008	10.0
Education	406	4.0
Sports	252	2.5
Arts/science/humanities	98	1.0
Religion	504	5.0
Cultural	504	5.0
Public service, etc.	504	5.0
Total	**10,080**	**100.0**

Source: RRI, Ministry of Information, 1998.

Table 4
Program Mix of TV Stations (Minutes per Week)

Program category	TVRI Public TV		TPI Private TV		SCTV Private TV		RCTV Private TV	
	L	F	L	F	L	F	L	F
Drama/movies	1495		1110	5206	750	3150	1058	1847
Pop music	800		503		390	30	611	31
Classical music					90			
Sitcom	100		1118		120	30	392	55
Light entertainment, e.g., Quiz shows, beauty contest	800		550	420	120		683	
Children's programs	725		60	530	90	390		125
News	290	161	730		1800	1954		
Information/education	865		60	30	30			
Sports	325			30	30	525	31	510
Art/science/humanities	200				30	30		
Religion/cultural/other	820		60	30	270		341	
Total	**6920**	**161**	**4191**	**6246**	**3720**	**4455**	**5723**	**2978**

Program time in minutes (Local/Foreign)

Source: TVRI, TPI, SCTV, & RCTI, Jakarta Press, 1998.

Table 5
Share of Advertising Revenue by TV Channel

TV Channel	1995		1996		1997	
	Million Rp	%	*Million Rp*	%	*Million Rp*	%
RCTI	624, 217	38.1	741,036	33.6	777,083	29.0
SCTV	332,863	20.3	464,262	21.1	548,211	20.5
IVM	229,326	14.0	361,804	16.4	490,803	18.3
TPI	297,638	18.2	343,801	15.6	466,796	17.4
AN-TV	154,075	9.4	291,699	13.2	395,123	14.8
Total	**1,638,119**	**100**	**2,202,608**	**100**	**2,678,016**	**100**

Source: PPPI, 1998.

Table 6
Indonesia's Top Newspapers: Circulation and Readership

Newspaper	Publishers	Established	Circulation ('000)	Readership
Kompas (am)	Kompas Media Nusantara	1965	525	2.04 million
Pos Kota (d)	Media Antarkota Jaya	1970	500	2.23 million
Jawa Pos (am) [Surabaya]	Jawa Pos	1949	120	-
Suara Pembaruan (pm)	Media Interaksi Utama	1987	250/387	802,000
Republika	Abdi Bangsa	1993	327	589,000
Media Indonesia	Citra Media Nusa Purnama	1969	294	590,000
Suara Merdeka (am) [Semarang]	Suara Merdeka Press	1950	192/200	402,000
Harian Pagi Memorandum (d) [Surabaya]	Jawa Post		190	
Pikiran Rakyat (am) [Bandung]	Pikiran Rakyat Bandung	1956	150/180	696,000
Suara Karya (am)	Suara Rakyat Membangun	1971	146	237,000
Surya [Surabaya]	Antar Surya Jaya	1986	141	
Berita Buana (am)	Berita Buana Press	1971	138/150	206,999
Merdeka (am)	Merdeka Press	1945	130	
Surabaya Post (pm) [Surabaya]	Surabaya Post	1953	101/115	209,000
Berita Yudha (d)	Yayasan Parikesit	1965	80	
English Lanugage Dailies				
Indonesia Times (am)	Wiwara Jaya	1974	41	
Indonesia Observer (am)	Indonesia Observer Ltd	1966	35	
Jakarta Post (d)	Bina Media Tenggara	1983	48	

Source: WAN, 1999; *Editor & publisher international yearbook*, 1999.

Table 7
Penetration of Selected Commercial Radio Stations
(Preferred Private Radio Stations in Jakarta)

Radio station	1995		1996		1997	
	('000)	%	('000)	%	('000)	%
Sonora	387	6.0	374	5.6	1,244	18.8
Kayumanis	327	5.1	338	5.1	988	14.9
Muara	N.A.	0.0	502	7.6	886	13.4
Prambors	190	2.9	224	3.4	829	12.5
Assyafiyah	101	1.6	132	2.0	659	9.9
Attahiriyah	173	2.7	187	2.8	653	9.9
TMI	N.A.	0.0	137	2.1	644	9.7
Bens Radio	163	2.5	206	3.1	584	8.8
Agustina	107	1.7	148	2.2	523	7.9
Safari	131	2.0	94	1.4	511	7.7

Source: PPPI, 1998.

9. USEFUL ADDRESSES

TPI Televisi Pendidikan Indonesia
Jl. Pintu II TMII
Jakarta 13810
Telephone: 62 21 8412473
E-mail: info@tpi.co.id

FORUM
Kebayoran Center Blok A No. 11
Kebayoran Baru Velbak
Jakarta 12120
Telephone: 7255625

Indonesia Observer
PT Indonesia Observer
Jl. Pecenongan No. 72 Blok C. 17
Jakarta
Telephone: 62 21 3500155

The Indonesia Times
PT Marga Pers Mandiri
Jl. Biak 31/C
Jakarta
Telephone: 62 21 3860113

The Jakarta Post
PT Bina Media Tenggara
Jl. Palmerah Selatan 15
Jakarta
Telephone: 62 21 53004676–478

Kompas Daily
Jl. Palmerah Selatan
Jakarta
URL: http://www.kompas.com

Media Indonesia
Komplek Delta Kedoya
Jl. Pilar Raya Kav. A-D
Kedoya Selatan
Jakarta Barat
Telephone: 62 21 5812088
URL: http://www.mediaindo.co.id

Merdeka
Jl. Raya Kebayoran Lama No. 17
Jakarta 12210
Telephone: 62 21 5349311

Pos Kota
PT. Media Antar Kota Jaya
Jl. Gajah Mada 100
Jakarta
Telephone: 62 21 6290384

Pro Paron
Pt Info Karya Aksara Sentral
Jl.,Dewi Sartika No. 357 Cawang
Jakarta
Telephone: 62 21 8001069

Republika
Jl. Warung Buncit Raya No. 37
Jakarta Selatan 12510
Telephone: 62 21 7803747
URL: http://www.republika.co.id

Suara Pembaruan
Jl Dewi Sartika No. 136 D
Jakarta
Telephone: 62 21 8034077

TEMPO
Gedung TEMPO
Jl. Proklamasi 72
Jakarta 10320
Telephone: 62 21 3916160
Fax: 62 21 3921947

Ummat
Jl. Kapten Tendean No. 85
Jakarta 12710
Telephone: 62 21 7988646
URL: http://www.ummat.co.id

10. REFERENCES

Agassi, J. (1969). *Mass media in Indonesia* (mimeographed). Cambridge, MA: Center for International Studies, MIT.

Anderson, M.H. (1982). Indonesia. In J.A. Lent (Ed.). *Newspapers in Asia: Contemporary problems and trends* (pp. 193–216). Hong Kong: Heinemann Asia.

APT (Asia-Pacific Telecommunity). (1998, 1999). *The APT yearbook*. Bangkok: APT.

Associated Press. (1999, April 14). Covering East Timor turmoil, Indonesian reporters find neutrality elusive [on-line]. *The Freedom Forum*. Available: ⟨http://www.freedomforum.org/international/1999/4/14indonesia2.asp⟩.

Astraatmadja, A. (1998). After Suharto, disillusionment among young Indonesian journalists. *The Freedom Forum* [On-line]. Available: ⟨http://www.freedomforum.org/international/1998/7/10suharto.asp⟩.

Basuki, T. (1998). Indonesia: The Web as a weapon. *Development Dialogue, 2*, 92–103.

Cohen, M. (1999, March 25). Fastest gun in the east. *Far Eastern Economic Review, 162* (12), 52–54.

Crawford, R. (1971). Indonesia. In J.A. Lent (Ed.), *The Asian newspapers' reluctant revolution* (pp. 158–178). Ames: The Iowa State University Press.

D'Haenens, L., Gazali, E., & Verelst, C. (1999). Indonesian television news-making before and after Suharto. *Gazette, 61*, 127–152.

Eapen, K.E., & Lent, J.A. (1978). Indonesia. In J.A. Lent (Ed.), *Broadcasting in Asia and the Pacific: A contemporary survey of radio and television* (pp. 163–176). Philadelphia: Temple University Press.

Eng, P. (1998, July/August). Economic woes pummel Thai, Indonesia media. *Columbia Journalism Review, 20* (4) [On-line]. Available: ⟨http://www.cjr.org/year/98/4/indonesia.asp⟩.

Freedom House Survey Team. (1998). *Freedom in the world: The annual survey of political rights and civil liberties, 199–98*. New York: Freedom House.

Hill, D.T. (1994). *The press in New Order Indonesia* (Asia Papers No. 4). Perth: University of Western Australia Press in association with Asia Research Center.

Idris, N. (1998). Indonesia. In A. Goonasekera & D. Holaday (Eds.), *Asian communication handbook 1998* (pp. 67–79). Singapore: AMIC & NTU.

Indonesia: DPPLN (Indonesia: Directorat Pelayanan Penerangan Luar Negeri). (1996). *The role of the Indonesian Parliament in the International fora*. Jakarta: Department of Information with the cooperation of the Secretariat General of the House of Representatives.

ITU (International Telecommunication Union). (1998, 1999). *World telecommunication development report*. Geneva: ITU.

Jakarta Press. (1998, November 14). Excerpts of the 12 decrees endorsed by MPR session. *Tempo* [On-line]. Available: ⟨http://www.tempo.co.id/harian/include/index.asp?file=14111998-jp-4⟩.

Lau, T.Y., & Ang, P.H. (1998). The Pacific Rim. In A.B. Albarran & S.M. Chan-Olmsted (Eds.), *Global media economics: Commercialization, concentration and integration of world media markets* (pp. 310–327). Ames: Iowa State University Press.

Luwarso, L. (1998). The liberation of the Indonesian press. *Development Dialogue, 2*, 85–95.

Maslog, C.C. (1985). *Successful Asian community newspapers*. Singapore: AMIC.

McBeth, J. (1998, September 17). Indonesia: Dawn of a new age. *Far Eastern Economic Review, 161* (38) [On-line]. Available: ⟨http://www.feer.com/Restricted/98sept_17/indonesia.html⟩.

National Commission on Human Rights [Komisi Nasional HAM]. (1999, January 4). *Annual evaluation of the implementation of human rights in Indonesia* [On-line]. Available: ⟨http://www.komnas.go.id/english/cases/cs_text04.html⟩.

NDI (National Democratic Institute). (1999, February, 23). *The new legal framework for elections in Indonesia: A report of an NDI assessment team* [On-line]. Available: ⟨http://www.ndi.org/indo_feb_23_99.htm⟩.

Neumann, A.L. (1998a, March/April). High price of secrecy: Restricting the press worsened the economic crash. *Columbia Journalism Review, 20* (2) [On-line]. Available: ⟨http://www.cjr.org/year/98/2/asia.asp⟩.

Neumann, A.L. (1998b, November/December). Bringing back a legend. *Columbia Journalism Review, 20* (6) [On-line]. Available: (http://www.cjr.org/year/98/6/indonesia.asp).

Oetama, J. (1989). The press and society. In A. Mehra (Ed.), *Press systems in ASEAN states* (pp. 135–146). Singapore: AMIC.

Parapak, J. (1998a, May). *Nusantara-21: Indonesian vision for 21st century global information society.* Paper presented at ITU meeting, Johannesburg.

Parapak, J. (1998b, May). *Global mobile personal telecommunication by satellite.* Paper presented at ITU meeting, Johannesburg.

PPPI (Advertising Association). (1998). *Media scene 1997/1998.* Jakarta: PPPI.

Pudjomartono, S. (1998). Indonesia. In A. Latif (Ed.). *Walking the tightrope: Press freedom and professional standards in Asia* (pp. 102–107). Singapore: AMIC.

Razak, A. (1995, April). *Information technology and newspaper publishing.* Paper presented at UNESCO Asia Pacific regional seminar on information technology and newspaper publishing, Singapore.

Razak, A., & Tobing, S. (1996). Media monitors in Indonesia. In K.S. Venkateswaran (Comp.), *Media monitors in Asia* (pp. 25–34). Singapore: AMIC.

Richardson, M. (1998, November 6). Economic and politics curb Asian press freedom. *International Herald Tribune,* pp. 1, 6.

Romano, A. (1998). Normative theories of development journalism: State versus practitioner perspectives in Indonesia. *Australian Journalism Review, 20* (2), 60–87.

Said, T. (1990). Indonesia. In C.J. Hamelink and A. Mehra (Eds.), *Communication development and human rights in Asia* (pp. 37–50). Singapore: AMIC.

Shah, H., & Gayatri, G. (1994). Development news in elite and non-elite newspapers in Indonesia. *Journalism Quarterly, 71,* 411–420.

Sinaga, E.J. (1989). Indonesia. In A. Mehra (Ed.), *Press systems in ASEAN states* (pp. 27–39). Singapore: AMIC.

Sorenson, K. (1996, May). Silencing the 'Net: The threat to freedom of expression on-line. *Human Rights Watch, 8* (2).

Sumadi, M.E. (1971). *Television and national development: The Indonesian experience.* Paper prepared for WHO workshop on development of health education media, New Delhi.

Sussman, L.R. (1999). *Press freedom 1999: News of the century.* New York: Freedom House.

UNESCO (United Nations Educational, Scientific and Cultural Organization). (1980). *Many voices, one world* (MacBride Report). Paris: UNESCO.

UNESCO (United Nations Educational, Scientific and Cultural Organization). (1999). *Statistical yearbook.* Paris: UNESCO.

Vanden Heuvel, J., & Dennis E.E. (1993). *The unfolding lotus: East Asia's changing media.* New York: The Freedom Forum.

Van der Kroef, J.M. (1954). The press in Indonesia: By-product of nationalism. *Journalism Quarterly, 31,* 337–346.

Widarto, S. (1998, February 17). *Public broadcasting in Indonesia* (Unpublished mimeograph). Paper presented at AMIC seminar on Research and Development Information Media, Singapore.

WAN (World Association of Newspapers). (1998a, 1999). Indonesia. In *World press trends* (pp. 123–125). Paris: WAN.

WAN (World Association of Newspapers). (1998b, August 8). *Proposed Indonesian press law draws fire* [On-line]. Available: (http://www.fiej.org/whats_news/news_articles/indonesia.html).

World factbook. (1999). Indonesia [On-line]. Available: (http://www.odci.gov/cia/publications/factbook/id/html).

World radio TV handbook. (1999). Amsterdam: Billboard.

Zakaria, K., Sunara, N., Karamoy, W.A., Idris, H., Suyatno, Noor, M., Hsin, A., & Dirgo, A.T. (Eds.). (1995). *Indonesia: 50 years of independence.* Jakarta: Department of Information.

Zeitlin, A. (1999). Indonesian journalists, government struggle to draft press law. [On-line]. *The Freedom Forum.* Available: (http://www.freedomforum.org/international/1999/4/14indonesia.asp).

♦

LAOS

Frank Morgan & Eric Loo

1. NATIONAL PROFILE

1.1 Geography

Laos is a small country of only 237,000 sq km, landlocked by China, Vietnam, Cambodia, Thailand, and Myanmar. It stretches for 2,500 km along the Mekong river and is seldom more than 100 km across. Beyond the Mekong valley plains, the terrain is ruggedly mountainous, largely forested and difficult to access (CofA, 1999; *World factbook*, 1999; Hatlavongsa, 1998; Panasia, 1998). Only 7 percent of the land is arable or suitable for grazing. The monsoonal climate is tumultuous and alternately prone to flood and drought. Consequently, most of the population lacks reliable drinking water (World Bank, 1998). Together, these geographical factors increase both the need for communication and the difficulty of achieving it.

1.2 People

The 5.4 million people of Laos are predominantly rural (US Census Bureau, International Data Base, 1999), scattered across the country at an average of only 23 per sq km (*World factbook*, 1999; Hatlavongsa, 1998). Only 20 percent of them live in the few main towns. Buddhists comprise 60 percent and others include animists. Their 70 distinct ethnic and linguistic communities divide into three broad groups (*World factbook*, 1999; CofA, 1999): The lowland Lao Lum, who form 68 percent of the population, speak the dominant language and live in the towns along the Mekong River plains; the upland Lao Theung, descended from the Mon-Khmer, comprise 22 percent of the population and have their own language; while the mountain-dwelling Lao Soung, made up of the diverse Hmong, Mien, and other hill tribes, comprise 9 percent of the population. In addition, there are significant merchant communities of ethnic Chinese, Vietnamese, Indians, and Pakistanis, each with its own language. English has overtaken both French and Russian as a second language, and Thai is also important. The media thus need to work domestically in three languages—Lao Lum, Hmong, and Khmou—and internationally in six—Cambodian, Chinese, Thai, Vietnamese, French, and English.

The Lao are a youthful people, with an average age of only 26 years and an average life expectancy of about 54 (*World factbook*, 1999; Hatlavongsa, 1998): Fewer than 4 percent live to the age of 65, and 45 percent of them are under 15. The majority having been born since 1975, they have no memory of life before the establishment of the Lao People's Democratic Republic (LPDR), or of the dreadful hardships of the independence struggle. Their worldview has been shaped largely by the contemporary media. When, shortly before his death in 1994, the aged revolutionary leader and intellectual Phoumi Vongvichit deplored "the lack of discipline and (patriotic) commitment" among young Lao (Stuart-Fox, 1998b), he blamed their perceived consumerism and sexual permissiveness on the pernicious influence of Thai television.

Lao history has been turbulent and divisive (CofA, 1999). For more than 1,000 years, since the T'ai peoples moved out of southwestern China to occupy large tracts reaching from eastern Burma (Myanmar), across northern Thailand and Laos to western Vietnam, Laos has been subject to the tides and eddies of continual immigration and invasion. The T'ai displaced the Mon-Khmer from the Plain of Jars and drove them into the hills. The Kingdom of Lane Xang ("one million elephants") began as a tributary state of the ancient Khmer Kingdom of Angkor, but flourished, became independent, and survived into the late 20th century. Lane Xang fought not only against the Burmese, Thais, and Vietnamese but also against the other Lao kingdoms of Vientiane and Champassak. Instead of establishing common cause in a Lao community, these kingdoms all mobilized outside forces to fight their internal rivals. Finally, in the early 19th century, the Vientiane monarchy was destroyed when its prince, Chao Anou, misled by a false rumor, attacked Bangkok, was captured, and died in Thai hands.

European imperialism soon engulfed Laos. The French, who had taken over Cambodia and Vietnam, believed mistakenly that Laos and the Mekong provided possible trade routes into China. They forcibly removed both the Thai and the marauding Chinese Ho. Then, they proceeded to rule by dividing, and staffed the Lao civil service with Vietnamese. Apart from a little tin mining (also done by the Vietnamese) and their own monopoly in opium (for sale to China), the French left the Lao economy to its own traditional devices. They neglected health, education, and social welfare, especially among the hill peoples, who had resisted the French as vigorously as they had the lowland Lao. They educated the children of the cultivated Lao elites in France or Vietnam.

1.3 Government and Politics

After 1,000 years of regional turmoil, a century of European colonization, and 30 years of civil war, Laos finally achieved its independence on December 2, 1975, when the victorious communist Pathet Lao established the LPDR (AFG, 1998; Sangkhane, 1997).

During World War II, the occupying Japanese initially allowed France to continue the civil administration of Laos. Then, in early 1945, they interned all French personnel and ordered the king of Luang Prabang to declare Laos "independent." France had used the war years to woo popular Lao support by improving schools and other amenities. They also attempted to foster national and cultural identity through music, dance, literature, and a Lao newspaper. Nevertheless, when Japan surrendered and the French returned as the colonial power at the end of 1945, they found the newly politicized Lao largely agreed on the need for independence but bitterly divided on how to achieve it.

Some Lao factions sought a moderate, neutralist path to self-government (AFG, 1998). Others, on the political right, joined forces with first France and later the United States of America. Those on the left allied themselves with the Vietnamese communists, under Ho Chi Minh, who, by the early 1970s would defeat both the French and the Americans. Consistent with past history, division among the Lao extended to the ruling class. While Prince Souvanna Phouma was elected as a neutralist prime minister, his half-brother Prince Souphanouvong led the communist Pathet Lao. In 1960, a US-backed coup briefly installed another prince, Boun Oum, as prime minister. That drove the neutralists to join the Pathet Lao. Both sides, again, sought foreign allies. Both also recruited the upland people. The Pathet Lao drew support from the Vietnamese, the Soviets, and Eastern Europe, and took to the hills and caves of the north and the east. The Hmong mobilized with American "special forces." The United States expanded the market for Hmong opium throughout Southeast Asia and beyond, and also bombed the Plain of Jars more heavily than it had all of Europe during World War II. Thai and other foreign forces fought with the Royal Lao military. Foreign media, such as the Voice of America, were directed against Pathet Lao Radio and other revolutionary media, compelling the latter to compete for audiences and their allegiance.

The civil war that raged in Laos throughout the 1960s and nearly 1970s was largely a proxy war between foreign forces. Vietnam supported the Pathet Lao in the east of the country, the United States and Thailand backed the Royal Lao government in the west, and China was active in the north. By 1975, when the Pathet Lao prevailed and the Americans withdrew, there was widespread social devastation and nearly a quarter of the Lao people were refugees in their own country. After 1975, the Pathet Lao successfully made "U.S.-imperialist aggression" a rallying point to unite the population in the new Lao People's Democratic Republic.

The dissonant forces of history, economics, and politics have always complicated nation building in Laos. Initially communist, LPDR remains a one-party state. Yet, its 1991 Constitution, adopted following the collapse of communism in the Soviet Union and Eastern Europe, formalizes a market economy, guarantees private property ownership, and protects both foreign and domestic investment. It also separates the powers of the executive, legislative, and judicial branches of government.

An 85-seat National Assembly, popularly elected every five years, elects the president who, in turn and subject to the approval of the Assembly, appoints the prime minister, the council of ministers, and the judiciary. The legal system is based on a mix of traditional custom, French norms and procedures, and socialist practice. Political parties, except for the Lao People's Revolutionary Party (LPRP), are proscribed. The LPRP Central Committee is the effective government. Laos thus has more in common with the dominant-party regimes that rule in various parts of Asia than with the more pluralist parliamentary democracies of Europe, North America, and Australasia (Stuart-Fox, 1998a).

After 1975, the LPRP imposed central control both on the economy and on information, restricting the press and broadcasting, and limiting freedom of speech and association. Dissidents were imprisoned, "re-educated," or driven into exile. Ninety percent of Laos' educated elite emigrated, via Thailand, to countries such as Australia, Canada, France, and the United States (Stuart-Fox, 1998a), reducing the population by 10 percent and decimating the urban middle class. When the rural population resisted attempts to set up cooperatives and agricultural production collapsed, the country again suffered economically.

The relaxation of economic policy and the development of market-based capitalism in LPDR began in 1986. At no time, however, has the LPRP relinquished its monopoly on power. Nor has the new, educated, and wealthy elite shown any sign of dissent. It is more likely to compromise and collaborate than to oppose the Party (Stuart-Fox, 1998a). Yet, the LPRP is a national party. For the first time, one party embraces and represents all ethnic groups in Laos, and allows debate. However, it insists on containing that debate within the Party rather than opening it up to the general public, to competing parties, to potentially partisan media, or (worst of all) to interfering foreigners.

The contentious and problematic nature of history and collective memory in Laos in evident in Kremmer's (1997) attempt to discover the fate of the king, queen, and crown prince after their internment in 1977, and also in Phoumi Vongvichit's frustrated attempts to write histories of the Lao people, the Kingdom of Lane Xang and the "30-years struggle," including the relationship between the Pathet Lao and the Vietnamese (Stuart-Fox, 1998b). Phoumi was less a Marxist than a Lao nationalist who found his cultural roots in Buddhism. He was thus caught between the Marxist view that "art, religion and duty have no real history" (Baudrillard, 1996) and the traditionally perceived divinity of the Lao monarchy along with the people's sense of duty.

1.4 Economy

Subsistence agriculture remains the basis of the Lao economy (ADB, 1998; ASEAN, 1998), making it particularly vulnerable to the tumultuous climate and the vagaries of international markets. In 1999, Lao PDR's gross domestic product (GDP) was only US$ 7 billion (at purchasing power parity) or about US$ 1,325 per capita. (The nominal per capita GNP was US$ 258). Annual exports, principally hydropower, timber, and forest products were a mere US$ 400 million and the reserves, excluding gold, only US$ 100 million (*Asiaweek*, December 17, 1999).

LPDR lacks transport and communication infrastructure (Hatlavongsa, 1998). It has 4,500 km of navigable waterways but no railways. Only 15 percent (2,000 km) of roads are sealed. Few civil aircrafts are serviceable and the standard of airports is poor.

Despite concerted efforts to improve the situation, Laos still lacks adequate and reliable telecommunications (ASEAN, 1998; Hatlavongsa, 1998; ITU, 1998; Panasia, 1998). The country has 5.5 mainline telephones and 1.2 cellular mobile subscribers per 1,000 people. Especially outside Vientiane, line quality is poor. These factors, together with widespread illiteracy, hampers not only economic activity in general, but also the gathering of news and the distribution of newspapers. The rural electricity system has been improved but broadcasting is likewise constrained by unreliable power supplies and a shortage of receivers (Silap, 1996; UNESCO, 1998b).

Following the initial failure of a command economy, the shift to market-based policies in 1986, along with a combination of aid and foreign investment, enabled the Lao economy to grow by 7 percent annually over the five years to 1998. Attracting foreign investment remains a government priority (Lao PDR, 1998). Manufacturing was never well developed; and extractive industries, such as forestry and mining, tend to be foreign-owned. Tourism, which had been a focal sector for foreign investment and had grown spectacularly during the 1990s, was hit hard by the 1998 crisis.

2. DEVELOPMENT OF PRESS AND BROADCASTING

2.1 Brief Early History

The press and radio were introduced into Laos in the early 20th century as arms of the French colonial empire. Their function was to serve the expatriate French and provide a public address system for their administration. The monthly *Bulletin Administratif du Laos* appeared first in 1902 (Nunn & Anh, 1971). *Chot Mai Het Lao* (1939), *Lao Nhay* (1941–45) and *Pathet Lao* (1941–44) were other early publications. Members of the ruling elite, returning from Vietnam or France after their education, brought with them a taste for the more sophisticated culture and media of the metropolitan centers there. That structure prevailed, largely unaltered, until after World War II.

2.2 Developments since 1945

The history of communication and the media in Laos, since 1945, has been inextricable from the struggle for political and cultural independence. In the classical Marxist tradition of *agitprop*, press and broadcasting became key propaganda weapons in the armory of the revolutionary movement, as they were for its opponents. The foundations of the present press and radio systems in LPDR were laid during the civil war. Television was not introduced until the 1980s, by which time the new regime was well established.

Prior to 1975, 41 newspapers or periodicals were published in Vientiane, including 11 dailies, 18 weeklies, one monthly, and 11 periodicals of undetermined frequency (Lent, 1974). Political factions or their supporters owned most of them. Sixteen were in Lao, three each in French and English, and one in all three languages (Lent, 1974, 1982). The leftist–neutralist Bong Souvannavong group published *Lao May* and *Santiphab*. The former Prime Minister Katay Don Sasorith controlled *L'Avenir du Laos, La Voix du Peuple,* and *La Tribune des Jeunes;* the Voravong family owned *Sieng Lao* and *Pratchatipatay*; and the Independent Party leader Phouy Sonanikone published *Mahasan* and *L'Hebdomodaire Independente*. Meanwhile, the royal government published its daily *Lao Presse* and the Nationalist Party put out its *Lao Lane Sang*. Six dailies—*Sat Lao* (Lao State), *Siang Seri* (Free Voice), *Lao Hua, Vientiane Post, Sai Kang,* and *Agence Lao Presse*—appeared during the early 1970s. By 1975, the right-wing *Sat Lao* and *Siang Seri* were the dominant Lao language papers. But the communists had also been active.

The central importance of the media to the revolutionary struggle in Laos is evident from the seniority of those who were responsible for them. Nouhak Phoumsavanh, who became the third president of the LPDR, was a publisher of *Samakhi Tham* (Solidarity Dharma) in eastern Laos, and the current president, Khamtay Siphandone, published *Lao Kou Sat* in the south. As the resistance movement united in 1950, their two publications were brought together to form the first communist newspaper in the country, *Lao Itsala* (Lao Freedom) (Kikuchi, 1996). *Lao Itsala* later became *Lao Hak Sat* (Lao Patriotism) and, as the official party paper, reached a circulation of 15,000 in 1959. The communists extended their media development throughout Pathet Lao-controlled areas, establishing Vithatyu Kajaisiang Khong Pathet Lao (Pathet Lao Radio Broadcasting) in August 1960 and the army paper *Khongtap Potpoi Pasason Lao* (Lao People's Liberation Army) in January 1965.

The Pathet Lao Committee on Information, Press, Radio, and Television Broadcasting established the present government news agency, Khaosan Pathet Lao (Pathet Lao News or KPL) on January 6, 1968. Operating initially from caves in Sam Nua Province (Lent, 1974), where it propagated the policies of Neo Lao Hak Sat, KPL moved its operations to the Neo Lao Hak Sat party offices in Vientiane in 1975. As a communist victory became imminent, virtually all non-communist papers closed. The Pathet Lao finally took over the last remaining Lao language daily in Vientiane, the right-wing *Vientiane Post*, and renamed it *Vientiane Mai* (Vientiane News). It was then the only daily newspaper in the capital.

In establishing the New Regime in 1975, the LPRP changed the name of *Neo Lao Hak Sat* to *Siang Pasason* (Voice of the People). In 1983, this became *Pasason* (People), which remains its current form. Yet, it retains the subtitle *Siang Khong Sunkang Phak Pasason* (The Voice of the Central Committee of the Lao People's Revolutionary Party) and continues to be administered by the Ministry of Information and Culture.

While KPL publishes its news bulletins in English, as well as in Lao and in French, there had been no English-language newspaper in Laos, following the closure of the *Vientiane News* in 1975, until the introduction of the *Vientiane Times* in 1994. The cover story of its first issue was the opening of the Australian-funded "Freedom Bridge" over the Mekong River, linking Laos with Thailand. Normally, however, both Lao- and English-language papers rely solely on KPL, which draws its world news from China's Xinhua news agency.

Broadcasting in Laos began in 1950 when the French installed a 1 kW shortwave radio transmitter. Lao National Radio started regular official broadcasting in April 1952. One regular program was titled "For Lao people in enemy hands." In addition to LNR services, the Royal Lao Army operated medium-wave stations in Vientiane, Savannakhet, and Pakse to disseminate propaganda. During the 1960s, Gen. Vangpao's CIA-backed army operated another station at Long Chen, using two 5kW transmitters to broadcast in Lao, Vietnamese, Hmong, Thai-Dam, and Mien. The Association of Lao Police set up a 20 kW transmitter at Thadeua in 1972 (Lichty & Hoffer, 1978). During the Civil War, the Pathet Lao broadcast from caves, using makeshift equipment, but could not reach the whole country.

3. THE PRESS

3.1 Policy and Legal Framework

In the absence of any formal media law, the press and broadcasting in LPDR continue to be administered by the Ministry of Information and Culture. Lao-language papers are expected "to link the party, the state and the masses" (M. Somsanouk, interview with E. Loo, May, 1998), and the English-language paper with its alluring Internet website (www.vientianetimes.com/Headlines.html) is expected to attract foreign investment and tourism.

Central censorship is no longer imposed on the press. Nevertheless, ambiguity and caution prevail; and individual journalists, many of whom lack any formal professional education, generally censor their own stories according to their perceptions of the government's sensitivities (K. Khamalavong and K. Kongvongsa, interviews with E. Loo, May 1998). Self-censorship is also widely evident among editors. "We must know where we stand as government officials. The journalists of Laos understand their duties.... It is necessary [that they] understand clearly what they can and cannot cover" (M. Somsanouk, interview with E. Loo, May 1998).

Without legislation or other clear guidelines, Lao journalists are especially cautious about overtly questioning government officials or policies. Although the 1991 Constitution provides for press freedom and civil liberties, few citizens feel free to exercise these rights fully. There are no legal safeguards, particularly where politics is concerned.

The anomalies that restrict the media in Laos derive from its political ideology and are enshrined in the 1991 Constitution. While Article 6 guarantees that "the freedom and democratic rights of the people...cannot be violated by anyone," Article 7 requires mass organizations to "unite and mobilize the people." Media organizations are still expected to raise political consciousness and mobilize support for the LPRP among all the diverse ethnic groups and social classes of Lao society. Another such anomaly is that while foreigners may now travel all over the country without official clearances and a wide range of information is available from the UN and other international agencies in Laos, its own media and public institutions remain largely uncommunicative.

3.2 Financial Aspects: Circulation, Advertising, Marketing Strategies

The Lao press has begun to diversify its revenue. In 1993, the LPRP resolved (Resolution 36) that the media should reduce their dependency on government and seek other sources of funding, and thus paved the way for the media to introduce advertising. The first Lao-language paper to do so was *Vientiane Mai*. The *Vientiane Times* continues to rely on the Ministry of Information and Culture to pay staff salaries and some operational expenses. Production costs, however, are offset by advertising and subscription fees. *Pasason Athit* (People Weekly) earns approximately US$ 4,000 (now more than 15 million kip) per page annually from the sale of advertising space to the utility authority, the Electricite de Lao (EDL). Although these developments appear to be consistent with the government's overall policy of economic liberalization, another anomaly arises. Resolution 36, in order to ensure that newspapers focus on news and information, limits advertising to only 10 percent of newspaper space.

There are some signs of an emerging private sector in the Lao media. *Dok Champa* (a Lao airline magazine named after the national flower) and *Discovery Lao* are privately owned. The sale of foreign publications, while still meager, is no longer strictly forbidden. Visitors can now bring in newspapers and magazines such as *Newsweek, Far Eastern Economic Review, The Times, Bangkok Post*, and *The Nation*. Thai newspapers are sold by subscription or in government-run bookshops in Vientiane. Hotel lobbies are often strewn with English and French novels, left behind by departing travelers. The proximity and ready availability of Thai radio and television provides the people of Laos, especially along the Mekong Valley, with a window on another media world and an alternative perspective on the news. Surveillance and jamming are impractical (K. Kongvongsa, interview with E. Loo, May 1998). The emerging middle class, which can afford to install satellite dishes, does so and tunes in to global television.

The *Vientiane Times* has expanded to produce a French-language paper at the end of 1998. It aims for a total domestic and overseas circulation of 5,000, compared with the 2,000 of the *Vientiane Times*. Drawing on *Agence France Presse* in Paris, the expatriate French production editor proposes to focus on French literary and cultural news and to train the local staff in writing and production. Financed by the Hanoi-based NGO, Association Francophonie, the new venture will promote French language, literature, and culture in Laos.

3.3 Structure and Organization

The Ministry of Information and Culture supervises the press, all academic publishing, and the national news agency in LPDR. All are also members of the Lao Journalists' Association, which is presided over by Vice Minister Bouabane Vorakhoun. A veteran journalist, who still contributes a regular column to *Vientiane Mai*, the vice minister has publicly disagreed with direct government involvement in news operations. Nevertheless, the Lao media, like those in Indonesia, Malaysia, and Singapore, remain subject to continual official scrutiny. *Vientiane Times* and *Pasason* are supervised by the national government while the Vientiane municipal government similarly controls *Vientiane Mai* (Vientiane News). Editors accept responsibility for fostering rural and economic development and reject both the "free-market" model of journalism and "infotainment" (M. Somsanouk, interview with E. Loo, May 1998), thus declining any direct responsibility to the general public.

Disputes over press coverage of public affairs are either resolved directly between complainants and editors or referred to the ministry. In "the Lao Way," confrontation is avoided. In 1997, a press report of corruption in local government attracted a complaint that was finally referred to the Lao Journalists' Association for adjudication. The journalist was found to be at fault for not seeking the comments of the accused official, and the ministry upheld the complaint. No "penalty" was imposed on the journalist except that he was transferred to another newspaper in another municipality.

Two documents provide a guide to professional media practice in Laos. One is Resolution 36. The other is the code of ethics formulated by the Lao Journalists' Association:

- to extend and protect the policy of the Party and the benefits of the people;
- to provide a forum for the exchange of constructive opinions by the people;
- to reflect the diversity of Lao culture and help implement the objectives of social and economic development;
- to solve cultural conflicts to lead to a better society and the public good;
- to improve the wisdom of the people by providing news and information that are beneficial to their development;
- to promote the language, culture, and independence of the state;
- to respect the culture, spiritual values, and wisdom of others;
- to be sensitive to new ideas;
- to have a sense of responsibility;
- to correct mistakes promptly;
- to realize the civil rights of the people in receiving news in accordance with the law; and
- to focus on making LPDR a country of peace, independence, democracy, unity, and prosperity.

Impartiality and fairness, both of which are highly valued in the rhetoric (if not always the practice) of the Western media, are conspicuously absent from this code. The emphasis, instead, is on the media as *"khuangmu an lemkhom"* (sharp instrument) and *"phasana"* (vehicle) for the Party. The notion of *"ve thi"* (forum) refers to *"sai nyai"* (linking the people to the party). The media are not included in the liberal policies applied to economic production and trade. They remain instruments for the dissemination of Party policy to the masses and the provision of *"suksa op-hom"* (education and training) in political ideology.

3.4 Quality and Popular Press

Except for the *Vientiane Times*, whose use of English, large readership, and website accessibility make it a flagship publication, the distinction between "popular" and "quality" media in Laos has little meaning. There is neither a privately owned newspaper industry seeking rapid profits nor any lucrative tabloid market for it to pursue. The major distinction is between the local media and those elsewhere.

Exposure to the relatively more liberal Thai media has made some Lao journalists question their approach to professional practice. Those trained in Bangkok, and the UN volunteers who work with them, in particular, observe a discrepancy between the dissemination of official, development-oriented information in Laos and the more inquisitive and interrogative approach to news among their private-sector counterparts in Thailand. Nevertheless, they see little option other than accepting the government position.

3.5 Distribution and Technology

In Laos, newspapers are essentially an urban phenomenon. Transport difficulties largely prevent their distribution in the rural and in the remote parts of the country. As a consequence, there are fewer newspapers per head of population (3 per 1,000 people), across the whole country, than there are television sets (10 per 1,000 people) (UNESCO, 1998b, 1999). Radio is, therefore, the medium of first report (145 receivers per 1,000 people) (Silap, 1996; UNESCO, 1999). There is no medium either of analysis and debate, or of record.

Virtually the sole source of news and information is the Lao News Agency (KPL), which distributes a daily bulletin in Lao, French, and English. Originally on mimeographed sheets, the bulletin is now produced on computer. KPL has traditionally used teleprinters to distribute its news but now has facsimile and electronic mail for both domestic and international distribution.

Despite the introduction of desktop publishing, the size, design, packaging, and circulation of Lao publications remain in their infancy. Magazines and newspapers, such as the *Vientiane Times*, are printed on sheet-fed, offset lithography machines. Full-color printing is used for glossy covers and center-spreads. The funds to upgrade printing machinery are sought continually from external sources.

4. BROADCASTING

4.1 Policy and Legal Framework

Like the press, radio and television broadcasting in Laos is controlled by the Ministry of Information and Culture and expected to promote national solidarity and government policy. Radio was introduced by the French, before World War II, and the current radio station in Vientiane was built by the Americans in 1966. Those in Luang Prabang, Pakse, and Savannakhet were added in 1968. During the civil war, the Pathet Lao broadcast from caves, using makeshift equipment, but transmission was difficult and could not reach the whole country.

4.2 Structure and Organization

4.2.1 Radio

The loudspeakers, which once adorned the street corners of Vientiane, testified to the difficulties that confronted the new regime after 1975, when it took over Lao National Radio (LNR). Radio has for long been the most accessible mass medium worldwide (*World radio TV handbook,* 1998; UNESCO, 1998a), with an unrivaled capacity both for message transmission and community building. It is cheaper and simpler to produce than television and easier to deliver than print. Nevertheless, LNR had to overcome not only a lack of money, of equipment, and of skilled personnel, but also an audience unable to procure receivers following the devastation caused by the war (Lichty & Hoffer, 1978; Morgan, 1991). These considerations, together with the government's programming policy, led to the installation of the public address system for radio. The Soviet Union donated an assortment of Hungarian and British taperecorders, microphones, mixing desks, and transmitters to help upgrade the radio stations. It also provided a portable generator and other equipment for a small outside broadcast vehicle, and expanded the range of the transmitter beyond the original 80 km. Nationwide coverage, however, remained impossible.

In 1994, Radio Australia donated some superceded studio equipment to LNR; and more recently UNESCO's International Program for the Development of Communication (IPDC) has approved funds to improve studios and install six 300W FM transmitters in provincial stations. Otherwise, LNR has had very little support to improve its services over the past 20 years.

4.2.2 Television

Lao National Television began in 1983, taking over studio space in the radio station and some adjacent houses in Vientiane. The first television studios thus had ceiling heights of only two meters. The cameras, control equipment and low-band U-matic video recorder that LNTV used for studio operations and the VHS camcorders that it used for news would have been below "broadcast standard" anywhere else. Television was extended in 1988 to include Savannakhet, Pakse, and Luang Prabang, again using former radio studios and low-band U-matic and VHS equipment.

The purpose-built Television Center, which the Japanese aid agency JICA established at Kilometer Six (the government precinct) in Vientiane in 1993, cost US$ 35 million. It is equipped with Betacam cameras and editing equipment, although it still uses Super-VHS for news gathering. Four new stations in the provinces and five relay stations have helped to extend national coverage. Improved facilities, together with staff development provided by Australia, other donor countries, and the Asia-Pacific Institute for Broadcasting Development (AIBD), have raised the standard of production. Program content, however, continues to follow the socialist style adopted during the 1970s.

4.3 Program Policies

The LPRP sees radio and television, like the press, as "the sharp instruments" and "vehicles" of Party and government policy, primarily responsible for creating a forum to link people to the Party. It does not see the media as free and independent agents in a democratic process, or as a part of the economy.

Most radio programming is studio-based: largely news, information, development programming, and music. Although journalists monitor BBC World Service, VoA and Thai services, they draw the news from the national news agency, KPL. Programs are also available for the ethnic minorities in their own languages. To assist English-language tuition in LPDR, the BBC program "Follow Me" is broadcast regularly, with the text printed in the *Vientiane Times*.

The broadcast media use even drama to focus on the reconstruction of society. Education, entertainment, and talk programs, including those especially for women and young people also serve the same purpose. Entertainment is seen as a socially constructive way of keeping the people happy and united, not (as in the West) as a "diversion" or as "distraction." Talks too are more likely to deal with the impact on Laos of other countries' policies rather than with domestic policy issues.

Each television station transmits three hours of programming each day (6.30 p.m.–9.30 p.m.), including a 15–20 minutes locally produced news bulletin. The remaining programs are either relays from Vientiane or prerecorded videotapes. The schedule typically includes Chinese children's programs, patriotic and traditional songs, cartoons, development programs, music, and dubbed Russian films. A network of 1-kW transmitters distributes programs.

4.4 Ownership and Financing

Advertising has been used to augment the revenues of LNR since 1987 but the country has never had any independent or commercial broadcasting to compete with the government service. Also, the volume of advertising is limited by both economic and policy constraints. LNR's principal role is to contribute to national development.

In 1993, LNTV and the Thai company Shinawatra IBC began TV3, a joint venture commercial television service. Staffed by former LNTV employees, it offered movies, music and entertainment programs, and commercials, all in Thai, along with a Lao-language news bulletin. There was widespread speculation at the time that "a lot of dollars" had "passed under the table" to obtain the necessary approvals. The programming, transmitted terrestrially in Laos, was uplinked to Shinawatra's satellite for broadcasting in Thailand. All advertising revenue and satellite service subscriptions were collected and retained in Thailand. When TV3 failed to obtain LPDR approval for its satellite uplink, the government cancelled the license and took over the operation in its entirety. It now operates as a second LNTV channel for four hours per day.

Satellite television was introduced in 1991, when a Lao–Australian electrical company began to import and market dishes and receivers, giving people access to STAR TV and BBC World Service from the Asiasat satellite. At first, only foreigners were allowed to install this equipment. In 1993, however, CNN, Discovery, Australia Television (ATV), and the national services from a number of ASEAN countries became available, free to air, on the Palapa 4 satellite. Satellite receiving equipment provided by Australia and France now allows LNTV to re-broadcast programs from ATV and TF1 free of charge.

The introduction of microwave (MMDS) television transmission from Thailand has been immensely popular in Laos. Since 1997, another 40 channels of television have been available by subscription (US$ 25 per month). This service also demonstrates the impossibility of excluding foreign programming by banning technology.

A widespread and active video-hire industry has supplemented the range of programming available on television for viewers in Laos. Some outlets supply English- and French-language titles. Most, however, originate in Hong Kong and the United States, and are dubbed into Thai. Their poor vision and sound quality and visible time-code windows indicate that many are pirated copies.

Laos has several private video production companies, including Lao Inter Arts (run by the former staff of the now defunct government Department of Cinematography), the Participatory Development and Technology Center (PADETC), and Indo-China Media Services (ICMS), a Lao–Australian joint venture that produces development programs for UN agencies and various non-government organizations (NGOs). Lao Inter Arts uses Hi8 technology to produce video documentaries on ethnic traditions for Francophone video festivals. PADETC works with Hi8 and VHS facilities to focus on health care and rural extension, within a broader community development framework. ICMS uses Betacam SP equipment and works extensively throughout Indo-China on public advocacy projects relating to drugs, HIV/AIDS, the repatriation of refugees, education, and gender issues. Despite its high quality and the lack of locally produced programming, LNTV broadcasts very little of this production output.

As elsewhere worldwide, Laos also has a burgeoning industry of private operators, chiefly camera people "moonlighting" from LNTV, producing videos of weddings, funerals, and other domestic events. Yet the industry has not reached a sufficient critical mass for that expertise to feed into the broadcast television system.

5. NEW ELECTRONIC MEDIA

5.1 Internet and On-line Media

Poor telecommunication infrastructure (Silap. 1996), high connection costs, low literacy, low fluency in English, and the inability of computer hardware to read Lao script have all hindered Internet communications in Lao PDR. The country had an estimated 5,000 personal computers in 1996 (ITU, 1999). PC usage is based mainly on a Lao version of DOS/MS Windows (APT, 1998). A lack of reading materials on computer applications and Internet developments has restricted the growth of a broad user base. Lao PDR only entered the Internet field in 1994 through a Usenet group (socio.culture.laos) formed by Lao expatriates. In the same year, a local group called LaoNet established the first fiber-optic public e-mail service, based at the National Polytechnic Institute (NPI) in Vientiane. The country now has a top-level domain designated ".la" that will allow the allocation of 64,000 individual e-mail addresses. LaoNet now operates through the organization "Globenet Professional Services" from the premises of the Hotel Lao Plaza (http://www.laonct.net). In July 1998, Lao Telecom Co. Ltd installed an Internet system to support the telecommunication services both domestically and internationally, starting with 1,000 general users and 10 corporate users (APT, 1999).

Prime Ministerial Decree 166 of November 28, 1997 (Lao PDR, 1997) requires the Internet to be used as a channel for "productive communication exchange to contribute to national socio-economic development." Article 5 requires the approval of the Ministry of Communication, Transport, Posts, and Construction for the establishment of networks, the importation and use of equipment and tools, and the control of communication systems. This responsibility has been given to the Science, Technology, and Environment Organization (STENO), which now regulates all e-mail and Internet use, and checks all software before users are allowed to go on-line. STENO also controls intellectual property rights on the Internet. The government is concerned particularly with preventing expatriate Lao factions from using cyberspace to establish propaganda channels back into LPDR. The Ministry of Interior, which includes the police, is responsible for inspecting "the content of information and data sent over the Internet network to ensure national peace and public order."

Private companies planning to provide Internet services must not only adhere to the country's foreign investment and commercial laws but also demonstrate that they are capable of "restricting information and data" that are in conflict with LPRP policies and directives or with Lao social and cultural values. Prospective Internet users must apply (under Article 8 of the Decree) for approval by the

Ministry of Information and Culture. The Ministry of Communication, Transport, Posts, and Construction registers approved users. Under Article 9, approved users then have "the right to be provided with and to send information and data for the benefit of their activities or business, via an Internet center approved by the Ministry of Information and Culture." Articles 11 and 12 provide for users and providers who use the Internet to "benefit national socio-economic development in accordance with the law..." to be commended. Those who do not "shall be educated, trained and fined" and shall have their registration withdrawn. They may even be prosecuted.

5.2 Telecommunications Infrastructure

Laos had a telephone density of 0.55 per 100 people in 1998 compared to 0.16 in 1990. The density of main lines per 100 households was 1.4 in 1996. In addition to the 28,500 mainline telephones, Laos had 6,500 cellular telephones (ITU, 1999). Thus, the country has one of the world's lowest teledensities. The country's main telecommunications operator is Enterprise of Telecommunications Lao (ETL). A joint-venture operator is the Lao Telecom Co. Ltd.

Laos' telecommunication network links Vientiane with Luangprabang in the north, Paksan and Thakhek in the central region, and Savannakhet and Pakse in the south. The rural communications project (RURTEL), two phases of which have been completed, has provided telephone services to districts in the northern province. The network is not capable of direct dial out of the country (APT, 1999).

6. POLICY TRENDS FOR PRESS AND BROADCASTING

Like their counterparts in many developing countries, the media in Laos have had to rely heavily on foreign aid to procure equipment and facilities. Often, this has meant being forced to work with superceded and inefficient machinery, which has been prone to breaking down and has been punitively expensive to repair. Another severe constraint has been the capability of their personnel.

During the Civil War and in the early days of the New Regime, the heroic efforts of pioneer media workers outweighed their lack of technical competence. Subsequently however, while there has been no formal audience research to measure media quality or effectiveness, the need to improve their human resources has become more evident (Goonasekera, 1993; Morgan, 1991, 1995). LPDR has been assisted in this effort by friendly countries such as Australia and France, regional organizations such as AIBD, and international agencies such as UNESCO.

In 1993, the Ministry of Culture and Information established a Mass Media Training Center (MMTC) (Kongvongsa, 1993, 1996). Housed in three bungalows on the premises of the former Department of Cinematography and the National Film Archive, MMTC was intended to provide professional education and training for practitioners in both the print and the broadcast media. It is beset, however, by precisely the same problem that afflicts the media themselves: a lack of capable staff, workable facilities, and sufficient funding. It has been equipped with VHS format video equipment for television work but has neither any radio facilities nor any computers or desktop publishing facilities for print media development. With no funds for spares and repairs, MMTC has had a perennial maintenance backlog. As a consequence, foreign training teams have had to fly in the facilities to support their courses or to make special arrangements to conduct those courses in professionally equipped media organizations, rather than at MMTC.

UNESCO recognizes (Morgan, 1995; UNESCO, 1997) that professional education for communication and the media must produce capable practitioners, and that capability includes personal attributes such as ingenuity, inventiveness, and worldly wisdom as well as particular skills and knowledge. It further recognizes that professional media educators also require similar capabilities. But, here lies a major obstacle for MMTC. None of its staff have had professional media experience; and consequently they have been unable to construct a comprehensive curriculum to meet the current and future needs of the media in Laos, and of the country itself.

7. MAIN ISSUES

In addition to the capability of personnel, the media in Laos are confronted by continuing economic, cultural, and political issues. The nation's economic future depends on an upturn in tourism and other lures to foreign investment. The print, broadcast, and on-line media have mobilized in support of this strategy. Global financial forces, however, have undermined these efforts, as has the domestic decision to exclude media and information from the more liberal policy framework applied to the economy. Nevertheless, inexorable forces are already at work to modernize the Lao economy and to make its society more complex and sophisticated (Stuart-Fox, 1998a). The opportunity exists to let the media invigorate both the economy and the politics of Laos. Since LPDR's admission to ASEAN, diplomatic observers have reported a greater self-confidence within the Lao government (ASEAN, 1998). The country is no longer so anxious about either its neighbors (who have, historically, rarely been friends) or its own people (who have historically so often been divided). Political change will inevitably follow. *Collaboration* between the media and the state (Nordenstreng, 1997) could soon grow into the *facilitation* and *surveillance* of government by the media, a process driven not by outsiders but by the Lao people themselves. Equally inevitably, they will use their own media to create their own future.

8. STATISTICS

Table 1
General Profile

Population	5.4 million
Area	236,800 sq km
Population density (1999)	23.4 per sq km
Urban population (1998)	22 percent
Per capita GDP (PPP) (1999)	US$ 1,325 per annum
Arable/grazing land (1998)	7 percent
Navigable waterways (1998)	4,500 km
Paved roads (1998)	2,000 km (15 percent)
Telephone lines/100 people (1998)	0.55
Cellular lines/100 people (1998)	0.12
Population under 15 years (1998)	45.2 percent
Average age	26 years
Average life expectancy (1999)	52.3 years
Population over 65 years (1998)	3.2 percent
Exchange rate (1999 average)	US$ 1 = 5,688 Kip

Source: *Asiaweek*, December 17, 1999; ITU, 1999; UNESCO, 1999; US Census Bureau (http://www.census.gov/cgi-bin/ipc/idbsum).

Table 2
Estimated Mass Media Penetration

	Radio receivers		TV receivers		Daily newspapers		
	Number ('000)	Per 100 people	Number ('000)	Per 100 people	Number	Circ'n ('000)	Per 100 people
1980	350	10.9	–	–	3	14	0.44
1985	430	12.0	–	–	3	13	0.36
1990	520	12.5	22	0.53	3	14	0.34
1995	630	13.2	45	0.94	3	14	0.29
1996	700	14.3	50	1.00	3	18	0.37
1997	730	14.5	52	1.00			

Source: UNESCO, 1999.

Table 3
Print Media (Publishers), Radio, Television

Print media		
Dailies	*Publisher*	*Circulation*
DAILIES		
Pasason (People)	Central Committee of LPRP	10,000
Vientiane Mai (New Vientiane)	Vientiane Party committee	5,000
TWICE WEEKLY		
Vientiane Times	Ministry of Information & Culture	3,200
WEEKLIES		
Pasason Van Athit (Sunday People)	CC of LPRP	2,000
Vientiane Thurakit Sangkorn (Business-Social)	Vientiane Party committee	2,000
Khao Thurakit (Business News)	Lao National Chamber of Commerce & Industry	
Khongtap (Army)	Lao Army	
MONTHLIES		
Haeng Ngan (Labor)	Lao Federation of Trade Unions	
Noum Lao (Lao Youth)		
Nyasvason (Pioneers)		
Vannasin (Literature) magazine		
Sieng Khaen Lao (Sound of Lao)	Lao Association of Writers	
Savannakhet Phatthana (Development)	Ministry of Information & Culture, Savannakhet Province	
Menhing Lao (Lao Women)	Lao Women's Union	
Khoueng Vientiane (Vientiane Province)	municipal government	
QUARTERLIES		
Seuksa Mai (New Education)		
Soukhaseuksa (Health Education)		
Pathet Lao (Lao Country)		
Aloun Mai (New Dawn)		
Khosana (Propaganda)		
Vithayasat Technic (Science and Technology)	Science, Technology & Environment Organization (STENO)	
Aham Lae Ya (Food and Drugs)		
Khosang Phak (Party Building)	LPRP	
Karn Ngeung (Finance)		
Houam Phattanha (Joint Development)		
Sang Khru (Teacher Training)		
Vai Dek (Children)		
Seumuanson Lao Lae Karn Phattanha (Lao Media and Development)		
Pathet Lao Khoueng Vientiane (Lao Country: Vientiane Province)	Vientiane municipality	
Champa Mai (New Champassak)	Champassak Province	
Thonthieo Laos (Lao Tourism)	Tourism Authority	
Discover Laos	Tourism Authority	
Dok Champa (Champa Flower)	Lao Aviation in-flight magazine	

Table 3 contd

Radio	
Lao National Radio	12 stations (AM/FM/SW) in Vientiane, Luang Prabang, Xieng Khouang, Luang Namtha, Oudomsay, Houaphan, Sayabouri, Khammoune, Laksao, Savannakhet, Champassak

Television	
Lao National Television (Ch. 3 and Ch. 9)	10 stations in Vientiane, Luang Prabang, Xieng Khouang, Luang Namtha, Oudomsay, Houaphan, Sayabouri, Khammoune, Savannakhet, Champassak.

9. USEFUL ADDRESSES

ORGANIZATION	CONTACT	TELEPHONE
MINISTRY OF INFORMATION & CULTURE		856.21.21.4307
PO Box 59, Monthatourath Road, Vientiane		
Vice Minister	Bounteng Vongsay	856.21.21.2898
Vice Minister	Bouabane Volakhoun	856.21.21.2402
Deputy Director,	Dy Sisombath	856.21.21.2424
Mass Media & Technical Planning		
Director,	Khamkong Kongvongsa	856.21.21.2455
Mass Media Training Institute		
PO Box 122, Vientiane		
Director,	Khamseng Soundara	856.21.21.2421
Publishing Library Sign Department		
Director,	Nithone Souliya	856.21.21.5901
State Printing House		
Director General.	Thongkham Onemanisone	856.21.21.2894
Dept of Literature & Mass Culture		
Director General,	Houmphan Rattanvong	856.21.21.2009
Cultural Research Institute		
Deputy Director,	Soradith Bounavong	856.21.21.2444
KPL News Agency		
PO Box 3770, Vientiane		
Director General,	Bounthanh Inthaxay	856.21.21.2428
Lao National Radio		
Director,	Khekheo Souisaoy	856.21.21.2467
Lao National Television		
Editor,	n/a	856.21.21.2467
Pasason Newspaper,		
PO Box 1110, Vientiane		
Editor,	Somsanouk Mixay	856.21.21.6364
Vientiane Times,		
PO Box 5723, Vientiane.		
Lao Journalists Association,	n/a	856.21.21.2420
PO Box 310, Vientiane		
OTHERS		
Science Technology & Environment		856.21.21.3740
PO Box 2279, Vientiane		

Foreign Investment Management Committee:		856.21.21.5636
Director, PADTEC	Sombath Somphone	856.21.21.5909
Lao Inter Arts	Som Ock	856.21.21.2156
Indo-China Media Services	Ron Hurrell	856.21.21.6223
Discover Laos Magazine		856.21.21.7294
PO Box 3770, Vientiane		
Vanasin Magazine,		856.21.21.2425
PO Box 163, Vientiane		
Noum Lao Newspaper,		856.21.21.2906
PO Box 1117, Vientiane		

10. REFERENCES

ADB (Asian Development Bank). (1998). *Statistical data of developing member countries* [On-line]. Available: (http://internotes.asiandevbank.org/notes/edr0004p/index.html).

AFG (ASEAN Focus Group). (1998). *Lao PDR timeline* [On-line]. Available: (http://www.aseanfocus.com/history/laos).

APT (Asia-Pacific Telecommunity). (1998,1999). *APT Yearbook.* Bangkok: APT.

ASEAN. (1998). *ASEAN transport and communication profile* [On-line]. Available: (http://www.aseansec.org/economics/tcstat5.html).

Baudrillard, J. (1996). Symbolic exchange and death. In L.E. Cahoone (Ed.), *From modernism to postmodernism: An anthology.* Cambridge, MA: Blackwell Publishers.

CofA (Commonwealth of Australia). (1999). *Laos brief* [On-line]. Available: (http://www.dfat.gov.au/geo/sea/laos).

Goonasekera, A. (1993). *Development of radio and television and national school for training in mass media in the People's Democratic Republic of Laos: An in-country evaluation of the projects.* Singapore: AMIC.

Hatlavongsa. (1998). *Laos Infosite* [On-line]. Available: (http://users.vmicro.com/laosinfosite/communications.html).

ITU (International Telecommunications Union). (1998, 1999). *World telecommunications development report.* Geneva: ITU.

Kikuchi, Y. (1996). *Rekishi teki haikei: motto shiritai raosu* (Historical background: want to know more about Laos?) S. Matsumoto, (Tr.), Sydney: University of Sydney Geography Department.

Kongvongsa, K. (1993, December 6–10). *Radio broadcasting in the Lao PDR.* Paper presented to AMIC Deutsche Welle Workshop on Radio Broadcasting Management 2000: Program trends and personnel development, Singapore.

Kongvongsa, K. (1996, August 18–22). *Media development in the Lao People's Democratic Republic.* Paper presented to the Professional Education Section of the 20th Biennial Conference of the International Association for Media and Communication Research, Sydney.

Kremmer, C. (1997). *Stalking the elephant kings: In search of Laos.* Sydney: Allen & Unwin.

Lao PDR. (1997, November 28). *Organization of a network: Importation, use and control of the Internet system* (Prime Ministerial Decree No. 166/PM) (Unofficial translation). Vientiane: Lao Government.

Lao PDR. (1998). *Lao embassy home page* [On-line]. Available: (http://laoembassy.com/indexlpdr.html).

Lent, J.A. (1974). Mass media in Laos. *Gazette, 20* (3), 171–179.

Lent, J.A. (1978). *Broadcasting in Asia and the Pacific: A continental survey of radio and television,* Philadelphia: Temple University Press.

Lent, J.A. (1982). Laos. In J.A. Lent (Ed.), *Newspapers in Asia: Contemporary trends and problems* (pp. 240–251). Hong Kong: Heinemann Asia.

Lichty, L.W., & Hoffer, T.W. (1978). Laos. In J.A. Lent (Ed.), *Broadcasting in Asia and the Pacific: A continental survey of radio and television* (pp. 120–123). Philadelphia: Temple University Press.

Morgan, F, (1991). *ASEAN–Australia media and information program—Phase two evaluation: Laos.* Report to the Australian International Development Assistance Bureau, Canberra: AIDAB.

Morgan, F. (1995). *UNESCO communication training activities, 1983–92: A critical evaluation.* Paris: UNESCO Communication Division.

Nordenstreng, K. (1997). Beyond the four theories of the press. In J. Servaes & R. Lie (Eds.), *Media and politics in transition: Cultural identity in the age of globalisation* (pp. 97–112). Louvain, Belgium: ACCO Publishers.

Nunn, G.R., & Anh, D.V. (1971). *Vietnamese, Cambodian and Laotian newspapers: An international union list.* Taipei: Chinese Materials & Research Aids Service Center.

Panasia. (1998). *Lao PDR country paper* [On-line]. Available: (http://www.panasia.org.sg/LAOPAPER.html).

Sangkhane, C. (1997). Communication policy and broadcasting in Laos. *Media Development, 44* (2), 15–16.

Silap, B. (1996, December 5). Wireless revolution in Laos. *I-Ways,* pp. 65–66.

Stuart-Fox, M. (1966) *Buddhist kingdom, Marxist state.* Bangkok: White Lotus.

Stuart-Fox, M. (1998a). *Laos: The post-Kaysone era* [On-line]. Available: (http://www.global.lao.net/laostudy/kaysone.html).

Stuart-Fox, M. (1998b). *Obituary: Phoumi Vongvichit (1909–1994).* [On-line]. Available: (http://www.global.lao.net/laostudy/phoumi.html).

UNESCO (United Nations Educational, Scientific and Cultural Organization). (1997). *UNESCO program and budget (29C/5, Technical Annex, p. 88).* Paris: UNESCO General Conference.

UNESCO (United Nations Educational, Scientific and Cultural Organization). (1998a) *World communication report,* Paris: UNESCO.

UNESCO (United Nations Educational, Scientific and Cultural Organization). (1998b) *Statistics* [On-line]. Available: (http://unescostat.unesco.org//Yearbook/Table6_3.html).

UNESCO (United Nations Educational, Scientific and Cultural Organization). (1999). *Statistical yearbook.* Paris: UNESCO.

Vientiane Times. (1998). News from Laos [On-line]. Available: (http://vientianetimes.com/Headlines.html).

World Bank. (1998). *Asia (South and East) tables: Access to safe water* [On-line]. Available: (http://www.worldbank.org/depweb/water/datasia1.html).

World factbook. (1999). Laos. Washington, DC: CIA [On-line]. Available: (http://www.odci.gov/cia/publications/factbook).

World radio TV handbook. (1998). New York: Billboard.

♦

12

MALAYSIA

H.M. Safar, Asiah binti Sarji, & Shelton A. Gunaratne

1. NATIONAL PROFILE

1.1 Geography

Malaysia is situated in Southeast Asia, bordering Thailand, Singapore, Indonesia, and the Philippines. It is a federation of 13 states, straddling the South-China Sea. Eleven of the states are in the peninsula, with Thailand to the north and Singapore to the south. The Straits of Malacca separate the peninsula from Indonesia to the west. Two states—Sarawak and Sabah—are on the island of Borneo, bordering Indonesia, Brunei Darussalam, the Philippines, and the South-China Sea.

1.2 People

Malaysia has a multiracial society. Slightly more than half of the people are *bumi-puteras* (culturally indigenous to the region), and the other half are non-*bumiputeras* (culturally non-indigenous). The three major ethnic groups are the Malay, the Chinese, and the Indian. This mix is the result of Malaysia's location between India and China at the center of *Nusantara*, the Malay world. The majority of Malaysia's 22.7 million people live in the states of Selangor, Johor, Perak, and Penang. Malaysia has an urban population of 47 percent and an adult literacy rate of 93.7 percent. The average life expectancy is 72 years (*Asiaweek*, December 17, 1999).

1.3 Government and Politics

Malaysia gained independence from Britain in 1957. The Portuguese became the first European power to conquer the Malacca Sultanate in 1511. Next came the Dutch, who defeated the Portuguese in 1641. The Portuguese and the Dutch kept very much to Malacca (Melaka) and left the other Malay states intact. The British acquired Penang in 1786 and, subsequently, established bases in Singapore (1819) and Melaka (1824) as well. These three events were collectively labeled the Straits

Settlements, which set off the process of political integration of the peninsula's Malay states into a modern nation-state. By 1914, the political picture of the present-day states of Malaysia was as follows:

- The Straits Settlements: British crown colony headed by a British governor, consisting of Singapore, Melaka, Penang, Labuan, the Cocos Isles, and Christmas Isle; capital: Singapore.
- The Federated Malay States: British protectorate headed by a British high commissioner (governor of the Straits Settlements) consisting of the states of Negeri Sembilan, Pahang, Perak, and Selangor.
- The Unfederated Malay States: British protectorate under the tutelage of a British adviser in each state responsible to the British commissioner, consisting of Johor, Kedah, Kelantan, Perlis, and Terengganu.
- Sarawak: British protectorate ruled by the Brooke family; capital: Kuching.
- Sabah: British protectorate, ruled by the Chartered Company of the British North Borneo; capital: Jesselton (Kota Kinabalu).

The Japanese took over Malaya and British Borneo in late 1941 and, subsequently, Singapore as well. After the defeat of the Japanese in 1945, the British rearranged the territorial set-up to form the Malayan Union and the crown colonies of Singapore, Sarawak, and British North Borneo. Malay opposition forced the British in 1948 to establish the Federation of Malaya in the peninsula, comprising the nine Malay states, Penang, and Melaka. The Alliance of the Malay, Chinese, and Indian political parties, which won the federation's first general election in 1955, succeeded in persuading Britain to grant independence in 1957. Malaysia formally came into being on September 16, 1963. Singapore, however, quit the federation in 1965, and Brunei opted to remain a separate sultanate.

Malaysia is a parliamentary democracy with a constitutional monarchy. Its head of state is the *Yang di-Pertuan Agong*, the supreme ruler of the country, elected every five years by the nine hereditary Malay rulers of the nine Malay states in Peninsular Malaysia. A governor known as the *Yang Dipertua Negeri* heads each of the other four states. An executive headed by a prime minister wields the actual power. The prime minister is the leader of the majority party in parliament, which comprises the 192-seat House of Representatives (the Lower House/*Dewan Rakyat*) and the 69-member Senate (Upper House/*Dewan Negara*). The members of the House are elected from single constituencies for a five-year term. The Senate has 26 representatives elected by the states for a six-year term and 43 appointed members.

Malaysia promulgated the *Rukunegara*[1] national philosophy following the racial riots of 1969. This stated that Malaysia should achieve greater unity among all its

---

[1] Woodiwiss, 1998, states that *Rukunegara* "combined patriarchic elements that were largely Malay and therefore Islamic in inspiration with modernistic American ones that promised positive discrimination to the Malays and economic progress to all" (p. 190).

citizens, maintain a democratic way of life, create a just society where people share the wealth of the nation equitably, ensure a liberal approach to the country's rich and diverse cultural traditions, and build a progressive society oriented towards modern science and technology. To achieve these objectives, it urged all Malaysians to pledge themselves to the five principles of the *Rukunegara*: belief in God, loyalty to the king and country, adherence to the constitution, adherence to the rule of law, and maintenance of good behavior and morality (Idid, 1989, p. 49).

The Barisan Nasional (National Front)—earlier called the Alliance—has governed the country since 1955, following the first general elections held before independence. This 14-party coalition's main components are the United Malays National Organization (UMNO), which leads the coalition, and its principal partners—the Malaysian Chinese Association (MCA) and the Malaysian Indian Congress (MIC). The other partners in Peninsular Malaysia are Malaysian People's Movement (GERAKAN) and the People's Progressive Party. The partners in Sarawak are Party Pesaka Bumiputra Bersatu (PBB), Sarawak United People's Party (SUPP), Sarawak National Party (SNAP), and Parti Bansa Dayak Sarawak (PBDS). The partners in Sabah are People's Justice Party (AKAR), Parti Bersatu Rakyat Sabah (PBRS), Sabah Democratic Party (PDS), and Liberal Democratic Party of Sabah (LDP). The original governing coalition comprising UMNO, MCA, and MIC expanded itself to form the Barisan Nasional by co-opting several other parties (because of the reduced majority the Alliance received in the 1969 general elections and the racial riots that followed in Kuala Lumpur).

In the November 1999 general elections, Barisan Nasional won 148 of the 193 Dewan Rakyat seats. The coalition of opposition parties, Barisan Alternatif, won 42 seats: the Pan Malaysian Islamic Party (PAS) 27 seats, the Democratic Action Party 10 seats, and the Parti Keadilan Nasional five seats. The Barisan Nasional held 166 seats in the previous parliament. BN's biggest success came in Sabah and Sarawak, where it won 45 of 48 seats (*Asiaweek*, December 10, 1999).

1.4 Economy

Malaysia has transformed itself from being a largely agricultural economy to a manufacturing one. Tin, rubber, and palm oil were traditionally Malaysia's major exports. The manufacturing sector, particularly electronics, has however superceded the traditional exports. The discovery of petroleum off Malaysian shores has boosted the country's economy. In 1999, Malaysia exported merchandise valued at US$ 76.9 billion and had reserves worth US$ 29.9 billion. Its gross domestic product (GDP) at purchasing power parity was US$ 163 billion (*Asiaweek*, December 17, 1999). Per capita income in nominal terms was US$ 3,092 in 1999 (Ringgit 11,750) a decline from US$ 4,284 (Ringgit 12,051) in 1997, reflecting the impact of the Asian economic crisis (*Bank Negara Malaysia annual report 1998*). Although Vision 2020 targeted that year for the country to reach the status of a developed economy, the 1998 Asian economic crisis might delay the process.

The private sector has played an active role in developing the country under Prime Minister Mahathir Mohamad, who came to power in July 1981. Malaysia's push for heavy industry has resulted in two national car projects, the Proton and the Perodua, the national motorcycle project, and the national truck project. A recent addition is the manufacturing of electrical goods. Mindful of the information economy, the country has set up a well-planned Multimedia Super Corridor, which has identified seven flagship applications for development: electronic government, smart schools, telemedicine, research and development, smartcard, borderless marketing, and worldwide manufacturing webs. Several cyber laws are already in place. The government has approved 189 companies, both local and foreign, for the corridor (*The Star In-Tech*, December 1, 1998, p. 3).

2. DEVELOPMENT OF PRESS AND BROADCASTING

2.1 Brief Early History

Merchant and auctioneer A.B. Bone started the country's first newspaper, *The Government Gazette*, on March 1, 1806, with the consent of Gov. Philip Dundas of the Prince of Wales Island (Penang). Bone came to Penang early in 1806 from Madras, where he was responsible for publishing and printing two newspapers, the *Hircarrah* and the *Madras Gazette*. Bone was trying his luck with the East India Company's fourth presidency set up in 1805. The other three presidencies were Bombay, Bengal, and Madras (Lent, 1982; Safar, 1996).

Bone had to agree to submit the proofs to a government secretary to allow undesirable news to be erased. This was the same censorship practice that the British had imposed on the other presidencies. In 1827, the colonial government attempted to replace censorship in the fourth presidency—which in 1826 had expanded to cover Penang, Malacca, and Singapore—with the 1818 Bengal Regulations or guidelines for editors. However, because Singapore and Malacca had been practicing censorship, the authorities had to drop the move.

In 1835, the British East India Company's government in Bengal passed the Indian Act XI, which amended all previous press laws, including censorship. In September 1835, this law also became applicable in the Singapore, Penang, and the Malacca residency.[2] The *Singapore Free Press* started publication to commemorate the enforcement of this passive law, which required only the registration of press machinery. The *Press* folded in 1869 but resurrected itself in 1884 to become a daily in 1887. Just before World War II, the *Straits Times*, a newspaper that started as a weekly on July 15, 1845, took over the *Press* and made it the *Times'* afternoon paper. The *Times*, which the Japanese renamed *Shonan Times* during the war, is the longest surviving newspaper in the region.

---

[2] In 1830, the fourth presidency was reduced in status to a residency. Singapore became the residency's new headquarters in 1832, when its economic development overtook Penang's.

In May 1939, a group of forward-looking Malays used Singapore as the launching pad for the first Malay newspaper in Jawi script, the *Utusan Melayu*. Several Chinese-language newspapers, including *Nanyang Siang Pau* (started in 1923) and *Sin Chew Jit Poh* (started in 1929) also appeared in Singapore (Lim, 1992; Tan, 1971).

Malaysia and Singapore share a common history of press and broadcasting services. Several leading Malaysian newspapers started in Singapore, and they continue to be published as separate entities in Singapore. A few have changed their names. Malaysia's *New Straits Times*, locally incorporated in 1972, is an off-shoot of the *Straits Times*, still published in Singapore under its original name. The *Malay Mail*, now an afternoon newspaper, started in 1896 in Kuala Lumpur as a morning newspaper. The *Straits Times* took over the *Mail* in the 1950s.

The longest surviving Tamil newspaper, *Tamil Nesan*, started in 1924 in Kuala Lumpur, is still operating today. Only one newspaper *Kwong Wah Yit Poh* (1910) that started in Penang before World War II has survived until today.

2.2 Developments since 1945

2.2.1 The Press

Six contemporary newspapers were started between 1945 and 1957: *China Press* (1946) that started in Kuala Lumpur; *Berita Harian* (1957), the first Malay newspaper to appear in Romanised script after World War II in preparation for Malaysia's independence; and four Sarawak newspapers—*Sarawak Tribune* (1945), which was the state's leading English newspaper; the *Chinese Daily News* (1945) of Kuching; the *Miri Daily News* (1945); and the *See Hua Daily News* (1952) of Sibu. The last three emerged to cater to the Chinese readership in three Sarawak locations, which then lacked road transportation connecting one another. A few Malay newspapers like *Suara Rakyat* (1945) of Ipoh, *Pelita Rakyat* (1946), and *Warta Negara* (1945) of Kuala Lumpur did not survive (Lim, 1992).[3]

As many as 36 of the newspapers in circulation today (in the four main languages) began after 1962. Twelve were started between 1963 and 1980, under three prime ministers; and 24 emerged under the pro-business policies of one prime minister, Mahathir Mohamad.

Notable among the newspapers established at the time of independence is the daily *Utusan Malaysia* (1967) and its Sunday edition *Mingguan Malaysia* (1964), the newspaper with the largest circulation, exceeding 500,000 copies. *The Star*, which started in Penang in 1971, is the other successful daily. It has become a national newspaper with its headquarters in Petaling Jaya, right next to the nation's capital. It has overtaken the *New Straits Times* as the country's largest English daily. The New Straits Times group's *Harian Metro* (1991), a Malay afternoon

[3] Lee and Sarachchandran, 1975, provide a useful bibliography on mass media in Malaysia.

daily with a breezy style, has become a newspaper popular beyond expectation. However, another Malay newspaper, *Harian Nasional* (which started in June 1984) failed after five months. Sabah and Sarawak account for the other newspapers, which have modest circulations. These two states distribute the national newspapers as well.

Malaysia also has smaller weeklies popularly called the "mosquito papers." These carry few advertisements and presumably have less impact. Political newspapers, like *The Rocket* of the Democratic Action Party and the *Harakah* of the Pan Malaysian Islamic Party, comprise another facet of the newspaper scene. As a party organ, *Harakah's* publishing permit limits its distribution to party members. However, it circulates freely as an alternative to the mainstream press. It had a circulation of 345,000 at the end of 1998, according to its editor (Zulkifli Sulong, interviewed on June 11, 1999). To meet the legal limitations of its permit, *Harakah* provides a special rack at the points of sale to notify people that as it is a party newspaper, only PAS members can purchase it. The paper carries a front-page notice that because it is "illegal" for non-members to read the paper, they should apply for party membership. Two tabloid weeklies—*Warta KL* (KL News) and *Ekslusif* (Exclusive)—made a successful debut in early 1999. These two mainly carry political news, giving prominent coverage to Anwar Ibrahim, the sacked deputy prime minister, and the activities of the newly formed National Justice Party led by Anwar's wife Wan Azizah Ismail and other opposition parties. *Ekslusif's* circulation was about 187,000 in June 1999 according to its editor (Abdul Jalil Ali, interviewed on June 15, 1999) and *Warta KL*'s was about 70,000. The contents of these weeklies, and of several magazines and books, are highly critical of the government, a trend unseen in previous years. Several other weekly tabloids concentrate on entertainment.

Malaysia's economic downturn caused the closure of a few newspapers, including *Watan*, a Malay-language tabloid daily, as well as the *Borneo Sun* and the *People's Mirror*, both of Sarawak (*The Sun*, January 3, 1999, p. 2). On the other hand, the defunct *Sabah Times* (first published in 1952), was re-published in March 1998, after a four-year hiatus, as *New Sabah Times*, with a circulation of 13,000 copies (interview with Anthony Wong, Managing Director, June 29, 1999).

Press laws affected the direction of the Malaysian press. Before World War II, the Straits Settlements and the Malay states had separate press laws, even though they were similar. In 1948, the Federation of Malaya, comprising the Malay states, Malacca, and Penang (two former Straits Settlements) promulgated a single Printing Presses Ordinance. Just before independence in 1957, the government of the Federation of Malaya amended the Ordinance. Newspapers published and printed in Singapore now had to apply for distribution permits to be sold in Malaya. The major newspapers like *Utusan Melayu*, the *Straits Times, Sin Chew Jit Poh*, and *Nanyang Siang Pau*, promptly set up their editorial and printing plants in Kuala Lumpur.

The law gave a boost to Malaysianize the press when the government passed another amendment in 1974 to ensure majority ownership in Malaysian hands. A major shake-up of the political and economic spheres followed the racial riots of May 13, 1969.

2.2.2 Radio

Malaysia was one of the earliest British colonies to operate a radio broadcasting service. However, the British government did not show much interest in radio in its early stage of development (Sarji, 1994). Amateurs, electric companies, telecommunication personnel, and radio enthusiasts were among those who started the ball rolling.

In 1921, A.L. Birch, the chief electric engineer of the Johore state government, experimented with a Peto Scott type of wireless set obtained from overseas (*Malay Mail*, July 30, 1921). In 1923, he formed the Johore Wireless Society, which triggered the formation of nearly one dozen radio societies throughout Malaya. News, music, and songs from the phonogram were among the first programs broadcast.

Institutionally and technically, the potential to set up radio broadcasting using the airwaves existed throughout the 1920s. However, the government failed to encourage the establishment of a broadcasting station until 1932. On April 1, 1933, it awarded a temporary license to Radio Service Company of Malaya (RSCM). In 1935, the British Malaya Broadcasting Company (BMBC), owned by a group of shareholders with participation by officers from the BBC, emerged as a full-fledged broadcaster. Following the award of the license to BMBC, the government withdrew RSCM's temporary broadcasting operating license at the end of 1936 (Sarji, 1994).

Owing to uncertainties in the political and economic environment at both the national and the international level, the parties agreed on March 2, 1940, to sell BMBC to the British government. At the end of 1941, just as the war in the Pacific began, the company changed its name to Malayan Broadcasting Corporation and began upgrading its organization and broadcasting equipment. The Japanese invaded and took control of Malaya and Singapore in February 1942 (Sarji, 1994).

Sarji (1994) contends that the broadcasting facilities came in handy for the Japanese during their occupation of three years and eight months. Although the Japanese used broadcasting for propaganda, they used the Malay language extensively, followed by English, Chinese, Tamil, and Japanese. However, the voices the people heard on air were those of their own people, especially the Malays.

After the Japanese surrender, the British military administration took charge of broadcasting. On April 1, 1946, the day the Malayan Union came into being, the government set up the Department of Broadcasting or Radio Malaya (Glattbach & Balakrishnan, 1978; Sarji, 1994). The sole function of broadcasting until the country's independence in 1957 was to help the government to control the social and political confusion that followed the war and the communist revolt of 1948. The political, educational, and national language policies planned during this period grew simultaneously with broadcasting, a process which helped to bring about social change (Karthigesu, 1998).

2.2.3 Television

Radio Television Malaysia (RTM) first introduced black-and-white television on December 28, 1963 (Adhikarya, 1977). A second black-and-white TV network followed in November 1969 (Glattbach & Balakrishnan, 1978). In 1970, RTM introduced an international standard satellite earth station in Kuantan, Pahang (on the east coast of peninsular Malaysia) to accommodate a TV link to Sabah and Sarawak, and also for overseas transmission. Color television came on December 28, 1978.

Malaysia continued with the government-controlled broadcasting system until 1983 when the government found it necessary to end its monopoly. Hashim (1995) says the reasons included budgetary pressures, emergence of new communication technologies, and competition from neighboring countries. The lucrative revenue potential of private television for the politically influential, especially with the ascendancy of television at the expense of the print media, expedited the privatization of broadcasting (pp. 236–261). Thus, in 1984, the government licensed the privately owned, profit-oriented Sistem Televisyen Malaysia Bhd., better known as TV3, to compete with the two government channels.

Ten years later, in 1995, the government licensed two more private TV stations: Metrovision and Mega TV. The first was a terrestrial UHF channel in the Klang Valley. The second was a 10-channel (initially five-channel) cable TV station. Astro, Malaysia's first satellite broadcasting station, with 23 TV channels and eight radio channels, joined the competition after Malaysia launched its first satellite, Measat 1, in January 1996. The government also approved another TV station with nationwide coverage, NTV7, which began operation in 1998. Had it not been for the economic downturn in 1998, another TV station, TV IMT-GT, would have started in northern Malaysia to cater for northern Indonesia and southern Thailand as well (Table 2).

Similar developments took place in radio broadcasting. In 1998, the Malaysian government operated 23 radio channels at national, regional, and local levels in various languages and dialects. Malaysia also had 14 private radio stations, including Astro's eight channels (Table 3).

Although two more TV channels—Nusantara TV and Medanmas—have received approval, they are unlikely to commerce soon because of the economic downturn. Nusantara TV, a joint venture of the Malaysian and Indonesian governments, will use Indonesia's Palapa satellite, Medanmas, a joint venture of Malaysian, Indonesian, and Thai business interests, will operate from Pulau Langkawi in the Indonesia–Malaysia–Thailand Growth Triangle (IMT-GT).

3. THE PRESS

3.1 Policy and Legal Framework

No published policy framework exists for the press. A panel chaired by veteran journalist Abdul Samad Ismail submitted a report on communication policy to the government in 1996, covering among other things, press and broadcasting. So far, nothing has come out of it, much like a similar initiative in 1983, when a seminar on national information policy mooted the idea of a media council but discarded it because of objections of the press representatives. Oon (1998) says that the National Union of Journalists, Malaysia, which has adopted an eight-point code of ethics, has opposed a government-run press council. The Malaysian Press Institute also promotes ethics through its 1989 Canons of Journalism, which uphold the precepts of *Rukunegara* and the national aspirations contained therein (Safar, 1996; Sulaiman & Che'Lah, 1996).

The legal framework, however, is more complex. Arbee (1990) points out that Malaysia has "no fewer than 42 pieces of legislation and ordinances regulating the mass media" (p. 58).[4] Foremost among them is the Printing Presses and Publication Act 1984, as amended in 1987, which requires anyone who wants to print, import, publish, sell, or distribute a newspaper to obtain a permit from the minister of home affairs, who can revoke or suspend the permit (which itself is valid for only one year). He can also confiscate any printing press used for unlawful purposes—such as to print or produce anything that is obscene, incites violence, or counsels disobedience to the law. The owner of the press is liable for a jail term of up to three years and/or a fine of up to 20,000 ringgit. A similar penalty exists for publishing "false news." The minister can proscribe any publication he considers undesirable—prejudicial to public order, morality, the relationship with any foreign country or government, or prejudicial to public or national interest (Cordingley & Oorjitham, 1998; Freedom House, 1998). Nain and Anuar (1998) point out that critics and human rights activists considered this law "draconian and very restrictive" (p. 14). The Act has its origin in the Printing Presses Ordinance 1920, promulgated in the Straits Settlements. The Federated Malay States followed it with the Printing Presses Enactment in 1924. The Federation of Malaya, established on February 1, 1948, enacted the Printing Presses Ordinance 1948. One could trace the development of this law to much earlier times—as far back as Penang in 1806 or even India in 1799.

Censorship laws and regulations that originated in India were extended to the British East India Company settlements in Penang, Singapore, and Malacca. In 1835, when Indian Act XI repealed such laws by requiring only the registration of printing presses for record purposes, Singapore greeted it with joy; and a

---

[4] Arbee attributes this finding to a survey by the School of Administration and Law of the MARA Institute of Technology. Faruqi and Ramanathan, 1999, have compiled a comprehensive list of the mass media laws and regulations in Malaysia.

newspaper established soon after the act came into force was named the *Singapore Free Press*.

The Official Secrets Act 1972, a carryover from colonial days, prohibits communicating, using, retaining, or endangering the secrecy of anything classified as an "official secret." Under a 1986 amendment, any one found guilty of violating the law can be imprisoned for one to five years; previously, a judge could impose either a fine or a jail term. Moreover, journalists can be prosecuted under the Sedition Act, 1948; sued under the Defamation Act; or held under the Internal Security Act (ISA), which provides for detention without charge or trial for inciting public unrest. The ISA keeps the local media in check (Associated Press, 1998). The 1970 Sedition Act amendments "prohibit discussion of privileges granted to Malays and other sensitive issues" (Freedom House, 1998, p. 301).

The International Press Institute (IPI, 1999) reported that the Malaysian press was "hamstrung by strict licensing regulations and a pattern of ownership that gives the ruling UMNO party overwhelming control of the popular press." The result, IPI claimed, "has been a media culture marked by self-censorship" and the "speak no evil" approach to sensitive issues. Freedom House has placed the press in Malaysia in the "not free" category primarily on the basis of two criteria: political pressures and controls on media content; and laws and regulations that influence media content (Sussman, 1999).

3.2 Financial Aspects: Circulation, Advertising, Marketing Strategies

Fourteen newspapers (dailies and Sunday editions) have a circulation exceeding 100,000 copies per issue (Table 1). Of these, four are Chinese dailies, four are English (dailies and Sunday editions), five are Malay (dailies and Sunday editions), and one is Tamil (Sunday edition). The newspaper with the largest circulation is the Sunday *Mingguan Malaysia*. Next comes the Sunday *Berita Minggu*. The *Sunday Star* has the largest circulation among the English-language newspapers. Four of the companies publishing these newspapers—the New Straits Times Press (Malaysia) Bhd., the Utusan Melayu (Malaysia) Bhd., The Star, and the Nanyang Siang Pau—are listed in the Kuala Lumpur Stock Exchange.

With regard to readership, all ethnic groups in Malaysia tend to read English and Malay newspapers. However, the Chinese and the Tamil newspapers are limited largely to the ethnic groups that speak these two languages (Arbee, 1990). Because Malay is the medium of instruction in schools, all ethnic groups are conversant in Malay. English is used widely and is becoming more important as Malaysia positions itself as a regional education center with several private universities using English as the medium of instruction. UNESCO (1999) has estimated that in 1996 more than 16 out of every 100 people in Malaysia bought a daily newspaper compared to six out of 100 in 1980.

Newspapers have consistently received the lion's share of advertising compared to other media. In 1998, the newspapers' share of advertising revenue was 58.2

percent of Ringgit 2.168 billion—down from the 1997 share of 61 percent of Ringgit 2.614 billion. Advertising revenue rose from 43 percent (of Ringgit 1.128 billion) in 1992 to 54 percent (of Ringgit 1.441 billion) in 1993, 54 percent (of Ringgit 1.674 billion) in 1994, 56 percent (of Ringgit 2.021 billion) in 1995, and 58 percent (of Ringgit 2.418 billion) in 1996 (*Advertiser's guide*, 1998; WAN, 1999; *Media guide*, 1999).

However, the 1998 economic crisis affected the advertising revenue of newspapers. For instance, The Star Group's profit (after paying tax) dropped by 30.7 percent to Ringgit 83.3 million in the 1998 calendar year. The Star attributed the decline in profitability to lower advertising revenue and an increase in newsprint costs (*New Straits Times*, February 11, 1999, p. 20). Other newspapers are also expected to show lower figures for profits and turnover. With the devaluation of the Malaysian currency, the price of newsprint (all imported) rose drastically. However, the Malaysian Newsprint Industries mill, which began operation in March 1999, is expected to produce 250,000 metric tons or 75 percent of domestic newsprint needs annually, thereby saving Ringgit 500 million in imports (*The Star*, December 27, 1998, p. 11).

The market strategy of large-circulation newspapers encompasses the whole country, whereas that of the small-circulation newspapers is confined to smaller regions. In the case of Sabah and Sarawak, some newspapers simply limit themselves to the towns where they are published and the immediate surrounding areas.

3.3 Structure and Organization

The major groups are the New Straits Times Press (Malaysia) Bhd., the Utusan Melayu (Malaysia) Bhd., and The Star Group—all listed in the Kuala Lumpur Stock Exchange.

The New Straits Times Press produces six dailies: the *New Straits Times*, the *Malay Mail, Business Times, Berita Harian, Harian Metro*, and *Shin Min Daily News*. It also publishes four Sunday newspapers: the *New Sunday Times, Berita Minggu, Sunday Mail*, and *Metro Ahad*. The magazine arm of the company, Berita Publishing, publishes more than a dozen titles, including *Anjung Seri, Dataniaga, Her World, Information Malaysia, Investors Digest, Jelita, Khidmar*, and *Malaysian Business*. The New Straits Times (Malaysia) Bhd. comes under the much bigger Malaysian Resources Corp. Bhd., which owns more than 48 percent of he NST shares through subsidiaries and associates. MRCB also owns more than 45 percent of the shares of TV3. In turn, TV3 owns 40 percent of Cableview Services, better known as Mega TV (Nain & Anuar, 1998). The present structure emerged following a management buyout of NSTP and TV3 by Realmild Sdn. Bhd., a company owned by four executives of NSTP, at a cost of Ringgit 800 million. NSTP and TV3 came under the umbrella of MRCB with Realmild becoming MRCB's ultimate holding company (Wang, 1998).

The flagship of the Utusan Group of companies is *Utusan Malaysia*. The Sunday edition of this newspaper *Mingguan Malaysia* has a printrun of more than one-half million, the biggest in the country. The original newspaper *Utusan Melayu*, still published in Jawi script, has a much smaller printrun of about 15,000. The group also publishes the weekly *Utusan Zaman*, in addition to about a dozen magazines: *Al Islam, Kawan, Mangga, Massa, Mastika, Pemikir, Pintar, Saji, URTV, Wanita*, and *Young Generation. Mastika* is the longest running of the magazines started before World War II. RHB Nominees Sdn. Bhd. owns almost 55 percent of the shares of Utusan Melayu (Malaysia) Bhd. The powerful Malaysian *bumiputera* banker and stock broker Rashid Hussein and his family own 32 percent of the shares of the RHB Group (Nain & Anuar, 1998).

The Star Group publishes the largest selling English newspaper in Malaysia, *The Star* and *The Sunday Star*. It also publishes *Day and Night* (a weekly entertainment guide), *Shanghai* (a business magazine in Chinese), and *Kuntum*, an educational magazine.

Analyzing the ownership and control of the country's media, Nain and Anuar (1998) assert that "these companies...not only have interests in other media-related activities such as distribution and broadcasting, but are also controlled by groups closely aligned to the political parties in the ruling coalition" (p. 9). Furthermore, they conclude that "all of the Malaysian media organizations—including RTM, TV3, Mega TV, Metro Vision, NTV7, Astro, *Berita Harian, Utusan Malaysia, New Straits Times*, and *Star*—are owned and controlled by [Barisan Nasional] parties or those associated closely with these parties. To a large extent, this allocated control helps to explain why these media organizations rarely—if ever—break ranks" (p. 16).[5] Freedom House (1998) confirms this conclusion: "The broadcast media and the major newspapers are all owned by individuals and companies close to the ruling National Front, and the opposition receives little coverage" (p. 349). Political parties do not own companies directly. They use proxies, and members own shares as individuals or through cooperatives.

3.4 Quality and Popular Press

Curran and Seaton (1981) contend that quality newspapers depend heavily on advertising (p. 117), and that they would not attract such advertising if their circulation were to expand to a non-elite audience, as illustrated by the case of *The London Times* from 1966 to 1969. Applying this yardstick, Malaysia's quality

---

[5] However, some Chinese newspapers published in the peninsula and some Chinese and English newspapers published in Sabah and Sarawak are not owned by any of the Barisan Nasional parties or their supporters. *Berita Sabah*, a bilingual weekly, is owned by Jefry Kitingan (brother of Pairin Kitingan, president of PBS, an opposition party). *Mingguan Waktu*, a Malay weekly, and *CBS Media*, a sensational tabloid, carry much opposition news. Moreover, the *Daily Express* is a family-owned newspaper. Nain & Anuar, 1998, base their analysis on the press groups that dominate the market. Because RTM is government-owned, it is not accurate to say that interests associated with Barisan Nasional own it.

newspaper should be the English broadsheet *New Straits Times*. However, *The Star*, a tabloid-size English daily with a higher circulation, earns the lion's share of advertising, and its popular appeal goes with a substantial amount of serious journalism.

The Malay dailies *Berita Harian* and *Utusan Malaysia*, which have large reader-ships, do not fall into the category of the popular press; yet they earn very much less in advertising. The popular dailies are the afternoon *Harian Metro* and the *Malay Mail* in the New Straits Times stable. Advertisers almost ignore the smaller newspapers, and these depend on circulation for their survival.

3.5 Distribution and Technology

The major newspapers are all published in the capital, Kuala Lumpur, or the nearby city of Petaling Jaya. In the 1960s and the early 1970s, trucks and vans carried the newspapers for distribution in the peninsula, while the airlines carried the news-papers to Sabah and Sarawak. Since then, the major newspapers have established regional printing plants. The NST Group has printing plants in Penang, Johor, and Terengganu. The Utusan Group has printing plants in Penang and Terengganu. The Star Group has a regional plant in Penang. *Sin Chiew Jit Poh*, now owned by a company in Sarawak, has a printing plant in Kuching. The *Sin Chiew Jit Poh* plant in Kuching also prints *Utusan Malaysia* and *Berita Harian* for distribution in Sarawak and Sabah.

Newspaper vendors have influenced the decision not to publish newspapers on four religious holidays: Christmas, Id-ul Fitr, Chinese New Year, and Deepavali. On these days the vendors are on leave, and newspapers are not published (except those of the NST Group, which uses other channels, including gasoline stations and convenience stores).

Computer technology has become part and parcel of the editorial and printing divisions of major newspapers for news processing and production. The NST Group has started using a new printing machine, the KBA Commander KS66 that can print 80,000 copies per hour, in the group's Shah Alam main plant and the regional plants. In mid-1998, the Utusan Group installed in its Bandar Baru Bangi plant a Man Roland printing machine that can print 70,000 copies per hour. The *Nanyang Siang Pau* began using the same machinery in early 1998 in its Petaling Jaya plant. The Star Group's Papyrus printing plant is using a Goss Urbanite that can print 36,000 copies per hour. *The Star* has also embarked on upgrading its printing machinery. The *Tamil Nesan* has been using a Harris V15C, which can print 25,000 copies per hour, for the last 14 years.[6]

---

[6] This information is based on interviews with the editors, printing operation managers, and supervisors of various newspapers.

4. BROADCASTING

4.1 Policy and Legal Framework

Prior to the privatization of broadcasting in 1984, the government determined the policy and legal framework for broadcasting. The Communication and Multimedia Act 1998 repealed the Broadcasting Act 1988, enacted four years after the establishment of TV3. These changes reflect the speed with which technology has changed the electronic media.

Radio and Television Malaysia presents the government's programs and policies. Purportedly, it aims to promote national unity, stimulate public interest, develop civic consciousness, and provide information and education (*Information Malaysia yearbook*, 1998). It emphasizes the concept of Infotainment—the presentation of information and entertainment as a "public service broadcasting station" (p. 231). However, with the advent of TV3, the government channels re-oriented their programming approach from an education-and-information bias to a greater entertainment bias (Sarji, 1998). *Rukunegara* provides the guidelines for RTM programs.

The Broadcasting Act 1988 governed private commercial radio and television. The Act empowered the minister of information to grant radio and TV licenses. It stated that no person shall broadcast any matter in Malaysia except under or in accordance with a license granted under the Act [Section 4(1)]. The license could contain such terms and conditions as the minister might determine [Section 4(3)]. The minister also had the power to control content. Section 10(1) empowered the minister, in the public interest, to prohibit the broadcasting of any matter.

The Communication and Multimedia Act 1998 (passed in July) repealed the Broadcasting Act, as well as the Telecommunications Act 1950. Following the passage of the new law, a "new" Ministry of Energy, Communications and Multimedia, as well as a new Malaysian Communications and Multimedia Commission, was formed on November 1, 1998. The new ministry has taken over from the Information Ministry all the functions related to the policy and regulatory aspects of broadcasting. The Information Ministry would continue to exist, but would share some duties with the new ministry. The new ministry will take over the issuing of broadcasting licenses.

The new commission, headed by Syed Hussein Mohamed, will be the single regulatory authority for the three industries that have converged: telecommunications, broadcasting, and computing (*The Star*, October 31, 1998, p. 1). The commission will take over some of the present technical functions of the old regulator, the Telecommunications Department. The regulatory functions of the Department of Posts would also go to the commission. Although discussions have taken place on the possibility of corporatization of Radio and Television Malaysia, this possibility is still remote (*The Star*, December 27, 1998, p. 1).[7]

---

[7] However, Jaafar Kamin, the director-general of broadcasting, had hinted on a "significant announcement" on the corporatization of RTM later in 1999 within the two-year deadline given to it to corporatize (*New Straits Times*, February 6, 1999, p. 2).

4.2 Structure and Organization

RTM, which has 24 radio stations in various parts of the country, operates six radio networks:

- R1: National Broadcast (24 hours),
- R3: Capital City Broadcast/Regional Broadcast (18 hours),
- R4: English Broadcast (24 hours),
- R5: Mandarin Broadcast (24 hours),
- R6: Tamil Broadcast (24 hours), and
- Radio Muzik in FM-Stereo (24 hours).

In Sarawak, RTM has a Yellow Network (Malay), a Red Network (Chinese and English), a Green Network (Iban), and a Blue Network (Bidayuh). Voice of Malaysia, RTM's overseas service, includes eight units broadcasting in English, Mandarin, Malay, Tagalog, Burmese, Thai and Arabic, and the Voice of Islam broadcasting in English and Malay. The government also operates Radio Penerangan (Information Radio) in the Kuala Lumpur area.

Time Highway Radio (THR) is a commercial radio network in the peninsula. BEST 104 is a commercial FM station operated from Johor Baru (*World radio TV handbook*, 1999). Other national radio broadcasters are Era, Hitz FM, Light & Easy FM, Mix FM, My FM, and the two satellite stations—Classic Rock Radio and Opus Radio. UNESCO (1999) has estimated that in 1997 Malaysia had 9,100,000 radio receivers or 43.4 per 100 inhabitants.

RTM also operates two TV networks: TV1, the Prime Network, which broadcasts in Malay; and TV2, the Golden Network, which broadcasts in Malay, English, Mandarin, and Tamil. The private commercial TV stations include TV3, Mega TV, Metrovision, NTV7, and Astro DTH. Astro's several services include: *Ria*, an all-Malay Channel; *Hua Li Dai*, an all-Chinese entertainment channel; *Wah Lai Toi*, another Chinese channel; and Super Sport.

RTM functions under the Broadcasting Department of the Ministry of Information. The director-general of broadcasting, whose immediate head is the secretary-general of the Ministry of Information, is responsible to the Minister of Information. A deputy director-general and several directors in charge of specific sections—including news and current affairs, programming and engineering—assist the director-general. Following the introduction of private commercial stations, RTM has become more businesslike.

The private commercial stations are organized on business lines. For instance, a chairman and an executive director (assisted by a general manager) are at the head of TV3. Several division managers—including those for news and current affairs, programming, and engineering—assist the general manager. The security of staff is one aspect that sets apart government-owned broadcasting from private broadcasting. Faced with rising cost and loss of advertising during the Asian financial crisis, TV3, Astro, and NTV7 retrenched their staff and cut down on broadcasting hours. TV3 halved its 24-hour-a-day service.

The following cable/satellite TV broadcasting services are also open to the Malaysian audience: Asian Entertainment Channel, Asia Business News, CNBC Asia/International, Cartoon Network and Variety, Channel V (music videos), Discovery Channel Southeast Asia, Disney Channel Malaysia, HBO Asia, Hallmark Entertainment Channel, MGM Gold, MTV Asia, NBC Asia, STAR (Movies, Plus, and Sports), TNT/Cartoon Network, and *Vaanavil* (Malaysia's only all-Indian entertainment channel).

4.3 Program Policies

4.3.1 Radio Television Malaysia

Malaysian laws and government policies determine the RTM program policy. RTM operationalized these in its objectives, which Adhikarya (1977) summarized:

- To explain in depth and with the widest possible coverage, government policies and programs to ensure maximum public understanding;
- to stimulate public interest and opinion in order to achieve its desired changes;
- to promote national unity—by using Bahasa Malaysia, the national language— in a multiracial society toward the preparation of a Malaysian culture and identity;
- to assist in promoting civic consciousness and fostering the development of Malaysian arts and culture; and
- to provide suitable elements of popular education, general information and entertainment (pp. 5–6).

Following independence, RTM's function was to help the government stabilize the country, promote unity, inculcate a sense of responsibility, and infuse the correct attitude and behavior towards nation building (Idid & Sarji, 1993; Hashim, 1989). All programs were supposed to contain developmental elements. However, with the influx of video entertainment, the government began to feel uncomfortable and began designing a better broadcasting policy (Sarji, 1998).

With the advent of private commercial television, RTM had to change its program policy to attract advertisers for both radio and television. It had to withdraw programs that failed to attract audience and advertisers. Thus RTM is slowly moving away from its original philosophy of programming. The competition it faced from private radio and TV stations became a major factor in changing its strategy (Sarji, 1994). Both RTM and private stations use audience rating as their guide for programming so much so that throughout the 1990s Malaysia experienced, for the first time, the real battle for airtime. RTM, however, continues to insist that even as a corporatized body, profits would remain its second priority (*New Straits Times*, February 6, 1992, p. 2).

4.3.2 Private Television Stations

The bottom line for private TV stations is profit. Sistem Televisyen Malaysia Bhd. (TV3), the leading private commercial station, has stated that its programs must have mass appeal because only such programs would attract sponsors. The competition among TV stations resulted in a great imbalance between local and foreign content on Malaysian television. A 1992 study revealed that about 70 percent of TV3 programs originated from abroad, compared to 58 percent of TV2 and 37 percent of TV1 (Sarji, 1994). These revelations caused the government to intervene; and in May 1991, the Ministry of Information instructed all TV stations to reschedule their programs and broadcast more local programs (*Berita Harian*, May 20, 1991, p. 1). Televising more local content had been an issue since the setting up of TV3 in 1984 (*Berita Harian*, October 12, 1984; July 17, 1984; September 28, 1987). Programs on Mega TV and Astro are also covered by government guidelines.

Generally, TV stations themselves censor films before broadcasting them. Officials of the Film Censorship Board stationed at TV3 also cover Mega TV, Metrovision, and RTM. However, Astro's own staff handles censorship of what Astro transmits. Initially, the Film Censorship Board trained Astro staff because of the special needs of the station, which had to re-transmit some programs within one hour.

4.4 Ownership and Financing

The government-owned Radio Television Malaysia operates TV1 and TV2, as well as national and regional radio stations in various languages. The largest private commercial station is STMB's TV3. Other private TV stations are Mega TV (a cable TV company), Metro Vision, NTV7, and Astro satellite TV station. Television, being an inexpensive source of entertainment, is available in almost every home, including in remote areas. UNESCO (1999) has estimated that in 1997 about 17.2 out of every 100 people in Malaysia owned a TV receiver. This translates into a penetration of about 85 percent of the population, taking five persons to a family. *ACNielsen Malaysia 1998 media index* shows that 96 percent of adults (15 years and above) live in homes with TV sets.

The government-owned broadcasting media derive "income" from three sources: government grants, radio and TV license fees, and advertising. In 1997, RTM received Ringgit 620 million (US$ 250 million) in grants and Ringgit 57.2 million (US$ 23 million) in television license fees. In 1998, however, RTM received only Ringgit 540 million (US$ 144 million) in grants (Ministry of Information, 1999). RTM's advertising revenue also declined to Ringgit 194.5 million (US$ 51.2 million)[8] in 1998 because of slashed promotional activities of the business sector (*New Straits Times*, February 6, 1999, p. 2). RTM's advertising revenue had risen from Ringgit 285.6 in 1993 to Ringgit 410.1 million 1996, but it has been on the decline thereafter. All the private TV stations depend on advertising for their income. Total advertising revenue of all TV stations, including RTM, was Ringgit 780.2 million (US$ 314 million) for 1997 (Table 12).

---

[8] This reflects the devalued exchange rate of the Malaysian ringgit during the 1998 financial crisis.

5. NEW ELECTRONIC MEDIA

5.1 Internet and On-line Media

Adjusted data based on the July 1999 Internet Consortium (www.isc.org) survey showed that Malaysia had 84,475 Internet hosts—4.0 hosts per 1,000 people—compared to 29,919 in January 1997. The country had an estimated 1 million computers in 1997—a computer density of 4.6 per 100 people. The estimated number of Internet users in 1996 was 63,945 (ITU, 1998). This number could now well exceed 166,000. *ACNielsen Malaysia 1998 media index* has estimated computer usage at 7 percent for adults (15 years and above), a comparatively high figure in relation to most neighboring countries. In 1997, MIMOS estimated Malaysia's IT literacy rate at 8.2 percent (*Economic report 1998/1999*).

Several newspapers are available on-line. The first to go on-line was *The Star*, followed by *Berita Harian, Utusan Malaysia, Sin Chiew Jit Poh*, and *Nanyang Siang Pau. New Straits Times* was the latest to join the rank. *Utusan Malaysia* is also available on-line in English, as is *Utusan Express*. Bernama, the national news agency of Malaysia, is also available on-line.

Malaysia has been at the forefront of promoting information technology in a big way as is evident from the Multimedia Super Corridor project. MIMOS and Telecom Malaysia are the country's two Internet service providers (ISP). Jaring (under MIMOS) became the first ISP in 1994. TMNet (Telecom Malaysia) followed in January 1996 (*Computimes Shopper Malaysia*, November 1998). Four more ISPs have received the green light: Bina Sat-Com Network Sdn. Bhd. (Binariang), Celcom Transmission, DiGi Telecommunications, and Time Telekom (*Asia Inc*, 1999).

Data from ISPs show a higher number of Internet users than the conservative ITU estimates. Jaring claimed a dial-up subscriber base of 150,000, and a customer base of 600,000. TMNet claimed a dial-up subscriber base of 200,000 (*Computimes Shopper Malaysia*, November 1998). By April 1999, Jaring and TMNet had about 500,000 subscribers (Daud, 1999). Jaring, started in 1987 as Rangkom, connected several major universities in Kuala Lumpur and Penang on an experimental basis using a 4.8 bps leased line network. MIMOS set up its first international leased circuit connection to the United States in 1992, when it had 28 educational subscribers (*Computimes Shopper Malaysia*, November 1998).

5.2 Telecommunications Infrastructure

The International Telecommunication Union (1999) reported that Malaysia had 4.38 million mainline telephones in 1998—a density of 19.8 per 100 people compared to the 1990 density of 9 per 100 people. In addition, in 1998, Malaysia had 2.2 million cellular mobile subscribers—a density of 9.2 per 100 people (ITU, 1999).

The government privatized the Telecommunication Department on January 1, 1987, as Syarikat Telekom Malaysia Bhd., under the Telecommunication Services (Successor Company) 1985 Act. Privatization opened up the telecommunication industry. Now, Malaysia, has five fixedline telecommunication providers—Telekom (the biggest), Celcom, Binariang, Time Telekom, and DiGi Telekom. In January 1999, Malaysia became the first country in Asia to provide equal access to all five fixedline operators (*Malaysian Enterprise*, January–February 1999). Under this arrangement, customers have a choice of making long-distance and international calls using different service providers. In 1993, Telecom Malaysia inaugurated the integrated services digital network (ISDN) on a commercial basis.

Celcom has established about 3,000 km of fiber backbone in the peninsula and another 1,800 km in Sarawak, while Time Telekom has laid another fiber-optic network of some 5,250 km. The fiber-optic network stretches more than 900 km along the North–South Expressway from Bukit Kayu Hitam to Johor Bahru. Plans are afoot to stretch it eastward from Kuala Lumpur to Kota Bahru via Kuantan and Kuala Terengganu. A submarine festoon cable with 25 landing stations complements the terrestrial trunk. Time Telekom's two earth stations in Labuan connect telecommunication traffic between the peninsula and East Malaysia. A fiber-optic submarine cable will eventually link the network to East Malaysia (APT, 1999). Internationally, Malaysia has joined the South Africa Far East Asia (SAFE) submarine cable system. Malaysia East Asia Satellite (MEASAT) system also serves the country's telecommunication structure.

6. POLICY TRENDS FOR PRESS AND BROADCASTING

The Multimedia Super Corridor's Bill of Guarantee stipulates that Malaysia will not censor the Internet. This stipulation is radical in the context of laws governing the traditional mass media. The Communication and Multimedia Act 1998, which came into force on April 1, 1999, contains the "no censorship" clause (Section 3[3]).

The use of the Internet as a source of information has proliferated. Malaysia made a landmark of sorts in Internet use following the dismissal of Anwar Ibrahim as deputy prime minister. An estimated 60 websites sprang up in his support in response to the perceived unfairness of the local media (Zeitlin, 1998). Rustam Sani, a former university lecturer and newspaper columnist, called for the boycott of mainstream newspapers. Sani is a committee member of *Adil*, a nongovernmental organization headed by Anwar's wife, Wan Azizah Ismail.

6.1 Press

The press has always been a private-sector enterprise. The government neither explicitly owns or operates newspapers. Even back in 1806, individuals like A.B. Bone, J.W. Court, and others (and not the government) owned the Prince of Wales Island's *Government Gazette*. One discernible shift in ownership was during the independent Malaya, when the United Malays National Organization bought a substantial stake in the small but influential newspaper company, *Utusan Melayu*, in 1961. That newspaper has since been associated with UMNO. Because UMNO is the backbone of the government, *Utusan* is considered close to the government.

In 1972, the UMNO youth called for Malaysian interests to hold a majority stake in the country's newspaper organizations. This affected the *Straits Times* and a few Chinese newspapers originally set up in Singapore. By August 1972, the *Straits Times* divided its operations: while the *Straits Times* remained in Singapore, its Malaysian operation became known as the *New Straits Times*. This arrangement resulted in 80 percent of the *New Straits Times* coming under local ownership, with 20 percent remaining in Singapore. Later, Malaysian interests bought that 20 percent as well. By 1973, the *New Straits Times* had become a public company listed in the Kuala Lumpur Stock Exchange, the first newspaper company to do so. In 1974, the government amended the Printing Press Act 1948 on ownership of newspapers to ensure that other newspapers would also follow the path of the *New Straits Times*.

Companies closely related to political parties in power own several mainstream newspapers in Malaysia. The majority stake in the *Star*, for instance, is owned by Huaren, a company closely related to the Malaysian Chinese Association, a partner of the ruling National Front. The ownership of certain Tamil newspapers is associated with certain personalities in the Malaysian Indian Congress, another partner of the National Front. In 1993, the *New Straits Times* was involved in a management buyout by two editors and two management personnel, a group close to the ruling UMNO (Gomez & Jomo, 1997). Nain & Anuar (1998) point out that the Malaysian Resources Corp. Bhd., which effectively controls NSTP, is closely associated with UMNO.[9]

Vanden Heuvel & Dennis (1993) say "direct censorship is relatively rare in Malaysia" (p. 151). They mention occasional blackouts of articles in foreign publications, and the censoring of imported television programs to purge them of sex and violence. However, they claim that Malaysia has "a tame media environment in which government influence and self-censorship inhibit probing, critical journalism" (p. 149). The degree of freedom of expression, they say, "is less dependent

<hr>

[9] IPI, 1999, reported that in July 1998 two leading Malaysian editors—Johan Jaafar of *Utusan Malaysia* and Ahmad Nazri Abdullah of *Berita Harian*—had to resign under pressure from UMNO before the prime minister removed his deputy Anwar Ibrahim, from office on September 3. The director of operations of TV3 also had to resign under similar pressure. All three were reputedly Anwar supporters. Of the original four owners of Realmild Sdn. Bhd. who staged a management buyout of the *New Straits Times* and TV3, only Abdul Kadir Jasin remains on the board of both. The *New Straits Times* (July 27, 1999) reported the resignations of Managing Director Mohd Noor Mutalib and directors Abdul Khalid Ahmad and Ahmad Nazri Abdullah from the board of *New Straits Times*, as well as their resignations as directors of TV3 and Malaysian Resources Corp. Bhd. These three were viewed as associated closely with the sacked deputy Prime Minister Anwar Ibrahim. The new board of NSTP includes P.C. Shivadas, a former NST group editor; while the new TV3 board includes Lee Lam Thye, a former politician and social activist.

on the law than on the political climate" (p. 151). Idid (1989), on the other hand, points out that one should not view the Malaysian press system within a continuum from an authoritarian to a Western (or libertarian) model because such a model is "ideological" (p. 49). Safar (1996), who proposes a perspective of power in studying press systems, suggests that ideology is merely a veneer, and that a configuration of powers lies beneath that veneer in any country's press system. Safar's perspective of power is based on a continuum from a fully integrated system to a fully separated system of power. The Malaysian press system, Safar contends, lies at the center of the two extremes with the executive branch playing a very dominant role. Mahathir (1989), who heads the country's executive, has argued the case for a socially responsible press that has an important role to play. He says the press "must be allowed much leeway to play this role, including to criticize authority" (p. 115).

The major newspapers are very supportive of government and act like partners in the nation's development agenda (Safar, 1998). The government has allowed the distribution of foreign newspapers, which are usually critical of the country, and has also permitted two global newspapers to be printed in the country. The Star Papyrus Printing Sdn. Bhd. and the Utusan Melayu Group print the *Asian Wall Street Journal* (*AWSJ*) and the *International Herald Tribune* respectively. *AWSJ* had been suspended from distribution in Malaysia for three months from September 1987. *AWSJ* (December 21, 1998, p. 10) carried an article on cronyism by K.S. Jomo, a University of Malaya professor. *Harakah*, the PAS organ, has reprinted the article. The government has taken no action. However, the information minister had announced in August 1998 that he planned to impose new rules and restrictions on the movements of foreign journalists, who already have to register with the Home Ministry to obtain a work permit (IPI, 1999).

6.2 Broadcasting

The main shift in broadcasting policy relates to privatization. Prior to privatization, the only private-sector participant in broadcasting was Rediffusion, which provided music and entertainment through cables. The policy shift has resulted in the emergence of several radio and TV stations. Karthigesu (1998), however, asserts that although "deregulation" has spawned "a few private radio and television stations, the government continues to be the main actor in domestic broadcasting by owning two television channels and an overwhelming number of national and local television stations" (p. 95).

Anuar & Wang (1996) point out that the official role assigned to Malaysian television (of fostering national unity) may create problems "particularly when the thrust of the dominant political culture is ethnic" (p. 276). They see the urgent need for "democratizing the access to mainstream mass media," particularly television, to bring about national unity and social justice so that people get equal opportunity to publicly express their ideas, anxieties and fears (p. 277). Nain (1996) has warned about the negative impact of the international marketplace on the organization of Malaysian television in the context of the country's internal tensions and contradictions.

7. MAIN ISSUES

● Retrenchment in media organizations

Retrenchment has occurred in several media organizations because of the economic downturn. TV3 retrenched about 600 of its personnel and Astro about 400. The latest to retrench was the new NTV7, which laid off 62 members of its staff. Retrenchment also affected the advertising agencies and the film industry.

● Rising cost of newsprint and increase in price of newspapers

The fall in the value of Malaysian ringgit against the US dollar, now pegged at US$ 1 to Ringgit 3.80, has caused these price increases. The price of *Berita Harian* has risen to Ringgit 1.20, and *Berita Minggu* (the Sunday edition) to 1.50. *Mingguan Malaysia* was the first to increase its price to RM1.50. *Utusan Malaysia* followed *Berita Harian* in increasing the price to 1.20

● Fall in advertising revenue

A significant drop in advertising took place in 1998 compared to Ringgit 2.6 billion in 1997. Table 11 shows total media revenue dropped 17.1 percent (from Ringgit 2.614 billion to Ringgit 2.168 billion). Newspaper revenues from advertising dropped by 16.3 percent and television revenue by 10.1 percent—considerably less than the 30 percent drop that Judy Lim, managing director of J. Walter Thompson Sdn. Bhd., had anticipated. JWT has reduced its work force from 100 to 50, beginning two years ago.

● Defamation suits

A spate of defamation suits has sprung up from press and broadcast reports involving corporate figures, politicians, and celebrities. One is a defamation suit against the printer of *Asian Wall Street Journal* (AWJS) in Malaysia, The Star Papyrus Printing Sdn. Bhd., by businessman Mirzan Mahathir, son of the prime minister, over an article printed on January 4, 1999. Businessman Vincent Tan, the majority shareholder of *The Sun*, has also sued the *AWSJ* printer over an article printed on December 21, 1998. Ousted Deputy Prime Minister Anwar Ibrahim has sued the Sun Media Corp. Sdn. Bhd., the publisher of *The Sun*, for Ringgit 100 million for reporting the comments of Prime Minister Mahathir Mohamad. Anwar has sued the prime minister also for the same amount. Another corporate figure, Tang Pek Khiing, has sued a journalist M.G.G. Pillai for Ringgit 100 million over an article in the *Sang Kancil* Listserv on the Internet. Former opposition leader Lim Kit Siang has sued Utusan Melayu (Malaysia) Bhd., the publisher of *Utusan Malaysia*, for publishing a story titled "Kit Siang unpatriotic—Malaysia ex-policemen's Association" (*New Straits Times*, February 24, 1999).

8. STATISTICS

General Profile

Area	329,758 sq km
Capital	Kuala Lumpur
Population	22.7 million
Population growth rate	2.3 percent (1998)**
Labor force	8.9 million (1998p)*
Major languages	Bahasa Melayu, English, Chinese, and Tamil.
Gross domestic product	Growth negative 6.7 percent (RM 131.3 billion in 1998p)*
Currency	US$ 1 = RM 3.80 (fixed as of September 1, 1998)*
Major industries	Electronics & electrical goods, textiles, clothing & footwear, chemicals, petroleum, wood products, metal products, and rubber.
Major exports	Electronics & electrical goods, petroleum & LNG, textiles, clothing & footwear, palm oil, sawn timber & wood products, rubber, cocoa & cocoa products.
Major imports	Manufacturing inputs, machinery & transport equipment, metal products, consumer durables & food, beverages & tobacco.

Source: ASEAN Secretariat, 1998; * *Bank Negara Malaysia 1998 annual report.*
Note: p = preliminary; ** Statistics Department of Malaysia.

Table 1
Newspapers

Newspaper	Year estb.	Place of publication	Language	Circulation
Kwong Wah Yit Poh	1910	Penang	Chinese	70,242
Nanyang Siang Pau	1923	Petaling Jaya	Chinese	175,339
Sin Chew Jit Poh	1929	Petaling Jaya	Chinese	264,283
Chinese Daily News	1945	Kuching, Sarawak	Chinese	16,075
Miri Daily News	1945	Miri, Sarawak	Chinese	24,230
China Press	1946	Kuala Lumpur	Chinese	171,636*
See Hua Daily News	1952	Sibu, Sarawak	Chinese	54,484
International Times	1968	Kuching	Chinese	36,170
Merdeka Daily News	1968	Sandakan, Sabah	Chinese	6,948*
Malaysia Daily News	1968	Sibu, Sarawak	Chinese	21,741
Berita Petang	1970	Kuching, Sarawak	Chinese	9,600*
New Life Post (bi-weekly)	1972	Petaling Jaya	Chinese	136,457*
Asia Times	1976	Kota Kinabalu	Chinese	15,729
Morning Post	1981	Tawau, Sabah	Chinese	8,730
Mun Sang Poh	1986	Ipoh, Perak	Chinese	79,138*
Overseas Chinese Daily News	1986	Kota Kinabalu	Chinese	18,505*
Guang Ming Daily	1987	Petaling Jaya	Chinese	100,475
See Hua Daily news	1993	Kota Kinabalu	Chinese	21,974
New Straits Times	1845	Kuala Lumpur	English	155,977
New Sunday Times				179,143

Table 1 contd

Newspaper	Year estb.	Place of publication	Language	Circulation
Malay Mail	1896	Kuala Lumpur	English	48,567
Sunday Mail				64,187
Sarawak Tribune	1945	Kuching, Sarawak	English	41,617
Sunday Tribune				
Daily Express	1963	Kota Kinabalu	English	26,558
The Star	1971	Petaling Jaya	English	220,493
Sunday Star				252,565
Business Times	1976	Kuala Lumpur	English	15,000*
Borneo Post	1978	Kuching	English	41,120
Sun	1991	Petaling Jaya	English	79,150
Borneo Post (Sabah)	1994	Kota Kinabalu	English	21,619
The Edge (weekly)	1994	Petaling Jaya	English	11,862
Borneo Mail	1988	Kota Kinabalu	English/BM/ Kadazandusun	17,007
New Sabah Times	1998	Kota Kinabalu	English	13,000 (c)
Utusan Melayu	1939	Kuala Lumpur	Malay	8,186
Utusan Zaman				8,963
Berita Harian	1956	Kuala Lumpur	Malay	249,756
Berita Minggu				391,813
Utusan Malaysia	1967	Kuala Lumpur	Malay	267,765
Mingguan Malaysia	1964			522,857
Utusan Sarawak	1983	Kuching	Malay	31,598
Harian Metro	1991	Kuala Lumpur	Malay	77,036
Metro Ahad				135,313
Tamil Nesan	1924	Kuala Lumpur	Tamil	35,000 (c)
Malaysia Nanban	1980	Kuala Lumpur	Tamil	45,000 (c)
				108,000 (c)
Thina Murasu	1987	Kuala Lumpur	Tamil	22,000 (c)
				85,000 (c)
Makkal Osai	1991	Kuala Lumpur	Tamil	28,000

Source: *Press guide*, 1998; *Media guide*, 1999.
Note: (c) = claimed circulation; * figures for 1997.

Table 2
Television Channels

Name of station	Mode	Year of operation	Coverage	Number of channels
Radio and TV Malaysia	Terrestrial	1963 (TV1)	National	1
Radio and TV Malaysia	Terrestrial	1969 (TV2)	National	1
Sistem Televisyen Malaysia Bhd.	Terrestrial	1984 (TV3)	National	1
Metrovision	Terrestrial	1995	Klang Valley (K. Lumpur and Selangor State)	1
Mega TV	Cable	1995	National	10
ASTRO	Satellite	1996	National/International	23
National TV	Terrestrial	1997 (NTV7)	National	1

Source: The Ministry of Information, 1999.

Table 3
Radio Channels

Name of station	Mode	Year of operation	Coverage	Number of channels
Radio Malaysia	Terrestrial	1946	national/regional/local	24
Rediffusion Network	Cable	1949	Malaysian Peninsula	2 Cable
Suara Johor (Best 104)	Terrestrial	1984	Malaysian Peninsula	1
Time Highway Radio	Terrestrial	1994	National	1
Suara Johor	Terrestrial	1994	Central Peninsular Malaysia	1
Radio Rediffusion	Terrestrial	1996	National	1
CATS Radio	Terrestrial	1996	Sarawak	1
ASTRO Radio	DTU/Satellite	1996	National/International	8

Source: The Ministry of Information, 1999.

Table 4
Population

Year	Population
1993	19.6
1994	20.1
1995	20.7
1996	21.2
1997	21.7
1998(p)	22.2*
1999(f)	22.7*

Source: *Economic report 1998/1999; * Bank Negara Malaysia 1998 annual report*, 1999.
Note: p = preliminary, f = forecast.

Table 5
Per Capita GNP

Year	GNP per capita (in US$)
1993	2,970
1994	3,515
1995	3,960
1996	4,463
1997	4,284
1998p*	3,013
1999f*	3,113

Source: *Economic report 1998/1999; * Bank Negara Malaysia 1998 annual report, 1999.*
Note: p = preliminary, f = forecast.

Table 6
Audited Circulation Figures Peninsular Malaysia
(English Newspapers)

	1993	1994	1995	1996	1997	1998*
New Straits Times	177,955	177,720	172,528	165,907	163,287	155,977
New Sunday Times	212,064	210,647	204,091	191,562	186,918	179,143
The Malay Mail	65,034	67,137	64,602	57,375	54,234	48,569
The Sunday Mail	93,941	91,821	80,435	75,641	70,664	64,187
The Star	180,043	190,944	192,022	192,059	206,832	220,493
The Sunday Star	215,801	225,167	230,148	232,790	244,176	252,565
The Sun	–	–	–	78,470	77,328	79,150

Source: Audit Bureau of Circulation (ABC) figures cited in *Press guide*, 1998; * *Media guide*, 1999.

Table 7
Audited Circulation Figures Peninsular Malaysia
(Bahasa Malaysia Newspapers)

	1993	1994	1995	1996	1997	1998*
Berita Harian	314,240	333,240	299,448	283,914	272,615	249,756
Berita Minggu	418,790	442,861	422,813	421,127	411,606	391,813
Utusan Malaysia	252,452	264,917	259,425	229,274	253,680	267,765
Mingguan Malaysia	514,677	546,330	541,174	493,523	503,759	522,857
Utusan Zaman	16,485	14,962	13,858	11,782	10,068	8,736
Utusan Melayu	15,560	14,380	13,440	11,618	9,922	8,816
Harian Metro	–	–	–	84,322	85,540	77,036
Metro Ahad	–	–	–	132,195	152,140	135,313

Source: Audit Bureau of Circulation (ABC) figures cited in *Press guide*, 1998; * *Media guide*, 1999.

Table 8
Audited Circulation Figures Peninsular Malaysia
(Chinese Newspapers)

	1993	1994	1995	1996	1997	1998*
Nanyang Siang Pau	182,926	191,002	189,280	183,801	184,279	175,339
New Life Post	148,372	136,457	–	–	–	–
Sin Chew Jit Poh	195,118	208,291	215,036	222,067	237,604	264,283
Kwong Wah Yit Poh	69,089	68,130	67,331	65,939	69,047	70,242
China Press	11,242	129,672	143,543	155,155	171,636	–
Mun Sang Poh	72,896	80,110	79,140	77,958	79,138	–
Guang Ming Daily	–	–	–	87,144	91,602	100,475

Source: Audit Bureau of Circulation (ABC) figures cited in *Press guide*, 1998; *Media guide*, 1999.

Table 9
Audited Circulation Figures Sabah and Sarawak
(English and Malay Newspapers)

	1993	1994	1995	1996	1997	1998*
Borneo Post (Sarawak)	26,736	29,890	44,421	53,587	58,659	41,120
Borneo Post (Sabah)	–	–	–	19,293	20,216	21,696
The Sarawak Tribune/Sunday	19,236	21,017	24,291	29,598	35,163	41,120
Daily Express	22,922	24,907	25,168	25,520	27,008	26,558
Borneo Mail	12,853	14,640	14,965	14,610	16,761	17,067
Utusan Sarawak (Bahasa Malaysia)	–	–	–	12,976	–	31,598

Source: Audit Bureau of Circulation (ABC) figures cited in *Press guide*, 1998; * *Media guide*, 1999.

Table 10
Audited Circulation Figures Sabah and Sarawak
(Chinese Newspapers)

	1993	1994	1995	1996	1997	1998*
Malaysia Daily News	20,283	20,901	22,006	22,735	23,104	21,741
Overseas Chinese Daily News	15,869	16,804	16,804	17,412	18,505	18,881
See Hua Daily News	43,465	48,029	63,215	72,112	74,504	59,484
Morning Post	7,725	7,860	8,287	8,353	8,590	8,370
Merdeka Daily News	6,364	6,223	6,948	–	–	–
Sandakan Jit Pao	4,553	4,908	–	–	–	–
Asia Times	13,586	14,172	15,101	15,349	15,396	15,729
Miri Daily News	19,753	20,697	21,526	22,431	23,335	24,230
Chinese Daily News	–	–	7,794	12,365	14,129	16,075
International Times	–	20,777	27,689	31,642	34,517	36,170

Source: Audit Bureau of Circulation (ABC) figures cited in *Press guide*; * *Media guide*, 1999.

Table 11
Advertising Revenue by Media

	1994 RM million	1995 RM million	1996 RM million	1997 RM million	1998 RM million
Newspaper	909.7	1,129.0	1,407.8	1,507.2	1,261.3
Television	528.2	653.8	772.4	772.2	694.4
Radio	42.1	59.3	76.0	91.1	55.7
Magazine	105.2	117.5	121.5	136.9	111.3
Cinema	6.4	7.1	6.8	9.3	10.3
Outdoor	49.6	–	–	–	–
Video	9.5	11.4	10.1	10.2	9.7
Point of Sales	14.0	14.4	17.4	20.1	20.6
Total Media	**1,644.7**	**1,992.5**	**2,412.0**	**2,547.0**	**2,163.3**

Source: *Media guide*, 1999.

Table 12
Advertising Revenue of Television

Year	Total revenue RM million	Market share %	Growth %
1988	222.4	42.4	34.5
1989	303.8	46.5	36.6
1990	353.6	43.2	16.4
1991	410.4	40.4	16.1
1992	446.9	39.6	8.9
1993	482.0	33.5	7.8
1994	528.2	31.6	9.6
1995	653.8	32.7	23.7
1996	772.4	32.0	18.1
1997	780.2	29.6	1.0
1998*	698.4	34.0	−11.2

Source: ACNielsen/MAA cited in *Advertiser's guide*, 1998: *Media guide*, 1999.

Table 13
Comparative Information Technology Usage

	1993	1997
USA	290	450
Singapore	120	316
Japan	100	228
Malaysia	21	65
Thailand		28
Indonesia		9

Source: *World competitiveness report 1994–98* cited in *Economic report 1998/1999*, p. 187.

Table 14
Comparative Internet Hosts

	Per 1,000
USA	122.00
Singapore	38.48
Japan	16.42
Malaysia	4.00
Thailand	0.99
Indonesia	0.22

Source: Internet Software Consortium (www.isg.org), July 1999.

Table 15
Cellular Penetration Rate (per 100)

Year	Percent
1998	13.0
1999	14.1
2000	15.6
2001	17.9
2020	55.0

Source: Asia Inc, June 1999.

Table 16
Top 10 Advertising Agencies, 1997

	Agency	Capitalized (in millions of ringgit)
1	Bates Malaysia	161.8
2	McCann	146.2
3	Naga DBB	135.0
4	DYR	133.9
5	Ogilvy & Mather	130.1
6	Leo Burnett	121.0
7	Grey	90.9
8	Peter Bourmount	89.0
9	Lintas	88.8
10	J. Walter Thompson	86.5

Source: *Advertiser's guide*, 1998.

9. USEFUL ADDRESSES

New Straits Times/New Sunday Times
Balai Berita
31 Jalan Riong
59100 Kuala Lumpur
Malaysia
Telephone: 603-282-3322
Fax: 603-282-1434

The Star
13, Jalan 13/6
46200 Petaling Jaya
Selangor
Malaysia
Telephone: 603-758-1188
Fax: 603-755-4039/755-2959
E-mail: editor@thestar.po.my

Berita Harian/Berita Minggu
Balai Berita
31 Jalan Riong
59100 Kuala Lumpur
Malaysia
Telephone: 603-282-2323
Fax: 603-282-2425
E-mail: bharian@bbnstp.com.my

Utusan Malaysia/Mingguan Malaysia
46M Jalan Lima
Off Jalan Chan Sow Lin
5200 Kuala Lumpur
Malaysia
Telephone: 603-221-7055
Fax: 603-222-7876/222-0911
E-mail: utusan@utusan.com.my

Nanyang Siang Pau
1 Jalan SS7/2
47301 Petaling Jaya
Selangor
Malaysia
Telephone: 603-777-6000
Fax: 603-777-6855
E-mail: editor@nanyang.com.my

Sin Chew Jit Poh
19 Jalan Semangat
46200 Petaling Jaya
Selangor
Malaysia
Telephone: 603-758-7777
Fax: 603-755-6881

Sistem Televisyen Malaysia Bhd. (TV3)
Sri Pentas
3 Persiaran Bandar Utama
Bandar Utama
47800 Petaling Jaya
Selangor
Malaysia
Telephone: 603-716-6333
Fax: 603-716-1333

Radio Television Malaysia (RTM)
Angkasapuri
506145 Kuala Lumpur
Telephone: (603) 282 5333
Fax: (603) 282 5103/282 4735

Astro
All Asia Broadcast Centre
Technology Park Malaysia
Lebuhraya Puchong-Sungai Besi
Bukit Jalil
57000 Kuala Lumpur
Malaysia
Telephone: 603-583-6688
Fax: 583-6868
URL: http://www.astro.com.my

Asia-Pacific Institute for Broadcasting Development (AIBD)
PO Box 1137, Pantai Post Office
59700 Kuala Lumpur
Telephone: (603) 282 4618/282 3719
Fax: (603) 282 2761
E-mail: admin@aibd.org.my ◆ devbroad@aidbd.org.my
URL: http://aibd.org.my

10. REFERENCES

ACNielsen Malaysia 1998 media index. (1999). Kuala Lumpur: ACNielsen Malaysia.

Adhikarya, R. (1977). *Broadcasting in Peninsular Malaysia.* London: Routledge & Kegan Paul.

Advertiser's guide. (1998). Kuala Lumpur: White Knight Communications.

Anuar, M.K., & Wang, L.K. (1996). Aspects of ethnicity and gender in Malaysian television. In D. French & M. Richards (Eds.), *Contemporary television: Eastern perspectives* (pp. 262–281). New Delhi: Sage Publications.

APT (Asia-Pacific Telecommunity). (1998). *The APT yearbook.* Bangkok: APT.

Arbee, A.R. (1990). Malaysia. In C.J. Hamelink & A. Mehra (Eds.), *Communication development and human rights in Asia* (pp. 51–67). Singapore: AMIC.

ASEAN Secretariat. (1998). *ASEAN macroeconomic outlook 1997–1998.* Jakarta: Asean Academic Press.

Associated Press. (1998, July 28). Malaysia makes fresh threats against news media. *The Freedom Forum* [On-line]. Available: (http://www.freedomform. org/international/1998/7/28malayjour.asp).

Bank Negara Malaysia annual report 1998. (1998). Kuala Lumpur: Bank Negara Malaysia.

Cordingley, P., & Oorjitham, S. (1998, November 13). How the media have fared: Mainstream newspapers take a beating. *Asiaweek, 24* (45), pp. 34–35.

Curran, J., & Seaton, J. (1981). *Power without responsibility: The press and broadcasting in Britain.* London: Routledge.

Daud, A.R. (1999, April 20). *Telecommunications access issues and challenges.* Paper presented at the Infotec 1999, Petaling Jaya, Malaysia.

Economic report 1998/99. (1998). Kuala Lumpur: Ministry of Finance.

Faruqi, S.S., & Ramanathan, S. (Comps.). (1999). *Mass media laws and regulations in Malaysia.* Singapore: AMIC.

Freedom House Survey Team. (1998). *Freedom in the world: The annual survey of political rights and civil liberties, 1997–1998.* New York: Freedom House.

Glattbach, J., & Balakrishnan, R. (1978). Malaysia. In J.A. Lent (Ed.), *Broadcasting in Asia and the Pacific: A continental survey of radio and television* (pp. 142–155). Philadelphia: Temple University Press.

Gomez, E.T., & Jomo, K.S. (1977). *Malaysia's political economy.* Cambridge: Cambridge University Press.

Hashim, R. (1989). *Accommodating national goals and conflicting societal need through privatization of television broadcasting: The Malaysian case.* Unpublished doctoral dissertation, Ohio State University, Columbus.

Hashim, R. (1995). Privatizing Malaysia: Rents, rhetoric, realities. In K.S. Jomo (Ed.), *Television programming* (pp. 236–249). Boulder: Westview Press.

Idid, S.A. (1989). Malaysia. In A. Mehra (Ed.), *Press systems in ASEAN states* (pp. 41–56). Singapore: AMIC.

Idid, S.A., & Sarji, A. (1993). *The role of mass media in bridging up the cultural understanding among various races in Malaysia.* Paper presented at the Consultative Council Meeting of the Ministry of Social Welfare and National Unity in Kuching, Sarawak, Malaysia.

Information Malaysia yearbook. (1998). Kuala Lumpur: Berita Publishing Sdn. Bhd.

IPI (International Press Institute). (1999, February 17). *Malaysia: 1998 world press freedom review* [On-line]. Available: (http://www.freemedia.at/archive97/malaysia.htm).

ITU (International Telecommunication Union). (1998, 1999). *World telecommunication development report.* Geneva: ITU.

Karthigesu, R. (1998). Malaysia. In A. Goonasekara & D. Holaday (Eds.), *Asian communication handbook* (pp. 95–107). Singapore: AMIC & NTU.

Lee, H.T., & Sarachchandran, V.V. (Comps.). (1975). *Mass communication in Malaysia: An annotated bibliography.* Singapore: AMIC.

Lent, J.A. (1982). Malaysia. In J.A. Lent (Ed.), *Newspapers in Asia: Contemporary trends and problems* (pp. 252–266). Hong Kong: Heinemann Asia.

Lim, P.H. (1992). *Singapore, Malaysian and Brunei newspapers: An international union list.* Singapore: Institute of Southeast Asian Studies.

Mahathir, M. (1989). The social responsibility of the press. In A. Mehra (Ed.), *Press systems in ASEAN states* (pp. 107–116). Singapore: AMIC.

Media guide. (1998, 1999). Kuala Lumpur: WhiteKnight Communications.

Nain, Z. (1996). The impact of the international market place on the organization of Malaysian television. In D. French & M. Richards (Eds.), *Contemporary television: Eastern perspectives* (pp. 157–180). New Delhi: Sage Publications.

Nain, Z., & Anuar, M.K. (1998). Ownership and control of the Malaysian media. *Media Development, 45* (4), 9–17.

Oon, E.S. (1998). The role of the press councils and journalists' unions. In A. Latif (Ed.), *Walking the tightrope: Press freedom and professional standards in Asia* (pp. 189–196). Singapore: AMIC.

Press guide. (1998). Kuala Lumpur: WhiteKnight Communications.

Safar, H.M. (1996). *The press and power.* Kuala Lumpur: University of Malaya Press.

Safar, H.M. (1998). The indigenization of the press in Malaysia: From adversary to partnership. In H.M. Safar, S.A. Rahim & B. Tukhtabayev (Eds.), *Mass media and national development: Experiences of Malaysia and Uzbekistan* (pp. 51–60). Kuala Lumpur: International Centre for Media Studies.

Sarji, A. (1994) *Factors influencing the development of broadcasting in Malaysia from 1920 to 1957.* Research report, Bangi: Department of communication, Universiti Kebangsaan Malaysia.

Sarji, A. (1998). Developing a broadcasting system in developing countries: The Malaysian experience. In H.M. Safar, S.A. Rahim & B. Tukhtabayev (Eds.), *Mass media and national development: Experiences of Malaysia and Uzbekistan* (pp. 107–124). Kuala Lumpur: International Centre for Media Studies.

Sulaiman, Z., & Che'Lah, N. (1996). Media monitors in Malaysia. In K.S. Venkateswaran (Comp.), *Media monitors in Asia* (pp. 41–46). Singapore: AMIC.

Sussman, L.R. (1998). *Press freedom 1999: News of the century.* New York: Freedom House.

Tan, P.S. (1971). Malaysia and Singapore. In J.A. Lent (Ed.), *The Asian newspapers' reluctant revolution* (pp. 179–209). Ames: The Iowa State University Press.

UNESCO (United Nations Educational, Scientific and Cultural Organization). (1998, 1999). *Statistical yearbook.* Paris: UNESCO.

Upwardly mobile: Malaysia's cellular telephone industry. (1999, June) *Asia Inc.*, [pull-out fact sheet].

Vanden Heuvel, J., & Dennis, E.E. (1993). *The unfolding lotus: East Asia's changing media.* New York: The Freedom House.

Wang, L.K. (1998). Malaysia: Ownership and control. *Development Dialogue, 2,* 61–83.

Woodiwiss, A. (1998). *Globalization, human rights and labor law in Pacific Asia.* Cambridge: Cambridge University Press.

WAN (World Association of Newspapers). (1999). *World press trends.* Paris: WAN.

World radio TV handbook. (1999). New York: BPI Communications.

Zeitlin, A. (1998, December 1). Web sites backing ousted Malaysian official evade government control. *The Freedom Forum* [On-line]. Available: (http://www.freedomform.org/international/1998/12/1anwar.asp).

♦

13

MYANMAR

Kalyani Chadha & Anandam P. Kavoori

1. NATIONAL PROFILE

1.1 Geography

One of the largest countries on the Southeast Asian mainland, the Union of Myanmar (Burma) covers an approximate area of 677,752 sq km. It shares borders with China in the north and northeast, Thailand in the east, and India and Bangladesh in the west and northwest. Historically, Myanmar's impassable periphery of mountain ranges effectively limited its interaction with neighboring nations.

1.2 People

Myanmar's population, estimated at 48.1 million, with a life expectancy of 60 years (US Census Bureau, International Data Base, 1999), comprises a number of ethnic groups, with the Burmans making up the majority. The others include the Shan, the Karen, the Mon, and the Kachin. The country's major language is Burmese, and most minority groups speak Burmese, as well as their own languages. Use of English is also widespread, particularly among the older generation (Bixler, 1971). About 89 percent of the population is Buddhist. The literacy rate is 83.6 percent (UNDP, 1999). The urban population is 29 percent (APT, 1999). For most of its history, a state of considerable isolation from the outside world characterized Myanmar. The first sustained break in Myanmar's isolation occurred in 1886 when, after a series of attacks, the British annexed the country to India (Bruce, 1973). Opposition to British rule, which emerged in the 1920s and early 1930s, gained momentum during the outbreak of World War II, when some nationalist Burmese groups turned to Imperial Japan for help against the British and assisted in the Japanese invasion of Myanmar in 1941. However, Burmese nationalists soon discovered that Japan had no intention of giving Myanmar real independence. Consequently, they shifted allegiance, established the Anti Fascist People's

Freedom League (AFPFL), and helped the British defeat the Japanese in 1945. After the war, AFPFL negotiated for independence from the British, and Myanmar became a free country on January 4, 1948 (Cady, 1958).

1.3 Government and Politics

Independent Myanmar (Burma) adopted a parliamentary form of government with a democratically elected civilian political leadership. This political system lasted until 1962, when Gen. Ne Win, a leader of the nationalist movement, staged a coup and replaced the democratic government with a military regime (Maung, 1969). Under Ne Win, the country adopted the so-called "Burmese way to socialism," which involved the establishment of a one-party military-socialist state that not only destroyed all private economic activity and prevented popular participation in politics, but also shut Myanmar off completely from the outside world again (Silverstein, 1977). Ne Win's reclusive regime collapsed in 1988 as the result of a countrywide movement of popular protest.

A democratic government eventually failed to emerge in Myanmar because the army managed to regroup under Gen. Saw Maung and seize control (Silverstein, 1998). The new regime, known as the State Law and Order Restoration Council or SLORC, brutally put down the popular uprising of 1988 and has since exercised absolute control. Despite the rejection of the SLORC-supported National Unity Party in the 1990 general elections, the military has refused to acknowledge the verdict and to transfer power to Aung San Suu Kyi's National League for Democracy (NLD), which swept the polls. SLORC, which renamed itself the State Peace and Development Council (SPDC) in November 1997, has shown no signs of giving up control of the country that it calls Myanmar (Yawnghwe, 1995).

1.4 Economy

Under colonial rule, the British opened up Myanmar through an extensive transport network and made the country an important source of teak, petroleum, rice, and tin for the British empire (Steinberg, 1982). Now, SPDC has abandoned the ineffective state socialism espoused by the previous regime and has attempted to stimulate exports and to attract direct foreign investment from other Asian countries, such as Malaysia and Singapore. However, it has failed to implement a program of comprehensive economic reforms. Consequently, the country's economy continues to suffer from a variety of structural problems, such as an overvalued official currency rate, severe energy shortages, and an underdeveloped infrastructure, all of which have constrained growth (Maung, 1992). Although the country is open to foreign investment, most large international companies have boycotted Myanmar because of the government's politically repressive practices. The inflow of external assistance has also been extremely limited as most international lending agencies have continued to withhold aid from the country (Vokes, 1998). These developments have decelerated the growth rate and caused deterioration in the living standard of the majority. Prospects for economic improvement remain poor. Substantial increases in external assistance are unlikely to come about without political liberalization. Myanmar's economy, with a gross domestic product estimated at US$ 57 billion at purchasing power parity, is one of the poorest in Southeast Asia. The country's per capita GDP at purchasing power parity is US$ 1,200 and its nominal per capita GNP is US$ 765. Its 1999 annual exports stood at US$ 1.2 billion, with a foreign debt of US$ 5.1 billion (*Asiaweek*, January 18, 2000).

2. DEVELOPMENT OF PRESS AND BROADCASTING

2.1 Brief Early History

Myanmar has a long-standing tradition of professional journalism (Allott, 1994a). Modern-style newspapers, similar to those existing in the West, were introduced around 1836 in what was then British-controlled territory: the English-language *Moulmein Chronicle*, the *Karen Morning Star*, and the Burmese-language *Moulmein Times*. The first newspaper in Burmese-controlled territory appeared in 1874. This was the Burmese-language *Ranabon Naypyidaw* (Mandalay Gazette) (Blackburn, 1982). Other Burmese-language newspapers followed. Among them were the nationalist newspaper *Myanmar Alin* (New Light of Burma), founded in Rangoon in 1919, and the *Ludu* (The People), published in Mandalay (Smith, 1994). Hollstein (1971) has traced the early history of the Burmese press in greater detail.

Compared to the print media, which had operated in Myanmar for a century and a half, the broadcast media did not make an impression until the 1940s. In 1937, the British started transmitting programs on a Marconi transmitter that had been used for wireless communication between India and Burma. In 1939, they set up a 10-kW transmitter at Mingaladon, near Rangoon (now Yangon), for broadcasting propaganda in English, Burmese, and Hindustani. During the Japanese occupation (1942–45), the invaders used both medium-wave and shortwave broadcasting, using additional languages like Japanese, Bengali, and Chinese. To counteract this, the underground Burmese Revolutionary Broadcasting Station carried programs for the resistance forces. The broadcasting operations returned to the British civil administration at the end of the war (Blackburn, 1978). Television was introduced in 1980.

2.2 Developments since 1945

From the 1940s, one can observe four phases in the development of the press that closely mirror the state of the country's polity.

2.2.1 First Phase: 1948–62

At the time of independence in 1948, Myanmar (then Burma) had more than 30 newspapers. These included, in addition to Burmese- and English-language newspapers, five Chinese newspapers, two Hindi newspapers, and one each in Urdu, Tamil, and Gujarati (Roberts et al., 1968). Politically, these newspapers fell into three main categories: pro-government, right-wing opposition, and left-wing opposition, and were published by a variety of presses. Although they were subject to occasional government restrictions, newspapers, for the most part, operated with considerable freedom during this period. In fact, in 1954, the Burma Journalists Association successfully prevented the government from passing a bill that made criticism of government leaders a criminal offence. The press generally served as "the unofficial public watchdog, keeping an eye on government policies" (Lintner, 1995, p. 67).

2.2.2 Second Phase: 1962–88

This situation changed dramatically in 1962 when the military under Gen. Ne Win seized power. As in most totalitarian regimes, the new Revolutionary Council established decisive control over the press (Maung, 1969; Win, 1998). To control the flow of information, the regime introduced a system of licensing that required the registration of all publications with the government. The government also established a system of censorship that required clearance of all printed material prior to publication, and it banned the foreign wire services from disseminating news in the country. It created the officially run News Agency Burma (NAB), which alone had the authority to select and distribute news from overseas wire services, such as UPI, AP, and Reuters (Blackburn, 1971, 1982).

In 1966, the Revolutionary Council decreed that newspapers could be published only in Burmese and English, a development that led to the closure of 12 Indian-, Pakistani-, and Chinese-language newspapers, some of which had been published since the late 19th century. By the early 1960s, the government had already banned several prestigious newspapers, including Edward Law Yone's centrist English daily, *The Nation*. The government also nationalized several independent dailies, which it placed under the Ministry of Information and Culture (Lintner, 1994). These newspapers included the English-language *Guardian*, which had a distinguished history as an independent paper, as well as the Burmese-language *Kyemon* (Mirror), the country's most widely read daily; the politically influential *Hanthawaddy*, named after a former capital in lower Myanmar; the widely respected *Myanmar Alin* (New Light of Burma), one of the oldest nationalist papers; and the more overtly ideological *Botahtaung* (Vanguard) (Roberts et al., 1968).

The government also established a daily newspaper, *The Working People's Daily*, as its official organ, published both in English and Burmese by the Ministry of Information and Culture. The Burmese edition bore the title *Loktha Pyithu Nazin*.

Initially, it covered both national and international news, and competed with the private media. Soon, however, no private media were left in the country (Lintner, 1995). In 1966, the government took over the Mandalay-based *Ludu* (The People), the last privately-owned newspaper in the country. The number of daily newspapers fell from 31 before 1962 to six in 1966 (*Editor & publisher international yearbook,* 1967). Having established total control over the domestic information flow, the Ne Win regime brought a decisive end to the post-independence era of a relatively free and professional press. This rigid control of the press prevailed until the middle of August 1988, when a widespread popular uprising against Gen. Ne Win's military government destabilized the entire state apparatus (Kyi, 1991).

2.2.3 Third Phase: Mid-August–Mid-September 1988

The press, unshackled for the first time in 26 years, experienced a brief resurgence during this period of unrest. By the end of August 1988, almost 40 independent newspapers and magazines had emerged in Yangon alone. Some were professionally printed while others were photocopied or handwritten. These lively new publications carried political commentary, editorials, and cartoons, as well as satires critical of the military regime. Their bold stance influenced even official papers, such as the *Guardian* and the *Working People's Daily*, which also began publishing outspoken political articles (Allott, 1990). However, this period of freedom was short lived. The military stepped in and regained control over the Burmese polity on September 18, 1988.

2.2.4 Fourth Phase: Mid-September 1988 Onwards

Once in power, the new junta moved swiftly to once again rein in the press. It reintroduced strict censorship and banned all non-government newspapers. To further bolster its control over the press, the regime closed even government-controlled papers like the *Guardian*, and decreed a single daily, the *Working People's Daily;* for the entire country. As in the third phase, it was to have two editions, Burmese and English. In 1993, the *Working People's Daily* was renamed *Myanmar Alin* after one of the country's oldest and most respected nationalist newspapers. For several years, the *Myanmar Alin*, along with its English-language edition, the *New Light of Myanmar*, was the only daily in the country. However, the *Editor & publisher international yearbook* (1997) indicates that in recent years the military regime has allowed the publication of additional newspapers, which include another government-controlled morning daily, the *Kyemon* (Mirror), as well as two afternoon daily tabloids, the Yangon-based *City News* and the Mandalay-based *Yadanabon Daily.*

Despite the few newspaper titles, the country's print media have shown some vibrancy, as is evident from the emergence of numerous monthly and weekly periodicals focusing on popular science, home and family, business, astrology, films and entertainment, as well as romantic and literary fiction. However, these periodicals, the majority of which are privately owned and published (only a few are government owned), are also subject to strict government censorship. The government has penalized many magazines and withdrawn the license of some for publishing material deemed unsuitable (Lintner, 1998; Allott, 1994a).

The government has also sought to monitor and restrict the activities of foreign press operations in the country. The state-controlled News Agency Myanmar, formerly the News Agency Burma, is the sole gatekeeper and distributor of news. Operating under the Directorate of Information, the News Agency Myanmar's domestic arm collects and disseminates national news and issues official pronounce-ments and announcements, while its external section "screens, reproduces, and provides the sole legal distribution channel of information from the international wire services" (Blackburn, 1982, p. 182).

Further, the government has made it extremely difficult for foreign journalists to enter and operate in the country, although some do manage to enter it cland-estinely. In fact, except for China's Xinhua, no other foreign wire service can post its own correspondents in Yangon. These agencies have to be staffed by local journalists who have obtained government approval. Journalist Khin Win, who worked as a stringer for the Agence France Presse in Myanmar, claims that often the government turns down applications filed by foreign agencies on behalf of Burmese journalists, and instead offers "acceptable" alternative candidates for the agencies to employ (personal communication, September 3, 1998). Typically, these candidates are journalists who have studied at the government's journalism school, which was established in 1967 as part of the government's effort not only to train journalists in the practical aspects of the profession, but also to influence them ideologically (Blackburn, 1982). Similarly, Burmese nationals who want to go abroad to work for the Burmese-language services of any foreign broadcasting station need approval from the government, although the VoA and the BBC do make an effort to hire their Burmese staff independently rather than from the pool of government-vetted correspondents.

2.3 The Broadcast Media

The BBC, which started a Burmese-language service as part of its war effort, laid the foundation for radio broadcasting in Myanmar. After independence, the govern-ment established the Burma Broadcasting Service (BBS), a government-owned and -operated agency, which transmitted medium-wave radio services in Burmese, English and several minority languages (Henderson et al., 1971). Programming was similar to that of any democratic country, and radio reporters and broadcasters operated quite freely (Blackburn, 1971). This freedom came to an abrupt end with the military takeover in 1962. The Ne Win government never gave up its control over radio, not even when personnel from the state-owned radio went on strike and demanded freedom during the 1988 uprising.

Compared to other Asian countries, Myanmar's radio network has always been quite limited, and it has one of the least developed national radio operations in the region at present. According to Blackburn (1978), this situation is the result of a combination of factors: the government's inability to finance the establishment of an extensive radio network and its strong desire to maintain centralized control of radio broadcasting, which has led it to prohibit the development of regional services and stations. For instance, until the fall of the Ne Win regime, the government did not allow Myanmar radio to carry any advertising because of the fear that commercialization would allow undesirable elements of the population (such as the country's Chinese and Indian minorities) to exert undue influence, and reduce state control over the medium. However, the country has always received both Burmese- and English-language broadcasts from a number of foreign radio services, including the BBC, the Voice of America, and Radio Free Asia, all of which are sources of independent news and information (Donow, 1995).

Television, established in 1980 with Japanese assistance, also came under government ownership and control. Originally, the transmission of the country's first television station was limited to Yangon and the nearby towns. However, both Myanmar Television and a second television station, set up by the military in 1990, are now available throughout the country. Initially these TV stations shared a single channel, but recently the military station has acquired its own channel (Military TV, 1997). The early 1990s witnessed the entry of satellite television networks such as Murdoch's STAR TV. However, government permission is required to own a satellite receiver dish. Large hotels in Yangon, as well as senior government and military officials, have received permits to install satellite dishes. Anecdotal evidence indicates that in some northern towns, such as Mandalay and Lashio, a small number of satellite dishes smuggled in form China are in use. Numbers remain small because of the expenses associated with the installation of dishes and the erratic supply of electricity in most upcountry areas (Donow, 1998).

3. THE PRESS

3.1 Policy and Legal Framework

The press operated in a state of comparative freedom during the first phase (1948–62). The main task of the small Press Review Department that U Nu's government established in the 1950s was to read through newspapers and periodicals to enable officials to respond to criticism. The military coup changed that situation dramatically in 1962, when control became the *leitmotif* of media policy (Blackburn, 1982). Most of the country's current press restriction policies originated during this period. The Printers and Publishers Registration Act of August 1962 was the first step taken by the military regime to control the press. The Act stipulated that publishers and printers of all printed material (such as newspapers, magazines, journals, calendars, posters, and the like could operate only after they had obtained a license from the Ministry of Information and had been registered with the newly formed Press Scrutiny Board (Allott, 1981).

This Act is still a crucial component of Myanmar's media policy. No publication is possible without explicit government authorization. In 1966, the government issued a policy directive that nationalized the country's newspapers and prohibited the publication of private newspapers. The present military regime continues to enforce this directive. Thus all newspapers in the country are government-owned and -controlled (Lintner, 1995). In the mid-1960s, the Ne Win regime also instituted a rigorous system of censorship, which was enforced by the Press Scrutiny Board, operating under the aegis of the powerful Ministry of Home and Religious Affairs. This censorship policy, a central aspect of Myanmar's press policy framework, is derived from Article 157 of the 1974 Burmese Constitution, which states that "every citizen shall have freedom of speech, expressions and publication to the extent that such freedom is not contrary to the interests of the working people and socialism." Essentially, the government's publication policy is to scrutinize every publication to deter views that might be detrimental to the ideology of the state, socialist economy, national solidarity and unity, national security, the rule of law, and peace and public order. The policy also aims to weed out obscenity, "non-constructive criticism," libel, and slander (Allott, 1981).

The unique characteristic of this system of censorship, and one that continues to define it, is the requirement to submit the publications to the Press Scrutiny Board not before, but rather after, printing (Allott, 1993). A publisher has to submit 20 to 30 copies of a publication to the censors, who examine them minutely for any reference to words such as "democracy" and "human rights," for any criticism of the SLORC or the country's military, as well as for any mention of the 1988 democracy movement and of its leaders. Censors also ensure that the work of writers who have been imprisoned or blacklisted is not published (Amnesty International, 1994). If the Press Scrutiny Board were to identify some material as objectionable, it could require the elimination of the objectionable matter before permitting the publication to enter the market. Publishers have to undertake this task at their own expense by "ripping out pages, gluing them together, inking over with silver paint or sticking opaque tape over the offending item" (Allott, 1993, p. 45). They have to send the tornout pages to the Press Scrutiny Board, which, after ensuring that none has been left in the publication or distributed separately, destroys the pages. The censors could also issue a blanket ban against the entire issue and demand the destruction of all copies of the publication (Allott, 1993). The Burmese press policy thus offers a powerful incentive for self-censorship. Editors and publishers tend to avoid potentially objectionable writing and select only such materials that are likely to please the Press Scrutiny Board. Stringent censorship applies not only to books, magazines, and other publications of private publishers, whether domestic or foreign, but also to state-owned periodicals and newspapers, although the latter are typically subject to less scrutiny.

The government's newsprint subsidy also relates to its press policy. This involves the Paper and Printing Corporation's monthly allocation of a fixed quantity of newsprint, priced at a rate lower than the market, to privately owned publications

(Blackburn, 1982). This subsidy is critical because the cost of imported newsprint in the open market is extremely expensive. Myanmar, which has only a few dozen small paper mills, mostly in the Yangon area, has to import most of the newsprint from countries like Bangladesh. Many journalists believe that the government's motivations in providing the subsidy stem from an ulterior motive: the ability to control the circulation of publications through the allocation of a fixed quota (Zaw, 1996).

The US State Department's (1999) human rights report on Myanmar for 1998 made the following points on freedom of speech and of the press:

- The government used the mass media as propaganda instruments. The media did not report opposing views except to criticize them.
- Editors and reporters remained answerable to the military authorities, who compelled them to publish pro-government articles in the non-official media.
- The *New Light of Myanmar* edited international wire service reports, as well as domestic news, to reinforce government policy.
- Citizens were generally unable to subscribe directly to foreign publications even though a selection of foreign newspapers was available for purchase in a few hotels and stores. Street vendors sold international newsmagazines illegally. Censors frequently banned issues or deleted articles that the government deemed unsuitable.
- Order 5/96, issued in 1996, prohibited the drafting of alternative constitutions, as well as speeches or statements that "undermine national stability."

3.2 Financial Aspects: Circulation, Advertising, Marketing Strategies

Newspaper readership is heavily concentrated in the country's urban centers. The estimated circulation of dailies exceeded 1 million copies in 1994. This was equivalent to 2.4 copies per 100 people. The circulation figure dropped to less than one-half million in 1995 and 1996. This represented a daily newspaper penetration of one copy per 100 people. The *Kyemon* has an estimated circulation of 100,000, while the *Myanmar Alin* has 400,000 and the *New Light of Myanmar* has 14,000.

Since newspapers in Myanmar are owned and controlled completely by the government, so the state finances them. However, the newspapers can also carry advertising, either on pages dedicated for this purpose or in special weekend advertising supplements. Unlike newspapers, more periodicals and magazines published in Myanmar are owned privately by individuals or by presses licensed by the government. U Thiha, who publishes a business magazine in Yangon, says that about four-fifths of the financing for magazines comes from a combination of subscriptions and newsstand sales, and the balance from advertising (personal communication, May 15, 1998). Publications in Myanmar do not appear to have developed the type of marketing strategies visible in less restricted media markets. The government's practice of allocating only a fixed quantity of newsprint has created a situation that enables magazines to print only a limited number of copies.

They are often not in a position to meet even the existing demand. Consequently, there has been little motivation for magazines to attempt an increase in circulation.

3.3 Structure and Organization

Myanmar has two morning dailies published in Burmese, the *Myanmar Alin* and the *Kyemon* (The Mirror); and one English daily, the *New Light of Myanmar*, which is the English version of the *Myanmar Alin* (Lintner, 1998). The SPDC itself is believed to put out some 15 journals. Both the *Kyemon* and the *Myanmar Alin* are tabloid-size publications that usually run to about 16 pages, while the *New Light of Myanmar* is an eight-page broadsheet. In addition, the municipal governments of Yangon and Mandalay each publish a 16-page afternoon daily tabloid, the *City News* and the *Yadanabon Daily* respectively.

The press in Myanmar also includes nearly 100 magazines and periodicals, mostly in Burmese, which appear weekly or monthly. They focus on a wide variety of subjects, including astrology, medicine, literature, films, business, and science and technology. The few English publications include *Myanmar Today* and *IT Myanmar: The Business and Technology Magazine*, which carry business news and features. The most popular magazines in the country include the Burmese-language *Myanmar Dana* (Burmese Wealth), *Dana* (Wealth), *Kyeebwaye* (Prosperity), and *Mahayathi* (The Lady) (Kaps, 1996a). The first three publications typically carry stories on business and society, while the last is a literary magazine that carries fiction and poetry. All, however, studiously avoid publishing controversial articles. These magazines have an estimated readership of 12,000 to 20,000 (Myanmar Directory, 1998). During the last few years, however, various periodicals and magazines that are either openly controlled by the government or enjoy its covert sponsorship have emerged. Such propaganda magazines include the *Myawaddy* and the *Ngwetryi*. Their stories and poetry reflect the state's ideology. These periodicals have a fairly low circulation ranging from 3,000 to 4,000 (Myanmar Directory, 1998).

Publications associated with the state also include journals owned by different government departments, either wholly or as joint ventures with private business interests. About 24 such publications exist, most of which started during the last two years (Kaps, 1996a). Typically, they focus on issues such as trade, tourism and entertainment, depending on which department owns them. Professional journalists, employed by the government departments on a contract basis, produce these publications.

The military government, in fact, runs some ostensibly private periodicals. The monthly *Myet Khin Thit* (New Sword) claims to be an independent publication but is widely believed to be controlled by Myanmar's secret police, the Directorate of Defense Services Intelligence. This publication largely contains articles attacking both the domestic and the foreign opponents of the military regime. It is perhaps the only publication in Myanmar to be completely exempt from the process of censorship (Zaw, 1996).

3.4 Quality and Popular Press

The Burmese press is not easily divisible into categories like "quality" and "popular." The policy of censorship, a fundamental aspect of the Burmese media, has fostered the sort of newspaper content that varies from outright propaganda about the regime to articles on sports, culture, and business. *Myanmar Alin* and *New Light of Myanmar* are essentially propaganda organs of the government, while the *Kyemon* occasionally carries some human-interest stories. Foreign news invariably tends to be a few days old because of the need to get clearance from the Press Scrutiny Board (Allott, 1994a).

3.5 Distribution and Technology

The majority of the magazines in Myanmar are internally produced and distributed. Typically, traditional printing presses such as the Hanthawaddy Press and the Myawaddy Press print the magazines. These presses tend to have extremely old and outdated equipment prone to frequent breakdowns. They also have to contend with almost constant shortages of spare parts and raw materials, such as ink and newsprint. These factors seriously hamper magazine production. Distribution problems saddle the foreign magazines, such as *Newsweek* and the *Far Eastern Economic Review*, although the government has permitted their entry into the country. They are not usually available on newsstands. Readers have to purchase them in the black market, usually from diplomats or government officials who subscribe to them. These magazines are also subject to censorship. They cannot be distributed without the approval of the Press Scrutiny Board. On many occasions the censors have not allowed these magazines into the country for carrying articles deemed to be objectionable.

4. BROADCASTING

4.1 Policy and Legal Framework

Unlike the press, the broadcast media in Myanmar have always been owned and operated by the government (Henderson et al., 1971). The Myanmar Television and Radio Department (MTRD) is responsible for radio broadcasting and for running the country's first television service. The Ministry of Information and Culture controls the MTRD. The military set up a second television service, which functions under the supervision of the Ministry of Defense (Demaine, 1998). Although television and radio services do not have to obtain licenses from the Ministry of Home and Religious Affairs, which controls the print media, their broadcasts, especially news, are subject to censorship by the Press Scrutiny Board.

The US Department of State (1999) reported that a 1996 amendment to the television and video law imposed additional restrictions and stiffer penalties on the distribution of videotapes not approved by the censor. Communication devices were rationed or licensed to limit people's access to information. Foreign broadcasts, such as those of the BBC, Voice of America, Radio Free Asia, and the Norway-based Democratic Voice of Burma, remained the main sources of information. Those who operated unlicensed satellite-TV receivers were subject to a prison sentence of up to three years.

4.2 Structure and Organization

Myanmar has only a single radio service: the government-run Myanmar Athan or Radio Myanmar (previously known as the Burma Broadcasting Service [BBS]), which broadcasts throughout the country with five transmitters located in Yangon, Radio is an extremely popular medium in Myanmar, and the ownership of radio sets is fairly widespread, even within the more remote regions of the country (Donow, 1995). A survey conducted in 1996 by Nielsen/SRG Myanmar, (a rather short-lived media research company affiliated with Nielsen/SRG Bangkok), showed that 95 percent of the radio audience listened to AM broadcasts while the remaining 5 percent listened to FM. (Yangon has three FM channels: 98MHz, 102MHz, and 104MHz). UNESCO (1999) has estimated that Myanmar had 4.2 million radio receivers, or 9.6 receivers per 100 people in 1997 (Table 1). This figure may not be accurate because it does not include the large number of receivers smuggled into the country from China and Thailand (Lintner, 1998).

Myanmar's first television broadcaster, the state-controlled Myanmar TV, was established in 1980 and was initially available only within the Yangon area. The addition of some 120 TV relay stations throughout the country and the use of the AsiaSat1 satellite have expanded the coverage of this channel to 82 percent of the country. Official data claim that 267 of the country's 324 townships can receive Myanmar TV (*Myanmar Today*, 1998; Donow, 1995). The second television broadcaster is the military-controlled Myawaddy Television, established in 1990. This service, transmitted via satellite, was originally intended only for the armed forces. Since March 27, 1997, it has been available to the general public as well. Its service is currently limited to three large townships, but expansion to other large towns is under way (*Myanmar Today*, 1998). UNESCO (1999) has estimated that in 1997, Myanmar had 260,000 sets in use or 0.6 sets in use per 100 people (Table 1). However, Donow (1995) puts this figure at about 500,000. Although the bulk of the TV sets are in urban areas, such as Yangon and Mandalay, many rural areas have had access to community television since the early 1990s.

4.3 Program Policies

4.3.1 Radio

In addition to Burmese-language programming, which comprises the bulk of the radio's day-long offerings, Myanmar Athan also transmits three half-hour English-language programs a day. It also broadcasts daily programs in minority ethnic languages—Shan, Mon, Arakanese, and Kachin (Myanmar Directory, 1998). A 1996 survey showed that the most popular programs in Myanmar were music programs, news broadcasts and radio plays (Nielsen/SRG, 1996).

4.3.2 Television

Myanmar TV broadcasts for approximately five hours on weekdays and for eight hours on weekends. Except for a nightly English news bulletin, all its programming is in Burmese. There are no programs in any of the minority languages. On average, Myawaddy TV transmits Burmese-language programming for about the same amount of time as Myanmar TV. Initially, both stations shared a single channel. In 1997, Myawaddy TV acquired its own channel (Military TV, 1997). Among those who have access to both radio and television, television usage rate is about twice as high as that for radio. The most popular television programs in Myanmar are Burmese films, international and domestic news programs, documentaries, and sports (Nielsen/SRG, 1996).

4.4 Ownership and Financing

The government and the military own and operate all domestic broadcasting in Myanmar. Although both Radio Myanmar and Myanmar TV are state-funded enterprises, they do carry advertising. The bulk of the advertising on television is sponsored by domestic businesses, except for a few advertisements placed by international conglomerates like Procter & Gamble, Nestle, and British Tobacco (Kilburn, 1996).

4.5 Foreign Radio and Satellite Services

4.5.1 Foreign Radio Services

Radio constitutes the only medium through which the ordinary people in Myanmar can obtain news from the outside world in uncensored form. This is a major reason for the popularity of radio. Listeners can access foreign radio services such as the BBC, Voice of America, Radio Free Asia, and Democratic Voice of Burma (which broadcasts Burmese-language programs) (Vanden Heuvel & Dennis, 1993). The most widely heard foreign radio service is the BBC, which began its transmission in 1942 with a modest 15-minute-per-fortnight broadcast. It now transmits more than 10 hours of Burmese programs every week, focusing on both domestic and international news. The BBC broadcasts of the pro-democracy movement in 1988 were so popular that TV Myanmar had to change the time slot of its international news bulletin to retain its audience. The BBC listenership has declined somewhat because of obstacles placed by the military regime on independent domestic sources (Kaps, 1996b).

The Voice of America service in Myanmar, also established as part of the war effort against the Japanese in the 1940s, now broadcasts about 90 minutes of Burmese-language programs daily. Although the VoA had almost as many listeners as the BBC during the 1988 uprising, the former never achieved the popularity of the BBC because the listeners felt that VoA contained too much US government propaganda (Donow, 1998). The Norway-based Democratic Voice of Burma—a relatively new service started in 1992 with a grant from the Norwegian government, as well as NGOs such as the US-based Open Society Institute and the National Endowment for Democracy—broadcasts for one and one-half hours daily. Its transmissions include news and news commentary related to Myanmar, as well as general segments devoted to health, women's issues, and song requests from listeners. Although DVB has a faithful audience, particularly among pro-democracy groups, its reception in Myanmar is poor, a fact that undoubtedly reduces its listnership. The Burmese broadcasts of Radio Free Asia started only in February 1997. With three hours of Burmese programs daily, it has become extremely popular, rivaling both BBC and VoA. The primary reason for its success is its network of domestic sources, which are considered better than that of any other foreign broadcaster (Lintner, 1998).

Because foreign broadcasters are vital sources of information for the Burmese and frequently broadcast material critical of the military regime, it is not surprising that the military government has jammed foreign broadcasts on several occasions. However, the government has not attempted to jam foreign radio services on a permanent basis, because the country's military rulers also depend on these services for news (Allott, 1994b).

4.5.2 Foreign Satellite Services

While satellite television is not banned explicitly, Myanmar does not have an indigenous satellite television service. Those who wish to install satellite reception dishes have to obtain a special permit or license for 10,000 kyats from the government. These are typically issued only to hotels and government officials (Donow, 1998). Similarly, government permission is required to establish a cable network. Recently, the military regime decided to stop issuing new licenses for reception dishes or for setting up cable networks, although the existing permits are still valid. Despite this, people continue to obtain dishes and to set up informal cable systems illegally, especially in the upcountry regions where restrictions are not enforced as rigorously as in the capital and its surrounding areas (Lintner, 1998).

The precise number of satellite dishes in Myanmar is not known, but it is probably significantly lower than that in Thailand or China because the costs of the license, the dish, and installation is relatively high at 80,000–100,000 kyats (Some thoughts, on satellite, 1994). Located squarely within the footprints of Thaicom and AsiaSat, Myanmar mostly picks up programming beamed from these satellites. Most viewers receive programs from Thai channels and Murdoch's STAR TV network, which includes the music video channel (Channel V), STAR Movies, STAR Sports, and

STAR Plus (a general entertainment channel which carries soap operas, sitcoms, and drama series). Some viewers can also pick up the Singapore-based Asia Business News network, while most of the large hotels also receive CNN and BBC news on their in-house cable systems (Donow, 1995). The general population, however, does not have access to these news-oriented channels. Moreover, ever since it dropped the BBC from its channel bouquet in 1994, the STAR TV network tends to have very little political content. As a result, the political impact of satellite television in Myanmar is very limited.

5. NEW ELECTRONIC MEDIA

5.1 Internet and On-line Media

The January 1999 Network Wizards Survey showed that Myanmar had only one Internet host (ITU, 1999). In 1998, the government began to offer Internet services to a small number of customers, with at least two government-affiliated companies providing e-mail services. However, the military regime has tightly restricted Internet communications. In 1996, the government had decreed that all computers, software and associated telecommunication devices would be subject to government registration (US Department of State, 1999).

The military regime has instituted a very restrictive policy on the Internet. Access to local Internet servers is off-limits to the general public. Even the possession of a computer with networking capability is illegal without government authorization. Moreover, obtaining or sending information over the Internet on subjects such as state security, the economy, and national culture or subscribing to an electronic mailing list is prohibited. In fact, ordinary citizens face prosecution and imprisonment if they risk accessing the Internet. Those privileged with access to the Internet in Myanmar are government and military officials (Bardacke, 1996). *New Light of Myanmar* has a Web presence (http://www.myanmar.com/nlm/).

5.2 Telecommunications Infrastructure

The country's sole telecommunication operator is the Posts and Telecommunications Department. By December 1998, Myanmar had 225,104 telephones, including the public switched telephone network, the wireless local loop, and cellular mobile telephones, and a telephone density of 0.49 per 100 people. The density of mainlines is 1.4 per 100 households. The number of cellular subscribers stood at 8,516. About 55,000 are on the waiting list for telephones. The country's seven 6GHz analogue microwave systems also serve as signal bearers to TV broadcasting stations in provincial towns. The number of digital microwave routes has increased to 10. No plans exist to introduce ISDN. Myanmar started to reap the benefits of the latest fiber-optic technology in August 1999 when it established direct links with SEA-ME-WE-3 member countries (APT, 1998, 1999; ITU, 1998).

In 1998, Myanmar had 523 local telephone exchanges, including 93 automatic ones, providing a capacity to communicate with 320 out of the 324 townships in the country. Moreover, it claims the successful establishment of the Code Division Multiple Access wireless local loop system (CDMA), as well as the installation of a 960-microchannel digital microwave link at the Thanlyin satellite communication station. Myanmar plans to use the Asia–Europe submarine cable to facilitate direct links with 32 countries by more than 10,000 channels (APT, 1998).

6. POLICY TRENDS FOR PRESS AND BROADCASTING

Although the Burmese media were once free and vibrant, now they are among the most repressed in the world. Heavy-handed control and censorship constitute the linchpins of the military government's media policy. In May 1998, the New York-based Committee to Protect Journalists (CPJ) named Gen. Than Shwe, who presides over Myanmar's ruling junta, as one of the 10 enemies of the press. As the CPJ put it, "Myanmar remains a nightmare for free expression. Fax machines, photocopies and computer modems are banned. There are absolutely no independent newspapers. In this climate of oppression, the Burmese people are kept in the dark even about the nature of their government" (CPJ, 1998, p. 50). Thus the media in Myanmar seem to have followed a curious trajectory, going, in the apt words of Allott (1994a) from "independence to unfreedom" (p. 88).

As a result, the country's media are largely untouched by the phenomenon of globalization, witnessing neither the proliferation in the technologies of distribution nor the emergence of multiple media outlets experienced by other nations. Instead, its restrictive and limited character presents a very stark contrast not only to the West, but also to other Asian nations, many of which have experienced some liberalization of their media in recent years. The likelihood of change under the current regime remains extremely limited. This is hardly surprising given the government's position that the media should restrain themselves from making statements that would disrupt public order, and that the government has the right to take appropriate steps to balance press freedom with domestic tranquility (Amnesty International, 1994). Thus the only way that the media in Myanmar could achieve greater freedom is through political change and the establishment of a democratic government, but that appears to be a distant prospect.

7. MAIN ISSUES

● Freedom of the press

Myanmar originally possessed a free and vibrant press with multiple newspapers in various languages. This era of press freedom came to end with the military takeover in 1962. Since then, both print and electronic media in Myanmar have been subject to stringent government control. Currently, the government owns and operates all newspapers, as well as radio and television services. The only privately-owned media in the country are magazines, but they too have to be licensed by the government. The only non-government controlled news sources for the country are the broadcasts of foreign radio services, such as the BBC, the VoA, and Radio Free Asia. Freedom House (Sussman, 1999) gave Myanmar a press restriction score of 97 out of 100 based on four criteria: laws and regulations, political pressures and controls, economic influences, and repressive actions that influence media content.

● Human rights

The government has turned a blind eye to Article 19 of the Universal Declaration of Human Rights. It has not ratified the two principal covenants relating to the declaration, the first on civil and political rights, and the other on economic, social, and cultural rights. In a 1999 report, the London-based International Center Against Censorship—known as Article 19—has condemned Myanmar's abuse of civil rights and freedom of expression (www.soros.org/burma/bn41699.html). The All Burma Federation of Students Union has claimed that three journalists have died in prison while another 10 are in detention (www.soros.org/burma/bn051299b.html). All media are subject to strict censorship by the country's Press Scrutiny Board. Foreign press operations are restricted severely since the military government banned the entry of foreign journalists into the country. International wire services are forced to hire government-approved journalists and cannot post their own staff. Moreover, the government-controlled Myanmar News Agency acts as the sole gatekeeper and distributor of international news within the country.

● Isolation

Myanmar does not have an indigenous satellite or cable television service. Those who wish to obtain satellite dishes or to set up cable networks can do so only with government permission. However, the high cost of licences and the uncertain supply of electricity have discouraged the use of satellite television and cable services on a large scale. Myanmar's telecommunication infrastructure is extremely limited. The country has only five telephone lines per 1,000 people, and access to the Internet is available only to senior military and government functionaries. The government has thereby deprived its people of the benefits of modern technology for its own preservation.

● Authoritarian rule

More than a quarter-century ago, Hollstein (1971) wrote: "For some 800 years Burma was ruled by absolute monarchs. For more than a century thereafter, parts, and ultimately all, of the country were controlled by the British. Since independence (January 1948), Burma has been dominated largely by a single political party or, as at present, a military dictatorship. Aspirations for achieving a democratic govern- ment and a free-press system have been frustrated, because Burma has managed to escape none of the now classic difficulties of the so-called emergent world" (p. 138). Very little has changed since Hollstein wrote those words.

8. STATISTICS

General Profile

Exchange rate (January 2000)	US$ 1 = 328 Kyat (market rate)
	US$ 1 = 5.91 (official rate)
Population (mid-1999)	48.1 million
Geographical size	657,741 sq km
Population density (mid-1999)	73.1 per sq km
Number of national television channels	2
Number of national radio channels	1
Life expectancy	60.1 years
Literacy	83.6 percent

Source: *Asiaweek*, January 14, 2000; UNDP, 1999; US Census Bureau.

Table 1
Estimated Mass Media Penetration

	Radio receivers		Television receivers		Daily newspapers		
	Number (millions)	Per 100 people	Number ('000)	Per 100 people	Number	Circ'n ('000)	Per 100 people
1980	0.8	2.3	1	...	7	350	1.0
1985	2.5	6.7	20	0.05	7	511	1.4
1990	3.4	8.4	101	0.25	2	700	1.7
1995	4.0	9.3	230	0.54	5	446	1.0
1996	4.1	9.6	250	0.58	5	449	1.0
1997	4.2	9.6	260	0.59			

Source: UNESCO, 1998, 1999; * ITU, 1999.

Table 2
Daily Newspapers

Title	Est.	Language	Circulation
Myanmar Alin [The New Light of Myanmar]	1963	Burmese	400,000
Kyemon [The Mirror]	1951	Burmese	100,000
New Light of Myanmar	1963	English	14,000
City News		Burmese	n.a.
Yadanabon Daily (Mandalay)		Burmese	n.a.

Source: *Editor & publisher international yearbook*, 1998.

9. USEFUL ADDRESSES

9.1 Broadcast

Myanmar Television and Radio Department (MTRD)
365–367 Bo Aung Gyew StÇ
Kyauktada Township
Yangon
Telephone: 95-1-289274

9.2 Newspapers

Myanmar Alin
212 Theinbyu Road
Botahtaung Township
Yangon
Telehpone: 95-1-73182

New Light of Myanmar
22–30 Strand Road
Yangon
Telephone: 95-1-89190

Kyemon
77 52nd St.
Pazundaung
Yangon
Telephone: 95-1-82777

9.3 Tabloids

City News
Third Floor, City Central Plaza
Shwedagon Pagoda Road
Yangon
Telephone: 95-1-74310

9.4 Magazines

Dana
189-B 33rd St.
Kyauktada Township
Yangon

Myanmar Dana
Building 7, Room 8
Lanthit Yeiktha Road
Yangon

Kweebwaye
Office of the Board of Editors

296 Bo Sun Pat St.
Pabedan Township
Yangon

Myanmar Economic Journal
1 Kinwun Mingyi Road
Dagon Township
Yangon

Oksa Dana Journal
Seven Dragon Myanmar Enterprise Co. Ltd.
37A U Tun Myat Road
Tamwe Township
Yangon

9.5 News Agencies

Myanmar News Agency
212 Theinbyu Road
Botahtaung Township
Yangon

9.6 Foreign Bureaus:

Agence France Presse
12L Pyithu Lane
7th Mile
Yangon

Associated Press
283 U Wisara Road
Sanchaung
PO Box 11111
Yangon

Xinhua News Agency
105 Leeds Rd.
Yangon

10. REFERENCES

Allott, A.J. (1981). Prose writing and publishing in Burma: Government policy and popular practice.
    In T.S. Chee (Ed.), *Essays on literature and society in Southeast Asia: Political and sociological
    perspectives* (pp. 1–35). Singapore: Singapore University Press.
Allott, A.J. (1990, December). The media in Burma and the pro-democracy movement of July–
    September 1988. *South-East Asia Library Group Newsletter, 34–35*, pp. 17–24.
Allott, A.J. (1993). *Inked over, ripped out: Burmese storytellers and the censors.* New York: PEN
    American Center.
Allott, A.J. (1994a). Independence to unfreedom. *Index on Censorship, 23* (3), 88–91.
Allott, A.J. (1994b). Letting the cat out. *Index on Censorship, 23* (3), 102–105.
Amnesty International. (1994, January). *Myanmar: Human rights developments: July to December
    1993.* New York: Amnesty International.

APT (Asia-Pacific Telecommunity). (1998, 1999). *The APT yearbook.* Bangkok: APT.

Bardacke, T. (1996, October 6). High price to pay for Internet use in Burma. *The Financial Times,* p. 6.

Bixler, N. (1971). *Burma: A profile.* New York: Praeger.

Blackburn, P. P. (1971). Communications and national development in Burma, Malaysia and Thailand: A comparative systematic analysis. *Dissertation Abstracts International, 32,* 04A. (University Microfilms No. UM 71–24938).

Blackburn, P. P. (1978). Burma. In J.A. Lent (Ed.), *Broadcasting in Asia and the Pacific: A continental survey of radio and television* (pp. 188–195). Philadelphia: Temple University Press.

Blackburn, P. P. (1982). Burma. In J.A. Lent (Ed.), *Newspapers in Asia: Contemporary trends and problems* (pp. 177–192). Hong Kong: Heinemann Asia.

Bruce, G.L. (1973). *The Burmese war 1824–1886.* London: Hart-Davis MacGibbon.

Cady, J. F. (1958). *A history of modern Burma.* Ithaca, NY: Cornell University Press.

CIA (Central Intelligence Agency). (1998). *World factbook* [On-line]. Available: (http://www.odci.gov/cia/publications/factbook/index.html).

CPJ (Committee to Protect Journalists). (1998, May). *Attacks on the press in 1997.* New York: CPJ.

Demaine, H. (1998). Myanmar: Physical and social geography. *The Far East and Australasia 1998* (29th ed., pp. 685–698). London: Europa Publications.

Donow, K. R. (1995). *East Asian media: Television, radio and information services in eight Asian markets.* Washington, DC: US Information Agency.

Donow, K. R. (1998). *Research memorandum: Notes for VOA Burmese program.* Washington, DC: US Information Agency.

Editor & publisher international yearbook. (1967, 1997, 1998). New York: Editor & Publisher.

Henderson, J.W., Heimann, J.M., Martindale, K.W., Shinn, R.S., Weaver, J.O., & White, E.T. (1971). *Area handbook for Burma.* Washington, DC: US Government Printing Office.

Hollstein, M. (1971). Burma. In J.A. Lent (Ed.), *Asian newspapers' reluctant revolution* (pp. 138–157). Ames: The Iowa State University Press.

ITU (International Telecommunications Union). (1998, 1999). *World telecommunication development report.* Geneva: ITU.

Kaps, P. (1996a, October 3). Vibrant magazine industry in Burma. *The Bangkok Post,* p. 12.

Kaps, P. (1996b, December 15). BBC's position weakened in Myanmar. *The Bangkok Post,* p. 7.

Kilburn, D, (1996, September). Sanctions may signal end of Burma's ad industry. *Media International,* 24.

Kyi, A.S.S. (1991). *Freedom from fear: And other writings.* New York: Viking.

Lintner, B. (1994). *Burma in revolt.* Boulder, CO: Westview Press.

Lintner, B. (1995). Burma repression continues. *Nieman Reports, 49* (4), 66–68.

Lintner, B. (1998). *The media environment in Burma.* Report prepared for the International Broadcasting Bureau, US Information Agency. Washington, DC: US Information Agency.

Maung, M. (1969). *Burma and Gen. Ne Win.* New York: Asia Publishing House.

Maung, M. (1992). *Totalitarianism in Burma: Prospects for economic development.* New York: Paragon House.

Military TV station to broadcast via AsiaSat 2. (1997, February 20). *Daily Variety,* p. 7.

Myanmar Directory. (1998). In *The Far East and Australasia 1998* (pp. 689–695). London: Europa Publications.

Myanmar Today. (1998). [On-line]. Available: (http://www.myanmar.com/today.htm).

Nielsen/SRG. (1996, October). *Myanmar media index.* Bangkok: Nielsen/SRG.

Roberts, T.D., Matthews, J.M., McMorris, D.S., Parachini, K.E., Raiford, W.N., & Townsend, C. (1968). *Area handbook for Burma.* Washington, DC: US Government Printing Office.

Silverstein, J. (1977). *Military rule and the politics of stagnation.* Ithaca, NY: Cornell University Press.

Silverstein, J. (1998). Myanmar: History. In *The Far East and Australasia 1998* (pp. 666–678). London: Europa Publications.

Smith, M. (1994). Unending war. *Index on Censorship, 23* (23), 113–118.

Some thoughts on satellite. (1994, March). *Burma Today*, p. 34.

Steinberg, D. (1982). *Burma: A socialist nation of South East Asia*. Boulder, CO: Westview Press.

Sussman, L.R. (1999). *Press freedom 1999: News of the century*. New York: Freedom House.

UNDP (United Nations Development Program). (1999). *Human development report*. New York: Oxford University Press & UNDP.

UNESCO (United Nations Educational, Scientific and Cultural Organization). (1999). *Statistical yearbook*. Paris: UNESCO.

US Department of State. (1999, February 26). *Burma: Country Report on human rights practices for 1998*. Washington, DC: Bureau of Democracy Human Rights and Labor [On-line]. Available: ⟨http://www.state.gov/www.global/human_rights/1998_hrp_report/burma.html⟩.

Vanden Heuvel, J., & Dennis, E. E. (1993). *The unfolding lotus: East Asia's changing media*. New York: Freedom Forum Center for Media Studies.

Vokes, R. (1998). Myanmar: Economy. In *The Far East and Australasia, 1998* (29th ed., pp. 678–684). London: Europa Publications.

Win, K.M. (1998). The Burmese way to muzzle dissent. *Development Dialogue, 2*, 48–59.

Yawnghwe, C. (1995). Burma, the depoliticization of the political. In M. Alagappa (Ed.), *Political legitimacy in Southeast Asia* (pp. 170–192). Stanford, CA: Stanford University Press.

Zaw, A. (1996, January 2). Myet Khin Thit, just another propaganda tool. *The Nation*, p. 8.

♦

14

PHILIPPINES

Crispin C. Maslog

1. NATIONAL PROFILE

1.1 Geography

The Philippines, the second largest archipelago in the world next to Indonesia, is composed of 7,150 islands with a land area of 301,000 sq km spread over its 2.2 million sq km of territorial waters. Only 2,803 of these islands are named and some 1,000 are inhabited. The major regions or island groupings are Luzon in the north, Mindanao in the south, and Visayas in between. The country is bound on the west and north by the China Sea, on the east by the Pacific Ocean, and on the south by the Celebes Sea and coastal waters of Borneo.

The Philippines is very rich in natural resources and, in fact, owns one-of-a-kind biogeographic zones. One example of its unique biogeographic zones is Palawan, popularly known as the Philippines' "last frontier." It has a very rich and diverse flora. Its forest ecosystem supports many of the Philippines' celebrated endemic flora and fauna. Environmentalists describe the Philippines as a "biodiversity superstar" (*Atlas of the Philippines*, 1998).

The climate of the Philippines is tropical, with two marked seasons: the dry season from December to May and the wet season for the rest of the year. Heavy rainfall and typhoons, especially from June to December, characterize the wet season.

1.2 People

The population rose from 60.7 million in 1990 to 68.6 million in 1995 at an annual rate of 2.35 percent (*Philippine yearbook*, 1995). The mid-1999 population was estimated at 79.3 million (US Census Bureau, 1999). The largest concentration of Filipinos is in Metro Manila, where about 8 million people live. Metro Cebu follows with about 2 million. The rural population is 54 percent. Life expectancy is 68.3 years.

The Negritos are believed to be the first inhabitants of the islands, but their origin is unknown. They live in scattered bands in the forested valleys and mountains. The Indonesians, who were the next to arrive, drove the Negritos away from the favorable lowlands. The Malays, the most recent people to reach the islands, took over all of the Philippines except the less desirable sections where the Negritos and Indonesians still live. The Spanish converted the people to Christianity. Today, the Christian Malays make up 91.5 percent of the population, Muslim Malays 4 percent, Chinese 1.5 percent and others 3 percent. The Roman Catholics make up the bulk (83 percent) of the population, with Protestants constituting 9 percent, Muslims 5 percent, Buddhists and others 3 percent (*World factbook*, 1999).

Filipinos speak some 89 major languages and dialects. The leading languages are Tagalog (spoken as mother tongue by 28 percent of the population), Cebuano (24 percent), Ilocano (10 percent), and Hiligaynon (9 percent). English, used by 20 to 30 percent of the population, is one of the two official languages. It is also the main medium of instruction in schools. The Philippines is reported to be the third largest English-speaking country in the world, next to the United States and India. The literacy rate (in any of the regional languages or English) is 94.6 percent (*Media factbook*, 1997).

Filipinos, it has been whimsically said, lived 350 years in a Spanish convent, 50 years in Hollywood, and four years in a Japanese concentration camp before they gained independence. An oversimplification perhaps, but it summarizes the country's history from 1521, when the Portuguese explorer Ferdinand Magellan, sailing in the name of Spain, "discovered" the Philippines for Europe. Although King Lapulapu of Mactan, Cebu, killed Magellan in battle, subsequent Spanish expeditions conquered the islands for Spain's King Philip, whose name the country still bears. Miguel Lopez de Legaspi, another Spanish explorer, established Manila as the country's capital in 1571 and subdued most of the Filipino chieftains in Luzon, the biggest island. The Spanish colonization stopped the conquest of the Philippines by the Muslims who had reached as far as Manila from their bases in the south. Thus the Philippines became the only Christian nation in Asia.

The Spanish ruled the country for about 350 years until a US fleet under Admiral George Dewey, who had come at first to help the Filipino rebels under Gen. Emilio Aguinaldo, defeated the Spanish at the Battle of Manila Bay in 1898. Independence from the Spaniards, however, was short lived because of the American decision to colonize the country. After two years of fighting, the Americans conquered the Philippines, and stayed until 1946 except for the four-year (1941–45) interlude under Japanese occupation.

Philippines became independent in 1946. While the Spanish gave the Filipinos Christianity, the Americans developed the country's democratic institutions. President Ferdinand Marcos, who imposed martial law from 1972 to 1986, interrupted the country's democratic tradition. The EDSA Revolution, so named after the main avenue in Metro Manila where it happened, ousted Marcos from power (see Section 2.2.2).

1.3 Government and Politics

The Philippines gained independence from Spain on June 12, 1898, and from the United States on July 4, 1946 (*World factbook*, 1999). With the ratification of the 1987 Consti-tution, the Philippines returned to the presidential form of government (*Philippine yearbook*, 1995).

The executive branch of the government consists of the president and the vice president—both elected on the same ticket for six-year terms—and the cabinet members, who are department secretaries. The legislative branch is the bicameral Congress or *Kongreso*, consisting of the Senate or *Senado* (24 seats—one-half elected every three years; members elected by popular vote to serve six-year terms) and the House of Representatives or *Kapulungan Ng Mga Kinatawan* (204 members elected by popular vote to serve three-year terms; and an additional 50 members appointed by the president). The Supreme Court—comprising the chief justice and 14 associate justices—and the inferior courts make up the judicial branch (*World factbook*, 1999).

The country is divided into 16 political regions for administrative purposes. As of April 1998, there were 78 provinces, 85 cities, and 1,525 municipalities. The smallest political unit is the *barangay*, of which there are 41,925. The local govern-ment units consist of the *barangays* and the municipalities. The *barangay* is the basic unit of the Philippine political system. It is composed of no fewer than 1,000 inhabitants residing within the territorial limit of a municipality and is headed by the *barangay* chairman. Clusters of *barangays* make up a municipality, which is a political corporate body headed by a mayor and a vice mayor. Groups of muni-cipalities make up a province headed by a governor and a vice governor.

1.4 Economy

The Philippine economy is primarily a mixture of agriculture (22 percent) and light industry (32 percent). Expansion of exports and investment enabled the eco-nomy to experience its fifth year of positive growth in 1997. Because of the spillover effects of the financial crisis in East Asia, the growth in 1998 dropped to 0.5 per-cent. The estimated Gross Domestic Product (at purchasing power parity) in 1999 was US$ 247 billion (*Asiaweek*, December 17, 1999). The per capita GDP (PPP) was US$ 3,390, while the nominal per capita GNP was US$ 907. The country exported merchandise valued at US$ 33.2 billion in 1999 and its reserves stood at US$ 12.6 billion (*Asiaweek*, January 14, 2000).

The country's principal farm products are rice, coconut, banana, sugar, abaca, corn, tobacco, and pineapple. It is one of the world's largest producers of coconuts and a major exporter of coconut products. It is also the second largest producer of pineapple in the world, next only to Thailand. In 1996, the total export of fresh and processed pineapples increased by 12 percent, breaking the constant downward trend since 1992. Banana is the leading fruit grown in the country, which ranks fifth among the world's top banana exporters (UAP, 1997).

The Philippines has established industrial zones in rural areas. The biggest of these is the Calabarzon industrial zone just outside Metro Manila. The Calabarzon is home to many multinational companies, quite a few of which are producing electronic products and computer chips. By November 1998, exports of electronics and components accounted for close to 53 percent of total exports (Delfinado, 1999).

2. DEVELOPMENT OF PRESS AND BROADCASTING

Philippine newspapers, radio, and television are essentially products of the very society of which they are a part, with all its virtues and vices. They also mirror the manners and mores of their owners, as well as of their readers. To read, hear, and view them is to get an education into Philippine life and culture.

2.1 Brief Early History

The Philippine mass media have roots that go back to the country's colonial past. Thomas Pinpin, a Spanish friar, printed the first book *Doctrina Cristiana* in the Philippines in 1593 (Castro, 1963). Pinpin is also credited with printing the first Philippine newsletter, *Sucesos Felices* (Glad Tidings), the equivalent of the European broadsheets, in 1637 (Lent, 1971; Fernandez, 1989). Portuguese explorer Ferdinand Magellan, sailing in the name of the Spanish Queen Isabella, "discovered" the Philippines for Europe in 1521. He presumably brought the first European books to the country, including the Bible. His chaplain and historian, Father Pigafetta, kept a diary, which has become a source book on early Philippine history. The Spanish missionaries came to the Philippines in successive waves, bringing with them printing presses and other paraphernalia for converting the Filipinos to Christianity. Religious orders owned the first printing presses in the country.

The first "formal" newspaper, *Del Superior Gobierno*, came out in 1811 on the initiative of Governor-General Mariano Fernandez de Folgueras, but it folded after 15 issues over a six-month period. *Ramillete Patriotico* appeared in 1821 followed by a number of short-lived newspapers. The Spanish censorship laws affected newspaper publication in the Philippines as well. The first daily newspaper of the country, *La Esperanza* (established on December 1, 1846), lasted only three years. *Diario de Manila*, started in 1848, lasted until 1899 (Lent, 1971; Fernandez, 1989).

El Pasig, a bilingual fortnightly in Spanish and Tagalog, came out in 1862, signifying the advent of the native press. *Diariong Tagalog*, the first native daily, appeared 20 years later but it lasted only three to five months. "The first newspaper that was genuinely native" (Fernandez, 1989, p. 60) was *EL Ilocano* (1889–96).

Englishman Thomas Gowan established the first English-language daily, *Manila Times*, on October 11, 1898. It lasted for 32 years. Franklyn Brooks, a New York journalist, established the second English daily, *The American*, four days later. The oldest existing newspaper in the Philippines is the *Manila Bulletin* (Lent, 1971; Fernandez, 1989). Carson Taylor, an American, started it as a shipping journal in 1900. In 1912, it widened its scope to include news of general interest. Its reputation as the mouthpiece of the American community remained even after independence in 1946 for as long as Taylor was its editor, publisher, and owner (Maslog, 1990).

Pro-American newspapers dominated the press during the early American period. It was not until 1920 that Manuel L. Quezon, who later became president of the Philippines, established the first pro-Filipino nationalistic newspaper, the *Philippines Herald*. Carlos P. Romulo, who eventually became president of the UN General Assembly and achieved fame in Philippine diplomacy, was one of the early editors of the *Herald* (Maslog, 1990).

Thus the two colonizing countries, Spain and the United States, introduced newspapers and magazines in the Philippines. The United States was also responsible for introducing movies and radio. Coronel (1998) points out that the Philippine press has had "a strong *samizdat* tradition" during periods of repression when "clandestine, anti-establishment newspapers were circulated and assiduously read" (pp. 27–28). Maslog (1990, 1994) has classified the periods of repression as the Spanish Period (1521–1900), the American Period (1900–46) and the Martial Law Period (1972–86).

Radio came to the Philippines in 1922 during the American period, only two years after the establishment of the first American radio station in Pittsburgh. Henry Hermann, an American, set up three 50-watt radio stations in Manila and in the neighboring city of Pasay in June 1922. Two years later, the 100-watt KZKZ station replaced them (Lent, 1978). The Radio Corporation of the Philippines introduced radio to the provinces in 1929, when it set up station KZRC in Cebu City. Americans owned most of the pre-World War II stations, which employed mostly Americans as their announcing staff. The language used was English. The programming included entertainment and news. Radio became mainly an entertainment medium. The quick public acceptance of the medium and its profitability led local distributors, such as department stores, to set up their own stations as channels for advertising their products.

The 1931 Radio Control Law set up the Radio Control Board that lasted until the 1972 declaration of martial law. Before World War II broke out, the Philippines had six commercial radio stations: KZRM, KZRF, KZIB, KZEG, KZRH—all in Manila—and the short-lived KZRC in Cebu City (Maslog, 1994). The Japanese shut down all radio stations except KZRH (renamed PIAM), which they used as a mouthpiece during the Japanese occupation. Lent (1978) asserts that "liberation from Japan in 1945 heralded the real birth of broadcasting in the archipelago" (p. 177).

2.2 Developments since 1945

2.2.1 Post-World War II Period (1946–72)

A number of newspapers sprang up right after World War II. However, most were fly-by-night tabloids that had short lives. Among those that survived was the *Manila Chronicle*, which a group of pre-war newspapermen started in 1945. They sold it a few years later to businessman Don Eugenio Lopez, brother of the then vice president, Fernando Lopez.

Meanwhile, publishers revived pre-war newspapers like the *Manila Bulletin* and the *Philippines Herald*. Joaquin Roces, who had taken over the newspaper business from his father, established the new *Manila Times* in place of the *Tribune*. Up to the time of martial law, the *Manila Times*, led all the Philippine-language dailies in circulation. The *Manila Chronicle*, on the other hand, with an average daily circulation of 250,000 copies, was building up a name as a paper of quality.

Radio broadcasting in the archipelago expanded during this period, with 30 stations operating just five years after the war. The 1946 Commonwealth Act of the US Congress permitted the president a four-year right to grant temporary permits to operate radio stations. Another act passed in 1947 required the Philippines radio stations to change the first call letter from K to D with DZ standing for Luzon stations, DY for Visayas and Palawan stations, and DX for Mindanao and Sulu stations. By 1968, the Philippines had 213 radio stations, with 40 in greater Manila. By 1972, the number of stations stood at about 350, with 55 in Greater Manila. Luzon alone had at least 120 stations, while Visayas had 90 and Mindanao 85. Many of these stations survived only with the backing of political parties because advertising alone could not support so many of them (Lent, 1978).

Although television had its beginnings way back in the 1930s when the British, Russians, and Americans were experimenting with it, it was not until the 1950s that it finally arrived in the Philippines. Two Philippine universities were experimenting with television before it turned commercial. In February 1950, a professor and his students successfully demonstrated their home-made receiver at the University of Santo Tomas. Two years later, Feati University opened an experimental television station.

Commercial television came to the Philippines in 1953, when Alto Broadcasting System in Manila opened the very first station, DZAQ-TV Channel 3. AQ in the station's call letters stood for Antonio Quirino, the owner of the station and brother of the then Philippine president, Elpidio Quirino. The station started on a four-hours-a-day schedule (6 p.m.–10 p.m.) limited to a 50-mile radius. The prospects then were dim for the future of television in the country. High production costs, the paucity of TV sets and of advertisers were big hurdles. By 1957, the Chronicle Broadcasting Network, owned by the Lopez family, operated the only two TV stations in the country—DZAQ and DZXL-TV Channel 9 (Lent, 1978). The Republic Broadcasting System opened DZBB-TV Channel 7 in 1960 (De Jesus, 1998). Despite problems, television continued to grow in the Philippines in the late 1960s and the early 1970s causing another problem, overcrowding. By 1966, Philippines had 18 privately owned TV channels with a peak-hour audience of more than 1 million (Maslog, 1994). ABS–CBN had become the country's biggest network by the time Marcos declared martial law (Coronel, 1998).

2.2.2 Martial Law Period (1972–86)

When President Marcos proclaimed martial law (Proclamation 1081, signed September 21, 1972), he quickly brought the mass media to heel. At that time, the press had been sharply critical of the graft, corruption, and human rights abuses attributed to the Marcos government. The very first presidential decree (issued on September 24, 1972) under martial law reorganized the government bureaucracy and created a Department of Public Information, a first in Philippine history. The president's very first letter of instruction issued on September 22, 1972 directed the press secretary and the secretary of national defense to "take over and control all media of communications for the duration of the present national emergency."[1]

Except for the *Manila Bulletin*, Marcos permanently closed down all the leading pre-martial law metropolitan newspapers and magazines. The victims included circulation-leader *Manila Times*; its sister publication in the afternoon, *Daily Mirror*; the anti-Marcos *Manila Chronicle*; the ultra-nationalist *Philippines Free Press*; the *Graphic*; and the *Nation*. The *Manila Bulletin* was revived on November 22, 1972, under the new name, *Bulletin Today*.

On the same day that Marcos ordered all mass media closed, he also authorized the continued operation of the government radio and TV stations in Manila—the Voice of the Philippines (operated by the National Media Production Center) and the stations of the Philippine Broadcasting Service. Additionally, he authorized the operation of two privately-owned mass media enterprises—the four-month-old *Daily Express* (published by Juan Perez, but reportedly owned by Roberto S. Benedicto, a crony of Marcos) and the Kanlaon Broadcasting System (also owned by Benedicto), which later changed its name to Radio Philippines Network, because they had not "participated in the communist conspiracy" to overthrow the Philippine government. The Far East Broadcasting System, owned and operated by Protestant missionaries in the Philippines, was allowed to resume operation on September 25, 1972.

Benedicto became Marcos' closest partner in manipulating the mass media, and the biggest mass media oligarch in Philippine history. He took control of Radio Philippines Network, with six TV and 15 radio stations; Banahaw Broadcasting Corp., with two TV and seven radio stations; and Inter-island Broadcasting Corp., with eight TV and four radio stations. He was also a major stockholder in various telecommunications enterprises—Domestic Satellite Corp., Nivico

---

[1] The martial law presidential decrees and letters of instructions implementing them have been published in a series of volumes by the National Media Production Center, 1973. Lent, 1982, provides a detailed account of the Philippines media in the early phase of the martial law period.

Philippines Inc. (TV set manufacturer), Oceanic Winders Corp., and Eastern Tele-communications Philippines Inc.

Under martial law, the Marcos government brought to the stockade dozens of top journalists on charges of subversion. Among those sent to jail were Joaquin Roces, publisher of the *Manila Times*; Eugenio Lopez Jr, publisher of the *Manila Chronicle*; his editor, Amando Doronila; Teodoro M. Locsin Sr, editor of the *Philippines Free Press*; Luis Mauricio, editor of *Graphic*; Max Soliven, top columnist of the *Manila Times*; Ernesto Granada, columnist of the *Manila Chronicle*; Napoleon Rama, staff writer of *Philippines Free Press*; and Juan L. Mercado, joint chief executive of Press Foundation of Asia. They were eventually released, except for Eugenio Lopez Jr, who made a dramatic escape from the military stockade and slipped out to the United States.

At the beginning of martial law in 1972, those who disagreed with the government were either in the stockades, in the hills, or six feet underground. Toward the end of the decade, a few brave souls began to test the waters when the government averred that things were back to normal. They cautiously began to criticize. The earliest of these brave souls was Jose Burgos Jr, who founded the *We Forum* on May 1, 1977, as a weekly for the youth (Maslog, 1990). It began publishing news that could not be found in the muzzled crony press—the newspapers owned by the Marcos business partners.

At about this time, the *Philippine Collegian*, the student organ of the University of the Philippines, had also been pursuing a critical brand of journalism that the professional media were unwilling to adopt. The *We Forum* and the *Philippine Collegian* were the forerunners of what was to be called the alternative press in the Philippines in the early 1980s. They provided an alternative source of information to the crony press, which printed only pro-government stories.

More than anything else, it was the assassination of former Senator Benigno Aquino, upon his return from three years of exile in the United States on August 21, 1983, that released the floodgates of press freedom in the Philippines. Among other things, it was Xerox journalism and cassette journalism that made it impossible for the authoritarian regime of Marcos to suppress information on this tragic event of national importance. The *Philippine Daily Inquirer*, founded on December 9, 1985, became the leading newspaper after the EDSA Revolution[2] in 1986 toppled the Marcos dictatorship (Flor, 1998).

3. THE PRESS

3.1 Policy and Legal Framework

The Philippines has no licensing requirement to publish a newspaper. The only requirement is a permit to operate a business. Press freedom is enshrined in the

---

[2] EDSA is the name of the main avenue in Metro Manila where the uprising happened.

1987 Philippine Constitution, which includes a Bill of Rights guaranteeing that "no law shall be passed abridging the freedom of speech, of expression, or of the people peaceably to assemble and petition the government for redress of grievances" (Teodoro & Kabatay 1998, p. 97; Coronel & Stuart, 1996, p. 56). This is similar to the First Amendment to the US Constitution. In addition, Article III Section 7 of the constitution recognizes "the right of the people to information on matters of public concern" (Teodoro & Kabatay, 1998, p. 107).

This guarantee has enabled the Philippines to have one of the "freest press [systems]" in Asia, if not in the world (Doronila, 1998a, p. 138). Its freedom is bound by few limitations, save for the laws of libel, national security, privacy, and obscenity. Most often these laws are interpreted liberally by the Philippine courts. Very few journalists have been convicted of libel and few movies are banned on grounds of obscenity. Investigative journalism is alive and well.[3] Freedom House (Sussman, 1999) has placed Philippines in the "free" press category with a restrictive score of 30 out of 100. On the criterion of laws and regulations that influence media content, Philippines' print and broadcast media each scored 5 out of 15. On the criterion of political pressures and controls on media content, the score was 7 out of 15 for broadcast and 3 out of 15 for print. On the criterion of economic influences on media content, the score was 3 out of 15 for broadcast and 5 out of 15 for print. The final criterion of repressive actions yielded a score of 2 out 5 for broadcast and zero for print.

Only Filipinos can own or publish newspapers. The Philippine Constitution states that "the ownership and management of mass media shall be limited to citizens of the Philippines, or to corporations, cooperatives or associations wholly owned and managed by such citizens." (Article XVI, Section 10). Philippine laws also frown on monopolies. The Philippine Constitution says, "Congress shall regulate or prohibit monopolies in commercial mass media when the public interest so requires. No combinations in restraint of trade or unfair competition shall be allowed" (Article XVI, Section 11). In practice, however, this provision of the new constitution, ratified only in 1987 after the lifting of martial law, has not yet been implemented. One problem encountered is the definition of press monopoly.

The Philippines has three press monitoring bodies set up on the initiative of publishers, editors, and independent journalists: the press council of the Philippine Press Institute, the ethics committee of the National Press Club, and the Center for Media Freedom and Responsibility. These three "have no legal or statutory basis but exist on the strength of a fragile consensus within the journalistic community that certain abuses need to be corrected if the press is to command any credibility" (Coronel & Stuart, 1996, p. 57).

---

[3] President Joseph Estrada sought US$ 2.6 million in damages from the *Manila Times* for defaming him in an investigative story (published February 17. 1999), which accused Estrada of being an "unwitting godfather" of a "rigged contract" for a hydroelectric-power deal. Estrada withdrew his case when the publisher carried an apology. Some believe this reflects the case of "a press that routinely abuses its freedom by publishing unsubstantiated allegations" (Tiglao, 1999, p. 25).

3.2 Financial Aspects: Circulation, Advertising, Marketing Strategies

The *Philippine media factbook* (1998) states that in 1997 the Philippines published 50 national dailies with a circulation of 7 million (Table 2), 418 community newspapers with a local circulation of 755,873 (Table 5), and 51 magazines with a national circulation of 4.6 million (Table 6). One national daily, *Manila Times*, folded on July 23, 1999, but reopened in November under a new management and with a new staff. Ten on-line dailies are operating as well. UNESCO (1999) estimated the daily newspaper circulation in the Philippines at 5.7 million in 1996—a penetration of 8.2 copies per 100 people (Table 1). The Print Media Audit Council, which first audited newspaper circulation in 1989, has conducted only 15 audits over a span of five years. No audits have been conducted in the last few years.

The country's top 10 dailies in 1998, according to PMAC data cited in WAN (1999) were *People's Journal* (circulation 382,000; readership, 441,000), *People's Tonight* (circulation 366,000; readership 825,000), *Manila Chronicle* (circulation 300,000), *Manila Bulletin* (circulation 280,000; readership 694,000), *Philippine Star* (circulation 271,000; readership 365,000), *Philippine Daily Inquirer* (circulation 248,000; readership 483,000), *Manila Standard* (circulation 210,000), *Manila Times* (circulation 209,000; readership 420,000), *Malaya* (circulation 178,000; readership 407,000), and *Today* (circulation 152,000). Thus the three leading Metro Manila broadsheets in circulation are *Manila Chronicle*, *Manila Bulletin*, and *Philippine Star*. The *Chronicle* has made a big leap from its 1997 circulation of only 80,000 with a readership of 200,000 (WAN, 1998). The *Star*, one should note, is not audited. Of the broadsheets published in Metro Manila, only four—the *Bulletin*, the *Inquirer*, *Business World*, and the *Chronicle*—are audited, according to the *Philippine Journalism Review* (Maslog, 1989). Other circulation breakdowns appear in Table 1 through Table 6. (Note the discrepancies between WAN data for 1997 and *Philippine media factbook* data for 1997 in Table 1.)

The 50 Metro Manila newspapers, however, claim a total circulation of 7 million. Roughly two-thirds of this circulation (by various estimates) is in Metro Manila—4.6 million for the 8 million Metro Manila residents. This is a ratio of 1.7 people for every daily newspaper copy, a high ratio compared to similar figures even in developed countries. In the provinces, however, the data are different. If we distribute one-third of this daily circulation (2.3 million) to 60 million Filipinos in the countryside, this will come out to 26 people per daily newspaper copy. The national (urban and rural) ratio of population to daily circulation is 10.7 people per copy on the basis of claimed, not audited, circulation.

The Philippine Information Agency states that the Philippines had 418 community publications in 1997, including 28 dailies with a circulation of 187,300, and 293 weeklies with a circulation of 438,623 (Table 5). Although the circulation of the community newspapers is small, they have a high pass-on readership of about five people per copy, and radio newscasters often read out of the newspaper pages, thereby considerably extending the reach of the newspapers.

Metro Manila also has 51 magazines, including 14 of general interest, 10 women's magazines, and 15 entertainment (or showbiz) magazines. The total circulation of these magazines in 1997 was 4.6 million (Table 6).

Comics comprise the main print medium with a wide readership in the rural areas, and therefore offer greater potential as a true mass medium in the Philippines, which today has 293 comic publications—14 dailies, 221 weeklies, eight semi-weeklies, 27 monthlies, 14 quarterlies, and nine others. They have a total circulation of 733,298 and a high pass-on readership of five per copy. This means that comics command a weekly readership of at least 3.7 million (Table 6).

Advertising expenditure in the Philippines has undergone rapid growth from 4.5 million pesos in 1990 to 20.4 million pesos in 1997—a compound annual growth rate of 24.1 percent. However, only 30 percent of advertising expenditure went into the print media, compared to 53 percent for television (WAN, 1999). The top 10 advertising sectors were communications, banks and financial institutions, vehicles, household appliances, property, department stores and supermarkets, entertainment, airlines and travel agencies, business machines/office equipment, and tobacco (WAN, 1999).

The price of the major dailies ranged from 24 US cents (7 pesos) for most, to 34 US cents (10 pesos) for the *Manila Bulletin*.

3.3 Structure and Organization

The Philippine press is privately owned and is independent of government control. It is multilingual, but the English-language press exercises leadership. Being Manila-centered, it is underdeveloped in the provinces. It is politically free, yet controlled by big business. Commenting on its sensationalism and on its lack of ethics and professionalism, Tuazon (1998) points out: "Mass media ownership remains in the control of a few vested interest groups, which exert considerable influence in the nations political and economic affairs" (p. 241). Vanden Heuvel and Dennis (1993) confirmed that although large business groups have been making inroads, "media ownership is concentrated in the hands of powerful Filipino families" (p. 105). The Roces, Soriano, and Lopez families were among those who owned the media.

Coronel (1998) asserts that an enduring American legacy in the Philippines, which was a US colony from 1898 to 1946, is "a free press run as a private enterprise" (p. 25). The press today is mostly privately owned because the Philippines is a democratic, capitalist country committed to free enterprise. Only four newspapers, sequestered with the downfall of the Marcos dictatorship in 1986, are government-controlled: the *Philippine Journal, People's Journal, People's Tonight*, and *Taliba*, all of which were owned formerly by Benjamin Romualdez, brother of the former First Lady Imelda Romualdez Marcos. Other newspapers are run as business enterprises, depending mostly on advertising and circulation for support.

A large number of them, however, are not making money. Their owners prop up these newspapers with profits from their other business enterprises.

3.4 Quality and Popular Press

Vanden Heuvel and Dennis (1993) assert: "The Philippines has achieved a media environment with a diversity of viewpoints, an idealism about the power of the media to improve society and an environment where media freedom is seen as a right.... Improving the quality of the media's offerings seems to be the course that Filipinos will pursue" (p. 97).

The Philippine press might be described as two-faced. One face is that of the Metro Manila press—coming out daily, highly developed, widely circulated with advertising support, well written, better edited, and using sophisticated technology. The other face is that of the community press in the provinces—mostly weekly, less endowed with financial resources, poorly edited with limited circulation, lacking advertising support, and using old-fashioned printing technology.

The number of newspapers in Metro Manila has proliferated from 12 dailies in 1986, when the Marcos dictatorship ended, to 50 in 1998. Of these, 24 are broadsheets and 26 are tabloids. The broadsheets in the Philippines are mostly the quality newspapers, read by the elite and the middle class. The tabloids are mostly the popular newspapers, read by the lower class, the masses (Table 2). Of the Metro Manila broadsheets, 19 are in English and five in Chinese. This is understandable because the quality press is read by the upper and middle class, who are financially well off and English-educated. On the other hand, most of the 26 tabloids are published in Filipino, the national language, while eight are in English. This, again, is understandable because the tabloids are read by the masses, whose education in English is limited.

About 85 percent of the community newspaper are published either simply in English or in English combined with a regional language. The reason for the use of English is that newspaper readers, even in the provinces, are the English-educated elite or the middle class, which can afford to buy newspapers. A typical community newspaper today is an eight-page weekly tabloid with a circulation of about 2,500, printed in English combined with Tagalog, Ilocano, Cebuano Visayan, or Hiligaynon. It is a small business enterprise, with a full-time staff of four operating in a city of about 181,000 people. Its annual volume of business is a little more than half a million pesos, with a net profit of 140,000 pesos. It usually has three or four competing newspapers in the town, and therefore hardly makes ends meet. At best it is making a small profit, most of the time it is breaking even, and at worst it is losing money (Maslog, 1993).

The majority (29 titles) of Metro Manila magazines is published in English, with 18 published in Filipino, and four in regional languages. Thirty six are weeklies and 13 are monthlies. The magazines are also the medium of the elite and the middle class.

Although comics command a high readership among the masses, their content comprises mostly fiction with trite love triangles, fantasy stories, sex and violence features, superstition, romance, and true confessions. Thus, they carry very little useful information and hardly any values that would enhance individual and social development.

3.5 Distribution and Technology

Maslog (1994) has documented that the distribution of tabloids is based mostly on street sales, as compared to broadsheets, which "vary in their pattern of distribution" (p. 51). For instance, while the top-end *Philippine Daily Inquirer* sells all its copies in the streets, two other top-end newspapers—the *Manila Times* and *Philippine Times Journal*—sell 97 and 92 percent of their copies respectively in the streets. The *Philippine Star*, on the other hand, sells 60 percent of the copies to subscribers, while the *Manila Chronicle* sells 55 percent to subscribers.

In a survey of nine broadsheets conducted as early as 1993, all nine papers said they were already using computers in their operations—seven in newswriting, eight in editing, nine in typesetting, and nine in accounting. All were using offset press printing (Maslog, 1993). Today, most of the broadsheets are using full-color printing for their front pages. The tabloids content themselves with color (mostly red) headlines. In addition, eight of the Metro Manila broadsheets and two provincial dailies have gone on-line.

4. BROADCASTING

4.1 Policy and Legal Framework

The broadcast media in the Philippines come under a greater degree of regulation than the press. Three main regulatory bodies are involved: the National Telecommunication Commission (NTC), the Kapisanan ng mga Brodkaster sa Pilipinas (KBP), and the Movie and Television Review and Classification Board (Coronel & Stuart, 1996).

Like the print media, broadcasting in the Philippines is mostly privately owned and free from government controls. This makes Philippine broadcasting unique in Asia, where radio and television are dominantly in the hands of government. The government owns one radio–TV network, PTV Channel 4, and still controls two privately-owned networks—Channel 9 and Channel 13—which it had sequestered after the overthrow of the Marcos dictatorship in 1986. Four other channels are privately owned—Channel 2, by ABS–CBN; Channel 5, by ABC Network; Channel 7, by GMA Network; and Channel 11, by a religious group, Jesus is Lord Church.

Unlike the print media, however, Philippine radio and TV stations need licenses from the NTC to operate. The NTC also assigns frequencies and promulgates and enforces guidelines for station operations. In addition, these radio and TV stations belong to the KBP (Association of Broadcasters in the Philippines), a self-regulating agency of the broadcasting industry. The responsibilities of the MTRCB include the review and classification of films and TV programs.

In the exercise of its power to issue licenses, NTC indirectly controls the quality of performance and standards of radio and TV stations. According to the law, the functions of NTC are:

- To establish and prescribe rules, regulations, standards, and specifications in all cases related to the issuance of the Certificate of Public Convenience, and to administer and enforce the same; and
- to promulgate such rules and regulations as public safety and interest may require, to encourage a more effective use of communications, radio and television facilities.

In practice, however, the KBP, regulates programming through its own codes of ethics (Maslog, 1992).

All the constitutional provisions and laws that govern the print media also apply to the broadcast media. In practice, however, the broadcast media are not as free and outspoken as the print media in criticizing government. They are more entertainment oriented and are more vulnerable to pressures from the government because of the licensing requirement.

4.2 Structure and Organization

Like the print media, the broadcast media have proliferated in recent years—from 338 radio stations in 1988 to 517 in 1998. Of the mass media, radio has the greatest reach in the Philippines, both in the urban and rural areas. It is well on its way to becoming the country's true mass medium, if it is not already one. The number of TV stations has also increased—from 75 in 1988 to 116 in 1998.

Radio set ownership by households in the Philippines is relatively high—88 percent (of households) in the National Capital Region (or Metro Manila) and 81 percent in the provinces. In 1988, only 77 percent of the Metro Manila households owned radio sets (Table 12).

Television set ownership, on the other hand, is lower compared to radio, except for the Metro Manila area, where 87 percent of the households own a TV set, compared to 78 percent in 1988. The average TV set ownership (by households) in the provinces is still a low 34 percent.

Another way to measure the reach of radio and television is to survey exposure of households to these mass media. In Metro Manila, the percentage of exposure to radio and television is even higher than the percentage of set ownership. This indicates that those who do not own radio or TV sets listen or watch outside their homes, probably in the homes of neighbors. According to the Philippine Information Agency, 83 percent of the Metro Manila households regularly tune in (are exposed) to radio while 91 percent regularly watch (are exposed to) television (Table 13).

Cable television is in the process of coming into its own after a decade of stunted growth. Under the martial law regime (1972–86), cable television was limited to four operators—the Nuevue Cable View in Baguio City, Sining Makulay in Manila, and two other CATV networks in Olongapo and Lucena cities in the provinces (Nazareno, 1997). With the fall of Marcos, cable television was thrown wide open to anyone with capital and entrepreneurship, and it soon swamped the airwaves.

The Lopez family's ABS–CBN, the leading local TV network, started SkyCable in 1992. Vision and aggressive marketing enabled SkyCable to capture 60 percent of the 500,000 or so cable subscriptions. This number is expected to double in the next four or five years, with SkyCable in the lead (Coronel, 1998). The country has about 300 registered cable television operators with hundreds more awaiting approval for their applications. Most are members of the Cable Television Association of the Philippines (CTAP). Commercial-free, 24-hour TV viewing made cable television popular, especially among urban middle classes with their Western tastes, fluency in English, and higher income. They can afford the average monthly subscription fee of US$ 15. Cable TV operators began to realize that the TV market was "segmenting on its own: The English-speaking middle- and upper-classes were opting for cable, while the Tagalog-speaking, lower-income groups now formed the main audience for the local networks" (Coronel, 1998, p. 26).

4.3 Program Policies

Coronel (1998) points out that when the ABS–CBN returned to the scene in 1986, following its shutdown under martial law, the network "made it to the top only in six months" and garnered an audience share of 62 percent by 1993 "through a combination of sensational news reporting, savvy marketing and sheer attitude" (p. 26). It made news and current affairs "an amalgam of gore, celebrity and scandal designed to titillate and entertain rather than educate or inform," a formula that the other networks followed soon. Thus local network programming has taken a tabloid orientation, with entertainment programs being "limited to soap operas, game shows and inane comedies" (p. 26). This situation persists despite the existence of a television code and self-regulation by the Kapisanan ng mga Broadcaster sa Pilipinas (KBP) (Association of Philippine Broadcasters).

The KBP's television code that governs TV broadcasting in the Philippines states: "Public affairs program shall be geared towards building an enlightened citizenry through the discussion and clarification of issues of national and international significance" (Teodoro & Kabatay, 1998, p. 415). The television code has guidelines for newscasts, public affairs programs, and commentaries. It stresses community responsibility, support for nationalism and development, and responsibility toward children. It prohibits sex, obscenity, and violence. It has regulations for contests, public participation programs and promotions, fund raising, showing of movies and movie trailers, and superstition and the occult. It has standards for general programs and for advertising. The radio code also covers similar ground (Maslog, 1992).

4.4 Ownership and Financing

Of the 517 radio stations, 90 percent (or 466) are privately-owned commercial stations—238 AM and 228 FM (Tables 7–9). The balance comprises 33 government stations, 11 stations owned by religious organizations, five educational stations, and two stations owned by the military. Of the 116 TV stations, 111 are privately-owned commercial stations and 15 are government stations. Of the privately-owned stations, 13 are under government sequestration because they were owned by business associates of Marcos.

Thirty-two broadcast companies own these radio and TV stations. The companies range in size from the single station to the largest networks with 34 radio stations, the Radio Mindanao Network; or with 30 TV stations, the GMA Network. Big businessmen own both networks. The 10 largest radio networks own 224 of the 517 radio stations (or 43 percent of all stations) and the two largest TV networks own 38 of the 116 television stations (or 32 percent of the total number of stations). These are fairly large concentrations of ownership in the Philippine broadcast industry (Table 9).

While cable TV depends on subscriptions as its financing mechanism, the overwhelmingly privately-owned TV networks depend on advertising. The TV networks have been getting the biggest slice of advertising revenue—60 percent in 1993 and 53 percent in 1998. The advertising share of radio was 14 percent in 1993 and 15 percent in 1998 (WAN, 1999).

5. NEW ELECTRONIC MEDIA

5.1 Internet and On-line Media

The Philippine Network Foundation Inc., a consortium of institutions from both the public and the private sectors, established the Philnet (later PHnet), the country's first Internet gateway, on March 29, 1994. It did so via a leased line from the Philippine Long Distance Telephone Co., linked to SprintLink (Gardner, 1995). Universities have eight of PHnet's main nodes. Before the enactment of the 1995 Telecommunications Act, ISPs had to obtain a franchise from the Congress and a certificate of public convenience and necessity. The 1995 Act de-regulated telecommunication value-added services, including the Internet (APT, 1998).

The first company to offer direct Internet access on a commercial basis was Mosaic Communications Inc. (Moscom). Internet connectivity was offered in May 1995 by IBM Philippines, while Globe Telecom GMCR Inc. offered Internet access a month later. Philcom started its Webquest Internet Service in 1996 while Capitol Wires Inc. (CAPWIRE) set up its own ISP named Wavenet to offer Internet business in April 1996 (APT, 1998). The country now has 139 full-service Internet service providers, six e-mail service providers, and 25 cybercafes. The ISPs have organized themselves as the Philippine Internet Service Organization. About 75 percent of Internet users have access to the World Wide Web, and this figure is expected to be 95 percent by the year 2002 (Paño, 1998). An estimated 6 percent of Internet users have bought products through the Web, and this number is expected to grow to 30 percent by the year 2002.

The International Telecommunication Union (1999) has estimated that the Philippines had 970,000 personal computers in 1997—a computer density of 1.3 per 100 people. Adjusted data based on Network Wizards' surveys showed that Philippines had an estimated 12,573 Internet host computers in January 1998 and 22,027 in January 1999—a 75 percent increase in one year. This figure jumped to 41,970 in July 1999. The compound annual growth rate during 1994–98 was 126.2 percent. The country has an estimated 200,000 Internet users today and their number is growing about 40 percent annually, according to a computer company consultant (Paño, 1998).

About a dozen Philippine newspapers have gone on-line as well. They include *Bohol Times, Business World, Chinese Commercial News of Manila, The Filipino Express, The Journal, Manila Bulletin, The Manila Times, Philippine Daily Inquirer, The Philippine Reporter, Tempo*, and *Today*. Two Cebu City newspapers, *The Freeman* and *Sun Star Daily*, also have Internet editions. The ABS–CBN network is also accessible on-line.

5.2 Telecommunications Infrastructure

From 1990 to 1997, the number of main telephone lines in the Philippines increased at a compound annual growth rate of more than 19 percent, from 610,000 to 2.08 million, thereby achieving a teledensity of 3.07 per 100 people by 1998 (ITU, 1999). The country also had close to 1.5 million cellular subscribers—a density of 2.19 percent (ITU, 1999). In Metro Manila, the telephone density rose from 9.28 lines in 1995 to 20.83 in 1996 (APT, 1998). In 1992, only 20 percent (309 out of 1,601 municipalities) had telephone service. By 1997, this went up to 37 percent (or 596 municipalities).

Until 10 years ago, the Philippines was lagging behind the other developing countries of Asia in telecommunications. Chua (1998) observed, "There were more names on the waiting list than there were in the telephone book" (p. 5). The reason for this was the PLDT's monopoly during the Marcos regime. President Ramos "broke down the PLDT monopoly in 1993 by decentralizing and liberalizing the telecommunication market" (Alumit, 1998, p. 15). Teledensity in the Philippines grew from 0.85 per 100 people in 1983 to 1.03 in 1992; and from 1.55 in 1994 to 2.06 in 1995. APT (1999) estimated the number of current main telephone lines at 5.7 million, that is, a density of 8.06 percent.

With the opening up of the industry, the number of companies operating international gateway facilities went up from one to nine; the number of cellular companies increased from two to five; paging companies grew from six to 15; and in the local telephone exchange segment, the number of companies increased from one to 11. The PLDT, however, still dominates the industry. In the local exchange market, it owned 45 percent of the total landlines in 1997 and cornered 80 percent of the subscribers. At present, foreign ownership of telecommunications companies in the country is limited to 40 percent.

In data communications, the country completed its first private frame relay network installation in late 1997. It inaugurated the Brunei–Malaysia–Philippines submarine fiber-optic system, in addition to the Guam–Philippines–Taiwan cable system opened in 1990. Moreover, satellite transmission facilities will expand with the addition of 500 channel units from the Demand Assigned Multiple Access (DAMA) system under a contract with Scientific-Atlanta. Meanwhile, Mabuhay Philippines Satellite Corp. (MPSC) operated two communication satellites, Agila 1 and 2, with a third satellite planned for 1999. The Philippine Agila Satellite Corp. (PASI) too was scheduled to launch two new satellites (APT, 1998).

6. POLICY TRENDS FOR PRESS AND BROADCASTING

The Philippine press and broadcasting are products of a democratic, free enterprise society. They, like the country (which was a colony of Spain for 377 years and of the United States for 46 years), reflect an enormous degree of Western influence. The press and broadcast media are privately-owned commercial ventures supported by advertising. They have the virtues and the vices of a free-enterprise society. As they need advertising, they have to cater to the tastes of the masses; and because they are free, they tend to skirt limits often bordering on license.

The Philippines, however, is also a developing country. Thus the government information apparatus, as well as the academe, has promoted the philosophy of development communication to harness communication, the mass media, and information for national development. Although the mass media and the government have an adversarial relationship in a free society, the media should also be concerned with the economic, political, social, and cultural development of a developing nation. The Philippines is perhaps the only country whose constitution "recognizes the vital role of communication and information in nation-building" (Article II, Section 24). Another section of the constitution—Article XVI, Section 10—says: "The State shall provide the policy environment for the full development of Filipino capability and the emergence of communication structures suitable to the needs and aspirations of the nation and the balanced flow of information into, out of, and across the country, in accordance with a policy that respects the freedom of speech and of the press." These new constitutional provisions were absent in the earlier 1935 and 1973 Philippine Constitutions.

The Philippine press today has the distinction (or notoriety) of being one of the freest in the world. It is a two-faced press—developed in Metropolitan Manila but underdeveloped in the provinces. The print media are aggressive critics of government, but the broadcast media are largely timid and uncritical, content to remain purely as an entertainment medium.

The country has a small group of sober, quality English-language broadsheets, but a majority are rip-roaring tabloids published in Filipino—rambunctious, sensational, freewheeling, and proliferating, and often reckless and irresponsible. It is a free, exciting press that lacks a sense of history and urgently needs to mature and become not only responsible, but also relevant and responsive to the needs of its society.

7. MAIN ISSUES

- Redressing the imbalance in the flow of information between rural and urban areas

Right now, information flows largely from the cities to the countryside. The mass media are too Manila-centered and report little of developments in the "outback," where the majority of Filipinos live.

- Establishing community newspapers in the countryside

Such newspapers cannot flourish without sufficient advertising. Advertisers, however, will not place their advertisements in these weeklies because they do not have a high circulation, which itself results from an inadequate income. The advertising industry faces the challenge of breaking this vicious cycle by placing goodwill advertising to help community newspapers survive.

- The rise of oligopolies in the print and broadcast industry

Oligopolistic ownership of the mass media (that is, where a few businessmen or politicians control the mass media), is dangerous for democracy. Although the constitution prohibits monopolies, the Congress has so far not enacted laws defining monopoly to implement this constitutional provision.

- Mass media ownership by the elite, whose interests and values are different from those of the masses

This is especially true for the print media, the majority of which is published in English. The elite also owns the radio and television stations. However, they are becoming more attuned to the needs and interest of the masses as they do more programming in Filipino or the regional languages.

- Access to the mass media

In a full-fledged democracy, the masses should have access to the mass media anytime. This, however, is not true in the Philippines, where the elite and the upper class monopolize access to the newspaper pages and to radio and television programs.

- The impact of proliferating sex and violence in the mass media on the children and the young

Sex and violence are dominating tabloids, movies, radio, television. The government and the industry have done very little to police this adverse development.

- Ethics and professionalism among practitioners

The Philippine Press Council (for the print media) and the *Kapisanan ng mga Brodkasters* (for the broadcast media) have done some policing. However, unethical practices among media practitioners have not abated. An example is the standard practice of movie page editors doubling as press agents of movie stars. Hofileña (1999) says that media corruption in the post-Marcos era has become more costly, and more pervasive and systemic. She adds that corrupt transactions have become much more sophisticated and have even been institutionalized through a network of journalists reporting to other journalists or to professional public relations people—a mafia of corrupt practitioners.

Hofileña asserts that during the 1998 presidential election campaign reporters received monthly bribes ranging from Peso 5,000 (US$ 128) to Peso 10,000 (US$ 256), and editors received Peso 10,000 to Peso 15,000 (US$ 384) from one candidate's payroll.

- Competition leading to deterioration of television programming

The need to get high ratings has forced TV stations to lower their news and entertainment program standards to cater to the tastes of the lowest common denominator.

> What took place in the Philippines in the last decade mirrors what has taken place in many other countries as the market for television programs is opened up to increased competition, both locally and globally. As the rivalry intensifies, networks do battle by aiming for the lowest common denominator of public taste. As the public becomes bombarded with increasingly "sexy" programming, the networks respond by providing even more titillation: more and more pieces of clothing are taken off, gorier and gorier crimes are shown; the exposes on the private lives of celebrities become ever more risqué. (Coronel, 1998, pp. 26–27)

- Politicians holding office getting actively involved in the mass media

In a country, which has elected a former movie star as president, politicians are taking advantage of other politicians, as well as of media practitioners, by getting actively involved in the media industry. The concentration of political as well as press power is unacceptable in a democracy. Examples include a senator (Vicento Sotto) who runs the weekly prime time TV program "Brigada Siete"; a cabinet secretary (Orlando Mercado) who runs a daily radio program on DZRH and a weekly TV program ("Kontak 5") with his wife; a cabinet undersecretary, who also has her own radio program; a senator (Renato Cayetano) who conducts the TV program "Compañero y Compañera"; a senator (Blas Ople) who has a newspaper column in *Manila Bulletin*; and another senator (Loren Legarda) who runs a monthly TV show "Loren" over ABS–CBN. Moreover, Vice President Gloria Macapagal-Arroyo has her own TV program "Dighay Bayan" and President Joseph Estrada himself is the star of the weekly radio-TV program "JEEP ni Erap." A mayor in Metro Manila (Joey Marquez) conducts a weekly sitcom "Cool Ka Lang" while a governor (Bong Revilla) is involved in making movies regularly. Another famous movie star (Vilma Santos) is a town mayor. Several former politicians who lost the last elections are also in mass media. Former Manila Mayor Alfredo Lim conducts the weekly TV program "Katapat," and former Sen. Ernesto Maceda writes a column for the *Philippine Star*.

A top columnist for the *Philippine Daily Inquirer* says:

> These officials are promoting self-serving points of view. There is uneasiness in the privately dominated media over whether this invasion of the press by officials is a healthy development for an informed public opinion and even for democracy. The tradition of the Philippine press frowns upon giving permanent platforms for politicians and officials to articulate their views (or agenda in the guise of public service). But this tradition has been breached as officials gain foothold inside the media, performing ambivalent roles as politicians and media persons.
>
> My concern is less about press freedom and more about why officials should squander their time being media practitioners when they have been elected to govern the country well. Equally problematic is the issue of classifying officials engaged in the media. It is hard to call them journalists since it is implicit in press freedom that journalists are independent of the government and are in fact performing an adversarial role as compared to officials—a role that requires journalists to disclose precisely what officials conceal. In effect, officials dabbling in media are nothing short of hacks—with a point of view, if not an agenda, to promote—using the private media as their platform.
>
> A fundamental contradiction therefore arises when officials enter the domain of independent media. Officials are elected to govern, not to double as commentators. When officials perform functions to which they are not elected—such as being media commentators—they are going beyond their mandate. They have to make up their minds whether they remain as officials or whether they enter professional journalism where ethics and social responsibility require journalists to observe certain norms of independence and to look after larger public interests. (Doronila, 1998b)

8. STATISTICS

General Profile

Exchange rate (1999 average)	US$ 1 = 39.20 Pesos*
Population (mid-1999)	79.3 million
Population density	266.1 per sq km
GDP (PPP)	US$ 247 billion
Per capita GDP (PPP)	US$ 3,350
Per capita GNP (nominal)	US$ 907

Source: *Asiaweek*, December 17, 1999; * OANDA Historical Currency Table [On-line]. Available: (http://www.oanda.com/converter/cc_table?lang=en).

Table 1
Estimated Mass Media Penetration

	Radio receivers		TV receivers		Daily newspapers		
	Number ('000)	Per 100 people	Number ('000)	Per 100 people	Number	Circ'n ('000)	Per 100 people
1980	6,000	12.4	1,050	2.2	22	2,000	4.1
1985	7,300	13.4	1,500	2.7	15	2,170	4.0
1990	8,600	14.2	2,700	4.4	47	3,400	5.6
1995	10,000	14.6	3,300	4.8	42	4,200	6.2
1996	11,000	15.7	3,500	5.0	47	5,700	8.2
1997	11,500	16.1	3,700	5.2	42*	4,712*	6.7*
			7,800*	10.8*	50**	7,011**	9.8**

Source: UNESCO, 1999; * ITU, 1999; • WAN, 1999; ** *Philippine media factbook*, 1998.

Table 2
Metro Manila Newspapers

BROADSHEETS

By Frequency	Number	Circulation
Daily	24	2,304,272
Weekly	0	0
Sub-total	**24**	**2,304,272**

By language	Number	Circulation
English	19	2,011,272
Chinese	5	293,000
Sub-total	**24**	**2,304,272**

TABLOIDS

By Frequency	Number	Circulation
Daily	26	4,706,784
Sub-total	**26**	**4,706,784**

By Language	Number	Circulation
Filipino	18	3,449,303
English	8	1,486,481
Sub-total	**26**	**4,706,784**
Total	**50**	**7,011,056**

Source: *Philippine media factbook*, 1998.

Table 3
Metro Manila Broadsheets: Dates of Founding and Circulation

Broadsheets	Date founded	Circulation
Malaya	January 17, 1983	80,000
Manila Bulletin	February 1900	240,000
Manila Times	October 11, 1945	200,000
Philippine Daily Inquirer	1985	240,000
Philippine Journal	October 21, 1942	131,000
Philippine Star	July 28,1986	268,000
Manila Standard	1987	184,650
Today	January 10, 1994	152,268
The Evening Paper	–	50,000
Business World	July 27, 1987	54,936
Business Daily	October 31, 1994	78,218
The Businessman	–	10,000
Manila Chronicle	1946, revived 1986	80,000
Money Asia	–	52,000
Chinese Com. News	–	50,000
China Times	–	12,000
United Daily News	–	85,000
Diario Uno	–	50,200
Kabayan	–	20,000
Universal Daily	July 2, 1986	58,000
World News	June 1, 1981	88,000
Sun Star Daily	–	130,000
The Philippine Post	–	–
The Journal	–	–
Total		**2,314,272**

Source: *Philippine media factbook*, 1998.

Table 4
Metro Manila Tabloids: Dates of Founding and Circulation

Tabloids	Date founded	Circulation
People's Journal	1978	382,000
People's Tonight	–	365,811
Taliba	–	226,635
Balita	December 1, 1971	150,000
Tempo	July 12, 1982	200,000
Bagong Pinoy	–	235,000
Abante	May 1, 1988	417,600
Abante Tonight	January 31, 1989	277,525
Bongga	–	236,000
Bandera	–	253,523
Ang Pilipino Star	–	296,000
Daily Balita	–	87,000
Remate	–	100,000
Balita Sa Hapon	–	35,000
People's Balita	–	120,000
Daily Aliwan	–	235,000
Daily Libangan	–	215,000
Bulgar	–	367,655
Philippine Pulse	–	20,000
Isyu	–	126,835
Metro Sun	–	100,000
Tribune		75,000
Pilipino Star Ngayon	March 17, 1986	150,000
Saksi Ngayon	–	45,000
Evening Tempo	–	10,000
Bandera Tonight	–	–
Total		**4,935,784**

Source: *Philippine media factbook*, 1998.

Table 5
Community Publications

By frequency	Number	Circulation
Daily	28	187,300
Weekly	293	438,623
Bi-monthly	11	27,100
Monthly	36	51,750
Quarterly	18	21,000
Others	32	30,100
Total	**418**	**755,873**

Source: *Philippine media factbook*, 1998.

Table 6
Metro Manila Magazines and Comics

MAGAZINES

By contents	Number	Circulation
General interest	14	1,040,758
Female-oriented	10	793,875
Male-oriented	1	29,890
Teen-oriented	1	25,000
Specialty	4	239,910
Sports magazines	3	522,494
Showbiz magazines	15	1,919,007
Regional magazines	3	33,000
Total	**51**	**4,603,934**

By language	Number	Circulation
English	29	2,273,412
Filipino	18	2,168,463
Dialect	4	162,059
Total	**51**	**4,603,934**

By frequency	Number	Circulation
Weekly	36	4,136,134
Monthly	13	432,800
Bi-monthly	2	35,000
Total	**51**	**4,603,934**

COMICS

By frequency	Number	Circulation
Daily	14	130,500
Weekly	221	395,723
Bi-monthly	8	21,700
Monthly	27	134,700
Quarterly	14	21,800
Others	9	28,875
Total	**293**	**733,298**

Source: *Philippine media factbook*, 1998.

Table 7
Number of Radio Stations by Type of Service

Type	AM	FM	Total
Commercial	228	260	488
Non-commercial			
Educational	4	3	7
Government	31	1	32
Military	2	0	2
Religious	8	2	10
Total	**273**	**266**	**539**

Table 8
Number of Radio Stations by Region

Region	AM	FM	Total
NCR	26	24	50
Luzon	100	92	192
Visayas	60	60	120
Mindanao	87	90	177
Total	**273**	**266**	**539**

Table 9
Top 10 Radio Station Networks

Broadcast network	AM	FM	Total
Radio Mindanao Network, Inc.	19	15	34
Philippine Broadcasting Service	31	1	32
Manila Broadcasting Co.	12	17	29
Nation Broadcasting Co.	15	14	29
Catholic Bishops Conference of the Phils	16	4	20
Radio Philippines Network, Inc.	20	0	20
Consolidated Broadcasting Systems, Inc.	8	9	17
Cebu Broadcasting Co.	7	9	16
ABS–CBN Broadcasting Network	2	12	14
Pacific Broadcasting System	7	6	13
Total	**137**	**87**	**224**

Source: *KBP media factbook*, 1996.

Table 10
Number of Television Stations by Region

Regions	Number
NCR	12
Luzon	53
Visayas	28
Mindanao	44
Total	**137**

Source: *Philippine media factbook*, 1998.

Table 11
Six Largest TV Networks

TV network	Originating	Relay	UHF	Total
GMA Network Inc.	1	28	1	30
ABS–CBN Broadcasting Corp.	10	8	0	18
Radio Philippines Network	8	0 .	0	8
Intercontinental Broadcasting Corp.	5	0	0	5
ABC Development Corp.	1	1	2	4
Southern Broadcasting Network	3	0	1	4
Total	**28**	**37**	**4**	**69**

Source: *Philippine media factbook*, 1995–96.

Table 12
Household Ownership of Radio, TV, VCR, and Personal Computers

	Radio (%)	TV (%)	VCR (%)	Personal computer (%)
Metro Manila	87.80	86.93	30.19	4.06
Provinces	81.15	34.43	10.71	0.67
National average	**84.50**	**60.68**	**20.45**	**2.40**

Source: *Philippine media factbook*, 1995–96.

Table 13
Household Population 10 Years Old and Over Exposed to Mass Media

	Newspaper %	Magazines %	Comics %	Books %	Radio %	Television %	Video tape %	Movies %
Metro Manila	69.12	20.94	24.75	41.22	83.34	91.11	18.89	17.35
Provinces	21.60	13.40	21.56	35.60	80.00	45.41	13.81	5.60
National average	**45.36**	**17.17**	**23.15**	**38.41**	**81.67**	**68.26**	**16.35**	**11.47**

Source: *Philippine media factbook*, 1995–96.

9. USEFUL ADDRESSES

Adboard
Secretariat - 2nd floor, L & F Bldg
107 Aguirre St., Legaspi Village
Makati City
Telephone: (02) 818-61-58

Advertising Suppliers Association of the Philippines (ASAP)
Secretariat - Unit S VI-C The Gallery Bldg
Amorsolo Street, Legaspi Village

Makati City
Telephone: (02) 843-21-20

Cinema Advertising Association of the Philippines (CAAP)
Secretariat - Unit 2-D Amorsolo Condominium
Amorosolo Street
Legaspi Village, Makati City
Telephone: (02) 818-73-32/892-6203

Kapisanan ng mga Brodkaster sa Pilipinas (KBP)
Secretariat - 6 floor, LTA Bldg
118 Perea St., Legaspi Village, Makati City
Telephone: (02) 815-19-89 to 93

Marketing and Opinion Research Society of the Philippines (MORES)
Secretariat - Unit 42 Martino Bldg
52 Liberated Corner Kanlaon Street
Mandaluyong City
Telephone: (02) 533-66-53

Outdoor Advertising Association of the Philippines (OAAP)
Secretariat - 5742 Kalayaan Ave., Corner EDSA
Pinagkaisahan, Makati City
Telephone: (02) 819-05-13

Philippine Association of National Advertisers (PANA)
Secretariat - Unit 2-D Amorsolo Condominium
Amorsolo St., Legaspi Village
Makati City
Telephone: (02) 892-62-03

Print Media Organization (PRIMO)
Secretariat - Mr & Mrs Publishing; Vibal Publishing House
Araneta Avenue, Corner Ma. Clara
Talayan Village, Quezon City

Foreign Correspondents Association of the Philippines (FOCAP)
Secretariat - Rm. 161, The Westin Philippine Plaza, CCP Complex
Roxas Blvd, Pasay City
Telephone: (02) 833-61-39

Philippine Association of Communication Educators Foundation Inc.
President - Ramon Tuazon
Unit 902, Annapolis, Wilshire Plaza
Annapolis, Greenhills
Telephone: (02) 724-4564/725-4227
Fax: (02) 725-4228

Association of Accredited Advertising Agencies – Philippines (4AS)
Secretariat - 2nd floor, L & F Building
107 Aguirre St., Legaspi Village, Makati City
Telephone: (02) 818-61-57

Philippine Press Institute
Secretariat - Rm. 308, BF Condominium Bldg
A Soriano Avenue, Intramuros, Manila
Telephone: (02) 527-44-78

Public Relations Organization of the Philippines
Secretariat - HRDD, 3rd floor, Philippine Information Agency Bldg
Visayas Avenue, Quezon City
Telephone: (02) 920-43-36

Public Relations Society of the Philippines
Secretariat - #30 San Pedro St
Bo. Capitolyo, Pasig City
Telephone: (02) 635-44-46

Manila Overseas Press Club
Secretariat - G/F Old Elks Club Bldg
Roxas Blvd. Corner T.M. Kalaw St.
Ermita, Manila
Telephone: (02) 571-252

Publishers Association of the Philippines Inc.
Secretariat - 4th floor, Domingo Bldg
2113 Pasong Tamo corner dela Rosa Street
Makati City
Telephone: (02) 819-12-15

National Press Club
Secretariat - NPC Bldg
Magallanes Drive, Intramuros, Manila
Telephone: (02) 527-0168

10. REFERENCES

Alumit, G.M. (1998). *Telecommunications reform in the Philippines: Successes, failures and challenges to Ramos' 2000 plan.* Paper presented at the BEA Convention, Las Vegas.
APT (Asia-Pacific Telecommunity). (1998, 1999). *The APT yearbook.* Bangkok: APT.
Atlas of the Philippines (1998). Manila: Environment Center of the Philippines Foundation.
Castro, J.L. (1963). *The Manila Times journalism manual.* Manila: Manila Times Publishing.
Chua, J. (1998). *Telecommunication industry in the Philippines.* Singapore: APEC Secretariat [On-line]. Available: (http://www.apecsec.org.sg/download/cti/cacphil.pdf).
Coronel, S.S. (1998) Media ownership and control in the Philippines. *Media Development, 45* (4), 25–28.
Coronel, S.S., & Stuart, T.H. (1996). The Philippines. In K.S. Venkateswaran (Comp.), *Media monitors in Asia* (pp. 55–72). Singapore: AMIC.
De Jesus, M.Q. (1998). Philippines: The problem with freedom. *Development Dialogue, 2,* 105–119.
Delfinado, R.D. (1999, January 6). Exports up 17% to $26.9 B in Jan–Nov '98. *The Philippine Star,* p. 17.
Doronila, A. (1998a). The Philippines. In A. Latif (Ed.), *Walking the tightrope: Press freedom and professional standards in Asia* (pp. 137–141). Singapore: AMIC.
Doronila, A. (1998b, November 2). Politicians as journalists. *Philippine Daily Inquirer,* p. 9.

Fernandez, D.G. (1989). Philippines. In A. Mehra (Ed.), *Press systems in ASEAN states* (pp. 57–84). Singapore: AMIC.

Flor, A. (1998). Philippines. In A. Goonasekera & D. Holaday (Eds.), *The Asian communication handbook* (pp. 135–146). Singapore: AMIC & NTU.

Gardner, C.E. (1995). The Internet and the Philippines [On-line]. Available: (http://super.nova.org/InternetPhil.html).

Hofileña, C.F. (1999). *News for sale: The corruption of the Philippine media.* Manila: The Philippine Center for Investigative Journalism and the Center for Media Freedom and Responsibility.

ITU (International Telecommunication Union). (1998, 1999). *World telecommunication development report.* Geneva: ITU.

KBP media factbook. (1996). Manila: One-Four-One Printing Supplies & Services.

Lent, J.A. (1971). The Philippines. In J.A. Lent (Ed.), *The Asian newspapers' reluctant revolution* (pp. 191–209). The Iowa State University Press.

Lent, J.A. (1978). The Philippines. In J.A. Lent (Ed.), *Broadcasting in Asia and the Pacific: A continental survey of radio and television* (pp. 176–188). Philadelphia: Temple University Press.

Lent, J.A. (1982). Philippines. In J.A. Lent (Ed.), *Newspapers in Asia: Contemporary trends and problems* (pp. 267–280). Hong Kong: Heinemann Asia.

Maslog, C.C. (1989). Philippine communication today: Profile and challenges. In *Communication for community: A resource book* (pp. 7–21). Manila: People in Communication.

Maslog, C.C. (1990). *Philippine mass communication: A mini-history.* Quezon City: New Day Publishers.

Maslog, C.C. (1992). *Communication, values and society.* Manila: Philippine Association of Communication Educators.

Maslog, C.C. (1993). *The rise and fall of Philippine community newspapers.* Manila: Philippine Press Institute.

Maslog, C.C. (1994). *The Metro Manila press.* Manila: Philippine Press Institute.

Media factbook. (1997). Makati: 4 A's Advertising.

Nazareno, R.G. (1997). The promise of cable TV. In C.C. Maslog, R.L. Navarro, L. Tabing and L. Teodoro (Eds.), *Communication for people power* (pp. 162–170). Diliman: Institute of Development Communication UP Los Baños & UNESCO National Commission, Philippines.

Paño, A.R. (1998, October 16). Internet use in RP growing 40% yearly. *The Philippine Star,* p. 24.

Philippine media factbook. (1995, 1996, 1998). Quezon City: Philippine Information Agency.

Philippine yearbook. (1995). Manila: National Statistics Office.

Sussman L. R. (1999). *Press freedom 1999: News of the century.* New York: Freedom House.

Teodoro, L.V., Jr., & Kabatay, R.V. (Comps.) (1998). *Mass media laws and regulations in the Philippines.* Singapore: AMIC.

Tiglao, R. (1999, May 13). Too much freedom? Manila media are accused of manipulation. *Far Eastern Economic Review, 162* (19), pp. 24–25, 28.

Tuazon R.R. (1998). Sociocultural factors as determinants of press freedom: The Philippine experience. In A. Latif (Ed.), *Walking the tightrope: Press freedom and professional standards in Asia* (pp. 238–250). Singapore: AMIC.

UNESCO (United Nations Educational, Scientific and Cultural Organization). (1999). *Statistical yearbook.* Paris: UNESCO.

UAP (University of Asia and the Pacific). (1997). *Food and agri-business yearbook '97.* Manila: Belgosa Publishing.

Vanden Heuvel, J. & Dennis, E.E. (1993). *The unfolding lotus: East Asia's changing media.* New York: The Freedom Forum Media Studies Center.

World factbook. (1999). Philippines. Washington, DC: CIA [On-line]. Available: (http://www.odci.gov/cia/publications/factbook).

WAN (World Association of Newspapers). (1998, 1999). *World press trends.* Paris: WAN.

◆

15

SINGAPORE

Eddie Kuo & Peng Hwa Ang

1. NATIONAL PROFILE

1.1 Geography

The Republic of Singapore consists of a small group of some 50 islands at the southern tip of the Malay Peninsula. Its land area of nearly 650 sq km is about 3.5 times the size of Washington, DC. As it is just a degree north of the Equator, Singapore is hot and humid all year round (Singapore InfoMap, 1998).

1.2 People

Singapore's residential population of 3.5 million includes 10 percent who are foreigners. It has a high population density of 5,660 people per sq km. Its multiethnic population is 76.4 percent Chinese, 14.9 percent Malay, 6.4 percent Indian, and 2.3 percent others. It recognizes four official languages: English as the dominant working language; and Chinese, Malay, and Tamil as languages of the respective ethnic groups. English is spoken by 20.3 percent of the population, while 26 percent speak Mandarin, 36.7 percent speak other Chinese dialects, 13.4 percent speak Malay, 2.9 percent speak Tamil, and 0.7 percent speak other languages (Goonasekera & Holaday, 1998, p. 163). The population is 100 percent urban. Literacy is 92.2 percent, and life expectancy 78.8 years. The people follow several religions: Buddhism (Chinese), Islam (Malays), Christianity, Hinduism, Sikhism, Taoism, and Confucianism (*World factbook*, 1999).

1.3 Government and Politics

Singapore's history[1] is most often traced to 1819 when Sir Stamford Raffles founded it as a trading post. The British saw the need for a strategic "halfway house" to

---

[1] Chew and Lee, 1991, provide a more detailed account. A succinct official summary is available at (http://www.sg/flavour/history.html).

secure and protect their line of trade from China to the colonies and to forestall any advances by the Dutch in the region. Raffles' policy of free trade attracted thousands of migrants. Singapore became a flourishing colony with a military and naval base. The population grew from a mere 150 in 1819 to 10,000 in 1824. Trade in that year surpassed that of Penang, an earlier colony. Peace and prosperity came to an abrupt end when the Japanese bombed the city in the wee hours of December 8, 1941 (Singapore InfoMap, 1998).

The Japanese captured Singapore on February 15, 1942. They renamed it *Syonan* (Light of the South). It reverted to the British in September 1945. The Japanese, who had demonstrated that an Asian power could overthrow a Western colonial power, had sown the seeds of nationalism during their occupation. The attempt of the Communist Party of Malaysia to take over Malaya and Singapore in June 1948 led to the declaration of a state of emergency, which lasted for 12 years. One legacy of this period was the Internal Security Act, which has been used to detain journalists without trial.

Singapore attained self-government in 1959. The first general election in May resulted in a victory for Lee Kuan Yew, a Cambridge-educated lawyer who headed an opposition People's Action Party (PAP). He became the republic's first prime minister, and his party has ruled the country since. In 1963, Singapore and Malaya merged to form the Federation of Malaysia, based on the belief that Singapore was too small to survive on its own. By 1965, however, the nascent federation was in tatters. Singapore separated from Malaysia and became a sovereign nation on August 9.[2]

Singapore is a republic with a parliamentary system modeled after Westminster, but with a written constitution. The president, as the head of state, has largely ceremonial powers. A cabinet, headed by the prime minister, exercises the powers of the government. The unicameral legislature has 83 seats. Lee stepped down as prime minister in 1990, handing the position to his protégé Goh Chok Tong. At the last general election, held on January 2, 1997, the ruling PAP received 65 percent of the votes in the 37 contested constituencies and won 81 parliamentary seats (*World factbook*, 1999).

1.4 Economy

Trade has been the backbone of Singapore's economy. It became a major port-of-call for ships plying between Europe and East Asia, thanks to the opening of the Suez Canal in 1869, and the new technology of the steamship. By the end of the 19th century, Singapore already enjoyed unprecedented prosperity, and trade expanded eightfold between 1874 and 1913.

Today, the country continues to look for ways to exploit new technologies to ensure its survival and well-being. Singaporeans enjoy one of the highest standards

[2] Lee, 1998, provides an account of the story behind the separation.

of living in the world with a per capita purchasing power parity (GDP) of US$ 27,740 and a nominal GNP per capita of US$ 21,828 (*Asiaweek*, February 4, 2000). The biggest sector of the economy is finance and business services, commanding almost 30 percent of the economic pie in 1997. Communications and transport had a 10 percent share (SDS, 1997b).

2. DEVELOPMENT OF PRESS AND BROADCASTING

2.1 Brief Early History

As a British colony, Singapore's press[3] evolved under a strong British influence. The first newspaper to circulate in Singapore was the *Prince of Wales Island Gazette*, founded in 1805 in Penang. The first local paper was the *Commercial Register* started by Christian missionaries. It merged with the *Singapore Chronicle*, but the joint paper closed down in 1837. William Napier founded the *Singapore Free Press* in 1885. The current *Straits Times* was founded in 1845. The first Indian paper, the *Singai Varthamani*, started in 1876. That same year, an association of locally-born Indian Muslims started the first Malay newspaper *Jawi Peranakan* with an initial pressrun of 250 copies (Tan & Soh, 1994). The well-edited *Jawi Peranakan* spun off other Malay newspapers (Lent, 1982). From the 1920s to 1930s, the Malay press moved out of Singapore to Malaya, reflecting growing Malay consciousness on the peninsula (Lent, 1982).

Christian missionaries based in Malacca in the peninsula published the first Chinese newspapers to circulate in Singapore. The *Chinese Monthly Magazine*, started in 1815, was a give away. Another early Chinese newspaper was the *T'en Hsia Hsin Wen* (The Universal Gazette) started in 1828. When the missionaries who started the latter moved their printing press and school to Hong Kong, they also took away the only Chinese periodical in Singapore and Malaya (Chen, 1967). The first Chinese daily in Singapore and Malaya, the *Lat Pau*, commenced on December 10, 1881 (Tan, 1971).

Broadcasting began in Singapore when a private enterprise, the British Malaya Broadcasting Corporation, began transmission in June 1936. The Singapore government bought the business in 1940. The "Broadcasting Station, Posts and Telegraph Department, Singapore and Federated Malay States" ran it for almost a year. In April 1941, the Malaya Broadcasting Corporation, a quasi-government enterprise, controlled jointly by the governments of the Straits Settlement and the United Kingdom, took over the radio station (Wong & Lian, 1978, p. 156). The radio station was named *Syonan Hoso Kyoku* under Japanese occupation (February 1942 to August 1945).

---

[3] Turnbull, 1995, provides a fuller account of the history of the *Straits Times*.

2.2 Developments since 1945

During World War II, the Japanese had published *The Syonan Shimbun*. The resurrection of the press began in the 1950s. The Chinese press was particularly active in the 1950s. Small publications described as "mosquito" or "yellow culture" newspapers came and went. They "dealt more in imaginative libelous stories than in factual reports" (Tan, 1971, p. 182). Reader protests led to their eventual closure by the government. Tabloids, which printed lottery results as lead articles, replaced them. Stiff competition among them cut their lifespan to between three and six months (Tan, 1971). Toward the late 1950s, some Chinese papers were started as a means to send remittances to support China (Tan & Soh, 1994).

The English press mounted more serious challenges among themselves. The *Singapore Tiger Standard*, established in 1949, lasted 10 years. Others in the fray were the now defunct *Malayan Times* (1961), *Eastern Sun* (1966), and *Singapore Herald* (1970).

Religious, economic, and political motives were behind the establishment of newspapers in Singapore. Christians and Muslims had religious motives in starting the early papers, while commercial and economic objectives spurred the establishment of English papers. The political motives of those engaged in politics in China often accounted for the establishment of the Chinese papers.

2.2.1 The Press

The evolution of the Singapore press into a monopoly started in the 1970s, when the government closed down two English dailies—*Eastern Sun* and *Singapore Herald*—and merged the two leading Chinese dailies (Lent, 1982).[4] Although the circulation of the Chinese newspapers was rising in the late 1970s, the government sensed that the readership of the Chinese dailies might fall eventually with an increasing number of students studying in English. The government, therefore, decided to allow Chinese papers to enter the English-daily market and also permitted *The Straits Times* to operate a Chinese daily (Tan & Soh, 1994).

In 1980, the two Chinese papers were merged to form Singapore News and Publications Ltd (SNPL) with a license to publish an English daily. (The paper, *The Singapore Monitor* folded in 1985, when Singapore had its first recession since independence.) *The Straits Times* had folded its afternoon paper, *New Nation*, so as not to compete with *The Singapore Monitor*. In turn, the government gave it a license to publish the Chinese daily, *Shin Min Daily News* (SPH, 1993). But in 1984, in a surprise move, the government merged *The Straits Times* group with the SNPL to form Singapore Press Holdings (SPH). The only newspaper outside the fold was the small Tamil daily, *Tamil Murasu*, which SPH later bought in the mid-1990s (Tan & Soh, 1994).

---

[4] Lent, 1982, gives a detailed account of the government–press relationship in Singapore during the 1970s. Seow, 1998; and Wong, 1999, provide other perspectives.

Singapore Press Holdings started *The New Paper*, an English-language afternoon paper, in 1988. Targeted at a blue-collar mass market, it filled the void left by *The Singapore Monitor*. The 1991 Gulf War gave *The New Paper* a circulation boost, and it has been profitable since.

2.2.2 Broadcasting

Following Japan's defeat, the British returned in 1946. They renamed the broadcasting service "Radio Malaya, Singapore and Federation of Malaya," with Singapore as its headquarters. The civil government ran a medium-wave and a shortwave service for the whole Malay Peninsula (Wong & Lian, 1978). When Malaya won independence in 1957, the radio service was split into Radio Malaya and Radio Singapore. The two services merged in August 1963 with the formation of the federation of Malaysia, only to split again on August 9, 1965, with Singapore's independence. The Department of Broadcasting, Ministry of Culture, took over the service now renamed Radio–Television Singapore. The government called on the radio service to "interpret...the government's objectives and policies...to enhance the people's political awareness...enabling the people to identify closely with the nation and to make the right choice at elections" (Ow, 1979, p. 140). This obligation discouraged the production of innovative programs (Chen, 1996).

Rediffusion, a private wired radio service relaying interference-free broadcasts, became the primary entertainment medium from the 1950s to the early 1980s. Rediffusion International London, a private operation that relayed broadcasts from BBC London to other parts of England, established Rediffusion (Singapore) Ltd as a branch. Rediffusion offered programs in Chinese dialects, English, and Malay, peaking at 120,000 subscribers in the early 1980s (SDS, 1983). Then, a government campaign to de-emphasize the Chinese dialects, coupled with a more lively radio industry, led to the decline of Rediffusion (Chen, 1996).[5] In 1975, Singapore became the location of the BBC relay station originally set up in Malaya in the 1940s (Wong & Lian, 1978).

Television arrived in 1963. Katz and Wedell (1978) suggest that Singapore introduced television to keep people off the streets following communal unrest (p. 82). Radio–Television Singapore started Channel 5 to televise English and Malay programs, and Channel 8 to feature Mandarin and Tamil programs. Full-color transmission came in mid-1974 (Wong & Lian, 1978).

3. THE PRESS

3.1 Policy and Legal Framework[6]

The Singapore press operates within a strict legal framework. Singapore does not subscribe to the libertarian or the US model of the press system that allows the

---

[5] Chen's 1996 study documents the reasons for the decline, including both technical and marketing problems.

[6] Ang and Yeo, 1998, provide a fuller account of mass media laws and regulations in Singapore.

press virtually unfettered freedom. The libertarian concept is deemed unworkable in Singapore because of racial, religious, and cultural differences (Vanden Heuvel & Dennis, 1993; Chua, 1998).

Singapore's Constitution provides the right to freedom of speech and expression in Article 14, which was modeled after that of the Indian Constitution. In both constitutions, it is a limited right. First, it guarantees freedom of speech and expression only to citizens of Singapore. Second, it gives the right only to convey expression, not the right to receive expression of any kind. Third, it does not deal expressly with the issue of prior restraint, thus implicitly allowing it. Fourth, the right is subject to parliament's power to legislate in the interests of national security, public interests and morality, and for the maintenance of foreign relations.

The Newspapers and Printing Presses Act of 1974, traceable to the colonial government's Printing Presses Act of 1920, is the dominant law affecting the press. The Act requires licenses for local printing presses, and local as well as foreign, newspapers and magazines. The law requires the annual licensing of daily newspapers, which only public companies, not individuals, can own. Such companies should have at least 50 shareholders, but no single shareholder can own more than 3 percent. All directors must be locals, and government approval is necessary to hold key positions. The company must create two kinds of shares: ordinary shares that make up 99 percent of the company, with one vote each; and management shares that make up just 1 percent of the company, with 200 votes each. The minister approves the ownership and transfer of the management shares. The 1986 amendment to the Act empowers the minister to restrict the circulation of publications that "engage in domestic politics." Since then, *Time, Asian Wall Street Journal, Far Eastern Economic Review, Asiaweek*, and *The Economist* have had their circulation restricted under the law.

In 1988, the *Far Eastern Economic Review*, in response to the restriction, stopped its circulation in Singapore. The Singapore government amended the Act to allow reproduction of the publication *in toto* without infringing copyright and on a cost-recovery basis. No advertisements were printed, so the copies appeared with white spaces where advertisements would otherwise have been. In 1990, the government amended the Act again to license newsweeklies produced outside Singapore with a circulation exceeding 300. The amendment empowered the government to specify the maximum number of copies that could be sold, to require the appointment of an authorized person to accept service of legal notice, and to require the publisher to furnish a deposit of S$ 200,000 (US$ 125,000). One publication, *Media*, a weekly from Hong Kong covering advertising, reduced its circulation in Singapore from 1,500 to 299 (Tan & Soh, 1994).

The Undesirable Publications Act prohibits the sale, import, or circulation of publications produced outside or within Singapore deemed "contrary to the public interest." More recently, the government has used this law against soft-porn and alternative lifestyle publications (Lim, 1996). Besides such universal issues as copyright and defamation, other laws pertinent to the media are the Criminal Law

(Temporary Provisions) Act, the Emergency (Essential Powers) Act, and the 1963 Internal Security Act. The latter allows for detention without trial although the last time a journalist was jailed was in the 1970s. More recently, the Official Secrets Act was used against journalists from *Business Times* for publishing news about economic growth before the data were released. This was the first time this law was used against journalists. Earlier, the presumption had been that the law targeted espionage. Other laws with provisions to regulate the press, but which have not been used against the press, are the Maintenance of Religious Harmony Act, the Parliament (Privileges, Immunities and Powers) Act, and the 1964 Sedition Act. Nair (1989) says: "Singapore reviews press laws regularly.... Laws are not meant to prevent the free flow of information, of differing views and expressions" (p. 90).

3.2 Financial Aspects: Circulation, Advertising, Marketing Strategies

3.2.1 Circulation

The daily newspaper circulation in 1993 was 977,846, or 34 copies per 100 people. Circulation rose from 20.9 per 100 people in 1976 to 27.2 in 1986 (SDS, 1993). In 1997, the total daily newspaper circulation increased to 1,087,551, but the circulation rate (27.4 copies per 100 people) remained the same because of population growth (SDS, 1998). In 1998, the circulation was estimated at 1,056,000 (WAN, 1999). Table 1 shows the circulation share among the papers in the four official languages. The English and Chinese press dominate the scene. Given the increasing importance of English among the younger population, the circulation of the English press is likely to grow further.

3.2.2 Advertising

Singapore's advertising market was about US$ 800 million in 1997. Unlike in most countries where television commands the lion's share of advertising, more than 50 per cent of the advertising revenue in Singapore goes to daily newspapers (Table 3). The bulk of the revenue goes to *The Straits Times*. Television gets about a third of total advertising expenditure. These two media command about 85 percent of the advertising market. The monopolistic control of newspaper and television holding companies becomes clear when the advertising revenue of their magazines is added.

The rest of the advertising pie goes mostly to magazines and radio. Magazines have seen their market share halved from about 10 percent to the current 5 percent. Radio, with more channels and greater competition, has seen its share increase recently. In 1998, advertising expenditure declined to an estimated S$ 1,150 million (US$ 689 million), with the share of newspapers at 48 percent, television at 38 percent, magazines and radio each at 5 percent, cinema at 1 percent, and other media at 4 percent (SRS Adex, cited in WAN, 1999).

3.3 Structure and Organization

The print media in Singapore are dominated by the local newspaper monopoly, Singapore Press Holdings (SPH). Its eight local dailies command a combined circulation of more than 1 million copies. English-language newspapers have the highest daily circulation, followed by Chinese, Malay, and Tamil newspapers.

Singapore Press Holdings is a listed blue chip stock and commands more than half of all advertising revenue in Singapore. It runs three English newspapers: *The Straits Times* (including *The Sunday Times*), *Business Times*, and *The New Paper*. It also publishes three Chinese newspapers: *Lianhe Zaobao* (United Morning News), *Lianhe Wanbao* (United Evening News), and *Shin Min Daily News*. It also owns the Malay newspaper *Berita Harian* (Daily News), including its Sunday edition *Berita Minggu* (Weekly News), and the Tamil newspaper, the *Tamil Murasu* (Table 2).

Singapore Press Holdings also publishes several periodicals, many of which are circulated widely in Singapore. The company, therefore, continues to be highly profitable. In 1998, the publicly listed SPH returned S$ 500 million (US$ 300 million) as a form of share buyback to its shareholders and still had a S$ 1.2 billion (US$ 718 million) stockpile to invest. It employs 3,000 (SPH cheers investors, 1998). The company is diversifying into property and telecommunications. It has bought both into the local cable television franchise and the second cellular phone provider, and is a partner in the third of three Internet licensees.

About 4,500 foreign publications also circulate in Singapore. Some 200 accredited correspondents representing 64 foreign news agencies, newspapers, and broadcasting stations are based in Singapore (Singapore InfoMap, 1998).

3.4 Quality and Popular Press

Singapore Press Holdings positions its papers to minimize competition. The only exceptions are the two Chinese-language evening newspapers, *Shin Min* and *Lianhe Wanbao*, which do compete for news and readers, and which often appeal to sensationalism. The business news of *The Straits Times* sometimes competes with the *Business Times* but this is more by accident than by design.

The Straits Times, or ST as it is known in acronym-favoring Singapore, is the oldest and longest running newspaper. It started in 1845 as a weekly and became a daily in 1858. Publication was interrupted when Singapore fell to the Japanese in 1942 but resumed with the end of the war in 1945. The company turned public in 1950 with a daily circulation of 50,000 copies and a Sunday circulation of more than 67,000 copies. In the 1950s, *The Straits Times* was published both in Singapore and Malaya by the Straits Times Press. But Singapore's separation from Malaysia in 1965 led to the establishment of *The New Straits Times* in Malaysia.

Today's *Straits Times* is a broadsheet daily with multiple sections for family reading. The news section is particularly strong on regional and international news. Besides sports, business, and regional news, a features section called "Life!" carries light articles on films, books, television, family, food, music, arts, culture, travel, and the like. It is as close to what can be considered a quality paper, as the term might generally be defined, in the Singapore setting. It is a local paper, a national paper, and a regional and international paper, all in one, and is billed as the national paper of record.

Until the economic crisis hit Singapore in 1998, ST was one of the few newspapers in the world that turned away advertising, chiefly because it had too many advertisers fighting for limited newspaper space. (The other two publications that turn away advertising, as far as the two writers know, are *The Economist* and *The South China Morning Post*.) Informal content analysis by the second author with students has shown that at its height, on some days, 80 percent of the *Times'* news pages contained advertising.

Singapore's only English-language afternoon tabloid, *The New Paper*, caters to the impulse buyer, and to the blue-collar and student readership. With bold headlines on sex, soccer, and such, it is more sensational than the other papers. But it barely approaches the level of sensation found in the Western press. It appeared first on July 26, 1988, three years after the afternoon daily *The Singapore Monitor* stopped publication. Its average daily circulation of more than 107,000 is way above its original target of 65,000.

The *Lianhe Zaobao* (*Lian-he* meaning "United" and *Zao-bao* meaning "Morning News") and the *Lianhe Wanbao* (United Evening News) were the products of a merger between two competing newspapers, the *Nanyang Siang Pau* and *Sin Chew Jit Poh*, which had merged in 1982 to form the Singapore News and Publications Ltd (SNPL). *Zaobao*, as it is known, is the leading Chinese newspaper in Singapore. This daily broadsheet focuses on issues of interest to the Chinese community, particularly the Chinese language and culture. Interestingly enough, its on-line edition is the most-read Chinese-language newspaper site in the world, with more than 30 million page-views a month. This ranks it among the 1,000 most-visited sites in the world. Significantly, more than 90 percent of the visits come from outside of Singapore, mostly from China and North America. The reason for its popularity is the readers' perception of it as a neutral voice on Chinese politics—not beholden to China or Taiwan.

Wanbao, which started in mid-1983, has adopted a bolder and less conservative editorial style because it has a direct competitor in *Shin Min Daily*, established just two years after Singapore's independence in 1965. It is a popular-reading evening paper that provides news on a wide range of local and international topics with added emphasis on the local entertainment scene. In the mid-1980s, with the formation of the Singapore Press Holdings, it looked as if *Shin Min* might have to fold. Now it thrives in competition with *Wanbao* in the same SPH stable.

3.5 Distribution and Technology

As with much of Singapore life, SPH employs new technologies in its production. It recently updated its printing plant at a cost of S$ 250 million (US$ 150 million). The new plant, intended to cope with the increased volume of advertising, was commissioned before the current economic crisis. In the early 1990s, the company also moved part of its layout and subediting team to Sydney, Australia. Less time-sensitive pages, such as entertainment and leisure features in the "Life!" section are subbed entirely in Sydney.

One area that has been less controlled is the distribution of its publications. Despite its virtual monopoly status, the company has only begun to take charge of its distribution. The distribution system is a legacy from the late-1960s. Independent newsvendors then were registered with the various newspaper companies and distributed a number of newspapers at one time. The newspaper companies did not bother with the distribution methods. Vendors carried out distribution only within their own territories, which were often marked out with the help of secret societies. Brawls often broke out when there was more than one vendor servicing the same territory. In as late as the mid-1980s, vendors would wait outside new flats to hand the owners their business cards (Lum & Khoo, 1998).

From 1988, the company started to control the vendors. First, it registered all 550 vendors. It then divided Singapore into four zones by postal district. Each zone has four area representatives, each typically handling between 30 and 40 vendors. The vendors then had to tender for the territories where they wished to distribute. Nevertheless, because of the carryover of the old system, some 20 percent of the areas in Singapore have more than one vendor (Lum & Khoo, 1998).

As the distribution system has several layers of managers, most of whom are not employees of the company, several layers of commissions are also involved. In 1990, some vendors met with the SPH to discuss the establishment of a distribution enterprise. But neither the company nor the vendors could agree on the terms. Eventually, the company drew up a joint distribution center scheme to distribute the papers in the new housing estates. The more than 100 vendors under the scheme collect the newspapers directly from the printing plant, instead of through a middleman. The profit margin for these vendors is lower but the delivery volume is guaranteed (Lum & Khoo, 1998).

Today's vendors are still independent contractors, not employees. Vendors generally get about 30 percent of the cover price of the newspapers. At that rate, a vendor who distributes to 1,000 homes (they are reluctant to distribute more) can expect a take-home pay of S$ 5,400 (US$ 3,300) (Lum & Khoo, 1998).

In 1990, the company started the system of direct outlet sales through outlets—which now exceed 400—such as petrol kiosk chains, supermarkets, convenience stores, and pharmacy chains. The vendors resisted the scheme because they got a delivery commission of only 6 Singapore cents. In 1997, the company started selling through vending machines, starting with two solar-powered ones. Currently, the company operates more than a dozen solar-powered vending machines in the more heavily trafficked areas (Lum & Khoo, 1998).

4. BROADCASTING

4.1 Policy and Legal Framework

The laws for the broadcast media are modeled after those related to the print media. Broadcasting, even over the Internet, is licensed. Unless regulations are waived by the Singapore Broadcasting Authority (SBA), no person can hold more than 3 percent of shares in a broadcasting company; the chief executive officer and at least half the board of directors must be Singapore citizens; and foreign funding is not allowed to exceed 49 percent of the capital of the company.

4.2 Structure and Organization

In 1980, an Act of Parliament transformed RTS into the Singapore Broadcasting Corporation (SBC), to provide the new entity with greater autonomy and flexibility in personnel, financial, and production matters. This marked the beginning of more locally produced programs. In 1984, SBC started Channel 12 to provide an extra dimension with documentaries, cultural performances and works, drama, art movies, educational programs, and sports.

In 1994, in a major exercise aiming to restructure the broadcasting industry to face a more competitive environment, SBC was corporatized to become Singapore International Media (SIM). This company controls all the broadcasting enterprises in Singapore, including the Television Corporation Singapore (TCS), Singapore Television 12 (STV12), and Radio Corporation Singapore (RCS). Currently, TCS operates Channel 5 (an all-English-language channel) and Channel 8 (an all-Chinese-language channel). TCS plays the role of the national station. Together, the two channels capture 80 percent of the market share (Table 4).

4.3 Program Policies

The Singapore Broadcasting Authority exercises censorship directly through a code of practice while the Ministry of Information and the Arts does so indirectly. Under a penalty framework, announced in November 1998, breaches of the codes may result in a fine from S$ 1,000 (US$ 600) to S$ 50,000 (US$ 30,000), depending on severity. To involve the community and to incorporate its views, SBA has set up several advisory committees. These include SBA's Program Advisory Committee, as well as three advisory committees with specific responsibilities for programs in the three ethnic languages—Chinese, Malay, and Tamil. The local TV industry has seen two major changes in recent years: the introduction of greater competition through cable television; and the restructuring of the SBC in 1994 through privatization, as well as the creation of several competitive companies.

The government has not dropped the ban on satellite dishes for private TV viewing despite its intent to enter the regional and international arena. Only foreign embassies and financial institutions have the privilege to install dishes. When the Gulf War broke out in 1991, Singapore's financial institutions learned of it 30 seconds later than other international markets—the time difference between the CNN news announcement and the wire service stories. The delay caused losses; and the government has allowed the financial institutions to use satellite dishes from then on (Hukill, 1996).

Cable television was introduced not only to provide such services but also to stave off competition from satellite TV broadcasters. Singapore CableVision (SCV) was formed in April 1992 to start and manage the new subscription television service. Its shareholders are the Singapore Press Holdings (20 percent), the government-linked Singapore Technologies Ventures or STV (24 percent), Singapore International Media (31 percent), and Continental Cablevision-USA (25 percent). SCV kicked off Singapore's first pay TV service on the UHF band in April 1992. As the public housing flats in which 80 percent of Singaporeans live had difficulty receiving the UHF signals, and also because of its high price, the service failed to do well. However, in June 1995, SCV was also licensed to operate cable television delivering 50 channels. By 1998, this service was offering 42 channels.

The trend in the TV industry is towards local productions, which increased by 60 percent between 1994 and 1995. TCS8, the Mandarin channel, produces an average of 600 hours of sitcoms, drama series, and variety shows per year, making it the TV station with the highest production record in the world. In recent years, TCS5, the English-language channel, has also begun to produce successful English comedies, modeled on US sitcoms but with a strong local flavor.

In 1997, TV12 began funding a series of local productions under a scheme to encourage independent local production houses to produce for the broadcasting industry. It funds each half-hour episode to the tune of S$ 20,000 (US$ 14,000). Although the amount does not match the minimum corporate video rates of S$ 40,000 for a half-hour, it is a start to get more local TV productions. The former SBC hardly used any independent local productions. The scheme is an attempt by the Singapore government to encourage local content so as to make Singapore a broadcasting and production hub. The SBA and the Economic Development Board are working to promote Singapore as a regional broadcasting hub. An influx of several international cable and satellite programmers has occurred since 1993.

4.4 Ownership and Financing

Television 12 owns and manages Prime 12, featuring Malay- and Indian-language programs; and Premier 12, featuring cultural, arts, sport, and public service programs, mostly in English. Both stations receive government subsidies for their services. The government—in line with its philosophy of minimal, if any, subsidies—has urged the companies to consider producing programs that they can sell to neighboring countries.

Radio Corporation Singapore (RCS), on the other hand, operates major radio stations to serve both local and international audiences. Singapore has 18 radio channels. RCS owns and manages 10 local and three international channels. Of the others, the umbrella union organization, National Trades Union Congress, operates two channels; a military-related organization, SAFRA (Singapore Armed Forces Reservist Association) Radio, operates two. The BBC World Service is the only foreign radio station in Singapore. It runs on FM channel on a 24-hour basis (the only 24-hour BBC station in the world) and uses Singapore as a base for shortwave relays to the region.

Singapore Cable Vision's subscription television service began in 1992 with three channels: a news channel (NewsVision), an English movie channel (Movie-Vision), and a Mandarin entertainment channel (Variety Vision). It also began operating a cable TV service in June 1995. Since February 1996, Singapore Telecom has been conducting trial runs of video-on-demand services.

Unlike the newspaper industry, Singapore's broadcasting industry has embraced competition. In 1997, some 26 companies—including ABN, BBC Worldwide, Discovery Asia, ESPN Asia, HBO, MTV Asia, and Walt Disney—were uplinking their programs from Singapore. Under the Singapore Broadcasting Authority Act, broadcasting licensees must have at least 51 percent local ownership; this rule is waived in the case of satellite broadcasters, whose main businesses are in regional markets.

5. NEW ELECTRONIC MEDIA

5.1 Internet and On-line Media

Singapore was the second country in Southeast Asia, after Malaysia, to offer public Internet access in July 1994. In typical Singapore style, however, once the decision was made, the Internet diffused very quickly. In March 1995, Singapore became the first country in the world to set up a national Internet website, *Singapore InfoMap* (http://www.sg). However, also in typical Singapore style, there was concern that Internet content could be destructive of the values that the country intended to uphold. In July 1996, the Singapore Broadcasting Authority announced new rules and the Class Licensing Scheme to censor the Internet. The new Internet regulations stirred a major controversy and received wide publicity all over the world. It portrayed Singapore as a country attempting to regulate what many described as impossible to regulate. However, after two years, no one has yet been prosecuted under the SBA rules.

Under the Class Licensing Scheme, those affected are first deemed to have a license to operate the website. SBA can withdraw the license of those who breach the regulations. Webmasters of political parties, religious organizations, and subscription electronic newspapers have to comply with the additional requirement that they must register with the authorities (SBA, 1998). The SBA set up the National Internet Advisory Committee (NIAC) in October 1996 to help with the task of regulating and promoting the Internet, and with addressing key issues of industry development, public education, and legal matters (SBA, 1997/1998). In September 1997, the NIAC released its first report, which recommended revising the Code of Practice for clarity and proposed strategies on creating multilingual content and the development of Singapore as an Internet hub. In response, SBA revised the code and issued a set of industry guidelines that explained the main features of the Internet regulatory policies. A policy switch that occurred has changed SBA's "tough" image to that of an "enlightened regulator." In its own words, "SBA sets in place a light-touch regulatory framework that is consultative, pro-business and transparent to the industry.... SBA encourages the industry to take the initiative to self-regulate and set [its] own standards" (SBA, 1997/1998).

As a part of the policy to encourage self-regulation, SBA required the three Internet service providers (ISPs) to offer a Family Access Network (FAN) in 1998. Currently, the new network offers the possibility of blocking out about 200,000, mostly pornographic, sites. The network purchases the domain names of the sites from commercial companies in the United States. Subscription is voluntary and costs more than the uncensored network (Hoong, 1998).

As of November 1998, more than half of the household in Singapore had personal computers (Mah, 1998). (Singapore is fifth in Asia after Japan, Taiwan, South Korea, and Hong Kong with more than 135,890 Internet hosts registered as of July 1999.) Singapore then had more than 500,000 Internet users—a penetration rate of more than 15 percent nationwide (Mah, 1998). An island-wide broadband network called Singapore ONE (One Network for Everyone) had 55,000 registered users in March 1999. The National Computer Board plans to increase this figure by training another 100,000 consumers within 12 to 18 months (Lombardo, 1999).

Cable television and Internet access are also merging in Singapore. Although initial projections envisaged wiring all 750,000 households for cable television by 2000, the country achieved that target ahead of schedule. Cable television is part of a wider attempt by the Singapore government to wire the island for the Information Age. In late 1998, the NCB was making trial runs of the cable system for Internet access. Singapore has four satellite earth stations owned by ST Teleport, Singapore Telecom, SIMCOM, and Asia Broadcast Center. Besides providing uplink and downlink services, these companies also provide full one-stop production and distribution services to the video programming industry. A high degree of digitization has made an active narrowband ISDN program possible in Singapore, which has laid 235,750 km of fiber-optic cable (APT, 1998). In January 1999, Singapore had more than 10,000 ISDN subscribers (Singapore Telecom, 1999). The country is also linked to four analog and four fiber-optic submarine cables linking it directly with 33 countries (APT, 1998).

5.2 Telecommunications Infrastructure

Singapore's mainline telephone density in May 1998 was 56.6 per 100 people (TAS, 1999), up from 39 per 100 people in 1990 (ITU, 1998). The market for mobile cellular and paging services was liberalized in April 1997, when one cellular phone company and three paging companies began service in competition with Singapore Telecom. In May 1998, Singapore had 1,139,600 mobile phone subscribers—a density of 36 percent (TAS, 1999). Singapore also had more than 1.2 million paging subscribers—a density of 40.3 percent (Ng, 1999).

No barriers exist against importing telecom equipment. The telecommunication industry is set for full liberalization in April 2000, when Singapore Telecom's monopoly on basic services ends and two more licenses will be granted for the provision of basic telecom services. Licensees will have to satisfy the criterion of having at least 51 percent local shareholding.

6. POLICY TRENDS FOR PRESS AND BROADCASTING

Singapore's demographic features of ethnic and linguistic diversity have a significant bearing on the media system. Living in a densely populated urban area, Singaporeans are known to be ardent media consumers. Singapore has the highest per capita cinema attendance in the world. Yet its small population base produces only a modest advertising revenue, which the various media categories have to share. The problem of a small population base is compounded by the division of audiences into various language streams, mainly English and Chinese. The media face the challenge of continuously competing with one another and of expanding their respective audiences. As the size of the pie can only grow to a certain extent, competition for each to claim a bigger share of the pie becomes more keen. Unfortunately, this is sometimes achieved at the expense of quality.

The opening up of Singapore society to the international media, with the introduction of cable television and the growing number of Internet users, compounds the challenge. Many major international media players are moving into Singapore, responding to the attractive policy measures, which the Singapore government has offered, to develop the country into a communication and telecommunications hub. Local media are responding to the challenge through diversification (an example being SPH) and internationalization (an example being TCS).

Meanwhile, many Asian countries are also competing against Singapore by positioning themselves as hubs for media and information services. Of immediate concern to Singapore is Malaysia's Multimedia Super Corridor—a project to build a Silicon Valley of high-technology companies on a tract of land larger than the whole of Singapore. Malaysian authorities have also indicated that they will adopt a more open approach, for example, by not attempting centralized control of the Internet and by offering incentive packages to companies. Such developments bring interesting challenges to Singapore and the region.

Against this background of vibrant competition and rapid development is the political culture of Singapore, often characterized as Confucian, paternalistic, and "neo-authoritarian." Singapore government enforces a set of strict media-related laws and maintains one of the most stringent censorship standards among the developed economies. (Circulation and possession of *Playboy* is illegal.) The leaders justify these laws and measures by stressing the uniqueness and vulnerability of Singapore society, as well as a set of characteristically Singaporean Asian values vis-à-vis Western or Western-influenced values.

One can summarize the rationale behind such a position thus: First, freedom is relative—not absolute, universal, or "inherent." No freedom exists without responsibility. Second, because an elected government receives the people's mandate, it can define the responsibility of the press, as well as the limits of press freedom. Ultimately, it is the government, not the media, that is accountable to the people. Hence, the government has both the legal and moral authority to act as the final arbiter when a disagreement arises between the government and the media. Moreover, this level of government control of the media is justifiable because Singapore, in particular, is vulnerable as a new nation with a multiracial and multireligious population. National survival and consensus building are accepted as top priorities at this stage of nation building (cf. Kuo, in press).

A process of evolutionary development has brought about a symbiotic relationship between the media and the state. Singapore media have adopted the development journalism model thereby playing an important role in nation building. The media take a pro-government and pro-establishment stance, and they justify it by pointing out that people have backed the good work of the government by re-electing it continuously since Singapore's self-government in 1959. A noted journalist has observed that "being pro-establishment is not only the most practical stand to adopt but also an intellectually and morally defensible one" (George, 1993, p. 132). It is as much out of conviction as of necessity.

More recently, however, signs have emerged to show that the prevailing system has become increasingly untenable.[7] First, the pressure on instituting a more open information system has come from a new generation of Singaporeans. They have lived through years of prosperity and development, are better educated and better informed, have traveled widely, and are more critical of government policies and more demanding of the role of the media. Although the PAP government should rightly be credited for the success of making Singapore a showcase of prosperity and development, it has to face a more demanding electorate, as a consequence of its own success.

Indeed some structural contradictions, and hence tensions, exist in Singapore. The current state of censorship and control of communication media is maintained against the backdrop of an open and mobile society, where citizens come into frequent contact with tourists and visitors of all national and cultural backgrounds. International travel has increasingly become a part of Singapore's middle-class

---

[7] The following discussion draws heavily form Kuo, 1994.

lifestyle. Moreover, no restrictions exist for Singaporeans who may choose to emigrate in search of greener pastures. Indeed, the younger generation of Singaporeans, who are well educated, fluent in English, and professionally mobile, will continue to exert pressure toward liberalization. They would want to make their votes count. Failing that, and if the environment becomes too stifling, they may pack up and leave.

Another dimension of structural contradiction is manifested in the tension between the open free-market economic system under which Singapore thrives and a media system that operates under external (government) and internal (self-imposed) constraints. The government has tried to manage these contradictions by separating different categories of information and treating them differently. It gives priority to financial news, which it considers essential for the economic system to remain globally competitive. The official attitude toward cultural and entertainment information, on the other hand, is ambivalent: an attitude founded in the belief that a "silent majority" support censorship in some areas of culture and entertainment as both justifiable and necessary.

This measure of "compartmentalization" is reflected in the current policy of granting permits for setting up satellite antennae to financial institutions (in addition to diplomatic missions) on the basis that they need such information to make themselves competitive internationally. In contrast, even hotels are denied permits to set up dishes to receive satellite broadcasting. Apparently, in the eyes of the decision-makers, the economic value of providing international broadcast channels to serve the tourist industry does not outweigh the unknown (and presumably undesirable) impact of allowing foreign programs from seeping into Singapore in a relatively uncontrolled manner.

Such ambiguity clashes head on with the government's goal of transforming Singapore into a global city, a center of international trade, finance, and banking, and an international hub for information, culture, and telecommunications. The government has encouraged foreign multimedia companies to set up operations in Singapore and to use it as a regional production or distribution center. The cultivation of an open and friendly media culture and environment is essential for Singapore to become competitive in playing such a regional role.

Meanwhile, the farsighted and successful National Information Technology Plan (National IT Plan), is fast moving Singapore into the Information Age with much emphasis on the information industry and knowledge economy (Low & Kuo, 1999). Advances and availability of new communication technologies have threatened the near monopoly of the traditional media in Singapore. The new Singapore CableVision (SCV) is already bringing a choice of more than 40 channels to the living rooms of many households. All major international news channels, including CNN, BBC, and CNBC, are available to cable TV subscribers. Even here, the hand of the government shows up: SBA, the regulatory authority, has to approve all SCV channels. This mild form of control may not be viable for very long because technology in satellite communications is advancing at such rapid speed that it will soon be impossible to censure the installation of miniature antennae to receive direct satellite broadcasting.

Perhaps more significant than others, the rapid expansion of the Internet is quickly changing the scene of communication and information management in Singapore. More than any other form of modern information technology, the growth of Internet users makes it blatantly obvious that censorship and control of information flow is becoming untenable and may well prove self-defeating (Yeo & Mahizhnan, 1998).

Government leaders have recognized the changing scene well. Senior Minister Lee Kuan Yew, in a landmark speech at the Asian Media Conference in Los Angeles in October 1998, stressed the impact of the new media on politics. He pointed out:

Information technology, in particular the Internet, has made it impossible for inconvenient news to be suppressed for long." Thus, governments "have to work with the technology, not suppress it. Governments that try to fight the new technology will lose.... Indeed, information technology is rapidly undermining whatever monopoly control of the media governments might have known. Thus, along with the official view, many other views are available and known.

He suggested that, under the circumstances, the best that governments can do is "to require the official view to be carried in the media, along with other views over which they have no control" (*The Straits Times*, October 31; November 2, 1998).

What was significant in Lee's speech was not so much his insights on the impact of new information technology, but the fact that he made it, suggesting a clear change in media policy and the direction Singapore media should go. The challenge ahead is the management of the process of liberalization, striking a balance between change and stability. This is as true of Singapore as of many other Asian countries.

7. MAIN ISSUES

One issue that Singapore and most other countries in the region face is the shortage of trained and experienced media personnel. Trained personnel are highly mobile, and talent often crosses borders. In Singapore's case, training of media personnel has so far been targeted at the entry level and in technical positions, while foreign expertise has been relied on to fill the managerial and creative positions. This dependency may continue for several years before local talent emerges to take the lead in the broadcasting industry, particularly in production and content creation. Measures to expedite the process through intraregional training courses are necessary. Singapore is positioned to offer such training through the School of Communication Studies at Nanyang Technological University and the Asian Media Information and Communication Center.

A major issue that Singapore will need to resolve is the tension between the tight regulation of the media, on the one hand, and the desire to be the media hub of Southeast Asia, to be an intelligent island, and to have a creative citizenry, on the other. Freedom House (Sussman, 1999) placed Singapore in the "not free" category of press restriction with a score of 66 out of 100—identical with Malaysia's 66 and higher than Indonesia's 53. This score is based on four criteria:

- laws and regulations that influence media content (on which Singapore scored 13 out of 15 each for the print and broadcast media);
- political pressures and controls on media content (on which Singapore scored 8 for broadcast and 10 for print, each out of a maximum of 15);
- economic influences over media content (on which Singapore scored 7 for broadcast and 15 for print, each out of a maximum of 15 each); and
- repressive actions (on which Singapore scored zero out of 5 each for the two media).

In March 1999, the Television Corporation of Singapore established a news channel to cover Asia. Censorship would have the effect of weakening the credibility of the new channel. As Yeo and Mahizhnan (1998) have argued, censorship and other similar forms of media regulation are ultimately incompatible with the kind of society that Singapore wants to develop: well-informed, cultured, and sophisticated. It is hard to envisage an "Intelligent Island" emerging from such controls.

A related tension is that between media control and commitment to free market economics. As Gunaratne (see Overview) points out, the World Economic Forum ranked Singapore (first) and Hong Kong (second) at the top in global competitiveness, both in 1997 and 1998, based on eight criteria: openness, government, finance, technology, infrastructure, management, labor, and institutions. Yet, in the Information Age, information companies in Singapore are concentrated and monopolistic, if not outright monopolies. Although the media monopolies in Singapore are well run, an issue debated internationally is whether economic efficiency is sufficient for a country. That is, can Singapore continue to thrive in the Information Age with concentrated albeit efficient media companies?

Lee Kuan Yew's 1998 landmark statement that censorship might be a futile exercise in the Information Age suggests another one of the regular reviews of the press law (Nair, 1989). Such a review could augur changes not just in the law but also in the structure of the Singapore media. The past decade has displayed a process of slow but sure liberalization of the media. We expect the process to continue and indeed accelerate in media structure, practice and laws, as Singapore enters the 21st century.

8. STATISTICS

General Profile

Exchange rate (1999 average)	US$ 1 = SS$ 1.69
Population (mid-1999)	3.5 million
male	1.76 million
female	1.77 million
Population density (1999)	5,660 per sq km
Population growth rate	1.2%
Urban population	100%
Life expectancy	78.8 years
male	75.8 years
female	82.1 years
Infant mortality	3.84 per 1000
	(live births)
Geographical size	647.80 sq km
Educational (1997)	
Primary	196 institutions; 261,648 students
Secondary	147 institutions; 181,548 students
Pre University	14 institutions; 22,114 students
University/Polytechnic	6 institutions; 83,914 students

Source: SDS, 1999 [On-line] Available: (http://www.singstat.gov.sg/FACT/SIF/sif1.html), (h⁺tp: //www.singstat.gov.sg/FACT/KEYIND/keyind.html); US Census Bureau, 1999; OANDA Historical Currency Table [On-line]. Available: (http://www.oanda.com/converter/ cc_table?lang=en).

Table 1
Daily Newspaper Circulation

Year	Total	English (%)	Chinese (%)	Malay (%)	Tamil (%)
1982	657,340	44.0	49.7	5.2	1.1
1983	694,711	43.4	50.6	5.1	1.0
1984	709,383	43.3	50.4	5.3	1.0
1985	713,866	43.2	50.3	5.6	0.9
1986	684,298	41.2	51.9	6.1	0.8
1987	700,927	41.8	51.5	6.0	0.8
1988	743,334	45.8	47.7	5.7	0.8
1989	777,052	46.7	47.1	5.5	0.7
1990	813,484	47.4	46.5	5.5	0.6
1991	877,523	48.2	45.7	5.5	0.6
1992	916,102	48.9	44.8	5.8	0.5
1993	977,846	49.2	44.4	5.9	0.5
1994	1,029,043	49.9	43.8	5.8	0.5
1995*	1,050,000	49.6	43.9	5.9	0.6
1996*	1,060,000	49.4	43.9	6.0	0.7
1997	1,087,551	49.1	43.9	6.2	0.8

Source: SDS, various years; Goonasekera & Holaday, 1998.
Note: * Estimated

Table 2
Daily Newspapers and their Sunday Editions

Newspaper	Year established	Frequency	Language	Circ'n	Per 1,000 population
The Straits Times	1845	Daily a.m.	English	369,773 (390,000)	123.81
Lianhe Zaobao	1983	Daily a.m.	Chinese	202,063 (201,000)	67.65
Lianhe Wanbao	1983	Daily p.m.	Chinese	129,715 (135,000)	43.43
Shin Min Daily	1967	Daily p.m.	Chinese	112,497 (118,000)	37.66
The New Paper	1988	Daily p.m.	English	107,080 (111,000)	35.85
Berita Minggu	1960	Sunday	Malay	67,377	22.56
Berita Harian	1957	Daily a.m.	Malay	56,438 (60,000)	18.89
Business Times	1976	Daily a.m.	English	34,446 (32,000)	11.53
Tamil Murasu	1935	Daily a.m.	Tamil	8,162 (9,000)	2.73

Source: Goonasekera & Holaday, 1998, p. 164; SRS Media Index circulation data for 1998 appear in parentheses (WAN, 1999).

Table 3
Advertising Share by Medium, 1997

Medium	S$ (M)	US$ (M)	Growth %	Share %
Newspapers	647.4 (50.8%)	397.2	12.1	50.8
Television	440.1 (34.5%)	270.0	16.1	34.5
Magazines	64.4 (5.1%)	39.5	−5.8	5.0
Radio	62.7 (4.9%)	38.5	−3.5	4.9
Cinema	15.1 (1.2%)	9.3	4.8	1.2
Rediffusion	1.6 (0.1%)	1.0	23.8	0.1
Bus-back/Taxi-top	18.4 (1.4%)	11.3	35.3	1.4
Posters	25.5 (2%)	15.6	18.1	2.0
Total	**1,275.3** (100%)	**782.9**		**100.0**

Source: ACNielsen quoted in *Asian Advertising & Marketing*, March 20, 1998.

Table 4
Television Audience Share

Television channel	Market share (%)
TCS Channel 5 (English)	20.7–24.8
TCS Channel 8 (Chinese)	56.7–59.6
TV Prime 12 (Malay and Indian)	4.3–5.7
TV Premiere 12	1.5–7.6

Source: Goonasekera & Holaday, 1998, p. 166.

Table 5
Television/Cable TV

TV licenses issued	668,671* (89% of households)
Cable Vision subscribers	104,027** (14% of households)

Source: * Goonasekera & Holaday, 1998, p. 166; ** SDS.

Table 6
Cinema Attendance (1998)

Cinema capacity and attendance	Number
Cinema halls	133
Cinema capacity	46,000
Cinema attendance	16,397,000

Source: SDS, 1998 [On-line]. Available: (http://www.singstat.gov.sg/FACT) (Accessed October 5, 1999).

Table 7
Telecommunications Facts

(May 1999)	
Telephone subscribers	1,791,000
Mobile phone subscribers	1,139,600
Pager subscribers (as in May 1999)	1,275,500

Source: TAS, 1999 [On-line]. Available: (http://www.tas.gov.sg/website/home.nsf/html/indexWhatsNew) (Accessed July 15, 1999).

Table 8
Number of Dial-up Subscribers

ISP	Established	Subscribers
SingNet	1994	140,000
Pacific Internet	1995	100,000
Cyberway	1995	50,000
Internet subscribers (May 1999)		441,900

Source: The Straits Times Interactive, June 29, 1998; TAS, 1999 [On-line]. Available: (http://www.tas.gov.sg/website/home.nsf/html/indexWhatsNew).

9. USEFUL ADDRESSES

Singapore Broadcasting Authority
1 Maritime Square, #09-59 (Lobby B) World Trade Center
Telok Blangah Road
Singapore 099253.
Telephone: (65) 270-8191
Fax: (65) 276-2238
URL: http://www.sba.gov.sg

The Straits Times/Sunday Times
390 Kim Seng Road, Times House
Singapore 239495.
Telephone: (65) 737-0011
Fax: (65) 732-0131
E-mail: straits@cyberway.com.sg
URL: http://straitstimes.asia1.com

The Business Times
390 Kim Seng Road, Times House
Singapore 239495
Telephone: (65) 737-0011
Fax: (65) 733-5271
E-mail: biztimes@asia1.co.sg
URL: http://biztimes.asia1.com

The New Paper
390 Kim Seng Road, Times House
Singapore 239495
Telephone: (65) 737-0011
Fax: (65) 737-5375
E-mail: tnp@asia1.com.sg
URL: http://web3.asia1.com.sg/tnp

Lianhe Zaobao
82 Genting Lane, News Center Level 3
Singapore 349567
Telephone: (65) 743-8800
Fax: (65) 748-2652
E-mail: zaobao@cyberway.com.sg
URL: http://www.asia1.com.sg/zaobao

Lianhe Wanbao
82 Genting Lane, News Center Level 3
Singapore 349567
Telephone: (65) 743-8800
Fax: (65) 743-2437

Shin Min Daily News
82 Genting Lane, New Center Level 2
Singapore 349567

Telephone: (65) 743-8800
Fax: (65) 747-6827
E-mail: shinmin@cyberway.com.sg

Berita Harian/Berita Minggu
390 Kim Seng Road, Times House
Singapore 239495
Telephone: (65) 737-0011
Fax: (65) 235-5402
E-mail: bharian@cyberway.com.sg
URL: http://web3.asia1.com.sg/cyBerita

Tamil Murasu
161 Kampong Ampat #05-03, Goldlion Building
Singapore 368329
Telephone: (65) 284-0076
Fax: (65) 284-2737

Television Corporation Singapore (TCS)
Caldecott Broadcast Center, Andrew Road
Singapore 299939
Telephone: (65) 256-0401
Fax: (65) 253-8808
URL: http://www.mediacity.com.sg

Radio Corporation Singapore (RCS)
Caldecott Broadcast Center, Andrew Road
Singapore 299939
Telephone: (65) 251-8622
Fax: (65) 254-8393
E-mail: Radio@mediacity.com.sg
URL: http://www.rcs.com.sg

Television Twelve Pte Ltd
12 Prince Edward Rd, #05-00, Bestway Building
Singapore 079212
Telephone: (65) 225-8133
Fax: (65) 225-7380
URL: http://www.tv12.com.sg

Singapore Cablevision Pte Ltd
2D Ayer Rajah Crescent, AOS Building
Singapore 139938
Telephone: (65) 773-5088
URL: http://www.scv.com.sg

Radio Singapore International (RSI)
1st Floor Annex Building, Caldecott Broadcast Center
Andrew Road, Singapore 299939
Telephone: (65) 353-5300
Fax: (65) 259-1380
E-mail: rsi@mediacity.com.sg
URL: http://rsi.com.sg

NTUC Voice
510 SLF Building, #B1-02
Thomson Road, Singapore 298135
Telephone: (65) 353-6100
Fax: (65) 353-6864

Rediffusion (S) Pte Ltd
6 Harper Road, #04-01/08, Leong Huat Building
Singapore 369674
Telephone: (65) 383-2633
Fax: (65) 383-2622
E-mail: rediprog@pacific.net.sg
URL: http://www.rediffusion.com.sg

SAFRA Radio
Tower B #12-04, Depot Road, Defence Technology Towers
Singapore 109676
Telephone: (65) 373-1917
Fax: (65) 373-1918
URL: http://power98.com.sg

SingNet
Singapore Telecommunications Ltd
20 Pickering St., #32-00 Picketing Operations Complex
Singapore 048658
Telephone: (65) 537-1800
Fax: (65) 535-8191
E-mail: help@singnet.com.sg
URL: http://www.singnet.com.sg

Pacific Internet
89 Science Park Drive, #04-09/12 The Rutherford
Singapore Science Park, Singapore 118261
Telephone: (65) 872-5055
Fax: (65) 872-6347
E-mail: help@pacific.net.sg
URL: http://www.pacific.net.sg

Cyberway Internet
82 Genting Lane, Singapore 349567
Telephone: (65) 843-4800
Fax: (65) 841-6153
E-mail: help@cyberway.com.sg
URL: http://www.cyberway.com.sg

10. REFERENCES

Ang, P. H., & Yeo, T. M. (Comps.). (1998). *Mass media laws and regulations in Singapore.* Singapore: AMIC.
APT (Asia-Pacific Telecommunity). (1998). *The APT yearbook.* Bangkok: APT.
Chen, K. (1996). *Staying on air: Rediffusion's survival in a competitive industry.* Honors thesis, National University of Singapore, Singapore.

Chen, M.H. (1967). *The early Chinese newspapers of Singapore, 1881–1912.* Singapore: University of Malaya Press.

Chew E.C.T., & Lee, E. (Eds.). (1991). *A history of Singapore.* Singapore: Oxford University Press.

Chua, L. H. (1998). Singapore. In A. Latif (Ed.), *Walking the tightrope: Press freedom and professional standards in Asia* (pp. 142–155). Singapore: AMIC.

George, C. (1993). Inside Singapore's successful, self-satisfied and sometimes smug establishment press. In J. Vanden Heuvel & E. Dennis, *The unfolding lotus: East Asia's changing media.* (pp. 132–136). New York: Media Studies Center.

Goonasekera, A., & Holaday, D. (Eds.). (1998). *The Asian communication handbook.* Singapore: AMIC.

Hoong, J. (1998, November 26). *Comment on the presentation of Ang Peng Hwa.* Presentation at ASEAN-COCI Conference on ASEAN Information Highway Infrastructure, Singapore.

Hukill, M. (1996). Structures of television in Singapore. In D. French and M. Richards, (Eds.), *Contemporary television: Eastern perspectives.* New Delhi: Sage Publications.

ITU. (International Telecommunication Union). (1998). *World telecommunication development Report.* Geneva: ITU.

Katz, E., & Wedell, G. (with M. Pilsworth and D. Shinar). (1978). *Broadcasting in the Third World: Promise and performance.* London: MacMillan.

Kuo, E. (1994, July 11–15). *Balancing credibility and accountability: Media and political liberalization in Singapore.* Paper presented at the 44th ICA Annual Meeting, Sydney.

Kuo, E. (in press). Mass media and management of ethnic relations: The case of Singapore. In Y. Ito & A. Goonasekera (Eds.), *Ethnicity in the global village: Mass media and cultural identity in Asia.* London: Pluto Press.

Lee, K.Y. (1998). *The Singapore story: Memoirs of Lee Kuan Yew.* Singapore: Singapore Press Holdings.

Lent, J. A. (1982). Singapore. In J.A. Lent (Ed.), *Newspapers in Asia: Contemporary trends and problems.* Hong Kong: Heinemann Asia.

Lim, I. (1996). Media monitors in Singapore. In K.S. Venkateswaran (Comp.), *Media monitors in Asia* (pp. 73–80). Singapore: AMIC.

Lim, J. (1986, June). *Media laws and regulations in Singapore.* Paper presented at the AMIC Seminar on Media Laws and Regulations in Asia, Singapore.

Lombardo, H. (1999, March 5). *Singapore invests heavily in e-commerce & broadband* [On-line]. Available: (http://www.internetnews.com).

Low, L., & Kuo, E. (1999). Towards an information society in a developed nation. In L. Low, (Ed.), *Singapore: Towards a developed state* (pp. 37–65). Singapore: Oxford University Press and The Center for Advanced Studies, National University of Singapore.

Lum, S., & Khoo, J. (1998). *A study into the distribution network of print media in Singapore.* Final-year thesis, School of Communication Studies, Nanyang Technological University, Singapore.

Mah, B. T. (1998, November 15). *Speech by Singapore's Minister for Communications at COMDEX International Marketing Forum,* COMDEX Fall '98, Las Vegas [On-line]. Available: (http://www.gov.sg/mita/sgnews/samplespeech/communications%20&%20IT.htm [15 July 1999]).

Nair, B. (1989). Singapore. In A. Mehra (Ed.), *Press systems in ASEAN states* (pp. 85–90). Singapore: AMIC.

Ng, C. K. (1999, June 17). *The regulatory framework in Singapore: Year 2000 and beyond.* Speech given at 7th Asian Multimedia Forum Plenary Meeting, Singapore [On-line]. Available: (http://www.tas.gov.sg/website/WEBTAS.nsf/b7c826d6c0a1f372c8256632003ceb30/0ba6dd355a526f584825679e00159162?OpenDocument [15 July 1999]).

Ow, C.II. (1979). Broadcasting in Singapore. In *People's action party 1954–1979* (pp. 134–145). Singapore: Central Committee, People's Action Party.

Seow, F.T. (1998). *The media enthralled: Singapore revisited.* Boulder, CO: Lynne Rienner Publishers.

Singapore. (1997). *Media guide*. Singapore: Ministry of Information and the Arts.

Singapore. (1998). *Arts, cultural & media scenes in Singapore*. Singapore: Ministry of Information and the Arts.

SBA (Singapore Broadcasting Authority). (Various years). *Annual report*. Singapore: SBA [On-line]. Available: (http://www.sba.gov.sg/).

SDS (Singapore, Department of Statistics). (Various years). *Yearbook of statistics, Singapore*. Singapore: Ministry of Trade and Industry.

SDS (Singapore, Department of Statistics). (1997a). *Statistics Singapore: Top-line indicators* [On-line]. Available: (http://www.singstat.gov.sg/FACT/SIF/sif1.html [1998, October 30]).

SDS (Singapore, Department of Statistics). (1997b). *Statistics Singapore: National income* [On-line]. Available: (http://www.singstat.gov.sg/FACT/SIF/sif5.html [1998, October 30]).

Singapore InfoMap. (1998). *Population profile* [On-line]. Available: (http://www.sg/flavour/profile/pro-people2.html [December 12]).

Singapore Telecom. (1999, January 27). *Singapore Telecom reduces ISDN rates by up to 44% and expects to increase penetration by 300%* [On-line]. Available: (http://www.singtel.com.sg/news_releases/1999/jan/news_1999_jan27.htm [July 15, 1999]).

SPH. (Singapore Press Holdings). (1993). *1923–1993, Our 70 years: History of leading Chinese newspapers in Singapore*. Singapore: Chinese Newspapers Division, Singapore Press Holdings Ltd.

SPH cheers investors. (1998, July/August 6). *Asian Newspaper Focus*, 5.

Sussman, L.R. (1999). *Press freedom 1999: News of the century*. New York: The Freedom House.

Tan, P.S. (1971). Malaysia and Singapore. In J.A. Lent (Ed.), *The Asian newspapers' reluctant revolution* (pp. 179–190). Ames, IA: Iowa State University Press.

Tan, Y. S., & Soh, Y. P. (1994). *The development of Singapore's modern media industry*. Singapore: Times Academic Press.

TAS (Telecommunication Authority of Singapore). (1998). *Annual report* [On-line]. Available: (http://www.tas.gov.sg).

TAS (Telecommunication Authority of Singapore). (1999). *Industry statistics* [On-line] Available: (http://www.tas.gov.sg/website/home.nsf/html/indexWhatsNew [July 15]).

Turnbull, C. M. (1995). *Dateline Singapore: 150 years of The Straits Times*. Singapore: Singapore Press Holdings.

Vanden Heuvel, J., & Dennis, E. (1993). *The unfolding lotus: East Asia's changing media*. New York: Media Studies Center.

Wong, K. (1999). *Media and culture in Singapore: A theory of controlled commodification*. Cresskill, NJ: Hampton Press.

Wong, S. C., & Lian, F. S. (1978). Singapore. In J.A. Lent (Ed.), *Broadcasting in Asia and the Pacific: A continental survey of radio and television* (pp. 155–162). Hong Kong: Heinemann Asia.

WAN (World Association of Newspapers). (1999). *World press trends*. Paris: WAN.

World factbook. (1999). Washington, DC: CIA [On-line]. Available: (http://www.odci.gov/cia/publications/factbook/sn.html).

Yeo, S.S.C., & Mahizhnan, A. (1998). Developing an intelligent island: Dilemmas of censorship. In M. Arun, & T.Y. Lee (Eds.), *Singapore: Re-engineering success* (pp. 138–149). Singapore: The Institute of Policy Studies.

◆

16

THAILAND

Daradirek Ekachai

1. NATIONAL PROFILE

1.1 Geography

Approximately the size of France, Thailand has a land area of 513,115 sq km. Located between the Andaman Sea and the Gulf of Thailand, it shares a 1,800 km border with Myanmar to the northwest, a 1,754 km border with Laos to the north and east, an 803 km border with Cambodia to the southeast, and a 506 km border with Malaysia to the south. It has a coastline of 3,219 km. The country has a tropical climate: rainy, warm, and cloudy during the southwest monsoon (mid-May to September); and dry and cool during the northeast monsoon (November to mid-March). The southern isthmus is always hot and humid. The Khorat Plateau lies to the east. The terrain comprises a central plain with mountains elsewhere. The highest point is the 2,576-meter Doi Inthanon. About 34 percent of the land is arable (*World factbook*, 1999).

1.2 People

About 10 percent of Thailand's 60.6 million people live in Bangkok, the capital. Ethnically, 75 percent of the people are Thai, and 14 percent are Chinese, while others make up the remaining 11 percent. According to 1991 data, Buddhists make up 95 percent, Muslims 3.8 percent, Christians 0.5 percent, and Hindus 0.1 percent, while others comprise 0.6 percent (*World factbook*, 1999). The Chinese and the Indians, who operate large and small commercial enterprises, account for nearly 10 percent of Bangkok's population. Thai is the national language, and English is widely understood in urban areas. The literacy rate is 94.1 percent, urban population 36 percent, and life expectancy 69 years (*Asiaweek*, December 17, 1999; UNDP, 1999).

Acknowledgments: The author wishes to express her sincere gratitude and appreciation to Professor Shelton A. Gunaratne who made significant contributions to this chapter.

Thailand—the kingdom of Siam until 1939—was an absolute monarchy for about 700 years after it was first established as a kingdom at Sukhothai in 1238. According to archaeological evidence, the Thai had established small states called *Lanna* and *Phayao* in the north by the early 1200s before the establishment of the kingdom. The creation of the Thai alphabet and the appearance of the first truly Thai elements of fine art and architecture occurred during the period of the Sukhothai kingdom, which declined during the 1300s and eventually became a vassal state of the young Ayutthaya kingdom.

During the next four centuries, Ayutthaya became a major power in Southeast Asia. Its ideal location as a commercial port and its richness in natural resources attracted numerous outsiders, including the Portuguese, the Dutch, the Spanish, the English, the French, the Arabs, the Chinese, and the Japanese. Ayutthaya remained the Thai capital until 1767, when the Burmese invaded and burned it. In 1782, the Thai found a new kingdom under the present Chakri dynasty's first king, who established a new capital south of Ayutthaya in the district of Bangkok (village of wild plums). Although Krungthep (city of angels) was the actual name of the city, Westerners preferred the name Bangkok (Warren & Invernizzi, 1994; National Identity Office, 1996).

1.3 Government and Politics

Thailand was an absolute monarchy until June 24, 1932, when a group of European-educated government officials staged a bloodless coup that set up a constitutional monarchy. Although Thailand has no colonial heritage, ever since the abolition of the absolute monarchy it has had a history of military coups and dictatorships: 22 prime ministers, 10 successful military coups (the latest in 1991), and 16 constitutions. Bhumibol Adulyadej, the ninth king of the Chakri dynasty, is the current monarch. He exercises legislative power through a bicameral National Assembly (*Rathasapha*), executive power through a cabinet headed by a prime minister, and judicial power through the courts. The *Rathasapha* consists of the Senate (*Wuthisapha*)—a 270-member appointed body, with members serving six-year terms—and the House of Representatives (*Sapha Phuthaen Ratsadon*)—a 393-member body with members elected by popular vote to serve four-year terms (*World factbook*, 1999). The current constitution, promulgated in October 1997, is called the "People's Constitution" because a special assembly elected from the grassroots drafted it to achieve thorough political reform (Rachawadi, 1998).

Since the downfall of the military-backed government in 1992, there have been four national multi-party elections. The much-revered King Bhumiphol continues to maintain strong informal influence, and he has never used his constitutionally mandated power to veto legislation or dissolve the elected House of Representatives. A coalition government, led by Prime Minister Chuan Leekpai's Democrat Party, was formed in November 1997, after the resignation of soldier-turned-politician Gen. Chavalit Yongchaiyudh.

1.4 Economy

Thailand's gross domestic product at purchasing power parity (GDP) stood at US$ 368 billion in 1999 with a corresponding per capita GDP of US$ 6,020. The nominal per capita GNP was US$ 1,850. The GDP showed a growth rate of 9 percent since the country began emerging from the 1997–98 recession. Thailand exported US$ 54.4 billion worth of merchandise during the year and had reserves of US$ 33.9 billion, excluding gold (*Asiaweek*, February 4, 2000). The main exports—manufactures (82 percent), and agricultural products and fisheries (14 percent)—went to the United States, Japan, Singapore, Hong Kong, Malaysia, and the United Kingdom. The main imports—capital goods (50 percent), consumer goods (10.2 percent), and fuels (8.7 percent)—came from Japan, the United States, Singapore, Taiwan, Germany, and Malaysia (*World factbook*, 1999).

2. DEVELOPMENT OF PRESS AND BROADCASTING

2.1 Brief Early History[1]

The "Thai moveable-metal type," the forerunner of the modern printing press, was first created in Burma (Myanmar) in 1816 and was not brought into Thailand until some 20 years later (Padmatin, 1970). Ann Judson, the wife of an American missionary, had been in Rangoon visiting Thai hostages who taught her the Thai language. She designed the Thai movable-metal type; and, with the cooperation of George H. Hough, the printer of the Baptist mission, used her invention to spread Christianity among the Thai hostages.

The Baptist mission moved the press to Calcutta in 1826. Captain James Low, a British soldier who learned the Thai language in Bangkok in the reign of King Rama II, printed the first Thai book, *A Grammar of Thai or Siamese Language*, in 1828. The London Missionary Society, which later established the Thai movable-metal type press in Singapore, sold the press to the American Board of Commissioners for Foreign Missions in 1832. When Dr Dan Beach Bradley, an American medical missionary, assumed his position in Bangkok in 1835, he moved the Thai printing press to Thailand. This press printed 9,000 handbills of the royal proclamation banning opium smoking and trade in 1839 (Teeravanich, 1977).

Bradley began publishing Thailand's first newspaper, *The Bangkok Recorder*, on July 4, 1844, during the reign of King Rama III (Teeravanich, 1983). The eight-page monthly lasted only a year because of low sales, and Bradley had to return to the United States with his three sons after his wife's death (Teeravanich, 1977). He returned to Thailand in 1850 and resurrected the paper as a fortnightly in 1864. But this venture also folded after two years because of various pressures, including the kingdom's first libel suit. The kingdom's second newspaper was

[1] Boonyaketmala, 1982; Chirasopone, 1989; Mitchell, 1971; and Muntarbhorn, 1998; among others, have sketched the early history of the press in Thailand.

Bangkok Calendar, published by Dr J.H. Chandler from 1847–50 (Teeravanich, 1977). Another newspaper, the *Siam Weekly Monitor*, appeared on May 22, 1867, but closed in September 1868 (Mitchell, 1971). The first government newspaper was the short-lived *Rajakijjanubeksa* (Royal Gazette), which came out in 1858 in the reign of the King Mongkut (Rama IV, 1851–68). It was revived as a government weekly in 1874 (Padmatin, 1984). Seven newspapers, mostly in English, appeared during this period (Teeravanich, 1977).

Samuel John Smith, a missionary, published the first daily in Thailand, the English-language *Bangkok Daily Advertiser*, in 1868—a single-sheet paper that printed shipping announcements and advertisements. Later, it expanded to four pages and carried obituaries, as well as news about foreign visitors. It folded after 10 years (Teeravanich, 1977). In 1869, Smith also started the English-language *Siam Weekly Advertiser* and the trimonthly *Siam Repository*, in which he wrote about the freedom of religion and of the press and about women's rights.

During this formative period, the press was foreign-owned, and its readership was confined to a few hundred people—foreigners, the Thai Royal Family, high-ranking government officials, and well-educated people (Padmatin, 1984). An exclusive group of Thai, most of whom were young members of the royal family who had been educated abroad, owned and edited the Thai press until well into the reign of King Chulalongkorn (Rama V, 1868–1910). The weekly *Darunnowat* (Instruction for Youngsters), which appeared in 1874 but failed to last out the year, contained government news, foreign news, academic articles, entertainment, and advertisements. Its readership was still confined to the court circle, and journalism was no more than a hobby of a few young members of the royal family. Other newspapers included the *Daily Court* (Thai, 1875–76), the daily *Siam Observer* (English, 1893–1932), the daily *China-Siam Varasup* (Chinese, 1907–30), and the daily *Thai* (Thai, 1908–32).

Several factors contributed to a greater interest in newspaper publishing and consumption during the Chulalongkorn era: higher literacy and education among commoners; increased trade with foreign countries that required trade news; and change in the political climate that sparked greater interest in the Western concept of free expression. People had become more enthusiastic about expressing their ideas and opinion in newspapers (Padmatin, 1984). Some 59 publications, including five dailies in Thai, Chinese, and English, appeared during this era.

Oddly enough, a Western observer (Mitchell, 1971) has commented that the Thai "press was freest under the absolute monarchy" (p. 215). The Golden Age of Thai Journalism came during the absolute monarchy of King Vajiravudh (Rama VI, 1910–25), when the press enjoyed much freedom. Even though the Newspaper Act of 1919 imposed the first formal censorship, its application was mild (Chirasopone, 1989; Mitchell, 1971). The king reached his people, especially through the opinion columns of the daily *Thai*. To show what a good newspaper should be, he founded the *Dusitsmit* in Dusit Thani (Dusit City), the model municipal city that he created (Teeravanich, 1977, p. 79). The press became a popular forum where writers and journalists expressed their political views freely. Some even went as far as to make personal attacks on the king. During this period, 22 new dailies and 127 periodicals appeared. However, many interest groups used the press as a propaganda tool, as was the case during World War I, when newspapers became propaganda mouthpieces. Because the press became so sensational and irresponsible, the king acted to define the rights, duties, and scope of publishing establishments with the promulgation of the 1992 Documents and Newspapers Law, which required every publication to obtain a permit before release (Padmatin, 1984; Teeravanich, 1977).

Some 60 daily newspapers and 160 periodicals appeared during the absolute reign of King Prachadhipok (Rama VII, 1925–32). As democracy was spreading throughout the Western world, the king recognized the importance of freedom of expression and the foundation of democracy for the Thai. But the Khana Rassadawn (People's Party) coup d'etat of June 24, 1932, ended the absolute monarchy and halted press freedom. The authorities closed down several newspapers and arrested many journalists. Ironically, the "democratic" regime enacted more press laws and restrictions than the absolute monarchy. The new Press Act of 1934 formalized censorship and prohibited publication of news from unapproved sources (Mitchell, 1971). It required editors to have an educational level no lower than high school. Some 30 newspapers closed down because of shortage of paper. The Press Act of 1941, under Prime Minister Pibul Songkram, imposed stiff restrictions and gave the interior minister wide powers of censorship (Mitchell, 1971). The law, however, allowed newspapers to be established legally, except for those in a foreign language, merely by informing the authorities (Padmatin, 1984; Pickerell, 1960).

2.2 Developments since 1945

2.2.1 The Press

Field Marshal Pibul Songkram, in his second stint as prime minister, allowed more press freedom. The press ignored the Press Act of 1941 (as amended in 1942 and 1945), which the government did not abolish. The press, at times, used its freedom with extreme irresponsibility until October 20, 1958, when Field Marshal Sarit Thanarat ousted Pibul Songkram. The "Dark Age of Thai Journalism" came with Sarit who declared martial law, suspended the constitution, and imposed press controls (Chirasopone, 1989). He closed down 14 newspapers for allegedly engaging in subversive activities and excessive criticism of his Revolutionary Party. The authorities arrested hundreds of opposition politicians and journalists for alleged communist involvement (Mitchell, 1971; Phayakvichien, 1971). Eleven dailies—five Thai, two English, and four Chinese—continued to appear (Lapira-tanakul, 1984). Seven laws and announcements, including Article 17 of the 1959 Constitution, empowered the prime minister to issue orders to repress or suppress actions that jeopardized national security or the throne (Mitchell, 1971). After Sarit's death in late 1963, his successor Field Marshal Thanom Kittikachorn continued the military dictatorship until the Student Revolution of October 14, 1973, which overthrew Thanom's nine-year government (Boonyaketmala, 1982).

The press celebrated the return to a free and rather chaotic publishing scene (Markham, 1974). Sanya Dhammasak, the first civilian prime minister since 1956, asked leading editors to tell him "what people wanted" and announced that he would resign if the press so desired (Lent, 1977). For the next three years, the Thai press enjoyed full freedom but, just as during the absolute monarchy period, it again misused its privileges, ignored its social responsibility, and engaged in sensationalism and personal muckraking. *Dao Siam*, *Thai Rath*, and *Daily News*, for instance, regularly published obscene columns and pictures. They used misleading headlines, doctored photographs, and failed to check "facts" (Markham, 1974). Columnists and journalists allegedly accepted bribes and blackmailed businesspeople (Lent, 1977). Press freedom had degenerated into corruption within the industry. What began with free meals and white envelopes stuffed with cash had grown into more sophisticated forms of ethical violation—acceptance of free merchandise and stocks and trips around the country and abroad. Changyai (1996), *Matichon*'s senior news editor, has exposed the darker side of Thai journalism. He has traced corruption among journalists to the post-World War II period. In the 1960s and the early 1970s, high-ranking military men began courting favors from newsmen. As the economy expanded, more and more entrepreneurs, politicians, and civil servants also began bribing journalists to get favorable publicity. Those with something to hide also paid to keep their misdeeds hidden.

The spree of irresponsible journalism ended on October 6, 1976, when the military seized power in a bloody coup. Decree 42, issued by the military, allowed the government to close down the press and to mandate the licensing of printers, publishers, editors, and newspaper owners (Vanden Heuvel & Dennis, 1993). In 1988, Chatichai Choonhavan of the Chart Thai Party formed the first democratically elected government after the 1976 coup. However, rampant corruption caused the military leadership to topple Chatichai's coalition in a bloodless coup in February 1991. Prime Minister Anand Panyarachun, who sought to liberalize media law, abolished Decree 42 in 1991. His draft Public Information Act failed to get through because of entrenched interests that did not want "a modern democratic legal structure for the media" (Vanden Heuvel & Dennis, 1993, p. 169). Elections in 1992 and 1995 led to weak coalition governments that collapsed over corruption allegations.

The press received credit for toppling the military dictatorship of Gen. Suchinda Kraprayoon after the May 1992 uprising. The *Nation*'s release of photographs showing the police clubbing a protester led to a public pro-democracy demonstration. The coalition government led by veteran politician Chuan Leekpai allowed media criticism of its leadership. The press and broadcast media became more staunchly independent in their coverage, thereby helping to shape the political agenda (Yong, 1995). But press freedom suffered setbacks in 1995 when Prime Minister Banharn Silapa-archa came to power and not only banned a number of critical radio and television talk shows but also increased pressure on newspapers through libel litigation. However, these threats turned out to be blessings in disguise because they forced editors to be more cautious and to adhere more strictly to professional standards (Sricharatchanya, 1998). The November 1996 elections brought to power a coalition led by former army commander Chavalit Yongchaiyudh, under whom Thailand adopted its liberal 1997 Constitution. Street protests during the economic crisis forced Chavalit to step down in November 1997, when veteran politician Chuan Leekpai took over again as prime minister.

2.2.2 Broadcasting

2.2.2.1 Radio: The Royal Thai Navy introduced telegraphic radio from Great Britain into the country in 1907 and set up two radio stations for official use. In 1913, King Rama VI officially opened the first radiotelegraph station in Bangkok and issued the country's first telegraph to his brother, Southern Viceroy Prince Lopburirames, in English. It read, "Greetings to you on this, which will be one of the most important days in our history" (Kitiwat, 1983). The Post and Telegraph Department established a 200-watt radio broadcasting station in 1928 with a 37-meter wavelength. Thailand's first public broadcasting commenced when King Rama VII delivered an inaugural speech to the Thai on February 25, 1930.

After the end of the absolute monarchy in 1932, the new government used radio as the main communication tool to educate the Thai about democracy. Although its initial mission as stated in King Prachadhipok's inaugural speech was to provide commerce, entertainment, and education for tradesmen and commoners, radio rapidly became a state propaganda machine for the government (Siriyuvasak, 1992). The Propaganda Department (later renamed the Public Relations Department [PRD]) founded in 1933, transferred all radio broadcasting away from the Department of Post and Telegraph (Lapiratanakul, 1984; Scandlen, 1978, Siriyuvasak, 1992). Radio Thailand, the official government broadcasting station established in 1941, came under the operation and control of the PRD. After the end of the World War II, various government agencies established more radio stations. Tor Tor Tor was the second state-run radio network established in 1952. Prompted both by economic and political imperatives, radio broadcasting proliferated. Radio stations jumped from 26 in 1959 to 252 in 1982 (Kitiwat, 1983) and to 480 in 1996 (National Identity Office, 1996). In 1997, 13.9 million radio sets were in use (UNESCO, 1999).

Unlike the print media, the government controls and operates the broadcast media (radio and television) as commercial enterprises through long-term leases to private companies. Except for the Ministry of Education and Radio Thailand stations, all other stations are commercial, entertainment-oriented ones, which rely heavily on advertising.

2.2.2.2 Television: Thailand was the first country in continental Asia to start regular television broadcasting. Although some have said that "it was Thai fascination with gimmickry and the traditional value of 'sanook' (fun) that explains the haste"

(Katz & Wedell, 1977, p. 11), others have observed that the Thai government conceived television with a definite political objective. Siriyuvasak (1996a) wrote that Prime Minister Pibul Songkram, who had a deep interest in using mass media for his political and cultural legitimization, conceived television. Legislation created the Thai Television Co. Ltd, a joint public- and private-sector venture, in 1953. It went into operation on June 24, 1955, as Channel 4 in Bangkok. The second TV station, Channel 7 of the Royal Thai Army, commenced in January 1958 as a commercial operation but started receiving a government subsidy since 1963 (Scandlen, 1978). TV broadcasting in its early days covered only the area around Bangkok, offering newscasts and entertainment programs such as drama, music, classical dances, movies, and games. Color transmission began in 1967.

Television in Thailand is a state monopoly often used for patronage. Although the state began to sell privileged franchises to the private sector in 1967, television has remained the main propaganda tool of the government. After the May 1992 political crackdown, during which the broadcast media toed the government line, the public demand for an independent broadcast media has forced the government to loosen its control.

Today, Thailand has six national TV stations, eight regional stations, and two cable stations. The government or the armed forces run five of the six national stations. The Army runs Channel 5 and the Mass Communication Organization of Thailand operates Channel 9. The Bangkok Entertainment Company and the Bangkok Television Company operate Channel 3 and Channel 7 respectively under government license. The PRD operates Channel 11 as an educational station. Independent Television (ITV), the country's first privately owned independent television station, began broadcasting in July 1996, stressing news, interviews and documentaries. Key staffers of ITV came from the English-language daily, the *Nation*. Hope exists for further liberalization of broadcasting.

3. THE PRESS

3.1 Policy and Legal Framework[2]

Muntarbhorn (1998) says, "To trace the history of mass media laws in Thailand is to be a witness to the history of democracy itself in the country" (p. 25). Chuensuksawasdi (1998), editor of *Bangkok Post*, says that even though Thailand did not evolve from a colonial past, the Thai press has experienced its fair share of highs and lows. Indirect government-military intervention and influence were common, especially during the 1960s, and even into the late 1980s. The government had the power to close newspapers indiscriminately for alleged national security reasons. Newspaper editors had to get their backgrounds cleared before they received licenses.

[2] Muntarbhorn, 1998, has compiled the media laws and regulations in Thailand. Also, see Chirasopone, 1989; Salayakanond, 1998; and Siriyuvasak, 1996b.

Assessing the situation in 1997, the Freedom House Survey Team (1998) observed that Thailand's 1997 Constitution ended the power of the authorities to close newspapers. Even though the press criticized government policies and publicized human rights abuses, journalists faced occasional intimidation and exercised self-censorship regarding the military, judiciary, and other sensitive subjects. The law prohibited defaming the monarchy (*lèse majesté*) and restricted freedom of expression in specific areas, such as in advocating a communist government and inciting disturbances. The 1998 US human rights report on Thailand noted the Thai media's common and vigorous criticism of political parties, public figures, and the government. Although the press practiced some self-censorship, especially concerning the monarchy and national security, journalists were generally free to comment on governmental activities without fear of official punishment. Morcover, consistent pressure from the media on the government's chronic corruption had spurred various governmental agencies to implement internal reforms (US Bureau of Democracy, Human Rights and Labor, 1998).

In Southeast Asia, Thailand has matched the level of press freedom in the Philippines (Eng, 1997). The 1999 Freedom House survey ranked both countries equally, with the lowest press restriction score of 30 among the 10 ASEAN countries. On the criterion of laws and regulations that influence media content, Thailand scored 7 for broadcast and 5 for print, each out of a maximum of 15. On political pressures and controls that influence media content, the score was 7 for broadcast and 3 for print, each out of a maximum of 15. On economic influences over media content, the score was 2 for broadcast and 5 for print, each out of a maximum of 15. On repressive actions, the score was zero for broadcast and 1 for print, each out of a maximum of 5 (Sussman, 1999).

Muntarbhorn (1998) points out that the enforcement of the media laws "depends upon the political climate of the day" (p. 4). In Thailand, the legal provisions affecting the print media in particular are the following:

- Constitutional provisions,
- Press Act of 1941 (as amended in 1942 and 1945),
- Copyright Act of 1994,
- Criminal Code of 1956 (as amended in 1992),
- Civil and Commercial Code of 1924,
- Civil Procedure Code of 1934, and
- Other laws and regulations such as the 1928 Suppression of the Dissemination and Trade in Pornographic Materials Act, the 1940 Protection of Official Secrets Act, the 1952 Prevention of Communist Activities Act (as amended in 1969 and 1979), the 1985 National (News) Intelligence Act, and the 1991 Youth and Family Courts Act.

The 1997 Constitution "is a breath of fresh air," Muntarbhorn (1998) says, because it is the most participatory of Thailand's 16 constitutions since 1932 (p. 40). Only five of those constitutions guaranteed the rights and freedom of the press. The 1997 Constitution aimed to promote greater accountability, transparency, and good governance. Its provisions on the mass media went further than those of the 1991 Constitution, which specified the Rights and Liberties of the Thai People in Chapter III and guaranteed freedom of expression. Chapter III of the 1997 Constitution includes the following sections most relevant to the mass media:

- Section 39 states, "Every person has the right to freedom of expression. Only laws enacted to protect "national security and public order or morals" can restrict this right. Section 39 also forbids the government from closing down the mass media; forbids officials from censoring news or articles before publication except, by virtue of the law, in times of war or fighting; prohibits state financial aid for private media; and requires media owners to be Thai nationals.
- Section 41 stipulates that the employees of both the private media and the state-owned media have rights and liberties that neither the state nor media owners can ideologically control.
- Section 58 states, "Every person has the right to receive information and news from government agencies unless their revelation is contrary to national security."
- Section 59 couples the right of access to information from government agencies with the possibility of public inquiries/hearings as permitted by law.

Sections 58 and 59 of the new constitution and the Official Information Act, passed in September 1997, give the public the right to access government or public information records. Thus Thai journalists now have vast opportunities to access official information and improve the quality and accuracy of their reports.

The Press Act of 1941 (as amended in 1942 and 1945) requires a Thai national seeking to become a printer, publisher, editor, or proprietor of a newspaper to notify the police of his or her intention to do so. This law gives broad powers to the authorities to ban publications, censor content, and revoke licenses. Muntarbhorn (1998) asserts, "In the light of the new Constitution, the Act is clearly outdated and needs reform, if not abrogation" (p. 44). A liberal interpretation of the constitutional provisions would mean the authorities would require a court order to censor, ban, or close publications. The Copyright Act of 1994 prevents violations of intellectually property. The law is an improvement on the earlier legislation because it now protects not only literary works but also computer programs. Violations can lead to both civil and criminal proceedings. The Criminal Code (as amended in 1942) requires the print media not to defame others, not to cast aspersions on various national institutions and not to cause unrest. Fair comment and truth, however, are defenses. The Civil and Commercial Code of 1924 stipulates the civil responsibility for defamation; it also pertains to violations of privacy. The Civil Procedure Code of 1934 contains provisions concerning contempt of court. Muntarbhorn (1998) points out that defamation suits in Thailand have become a common phenomenon reflecting at least three trends: claims for high damages against the press; imposition of suspended sentences and fines on editors; and use of the broad criminal law provision of public interest—Section 116 of the Criminal Code—for prosecution of newspapers.

Muntarbhorn (1998) argues that reform and abrogation are most relevant to other laws such as the 1985 National (News) Intelligence Act, which empowers the authorities to monitor news detrimental to national security. He says that the world's concern today has shifted to human security. The 1952 Prevention of Communist Activities Act allows not only censorship of news but also long periods of detention of the accused without trial.

The press has occasionally come under fire for its sensational approaches and its misguided crusading journalism (Yong, 1995). For the first time, the print journalists, whom the public saw as watchdogs of past oppressive regimes, have come under close scrutiny. The tabloids' increasing coverage of scandalous and lurid stories resulted in the call for an independent and self-regulating body to oversee journalistic ethics and to enforce a code of conduct. After 34 years of attempting several times to establish such an organization, publishers and editors of national and provincial newspapers formed the National Press Council on July 4, 1997. A committee headed by Prawase Wasi drafted the council's charter in August 1997. The council comprises 14 representatives from the press and seven intellectuals in various disciplines (*Bangkok Post*, July 5, 1997). Previous attempts by journalists failed because newspapers did not see its importance and the state tried to prevent its creation.

Today, quality newspapers such as *Matichon* and *Bangkok Post* have adopted a policy of rejecting gifts and bribes. The Reporters Association of Thailand has also disapproved the practice followed by companies of giving expensive presents at their thank-you press parties. The Thai press, which still maintains its independent philosophy and practice, has become more critical of the country's political leadership. More and more Thai journalists are demanding greater freedom in their professional work (Thongpao, 1990). The corrupt political and economic system and its deep-rooted practices of patronage and cronyism have come under close scrutiny. Freedom House observed:

> Because the Asian media had failed to warn of the [financial] crisis, the press, parti-
> cularly in Thailand, was regarded as a necessary element in improving the country's
> financial position. Lively political and economic news has become routine fare in
> many newspapers and magazines whose content had traditionally been entertainment
> news and fiction. The papers have also been investigating the social implications of
> the economic crisis. (Sussman, 1999, pp. 31–32)

3.2 Financial Aspects: Circulation, Advertising, Marketing Strategies

From 1997 to 1998, the number of dailies went down from 44 to 33, and the number of magazines from 237 to 216. The number of Thai-language newspapers dropped from 34 to 25, and the number of English-language newspapers from four to three, while the Chinese-language newspapers remained unchanged at six (WAN, 1999).[3] According to the Reporters Association of Thailand, in June 1999,

[3] *World press trends* mentions an estimated daily circulation of 11.7 million (19.4 copies per 100 people) for 1998. This is far above the UNESCO estimates up to 1996. The following newspapers

the country had 25 daily newspapers: 15 in Thai, two in English, five in Chinese, and three in Japanese. Thailand has no independent audit bureau. The total claimed daily circulation was 4.46 million—a penetration of 7.2 per 100 people.[4] Non-dailies included six monthly newsmagazines, 12 biweekly newspapers, and 205 provincial newspapers.

In 1996, Thailand had 30 dailies with a circulation of 3.8 million—a penetration of 6.4 per 100 people (Table 1); and 320 non-dailies with a circulation of 2.5 million—a penetration of 4.3 per 100 people (UNESCO, 1999). In 1998, the daily *Thai Rath* had a circulation of about a million and a readership of 8.9 million. Its nearest competitor was the *Daily News* with a circulation of 750,000 and a readership of 6 million. *Khao Sod* (Fresh News) and *Matichon* each had a circulation of 400,000 with a readership of 1.1 and 1.8 million respectively. While *Phoo Jad Karn Daily* had a circulation of 260,000, *Naew Na, Wattachak, Baan Muang*, and *Siam Keela* each had a circulation of about 200,000 (Deemar Media Index cited in WAN, 1999; also see *Editor & publisher international yearbook*, 1998; and Tasker, 1998).

The *Bangkok Post*, founded in 1946, had a circulation of 65,000—the highest among the English-language dailies. Following it were the *Nation* (54,000), and *Business Day*—begun in January 1992 as a joint venture of Thai Premier Publishing, United Cinema Holding and Management Company of the Crown Property Bureau, and Singapore Press Holdings. The *Bangkok Post*, a member of the London-based Audit Bureau of Circulation, claimed to be the first newspaper in Thailand to audit circulation. It made a net profit of US$ 572,340 (26.9 million baht) in 1997. *Tong Hua Yit Pao* led the Chinese-language newspapers with a circulation of 100,000, followed by *Sirinakorn* (90,000), *Sin Sian Yit Pao* (50,000), and the *Universal Daily News* (40,000) (http://www.thaiadvertising.com).

Successful newspapers, which are generally financially independent, derive about 80 percent of their revenue from advertising. The law prohibits government subsidy of newspapers or foreign ownership (more than 49 percent) of the media. Second to television, which is the most popular medium for advertisers, newspapers topped their advertising revenue in 1992 at US$ 219.4 million or 27 percent of the total advertising expenditures (*The Leo Burnett worldwide advertising and media factbook,* 1994). *Thai Rath*, the daily with the largest circulation, charged the highest, with one full-page black and white advertisement costing US$ 9,048. The economic downturn that began in 1997 affected press income considerably. According to the Thailand Advertising Association (cited in WAN, 1999), the total advertising spending in 1998 was 38 billion baht: 22.4 billion on television, 6.4 billion on newspapers, 4.9 billion on radio, 1.5 billion on magazines, and the remainder on other media (Table 2). Television's share of advertising revenue

---

folded in 1997–98: *Bangkok Post Weekly Review, Financial Day, Hunn Siam Daily, Hunn Thai Weekly, Khoo Khaeng Daily, Luk Sup Siam, Siam Post, Sue Thurakij, Thai Financial, Thailand Times, Thai Thurakij Finance, Tham Sethakis Artit Wikroa,* and *Wattachak Luk Sup.*
[4] Data obtained from personal communications with the Reporters Association of Thailand and Zenith Media Thailand.

increased from 30.5 percent in 1992 to 59 percent in 1998 while the press lost its share from 27 percent in 1992 to 17 percent in 1998 (*The Leo Burnett worldwide advertising and media factbook*, 1994; WAN, 1999).

The economic and financial crisis has clearly hurt the newspaper industry. The devaluation of the Thai baht in July 1997 set off the Asian financial crisis and sent costs skyrocketing. The price of newsprint soared, and advertising revenues declined. More than 3,000 journalists and other media employees have lost their jobs, and 12 out of 25 daily and weekly newspapers have closed. These included the Thai-language *Siam Post*, known for crusading against government scandals, and two English-language dailies—Manager Media Group's *Asia Times*, which folded in June 1997; and Wattachak Group's *Thailand Times*, which folded in September 1997 (Eng, 1998; Schidlovsky, 1999). Several newspapers have downsized. For example, the *Nation*, the English-language daily that defied military censorship during the pro-democracy uprising in 1992, laid off 500 employees, including 120 editorial and production staffers, reduced its number of pages by half, and allowed foreign interests to own up to 49 percent of the company. The *Bangkok Post* closed its bureau in Hanoi, merged or reduce sections of the paper, cut down the editorial staff from 270 to 226, and cut salaries, benefits, and leave time (Schidlovsky, 1999). It also opened itself up to foreign shareholders. The Manager Group, which Sondhi Limthongkul founded in 1983 with a monthly business and economics magazine, came to an abrupt halt, forcing it to close or sell all but three publications.

The *Bangkok Post* (1998) surmised that the print media would remain in difficulty because most advertisers did not plan to increase their advertising budget in 1999. The print media would have to work harder to attract specific groups of readers, to be better segmented, and to attain a larger circulation (http://www.bangkokpost.net/yere/98yre12.html).

3.3 Structure and Organization

The Thai press is predominantly privately owned and has little concentration in ownership. Daily newspapers are concentrated in Bangkok, where at least 65 percent of the adults read a daily, compared with about 10 percent in rural areas (Vanden Heuvel & Dennis, 1993). Almost all of Thailand's 76 provinces have local newspapers.

The Thai Press is mostly owned by media barons and entrepreneurs. The late Kampol Watcharapol, who founded *Thai Rath* in 1962, used his sharp business skills and strong work ethic, to make the paper one of the widely read and most influential in the country. Unlike other media owners, however, the Watcharapol family has not expanded into other media. The *Daily News* belongs to the Hetrakul family. Veteran journalists Kanchai Boonpaan and Pongsak Phayakvichien manage the Matichon Company Ltd, a public company in which they hold the majority stock. The company also owns *Khao Sod* daily and *Matichon Weekly*, as well as Matichon Publishing, which produces several books each year. Prominent journalist Suthichai Yoon heads the Nation Multimedia group, which owns the *Nation*, the group's flagship that has also started an Asian edition; *Krungthep Thurakij* (Bangkok Business); and the *Nation Weekly*. It also has a 10 percent share in Independent Television (ITV), the country's sole independent TV channel (Tasker, 1998–99).

Salayakanond (1998) reported that seven print media groups, which publish dailies and weeklies, have become public companies listed in the Security Exchange of Thailand. The top publishing companies (ranked by total circulation) are the Watcharapol Company, publisher of *Thai Rath*; Si Phraya Publishing Company Ltd, publisher of *Daily News*; Matichon PCL, publisher of *Matichon*; Khao Sod Company Ltd, publisher of *Khao Sod*; the Manager Media Group, publisher of *Phoo Jad Karn Daily*; Naew Na Company, publisher of *Naew Na*; Wattachak Public, publisher of *Wattachak*; Bahn Muan Publishing Company, publisher of *Bahn Muan*; and Siam Sport Syndicate PCL, publisher of *Siam Keela*. The ranks of National Multimedia PCL—publisher of *Krungthep Thurakij*—and Than Settakij Company Ltd, the publisher of *Prachachart Thurakij* went down from the previous year (WAN, 1999).

3.4 Quality and Popular Press

Thailand has a handful of quality Thai-language dailies. *Matichon* had a long reputation as a serious newspaper read by the educated elite. But with increasing competition from other tabloids, the paper has loosened up its coverage, adding more soft news stories to attract a wider audience. Its parent company, the Matichon Company Ltd, established its sister paper *Khao Sod* (Fresh News) to compete with other sensational, popular papers. It has increased its circulation fourfold to 350,000 copies since 1994 with investigative economic reporting, related editorials, and special columns (Tasker, 1998). *Siam Rath* lost its reputation of high-quality coverage and analytical reporting when its owner Kukrit Pramoj died, and the paper was sold to a politician.

Well-educated and influential members of the Thai society read the two English-language dailies, the *Bangkok Post* and the *Nation*, which they regard as more reliable than the Thai dailies. The *Post*'s readers are highly educated (84 percent with university degrees), young (typically between 24 and 44 years of age), and predominantly male (73 percent) (http://www.bangkokpost.net.net/rate/ratecard.html).

Thai Rath and *Daily News* are synonymous with the Thai-language popular press whose hallmarks are their "brash headlines, use of color and unabashedly sensational reporting" (Vanden Heuvel & Dennis, 1993, p. 169). Crime, sex, scandal, and sport are their regular fare, along with summaries of popular television series, semi-nude pictures, and entertainment news reported almost verbatim from press releases. Scandlen and Winkler (1982) reported almost two decades ago that "soft news" published in these two newspapers were "most frequently mentioned in readership surveys as read daily" (p. 333). Today, competition has forced

Thai Rath to report political and economic, news as well (Tasker, 1998). Other popular newspapers include *Naew Na* (Frontline), *Khao Sod*, and *Ban Mueng*.

Mitton (1998) wrote that some of the coverage of the Thai popular press could often shock readers new to Thailand. The popular press portrayed former Thai Prime Minister Chavalit Yongchaiyudh as inept, with headlines suggesting he might be suffering from Alzheimer's disease. The popular press also called the current soft-spoken Prime Minister Chuan Leekpai "effeminate." Some might construe such criticism in the Thai media as thoughtless and destructive, if not outright malicious. However, Vanden Heuvel and Dennis (1993) point out that tabloid journalism is immensely popular among the Thai so much so that "if a paper becomes too serious or too tame, its readers will complain" (p. 167).

3.5 Distribution and Technology

Some Bangkok dailies are considered to be national newspapers because of their countrywide distribution. Many, such as *Thai Rath, Matichon,* and *Daily News,* publish at least two editions each day. Although most dailies are morning papers, one can buy the first edition of the next day's papers in the afternoon. *Thai Rath* has a sophisticated distribution system that gets the 40-page daily—sold at 8 baht (20 US cents)—to the provinces with great speed. Its multimillion-dollar presses were claimed to be able to print 60,000 copies per hour. The *Bangkok Post* has installed a new computer pagination system for the editorial and advertising departments.

Overall, the Thai press outsells newspapers in the other Southeast Asian markets (Vanden Heuvel & Dennis, 1993). Thai-language papers are sold both by subscription and newsstand. Their English-language counterparts rely more on subscription. *Bangkok Post*, for example, sold 78 percent by subscription and 22 percent at newsstands.

4. BROADCASTING

4.1 Policy and Legal Framework

The provisions in Chapter III of the 1997 Constitution (see Section 3.1) relate to the broadcast media as well. Because Section 39 of the Constitution guarantees "the right to freedom of expression," it forbids officials to censor news before its publication, except "in time of war or fighting; but this is only possible by virtue of law." Section 39 also forbids the government "to close down the mass media (the press, radio and television stations)." The inclusion of the broadcast media, controlled by the government (except for ITV) is a refreshing development because previous constitutions only protected the rights of the print media (Khachayudhadej, 1998). Section 40 states: "The frequency bands of radio, television and telecommunications are public resources.... An independent public agency [will] allocate bands and oversee relations with the mass media under the law."

The House of Representatives unanimously passed the Frequencies Allocation and Broadcasting and Telecommunication Supervision Organization Bill (FABTS) on its first reading on April 7, 1999, despite protest from academic and civic groups who contended that the one regulator to be established would still be under government control. The bill requires the appointment of a 15-member national communications resources management commission to allocate radio, television, and telecommunication frequencies and to oversee services in these fields (*Bangkok Post*, April 8, 1999). The legislation must become law within three years of the 1997 Constitution. The law must set up a new, independently run, and publicly supervised body to oversee broadcasting and telecommunications enterprises (*The Nation*, April 22, 1999).

The opponents of the approved bill preferred another version drafted by a panel chaired by Supatra Masdit, a minister in the Office of the Prime Minister. The panel, composed of mass communication experts and media representatives, called for the establishment of two independent regulators: a National Broadcasting Commission to administer radio and television frequencies; and a National Telecommunications Commission to oversee telecommunications services and frequencies. Both would comprise seven commissioners. Public hearings were scheduled to iron out some problematic issues (The *Nation*, April 22, 1999).

The major laws and regulations that currently govern broadcasting in Thailand are:

- The 1955 Broadcasting Act (as amended in 1965, 1978 and 1987),
- the 1955 Radiocommunications Act (as amended in 1961 and 1992),
- the 1987 Act for the Control of Business concerning Tape and Television Material, and
- other legal provisions in Copyright Act, Criminal Code, Civil Code, Consumer Protection Act, and the like.

The Broadcasting Act, which covers cable television as well but does not apply to government channels, gives the state substantial control over the allocation of channels and of program content. It requires private broadcasters to obtain a license from the Public Relations Department, which can revoke the license subject to appeal. Muntarbhorn (1998) argues that the law is antiquated because "it perpetuates a state monopoly" (p. 47). Decree Nos 15 and 17 of 1976, which were revoked in the early 1990s, obliged radio and TV stations to broadcast state news, and imposed strict conditions on program and advertising content. Ministerial Regulation No. 14 of 1994, issued under the Act, allowed for censorship on grounds of public order or good morals. The regulation also set up the National Broadcasting Commission, which replaced the National Broadcasting Executive Board set up in 1974 as a pre-censorship organ to control all aspects of broadcasting (Siriyuvasak, 1996b). FABTS will replace the NBC under the new constitution.

The 1955 Radiocommunications Act covers radiocommunications and related equipment other than radio and TV broadcasting. The 1987 Act for the Control of

Business concerning Tape and Television Material applies to videotapes and the videotape business. Inspecting officials can order the erasure of material that violates the act. The provisions of the criminal and civil codes and other laws (see Section 3.1) also apply to broadcasting in regard to copyright and consumer protection.

4.2 Structure and Organization[5]

4.2.1 Radio

In mid-1999, the nation had 523 radio stations.[6] In 1997, the *Nation* (February 2, 1997) reported the existence of 493 national and local stations, about two-thirds of which belonged to the government's Public Relations Department (109 stations), the Ministry of Defense (128 stations), and the Mass Communications Organization of Thailand (62 stations). The PRD owned and operated 52 AM radio stations, 54 FM radio stations and three shortwave stations. Of the 109 radio stations, 12 were in Bangkok and 97 in the provinces. It also operated 11 AM/FM radio stations for educational purposes—one in Bangkok and the rest in the provinces. Radio stations used their initials to identify themselves. For example, the Air Force stations are identified as Tor Or; the Navy stations as Sor Tor Ror; the Army stations as Wor Por Tho; the Police stations as Sor Wor Por; the PRD stations as Por Cho Sor; and the Radio Thailand stations as Sor Wor Tor. Thailand is also host to three international relay stations: Voice of America, BBC East Asian, and Radio France Internationale.

The Broadcasting Directing Board, which reports to the prime minister, determines all aspects of radio broadcasting, such as operating hours, content, programming, advertising, and technical requirements. The Office of the Prime Minister, through the PRD, manages Radio Thailand and the National Broadcasting Services of Thailand (NBT). All stations are required to broadcast NBT-transmitted 30-minute local and international newscasts daily at 7 a.m. and 7 p.m. Government transmitters broadcast the signals of all private radio stations, which must renew their licenses annually.

Since the May 1992 uprising, radio journalists have become more aggressive in criticizing the government. Public-affairs talk shows with audience participation appeared on radio for the first time (Eng, 1997).

4.2.2 Television

All television broadcasting was under state monopoly and control until July 1996, when the first non-government television station, Independent Television, went

[5] Scandlen, 1978, provides the historical background. Also see Siriyuvasak, 1996b; and Salayakanond, 1998.
[6] Figure supplied by Professor Joompol Rodcumdee who is the dean of the Faculty of Communication Arts, Chulalongkorn University.

on air with promises of in-depth and aggressive news coverage. This UHF channel was a direct legacy of the 1992 public uprising that toppled the military government and led to demands for political reform, as well as for liberalization and privatization of broadcast media.

Of the five state-owned national TV stations, the PRD owns and operates the Television of Thailand (Channel 11) network of 29 stations, covering all regions of the country. The Mass Communications Organization of Thailand (MCOT) controls two stations (Channel 3 and Channel 9), and the Army controls the other two stations (Channel 5 and Channel 7). Two private groups—Bangkok Entertainment Co., and Bangkok Broadcasting & TV Co.—operate Channels 3 and 7 respectively with a license from the government. A decade ago, Chirasopone (1989) wrote, "Three of the state-owned television stations (Channels 5, 9 and 11) have given franchises to private groups to run their evening programs because production of quality TV new programs requires very large investments, which they cannot afford" (p. 99).

Thailand had two cable TV operators until 1998 when Thai Sky Cable Television stopped its operation. The country's sole cable operator at present is the United Broadcasting Corporation (UBC), which is an outgrowth of the merger of two leading cable television operators—International Broadcasting Corporation (IBC) and UTV Cable Network. They enjoy almost complete autonomy under the indirect oversight of the Mass Communications Authority of Thailand.

4.3 Program Policies

Radio Thailand has been broadcasting special programs from Chiang Mai for more than three decades. These are aimed at hill tribes—Yao, Akha, Karen, Lisu, Lahu, and the like. These programs, prepared by PRD officials in collaboration with representatives of hill tribes, consist of "news, takes on various subjects, as well as the hill tribes' culture and tradition" (Tiam-Tong, 1997, p. 9).

Private operators of TV stations are free to determine entertainment programming even though the state owns and controls all broadcasting. However, all TV stations must carry the state-run Television of Thailand's evening news at 7 p.m. Programmers are generally free to determine the content and nature of other programs without government intervention (Vatikiotis, 1996). However, as with the print media, self-censorship exists, especially in reporting, commenting on, and analyzing current events because private concession holders do not want to risk losing their license. Stations occasionally edit or "blackout" portions of programming deemed politically sensitive or pornographic.

Programming resembles the commercial format in other countries. The TV networks provide viewers a steady diet of local serial drama, talk shows, quiz and game shows, and imported movies from the United States, Japan, and Hong Kong. Sports programs, particularly local and overseas soccer, boxing, golf, NBA basketball tournaments, and snooker, are popular among the Thai. US and Japanese cartoons, as well as local children's programs, also attract a sizable audience of younger viewers.

Until recently, news and information programs accounted for the least airtime—about 6 percent to 15 percent for news, and between 7 and 14 percent for information programs (Siriyuvasak, 1996a). Media research in the 1990s, however, showed that news programs ranked among the top three popular programs as a result of the changing socio-political context and a new format of TV news reporting initiated by a private media group on Channel 9. Thus, stations began to expand the half-hour newscasts into one and one-half to two-hour ones, and to air news-in-brief every few hours. In 1994, the news and information programs took up more than 12 percent of program time on commercial stations and almost 50 percent on the education channel (Table 5).

After May 1992, leading broadcast journalists and academics started to push for the autonomy of the state media. A more liberal climate has encouraged the news broadcasters to openly criticize current political and social affairs. The most popular format on every channel has been panel discussion among experts with openline commentaries from the audience. Among the favorites are "Mong Tang Moom" (Different Perspectives), "Nation News Talk," "Trong Praden" (Right to the Point) and "Koe Wela Nok" (Time Off). The new trend of the current affairs programs came to a halt, however, when Banharn Silapa-archa's government suspended "Mong Tang Moom" on the state-run Channel 11 in February 1996. Officials alleged that the show's founder and moderator, Professor Chermsak Pinthong, was biased. Later, they removed all his radio shows as well (Fairclough, 1996).

Radio Thailand (Sor Wor Tor), the external service, broadcasts regular programs in Burmese, Cambodian, Chinese, English, German, Indonesian, Japanese, Laotian, Malay, Thai, and Vietnamese. The Voice of Free Asia (Wor Or So) broadcasts in Cambodian, English, Laotian, Malay, and Vietnamese.

4.4 Ownership and Financing

The Broadcasting Act of 1955 and subsequent ministerial regulations have limited radio and television transmission exclusively to 11 state agencies, whose two principals are the PRD and the military. The military owns two television stations and a substantial number of the country's 523 national and local radio stations (*Nation*, February 27, 1997). Although independent companies operate the broadcast media on a concession basis and the recent governments have tried to abolish outdated regulations, the government can revoke the concessionary license if the stations step on its toes.

Siriyuvasak (1992) wrote that three models of commercial radio have developed because of the contradiction between the structure of ownership and financial constraint. As the owner of all broadcasting stations, the state allowed three types of stations: those with (*a*) allocative control, (*b*) operational control, and (*c*) revenues and franchise. Stations controlled and operated by the state that receive revenues from state budget allocation and advertising come under the first model.

Stations that contract all air time to the highest bidder for 5–10 years come under the second model, with the state agencies receiving an initial lump sum installment and a percentage share of monthly revenue. Stations that operate like business corporations come under the third model, with the licensee supplying the capital investment to establish the station, and also paying an installment fee and a percentage of monthly revenue to the involved state agency.

The structural differences between state ownership and media entrepreneurship in commercial radio has created issues over the control of airtime and the quality of program production. Furthermore, because the government typically gives contracts to private media operators or advertisers who are prepared to meet the kickback requirement, no clear station policies exist on how to serve the needs of the audience (Siriyuvasak, 1992).

5. NEW ELECTRONIC MEDIA

5.1 Internet and On-line Media

In July 1999, Thailand had an estimated 59,718 Internet hosts—a density of 9.9 per 10,000 people (Internet Software Consortium, 1999), a substantial increase from 29,473 hosts in January 1998, when the country had an estimated 1.2 million personal computers (ITU, 1999a). Internet began in Thailand in 1987, when Prince of Songkla University and Asian Institute of Technology started the Thai Computer Science Network (TCSNet) via an electronic mail connection with the University of Melbourne. The same year, the Ministry of Science's National Electronics and Computer Technology Center (NECTEC) initiated the Inter-University Network Project, which, in 1991, expanded to include other major universities in Bangkok—Chulalongkorn, Thammasat, and Kasetsart. In 1993, the Thai Social/Scientific, Academic and Research Network (ThaiSarn) established the country's first World Wide Web server (www.nectec.or.th) in the second phase of the Inter-University Network Project. The ThaiSarn III project will use a government allocation of 4.2 billion baht (about US$ 11 million) to upgrade the ThaiSarn network to support thousands of schools for Internet access (Koanantakool, 1998a).

Three companies already provide commercial Internet service: Internet Thailand, KSC ComNet, and Loxinfo. Three more companies—Ucomm, Acumen, and Shinawatra—have begun work on providing satellite-based Internet service (APT, 1998). The Internet Thailand Service Center was established in 1994 as the first commercial service—a joint-venture company of the Communications Authority of Thailand (CAT), the Telephone Organization of Thailand (TOT), and NECTEC. Internet Thailand received its operating license from CAT in 1995, when it started accepting applications for commercial use of the Internet. Newspapers adopted the new technology quickly. The *Bangkok Post* started its Internet edition (http://www.bangkokpost.net) on April 1, 1996. In March 1999, 100hot.com (http://www.100hot.com/newspaper) ranked it the world's sixth most popular newspaper website. Among the newspapers available on-line are *Bonjour Siam* (Phuket),

Business Day, Daily News, Financial Day, Nation, Pattaya Mail, Phuket Aktuell, Phuket Gazette, Phuket Walk, Siam Post, Thai Rath, and *Tharn Settakij* (http://www.sanook.com/link/News_and Media). The press had to adopt the new media technology primarily to maintain its leadership, effectiveness, good image, and market competition (Kaewthep, 1998).

In July 1997, with the cooperation of several media and telecommunication groups, Thailand's first commercial radio station commenced broadcasting live on the Internet. Today, several Bangkok radio stations have established websites: Business Radio, City Radio, FM 94, FM 97, Love FM, National Radio Network, Radio Thailand, Sport Radio, V-FM, and Z-FM. Hatyai's Escati Magic Radio also has a website. On August 1, 1997, the Royal Thai Army Radio and Television Channel 5 (www.tv5.co.th) became the first TV station to broadcast live on the Internet. Today, all national TV stations have gone on-line: Bangkok Broadcasting & TV (BBTV 7), Television of Thailand (Channel 11), ITV and Bangkok Entertainment (TV 3). The UBC cable group also has a Web presence.

In 1998, the government set up the *SchoolNet Thailand* (SchoolNet@1509), a nationwide access service, to enable Internet access to more people, especially the youth. This new network permits secondary schools nationwide to use the local access number 1509 to connect to the Internet free of charge.

Despite the economic crisis, Thailand continues to implement the national-level projects aimed at promoting Internet use. Under the rural-area telephone project, TOT will expand the telecommunication infrastructure to all 60,000 villages in the country (Koanantakool, 1998b). The Ministry of University Affairs will implement its "IT Campus" project, started in 1999, to cover 30 provinces so that college students could go on-line and expand their research globally. The government's computerization program, which aims at ensuring that government agencies and their staff are well equipped with office automation and the Internet, has continued. Today, all the Thai government agencies have their websites featuring up-to-date information (www.nectec.or.th/directories/government.html).

5.2 Telecommunications Infrastructure

In 1998, Thailand had 7.1 million main telephone lines—the equivalent of 11.83 lines per 100 people (APT, 1999), as well as 3.48 cellular subscribers per 100 people. In 1997, Thailand had 6.1 million main telephone lines. The rural telephone density was only 5.3 percent (APT, 1998). However, TOT, through contract with Acumen, runs one of the world's largest VSAT telephone networks to serve the country's 48,000 remote villages (APT, 1999). In 1997, the country also had two million cellular subscribers—a density of 3.3 per 100 people (ITU, 1999a). The cellular network, which was showing growth rates of about 40 percent, has begun to penetrate the rural areas as well.

The Post and Telegraph Department (PTD) and two state enterprises—the Telephone Organization of Thailand (TOT) and the Communications Authority of

Thailand (CAT)—are responsible for the country's telecommunications.[7] TOT provides domestic telecommunications while CAT provides international telephone services. PTD controls and manages radio frequencies, and regulates and co-ordinates domestic communications via satellite. In 1991, the government allowed private-sector participation in telecommunications on a build, transfer, and operate basis. TelecomAsia was the first private company to participate, followed by Thai Telephone & Telecommunication. The private-sector cellular operators are Advanced Info Services and Total Access Communications (APT, 1998, 1999).

TOT has already installed two fiber-optic cable networks: a railway fiber-optic network running through the northeastern, eastern, and southern regions; and a submarine fiber-optic cable along the east coast. Fiber-optic cable networks are also being installed along 3,000km of the four main railway routes. TOT has expanded ISDN services to all major provinces. CAT has international telephone switching centers at Bangkok, Nonthaburi, and Sri-Racha. Thailand's international submarine links include the 1,340km Malaysia–Thailand (M–T) fiber-optic network with landing points in Kuantan (Sarawak) and Phetchaburi; the back-up Thailand–Vietnam–Hong Kong (T–V–H) fiber-optic network; and the fiber-optic Asia Pacific Cable Network (APCN) linking Thailand, Malaysia, Singapore, Indonesia, the Philippines, Hong Kong, Taiwan, South Korea, and Japan (APT, 1998).

Thailand began domestic satellite communications in 1984, using Indonesia's Palapa system and 10 earth stations. In 1991, Shinawatra Satellite won the exclusive rights for eight years to operate the Thaicom domestic satellites, the first of which was launched in December 1993. In addition to the original four orbital positions, Thailand has filed for 12 more orbital locations. The domestic satellite communication center is in Nonthaburi, just southwest of Bangkok. Thailand has also invested in the Iridium low-earth-orbit project to improve mobile phone and paging services (APT, 1998).

6. POLICY TRENDS FOR PRESS AND BROADCASTING

As the Thai House of Representatives was trying to iron out some contentious issues in the new broadcasting and telecommunication bills, the road toward media liberalization and privatization seemed far away. The 1997 Constitution that stipulates transparent regulations on broadcasting and telecommunications has apparently caused some confusion.

Although the government has been giving concessions to private companies, the broadcast media are not really out of government control. Despite ITV's claim to be the first independent TV operation, the Office of the Prime Minister still owns the station's license. Media analyst and educator Ubonrat Siriyuvasak has argued that if ITV were truly independent, it would not need a government agency to act as its overseer. As long as the concession system remained in place, she said, broadcasting in Thailand would be subject to state control (Vatikiotis, 1996).

---

[7] The US$ 17.2 billion IMF bailout required Thailand to privatize TOT and CAT in 1999.

The press situation in Thailand, however, is different. Although the primary concern of the Thai press is no longer state intimidation or control, the economic downturn has become a devastating force affecting the future of the press (Chongkittavorn, 1998b). For the first time, the pattern of press ownership in Thailand has changed with the onset of foreign investment. Press proprietors, just like other business entrepreneurs, have sought foreign capital to survive the financial ordeal. The implications of this development on the Thai press are not yet clear.

On the brighter side, the Thai media have become freer, more responsible, and more accountable as a result of the 1997 Constitution that guarantees freedom of the press, the establishment of the Press Council, and the implementation of the 1997 Official Information Act. The key challenge for the press is to respond to the rising expectation of the public for a more responsible press. As Sricharatchanya (1998), managing director of the (defunct) *Siam Post*, points out, "growing debate in Thailand today is how to strike a proper balance between freedom and better professional standards" (p. 185). Lertchanyarak (1998) argues that the Thai value system—dominated by "personalism and fun-loving values"—is such that "it is hard to control freedom of the press by means of self-regulation" (p. 259).

Chongkittavorn (1998a), executive editor of the *Nation*, wrote that to survive amidst fierce competition during the harsh economy, Thai journalists should improve their professionalism and ethics and keep abreast of new developments. He added that the Thai press should provide more civic elements in their newspapers to gain respect both inside and outside the region. If it merely continued to report the problems and scandals without offering alternatives or solutions, it would only be considered a part of the social malaise.

The Chuan Leekpai government should get credit for creating and promoting greater press liberty. Chuan has literally left the press untouched, unlike many of his predecessors who not only tried to tamper with the press but also sought to manipulate it and its owners. Further, the Interior Ministry's media advisory group has already recommended the abolition of the infamous Press Act of 1941.

7. MAIN ISSUES

● Demonopolizing broadcasting

Although the 1997 Constitution mandates the establishment of an independent public agency to allocate frequencies, whether the proposed Frequencies Allocation & Broadcasting and Telecommunication Supervision Organization will help demonopolize Thai broadcasting is yet to be seen.

● Ethics and responsibility

The 1997 Constitutional guarantee of freedom of expression has given the mass media the opportunity to prove that they can go beyond "yellow journalism" and become the watchdog of the public. Inculcating ethics and responsibility among journalists in a "fun-loving" society requires ongoing professional training. The establishment of the Press Council of Thailand in 1997 was a historic event but its role in improving journalists' professional conduct and ethics is too early to tell.

● Media economics and foreign ownership

The economic debacle has forced the media to seek foreign investment as a matter of survival. How much these economic influences are likely to affect the content of the Thai media is no longer a mere rhetorical question. The "watchdog" cannot afford to be a creature in the service of aliens.

8. STATISTICS

General Profile

Exchange rate (1999 average)	US$ 1 = Baht 37.82
Geographical size	513,115 sq km
Population (mid-1999)	60.6 million
Population density (1999)	118.4 per sq km
Urban population	36%
Life expectancy	69 years
No. of households (1997)	14.4 million
Literacy rate	94.7%

Source: *Asiaweek*, December 17, 1999; US Census Bureau's International Data Base (http://www. census.gov/cgi-bin/ipc/idbrank.pl); OANDA Historical Currency Table (http://www. oanda.com/converter/cc_table?lang=en).

Table 1
Number and Circulation of Daily Newspapers

	1980	*1990*	*1995*	*1996*	*1997**	*1998***
No. of dailies	27	34	35	30	44	25
Total circulation	2,680,000	4,500,000	2,700,000	3,800,000		4,460,000
Circulation per 100 people	5.7	8.1	4.6	6.4		7.2

Source: UNESCO, 1999; * WAN 1999; ** Reporters Association of Thailand and Zenith Media Thailand (personal communication, June, 1999).

Table 2
Display Advertising Revenue Share by Medium

	Total Baht (millions)	*Newspapers* %	*Magazines* %	*TV* %	*Radio* %	*Cinema* %	*Outdoor* %
1993	27,519	27	9	48	11	0	5
1994	36,130	30	9	45	11	0	5
1995	41,969	28	9	44	11	0	8
1996	47,087	24	8	49	11	0	8
1997	47,088	20	7	52	12	0	9
1998	38,095	17	4	59	13	0	5

Source: WAN, 1999; *Bangkok Post*, 1999.

Table 3
Number and Penetration of Radio Receivers

	1980	1985	1990	1996	1997
No. of receivers ('000s)	6,550	8,000	9,950	12,000	13,959
Receivers per 100 people	14.0	15.6	17.1	20.3	23.4

Source: UNESCO, 1999.

Table 4
Number and Penetration of Television Receivers

	1980	1985	1990	1996	1997
No. of receivers ('000s)	1,000	4,122	5,150	11,150	15,190
Receivers per 100 people	2.1	8.1	10.8	18.8	25.4

Source: UNESCO, 1999.

Table 5
Percentage of Five Program Types on Four Commercial TV Channels and One Non-commercial Channel in January 1994 (Weekday Program)

Program type	Ch. 3 (%)	Ch. 7 (%)	Ch. 5 (%)	Ch. 9 (%)	Ch. 11 (%)
Entertainment	71.38	59.26	72.42	50.92	15.9
Advertising	14.63	16.26	14.81	13.88	–
News	12.19	17.31	11.93	11.11	20.45
Information	1.78	7.15	0.82	24.07	27.27
Education	–	–	–	–	36.36

Source: Siriyuvasak, 1996a.

Table 6
Telecommunications Data

	1997	1998
Main telephone lines per 100 people	7.96	11.83
Cellular subscribers per 100 people	3.31	3.48
ISDN subscribers	1,010	1,400
TV receivers per 100 people	23.43	–
Personal computers per 100 people	1.98	2.16
Internet hosts per 10,000 people	4.86	7.25

Source: ITU, 1998, 1999a, 1999b; APT, 1999; *Asiaweek*, December 17, 1999.

9. USEFUL ADDRESSES

9.1 Daily Newspapers (Thai)

CIRCULATION

Baan Muang   200,000
Baan Muang Printing
1 Soi Pleummanee Vibhavadi-Rangsit Chatujak
Bangkok 10900
Telephone: 5130230-3, 5138114-6,
                  5133118, 5138120
Fax: 5133106

Daily News   750,000
Si-Phya Publishing
1/4 Vibhavadi-Rangsit Don Muang
Bangkok 10210
Telephone: 5610456, 9409800
Fax: 5611329, 5611343
URL: http://www.dailynews.co.th

Khao Sod   400,000
Khao Sod Co., Ltd.
40/9 Tessabannimitmai Ladyao Chatujak
Bangkok 10900
Telephone: 9544999, 5804030
Fax: 9543992

Krungthep Turakij   75,882
Nation Multimedia Group
44 Moo 10 Bangna-Trad Km 4.5 Prakhanong
Bangkok 10260
Telephone: 3170042, 3172131
Fax: 3171414
URL: http://www.nationgroup.com/bkk/bkk.html

Matichon Daily   400,000
Matichon
12 Tessaban-Narumarn Prachanivej 1 Chatujak
Bangkok 10900
Telephone: 5890020, 5800021
Fax: 5895674, 5890522

Naew Na   200,000
Naewna Newspaper
96 Moo 7 Vibhavadi-Rangsit Bangkhen
Bangkok 10210
Telephone: 5214647-9, 5215120-4
Fax: 5214949, 5523800, 5214651

Poojadkarn   260,000
The Manager Media Group

101/1 Baan Pra-Arthit Chanasongkham Pranakhon
Bangkok 10200
Telephone: 2884000
Fax: 2884118-9
URL: http://www.manager.co.th

Siam Rath   100,000
Siam Rath
6th Bldg 12 Rajdamnoen
Bangkok 10200
Telephone: 6221810-41
Fax: 2242187, 2242287

Siam Sports Daily   200,000
Siam Sports Syndicate
1776-1784 Rama IV Kasemrat Prakhanong
Bangkok 10110
Telephone: 2490447
Fax: 2494251

Sports World Daily   180,000
Wattachak Public
88 Boromrajachonnee Taling Chan
Bangkok 10170
Telephone: 4340330-70, 8808989
Fax: 8809110

Sports Game Daily   98,000
Wattachak Public
88 Boromrajachonnee Taling Chan
Bangkok 10170
Telephone: 4340330-70, 8808989
Fax: 8809110

Thai Post   30,000
Thai General Group
12/F1 Sorachai Bldg
23/15-19 Ekamai Sukhumvit 63 Klongtoey
Bangkok 10110
Telephone: 7143010
Fax: 7143048-9

Thai Rath   1,000,000
Vacharaphon
1 Vibhavadi-Rangsit Ladyao Chatujak
Bangkok 10900
Telephone: 2721030
Fax: 2721350-2, 2731342
URL: http://www.thairath.com

Wattachak Daily   200,000
Wattachak Public
88 Boromrajachonnee Taling Chan

Bangkok 10170
Telephone: 4340330-70, 8808989
Fax: 8808316

9.2 Daily Newspapers (Chinese)

Kia Hua Tong Nguan (Sirinakorn)   90,000
Sirinakorn Newspaper
108 Suapa Pomprab
Bangkok 10100
Telephone: 2214181-2, 2222838-9, 2238172-3,
             2219142-5, 6231210-2
Fax: 2254073

Sing Sian Yit Pao   90,000
Sing Sian Yit Pao
267 New Road
Bangkok 10100
Telephone: 2250070, 2254650-62
Fax: 2254663
E-mail: singpao@loxinfo.co.th

Tong Hua Yit Pao   90,000
Tong Hua Newspaper
877-879 Charoenkrung Talad Noi Samphantawong
Bangkok 10100
Telephone: 2369172-6
Fax: 2385286

The Universal Daily News   40,000
Universal Press
21/1 Charoenkrung Wangburapa Phirom Pranakorn
Bangkok 10200
Telephone: 2260040, 2264849
Fax: 2247968

9.3 Daily Newspapers (English)

Bangkok Post   65,000
The Post Publishing
136 Na Ranong Off Sunthorn Kosa Klongtoey
Bangkok 10110
Telephone: 2403700
Fax: 2403790-91
E-mail: webmaster@bangkokpost.net
URL: http://www.bangkokpost.net

Business Day   40,000
Business Day
22/F1 Olympia Thai Tower
444 Ratchadapisek Samsennok Huaykwang
Bangkok 10320

Telephone: 5123579
Fax: 5123565
URL: http://www.bday.net

Nation   55,000
Nation Multimedia Group
44 Moo 10 Bangna-Trad Km. 4.5 Prakhanong
Bangkok 10260
Telephone: 3170420, 3172131
Fax: 3171414
URL: http://www.nationmultimedia.com

9.4 Television Channels

Bangkok Entertainment (Thai TV Color Channel 3)
1126 Vanich Bldg New Petchburi
Bangkok 10400
Telephone: 2539940-3
Fax: 2539978
URL: http://www.tv3.co.th

Bangkok Broadcasting & TV (Channel 7)
998/1 Phaholyothin Chatujak
Bangkok 10900
Telephone: 2720201
Fax: 2720227
URL: http://www.ch7.com

Mass Communications Organization of Thailand
(Thai TV Color Channel 9)
63/1 Rama IX Huaykwang
Bangkok 10320
Telephone: 2016000-3
Fax: 2461960
URL: http://www.mcot.or.th

Royal Thai Army Television Station (TV 5)
210 Phaholyothin Sanampao
Bangkok 10400
Telephone: 2710060-9
Fax: 2701510
URL: http://www.tv5.co.th

Television of Thailand (Channel 11)
New Petchburi Bangkok 10310
Telephone: 3144006, 3184545, 3182110, 3144008
Fax: 3182991
URL: http://tv11.iirt.net

Independent Television (ITV)
SCB Park Plaza, Tower 2 West
18 Ratchadapisek Road
Bangkok, 10900

Telephone: 9376097-111, 9376315
URL: http://www.itv.co.th

World Cable TV (UCOM)
Benjachinda Bldg
499/5 Vibhavadi-Rangsit Chatujak
Bangkok 10900
Telephone: 9531111
Fax: 9532240

9.5 Radio Networks/Groups

Radio Thailand
236 Vibhavadi Rangsit Highway
Huaykwang, Bangkok 10400
URL: http://www.radiothailand.com

Nation Radio Network
44 Moo 10 Bangna-Trad Km. 4.5 Prakhanong
Bangkok 10260
Telephone: 3170420
Fax: 3172070

Pacific Group
1400 Thai Bldg Rama IV
Bangkok 10110
Telephone: 2499449
Fax: 2491837

Pirate Radio
573 Ramkhamhaeng 39 Wangthonglang Bangkapi
Bangkok 10310
Telephone: 5590964-6
Fax: 5590967

Plan Publishing
1532/40-43 Soi Pracharat 36 Krungthep-Nonthaburi
Bangkok 10800
Telephone: 9114211, 5869555
Fax: 9114251, 5874600
E-mail: harn@ksc7.th.com

R.S. Promotion 1992
419/1 Chetchotisak Bldg
Ladprao 15 Soi Jompol Chatujak
Bangkok 10900
Telephone: 5112024, 5139729
Fax: 5112324, 5132320

Star Bright Entertainment 1899
Pattanakarn Suan Luang
Bangkok 10250

Telephone: 3210041-4
Fax: 3213116

Star Bright Entertainment 1899
Pattanakarn Suan Luang
Bangkok 10250
Telephone: 3210041-4
Fax: 3213116

Universal United
296 St Louis 3 Sathorn Tai Yannawa
Bangkok 10120
Tel/Fax: 6759006-7, 2122225, 2112215

Watch Dog
Room #671-672 Imperial Queen's Park Hotel
199 Sukhumvit 22
Bangkok 10110
Telephone: 2621743-4
Fax: 2621743

You & I Corporation
2/F1 Vanij 2 Bldg
1126/2 New Petchburi Makkasan Rajthevi
Bangkok 10400
Telephone: 2558500-9
Fax: 2558513-14

10. REFERENCES

APT (Asia-Pacific Telecommunity). (1998, 1999). *The APT yearbook*. Bangkok: APT.
Bangkok Post 1998 year-end economic review. (1998). [On-line]. Available: (http://www.bangkokpost.net/yere/98yere12.html).
Boonyaketmala, B. (1982). Thailand. In J.A. Lent (Ed.), *Newspapers in Asia: Contemporary trends and problems* (pp. 334–367). Hong Kong: Heinemann Asia.
Changyai, B. (1996). *Song Khao Nangsue Phim* (Newsmen's white envelopes). Bangkok: Matichon Publishing.
Chirasopone, P. (1989). Thailand. In A. Mehra (Ed.), *Press systems in ASEAN states* (pp. 91–100). Singapore: AMIC.
Chongkittavorn, K. (1998a, April 21). Economy threatens media freedom. *The Nation* [On-line]. Available: (http://203.146.514/nationnews/1998/199804/19980421/25315.html).
Chongkittavorn, K. (1998b, December 28). Press emerges stronger after crisis. *The Nation* [On-line]. Available: (http://203.146.51.4/nationnews/1998/199812/19981228/36824.html).
Chuensuksawasdi, P. (1998, October 1). *It's making a difference that matters*. Arthur Norman Smith Memorial lecture to the Australian Journalists Association, University of Melbourne, Melbourne.
Editor & publisher international yearbook. (1998). New York: E&P.
Eng, P. (1997). Media rising: How the press is bolstering democracy. *Columbia Journalism Review, 36* (1), 20.
Eng, P. (1998). Economic woes pummel Thai, Indonesia media. *Columbia Journalism Review, 37* (2), 58–60.

Fairclough, G. (1996, February 29). Shut up or shut down: Government pulls plug on current affairs show. *Far Eastern Economic Review, 59* (9), 20.

Freedom House Survey Team. (1998). *Freedom in the world 1997–1998: The annual survey of political rights and civil liberties.* New York: Freedom House.

ITU (International Telecommunication Union). (1998). *World telecommunication development report.* Geneva: ITU.

ITU (International Telecommunication Union). (1999a). *Yearbook of statistics: Telecommunication services 1998–1997.* Geneva: ITU.

ITU (International Telecommunication Union). (1999b). *Challenges to the network: Internet for development.* Geneva: ITU.

Katz, E., & Wedell, G. (1977). *Broadcasting in the Third World: Promise and performance.* Cambridge, MA: Harvard University Press.

Khachayudhadej (Changyai), B. (1998). Sitti lae sereepaab khong sue *Matichon* (Press freedom and rights). In Constitution Draft Assembly, *Ruam sara rattammanoon chabab prachachon* (People's constitutions handbook) (pp. 185–200). Bangkok: Mathichon Publishing.

Kaewthep. K. (1998, November 12). *Kaan nam ow technology saan sontate ma chai nai ngarn sue muanchon* (Use of information technology in mass media). Paper presented at a seminar on research directions and applications of information technology in the next century, Bangkok.

Kitiwat, K. (1983). Radio broadcasting. In *The Thai mass media development* (pp. 103–136). Bangkok: Faculty of Communication Arts, Chulalongkorn University.

Koanantakool, T. (1998a). The perpetual chronicles of Internet events in Thailand. *Internet in Thailand: Our Milestones* [On-line]. Available: http://www.nectec.or.th/users/htk/milestones. html).

Koanantakool, T. (1998b). National IT projects in Thailand. *Thailand the big picture* [On-line]. Available: (http://www.nectec.or.th/it-projects).

Lapiratanakul, W. (1984). *Public relations.* Bangkok: Chulalongkorn University Press.

Lent, J.A. (1997, July–August). Thailand's brief press freedom. *Index on Censorship, 6* (4), 45–50.

Lent, J.A. (1978). Press freedom in Asia: The quiet but completed revolution. *Gazette, 24* (1), 41–60.

The Leo Burnett worldwide advertising and media factbook. (1994). Chicago: Triumph Books.

Lertchanyarak, O. (1998). Social and cultural factors affecting press freedom: Thailand's perspective. In A. Latif (Ed.), *Walking the tightrope: Press freedom and professional standards in Asia* (pp. 251–259). Singapore: AMIC.

Markham, J.M. (1974, June 2). Thailand's press plays wider role. *New York Times*, p. 19.

Mitchell, J.D. (1971). Thailand. In J.A. Lent (Ed.), *The Asian newspapers' reluctant revolution* (pp. 210–233). Ames: The Iowa University Press.

Mitton, R. (1998, December 25). On the attack: Thai media go for blood at home and abroad. *Asiaweek* [On-line]. Available: (http://www.pathfinder.com/asiaweek/98/1225/nat7.html).

Muntarbhorn, V. (Comp.). (1998). *Mass media laws and regulations in Thailand.* Singapore: AMIC.

National Identity Office. (1996). Office of the Prime Minister [On-line]. Available: (http://www.mahidol.ac.th/Thailand).

Padmatin, S. (1970). *Typography.* Bangkok: Thammasat University Press.

Padmatin, S. (1984). *Mass communication in Thailand.* Singapore: Asian Mass Communication Research and Information Center.

Phayakvichien, P. (1971). *The comparative content analysis of the Thai newspapers from 1960–1969.* Master's thesis, School of Journalism and Mass Communication, University of Wisconsin at Madison.

Pickerell, A.G. (1960). The press of Thailand: Conditions and trends. *Journalism Quarterly, 37*, 83–96.

Rachawadi (pen name). (1998). Constitution day: 10 December. *Thaiways, 25* (17), 24–26.

Salayakanond, W. (1998). Thailand. In A. Goonasekera & D. Holaday (Eds.), *Asian communication handbook* (pp. 183–195). Singapore: AMIC and NTU.

Scandlen, G. B. (1978). Thailand. In J.A. Lent-(Ed.), *Broadcasting in Asia and the Pacific: A continental survey of radio and television* (pp. 123–142). Philadelphia: Temple University Press.

Scandlen, G. B., & Winkler, K. (1982). Thailand. In J.A. Lent (Ed.), *Newspapers in Asia: Contemporary trends and problems* (pp. 302–33). Hong Kong: Heinemann Asia.

Schidlovsky, J. (1999, March). Hard times for Thai journalists. *American Journalism Review, 21,* 18–19.

Siriyuvasak, U. (1992). Radio broadcasting in Thailand. *Media Asia, 19* (2), 92–99.

Siriyuvasak, U. (1996a). Television and the emergence of "civil society" in Thailand. In D. French & M. Richards (Eds.), *Contemporary television: Eastern perspectives*. New Delhi: Sage Publications.

Siriyuvasak, U. (1996b). Media monitors in Thailand. In K.S. Venkateswaran (Comp.), *Media monitors in Asia* (pp. 105–110). Singapore: AMIC.

Sricharatchanya, P. (1998). Thailand. In A. Latif (Ed.), *Walking the tightrope: Press freedom and professional standards in Asia* (pp. 183–186). Singapore: AMIC.

Sussman, L.R. (1999). *Press freedom 1999: News of the century.* New York: Freedom House.

Tasker, R. (1998, December 24). The watchdog bites: Thailand's press increasingly shows its teeth, helped by greater official transparency. *Far Eastern Economic Review, 161,* 25–26.

Tasker, R. (1998–99, December 31–January 7). Back to basics: Thai leaders focus on what they know best. *Far Eastern Economic Review, 162* (1), 86–87. [On-line]. Available: (http://www.feer.com/Restricted/rev200/thailand.html).

Teeravanich, S. (1977). *History of the Thai press under absolute monarchy* (1782–1932). Bangkok: Thai Wattanapanich Press.

Teeravanich, S. (1983). Kaan nungsuepim nai pratate Thai (Newspapers in Thailand). In *Wiwattanakaan suemuanchon Thai* (Thai mass media development) (pp. 3–20). Bangkok: Faculty of Communication Arts, Chulalongkorn University.

Thongpao, T. (1990). Thailand. In C.J. Hamelink & A. Mehra (Eds.), *Communication development and human rights in Asia* (pp. 123–127). Singapore: AMIC.

Tiam-Tong, C.S. (1997). How communication preserves cultural identity in northern Thailand. *Media Development, 44* (2), 7–10.

UNDP (United Nations Development Program). (1999). *Human development report.* New York: Oxford University Press & UNDP.

UNESCO (United Nations Educational, Scientific and Cultural Organization). (1998, 1999). *Statistical yearbook.* Paris: UNESCO.

US Bureau of Democracy, Human Rights and Labor. (1998). *Thailand: Country report on human rights practices for 1998* [On-line]. Available: (http://usa.or.th/usis/hr98-ind.htm).

Vanden Heuvel, J., & Dennis, E. (1993). *The unfolding lotus: East Asia's changing media.* New York: The Freedom Forum.

Vatikiotis, M. (1996, July 4). Freeing the waves: Independent TV has to fend off the government. *Far Eastern Economic Review, 59* (27), 20–22.

WAN (World Association of Newspapers). (1999). *World press trends.* Paris: WAN.

Warren, W., & Invernizzi, L. (1994). *Arts and crafts of Thailand.* Bangkok: Asia Books.

World factbook. (1999). Washington, DC: Central Intelligence Agency [On-line]. Available: (http://www.odci.gov/cia/publications/factbook).

Yong, T. (1995). Thailand: Media's growing influence. *Nieman Reports, 49* (4).

◆

17

VIETNAM

Zeny Sarabia Panol & Yen Do

1. NATIONAL PROFILE

1.1 Geography

The Socialist Republic of Vietnam is a peninsula located in Southeast Asia. Occupying a total landmass of 325,360 sq km (125,472 sq miles), it is bounded to the north by China, to the west by Cambodia and Laos, and to the east by the South China Sea. Geographically, a rugged mountainous region in the central part of the country divided what used to be North and South Vietnam (Reddy, 1994). About 40 percent of the country has forest cover; 35 percent is used for other purposes; and 22 percent is arable land of which 2 percent is under permanent cultivation.

1.2 People

Vietnam had a mid-1999 population estimated at 77.3 million, 21 percent of which is urban and 91.9 percent literate. (US Census Bureau, International Data Base). Life expectancy is 68 years (*Asiaweek*, January 14, 2000). About 85 to 90 percent are Vietnamese while 3 percent are Chinese. Religions include Buddhism, Taoism, Roman Catholicism, Islam, Protestantism, Cao Dai, Hoa, and indigenous beliefs. Vietnamese is the official language but French, Chinese, English, Khmer, and various tribal languages are also spoken (Reddy, 1994). The country has 60 provinces and two densely populated cities—Ho Chi Minh City (formerly Saigon), where 6 percent or 4.5 million of the nation's people live; and Hanoi (the capital) with a population of 2.2 million (*The Europa world yearbook*, 1997).

Primary education, which lasts for five years, is compulsory. The seven-year secondary education phase is completed in two cycles with the first requiring four years and the second three. In 1994, about 40 percent of the relevant age group was enrolled in secondary education classes. The country has 104 colleges and universities and 451 vocational and technical schools. The first private college,

Thang Long College, opened in 1989 in Hanoi. About 8.2 percent of the government's 1996 budget went to education (*The Europa world yearbook*, 1997).

Vietnam has a long colonial history. China conquered it in 111 B.C. It became independent in A.D. 939 but subsequently fell back to the Chinese. From 1867 to 1945, it was a French colony. After the 1945–46 Japanese occupation, it reverted to French rule until 1954 with the country divided into two military zones at the 17th parallel: the French in charge of the south, and the Democratic Republic of Vietnam headed by Ho Chi Minh in charge of the north. When France withdrew in 1954, Ngo Dinh Diem became the first prime minister of South Vietnam. The Vietcong, with the support of the DRV, persistently opposed Diem's anti-communist regime. These insurgents established the communist-led National Liberation Front in 1960. American involvement in the war began in 1961 and ended in 1973 with the Paris Peace Agreement that stipulated a cease-fire and withdrawal of US military forces. Saigon fell to the communists in April 1975. The country was reunified in 1976 with the declaration of the Socialist Republic of Vietnam (*The Europa world yearbook*, 1997). It became a member of the United Nations and the Association of Southeast Asian Nations in 1995.

1.3 Government and Politics

Vietnam's legal system is based on communist dogma and French civil law (*The Europa world yearbook*, 1997). It has a communist government and a market-socialist economy (*Statesman yearbook*, 1997–98). Its 1992 constitution vests political power in the Communist Party. The executive branch consists of the president, the prime minister, the deputy prime minister, and a council of ministers. The president, who is elected by a unicameral 450-seat National Assembly (*Quoc-Hoi*), serves as the head of state. At the helm of the judiciary is the Supreme People's Court.

1.4 Economy

Vietnam is attempting to increase productivity through *Doi Moi*, a reform program based on the principles of free enterprise and reduced central control. The country's nominal per capita gross national product in 1999 was US$ 310. The per capita gross domestic product at purchasing power parity was US$ 1,705. The GDP at purchasing power parity stood at US$ 137 billion (*Asiaweek*, February 4, 2000). Predominantly agricultural, with rice as the staple crop, Vietnam, which used to import the commodity, became the world's second biggest rice exporter in 1996 (*World factbook*, 1999). The agriculture sector accounts for 28 percent of the country's GDP and employs 72 percent of its labor force (*The Europa world yearbook*, 1997).

Government efforts are geared toward merging the agricultural resources of the south with the industrial resources of the north. Coal, a major export item, is abundant in the north, but in 1986 oil was discovered on the country's southern coast. Inflation has come down from 30 percent in 1991 to 1.4 percent at present

(*World factbook*, 1999; *Asiaweek*, February 4, 2000). Vietnam's currency is the Dong, which had an average exchange value of 13,941 dong to US$ 1 in 1999.

2. DEVELOPMENT OF PRESS AND BROADCASTING

2.1 Brief Early History

2.1.1 The Vietnamese Press during Colonial Times (1860–1920)

The earliest newspapers in Vietnam appeared in the 1860s. In 1861, Admiral Paul Bonard, a pioneering French governor of Cochinchina (southernmost Vietnam), published the first bulletin-type newspaper, *Bulletin de 1 'Expedition de la Cochinchine*. Because this bulletin was in French, Bonard, in an attempt to reach the local readers, also published the Chinese-language *Bulletin of the Communes* later that same year. The early newspapers catered primarily to the information needs of the French colonialists. The bulletins reported news stories about the home country and official decisions of the French authorities (Thai, 1971).

Simultaneous attempts to publish Vietnamese-language newspapers failed because of delays in getting the required special fonts from France. Thus the publication of the first Vietnamese newspaper *Gia-Dinh Bao* (Gia-Dinh Journal) had to wait until 1865. Its founder, Petrus Truong Vinh Ky, is known as Vietnam's first indigenous journalist (Thai, 1971). The weekly *Gia-Dinh Bao*, which measured 10 by 12 inches, mostly carried announcements about the colonial government's activities and advertisements. It served both as a propaganda instrument of the colonial government and as a tool for promoting the journalistic use and appreciation of Vietnamese (Thai, 1971). Six other newspapers followed: *Phan Yen bao* (1868), *Nhut Trinh Nam Ky* (1883), *Nong Co Min Dam* (1901), *Luc Tinh Tan Van* (1907), *An Ha Nhat Bao* (1912), and *Nam Trung Nhat Bao* (1917) (Thai, 1971, Guimary, 1982).

The first newspaper in North Vietnam (Tokin) was *Dai Viet Tan Bao* (New Journal of Greater Vietnam) published in 1892. Its editor was Dao Nguyen Pho and the publisher Ernest Babut. It contained a Chinese and a Vietnamese section (Thai, 1971).

Other luminaries in journalism during the early 20th century were Henri Schneider, a retired official of the colonial government, and Nguyen Van Vinh, a pro-French writer who previously worked as a civil servant in the colonial administration. Schneider, who owned printing shops in North and South Vietnam, had two successful publications: the *Dai Nam Dong Van Nhut Bao*, a literary journal first published in 1907, and *Dong Duong Tap Chi*, a weekly initiated in 1913. The latter attracted regular contributions by Vietnamese scholars whose agenda was the promotion of *quoc-ngu* as a national language. Both Schneider and Vinh collaborated on another successful publication in 1913, the *Trung Bac Tan Van* (Thai, 1971). *Nam Phong Tap Chi*, a pro-French newspaper published by Louis Marty and edited by Pham Quynh, became noted for rallying the Vietnamese to the side of France during World War I.

During this period French colonial policy made newspapers subservient to the interests of France and thus made them instruments of the colonial regime. This was done through censorship and licensing of newspapers. A double-standard regulatory system favored French-language newspapers owned by French citizens. The Fundamental Press Law of July 28, 1881, for instance, allowed the publication of such newspapers without prior authorization by the government. Only the filing of an application and compliance with the legal deposit were required (Guimary, 1982). The decree of December 30, 1898, on the other hand, required Vietnamese newspapers to seek prior authorization. As a result, newspaper publishing became an exclusive club of French citizens or Vietnamese who were naturalized French citizens (Thai, 1971). During this period, newspapers fluctuated constantly in number, were of inferior quality, and usually consisted of four pages.

2.1.2 The Era of Nationalism (1920–40)

Opposition to French colonial policies and a rapid increase in Vietnamese national-istic fervor marked this period. Naturally, newspapers reflected the country's mood. The French regulatory regime at this time was, at best, ambivalent. The regime's initial liberal approach might have spawned nationalistic journalism, but the reimposition of press controls soon followed. For instance, the decree of October 4, 1927, which exempted French newspapers from prior authorization, was rescinded by the decree of August 30, 1938, thereby extending the privilege to Vietnamese- and Chinese-language newspapers. This liberal press climate soon disappeared when the regime reimposed press restrictions by the decree of August 24, 1939. Two years later, the French enacted the law of December 31, 1941, abolishing the freedom of publication and requiring prior authorization of all local papers (Thai, 1971).

The well known nationalistic papers during this era included *La Cloche Felee* (1924) published by Nguyen An Ninh in Cochinchina; *Huu Thanh* (1921) and *Than Chung* (1929) in the south; *Tieng Dan* (1927) in central Vietnam; and *Phong Hoa* (1932) and *Ngay Nay* (1935) both published by Tu Luc Van Doan (Self-Help Literary Group) in the north (Thai, 1971).

Another characteristic of this period was the rise in Vietnam's feminist movement and with it the emergence of a number of newspapers for women. Examples are the *Phu Nu Tan Van* (1929), *Phu Nu Thoi Dam* (1930), *Phu Nu Tan Tien* (1932), and *Dan Ba Tuan Bao* (1939) (Thai, 1971).

During World War II, the Vietnamese press went with the shifting political tides as the country successively came under the Vichy (French) regime, Japanese occu-pation, and the communist government under Ho Chi Minh. Communist papers such as *Tien* in the south and *Cuu Quoc, Su That*, and *Tien Phong* in the north began to appear at this time (Thai, 1971).

2.2 Developments since 1945

Vietnam's colonizers left indelible influences on the country's mass media. Chinese-, French-, and English-language newspapers continue to be published to this day. Of the current seven major dailies, at least one, the Hanoi-based *Le Courrier du Vietnam* is in French; and two, *Vietnam News* and *Saigon Times*, are in English. At one point, 13 Chinese-language dailies served about a million Chinese in Cholon, now part of Ho Chi Minh City. Printing technology is another foreign contribution. France is credited with introducing the Linotype in Vietnam. The current practice of placing the editorial on the front page is also considered a French legacy.

The French initiated radio broadcasting in the country while the Americans introduced television. The erstwhile Soviet Union, France, Japan, and Germany assisted the development of the telecommunication network. The French also left vestiges of government control on the press. The series of edicts that the French issued provided the prototypes of Vietnam's subsequent forms of government regulation and supervision of the press.

2.2.1 Print Media

Vietnam's 137-year old press history may be relatively short but it is certainly long on struggles for survival under repressive governments and in conditions of political, social, and economic instability.

Despite numerous handicaps, the number of newspapers and periodicals has grown phenomenally—from roughly 10 in 1939 to 64 in 1965, 135 in the mid-1970s (Van Dinh, 1982) and around 449 at present (WPV 1997). This steady growth in number tells only part of the story because suspensions and other factors had led to the closure of several newspapers. For a long time the government suspended 30 to 40 publications every year for negative reporting and other violations (Thai, 1971). A proliferation of fly-by-night publications, particularly in South Vietnam, was another noteworthy aspect. Guimary (1982) noted that historically "there was no continuity or firm tradition of newspapers in South Vietnam" (p. 371). The *Editor & publisher* listings between 1959 and 1975 indicate wide fluctuations in the number of periodicals—from a low of 16 to a high of 81 and an average of 37 over the 16-year period. The number of newspapers jumped from 13 in 1965 (10 Vietnamese, two English, and one Chinese) to 37 in 1996 (23 Vietnamese papers, two French, 10 Chinese, and two English).

The contemporary Vietnamese press has been through three stages since the end of World War II.

2.2.1.1 From 1947 until 1954: When the first Indo-China War ended in 1954 with the Vietnamese victory against the French at Dien Bien Phu and the partitioning of Vietnam, the communist press in the north operated clandestinely in support of the communist revolution. Only a few newspapers existed at that time because winning the war took precedence over newspaper publishing. In 1949, the first

Vietnamese Ministry of Information came into being soon after the creation of the Associated State of Vietnam in the French Union under the leadership of Bao Dai (Thai, 1971). The few newspapers that existed in French-controlled areas during this period were not only short-lived but also mediocre. Two journalistic developments were noteworthy: the publication of the political-religious newspapers *Chien Dau* (Struggle) and *Thoi Dai* (Times); and the publication of *Doc Lap* (Independence), which pioneered the practice of leasing newspapers (Thai, 1971).[1] Censorship prevailed during the Bao Dai period.

The first press service in Vietnam began in 1946. This was the Vietnam News Agency (VNA) or Thong Tan Xa Viet Nam, set up by the Ho Chi Minh government at the beginning of the first Indo-China War. Three years later, those opposing the Bao Dai government set up another news agency, the Vietnam Press (VNP). The non-communist Vietnam Thong Tan Xa (Vietnam Press) served as the official press agency of South Vietnam until the collapse of Saigon. It produced a morning and evening news bulletin in Vietnamese, French, and English (Nhan, 1970). With the fall of the south, the Vietnam News Agency became the only press service in reunified Vietnam.

2.2.1.2 From 1954 to 1975: Two different press systems developed between 1954 and 1975 under a divided Vietnam: the communist press in the north and the authoritarian press in the south. The former officially espoused the proletarian ideology to serve the state. The latter was subject to heavy regulation to prevent infiltration from the north.

When the second Indo-China War began in 1960, the National Liberation Movement, a communist front of Vietnam's Labor Party, secretly organized press and radio operations in the south to rally the people against the United States and the Diem regime. The communist press in the north appeared to be relatively more organized, stable, and ideologically focused. It was also generally informative and analytical (Van Dinh, 1982). The press was likewise considered national in circulation and content, "providing information on national development and emphasizing national history and traditional culture" (p. 391).

The more "chaotic" press in the south suffered from repressive policies—censorship, seizures, and even suspensions or closures—of successive rulers from Diem to Thieu. Newsprint shortages made continuous publishing difficult but the pro-government papers received subsidies. The degree of hostility between the government and the press determined the number of publications. Although Diem had placed rigid press censorship between 1954 until his overthrow in 1963, a "relative free press" prevailed during the next five years (1964–68) when, according to a veteran Vietnamese journalist, "some five to 10 new newspapers appeared on the scene" each time a change occurred in the cabinet. "The premier himself, or his friends, supporters, or the newly appointed ministers would put up some new dailies to make money or to support the new cabinet" (quoted in Guimary, 1982,

---

[1] This refers to the practice of leasing the publication permit to the highest bidder.

p. 370). Some South Vietnamese journalists tested the boundaries of press restrictions by reporting government corruption and smuggling. The politically independent *Chinh Luan* (Right Opinion), founded in 1964 by former Senator Dang Van Sung, emerged as a respected daily. It carried 10 pages unlike many other newspapers, which had between four and eight pages (Guimary, 1982; Thai, 1971).

Underpaid journalists often had second jobs. "A journalist is a man who lies to make money," was an apt local saying (Guimary, 1982). A unique practice in Vietnam was the "hiring out" or renting of daily newspapers at half the sale price and returning them to the vendor later in the day (Guimary, 1982; Thai, 1971). Guimary (1982) reported that about half of the estimated newspaper circulation of between 200,000 to 300,000 before 1975 were rentals. The French term *feuilleton* describes another Vietnamese media practice of this period: the serialization of novels to fill up newspaper pages and boost newspaper sales.

In 1976, the government named the Vietnam News Agency (VNA) as the official press service of the reunified country. It produced 40 to 60 news bulletins a day. The only privately owned press service, the Mekong Features, put out stories on a biweekly basis. Established during the early years of American intervention (1965–66), it served the foreign-language media but closed shop in the early 1970s. Two news-photo services—Saigon Anh Xa (Saigon News Pictures Agency), set up during the later years of the Vietnam War by the Vietcong or Vietnamese communists in South Vietnam as a minor auxiliary branch of the Vietnam News Agency, and Vietnam Anh Xa (Vietnam News Picture Agency) based in Hanoi—were also on the scene. The Vietnam Press, South Vietnam's press service, ceased operations in April 1975.

2.2.1.3 From 1976 to the Present: The reunification of the country in May 1976 resulted in the gradual integration of the press in the south and the north. The Thong Tan Giai Phong (Liberation Press Agency), which started operating clandestinely in the south in 1961, merged with the Vietnam Thong Tan Xa (VNTTX), a government monopoly of news distribution set up in 1945 (Van Dinh, 1982). Two dailies continue to operate in the south—*Saigon Giai Phong* (Liberated Saigon), established in 1975, and the *Saigon Times*, established in 1995—after the demise of the Vietnamese daily *Tin Sang* (Morning News).

At the time of reunification, North Vietnam had 139 newspapers and about 54 monthlies (Van Dinh, 1982). South Vietnam also had a large number of publications. Of the current dailies, only four are more than 20 years old. *Nhan Dan* (The People), established in 1946 as the official organ of Vietnam's Communist Party, is the oldest. *Quan Doi Nhan Dan* (People's Army), published by the political section of the armed forces since 1950, is the second oldest. A distant third is *Saigon Giai Phong* (1975), and the fourth is *Hanoi Moi* (New Hanoi) started in 1976 as the organ of the Hanoi Committee of the Communist Party of Vietnam.

Among the weeklies, *Lao Dong* (Labor), the official publication of the Vietnam General Confederation of Labor, is the oldest. It first appeared in 1929. Six other weeklies are more than 20 years old: *Van Nghe* (1949), *Khoa Hoc va Doi Song* (1959), *Giao Duc Thoi Dai* (1959), *Giao Thong-Van Tai* (1962), *The Thao Vietnam* (1968), and *Dai Doan Ket* (1977).

In fact, of the 42 or so periodicals in circulation, 38 percent were started in the 1980s and the 1990s. Four of the latest are *Tap Chi Tu Tuong Van Hoa, Thoi Bao Kinh Te Vietnam, Thuong Mai*, and *Vietnam Renovation*. The newest among the dailies in the north is *Vietnam News*, which began publication in 1991.

International publications are available at hotels catering to foreign business visitors. Newsstand availability is limited. Some of the international publications with limited circulation are the *Financial Times, International Herald Tribune, Newsweek, Time, USA Today, U.S. News and World Report*, and the *Wall Street Journal* (FFWC, 1993).

Two press agencies are in operation today: the state-owned Vietnam News Agency (VNA) and the non-governmental Vinapress established in 1988. VNA is a member of the Organization of Asian and Pacific News Agencies. Some eight foreign news agencies operate from Hanoi: AFP (France), ITAR-TASS (Russia), Kyodo (Japan), PAP (Poland), Prensa Latina (Cuba), Reuters (UK), RIA-Novosti (Russia), and Xinhua (China).

2.2.2 Broadcasting

2.2.2.1 The Early Years of Broadcasting: Both radio and television broadcasting preceded the country's reunification in 1976. The two developed independently, following different patterns in both programming and reach. The French brought radio broadcasting to Vietnam, but the modernization of broadcasting in the south was mainly the result of US investments of about US$ 12.5 million between 1956 and 1972. The United States was also largely responsible for building the television infrastructure and upgrading radio facilities in South Vietnam (Hoffer & Lichty, 1978).

Radio: The first official broadcast of the Voice of Vietnam (VoV) went on air from Hanoi on September 7, 1945, using old French equipment. The Voice of Vietnam was established during the August 1945 revolution led by Ho Chi Minh. The initial broadcast carried news bulletins on the Declaration of Independence and other public affairs in Vietnamese and four other languages: English, French, Cantonese, and Esperanto (WPV, 1997). In January 1950, Vo Tuyen Vietnam (VTVN) or Radio Vietnam began operating in the south, originally under French control. In 1955, with the cessation of all French broadcasting, the South Vietnamese assumed full control (Hoffer & Lichty, 1978).

Because of renewed hostilities in 1946, the Voice of Vietnam broadcast from various places in Viet Bac—the northwest provinces. In 1954, the North Vietnamese merged the four other broadcasting stations that the Viet Minh operated in central and south Vietnam with the Hanoi-centered Voice of Vietnam. In the early 1960s, the Voice of Vietnam had nine medium-wave and shortwave transmitters. With the country's reunification in 1976, the Broadcasting Department managed Radio

Hanoi as a government agency. Its two networks of both shortwave and medium-wave stations broadcast a 12-hour domestic program targeting farming communities as part of an extensive campaign to introduce modern farming techniques and collective agricultural practices. By 1972, the other network provided about 300 hours of weekly international broadcasts using one medium-wave and 11 shortwave transmitters (Lichty & Hoffer, 1978).

The number of radio receivers in North Vietnam increased from 130,000 in 1963 to 550,000 in 1975. However, penetration of radio broadcasts was much higher because of the megaphone system installed in densely populated cities and towns. The existence of such a wired distribution system and other private relay broadcasting facilities in collective farms, factories, schools and hospitals boosted penetration rates to about 20 percent of the population in the north (Lichty & Hoffer, 1978).

As US involvement in the Vietnam War escalated in the mid-1960s, Radio Hanoi broadcast special half-hour "Hanoi Hannah" programs designed for American servicemen. These programs contained anti-war propaganda, American popular music, and political commentaries reflecting psychological warfare (Lichty & Hoffer, 1978). The National Liberation Front, which led the communist presence in the south, also started radio operations in the early 1960s. Radio Giai Phong went on air in February 1962 to promote the aims of the revolutionary movement in the south (Van Dinh, 1982).

VTVN's facilities included three channels. The Channel A network, which comprised four medium-wave stations in Danang, Qui Nhon, Nha Trang, and Saigon, targeted a civilian audience. It had apparently the most popular stations. Channel B, which used programming by the Armed Forces Vietnam Network (ARVN), targeted the military audience. Channel C, which broadcast in Chinese, French, Thai, Cambodian, and English, targeted minorities. In Saigon, both A and B channels were on air for 24 hours every day. Almost half of VTVN's programming content in mid-1969 consisted of music and news. All stations carried hourly network news broadcasts. Religious and pacifist programs—along with dramas, commentaries, and development-oriented feature—made up the rest (Hoffer & Lichty, 1978). At least one radio signal was potentially available to 95 percent of the South Vietnamese by the early 1970s. A 1967 study showed that 65 percent of the radio audience owned radio receivers (Hoffer & Lichty, 1978).

Prior to reunification, radio broadcasting possessed the following features:

● **External broadcasting:** The Voice of Freedom (VoF), South Vietnam's external service, had 24-hour daily programming aimed at North Vietnam. The ARVN Political Warfare Department operated this service with major financial support from the United States. VoF carried news, commentary, drama, and music that appealed to the North Vietnamese. The NLF and the North frequently jammed these broadcasts (Hoffer & Lichty, 1978).

● **Radio Giai Phong (Liberation Radio) broadcasts:** RGP was the North Vietnamese version of VoF. Its largely clandestine operations, along with Radio

Hanoi, originally disseminated party propaganda, news, and music to the South Vietnamese. Later, it targeted US forces as well. With initial 90-minute daily broadcasts (later increased to five hours) in four languages, about 60 percent of Radio Giai Phong was audible in Saigon (Lichty & Hoffer, 1978).

● **American military broadcasting:** The US Armed Forces in Vietnam Network (AFVN) began its 18-hour (later 24-hour) daily broadcasting of news and music from Saigon on August 15, 1962. Eight years later, AFVN's facilities included six combined AM and FM stations, including two with stereo quality. The AFVN also aired programs for the military personnel of other countries in the area (Hoffer & Lichty, 1978).

Television: Lichty and Hoffer (1978) wrote: "South Vietnam may be the only country where television was introduced, in part, with the hope it would interest people in buying sets, thus inducing them to spend money and reduce inflation" (p. 99). In February 1966, the first broadcast of the Vietnamese THVN Channel 9 went on air with a 30-minute segment of news, comedy skit, two short films, and a brief introduction by Prime Minister Nguyen Ky and US Ambassador Henry C. Lodge. Immediately following the signing off of this Vietnamese channel, the AFVN-TV channel made its debut with remarks from Gen. William Westmoreland and Defense Secretary Robert McNamara and a KTLA-produced videofilm. That day the PX store reportedly sold some 800 TV sets. These broadcasts were, however, done on board a US Navy Super Constellation (C-121) at phenomenal costs (Hoffer & Lichty, 1982).

Later that year—with the United States providing the equipment, training, and receivers and the South Vietnamese providing the land, buildings, staff, and operating budget—the first ground stations in Saigon and Hue became operational. Half of THVN's programming was entertainment, about 30 percent public affairs (psychological warfare programs), and 18 percent news and commentary. This Vietnamese TV station survived the 1975 events that led to the change of government in the south and soon resumed operations following the programming of the Hanoi TV station (Hoffer & Lichty, 1978).

The AFVN station, on the other hand, had popular programs such as comedy, sports, drama, and Westerns. The station also provided updates on the GI Bill, health- and safety-related information, as well as exhortations to promote good American–Vietnamese relations. A 1968 survey showed that 20 percent of American soldiers in Vietnam owned TV sets. Television reached about 75 percent of the South Vietnamese public in 1970 but only 40 percent owned TV sets. Group TV viewing, especially in the provinces, was not uncommon (Hoffer & Lichty, 1978).

North Vietnam built its television system in Hanoi with the help of East Germany and other socialist countries. Its first broadcast was on September 7, 1970 (WPV, 1997). It was forced to evacuate its equipment to the countryside and remain at an experimental stage until the end of US bombing. Broadcasting two nights a week to some 1,000 sets in public places in the early 1970s, the station used educational, health, and children-oriented programs (Lichty & Hoffer, 1978).

3. THE PRESS

3.1 Policy and Legal Framework

The Ministry of Culture and Information based in Hanoi supervises the activities of newspapers and periodicals, as well as of the news agencies. The 1960 Constitution of the former Democratic Republic of North Vietnam, which formed the basis of the constitution of reunified Vietnam, protects freedom of speech and the press but "these freedoms are to serve the interests of the revolution of the people" unlike "freedoms in the bourgeoisie press of the West" (Van Dinh, 1982, pp. 390–391).

Consistent with this philosophy and in accordance with the 1992 Constitution, the government passed a Publishing Law in 1993 defining publishing as part of the cultural and ideological activity of the nation, hence not a purely commercial venture. Consequently, the press is subject to state management and regulation.

Among the major provisions of the Publishing Law are copyright protection by the government; pre-publication approval of periodicals; ownership of publishing houses by state agencies or social and political organizations; Vietnamese citizenship or permanent residency as prerequisites for directors and editors-in-chief of publishing houses; submission of an application form, issuance of permit, and payment of a copyright deposit to start publishing operations; and provision for joint ventures with government approval. The Law also prohibited the publication of any material detrimental to the republic—such as those that incite violence, hatred, and aggression, or damage the morals and unity of the Vietnamese people; articles that reveal "party, state, military, national security, economic and foreign affairs secrets"; and material that distorts history and revolutionary achievements, discredits the achievements of the country's heroes, or maligns the reputation of organizations and citizens (Article 22). The Law likewise provides government assistance for the distribution of publications to remote locations.

Immediate precursors to this Law were the 1989 Press Law, which allowed a free press in theory but not in reality (FFWC, 1993); the 1943 Party Cultural Program in North Vietnam; and the Press Law of 1969 in South Vietnam, which was amended in 1970. The Press Law adopted in 1989 declared that the press should advance party policy and also provide a "forum" for the citizens. Providing a theoretical foundation to this Law was the 1943 document that enunciated a consistent policy on culture, including the press and other publications, based on the principles that it must be "national, scientific, popular and led by the Party" (Van Dinh, 1982, p. 387). South Vietnam's Press Law of 1969 or "007" required, among other things, a publishing deposit that drove "nearly two-thirds of the nation's dailies out of business" (Guimary, 1982, p. 376). It imposed penalties—imprisonment or a fine—for violations such as insulting government officials. Instead of direct censorship, it specified guidelines on what publications should avoid. The same law, however, upheld press freedom as a fundamental right and stated that no suspension was possible except through the judicial process. Press Law 007 also addressed such practical problems as the distribution system and banned the practice of renting newspapers (Thai, 1971).

Freedom House (1999) has placed the Vietnam press in the "not free" category with the highest restrictive scores on two criteria: laws and regulations that influence media content, and political pressures and controls on media content. The Freedom House Survey Team (1999) observed that in recent years the government had "shut down several newspapers for violating the [narrow] limits on permissible reporting" (p. 496) and had imprisoned five journalists including Nguyen Hoang Linh, the editor of *Enterprise*, a state-controlled business newspaper, for revealing state secrets and writing about corruption. His arrest and conviction sparked protests within and outside the country. Throughout 1998 and 1999, commercialization of the press continued "under a system in which editors also remained responsible for vetting material published in newspapers and magazines" (Sidell, 1999, p. 95)."

In mid-May 1999, the National Assembly amended the Press Laws to tighten state control over the official media. The amendment emphasises "accurate reporting" that must "benefit the country and the people" (*Nhan Dan*, May 17, 1999). However, in late 1998, Vietnam freed the country's best known dissident, Doan Viet Hoat, who was serving a 15-year sentence for publishing pro-democracy newsletters (Associated Press, September 1, 1998).

3.2 Financial Aspects: Circulation, Advertising, Marketing Strategies

As in other communist systems, the party and the government or its agencies fund most of the publications in Vietnam. The two largest-circulating dailies are the Hanoi-based *Nhan Dan*, with 180,000 copies, and the Ho Chi Minh City-based *Saigon Giai Phong*, with a reported circulation of 100,000. Among the 17 weeklies, the top four in terms of circulation are *Thieu Nien Tien Phong* (Young Pioneers), 150,000; *Hoa Hoc Tro* (Pupils' Flowers), 100,000; *The Thao Van Hoa* (Sports and Culture), 100,000; and *Lao Dong* (Labor), 80,000. For other periodicals, circulation ranges from 10,000 to 165,000. The periodical with the largest circulation is *Tien Phong* (Vanguard) published four times a week by the Ho Chi Minh Communist Youth Union and the Forum of Vietnamese Youth. Although a complete and updated list of publications is difficult to find and estimates of circulation figures vary, the best approximation of daily newspaper circulation in 1996 ranged from the UNESCO (1999) estimate of 300,000 to 570,000. In 1996, Vietnam also had 214 non-daily publications with a circulation of 4 million (UNESCO, 1999).

Even though all the newspapers are affiliated to state agencies, they compete in the emerging free market for advertising and readers. The business weekly, *Vietnam Investment Review*, devotes a third of its issues to advertising (Sherry, 1991) and it made a profit in 1992. In 1998, the newspapers' share of display advertising revenue was 35 percent compared to television's 42 percent, outdoor's 20 percent, and radio's 2 percent. In 1993, these percentages were 20 (newspapers), 33 (television), 39 (outdoor), 7 (magazines), and 2 (radio) (WAN, 1998, 1999).

Dentsu Inc., Vietnam's media planner, has determined that only 33 of the 450 state-run publications offer value for money. Government regulations allow print advertising to take up only 10 percent of the space in local newspapers and 30 percent in foreign-language publications. A three-tiered advertising rate system exists based on categories like local firms, joint ventures, and foreign firms, with the latter two billed twice or thrice what the locals pay (Frith, 1998).

3.3 Structure and Organization

Under a purely communist system, the press is an instrument of the state, which owns and controls it. Vietnam deviates slightly from this model because, with the shift toward a market economy, it has permitted some form of private ownership of periodicals. The condition for ownership is that the publication should be a joint undertaking between the owners and the relevant state agency. A case in point is the *Vietnam Investment Review*, the first foreign-owned, Western-style periodical in the country (Sherry, 1991). An Australian entrepreneur in Ho Chi Minh City reportedly owns it while the State Committee for Cooperation and Investment publishes it. Established in 1990, it is the country's main English-language business weekly with half its circulation overseas (Rogers, 1993).

Today, all newspapers, including the seven dailies—five in Hanoi and two in Ho Chi Minh City—are either state-owned or affiliated with a government agency. The same is true for weeklies and other periodicals, excepting a few business publications. The FFWC (1993) noted that generally there seems to be a greater tolerance for freer business and economic reporting because of the country's desire to participate more actively in the world market.

3.4 Quality and Popular Press

In Vietnam's vast media landscape with some 350 newspapers and periodicals in 1994 (*Statesman yearbook* 1997–98) increasing to 449 in 1995 (WPV, 1997), it is the low-quality tabloids that dominate the market. There is no viable underground press, but occasionally overseas Vietnamese publications are allowed in the country (FFWC, 1993).

Among the quality newspapers are *Phu Nu* (Women), *Van Hoa* (Culture), and *Van Hoa-The Thao* (Culture and Sports). All are monthlies printed on good newsprint and have informative content with a little propaganda. In addition to the *Vietnam Investment Review*, the *Saigon Economic Times* also provides quality economic news.

The three most popular tabloids are *Cong An* (Public Police), *Tuoi Tre* (Young Age), and *Than Nien* (Youth). *Cong An*, considered the only infotainment paper for general readers, reports on crime and spy- or war-related stories that are either factual or fictitious for propaganda purposes. It enjoys exclusive access to and reporting of news concerning the police and secret service agencies.

Tuoi Tre, on the other hand, is a weekly magazine that thrives on humor and campaigns for charity, community involvement, and promotion of youth services.

It reports news events from the perspective of the youth, using an investigative style and a community angle.

Competing with *Tuoi Tre*, *Thanh Nien*, published four times a week, reports on national and world sports, movies, fiction, and literary activities. Its circulation has reached 300,000 when reporting on special sports events such as the Asiad and World Cup Soccer (Interview with Le Thuy, former librarian of *Tin Sang Daily News*, California, December 20, 1998).

3.5 Distribution and Technology

Although the government has tried to improve the distribution of publications and extend the reach of the media, the press in Vietnam is still a largely urban phenomenon with sources, facilities, and readership centered in the huge urban areas. Except for two dailies, all the newspapers and other periodicals originate in Hanoi, the capital, and the majority happen to be official organs of government or party agencies. Provincial and regional papers are few.

The use of typographic machines continued after World War II. These were the workhorses of newspaper printing enhanced by some local innovations like using lead for typesetting. In 1954, rotative typesetting was introduced in Saigon. Offset printing became the most popular method for magazines after 1958 while almost all dailies continued to use typographic machines. Web printing was introduced in mid-1971, while desktop publishing began in the mid-1980s, improving quickly during the early 1990s (Interview with Le Thuy, former librarian of *Tin Sang Daily News*, California, December 20, 1998).

4. BROADCASTING

4.1 Policy and Legal Framework

The Ministry of Culture and Information is the government body in charge of the overall management and supervision of radio and television broadcasting services. Two other agencies—the Central Television and the State Committee for Radio and Television—also exercise some regulatory control and oversight of broadcasting activities. The laws and political ideology that guide the print media apply to radio and television as well because their main function is to promote the interests of the state and the programs of the Communist Party.

4.2 Structure and Organization

Radio and television are government monopolies, owned, operated, and financed by the state (FFWC, 1993). Since its inception in 1945, the Voice of Vietnam has increased both its airtime and the power of its transmitters to serve domestic and overseas listeners including overseas Vietnamese (WPV, 1997). In 1991, Vietnam had 288 FM stations and 8,365 radio-relay stations (*The Europa world year-book*, 1997).

Television Vietnam with three main channels broadcasts via satellite from Hanoi to the entire country and the Asian region. Broadcasts are in Vietnamese, French, and English. Other regional broadcasting centers are in Tam Dao (for the provinces in the Hong (Red) River delta, the Midlands, and Highlands), Ho Chi Minh City, Hue, Nha Trang, and Can Tho (WPV, 1997). At the end of 1994, Vietnam had 53 provincial television stations and 232 relay stations.

Local radio programs reach about 70 to 80 percent of the nation's populated areas (*The Europa world yearbook*, 1997). Television penetrates about 40 percent of the population. According to UNESCO (1999), Vietnam had about 3.5 million TV receivers and 8.2 million radio receivers in use in 1997, a density of 4.7 and 10.7 per 100 people respectively. ITU (1999) data, on the other hand, show 13.5 million TV receivers with a penetration of 18 per 100 people in 1996.

4.3 Program Policies

Since July 1, 1994, the Voice of Vietnam has been broadcasting simultaneously in three networks on its national service. Network 1 programs include news, current affairs, and music, which it broadcasts daily for 18 hours on seven medium-wave (AM) and two shortwave (SW) stations. Network 2 provides economic, cultural, social, literary, art-related, and educational programs on six AM and two SW stations with a daily 18-hour airtime. Network 3, on the other hand, serves the minority population and broadcasts in ethnic languages—Bana, Ede, Giarai, Hmong, and Khmer. The networks broadcast news in English, French, and Russian as well. Provincial stations broadcast in Vietnamese, as well as in the major ethnic language of the region (*World radio TV handbook*, 1998).

Voice of Vietnam's international service broadcasts target audiences in Asia, Europe, the Americas, the Caribbean, and Russia, as well as foreigners living in Hanoi (WPV, 1997). The languages used are Cambodian, Cantonese, English, French, Indonesian, Japanese, Laotian, Mandarin, Spanish, Thai, and Vietnamese (*World radio TV handbook*, 1998; *The Europa world yearbook*, 1997).

Domestic television programming has remained largely educational in content although lately there have been indications of a liberalizing trend. The state-run Television Vietnam, the only nationwide network, for instance, began airing entertainment-oriented programs such as quiz shows. Because of the dearth of interesting domestically produced television shows, some foreign dramas such as the favorite Taiwanese period drama "Bao Cong," find their way on to Hanoi Television.

The Vietnamese also have access to foreign-operated satellite channels, such as CNN and Hongkong's STAR TV, through the use of satellite dishes, which require government approval. Because many households seemed to be ignoring this regulation, the government made it illegal in early 1997 for the general public to receive satellite programs. Communist Party officials and other high-ranking government officials are, however, exempt from this law (Hanoi's Doi Moi should encompass TV, 1997).

4.4 Ownership and Finance

Even though the broadcasting system operates under a communist model, the World Association of Newspapers (WAN, 1998) reported that 48 percent of display advertising revenue in the country went to Television Vietnam in 1997. Thus advertising-financed television appears to be emerging in the country. However, with only 3 percent of display advertising to its credit, radio appears to maintain its non-commercial character.

Despite advertising revenues that have made television the dominant medium since 1966, the state-owned provincial relay stations do not have the budget or facilities to create their own programming. Officially, television commercials can only take up 5 percent of total broadcast time but local stations seemed to apply their own rules (Frith, 1998).

Patterned after China's media buying system, advertisers purchase television spots through a local agency. A three-tier price method is used where the locals get the cheapest; while foreigners, as well as joint partnerships, are charged higher rates (Marshall, 1995).

5. NEW ELECTRONIC MEDIA

5.1 Internet and On-line Media

Personal computers came into Vietnam in the early 1980s. The country had an estimated 250,000 computers in 1996, a computer density of 0.33 per 100 people (ITU, 1998). In 1997, the number increased to 350,000, about 70 percent of which were imported and the balance assembled at the nation's 160 information technology centers (Ha, 1998). ITU (1999) estimated the number of personal computers at 500,000 in 1998, or 0.64 per 100 people.

In 1993, the government initiated a national program for the development of information technology. Relevant ministries and policy groups such as the IT 2000 have pitched for investment in localized production of hardware, as well as software development through incentives such as tax exemption, investment assistance and shared cost schemes (Mansell & Wehn, 1998). The country now has 2,000 IT engineers. Seven newly established IT faculties in universities aim to produce about 1,500 IT engineers annually (Ha, 1998).

Vietnam was officially connected to the Internet in November 1997 (Ha, 1998). In March 1998, the government announced plans to regulate local Internet use but in October stated that Internet access would be unrestricted (Freedom House, 1998; Vietnam to further open access to Internet, 1998). The number of Internet users is estimated at between 11,000 (Vietnam to further open access to Internet, 1998) and 40,000 (*Asia Pulse*, 1998). In 1996, the number of Internet hosts stood at five, with 100 users (ITU, 1998). The Network Wizards' surveys show that the number of Internet hosts increased from 25 in July 1998 to 34 in July 1999. Most of the Internet subscribers are businesses, 44.2 percent of which are in the private sector, 34.4 percent in the foreign-invested sector, 13.7 percent in the state sector, and 4.7 percent in other sectors located in larger cities (Levine, 1998). Factors that have restricted the diffusion of the Internet are the lack of proper infrastructure, slow transmission lines, and the high cost of on-line services.

The English-language *Saigon Times Daily* has gone on-line (http://www.saigon.news.com). *Nhan Dan* went on-line on June 21, 1998, and added an English on-line edition on March 11, 1999. It claims an Internet readership of 100,000 of which 85 percent is from outside Vietnam (*Nhan Dan*, June 14, 1999). Three Vietnamese magazines also have on-line editions: *Hop Luu* (http://www.kicon.com. hopluu), *The Key 21* (http://kicon.com/thekey21/), and *Phu Nu Viet* (http://home. earthlink.net/~phunuviet/). The first two are general-interest magazines while the third is a women's magazine.

Vietnam is engaged in the construction of a broadband integrated service digital network (B-ISDN) to meet all the telecommunication requirements of the country and to join the global information infrastructure (APT, 1998). The Vietnam Electronics and IT Association has said that the country needs to invest US$ 1.7 billion information technology but, from 1995 to 1998, investments in this field amounted to only US$ 7.2 million or VND 100 billion (Ha, 1998).

5.2 Telecommunications Infrastructure

The French laid the foundations for Vietnam's first telephone system. In 1998, Vietnam had 2 million mainline telephones, a density of 2.58 per 100 people—showing a compound annual growth rate of almost 49 percent since 1990. The country also had 157,000 cellular subscribers in 1998, a density of 0.24 per 100 people (ITU, 1998, 1999; APT, 1998).

In July 1995, the Vietnam Posts and Telecommunications Corporation, a state-owned monopoly reporting to the Department General of Posts and Telecommunications, took over the operation of telecommunications. Under the corporation, two separate companies manage the national and the international networks. Other companies within the corporation handle data communications, mobile services, postal services, import–export operations, and the like (APT, 1998). Business corporation contracts allow private-sector involvement in telecommunications. Participating foreign companies include Telstra (Australia), Kennevik (Sweden), and Sapura (Malaysia) (APT, 1998).

Vietnam has modernized its national telecommunication backbone network with one digital microwave and two fiber-optic cable links, each running along the entire length of the country. Vietnam has three gateways and eight Intersputnik and Intelsat earth stations. The Thailand–Vietnam–Hong Kong fiber-optic submarine cable began operating in 1996. Vietnam is also a participant in the SEA-

ME-WE-3 fiber-optic submarine cable. It is also involved in the CSC terrestrial fiber-optic cable link connecting China, Vietnam, Laos, Thailand, Malaysia, and Singapore (APT, 1998).

6. POLICY TRENDS FOR PRESS AND BROADCASTING

Since 1988, Vietnam has shown a trend toward allowing private ownership of some media organizations in conjunction with the country's reform policy to increase privatization. Although a majority of the print media are still government-owned or -affiliated and all broadcast media are government monopolies, the country has one non-governmental news agency, Vinapress, as well as a private, foreign-owned, Western-style periodical, the *Vietnam Investment Review*. Australian-born media baron Rupert Murdoch has also expressed interest in starting some publications in Vietnam. In general, the government seems to be showing a more tolerant attitude toward business and economic journalism because Vietnam wants to become an important player in the world market.

The proliferation of newspapers and periodicals is bewildering but the government has stepped in and closed down redundant publications. The trend toward streamlining may continue as the media industry matures and either market forces or the government dictate what publications should be supported.

Radio will remain an influential medium and a tool used by the government to pursue national development. As the quality and reach of the print media and television improve, along with a prospering market-driven economy, they are likely to have a greater impact. However, sustained efforts and clear-cut policies are vital to establish priorities for the country's communication and basic infrastructure in readiness for the Information Age.

The role of universities and professional organizations in the establishment and enforcement of standards, as well as in the re-education and training of journalists, will be significant. According to a Freedom Forum report, few Vietnamese journalists receive formal training because of the limited availability of journalism education.

In 1964, the University of Dalat—a private, Catholic school—established the first journalism department with about 30 students. The university's founder, Nguyen Ngoc Linh, a graduate of American higher education, served as a *New York Times* stringer. A Buddhist university in the south has established a second journalism department. Today the University of Hanoi and the University of Ho Chi Minh City also have schools of journalism. Instruction though is on a modest scale with only a handful of courses offered. In fact, the Freedom Forum reported the need to raise the standards of journalism education to international levels.

The Vietnam Journalists' Association also offers some journalism training. First established in 1950, it is an organization of Vietnamese editors, reporters, and photographers working in the press, radio, television, and news agencies in the country. In 1996, it had 8,000 members (*The Europa world yearbook*, 1997).

7. MAIN ISSUES

● Vietnam's press shares a number of problems associated with many developing nations: low income resulting in low newspaper readership per capita, a lack of technology and technical expertise, and a low level of economic development. The latter translates directly into the lack of a basic and reliable infrastructure of electricity supply, roads and transportation facilities, and the like, which are essential for media development and distribution. The absence of an adequate infrastructure is particularly critical for the country to take advantage of new information technologies associated with the Internet. Although Vietnam has shown robust economic growth for the past few years (8.8 percent between 1991–95 increasing to 9.5 percent in 1995), it easily lags behind its ASEAN neighbors by about 15 years in terms of the country's level of economic and media development.

● The country's topography—in addition to infrastructure and economic problems—also hampers media distribution. The government has subsidized circulation of publications in an effort to extend their reach to remote villages. However, to achieve success, it is necessary to reduce the existing inequities by closing the media consumption and literacy gap between urban and rural population.

● The country's dual system—a communist government and a quasi-market economy—poses unique problems for the press. Historically, the press in Vietnam has not been either politically or financially independent. Although today's newspapers do not have to depend on advertising income because they are either government-owned or -affiliated, yet they are competing aggressively for advertisers and readers. Already, the problems spawned by commercialism, such as the dominance of low-quality tabloids chiefly carrying stories on sex and crime in order to increase circulation, are beginning to show. Also, the government's ambivalence regarding the degree of control over the press and advertising has resulted in the sporadic changes in regulations and enforcement procedures. After experimenting with "renovation, openness and democracy" in 1986, the government once again began clamping down on the press in 1989. As the country continues to move toward a market economy, these issues may become more pronounced if not addressed.

● The Freedom Forum has brought up the issue of raising the standards of journalism and media training to international levels. A need exists to increase not only the number but also the quality of courses to supply knowledgeable and skilled manpower to the editorial and technical side of a growing media industry. Upgrading of technical and production facilities, along with training of media personnel is necessary to alleviate the shortage of professional journalists and technical people.

8. STATISTICS

General Profile

Population (1999)	77.3 million*
Population density (1999)	237.6 per sq km
GNP per capita (1999)	US$ 310
GDP per capita (PPP)	US$ 1,755
Adult literacy	91.9 percent
Urban population	21 percent
Geographical size	325,360 sq km
Exchange Rate (1999 average)	US$ 1 = Dong 13,941**

Source: * US Census Bureau, International Data Base (http://www.census.gov/cgi-bin/ipc/idbrank.pl); ** OANDA Historical Currency Table (http://www.oanda.com.converter/cc_table?lang=en); *Asiaweek*, February 4, 2000.

Table 1
Number and Circulation of Daily Newspapers

	1980	1985	1990	1995	1996
No. of dailies	4	4	5	10	10
Total circulation	520,000	540,000	560,000	294,000	300,000
Circulation per 100 inhabitants	0.97	0.9	0.84	0.4	0.4

Source: UNESCO, 1999.

Table 2
Daily Newspapers: Circulation, Language, and Other Data

Name	Date established	Place of publication	Language	Circulation
Le Courrier du Vietnam	N.A.	Hanoi	French	N.A.
Hanoi Moi	1976	Hanoi	Vietnamese	35,000
Nhan Dan	1946	Hanoi	Vietnamese	180,000*
Quan Doi Nhan Dan	1950	Hanoi	Vietnamese	60,000
Vietnam News	1991	Hanoi	English	10,000
Saigon Giai Phong	1975	Ho Chi Minh	Vietnamese	100,000
Saigon Times	1995	Ho Chi Minh	English	N.A.

Source: *The Europa world yearbook*, 1997; * *Nhan Dan* website.

Table 3
Number and Penetration of Radio Receivers

	1980	1985	1990	1995	1996	1997
No. of receivers ('000s)	5,000	6,000	6,900	7,800	8,000	8,200
Receivers per 100 inhabitants	9.3	10.0	10.3	10.6	10.7	10.7

Source: UNESCO, 1999.

Table 4
Number and Penetration of TV Receivers

	1980	1985	1990	1995	1996	1997
No. of receivers ('000s)	1,800	2,000	2,600	3,200 (12,000)	3,500 (13,500)	3,570
Receivers per 100 inhabitants	3.4	3.3	3.9	4.3 (16.3)	4.7 (17.9)	4.7

Source: UNESCO, 1999.
Note: Figures in parenthesis are from ITU, 1999.

Table 5
Top Circulating Periodicals

Name	Date established	Place of publication	Publisher	Frequency	Language	Circulation
Hoa Hoc Tro (Pupil's Flowers)	N.A.	Hanoi	N.A.	weekly	Vietnamese	100,000
Lao Dong (Labor)	1929	Hanoi	VN Confed. of Labor	weekly	Vietnamese	80,000
Tap Chi Cong San (Communist Review)	1955	Hanoi	Communist Party of Vietnam	fortnightly	Vietnamese	50,000
The Thao Van Hoa (Sports and Culture)	1982	Hanoi	N.A.	weekly	Vietnamese	100,000
Thieu Nhi Dan Toc (The Ethnic Young)	N.A.	Hanoi	N.A.	monthly	Vietnamese	60,000
Thieu Nien Tien Phong (Young Pioneers)	N.A.	Hanoi	N.A.	weekly	Vietnamese	150,000
Tien Phong (Vanguard)	1953	Hanoi	Ho Chi Minh City Communist Youth Union & Forum of Viet. Youth	4 x per week	Vietnamese	165,000
Van Nghe Quan Doi (Army Lit. & Arts)	1957	Hanoi	Army	monthly	Vietnamese	50,000
Vietnam Pictorial	1954	Hanoi	N.A.	monthly / bimonthly	Vietnamese, English, French, Chinese Spanish, Lao	120,000

Source: *The Europa world yearbook*, 1997.

Table 6
Telecommunications Profile

Number of mainline telephones (1998)	2,000,000
Number of mainline telephones per 100 people	2.58
Number of cellular/mobile subscribers (1998)	157,000
Number of cellular/mobile subscribers per 100 people (1998)	0.24
Number of fax machines (1996)	19,800
Number of Internet hosts (1999)	34*
Number of personal computers (1998)	500,000
Number of personal computers per 100 people (1998)	0.64

Source: ITU, 1999; * Internet Software Consortium (www.isg.org).

9. USEFUL ADDRESSES

9.1 Vietnam Dailies

Le Courrier du Vietnam
33 Le Thanh Thong, Hanoi
Telephone: (4) 8214587
Fax: (4) 82583368

Hanoi Moi (**New Hanoi**)
44 Le Thai To, Hanoi
Telephone: (4) 8248054
Fax: (4) 8248054

Nhan Dan (**The People**)
71 Hang Trong, Hanoi
Telephone: (4) 8254231
Fax: (4) 8255593

Quan Doi Nhan Dan (**People's Army**)
7 Phan Dinh Phung, Hanoi
Telephone: (4) 8254118

Vietnam News
79 Ly Thuong Kiet, Hanoi
Telephone: (4) 8248181
Fax: (4) 8246908

Saigon Giai Phong (**Saigon Liberation**)
432 Nguyen Thi Minh Kai, Ho Chi Minh City
Telephone: (8) 8395942
Association Fax: (8) 334183

Saigon Times
35-37 Nam Ky Khoi Nghia St. District 1

Ho Chi Minh City
Telephone: (8) 8295936
Fax: (8) 8294294

9.2 Selected Periodicals

Lao Dong **(Labor)**
51 Hang Bo, Hanoi
Telephone: (4) 8252441
Fax: (4) 8254441

Hoa Hoc Tro **(Pupils' Flowers)**
5 Hoa Moa, Hanoi
Telephone: (4) 8211065

Van Nghe **(Arts and Letters)**
17 Tran Quoc Toan, Hanoi
Telephone: (4) 8264430

Tien Phong **(Vanguard)**
15 Ho Xuan Huong, Hanoi
Telephone: (4) 8264031
Fax: (4) 8225032

9.3 News Agencies

Vietnam News Agency
5 Ly Thuong Kiet, Hanoi
Telephone: (4) 8255445
Fax: (4) 8252984

Vinapress
79 Ly Thuong Kiet, Hanoi
Telephone: (4) 8253508

9.4 Radio

Voice of Vietnam
58 Quan Su, Hanoi
Telephone: (4) 8261122

9.5 Television

Vietnam Television
59 Giang Vo Ave., Hanoi
Telephone: (4) 8355933
Fax: (4) 8355332

9.6 Press Association

Vietnam Journalists
59 Ly Thai To, Hanoi
Telephone: (4) 8253608
Fax: (4) 8250797

10. REFERENCES

APT (Asia-Pacific Telecommunity). (1998, 1999). *The APT yearbook*, Bangkok: APT.
Businesses line up to subscribe to Internet in Vietnam. (1998, July 8). *Asia Pulse*, pp. 10–11.
Editor & publisher international yearbook. (1959–1975). New York: E&P.
Europa world yearbook, The. (1997). London: Europa Publications.
FFWC (The Freedom Forum World Center). (1993). *Summary of roundtable on the state of the media in Vietnam*. Arlington, VA: The FFWC.
Freedom House Survey Team. (1999). *Freedom in the world: The annual survey of political rights and civil liberties, 1998–1999*. New York: Freedom House.
Frith, T.K. (1998). Advertising in Vietnam during the Doi Moi period. *Media Asia, 25*, 156–160, 169.
Guimary, D. L. (1982). South Vietnam: Before 1975. In J.A. Lent (Ed.), *Newspapers in Asia: Contemporary trends and problems* (pp. 368–385). Hong Kong: Heinemann Asia.
Ha, P.N. (1998, June 29). Profile: Vietnam's computer industry. *Asia Pulse*, pp. 55–59.
Hanoi's Doi Moi should encompass TV. (1997, March 5). *The Daily Yomiuri*, pp. 20–21.
Hoffer, T.W., & Lichty, L.W. (1978). Republic of Vietnam (South Vietnam). In J.A. Lent (Ed), *Broadcasting in Asia and the Pacific: A continental survey of radio and television* (pp. 93–111). Philadelphia: Temple University Press.
ITU (International Telecommunication Union). (1998, 1999). *World telecommunication development report*. Geneva: ITU.
Levine, J. (1998, October 1). Internet in holding pattern. *The Vietnam Business Journal, 18*.
Lichty, L.W. & Hoffer, T.W. (1978). North Vietnam. In J.A. Lent (Ed), *Broadcasting in Asia and the Pacific: A continental survey of radio and television* (pp. 111–118). Philadelphia: Temple University Press.
Mansell, R., & Wehn, U. (Eds.). (1998). *Knowledge societies: Information technology for sustainable development*. New York: Oxford University Press (for UNDP).
Marshall, A. (1995, April 21). Vietnam. *Asian Advertising and Marketing*, pp. 26–27.
Nhan, T. (1970, July 18). Press agencies in Vietnam. *International Relations Newsletter* (Saigon), p. 21.
Reddy, M. (Ed). (1994). *Statistical abstract of the world*. Detroit: Gale Research
Rogers, J. (1993, September 9). War on the weeklies starts in Vietnam. *Reuters News Agency*.
Sherry, A. (1991, August 5). First foreign-owned newspaper to appear in September. *Far Eastern Economic Review*, p. 33.
Sidell, M. (1999). Vietnam in 1998: Reform confronts the regional crisis. *Asian Survey, 29* (1), 89–97.
Statesman yearbook. (1997–98). New York: St. Martin's Press.
Sussman, L.R. (1999). *Press freedom 1999: News of the century*. New York: Freedom House.
Thai, N. (1971). South Vietnam. In J.A. Lent (Ed.), *Asian newspapers' reluctant revolution* (pp. 234–254). Ames: The Iowa State University Press.
UNESCO (United Nations Educational, Scientific and Cultural Organization). (1999). *Statistical yearbook*. Lanham, MD: UNESCO Publishing and Bernan Press.
Van Dinh, T. (1982). Vietnam after 1975. In J.A. Lent (Ed.), *Newspapers in Asia: Contemporary trends and problems* (pp. 386–394). Hong Kong: Heinemann Asia.

Vietnam to further open access to Internet. (1998, September 10). *Bernama*, p. 4.
World Bank. (1999). *World development report 1998–99*. New York: Oxford University Press.
WPV (World Publishers in Vietnam). (1997). *The press, radio and television*. Hanoi: WPV.
WAN (World Association of Newspapers). (1998, 1999). *World press trends*. Paris: WAN.
World factbook. (1998). Washington, DC: US Central Intelligence Agency [On-line]. Available:
    (http://www.odci.gov/cia/publications/factbook).
World radio TV handbook. (1998). Amsterdam: Billboard.

♦

East Asia

INTRODUCTION

Shelton A. Gunaratne

1. MULTIMEDIA ACCESS

East Asia is better prepared for the Information Age than all of South Asia and much of Southeast Asia. With the exception of China, Mongolia, and North Korea, all other East Asian economies have a telephone density (that is, mainline telephones per 100 people) exceeding the world average of 18.9 (Table 1). The scenario is even better in relation to TV sets per 100 people, with only Mongolia and perhaps North Korea below the world average of 24.1. In Internet-host density (that is, hosts per 10,000 people), however, only Hong Kong, Japan, and Taiwan are ahead of the world average with South Korea trailing closely. (By January 1999, Internet density had increased to 356.67 in Hong Kong, 142.75 in Taiwan, 133.64 in Japan, and 60.47 in South Korea, with the world average at 74.1.)

2. STATE OF THE PRESS AND OF BROADCASTING

North Korea stands out as the only country in Asia with a perfect press restriction score on all four criteria that Freedom House has been using to conduct its annual surveys (Table 2). China comes next except for its relative relaxation of economic influences on media content—perhaps a reflection of the economic policies that China has adopted for global competitiveness. China appears to have relaxed repressive action on the broadcast media as well. Because Freedom House has placed China's two SARs—Hong Kong and Macau—in the "partly free" category on governance, one may presume that they also have a "partly free" press. Japan, Taiwan, South Korea, and Mongolia head East Asia in press freedom. This introduction uses Freedom House's press freedom ranking to list the countries/economies for the discussion of highlights.

2.1 Japan

In this section, Saito points out that Japan has no press law that exclusively regulates newspapers even though several legal provisions relating to newspapers do exist. Article 21 of Japan's Constitution bars censorship and protects the secrecy of communication. On the negative side, as Freedom House states, the press clubs associated with government ministries and the police tie journalists closely to officials. Five mainstream dailies and some TV stations belong to these groups. The tabloid press, excluded from the clubs, breaks most scandals. The 1950 Broadcast Law and the Radio Wave Law (as revised in 1989) regulate Japan's two separate radio and television broadcasting systems. NHK, the public entity, runs three nationwide radio networks. Subscriptions finance two nationwide television networks. Advertising revenues finance about 6,900 private radio and TV stations. The ruling Liberal Democratic Party has revealed a plan to establish a 24-hour system to monitor radio, newspapers, and television for incorrect or biased reports about the party. Although this plan could limit certain types of political coverage, the mainstream press has paid scant attention to it. Freedom House says that constraints already at work within the press suggest that little uproar is likely.

2.2 Taiwan

Since the lifting of martial law in 1987, the Taiwan press has acquired a freedom never enjoyed before, claim Wang and Lo in this section. In 1992, the government amended the Sedition Law to cover only direct advocacy of violence. It legalized the promotion of political independence from China. With most of the controlling measures getting outdated, the government abolished the 1930 Publications Law, which required licensing. New legislation has aimed to help the print industry maintain stable development. Taiwan has some 233 news agencies, as well as some 350 regularly published newspapers and more than 243 magazines. A national press council operates to deal with criticism. Freedom House says that for social and political reasons, some self-censorship prevails. Foreign investors are moving into the flourishing electronic media field. Broadcast and print media reflected the country's transition to democracy in 1996. Four TV channels, more than 140 cable TV stations, and 44 radio stations reflect the marked diversification occurring after decades of restrictive Kuomintang (KMT) rule. The KMT still operates some of these outlets but must face competition for its dwindling share of the audience.

2.3 South Korea

Freedom House states that the news media have not fully felt the freedom that the political system has provided after the election of reformist President Kim Dae Jung. In this section, Heo, Uhm, and Chang point out that the Kim administration has pushed for the independence of the press from *chaebols*, media barons, and political pressure. Moves have been afoot to revise the 1997 Periodicals Act, which replaced the 1980 Basic Press Act, to de-regulate the industry and allow greater competition. Even though three laws allow the government to control broadcast ownership and programming, news broadcasters enjoy a large degree of autonomy and offer diverse views. The mainly private newspapers, however, still practice self-censorship even though the government has ceased to exert direct pressure. Freedom House says that officials, as in most democracies, now seek to prevent critical and unflattering reports of the government through persuasion. A case of defamation of the president resulted in a two-year prison sentence on a journalist in 1998.

2.4 Mongolia

Chapter 2 of Mongolia's 1992 Constitution guarantees human rights and freedoms, including press freedom. The country's libel laws, however, make it relatively easy for officials to prove damages. But the authorities did not use the courts to harass journalists during the last decade. A law enacted on January 1, 1999, aimed to unshackle, from government control, those newspapers, radio and TV stations, and other media not already in private hands. In this section, Lowe and Gunaratne assert that since the transition to democracy, Mongolia has encouraged private interests to enter the broadcasting market. Although more than 100 private newspapers and magazines exist, poor financing allows most to publish only sporadically. Each party has at least one paper. The largest independent paper is a former government organ that has been privatized. Mongolia has more than 300 TV stations. The state broadcast media, the best funded, are the most watched. State-run broadcast media occasionally favor the ruling party. In the January 1999 survey, Freedom House gave Mongolia a press restriction score of 30, four notches lower than in the previous year.

2.5 Hong Kong SAR (China)

Freedom House has ranked Hong Kong as "partly free" in relation to governance: political rights and civil liberties. In this section, however, So, Chan, and Lee maintain that Hong Kong is a capitalist society with the government firmly wedded to a *laissez-faire* policy on commercial activities. They say that after the 1997 handover to China, the press has continued to be more vocal than most people had envisaged. However, it remains to be seen whether this desirable trend will remain in the long run. Broadcasting regulation at the highest level rests with the chief executive and his advisory body, the Executive Council. Under the name of market-driven journalism, yellow journalism has become the order of the day for the popular press, as well as for some so-called "infotainment" type of TV programs.

2.6 Macau SAR (China)

Freedom House has placed Macau also in the "partly free" category in relation to governance. It is on par with Hong Kong on limits to political rights and civil liberties. Macau has eight Chinese dailies and 10 weeklies. The most influential is the communist organ *Macao Daily News*, which claims a circulation of 100,000 copies. This daily, which reaches some coastal cities in Guangdong as well, is a "semi-official" paper reflecting the views of the Chinese government. So, Chan, and Lee point out that because the majority of Macau's press was already pro-communist, little has changed since Macau reverted to China in December 1999.

2.7 China

Yan, in this section, asserts that China's economic reforms have brought about great changes in the media scene. She says much of the content of the weekend editions and evening papers—which are flourishing while the party papers are declining rapidly—has deviated from the notion that the media should serve the party. "Several small weekly newspapers provide avant-garde coverage of news that the Communist dailies and government sources do not reveal," the Freedom House points out. "[They] write about local corruption, faulty public services, and investigative news that does not implicate top Communist policy makers" (Sussman, 1999, p. 12). Plans were afoot in mid-1999 to start an independent English-language daily for expatriates in Shanghai with no central government subsidy or links to the Xinhua news agency. Independent English-language dailies are also published in Shenzhen and Guangzhou. On the negative side, editors resort to self-censorship because they are uncertain just how far they can go. In 1998, the government withdrew visas of Hong Kong journalists who wanted to cover the Clinton visit, arrested a CBS correspondent and seized her videos, deported a Japanese journalist, and ordered a German reporter to leave China. Moreover, the authorities jammed the Voice of Tibet broadcasts and monitored "harmful information" on the Internet, with 2.1 million accounts and 6 million users, through a special office in the Shanghai police.

2.8 North Korea

North Korea exemplifies complete government control over every aspect of the mass media. The party and the government strictly monitor all information entering the country. The penalty for repeating views critical of the regime, or its head, can be execution or a sentence to a "corrective labor camp." Gunaratne and Kim, in this section, assert that the country's mass media, as organs of the communist political and social structure, promote the state philosophy of *Jucheism* (self-help) to a degree that has hampered international cooperation and the introduction of foreign capital and advanced technology. They argue that because the survival of the current regime and reform are incompatible, press freedom is unlikely to emerge in North Korea in the near future.

3. PROBLEMS AND PROSPECTS

By 2025, East Asia would have a population of 1.64 billion: 20.8 percent of the world population (Table 3) or 38.8 percent of Asia's population. (Currently, East Asia accounts for 45.2 percent of Asia's population.) Japan's population would have declined by 6.6 million from its current size while China's population would have increased by 153.3 million. However, China's population will start declining from then onwards. South Korea would have 7.7 million more, Taiwan 4 million more, North Korea 2.7 million more, and Hong Kong and Mongolia would each have 1 million more. Nonetheless, these increases are unlikely to impose tremendous burdens inasmuch as illiteracy and infrastructure problems do not exist to the extent that they do in South Asia and in parts of Southeast Asia. The mass media are more likely to enjoy greater freedom as more of East Asia prospers economically.

4. STATISTICS

Table 1
Multimedia Access in South Asia

Overall world rank	Country	Main telephone lines per 100 people		TV sets per 100 people		Internet hosts per 10,000 people	
		1997	*Rank*	*1997*	*Rank*	*1997*	*Rank*
18	Japan	48.9	24	70.6	6	92.58	27
21	Hong Kong SAR	56.1	14	41.2	38	250.20	15
34	Taiwan	46.6	28	32.7	51	81.81	30
40	South Korea	44.4	33	34.2	50	39.35	40
63	Macau	40.5	39	28.8	70	3.62	84
107	North Korea	4.9	133	N/A	0	0.00	176
119	China	5.6	129	27.0	76	0.58	136
153	Mongolia	3.3	142	5.9	146	0.05	147
World average		**18.9**		**24.1**		**52.79**	

Source: ITU, 1999.

Table 2
Press Freedom in Asia–January 1999
(Freedom House Ratings)

East Asia		A	B	C	D	Total	Rating on political rights ❶ and civil liberties ❷
Japan	Broadcast	1	6	0	0	19	
	Print	1	6	5	0	F	F 1, 2
Taiwan	Broadcast	5	6	4	0	25	
	Print	2	4	4	0	F	F 2, 2
Korea (S)	Broadcast	2	7	0	0	28	
	Print	4	9	5	1	F	F 2, 2
Mongolia	Broadcast	7	6	0	0	30	
	Print	6	3	8	0	PF	F 2, 3
Hong Kong SAR				N/A			PF 6, 4
Macau SAR				N/A			PF 6,4
China	Broadcast	15	15	7	2	81	
	Print	15	14	8	5	NF	NF 7, 6
Korea (N)	Broadcast	15	15	15	5	100	
	Print	15	15	15	5	NF	NF 7, 7

Source: http://freedomhouse.org/pfs99
Note: Press freedom criteria:
A = Laws and regulations that influence media content; scale: broadcast, 0–15; print, 0–15
B = Political pressures and controls on media content; scale: broadcast, 0–15; print, 0–15
C = Economic influences over media content; scale: broadcast, 0–15; print, 0–15
D = Repressive actions (killing journalists, physical violence, censorship, self-censorship, arrests, etc.); scale: broadcast, 0–5; print, 0–5
RATING: free: 0–30; partly free: 31–60; not free: 61–100
GOVERNANCE:
❶ First number in column = rating on political rights
❷ Second number in column = rating on civil liberties
RATING: 1 = most free; 7 = least free

Table 3
East Asia: Estimated Population in 2025

World rank	Country	Population
2	China	1,407,739,146
12	Japan	119,864,560
26	South Korea	54,256,166
54	Taiwan	25,897,118
55	North Korea	25,485,239
105	Hong Kong SAR	7,816,391
134	Mongolia	3,555,370
167	Macau SAR	644,217
	Total	**1,645,258,207**

Source: US Census Bureau, 1998.

5. REFERENCES

ITU (International Telecommunication Union). (1999). *Challenges to the network: Internet for development*. Geneva: ITU.

Sussman, L. R. (1999). *Press freedom 1999: News of the century*. New York: Freedom House.

US Census Bureau, International Data Base. (1998, December 28). *IDB: Countries ranked by population* [On-line]. Available: (http://www.census.gov/cgi-bin/ipc/idbrank.pl).

18

CHINA

Liqun Yan

1. NATIONAL PROFILE

1.1 Geography

China has a total area of 9.6 million sq km, next only to Russia, Canada, and the United States in size. It is situated in Eastern Asia, bordering the East China Sea, Korea Bay, Yellow Sea, and the South China Sea, between North Korea and Vietnam. It shares borders with 14 countries: Mongolia, Russia, and North Korea in the north and northeast; Afghanistan, Kazakhstan, Kyrgyzstan, Pakistan, and Tajikistan in the east; and Bhutan, India, Laos, Nepal, Myanmar, and Vietnam in the south.

China has an extremely diverse climate—tropical in the south to sub-arctic in the north. Its terrain comprises mostly mountains, high plateaus, and deserts in the west; and plains, deltas, and hills in the east. About 10 percent of the land is arable (*World factbook*, 1999).

1.2 People

Although China has 56 ethnic groups, the Han people make up more than 91 percent of the country's 1.247 billion people. The other 55 ethnic groups make up less than 9 percent. The Han language is Chinese: standard Chinese or Mandarin (*Putonghua*, based on the Beijing dialect), as well as the *Yue* (Cantonese), *Wu* (Shanghaiese), *Minbei* (Fuzhou), *Minnan* (Hokkien-Taiwanese), *Xiang, Gan*, and *Hakka* dialects (*World factbook*, 1999). The Hui and Manchu ethnic groups also use the Han (Chinese) language. The other 53 ethnic groups have their own languages. China is a country with many religious beliefs. Buddhism is the most influential, followed by Islam, Catholicism, Protestantism, and Taoism.

Acknowledgments: The author would like to thank Chin-Chuan Lee, who is a professor of journalism at the University of Minnesota, for his help in the preparation of the manuscript; and Anthony Blasi, who is an associate professor of sociology at Tennessee State University, for his valuable suggestions. Editor Shelton A. Gunaratne also contributed to this chapter.

The country has an adult literacy rate of 84 percent. Life expectancy at birth is 70 years. By 1997, China had 1,032 regular higher-education institutions and 1,107 adult higher-education institutions with a total enrollment of 5.9 million, including regular undergraduates and those in three-year programs (China, 1998a).

1.3 Government and Politics

The People's Republic of China (PRC) was founded on October 1, 1949, after the Chinese Communist Party (CCP) took over power from the Kuomintang (Nationalist) government. Its political system has two components. One is the National People's Congress, the highest legislative body of the country. The other is the multi-party cooperation and political consultation system, under which the CCP, as the party in power, consults with other political parties to make major decisions. The latter system operates through (*a*) the Chinese People's Political Consultative Conference and (*b*) the system of consultative meetings and forums of democratic parties and non-party personages convened by the CCP Central Committee or the local party committees at different levels. These meetings and forums, which used to be mostly formalities, are beginning to play an influential role as political reforms slowly unfold.

With a history of more than 5,000 years, China has a rich culture enmeshed deeply with the feudalism that dominated the country for more than 2,000 years. After 1949, China went through a socialist transformation aiming to break the shackles of feudalism and to institute state ownership. From 1957 to 1966, China consolidated its socialist reconstruction. In the wake of that period of great development came a decade of enormous destruction: the 1966–76 "Cultural Revolution," which almost brought China to the brink of collapse. A new era in Chinese history began at the end of 1978, when China instituted a policy of reform and opened itself to the outside world. Economic development and the building of social morality became China's main foci.

China's administrative divisions comprise 23 provinces (*sheng*), five autonomous regions (*zizhiqu*), and four municipalities (*shi*)—Beijing, Shanghai, Tianjin, and Chongqing. China considers Taiwan to be its 23rd province.

1.4 Economy

China's gross domestic product at purchasing power parity stood at US$ 4,114 billion with a corresponding per capita GDP of US$ 3,275. However, the nominal per capita GNP was only US$ 783 (*Asiaweek*, February 11, 2000). The sector composition of the economy was industry, 49 percent; services, 31 percent; and agriculture, 20 percent (*World factbook*, 1999).

In 1999, the country's total import and export volume reached US$ 324 billion, with a trade surplus of US$ 44 billion. China has been ranked the 11th among the world's major trading countries and regions since 1992 (China, 1998b). The most common exports are textiles, miscellaneous consumer goods, footwear, food products, radio receivers, watches, bicycles, and computer parts.

2. DEVELOPMENT OF PRESS AND BROADCASTING

2.1 Brief Early History

2.1.1 Beginnings

An authorized gazette—a sort of court circular, *bao*, or "report"—that came out during the Tang Dynasty (A.D. 618–907) was China's earliest newspaper. It appeared continually under a variety of forms and names until the end of the Qing Dynasty in 1911. An English missionary, Robert Morrison (1782–1834), published the first modern Chinese newspaper in 1815. In the 50 years following the Opium War in 1840, foreigners established more than 300 newspapers, most of which were published in Chinese in Shanghai. They included *Shanghai Xinbao* (Shanghai News), *Wanguo Gongbao* (International Review), *Shen Bao, Xinwen Bao* (News Gazette), and *Min Bao* (People's Journal). It is clear that Western powers tried to use media to control and influence the Chinese from early times (Fang & Chen, 1992).

Zhaowen Xinbao (Clarity News), published in Hankou in 1873, and *Xun Huan Ribao* (Cycle Daily), published in Hong Kong in 1874, were the earliest Chinese newspapers run by the Chinese in modern times (Tseng, 1971).

Following China's defeat in the Sino-Japanese War of 1895, many reform-minded intellectuals used newspapers to spread their ideas. Some 94 newspapers and periodicals appeared throughout the country from 1895 to 1898 (Gong, 1997). The most influential of them was the *Shi Wu Bao*, edited by the well-known reformer Liang Qichao. The failure of the reform movement in 1898 brought about more newspapers advocating violent revolution. In 1905, more than 160 revolutionary newspapers were published (Gong, 1997), both overseas and at home. The first newspaper run by Sun Yat Sen's revolutionary party was the *Zhongguo Ribao* founded in Hong Kong in January 1900. One of the most influential papers was the *Min Bao*, which the China Revolutionary League founded in Tokyo in 1905 (Chang, 1989).

The development of China's modern press clearly indicates the close relationship between the press and politics. From early times, the Chinese have used the press to advocate their ideas and to mobilize the people to support their cause. This legacy continued throughout the years of the CCP's revolutionary struggle and in the PRC's political struggles and efforts to promote economic development.

2.1.2 Creation of the Communist Media System (1919–49)

The creation and development of China's current media system paralleled the founding and development of the CCP. The party built and expanded its propaganda force, which in return promoted the party's cause and played a key role in the party's growth and its propulsion to power in 1949.

Following in the footsteps of their revolutionary predecessors, communist leaders used the press to advocate their ideas early on. Chen Duxiu and Li Dazhao, founders of the CCP, were the chief editors of the famous *Xin Qingnian* (New Youth) magazine, which vigorously propagated Marxism-Leninism in China during the May Fourth Movement in 1919. Mao Zedong, the founder of the PRC, was the editor of the *Xiangjiang Pinglun* (Xiang River Review); and Zhou Enlai, the first premier of the PRC, was the editor of the *Tianjin Xuesheng Lianhehui Bao* (Bulletin of the Tianjin Students' Federation in Tianjin).

From the very beginning, the CCP attached great importance to the role of the press in its revolutionary cause. Soon after its founding in 1921, the party set up newspapers in the major cities, the most influential of which were the *Laodong Zhoukan* (Labor Weekly) in Shanghai and *Gongren Zhoukan* (Worker's Weekly) in Beijing. The party started its first central organ, *Xiangdao Zhoukan* (Guide Weekly) in 1922.

After the failure of its first attempt at cooperation with the Kuomintang in 1927, the CCP made greater efforts to build its propaganda system. One year after it set up its central revolutionary base in Jiangxi Province in the south in 1930, the party established its first news agency—the Red China News Press—predecessor of today's Xinhua (New China) News Agency. Two months later, the provisional central government established its organ, *Hongse Zhonghua* (Red China News).

During the War of Resistance against Japan (1937–45), the communists further developed their media institutions both in the base areas and elsewhere. They published in the liberated areas more than half a dozen newspapers, including the *Jiefang Ribao* (Liberation Daily) in 1941. During the same year, under the direct leadership of Zhou Enlai, the CCP established its first radio station, the Yan'an Xinhua Broadcasting Station, which has become the Central People's Broadcasting Station today. Outside their base areas, the communists published several editions of the *Xinhua Ribao* (New China Daily) in several Kuomintang-controlled cities. Meanwhile, underground communists in Shanghai and Hong Kong brought together some left-oriented intellectuals who helped publish many other newspapers and periodicals in those cities. Some of these papers became major propaganda forces against the Kuomintang soon after Japan's surrender in 1945.

2.2 Developments since 1945

Because the CCP used the media as a party tool from the very beginning, political changes in the party greatly influenced the development of the media. The CCP has gone through a tortuous road over the last half century, and so have the media.

The communist media developed rapidly during the civil war between the communists and the Kuomintang (1945–49). (The Xinhua News Agency had 53 military and local offices with 33 branches comprising some 3,000 people [Chang, 1989]. In May 1946, the CCP Central Committee designated the Xinhua News

Agency and *Jiefang Ribao* as the party's official news agency and official newspaper. Meanwhile, the number of radio broadcasting stations had increased to 16 by the end of 1948 [Chang, 1989]. In March 1949, Xinhua News Agency established itself in Beijing, as did the party's central committee. The Xinhua Radio Station became independent in June). *Renmin Ribao* (People's Daily), the organ of the North China Bureau of the Party Central Committee, became the organ of the Central Committee.

Thus, by the time the communists assumed power, they had already built a foundation for the media system for the New China, with the key institutions well established. Strongly influenced by Lenin's media theories adopted in the Soviet Union, the Chinese media system emphasized service to the party, under complete party control. This characteristic was to manifest itself throughout the process of media development in the PRC. Liu (1971) asserted that the Chinese press reflected "the Leninist or (Soviet) and the Maoist conceptions of mass persuasion and the press" (p. 43).

2.2.1 Press

Right after the CCP assumed power in 1949, it began establishing a national press system to consolidate its power. It gave priority to establish a network of party organs. The press workers and the material and technological infrastructure left over from the old regime provided the base for building the network (Zhao, 1998). The CCP moved some of the old party organs, established in the revolutionary base areas, to the big cities as central and provincial party organs. Meanwhile, local party organizations expropriated the existing press facilities and transformed them into communist newspapers. Thus, at the national level, the *People's Daily* became the organ of the CCP Central Committee. Similarly, the CCP committee in each province, autonomous region, or city, also established its official party organ.

In addition to CCP's own organs, the party agencies set up a variety of other publications throughout the country. Some political and social organizations, as well as government departments, started special-interest newspapers, such as those for workers, youth, and intellectuals. In 1957, China had 341 provincial-level papers, almost all dailies; more than 936 county papers; and 31 minority-language newspapers (Chang, 1989). From 1957 to 1966, farmers' papers emerged in many provinces. Some appeared as the peasants' edition of the central organ of the provincial press. At the same time, about a dozen evening papers were established in the major cities—Shanghai, Tianjin, and Beijing—and other cities.

During the "Cultural Revolution" (1966–76), the press suffered enormous setbacks, as newspapers became the battlefields of different groups in the party. All major papers, including the *People's Daily* and the *Liberation Army Daily*, became much involved in the political struggle. They inflamed the "Cultural Revolution" and pushed it to the extreme. Meanwhile, those in power suspended or closed many newspapers, including the 13 evening papers, because those papers had a human-interest or non-political orientation. Thus, the number of regular newspapers shrank to a mere 43 in 1967 (Zhao, 1998).

The economic reforms that followed the "Cultural Revolution" produced a comparatively relaxed political atmosphere that set the pace for a boom in the press. Many papers that had fallen victim to the "Cultural Revolution" resumed publication and numerous other publications sprouted, including specialized and enterprise-oriented newspapers. By the end of 1988, China had 1,579 newspapers distributed openly throughout the country (Fang & Chen, 1992).

Following the crackdown on the pro-democracy movement in June 1989, the press suffered some major setbacks. Some papers had to fold for political reasons. The oppressive period, however, did not last long. By 1990, the last year for which UNESCO (1999) provides daily newspaper data for China, the country had 44 dailies with a circulation of 48 million and 729 non-dailies with a circulation of 68 million. With the publication of Deng Xiaoping's talks during his inspection tour of south China in early 1992, the press entered a second period of boom. The number of non-dailies rose to 1,015, with a circulation of 131.5 million in 1994 (UNESCO, 1999). Polumbaum (1997) has referred to 6,000 or so "internal" publications as well, in addition to the official count of 2,053 newspapers for 1998.[1]

2.2.2 Broadcasting

2.2.2.1 Radio: As with the press, the Chinese government developed broadcasting largely for political infiltration. At the end of 1949, mainland China had 49 state-owned and 30 privately-owned radio stations (Fang & Chen, 1992). The new China government took a series of actions to restore and develop broadcasting. First, it established a four-tier broadcasting network—central, regional, provincial (municipal), and city—with the Central People's Broadcasting Station (CPBS) as the apex. At the end of 1957, the network had 59 local stations. Meanwhile, in 1950, CPBS had begun programs in minority languages, including Tibetan, Mongolian, and Uygur. In addition, in 1954, it had started broadcasts targeted at Taiwan. Second, it permitted CPBS to begin official overseas broadcasting in April 1950. The station's international department inaugurated "Radio Peking," which broadcast programs in seven foreign languages—English, Japanese, Korean, Vietnamese, Burmese, Thai, and Indonesian. In addition, it targeted overseas Chinese with programs in Cantonese and other Chinese dialects. Third, it transformed all 33 privately-owned radio stations, which it had allowed to operate during the earliest stage of the communist regime, into state-owned ones (Chu, 1978; Fang & Chen, 1992).

---

[1] Data supplied by China's Institute of Journalism and Communication (WAN, 1999), however, show that China had 647 dailies (with a circulation of 41.76 million) and 1,516 non-dailies (with a circulation of 137 million) in 1996. In 1998, the number of dailies had increased to 740 (with a circulation of 44.35 million) and the number of non-dailies had decreased to 1,313 (with a circulation of 137.76 million).

Despite a shortage of equipment and professional personnel, provincial, municipal, and local stations developed steadily. In June 1959, China reported 107 stations in operation. That number increased to 122 at the end of 1959 (Chang, 1989). To solve the problems of insufficient radio facilities and the limited number of radio receivers, as well as the problems of illiteracy and newspaper shortage for mass education and propaganda in the early 1950s, the government developed a wired broadcasting system in the countryside. The system contributed a great deal at the local level to the political and cultural education of the peasants, the dissemination of information, and the advancement of cultural life in rural areas.

During the "Cultural Revolution," radio suffered severe setbacks. Many radio programs went off the air because staff members had to participate in the "revolution." Political, economic, and technological developments in the 1980s, however, brought about enormous growth in radio broadcasting. Radio's reach rose from 53 percent in 1981 to 70.6 percent in 1988 (Fang & Chen, 1992). By the early 1990s, more than 1,200 radio stations were operating in the country. In addition, more than 2,000 cities and counties had wired "broadcast stations" (*guangbozhan*) (Polumbaum, 1997). In 1997, China had 417 million radio receivers, or 33.5 receivers per 100 people (UNESCO, 1999).

Although television had taken the lion's share of the audience during the 1980s, radio made a successful comeback in the 1990s, when it caught the audience's attention again with innovative programs, including talk radio. Call-in shows on topics such as marriage, family life, legal affairs, consumer complaints, and the like, have become very popular.

2.2.2.2 Television: On May 1, 1958, China's first television station, the Beijing Television Station, renamed China Central Television Station (CCTV) in May 1978 to reflect its nationwide reach, started operation (Chu, 1978). Soon TV stations emerged in Shanghai and Haerbin. By 1961, China had 26 TV stations. Political interference and economic setbacks slowed down China's television development during the next decade or so.

Color television came in 1973. By 1978, a national TV network of more than 30 stations located in each of the provincial and autonomous regional seats, as well as in Shanghai, Beijing, and Tianjin, was in operation. When Beijing Television Station became CCTV, Beijing got its own local station, BTV. The first ground satellite-reception station was set up in Beijing in 1972 to assist in domestic and international program exchanges. Thus, by the early 1980s, a complete national television network was in place, linking provincial stations to transmitting, channel-switching, and relay stations (Yu, 1990).

In 1985, the Ministry of Radio, Film, and Television (MRFT), which subsequently became the State Administration of Radio, Film, and Television (SARFT), adopted a strategy to enhance TV penetration, similar to the one for radio development. Under this strategy, stations were to be set up at four levels (national, provincial, municipal and county) "to have mixed coverage of television, aimed particularly at extending television into rural areas and inland provinces" (Yu,

1990, p. 72). By November 1998, China had more than 1,000 broadcast TV stations, more than 1,000 cable stations and an additional 1,000 educational TV stations. Television's reach exceeded 90 percent. Almost all provincial-level TV stations offer satellite channels (Remarkable accomplishments, 1998).

UNESCO (1999) estimated that in 1997 China had 400 million TV receivers—almost 32.1 per 100 people. By 1999, with almost 90 percent of the households owning at least one TV receiver and a regular TV audience of 1.1 billion, China has become the world's largest television market. Television has become a key medium from which people learn, understand, and feel Chinese culture.

3. THE PRESS

3.1 Policy and Legal Framework

The 1982 Constitution contains some articles similar to a Bill of Rights. Article 35 guarantees the freedom of expression, press, assembly, association, demonstration, and protest. Article 94 of the Civil Law also states that citizens have the right to sign, express, and publish. But as Trionfi (1999) points out, these rights have been mostly overridden in practice by other clauses relating to national security, interests of the state, and the primacy of the Communist Party. Three other articles are often used by the state when dealing with the media:

- Article 51: "Citizens of the P.R. of China, in exercising their freedom and rights, may not infringe upon the interests of the state, of society or of the collective or upon the lawful freedom and rights of other citizens";
- Article 53: "Citizens of the P.R. of China must abide by the constitution and the law, keep state secrets, protect public property, observe labor discipline and public order and respect social ethics";
- Article 54: "It is the duty of citizens of the P.R. of China to safeguard the security, honor and interests of the motherland; they must not commit acts detrimental to the security, honor and interests of the motherland" (p. 13).

Furthermore, the government of China considers the media a branch of its own; therefore, there is no need to create legislation regarding the media. The direction of the CCP is more important in determining the status of the media than any legal codes. The party's press policies, which claim to serve as the guiding principles, are more or less regarded as laws in practice. China's press policy, therefore, is characterized by the "party journalism" emphasizing the "party principle."

The central concept of "party principle" underlies the CCP's domination over the media. The principle comprises three elements: that the news media must accept the party's guiding ideology as their own; that they must propagate the party's programs, policies, and directives; and that they must accept the party's leadership and stick to the party's organizational principles and press policies (Zhao, 1998, p. 19). In a widely publicized speech in 1985, former CCP General Secretary Hu Yaobang said, "The party's news media are the party's mouthpiece, including 'both party and non-party news outlets. They are all under the leadership of the party and must follow the party lines, principles and policies" (quoted in He, 1994, p. 45).

In practice, all important media expressions must go through the collective discussion of the party committee before publication. Any deviation from such practice is called "bourgeois liberalization." In a 1990 speech, President Jiang Zeming urged journalists to stick to the party principle and steadfastly and consistently oppose bourgeois liberalism. He said, "Our newspapers, periodicals, radio and television stations should never be allowed to provide grounds for bourgeois liberalization" (quoted in Vanden Heuvel & Dennis, 1993, p. 31). Since 1987, the party has expelled a number of reporters and writers and closed several newspapers, such as *Shenzhen Youth Daily, Modern Man,* and *the World Economic Herald,* for their bourgeois liberalism.

The party principle determines all other issues in media work. Freedom of the press, truthfulness, objectivity, and "news values" are all subordinate to the party principle. Thus expression of different voices other than the party's is tantamount to "bourgeois freedom of the press.... [T]ruthfulness in news reporting means precisely to uphold the party's ideological line" (Jiang, 1990, quoted in Vanden Heuvel & Dennis, 1993, p. 31). Thus the media could fabricate news to serve the party irrespective of the impact; and "whether a piece of news should be published sooner or later depends on political consideration" (Hu, 1985, cited in He, 1994, p. 55).

The "party principle" reflects the views of many Asian leaders about journalism. Trionfi (1999) says that for most Asian leaders, a fundamental aspect of journalism "is the social responsibility to contribute to the country's political and economic stability" (p. 5). The constant shift of China's press policy accurately mirrors the government's concern for stability. For instance, when the country was politically stable during Deng Xiaoping's leadership in the 1980s, development took priority over stability. So Deng allowed the press to write about economic inefficiencies and political corruption in the belief that a freer media would help to promote economic reforms, and China's press enjoyed a brief period of relative freedom. However, the unrest that accompanied the Tiananmen Square protest in 1989 made stability the government's highest concern, and media became a central target for control.

As the CCP prepared for the transition of political leadership from Deng Xiaoping to Jiang Zeming, it tightened its grip on the media. During a series of top-level conferences on media control, held between 1994 and 1998, Jiang and his propaganda chief Ding Guangen spelled out the boundaries of press autonomy and re-stated the obligation of the media to follow the guidelines set by the CCP.

Starting in the late 1980s, Chinese leaders adopted a new strategy for controlling the news media, a shift from informal to formal regulatory mechanisms. The new strategy became evident with the establishment in early 1987 of the State Press and Publications Administration (SPPA), a ministry-level agency with corresponding agencies at provincial and municipal levels. Among other things, it drafts and enforces press regulations and policies, licenses publications, and monitors texts. (SPPA also overseas issuance of press credentials and permits for news organizations to operate "journalism stations" or local news bureaus.) In December 1990, it promulgated the Provisional Regulations on Newspaper Management (China, 1990), spelling out its first set of formal detailed regulations governing newspaper registration, operation and content.

The general principles of the regulations state that newspapers must uphold the principle of serving socialism and the people; propagate Marxism, Leninism, and Maoism, and the party's and the government's principles and policies; disseminate information, science and technology, and cultural knowledge; provide healthy entertainment for the people; reflect people's opinions and suggestions; and monitor public opinion. The regulations list several taboo areas for the media:

- Inciting and sabotaging the constitution and the implementation of laws;
- inciting to overthrow the regime of the people's democratic dictatorship and sabotaging the socialist system;
- dividing the country or inciting armed rebellion or riot;
- inciting opposition to the leadership of the CCP;
- inciting racial discrimination and sabotaging national unity;
- sabotaging social stability and instigating chaos;
- promoting violence, obscenity, sex, superstition or pseudo-science, and subordination or content harmful to adolescents' physical and psychological health;
- disseminating libel or defamation and other material prohibited for publication by law.

Article 50 states that any violation of the prohibited material is a prosecutable breach of the law. Penalties include fines, confiscation or destruction of the paper, termination of publication and closure.

In mid-1991, the government set up an "information office" to supervise propaganda targeted at foreign audiences. Still another agency that keeps an eye on the press and publication is the Ministry of Public Security, which monitors the leaking of sensitive information.

In the 1980s, some reform-minded journalists started a movement to draft a national press law. "They hoped the law would carve out explicit safeguards beyond the vague 'freedom of the press' provision in Article 35 of China's Constitution, as well as clearly spell out the limits of press freedom" (Polumbaum, 1994, p. 120). But ideological differences over the press law made the drafting process drag on for so long that the latest draft in circulation was shelved indefinitely following the demonstration of spring 1989. Meanwhile, in mid-1999, Zhuhai, a special economic zone in southern China, became the first Chinese city to issue rules lifting restrictions on the media, and it has attracted interest from journalists in other parts of China.[2]

---

[2] Chinese district allows more press scrutiny to lure investors (http://www.freedomforum.org/international/1999/7/1china.asp).

3.2 Financial Aspects: Circulation, Advertising, Marketing Strategies

Since China's media were deemed to be governmental units, they had to perform public functions, which included publicizing government and party policies, educating the public, and mobilizing the masses. They were assessed by how well they produced social benefits as defined by the state, rather than by how much profit they made (To, 1998, p. 268). Therefore, until economic reforms began in 1978, the state completely subsidized the media, except briefly in the early 1950s, when some party organs were financially independent (Zhao, 1998). The estimated circulation of China's major newspapers appears in Table 1.

Economic reforms made commercialization not only possible but also necessary. Reform and openness had created a growing demand by foreign and domestic enterprises for effective advertising channels. Moreover, the party's policy of economic decentralization had caused the state revenues to drop sharply as a portion of national income. The state found it "imperative to shed part of its mammoth financial obligations, urging all media to achieve financial self-reliance and even taking measures to curtail traditional aid to them" (Chen & Lee, 1998, p. 580). In addition, the public's growing demand for more media services stimulated investment in the media industry.

Although the first appearance of advertising on Shanghai Television in February 1979 is often considered the beginning of media commercialization in China, market mechanisms in the media actually began a year earlier (Zhao, 1998). In 1978, the Ministry of Finance approved the introduction of a business management system at the *People's Daily* and several other newspapers published in Beijing. Although these newspapers were still considered non-profit institutions and received subsidies, they began to be managed as business enterprises. The government adopted a policy of gradually cutting subsidies and encouraging commercialized financing. Some newspapers lost all subsidies in the early 1980s.

China's newspapers today operate under three types of financing—fully subsidized, partially subsidized, or unsubsidized—based on the decision of the state. Specifically, most of the internally circulated newspapers published by industries, enterprises, colleges, and universities do not have state subsidies. They operate within the unit's overall budget plan. The majority of the publicly available newspapers receive partial state subsidies, with the balance coming from circulation and advertising. The third type is the increasing number of profitable newspapers permitted to be run entirely on their own without state subsidies, even though their financing must still observe state regulations (Chen & Lee, 1998). In 1992, the Newspaper and Publication Bureau (NPB) under the State Council announced a new policy, which called for all newspapers but a few chief organs such as the *People's Daily* and the *Economic Daily* to achieve self-reliance by 1994. In spite of the call, only an estimated one-third of the press was financially self-reliant by 1997. Most of the central-level papers and some of the major provincial-level newspapers were said to be self-supporting (Chen & Lee, 1998).

The government adopted a series of policies to loosen the control over the media and to encourage them to create their own revenues. In 1998, the NPB authorized newspapers to undertake media-related business such as printing, advertising, and photographic services. Following these policies, many newspapers plunged not only into media-related business but also into other activities—real estate, hotels, and restaurants. Most papers lost money because of poor management, but some made tremendous profits. *The Guangzhou Daily* (1998 circulation: 870,000) generated an advertising income of RMB$ 500 million in 1995. The newspaper later became a press group, operating six special-interest newspapers based on themes as divergent as child care and football. The group also runs newsprint companies, printing plants, retail chain stores, and an advertising agency (To, 1998, p. 274).

Circulation and advertising now constitute the most important sources of income. In newspaper pricing, the state sets the price for seven national newspapers. Provincial authorities set the price or price threshold for provincial-level newspapers. Only professional newspapers, or those with a small circulation, are allowed to set the price on their own. To add new supplements or pages, publishers must seek NPB's prior consent (To, 1998, p. 275).

However, Chen and Lee (1998) point out that "newspaper subscriptions are for the most part approved and paid by government units and thus should be seen as an essential ingredient of state subsidies" (p. 590). China's government units at various levels reserve funds exclusively for subscriptions to party newspapers. Chen and Lee (1998) estimate that across China, for every private subscription, there are 19 state subscriptions.

Market reform has generated an advertising bonanza for the Chinese press. In the early 1980s, newspaper advertising was virtually insignificant. Nationally, the growth rate of both newspaper circulation and advertising revenue from 1986 to 1996 surpassed that of the gross national product several times. Advertising grew 31 times whereas circulation grew 10 times over the decade (Chen & Lee, 1998).

By 1997, total advertising expenditure in China had reached RMB$ 30.6 billion (US$ 3.7 billion); and 36 percent of that went to newspapers, 44 percent to television, 4 percent to radio, 2.5 percent to magazines, and the balance to other media (Table 2). Advertising expenditure in China has shown a compound annual growth rate of 47 percent over the seven-year period from 1990, when the total was a mere RMB$ 2 billion (WAN, 1999). Dependence on advertising revenues is expected to intensify as the state reduces its subsidies, including newspaper subscriptions.

The increased dependence on advertising has made great changes in press operations. First, party control over the press has decreased. Thus, the old party organs are placing less and less emphasis on political issues while the new newspapers and supplementary pages of other newspapers are carrying more business information. Second, the party press has declined, and mass-appeal papers have increased. Ranked by total revenue, China's top publishing companies in 1998 were the Wenhui and Xinmin United Newspaper Group of Shanghai; Guangzhou

Daily News Group and Yangcheng Evening News Group of Guangzhou; Beijing Daily and Evening News Group; Shenzhen Special Zone News of Guangzhou; and Liberation Daily of Shanghai (WAN, 1999).

3.3 Structure and Organization[3]

Party control has characterized China's press policy, as well as its press system. The whole structure and organization of the press ensured maximum party penetration and control (until commercialization set in). Patterned after the old Soviet system, China's newspapers "functionally and organizationally" fell into five types that formed "an interwoven web of targeted and overlapping readership, with profound implications for their financial control, social influence, and editorial content" (Chen & Lee, 1998, p. 581).

At the apex were the party organs at national, provincial, and local levels, corresponding to the organizational structure of the party. They performed as the mouthpiece of the party committees at various levels and became the most authoritative in propagating the party's policies. At the national level, the most influential was the *People's Daily*, the organ of the central committee of the CCP. At the next level were the municipal or provincial CCP committee organs, which closely followed the *People's Daily* propaganda policies and direction. Usually, they reported the activities and important policies of the provincial CCP committee, as well as the important provincial happenings. At the third level were the organs of county or city CCP committees.

The second group of newspapers was the "target press" that official or semi-official organizations published for specialized readers of various occupational backgrounds or socio-economic interests. These included *Gongren Ribao* (Workers' Daily) of the All-China Trade Union Federation; *Zhongguo Qingnian Bao* (Chinese Youth Daily) of the Chinese Socialist Youth League (and later the Chinese Communist Youth League), and *Guangming Ribao* (Guangming Daily) of the Chinese Democratic League.

The third group comprised the enterprise/industry press published either by government departments (for example, the *Chinese Petroleum Daily*) or by large state enterprises (for example, the *Baoshan Steel Daily*). This group accounted for 15 percent of the circulation of national newspapers in 1996 compared with 1.2 percent a decade earlier (Chen & Lee, 1998). Specialized publications, such as the *Jingji Ribao* (Economic Daily), *Jingji Cankao* (Economic Reference), *Zhongguo Jiaoyu Bao* (Chinese Education Daily), and *Zhongguo Fazhi Ribao* (China's Legal System Daily) also fell into this category.

The fourth type was the mass-appeal press that comprised the evening press, the municipal press, the tabloids, and the general-content press with more than 50 percent of private subscription (vis-à-vis state subscription). The evening press surged with the commercialization of the press in the 1990s. By the end of 1994,

[3] See Giles and Snyder, 1999, for changes taking place in the Chinese media system.

their total had reached 128 (Zhao, 1998). In major cities, the circulation of evening dailies was higher than that of the morning party organs. The tabloids, called "small papers on the streets" (*jietou xiaobao*), were very similar to Western tabloids. They emphasized sex, crime, gossip, and entertainment; and they thrived on sensationalism, fabrication, and vulgarity. The first wave of tabloids emerged in 1984–85. Although they came under party attack during the campaign against "spiritual pollution," they flourished even more after Deng's trip south in the spring of 1992.

The fifth type comprised digests such as the *Cankao Xiaoxi* (Reference News), which printed selections from the foreign press. Because of freer access to foreign media, the circulation of *Reference News* has declined from 7 million in the 1970s to about 2 million today (FlorCruz, 1999).

This structure of the Chinese press reflected the CCP's basic principle of integrating the press with the party structure (Liu, 1975). Even though some papers were not party organs, all came under the Propaganda Department of the CCP, and simultaneously under their respective sponsoring party organizations. Therefore, they were the voice of the party in different fields because they followed the same general direction and principles of reporting. This structure facilitated the party to control the media through a nationwide hierarchical system. The leaders of the Political Bureau of the Central Committee oversaw the activities of the party's Propaganda Department, which, among other things, appointed the chiefs of national newspapers. Local Communist Party leaders appointed the chiefs of provincial newspapers. The ministries associated with a particular trade appointed the chiefs of trade papers.

The increasing commercialization of the press, as evident from the surge of "weekend editions" (*zhoumo ban*) and tabloids, has challenged this structure. That challenge has forced many official party and government organs to publish weekend editions and experiment with the market to attract and retain readers. Concern with the bottom line has caused the "weekend-edition craze." Between 1981 and 1990, fewer that 20 newspapers had weekend editions. By the end of 1994, the number had jumped to 500, or one-fourth of the total (Zhao, 1998).

Zhao (1998) says the flourishing of tabloids and weekend editions, as well as their distribution through private networks, has posed a serious challenge to the political and moral codes of party journalism. Publication of "high-class complaints" (*gaoji laosao*), that is, well-written and highly implicit political and social critiques, has challenged the political code. Publication of nude pictures has challenged the moral code. "In short, the tabloids, especially some of the weekend editions, have violated many aspects of party journalism in their pursuit of market success. Principles of party journalism such as positive propaganda, 'correct' guidance of public opinion, as well as conventional party definitions of news, have been disregarded or subverted" (Zhao, 1998, p. 139). *Time* correspondent James FlorCruz (1999) says: "As the media market continues to grow, the news media have become increasingly open and responsive to public demand. To the people in China, the press and broadcasters are now a real source of information and food for thought, rather than a skimpy compendium of sterile polemic and abstruse dogma. The vibrancy, diversity and enterprise of newspapers, magazines and television shows reflect growing pluralism and Beijing's inability to control it" (http://www.mediastudies.org/china1.html#florcruz).

A trend toward press conglomeration is also becoming visible as increasingly more official newspapers publish spin-off publications, such as "weekend editions" and specialized supplements, to attract more readers and more advertising. In 1996, the Newspaper and Publication Bureau approved the *Guangzhou Ribao* (Canton Daily) to develop itself as China's first press group. Ten more newspapers received approval in 1998, including the *Nanfang Ribao* (South Daily), the *Yangcheng Wanbao* (Yangcheng Evening News), and the *Shenzhen Special Zone Herald*.[4]

3.4 Quality and Popular Press

China does not have a quality versus popular press as in the Western world; instead, it has an influential and a mass-appeal press. Major national newspapers, all broadsheets, are the most influential. *People's Daily*, which carries the party's policies and important directives, is the most influential. It sets the tone for all other newspapers to follow throughout the country. With modern technology, *People's Daily* is now printed in 25 places in the country and circulated in 132 countries and regions. It also prints numerous magazines and periodicals, and publishes more than 100 varieties of books. It is developing into a new newspaper conglomerate (He, 1994).

Guangming Daily, a paper mainly reporting science, education, theory, literature, and art, is second only to the *People's Daily* in terms of influence, and probably even more popular with ordinary Chinese. Because of its academic nature, it enjoys more freedom in discussing new ideas, often setting ideological and cultural trends. *Economic Daily*, a paper mainly reporting on economic development, is particularly influential today. It carries news on economic policies, reform of enterprises, consumer trends, and the like. To some extent, it is similar to *The Wall Street Journal*. *Zhongguo Qingnian Bao* (China Youth Daily) is the most influential among the young people. Its content is more diverse and its style more lively. It often triggers national discussion of sensitive and profound issues among both young and old people.

China Daily, until recently the only English-language daily in China, reports on the country's progress to foreigners in China. Chinese intellectuals also read it. (*China Daily* also publishes the *Shanghai Star*, a semiweekly newspaper in English. *Shanghai Times*, an independent English daily backed by the Shanghai Municipal Corporation, made its debut in mid-1999.)

[4] Five new newspaper groups were established in 1998: South Daily Newspaper Group and Yangcheng Evening News Newspaper Group in Guangzhou; Guangming Daily Newspaper Group and Economic Daily Newspaper Group in Beijing; Wenhui & Xinmin United Newspaper Group in Shanghai (WAN, 1999).

The most popular mass-appeal newspapers are the local evening papers, usually general-interest dailies. They offer more entertainment-oriented soft news than the morning party papers. Their content is more diversified and closer to everyday life. The best known evening papers are *Beijing Evening News, Xinmin Evening News* of Shanghai, and *Yangcheng Evening News* of Guangzhou. The Guangzhou-based *Nanfang Zhoumo* (Southern Weekend) has become a bold vanguard serving the watchdog role of the press.

3.5 Distribution and Technology

The reforms of the early and mid-1980s have led to a diverse distribution system. From the 1950s to the 1980s, the post office monopolized press delivery, charging one-quarter of the newspaper's sale price for the service. This practice began to change when, faced with increasing postal charges for the service, as well as market challenges in the mid-1980s, many large newspapers began to organize their own delivery system. In 1995, postal delivery accounted for 60 percent of the nation's newspapers, with the newspapers' own delivery systems accounting for the balance (Chen & Lee, 1998). In 1998, postal deliveries accounted for 65 percent of newspaper sales whereas home deliveries accounted for 28 percent and single copy sales 7 percent (WAN, 1999). The most notable change in the distribution system, however, was the "creation of a newspaper market literally on the streets" (Zhao, 1998, p. 128). In 1992, Beijing alone had approximately 1,200 individual newspaper vendors. The street outlets are the major suppliers of popular newspapers to private homes.

Zhao (1998) says that major national party and government organs, including the *People's Daily, Guangming Daily*, and *Economic Daily*, are seldom available on the streets. The sale of these "official" papers is through subscriptions for consumption in offices, classrooms, and factory workshops. The public reads these papers on press boards—glass-framed bulletin boards in public places—on which the local party committees displays them.

4. BROADCASTING

4.1 Policy and Legal Framework

The policy and legal framework for the press is also largely applicable to the broadcasting media. Party propaganda and control is the prevailing character in the policy governing the broadcasting industry (see Section 3.1).

4.2 Structure and Organization

Under the strict communist system, the party (in the name of the state) was concurrently the owner, the manager, and the practitioner of radio and TV broadcasting. All stations were under the dual jurisdiction of the party's Central

Propaganda Department and the SARFT. The party's propaganda department was under the supervision of the secretariat and the political bureau of the party's Central Committee. Local supervision came from the various provincial, municipal, and local party-propaganda departments. The Propaganda Department set media policies, determined programming content and themes, and issued operational directives (Hong, 1997). The SARFT supervised the management of radio and television industries throughout the country. It was in charge of running the Central Radio Broadcasting Station, the CCTV, and external broadcasting. Local administrations were in charge of the management and construction of radio and television at the provincial and municipal levels.

For decades, China's broadcasting system had a monopolistic structure, in addition to being highly hierarchic (Zhao, 1998). Each level of governmental administration had only one "people's radio station" and one "people's television station."

Market reform caused a change in this monopolistic structure. Since 1992, many provinces have created an "economic station" in addition to the "people's station." The number of "economic" radio and TV stations rose from 32 in 1992 to more than 100 in 1994 (Zhao, 1998). Many "economic" stations are actually general-interest commercial stations with a higher degree of autonomy than the "official" stations. Some provinces have established more specialized stations for art and entertainment, music, and education. Other specialized stations focus on such areas as traffic, children's programming, and even the stock market.

The trend toward decentralization and specialization is most likely to grow despite some problems. Zhao (1998) says, "The new types of stations counterbalance the lopsided political and propagandist orientation of the 'official model' and give fuller play to the economic, cultural and entertainment functions of broadcasting" (p. 125). As they gradually mature, they may serve as seeds for fully independent, commercialized broadcasting in China.

4.3 Program Policies

The nature and content of broadcasting in China were closely linked to newspapers. All radio and TV stations had the function of disseminating news, social education, and entertainment, and they relied heavily on the Xinhua News Agency and *People's Daily* for news and editorials.

The government also had specific policies on radio and TV programs. For instance, the MRFT (now SARFT) spelled out policies on programs in its 1994 Regulations on the Management of Cable Television (China, 1994a). These policies included conformation to national laws and regulations; and exclusion of reactionary, indecent programs and video products that obstructed national security and social order. The regulations required all cable stations to set a special channel for relaying programs of the central television station, the provincial station and local station, as well as the educational TV programs of the education ministry.

Radio and TV programs in China comprise four main categories: news, education, literature and art, and public service. CCTV, which now operates nine channels, including three pay channels, shows how the program mix works nationally. Channel 1 emphasizes news and current affairs; Channel 2 focuses on economic, social, and educational topics; pay Channel 3 specializes in opera and music; pay Channel 5 in sports; pay Channel 6 in movies; Channel 7 concentrates on children, agriculture, military, and science; and Channels 4 and 8 on art and entertainment. Channel 4 and 9 target overseas viewers, the latter providing English-language satellite feeds. Most channels relay signals via the satellites Apstar and PanAmSat using digital compression technology.

Television was "an important publicity tool" under China's Leninist-Maoist media philosophy, which considered television news to be "a major source of information" and a window for the Chinese audience to know their country and the rest of the world" (Li, 1994, p. 348). Since the initiation of market reforms, the media have expanded the coverage of both domestic and foreign news. Broadcast news has regularly highlighted crime, disasters, human-interest pieces, problems of economic reforms, public opinion, and the like. Since 1993, in particular, "there have been many more stories both closer to the lives of ordinary people and more reflective of the society" (Burgh, 1998, p. 64).

The outstanding examples include CCTV's magazine programs *Dongfang shikong* (East Time and Space), a one-hour morning show started in May 1993; and *Jiodian fangtan* (Focus), introduced in April 1994. By presenting in-depth reports and discussion of some key issues, and by conducting personality-profile interviews with distinguished individuals, as well as ordinary people, these programs provide "follow-ups to current affairs, background analysis, perspectives on hot social issues, and discussions of topics of common concern" (Zhao, 1998, p. 112). FlorCruz (1999) says these shows probe beyond the headlines, using legwork and man-on-the-street interviews to uncover riveting tales; and their targets of exposés include corrupt local officials, enterprise managers, customs employees, and tax collectors. These programs have enjoyed enormous popularity and high audience ratings.

In 1980, CCTV signed an agreement with Visnews (renamed Reuters TV) and UPITN (later Worldwide Television News) to receive international news via satellite. Now, CCTV also receives international news from Asiavision and CNN (Hong, 1997, p. 361).

The Chinese government pays great attention to the educational function of television. It has expanded educational programs to include college courses offered by TV universities. More than 5,000 ground receiving terminals have been installed to receive educational programs, thereby allowing 1 million college students to study at home. In 20 years, 5 million people received continuing education through TV networks and 20 million farmers learned practical farming techniques in this way. Currently, 2 million students get their education or training via television, including 1.2 million primary- and middle-school teachers (Hong, 1997).

The entertainment programs fall into four types based on their functions: appreciation (of arts and literature); knowledge and education; service; and critiques and recommendations. China's entertainment programs are expected to serve social education. Therefore, entertainment programs must have moral and educational elements. In 1986, CCTV opened an English-language channel to serve foreigners in China. A dozen municipal and provincial stations also have English channels. Service programs failed to make much progress until the last 10 years.

According to China (1994b), SARFT has also issued specific regulations governing the use of imported programs, which includes all TV programs, cartoons, TV series, videos, or CDs that come from Taiwan, Hong Kong, Macao, and other foreign countries through purchase, exchange, or as gifts. The regulations state that all such imports must get the approval of the relevant supervising department, and that no TV station can broadcast imported products for more than 25 percent of its program time. In March 1999, Murdoch's News Corporation opened a representative office in Beijing to expand its satellite channels in China by investing in new programming (Holland, 1999).

4.4 Ownership and Financing

The communist set-up implied state ownership of all radio and TV stations in China. No private ownership of any station—domestic or foreign—was permitted. The onset of economic reforms in the late 1970s drastically changed the financing of the media. Beginning 1979, advertising has become the main source of revenue for television. In the late 1980s, advertising and other commercial activities funded about 40 to 70 percent of most of Chinese TV stations. CCTV, for instance, is receiving only a quarter of its operational expenses from the central government (Huang, 1994).

Since China's advertising industry started developing on a large scale in 1981, TV advertising revenues have risen at an annual average of 30 to 40 percent (BTV Enterprises, 1998a). In 1997, TV advertising accounted for 45 percent of China's total advertising revenue (Table 2).

Fully commercialized TV services are emerging. The Oriental TV Station in Shanghai, funded entirely by the sale of shares and advertising profits, does not receive state financial support. The station issued its initial shares at the end of 1992 (Huang, 1994).

The TV industry has also engaged in many other forms of commercial sponsorship and businesses to create revenue. Core businesses are mostly information or media related. These include electronic databases, audiovisual production, business consultation, and cable TV stations. Some television stations even engage in businesses such as restaurant, hotel, and property.

Still another form of creating revenue is through the exchange of programs between the central station and local stations and among the local stations. CCTV offers two types of compensation for the programs it receives from local stations. First, since 1982, CCTV has granted financial awards to local stations that produce high-quality TV drama. Second, CCTV subsidizes local stations with funds for drama production provided CCTV gets the rights for premier exhibition nationwide. The amount of the award varies according to the quality and length of the program (Yu, 1990).

To reduce the reliance on the vertical flow of TV programs from higher-level stations, inter-provincial and inter-city stations each formed an organization to facilitate program exchanges among member stations. More than 30 stations have joined the former, called the China Provincial-Level TV Stations Shareholding Co.; and more than 200 stations have joined the latter, called the City Stations' Cooperative (To, 1998, p. 276).

China has five major TV fairs to facilitate program trading: the annual Beijing International TV Week sponsored by Beijing Television (BTV) every spring since 1992; the biennial Shanghai International TV Festival; the Chinese TV Program Fair sponsored by the MRFT (now SARFT); the biennial Sichuan International TV Festival; and the biennial Guangdong Chinese TV Week held since 1993.

5. NEW ELECTRONIC MEDIA

5.1 Internet and On-line Media

Internet service, which began in Beijing and Shanghai only in 1994, is spreading rapidly throughout the country. ITU (1999) has estimated that China had 7.5 million computers in 1997 with 400,000 Internet users. The number of Internet hosts reached 191,056 in July 1999—a density of 1.53 per 10,000 people (Internet Software Consortium, 1999). China also had 3,700 websites (Zhang, 1998).

Following the establishment of CAnet, China's first computer network, in 1987, the Internet spread rapidly in a decentralized manner throughout many sectors of Chinese society. In February 1996, the State Council issued Order No. 195, "Interim Regulations on International Interconnection of Computer Information Networks in the PRC," authorizing four organizations to operate interconnecting networks. Thus, the Ministry of Posts amd Telecommunications (MPT) set up ChinaNET; the State Education Commission (SEC), CERNET; the Ministry of Electronics (MEI), China GBN; and the Chinese Academy of Science (CAS), CSTNet (Tan, 1998). MPT's ChinaNET covered all the provinces by the end of 1997. Eight regional centers and some 200 nodes operated across the country, covering all 28 provincial capitals and four province-level cities. CERNET provided access to about 270 universities. CSTNet provided interconnections to several hundred research institutes (Tan, 1998).

It was reported that 82 newspapers had started Internet sites in 1998, bringing the number of on-line newspaper editions to 128 (WAN, 1999). These included the *People's Daily*, which went on-line in January 1997, and leads the electronic dailies with 1.1 million daily hits; the *Guangzhou Daily* (850,000 hits); *South Daily* (600,000 hits); *Xinmin Evening News* (570,000 hits); and *Yangchen Evening News* (450,000 hits). *China Daily, Economic Daily, China Trade News, China*

Consumer News, Farmer's Daily, and *China Business Weekly* (Zhang, 1998), among others, have also gone on-line together with several radio and TV stations.

Despite its ardor to catch up with the world in cyberspace, China also wants to control and monitor computer networks. Mueller and Tan (1997) point out that the penetration of market forces has created a strong demand for information technology and telecommunications in China's economy. However, they say, the free play of the forces of information has not been possible because "China's government is jealous of its sovereignty and obsessed with the problems of stability, order, unity, and micro-economic control" (p. 33). In December 1997, the Ministry of Public Security promulgated the "Regulations on the Security and Management of Computer Information Networks and the Internet." The government attempts to block the websites with politically sensitive or sexually explicit content. As Kees (1999) puts it, China is concerned with "the contagion of certain outside forces, even some corrupting cultural forces" (p. 2). Thus, it has banned several websites, including those of CNN, *The New York Times*, and human rights NGOs.[5]

5.2 Telecommunications Infrastructure

China hardly had any telecommunications infrastructure 20 years ago; very few families had telephones. But since the initiation of reforms, the industry developed on large scale, growing at annual rates of between 30 and 50 percent. By the mid-1990s, fax machines, an estimated 270,000 in 1996 (ITU, 1998), had become commonplace in urban areas.

By 1996, the majority of China's large cities had direct-dial automated service for long-distance and overseas calls, with more than 24 million customers; and more than 25 million Chinese-owned pagers (*China economic almanac*, 1997). By 1998, China had 108.6 million mainline telephones and an overall telephone density of 7.3 percent. However, the rural telephone density was 1.3 percent. The number of cellular subscribers was 6.8 million in 1996 (APT, 1998). China's Ninth Five-Year Plan (1996–2000) envisaged increasing the number of telephone subscribers to 123 million and the number of cellular subscribers to 18 million (APT, 1998). By April 1998, more than 16 million Chinese had mobile phones, a figure that is expected to rise more than 100 percent annually ("Structural excess," 1998).[6]

The state's monopoly of providing telecommunication services is also going through changes. In 1993, the government incorporated much of the alternative network into two new national services—Liantong and Jitong—with the latter allowed to provide Internet services. Provisional regulations issued by the State Council in November 1993 permitted collective as well as state-owned enterprises

---

[5] In June 1999, police closed some 300 of the 2,000 Internet cafes in Shanghai for operating without licenses. Only about 350 of those cafes are known to have licenses (http://www.freedomforum.org/international/1999/6/8internetcafes.asp).

[6] ITU, 1999, estimated the number of mainline telephones at 87.5 million in 1998 (6.96 per 100 people) and the number of cellular subscribers at 23.9 million (1.9 per 100 people).

to offer telecom services under license from the Ministry of Post and Tele-communication. In 1999, Murdoch's News Corp. started its Internet services in China. The China Byte, a website run jointly with the *People's Daily*, specializes in information-technology news (Holland, 1999).

China has expedited the construction of international fiber-optic cables, such as the South Asia route. In 1997, China joined the Trans-Asia–Europe (TAE) optical cable trunk and the fiber-optic link around the globe (FLAG). In 1998, China set up a joint venture called China SpaceCom (*Zhong Yu*), which will build four gateway stations in Beijing, Guangzhou, and Lanzhou to become part of the Iridium and Globalstar mobile satellite telecommunication system (APT, 1999).

6. POLICY TRENDS FOR PRESS AND BROADCASTING

Because of the government's belief that the media must help keep social stability, China's media policy has tightened or loosened with the country's state of stability. After the initiation of market reform, the media enjoyed more freedom and flex-ibility but also experienced greater volatility. In the 1980s, when the focus was on economic development and opening up to the outside world, the media enjoyed a great deal of freedom. The Tiananmen Square incident brought that to a halt. Since then, media freedom in China has loosened or tightened like a pendulum.

Following the late paramount leader Deng Xiaoping's remarks made during an inspection tour of south China in 1992 and the official beginning of the era of the market economy, China's media policy became more complicated than before. As Polumbaum (1994) points out, press supervision underwent a bifurcated change in 1992, most noticeably at the end of that year, when Ding Guangen replaced Li Ruihuan as the Politburo member in charge of propaganda. On the one hand, the party and government seemed willing to relinquish control over certain categories of specialized, professional, lifestyle, and entertainment publications. On the other hand, the authorities seemed determined to get a better grip on media that trafficked in political content (pp. 113–128). That explains the rich and colorful scene in entertainment sections of the media and the rigid and prudent style and content in other sections. Political considerations are behind media control. As the market economy took on many capitalist practices, the government considered it very important for the people to back the party's leadership, follow its policies, and uphold social morality. Such tasks naturally fell on the news media.

The most encouraging sign of improvement in press freedom appeared in 1998. At his inaugural news conference in March, Premier Zhu Rongji set the new tone by asserting that he favored democracy. In October, he visited CCTV and presented a calligraphic scroll, which said that the Chinese news media represented the "vanguard of reform; a mouthpiece of the masses; a mirror and watchdog of the government and supervisor of government through public opinion" (Zeitlin, 1999, p. 1). Observers considered the scroll a call to radically change the official media. Before his visit to CCTV, Zhu had conducted a series of meetings with Communist Party officials, news media, and propaganda chiefs, urging the freeing of the news media to support the country's far-ranging economic reforms. During the year, China signed the human rights covenants and released a number of well-known dissidents. The Chinese government's willingness to loosen its grip on the media was also evident in the somewhat surprisingly open approach to the coverage of President Clinton's visit to China in June 1998. The open access to the live coverage of the Jiang–Clinton press conference and Clinton's speech at the Beijing University left an impression that the Chinese government had confidence in a more relaxed media environment.

But the year ended with President Jiang Zeming's speech on the 20th anniversary of Deng Xiaoping's economic reforms. "From beginning to end, we must be vigilant against infiltration, subversive activities and separatist activities of international and domestic hostile forces," Jiang said. At the end of the year, Chinese authorities announced that newspaper, book, and magazine publishers, as well as music producers and filmmakers, would face life in prison if found guilty of "inciting to subvert state power." Consequently, several publications were closed.

Stability was the watchword for the Chinese government in 1999, a year full of anniversaries—the 10th year of Tiananmen Square incident; the 70th year of the May Fourth movement; and the 50th year of the founding of PRC. At the end of January, the propaganda department censored two magazines, *News Weekly* and *Shenzhen Pictorial Journal*, for mentioning the June 4 incident.

As volatility is likely to continue in China's political scene in the next few years, stability will be a high priority of the Chinese government. The phenomenon of the swing between looscning and tightening in China's media policy will continue.

7. MAIN ISSUES

China's economic reforms have, most probably unintentionally, brought about great changes in the media scene. The economic reforms in the mass media have resulted in an unprecedented media market, but they have also brought many new problems for the CCP and the Chinese government.

First, economic reforms in the media have created a need to redefine the role of the media. For decades, Chinese journalists have been told that the media are the tools of the party, and everything they do should serve the party. However, the commercialization of the media has made them more oriented toward the consumers than the party. For instance, much of the content of the weekend editions and evening papers—which are flourishing while the party papers are declining rapidly—has deviated from the notion of party journalism. Apparently, the role of the media needs a redefinition.

Second, economic reforms in the media are threatening the party control of the media. Economic reform and media commercialization have made party control of the media increasingly difficult (Zhao, 1998). Although the party can still control the party papers, such control only makes them monotonous and detached from the people, thereby losing circulation. Moreover, with the proliferation of outlets, monitoring becomes increasingly difficult. Although central and provincial authorities maintain control of news organs under their direct supervision, their grip on other media outlets has become much looser.

Third, economic reforms in the media have opened the floodgates for malpractices that undermine market principles. As the dependence on advertising grows, media are open to abuse by the advertisers internationally or otherwise. Misleading advertisements with exaggerated or even false claims are widespread (To, 1998, p. 278).

Fourth, the rise of "red-packet" journalism is corrupting the integrity of the media. Business entrepreneurs are known to reward journalists with "red packets" for favorable publicity. Newspapers also often organize special supplements or features to promote a region, an enterprise or an entrepreneur and, in return, solicit sponsorship from those interviewed (To, 1998, p. 278).

Fifth, the old issue of freedom of the press remains. Although press freedom stalled during the 1989 crackdown, commercialization of the press has generated the demand for more freedom. As more journalists enjoy more freedom, they will eventually require a legally guaranteed freedom. Thus the call for a press law is certain to resurface.

Sixth, the issue of dealing with the influence of the external media, both political and commercial, on China has become a matter of major concern (Zhao, 1998). The news media of Hong Kong and Taiwan are increasingly influential among the Chinese. Moreover, Western media influences come in many technological forms—shortwave radio to satellite television to the Internet. How to deal with such external influences is under debate.

Last, the need for the CCP and the Chinese government to formulate clear policies to deal with the foregoing issues has become increasingly urgent. Currently, there is no coherent policy on news media and information. Moreover, there is a lack of agreement among the top political leadership over media policy. Media policies in the 1990s have been rather chaotic and confusing.

As economic reform deepens and media commercialization increases, the contradictions and tensions in the news media system are likely to intensify further. As Zhao (1998) says, "The party cannot simply pretend that nothing has happened and that it can resort to old forms of control by simply reiterating the party line. The enormous energy for commercialization and democratization will find outlets one way or another" (p. 179).

8. STATISTICS

General Profile

Exchange rate (1999)	US$ 1 = 8.28 Renminbi (RMB)*
Population (mid-1999)	1.247 billion**
Number of dailies (1998)	740
Number of non-dailies (1998)	1,313
TV receivers/100 people (1999)	32.1***
Main telephone lines/100 people (1998)	6.96****
Cellular subscribers/1000 people (1998)	1.9****
Internet host computers (July 1999)	191,056*****

Source: * OANDA Historical Currency Table (http://www.oanda.com/converter/cc_table?lang=en).
** US Census Bureau, International Data Base; *** UNESCO, 1999; **** ITU, 1999;
***** Internet Software Consortium (www.isc.org).

Table 1
China's Top Dailies

Selected titles	Established	Estimated circulation
Sichuan Ribao (Sichuan Daily)	1952	8 million
Cankao Xiaoxi (Reference News)		2.90 million*
Renmin Ribao (People's Daily)	1948	2.13 million*
Xinmin Wanbao (Xinmin Evening News)	1903	1.72 million*
Wenhui Bao (Wenhui Daily)	1938	1.7 million
Jingji Ribao (Economic Daily)	1983	1.5 million
Yangcheng Wanbao (Yangcheng Evening Post)	1957	1.29 million*
Nongmin Ribao (Peasant Daily)	1980	1 million
Jiefang Ribao (Liberation Daily)	1949	1 million
Guangming Ribao (Guangming Daily)	1949	950,000
Hubei Ribao (Hubei Daily)	1949	900,000
Guangzhou Ribao (Guangzhou Daily)	1952	870,000*
Zhongguo Fazhi Bao (China Legal Daily)		830,000*
Gongren Ribao (Workers Daily)	1949	820,000*
Jiefangjun Ribao (Liberation Army Daily)	1949	800,000
Zhongguo Tiyu Bao (China Sports Daily)		800,000
Beijing Wanbao (Beijing Evening News)	1958	800,000
Zhongguo Qingnian Bao (China Youth Daily)	1951	790,000*
Beijing Ribao (Beijing Daily)	1952	700,000
Nanfang Ribao (South China Daily)	1949	670,000*
Guangxi Ribao (Guangxi Daily)	1949	650,000
Tianjin Ribao (Tianjin Daily)	1949	600,000
Liaoning Ribao(Liaoning Daily)		600,000
Fujian Ribao (Fujian Daily)	1949	600,000
Dazhong Ribao (Masses Daily)	1939	550,000
Jingji Xinxi Bao (Economic Information Daily)		500,000
Weisheng Bao (Health Daily)		500,000
Shaanxi Ribao (Shaanxi Daily)		500,000
Jilin Ribao (Jilin Daily)	1948	500,000
Heilongjiang Ribao (Heilongjiang Daily)		500,000
Guizhou Ribao (Guizhou Daily)	1949	300,000
Hunan Ribao (Hunan Daily)		300,000
China Daily	1981	150,000

Source: *Editor & publisher international yearbook*, 1999; * WAN, 1999.

Table 2
Media Share of Advertising Revenue: 1993–98

	Total (RMB in billions)	Newspapers	Magazines	Television	Radio	Outdoors
1993	8.79	43	2	33	4	18
1994	12.97	39	3	34	4	20
1995	16.61	39	2	39	4	15
1996	20.99	37	3	43	4	13
1997	30.63	36	2	44	4	14
1998	34.49 (est.)	37	2	44	4	12

Source: State Administration of Industry & Commerce (WAN, 1999).

Table 3
Estimated Mass Media Penetration

	Radio receivers		TV receivers		Daily newspapers		
	Number ('000)	Per 100 people	Number ('000)	Per 100 people	Number	Circ'n ('000)	Per 100 people
1990	372,866	32.3	309,001	26.7	44	48,000	4.2
1995	408,000	33.4	374,410	30.7	...	...	...
1996	412,797	33.5	393,630	31.9	...	...	...
1997	417,000	33.5	400,000	32.1	...	...	....

Source: UNESCO, 1999.

9. USEFUL ADDRESSES

9.1 Media-Related Organizations

Ministry of Culture
A83 Donganmen
Beijing
Telephone: 6401-2255

State Press and Publication Administration
85 Dong Si Nan Da Jie
Beijing
Telephone: 6512-4433

The State Administration of Radio, Film & TV
2 Fuwaidajie
Beijing 100866
Telephone: 6609-3114

All China Journalists Association
Xi Jiao Min Xiang, Beijing
Telephone: 6603-3862

9.2 Newspaper Organizations

Renmin Ribao (People's Daily)
2 Jin Tai Xi Lu
Beijing, 100733
Telephone: 6509-2121
Fax: 6500-3109

Jingji Ribao (Economic Daily)
277 Wang Fu Jin Da Jie
Beijing, 100746
Telephone: 6512-5035

Gongren Ribao (Worker's Daily)
An Ding Men Wai, Liu Pu Kang
Beijing, 100718
Telephone: 6421-1561

Zhongguo Funu Bao (Chinese Women's Daily)
50 Deng Shi Kou Da Jie,
Dong Cheng District
Beijing, 100730
Telephone: 6512-7711

Wen Hui Bao (Wen Hui Daily)
50 Hu Qiu Lu
Shanghai, 200002
Telephone: 6321-1410

Guangming Ribao (Guangming Daily)
106 Yong An Lu
Beijing 100050
Telephone: 6301-7788

Zhongguo Ribao (China Daily)
15 Hui Xin Dong Jie, Chaoyang District
Beijing 100029
Telephone: 6422-4488

Zhongguo Qingnian Bao (Chinese Youth Daily)
2 Dong Zhi Men Nei Hai Yun Chang
Beijing, 100702
Telephone: 6403-2233

Beijing Wanbao (Beijing Evening News)
34 Dong Dan Xi Biang Bei Hu Tong
Beijing, 100734
Telephone: 6529-8322

Xinmin Wanbao (Xin Min Evening News)
839 Yan An Zhong Lu
Shanghai, 200040
Telephone: 6279-1234

Yangcheng Wanbao **(Guangzhou Evening News)**
733 Dong Feng Dong Lu
Guangzhou. 510085
Telephone: 8777-6211

Fazhi Ribao
A1 Hua Jia Di, Chaoyang District
Beijing
Telephone: 6436-1144

9.3 Electronic Media Organizations

China Central Television
No. 11 Fuxing Rd.
Beijing, 100859
Telephone: 6850-0114

Central People's Radio Station
2 Fuxingmenwai Dajie
Beijing 100866
Telephone: 6851-5522

Tianjin TV Station
143 Wei Jin Lu, He Ping Qu
Tianjin, 300070
Telephone: 2335-9514

Shanghai TV Station
Nanjing Xi Lu
Shanghai
Telephone: 6256-5899

Beijing TV Station
3 Xi San Huan Bei Lu, Hai Dian Qu
Beijing, 100081
Telephone: 6841-9922

China Radio International
2 Fuwaidajie
Beijing 100866
Telephone: 6852-8471

Shanghai Dongfang TV Station
627 Nanjing Dong Lu
Shanghai, 20001
Telephone: 6322-3007

Shanghai People's Broadcasting Station
1376 Hong Qiao Lu
Shanghai
Telephone: 6278-8177

Source: *Editor & publisher international yearbook*, 1999, and personal contacts.

10. REFERENCES

APT (Asia-Pacific Telecommunity). (1998, 1999). *The APT yearbook.* Bangkok: APT.

BTV Enterprises. (1998a, July 28). A brief introduction to China's TV advertising industry. *Beijing TV Express* [On-line]. Available: (http://www.beijing-tv.cn.net/btvexp/tvabc.htm).

BTV Enterprises. (1998b, July 28). China's five major TV markets. *Beijing TV Express* [On-line]. Available: (http://www.beijing-tv.cn.net/btvexp/tvabc.htm).

BTV Enterprises. (1998c, November 7). China's TV ABC: China Central Television. *Beijing TV Express* [On-line]. Available: (http://www.beijing-tv.cn.net/btvexp/tvabc.htm).

Burgh, H. (1998). China: New public sphere, new TV journalists? *Media Development, 45* (4), 64–67.

Chang, W.H. (1989). *Mass media in China.* Ames: Iowa State University Press.

Chen, H. & Lee, C.C. (1998). Press finance and economic reform in China. In J. Cheng (Ed.), *China review, 1998* (pp. 577–609). Hong Kong: Chinese University Press.

China. (1990). *Provisional regulations on newspaper management.* Beijing: State Press and Publications Administration.

China. (1994a). *Regulations on the management of cable television* (Promulgation No. 11). Beijing: Ministry of Radio, Film, and Television.

China. (1994b). *Regulations on the management of importing and broadcasting foreign television programs* (Promulgation No. 10). Beijing: Ministry of Radio, Film, and Television.

China. (1998a). Educational development in China. *China march toward 2000.* Beijing: China Intercontinental Press.

China. (1998b). China's foreign trade and economic cooperation. *China march toward 2000.* Beijing: China International Press.

China economic almanac. (1997). Beijing: Publishing House of China Economic Almanac.

Chu, J.C.Y. (1978). People's Republic of China. In J.A. Lent (Ed.), *Broadcasting in Asia and the Pacific: A continental survey of radio and television* (pp. 21–41). Philadelphia: Temple University Press.

Ding, G. (1990). *History of Chinese journalism.* Wuhan, China: Wuhan University Press.

Editor & publisher international yearbook. (1999). New York: E&P.

Fang, H., & Chen, Y. (1992). *History of contemporary Chinese journalism.* Beijing: Xinhua.

FlorCruz, J.A. (1999). Chinese media in flux: From party line to bottom line. *Media Studies Journal, 13* (1) [On-line]. Available: (http://www.mediastudies.org/china1.html#florcruz).

Giles, R., & Snyder, R.W. (Eds.). (1999). Covering China. *Media Studies Journal, 13* (1) [On-line]. Available: (http://www.mediastudies.org/china1.html).

Gong, D. (1997). *History of Chinese journalism.* Changsha, China: Hunan Normal University Press.

He, C. (1994). *Analysis of the press system under the Chinese Communists* (Chinese). Taipei: Chongchung Publishing House.

Holland, L. (1999, April 1). Tuned in to China: Murdoch beefs up business in China—Again. *Far Eastern Economic Review*, p. 50.

Hong, J. (1997). China. In H. Newcomb (Ed.), *Encyclopedia of television* (Vol. 1, pp. 360–362). Chicago: Fitzroy Dearborn Publishers.

Huang, C. (1998). China. In A. Goonasekera & D. Holaday (Eds.), *Asian communication handbook* (pp. 17–33). Singapore: AMIC & NTU.

Huang, Yong. (1993). New waves of reform are quietly surging in the radio and television field. *Journal of Beijing Broadcast College, 1,* 1–34.

Huang, Yu. (1994). Peaceful evolution: The case of television reform in post-Mao China. *Media, Culture & Society, 16,* 217–241.

ITU (International Telecommunication Union). (1998, 1999). *World telecommunication development report.* Geneva: ITU.

Kees, B. (1999, March 10). Panel: China's Jiang has 'split' in approach to press. *The Freedom Forum* [On-line]. Available: (http://www.freedomforum.org/international/1999/3/10china.asp).

Li, X. (1994). The Chinese television system and television news. *China Quarterly, 126,* 340–355.

Liu, A.P.L. (1971). Communist China. In J.A. Lent (Ed.), *Asian newspapers' reluctant revolution* (pp. 43–54). Ames: The Iowa State University Press.

Liu, A.P.L. (1975). *Communications and national integration in Communist China.* Berkeley: University of California Press.

Liu, A.P.L. (1982). People's Republic of China. In J.A. Lent (Ed.), *Newspapers in Asia: Contemporary trends and problems* (pp. 31–50). Hong Kong: Heinemann Asia.

Mueller, M., & Tan, Z. (1997). *China in the information age: Telecommunications and the dilemmas of reform.* Westport, CT: Praeger.

Polumbaum, J. (1994). Striving for predictability: The bureaucratization of media management in China. In C.C. Lee (Ed.), *China's media, media's China* (pp. 113–128). Boulder, CO: Westview Press Inc.

Polumbaum, J. (1997). Political fetters, commercial freedoms: restraint and excess in Chinese mass communications. In C. Hudson (Ed.), *The China handbook.* (pp. 211–226). Chicago: Fitzroy Dearborn.

Remarkable accomplishments in China's television industry in 20 years. (1998, November 2). *People's Daily,* p. 1.

Structural excess of electronic products. (1998, June 22). *People's Daily,* p. 2.

Tan, Z. (1998, March). People's Republic of China. In *The global diffusion of the Internet* (pp. 109–145). Tempe, AZ: Arizona State University Press.

Tseng, H.P. (1971). China prior to 1949. In J.A. Lent (Ed.), *Asian newspapers' reluctant revolution* (pp. 31–42). Ames: Iowa State University Press.

To, Y.M. (1998). The marketization of media in China: Economic freewheeling in a political straitjacket. In A.B. Albarran & S.M. Chan-Olmsted (Eds.), *Global media economics: commercialization, concentration of world media markets* (267–283). Ames: The Iowa State University Press.

Trionfi, B. (1999). Growing media repression & self-restraint in China. *IPI Survey* [On-line]. Available: (http://www.freemedia.at/china.htm).

UNESCO (United Nations Educational, Scientific and Cultural Organization). (1999). *Statistical yearbook.* Paris: UNESCO.

Vanden Heuvel, J., & Dennis, E. E. (1993). *The unfolding lotus: East Asia's changing media.* New York: The Freedom Forum Media Studies Center.

WAN (World Association of Newspapers). (1999). *World press trends.* Paris: WAN.

World factbook. (1998). [On-line]. Available: (http://www.odci.gov/cia/publications/factbook/country-frame.html).

Yu, J. (1990). The structure and function of Chinese television, 1979–1989. In C.C. Lee (Ed.), *Voices of China: The interplay of politics and journalism* (pp. 69–87). New York: The Guilford Press.

Zeitlin, A. (1999, January 20). After brief relaxation, China moves to bring news media into line. *The Freedom Forum* [On-line]. Available: (http://www.freedomforum.org/international/1999/1/20china.asp).

Zhang, Q. (1998, July 20). Update of our country's Internet. *Info Web* [On-line]. Available: (http://ciw.ccid.cn.net/ccu/325/01106.htm).

Zhao, Y. (1998). *Media, market, and democracy in China: Between the party line and the bottom line.* Urbana and Chicago: University of Illinois Press.

◆

19

HONG KONG SAR (CHINA)

Clement So, Joseph Man Chan, & Chin-Chuan Lee

1. NATIONAL PROFILE

1.1 Geography

Hong Kong, a 1,092-sq km-city, about six times the size of Washington, DC, comprises more than 200 islands including Lantau to the southwest. Located at the southeast border of China, it has a tropical monsoon climate: cool and humid in winter; hot and rainy from spring through summer; and warm and sunny in the fall. Only 6 percent of the land is arable. Its terrain ranges from hilly to mountainous with steep slopes. Lowlands lie to the north.

1.2 People

Asiaweek (December 11, 1998) ranked Hong Kong as Asia's seventh best city on a "quality of life" index. 92.4 percent of its 6.8 million people are literate, while 95 percent live in urban areas. The life expectancy of its people is among the highest in the world: 76.2 years for males and 81.9 years for females (Howlett, 1998).

Hong Kong is a meeting point of the cultures of the East and the West. Although 95 percent of the population is of Chinese descent, its composition also includes those who arrived from countries like Indonesia, Philippines, Thailand, and Malaysia. Immigrants from Japan, India, Canada, Australia, the United Kingdom, the United States, and other countries comprise the balance. Cantonese is the most commonly used Chinese dialect, but many people also speak English and *Putonghua* (Mandarin), the official Chinese language. Buddhists and Taoists make up the vast majority of the population. Christians (9 percent), Muslims (1 percent), and Hindus (0.2 percent) represent the minority religions.

Hong Kong has little natural resources, but a combination of hard work, a strategic locations as a gateway to China, and its unique social system has enabled it to become a vibrant economy and an advanced society. In the mid-19th century, Hong Kong was just a village occupied by a few thousand fishermen who lived on board their boats in the harbor. When Imperial China lost the Opium War in 1841, it ceded the island of Hong Kong, the neighboring Kowloon, and the New Territories to Britain. Thereafter, Hong Kong gradually became a trade and commercial entrepot between China and the outside world. It remained a backward small town until after 1949, when it became the home for refugees from mainland China following the communist takeover. This influx brought manpower, capital, and entrepreneurial skills from Shanghai and the neighboring Canton (Guangdong) province. Hong Kong began to industrialize, especially in the textile and garment industries. Later on, its electronic products and printing industries became major exporters in the world market.

1.3 Government and Politics

Hong Kong became the world's media spectacle with some 8,000 journalists converging there on July 1, 1997, to cover the return of sovereignty to China after 156 years of British rule. It became a special administrative region (SAR) of China as stipulated in the Sino-British Joint Declaration of 1984 and the subsequent Basic Law. These legal instruments allowed Hong Kong to enjoy a high degree of autonomy, except in foreign and defense affairs. China agreed to implement the principle of "one country, two systems" and allow the SAR "a high degree of autonomy" so that "the people of Hong Kong would administer Hong Kong." Thus, Hong Kong has continued to enjoy the same political and civic rights and freedoms as before. It has, so far, maintained its free and open economic system.

1.4 Economy

Free trade and low taxation, coupled with the rule of law and an efficient civil service, enabled the Hong Kong economy to take off in the early 1970s. In the 1990s, it became one of the most important financial and transport centers in the world. In 1999, Hong Kong's gross domestic product stood at US$ 146 billion; its per capita GDP (at purchasing power parity) at US$ 21,830 and its nominal per capita GNP at US$ 24,716. It exported merchandise valued at US$ 171 billion in 1999, while its reserves stood at US$ 96.3 billion (*Asiaweek*, February 11, 2000).

2. DEVELOPMENT OF PRESS AND BROADCASTING

2.1 Developments since 1945

2.1.1 The Press

The most vital characteristic of the Hong Kong press is its close connection with Chinese politics. The British colonies of Shanghai and Hong Kong were the birthplaces of the modern Chinese press. In the 1850s, missionaries first published a Chinese edition of the English-language press. A Chinese-owned press followed in the 1870s. At the turn of the century, both Manchurian loyalists and revolutionaries published newspapers in Hong Kong as their propaganda organs. From Hong Kong, they aimed to reach the Chinese intellectuals on the mainland, not so much to provide news but to promote enlightenment and advocate reform or revolution.

For almost three decades after 1949, politics in Hong Kong followed the line of division between the Chinese Communist Party (CCP), which ruled mainland China, and the Nationalist Party (Kuomintang or KMT), which ruled Taiwan. The press reflected this rift, spanning the entire ideological spectrum in ways akin to what Seymour-Ure (1974) calls "party-press parallelism" (pp. 192–195). The colonial government discouraged political activism in Hong Kong, while the general population, many of whom were refugees from communist rule, aspired to return to the mainland some day and regarded Hong Kong as a temporary sanctuary. In the 1950s and the 1960s, the CCP–KMT struggle dominated the press to the relative neglect of local affairs.

By 1970, the proportion of local-born residents had begun to overtake that of mainland immigrants. Unlike the preceding generations, the native-born had their roots in Hong Kong. China signified to them a geographical, cultural, and political entity about which they felt intensely ambivalent because most of them had not lived there. A pristine Hong Kong identity began to form in the early 1970s as the epitome of the growing local autonomy vis-à-vis China. Local and immediate concerns took precedence over the distant and perennial CCP–KMT fights. As a natural consequence, market-oriented newspapers emerged and prospered with no binding partisan allegiance to either the CCP or the KMT. Benefiting from Hong Kong's thriving economy and its formidable advertising industry, they focused on local coverage that inspired the immediate concern of their readers. The result has been a weakened relevance of the partisan or party press and its peaceful coexistence with the increasingly robust commercial, "professional" press (Chan & Lee, 1991; Chang, 1982; Clayton, 1971; Lee, 1997; Vanden Heuvel & Dennis, 1993).

Acquiescing to historical legacy and power reality, the British allowed the CCP to set up schools, organize trade unions, publish newspapers, and distribute propaganda in the colony. They were more guarded in giving this privilege to the Nationalists. The British acquired Hong Kong at the close of their colonial expansion; trade became more important to them than territorial ambition. Just as China was too big, Hong Kong was too small. Hong Kong Gov. (Sir) Alexander Grantham (1947–58) said, "We are just simple traders who want to get on well with our daily round and common task. This may not be very noble, but at any rate it does not disturb others" (HKLC, 1950, p. 41). The only sure route to absorb the pervasive pressure of the China factor was to depoliticize Hong Kong by taking a neutral stand on the CCP–KMT feud. Therefore, the British were content with setting the rules of the game and making sure that exogenous political forces obeyed Hong Kong's legal framework and did not undermine the legitimacy of British rule in the colony. Hong Kong's press freedom, said to be second only to that of Japan in Asia (Lent, 1982), should be understood as an absence of explicit government censorship and a right to criticize the contending Chinese regimes, rather than as a right to participate in democratic politics or to criticize the colonial government itself.

Consistent with the British colonial style, the Hong Kong government co-opted the Chinese elite into the administrative machine but deprived the huge masses of political participation (Lau, 1982). The media performed the crucial role of aggregating popular interests and channeling public opinion at the boundary between the polity and the civil society. Because the native-born were more assertive about their legitimate rights in Hong Kong, the 1970s and the 1980s saw an outburst of civil protests that sought to harness the mainstream media to reformist causes. After the 1967 communist riot, the colonial government felt a strong need to "close [the] communication gap" with the people. It upgraded the Government Information Services (GIS) to play the double role of news producer and news distributor to the press, both controlling and facilitating press access to government information (Lee & Chan, 1990). The colonial regime claimed itself to be a government "for the people" and "of the people" if not "by the people"; and, as part of the effort to bolster its legitimacy, it entrusted the GIS to gather and translate press opinions for policy-makers. The GIS also used the media to send out trial balloons for government policy.

When China and Britain held negotiations in the early 1980s over the future of the colony, a majority of the Hong Kong press sided editorially with the British position and cast serious doubt about the "one country, two systems" policy proposed by the Chinese regime, which had just emerged from the wreckage of the Cultural Revolution. The colonial government enlisted the support of the media to play what it saw as a "public-opinion card" against China's "sovereignty card." The British effort failed, and China insisted on resuming sovereignty over Hong Kong in 1997. Both sides signed the Sino-British Joint Declaration in 1984. From 1984 to 1997, the press had to cope with a dualistic power structure consisting of the colonial regime and the Chinese authorities, while both power centers tried very hard to co-opt the media in their favor. The Chinese side had considerable success in calming public doubt and in incorporating the elite, including media owners and editors, into special bodies set up to formulate the Basic Law as a legal framework for post-handover Hong Kong. The colonial regime became increasingly defensive. China's bloody Tiananmen Square crackdown in 1989, however, reopened the old wound (Chan & Lee, 1991). Throughout much of the 1990s, the Hong Kong press largely supported Britain's last effort to undertake democratic electoral reforms under Gov. Chris Patten, partly as a way to forestall future communist intervention. China objected vehemently to the reforms and abolished them immediately upon taking over in 1997. Under the Basic Law, however, China is obliged to let Hong Kong keep its present way of life, including press freedom, for at least 50 years.

In 1997, 30 Chinese-language dailies, 10 English-language dailies, one bilingual daily, and four dailies in other languages had registered with the Hong Kong government (Howlett, 1998). On March 18, 1999, the Oriental Press Group's *The Sun* joined the already fierce mass newspaper market. Excluding those publications covering only entertainment news or horseracing information, as well as news agency bulletins registered as newspapers, Hong Kong published 15 major dailies in 1999. Some have distribution networks and print editions overseas, particularly in the United States, Canada, the United Kingdom, and Australia. Some regional publications such as the *Asian Wall Street Journal, Asiaweek*, the *Far Eastern Economic Review*, and the *International Herald Tribune* have chosen Hong Kong as their base or printing location. Many international news agencies, newspapers, and overseas broadcasting corporations have established regional headquarters in Hong Kong because of its advanced telecommunications infrastructure and the availability of the latest technology, as well as its strategically important location in Asia.

2.1.2 Broadcasting

In 1928, a station using the call letters GOW provided the first radio broadcasting in Hong Kong. Charging of license fees on radio receivers also began in the same year. In 1948, GOW officially became Radio Hong Kong (RHK). With the introduction of FM channels in 1960 and the establishment of a public affairs television unit in 1970, RHK changed its name to Radio Television Hong Kong (RTHK). Commercial Radio had been operating as another broadcasting service since 1959.

Rediffusion, a cable broadcaster, had begun operation in 1949 to serve listeners who were willing to pay a subscription. Rediffusion had two channels, one solely for its own programs and the other for RHK programs. This cable radio service was popular in the 1950s and 1960s but it could not survive the growing popularity of transistor radios. The affordability of transistor radio sets and the abolition of the license fees in 1967 allowed people to access free radio broadcasts from RHK and Commercial Radio (Everest, 1978). Rediffusion closed down in 1973 (Ho, 1975). Metro Radio began in 1991 as another commercial radio broadcaster.

Commercial television in Hong Kong began in 1957, when Rediffusion introduced a closed-circuit bilingual TV channel (Everest, 1978; RTHK, 1988; Vanden Heuvel & Dennis, 1993). With the advent of the first wireless TV broadcaster, Television Broadcasts Ltd (TVB), in 1967, the closed-circuit service dwindled in importance and closed down in 1973. Rediffusion immediately obtained a license to run a wireless television service. This service changed its name to Asia Television Ltd (ATV) in 1982, when ownership changed hands. Briefly, between 1975 and 1978, Hong Kong had a third private TV station, the Commercial Channel. However, financial difficulties forced it to close down.

Each of the two TV broadcasters, TVB and ATV, carries one Chinese- and one English-language channel. In 1998, they provided more than 550 hours of programming per week (BA, 1998; Lau & Ang, 1998). Nearly all the local programs are in-house productions that include drama series, magazines, music, news, infotainment, and the like. TVB Jade, the Cantonese channel, has come to dominate the local TV industry ever since its inception. It has consistently secured 70 percent to 90 percent of the prime time rating share (Chan et al., 1997). Wireless television as presented by TVB Jade achieved quick penetration, snatched a major audience share from radio and movies, and became the predominant mass medium in Hong Kong.

Radio and Television Hong Kong, a quasi-public broadcaster, supplements commercial television (Chan et al., 1997; Ma, 1992). RTHK does not have a TV channel of its own, but the law requires the two commercial TV broadcasters to carry some of its programs during prime time. Organizationally, RTHK is a government department with civil servants comprising most of its staff. Its official mission is to inform the public of government policy and to provide non-commercial programming. However, the social changes in the last two decades have enabled RTHK to operate with a high degree of editorial autonomy since the mid-1980s, allowing it to slowly assume the role of a public broadcaster. Following the BBC model, RTHK has evolved itself less as a government mouthpiece but more as public television run by a politically neutral team of civil servants. It is, therefore, not difficult to find some RTHK programs critical of the Hong Kong government.

Wharf Cable Ltd (renamed Hong Kong Cable Ltd at the end of 1998), formed in 1993, at first monopolized subscription television in Hong Kong. Five years later, Cable TV had a household penetration of about 20 percent. It offered 37 channels, including the pay-per-view and the Near Video on Demand channels (BA, 1998). In 1998, the subscription TV market became more crowded with the entry of Hong Kong Interactive TV, a subsidiary of Hong Kong Telecom.

3. THE PRESS

3.1 Policy and Legal Framework

Hong Kong is a capitalist society with the government firmly wedded to a *laissez-faire* policy on commercial activities. The Hong Kong government has traditionally treated the newspaper industry as a private enterprise. Before 1997, the government allowed the press to operate on its own as long as the latter did not pose any real threats to social stability and to colonial rule. The government did not exercise press censorship or any other forms of direct control outside of the general laws such as those on libel and obscenity. It had no specific regulatory body to control the press, save for the process of registering publications and handling complaints from citizens. After 1997, the situation has remained more or less the same.

3.2 Financial Aspects: Circulation, Advertising, Marketing Strategies

The *Oriental Daily News* and *Sing Pao Daily News* led the mass-circulation press—until the *Apple Daily* entered the fray in 1995—pampering the audience with vivid, vulgar, and sensational stories on crime, a large dose of entertainment and gossip, and daily tidbits of soft pornography. A garment tycoon spent approximately US$ 100 million to found the *Apple Daily*, which became an instant success. With its huge financial resources, the paper was able to lure away talent, launch expensive promotional campaigns, and offer not only a better graphic design but also concise writing. From the beginning, the paper sought to lower its price and cut quickly into the commanding circulation lead of the *Oriental Daily News*, which responded with several price cuts of its own (So, 1996; Lee, 1997). These price wars have squeezed at least five financially weaker newspapers out of the market. In the past, Hong Kong was noted for having a larger number of small, diverse, and family-owned newspapers. However, the new publishing economics—as symbolized by the *Apple Daily*—has made it difficult for newspapers to survive. Newspaper publishing has thus become the prerogative of those individuals or corporations with substantial economic means (Lee, 1997).

Ming Pao Daily News too has lost many of its readers and reporters to the *Apple Daily*. To a certain extent, the formidable economic pressure has driven the former to pursue sensationalism at the expense of serious political analysis. Some journalists and media are exercising self-censorship for fear of real or imagined pressure from China. The Hong Kong Journalists Association (HKJA, 1997) has identified three broad categories of self-censorship: direct and indirect external pressure on a media organization, pressure within a media organization, and assimilation of values by journalists (pp. 50–57). The *South China Morning Post* has hired a Beijing journalist to be its editorial consultant, and its China reporting has been less vigorous. *Ming Pao Daily News* has refrained from editorial criticism of Beijing in recent years, particularly since 1996. It has tried instead to promote conservative nationalistic feelings, create sensational issues, and substitute crime stories for political ones (Lee, 1998).

The mass press was apolitical from the beginning; now the elite press has embarked on the road of growing depoliticization. Surveys (So et al., 1996, 1999). Indicate that journalists, as well as citizens, have perceived a steady erosion in media credibility in the 1990s. In fact, many outlets (including the prestigious *South China Morning Post* and *Ming Pao Daily News*) have lost significant ground. Press freedom is likely to erode seriously without conscious measures to safeguard press integrity. UNESCO (1999) data showed that in 1996 Hong Kong published 52 dailies with a circulation of 5 million—a penetration of 78.6 copies per 100 people.

In 1999, the newspapers' share of display advertising revenue was 36 percent, compared to television's 45 percent, magazines' 12 percent, radio's 4 percent, and outdoor's 3 percent, according to ACNielsen's Adex data for Hong Kong.

3.3 Structure and Organization

Hong Kong's press is an amalgamation of privately owned and party-financed newspapers. Most newspapers in Hong Kong are owned and operated by private investors whose main goal is profit. The ideological struggle between the CCP and the KMT is no longer their concern. These commercial newspapers are further divisible into quality press and popular press. In the past, the KMT backed a few "rightist" newspapers published in Hong Kong, but such papers folded in the early 1990s. Only the CCP-financed "leftist" papers remain in Hong Kong. They serve as mouthpieces for the Chinese government. Foreign investors own quite a number of prominent newspapers, including the *South China Morning Post, Ming Pao Daily News, Sing Tao Daily*, and *Hong Kong Standard*. Because of financial difficulties, Sally Aw Sian was forced to sell Sing Tao Holdings (which owns *Sing Tao Daily* and *Hong Kong Standard*) to a foreign investment bank, Lazard Asia Investment Management, in March 1999.

Overall, Hong Kong's newspapers have enjoyed a high degree of freedom, perhaps because of the British tradition. Although the colonial government had a number of laws in hand to control the press, it seldom used them. Contrary to widely held predictions, Hong Kong has continued to enjoy a high degree of press freedom as China seems to have kept its promise of not interfering with the SAR's internal matters.

3.4 Quality, Popular, and Party Press

Hong Kong newspapers had evolved into the party press, the partisan press, and the popular-centrist press. An immediate impact of the political transition has been the marginalization, and eventual demise, of the pro-KMT newspapers in rapid succession (Lee, 1997). The pro-KMT press, which had a substantial anti-communist following in the 1950s, began to weaken in the subsequent decades as it became apparent that Chiang Kai-shek was unlikely to recover mainland China. After the conclusion of the Sino-British Joint Declaration in 1984, the KMT institutions became even more irrelevant to Hong Kong's political life. *Kung Sheung Daily News*, owned by the pro-KMT Ho family, ceased publication in the wake of the declaration; and the KMT organ, the *Hong Kong Times*, followed suit a decade later. On the opposite side, the China-controlled *Ta Kung Pao* and *Wen Wei Po* enjoyed a high degree of autonomy under China's localization policy in the late 1980s. However, when these newspapers rebelled against the hard-line Chinese authorities during the Tiananmen crackdown in 1989, China tightened its control to ensure that they toed the party line. Despite their low credibility and dismal circulation in Hong Kong, they are well financed by advertising revenues from the China-related companies. Investment mistakes, however, have resulted in financial losses. Prior to the 1997 handover, these organs attacked the colonial government, and China's critics, extremely harshly.

Moreover, a progressive blurring of boundaries between the centrist (popular) and rightist (partisan) newspapers have occurred (Lee, 1997). Both catered to the market and allied with the colonial regime. But the rightist newspapers, founded long before the communists took power in China, historically supported the KMT.

The popular-centrist press, which did not emerge until 1970, owed no loyalty to the KMT. China began to co-opt *Wah Kiu Yat Po* (Overseas Chinese Daily News) and *Sing Tao Daily* in the mid-1980s. These two papers tried to play duplicity with the Chinese and the Hong Kong authorities, while gradually loosening their traditional ties with the KMT. Market competition was not kind to the weaker of the two, and *Wah Kiu Yat Po* struggled unsuccessfully in the hands of different editors until its closure in 1995. Pessimistic about Hong Kong's future, *Sing Tao Daily* moved its headquarters to Australia in 1985. It made money from real estate in Hong Kong and abroad before accumulating a mountain of debt. In 1992 its publisher responded to China's overture and was received warmly by Chinese leaders in Beijing. She began to invest in a variety of publishing projects in mainland China, but to no avail. Financial woes and declining readership have relegated this once influential paper to being an insignificant organ. It was almost sold to a pro-China businessman in 1998.

The ascendance of the popular-centrist press since the late 1960s brought about a weakening of the partisan press and a progressive de-linking of the traditional party–press ties. This group comprises two orientations: those representing the elite culture (notably, the *South China Morning Post, Ming Pao Daily News*, the *Hong Kong Economic Journal*, and the *Hong Kong Economic Times*); and those representing mass culture (notably, the *Oriental Daily News, The Sun*, the *Apple Daily, Sing Pao Daily News, Hong Kong Daily News*, and *Tin Tin Daily News*). The elite papers are influential opinion leaders despite their small circulation. The mass press controls two-thirds of newspaper circulation and advertising with profound influence on shaping popular culture.

The English-language *South China Morning Post* serves the small but powerful constituencies of the expatriate community and the Chinese elite. Rupert Murdoch briefly owned the paper, which he sold to a Chinese-Malaysian tycoon, Robert Kuok, who has considerable investment in China. On the Chinese-language press side, *Ming Pao Daily News* was widely acclaimed for its expertise on China-watching and insightful political analysis during the Cold War. Having been scathingly critical of China's radical-left leadership faction during the Cultural Revolution, its publisher Louis Cha entered the 1980s as a firm supporter of Deng Xiaoping's economic reform policy, even forbidding his paper to criticize Deng by name. As an active member of the committee charged with formulating the Basic Law, he opposed any hasty move to hold full democratic elections in Hong Kong. Cha sold the paper to Yu Pun-hoi in 1991. Yu fancied himself to be a Chinese media empire builder but his investment, including a global Chinese Television Network (CTN) and other newspaper ventures, all suffered from considerable financial losses. He also had a strained relationship with Beijing despite his effort to ingratiate himself with the Chinese authorities. He sold the paper in 1995 to the Chinese-Malaysian tycoon and publisher Tiong Hiew King, who is known to have significant business investment in China.

3.5 Distribution and Technology

Because of Hong Kong's high concentration of population and abundance of towering residential and commercial buildings, mailing and hand delivery are not efficient methods for newspaper distribution. Therefore, the press relies on a street hawker system comprising numerous individuals who operate small but fixed spots near restaurants or at busy street corners selling all kinds of newspapers and magazines (Li, 1983). People have the habit of buying newspaper copies from these street hawkers. Subscriptions constitute only a minute percentage of the total newspaper sales. Every day, very early in the morning, the major newspaper wholesalers gather in the central district and await the newspapers to arrive from the printing plants. Then they transport the newspapers to various areas by trucks. Newspaper distribution in Hong Kong does not involve much modern technology.

4. BROADCASTING

4.1 Policy and Legal Framework

Broadcasting regulation at the highest level rests with the chief executive and his advisory body, the Executive Council. Other key players in implementing the policy objectives include the Information Technology and Broadcasting Bureau (ITTB), the Broadcasting Authority (BA), and the Office of the Telecommunications Authority (OFTA).

The ITBB, established after the handover in 1997, is the government department responsible for the regulation of the broadcasting industry in Hong Kong. Earlier, the regulation of broadcasting, telecommunications, and information technologies was under different government departments. The SAR government created the ITBB to coordinate and regulate the converging industries of broadcasting, tele-communications, and information technology. The ITBB reviews the broadcasting regulatory framework in keeping with the ever-changing broadcasting environment.

The Broadcasting Authority is a statutory body set up in 1987 to control and regulate licensed TV and sound broadcasters in Hong Kong through provisions in the Television Ordinance, the Telecommunication Ordinance, and the Broadcasting Ordinance (BA, 1997). The BA makes recommendations to the government-in-council on applications for and renewal of licenses. It monitors radio and TV broadcasts to ensure compliance by the licensees. It keeps abreast of developments in the industry and deals with complaints about broadcasting. It also prepares and revises codes of practice for TV and radio broadcasts. It comprises 12 members, all appointed by the chief executive—three are official members; the rest, including the chairman, are drawn from the community.

The OFTA regulates all telecommunication services in Hong Kong. It provides advice to the BA on the technical aspects of broadcasting and assists it in drafting the codes of practice on technical standards.

4.2 Structure and Organization

4.2.1 Radio

Hong Kong has two commercial radio broadcasters, Commercial Radio (CR) and
Metro Radio (MR), as well as a quasi-public radio, Radio Television Hong Kong
(RTHK). CR and MR each has three channels, two of which use Chinese, while
the third uses English. These two commercial stations broadcast an aggregate of
more than 550 hours of programming per week (BA, 1997). RTHK is organizationally a government department but the editorial independence gained by it in
the last decade qualifies it as a quasi-public broadcaster. It broadcasts more than
1,100 hours of weekly radio programs over seven channels.

Regionally, Hutchvision started "The Wave" satellite radio service in 1995. It
carries two 24-hour music channels, one targeting Greater China and Northeast
Asia, and the other targeting India and the Middle East (BA, 1996). Apart from its
own programs, the service also offers two BBC World Service Radio channels.

4.2.2 Television

Virtually all Hong Kong households have access to television—about 2 million
TV households, constituting 6.3 million viewers aged 4 or above (BA, 1997).
More than 35 percent of TV households own more than one TV set. In late 1995,
more than 78 percent also had a videocassette recorder. Although the average
time people spent on daily TV viewing has decreased from 4.2 hours in 1990 to
3.5 hours in 1994, TV viewing remains Hong Kong's most popular leisure activity
(Chan et al., 1997).

Altogether, the TV industry in Hong Kong provides more than 38 channels. It
consists of two commercial TV broadcasters, a quasi-public broadcaster, a cable
television operator, an interactive TV service, and a number of regional satellite
TV broadcasters. Hong Kong is also the home of some regional TV broadcasters,
including Satellite Television Asian Region Ltd (STAR TV), Chinese Television
Network (CTN), and Chinese Entertainment Television (CETV). Using primarily
AsiaSat 1 as its satellite platform, STAR TV transmits more than 45 programming
services in eight languages on 25 channels, reaching more than 260 million viewers
across Asia (BA, 1998). It offers both subscription and free-to-air TV services.
CTN is a 24-hour news and information channel targeting the Greater China market.
STAR TV operates a Chinese "Phoenix" channel, which is popular in China.
Murdoch has reportedly exercised editorial control on this channel, backed by
Chinese investment, to avoid offending Beijing.

The most important socio-political factor that influenced Hong Kong television
and other media in the 1990s was the pending reunification with China in 1997
(Chan & Lee, 1991; Chan et al., 1997). Since the early 1980s, when the issue of
sovereignty reversion emerged, the proportion of advertising money connected
with Chinese interests increased steadily. The political influence of China has

inhibited ideological options and encouraged new nationalistic discourse. How far such changes will have an impact on the local TV industry remains to be seen.

As a communication hub of the Asia-Pacific, Hong Kong has the world's largest Chinese TV program library. It is also an important exporter of audiovisual products (Chan, 1997). The distribution channels include videos, cable and satellite television, and piracy. TVB marketed 1,000 hours of its 2,000–3,000 hours of annual production to 25 countries while ATV marketed 520 hours overseas in 1987 (Pomery, 1988). These exports have increased with the growth in output. TVB produced more than 5,000 hours of programming in 1993. It now owns a library of more than 80,000 hours of Chinese programming that ranges from classic Cantonese films and soap operas to musicals and sports (To & Lau 1994).

Although the Hong Kong TV industry has been suffering from an economic slowdown since the handover, the operating environment remains free, and the industry is still vibrant. With the aggressiveness of ATV's new owner and management, competition among terrestrial stations has intensified. Joining this competition are the relatively new media players such as cable television, interactive television, satellite television, and other video-service providers. As competition intensifies, Hong Kong's broadcast television has to control its costs, streamline its operations, and expand its distribution networks and regional services.

So far, the small domestic market of Hong Kong has not stopped its media industry from thriving because its has successfully drawn an audience from overseas Chinese in Taiwan, Southeast Asia, and other parts of the world (Chan, 1996, 1997). If China were to open its market, the economies of scale of the Hong Kong media would expand greatly. While Hong Kong media will gain from China's vast market and stocks of talent and scenes, the Chinese media industry will benefit from the capital, ideas, and marketing know-how from Hong Kong. Hong Kong TV broadcasters have long been supplying Asian broadcasters with production expertise and TV programs. With the competitive edge of proven management approaches and voluminous program libraries, the local TV broadcasters could emerge as strong media players when the Greater China TV market becomes a reality.

4.3 Program Policies

Less than half of the population of Hong Kong listens to radio every day. When people do listen, the highest number is no more than one-fifth of the total population at one time (Chan & Lee, 1992): Radio is much less important than television as a mass medium in people's daily life. In 1995, a large audience survey found that 69 percent of the population listened to radio within seven days prior to the interview (BA, 1997). These "past-week listeners" spent an average of 2.2 hours per day listening to radio.

Both RTHK and CR are competing neck-to-neck as both are popular with the audience. MR is a distant third. The three stations together offer a wide range of radio programs, including public affairs, news, magazines, music, talk show, drama, and sports. In the last decade, call-in programs on public affairs have gained wide popularity. Radio has become an important forum for the people, government officials, and social leaders to exchange their thoughts on current issues. This function was particularly important for Hong Kong as it went through the process of political transition.

Foreign programs have never dominated Hong Kong's Chinese TV channels (Chan & Lee, 1992). They have, at most, taken up only one-third of the airtime at most since the 1970s. As Table 3 shows, in 1969, two years after the inauguration of broadcast television, 62.7 percent of the programs of TVB Jade were already locally produced, and foreign programs accounted for only 33.8 percent of the total. By 1985, local production had increased to 80.2 percent and foreign programs had decreased to 19.3 percent. This pattern has remained relatively stable in the 1990s. In 1995–96, TVB Jade's local production had increased further to 82.5 percent. The same pattern applies to ATV and its predecessor RTV (BA, 1997; Lee & Yung, 1990).

Hong Kong's wireless television developed rapidly in the 1970s and 1980s. During this period, this medium absorbed Western ingredients, transformed Chinese cultural particulars, articulated local experiences, and crystallized a distinct Hong Kong way of life (Chan et al., 1997). It provided a distinctly popular culture that helped to integrate Hong Kong society. One can, therefore, say that Hong Kong television in the 1970s was more cultural than industrial. Since the 1980s, Hong Kong television has institutionalized its industrial process to cope with the commercial and political changes in the 1990s.

4.4 Ownership and Financing

In the absence of much government intervention, the operation of Hong Kong's media market depends on the state of the advertising industry. Because of Hong Kong's vibrant economy, heavy advertising expenditure has become the lifeblood of Hong Kong's many communication media. As shown in Table 7, newspapers, the dominant advertising medium in the early 1970s, accounted for more than 50 percent of the total advertising expenditure in 1972 (Chan & Lee, 1992). Its importance declined over the years to a low of 23.5 percent in 1985. In contrast, broadcast television, the second advertising medium in the early 1970s (shortly after its introduction in 1967), climbed to take up 60.2 percent of advertising expenditure in 1985. Television has remained the dominant medium since 1985, despite the fact that newspapers and magazines have nibbled its share. In 1999, television advertising still registered 45.2 percent of the advertising revenue. In contrast, radio has been a relatively unimportant outlet for advertising. In 1987, for instance, it got a mere 2.5 percent of the total advertising expenditure. But it improved to 3.9 percent in 1999. The emergence of new media such as cable television, interactive television, and the Internet will force the advertising agencies to rethink their policies on advertising expenditure.

Broadcast television was at its peak around mid-1980s when it registered the highest prime time ratings. As Table 4 shows, the prime time ratings started to slide after a decade of popularity in the mid-1980s. The reasons for the decline include the loss of the novelty of television, the lack of TV competition and the rise of new domestic entertainment media such as Karaoke and video players. This audience erosion has resulted in declining advertising revenue. ATV, the weak station, has been running a loss most of the time; TVB also has had to face the challenge of negative profit growth since the early 1990s.

5. NEW ELECTRONIC MEDIA

5.1 Internet and On-line Media

The development of information technology in Hong Kong has been very rapid in the past decade. ITU (1999) estimated that in January 1999, Hong Kong had 231,912 Internet host computers showing a density of 356.7 per 10,000 people. The July 1999 survey of the Internet Software Consortium (www.isg.org) shows that the figure has risen to 322,376 or 470.8 per 10,000 people. About 125 Internet Service Providers (ISPs)—including major ones like HKT-IMS, Star, HKNeT, and CTInets—were in operation in mid-1998 serving 25 percent of Hong Kong's households. More than half of all households had personal computers and the estimated number of Internet users stood at 850,000 (ACNielsen, 1998). The ACNielsen survey also shows that the average home users access the Internet three to four times a week for e-mail and for surfing the Web. In 1996, only 4.5 percent of the households had their personal computers connected to the Internet, but the figure more than doubled to 10.6 percent in 1997 and then to 16 percent in 1998. The number of Internet users in Hong Kong increased rapidly from 270,000 in 1996 to 500,000 in 1997 (Breakthrough, 1998). The current number of Internet users is believed to be more than 1 million (ACNielsen, 1998).

In his 1997 annual policy speech, Chief Executive Tung Chee-hwa announced an ambitious plan to upgrade information-technology education in primary and secondary schools. With generous government funding, the schools could now purchase more computers and hire related staff. In 1998, eight universities colle-ctively created the "Hong Kong Cyber Campus" (1998), which aims to connect schools at all levels in Hong Kong via the Internet. Programs offered by this Cyber Campus include an electronic magazine, a virtual campus, software demonstration, teacher training, and student information.

In March 1999, Hong Kong's finance secretary announced plans for establishing a US$ 13 billion ultra-modern intelligent building complex known as Cyberport, equipped with state-of-the-art telecommunication and information backbone to meet the needs of leading multinational and local information services companies. Business tycoon Richard Li's Pacific Century Group (PCG), a leader in developing interactive information services, will make a capital contribution of about US$ 7 billion to the Project. PCG has recruited eight multinational companies—Hewlett-Packard, Hua Wei, IBM, Oracle, Pacific Convergence Corp., Softbank, Sybase, and Yahoo!—to become anchor tenants at the Cyberport, which will be built on 26 hectares of land in Telegraph Bay, Pok Fu Lam. The Cyberport will accommodate more than 30 large- to medium-sized companies and about 100 smaller companies (ITBB, 1999).

5.2 Telecommunications Infrastructure

When the franchise for the local telephone service granted to Hong Kong Telephone Co. Ltd (HKTC) expired on June 30, 1995, four companies—HKTC, New World Telephone Ltd, New T & T Hong Kong Ltd, and Hutchison Communications Ltd—received licenses to provide local fixed telecommunication services on a competitive basis. By March 1998, Hong Kong had 4.7 million telephones served by more than 3.6 million mainlines. The telephone density was 72.2 telephones or 56.5 mainlines per 100 people—the highest in Asia. By December 1999, the number of main telephone lines stood at 3.84 million. In addition, Hong Kong also accommodated 3.70 million cellular subscribers as of November 1999 (OFTA, 1999).

Hong Kong provides satellite-based telecommunications and television broadcasting services via 36 satellite earth antennas operated by Hong Kong Telecom, Asia Satellite Telecommunications Co. Ltd, APT Satellite Co. Ltd, and Hutchvision Hong Kong Ltd. Hong Kong is also connected directly to eight submarine cable systems. The Okinawa–Luzon–Hong Kong submarine cable system connects Hong Kong to the Philippines, Japan, and North America. The Singapore–Hong Kong–Taiwan submarine cable system links Hong Kong with ASEAN countries, Australia, and Europe. The Hong Kong–Japan–Korea (H–J–K) optical fiber cable system connects Hong Kong, Japan, Korea, and North America. The Hong Kong–Taiwan (HONTAI-2) optical fiber cable system connects Hong Kong and Taiwan. The Asia Pacific Cable (APC) system links Hong Kong to Malaysia, Singapore, Taiwan and Japan. The T–V–H optical fiber submarine cable system connects Hong Kong to Thailand and Vietnam. In 1997, two new optical fiber submarine cable systems came into operation: the Asia Pacific Network (APCN) connecting Hong Kong to Taiwan, Korea, Japan, Thailand, the Philippines, Malaysia, Singapore, Indonesia, and Australia; and the Fiber-optic Link Around the Globe (FLAG) connecting Hong Kong to South Korea, Japan, Thailand, and other countries around the world (OFTA, 1999).

In early 1998, the Hong Kong government formally granted two separate video-on-demand program service licenses to Hong Kong Telecom VOD Ltd (HKTVOD) and STAR Interactive Television Ltd (STAR TV). They are the world's first commercially available interactive TV services. Hong Kong's people have a choice of hi-tech, interactive multimedia service added to their family entertainment programs. Apart from home entertainment, the services also include video, radio, music, education, and racing on demand, home banking and shopping, and broadband Internet. An HKTVOD subscriber pays a basic monthly fee of about US$ 26, in addition to the pay-per-view charges (Hongkong Telecom IMS, 1998).

6. POLICY TRENDS FOR PRESS AND BROADCASTING

6.1 Press

British common law governs the Hong Kong press. Despite its vaunted press freedom, however, the colony also had notoriously illiberal ordinances. Considered
an outpost of the "free world" during the Cold War of the 1950s, Hong Kong
deeply feared the formidable communist threat from China. The colonial government passed the Control of Publications Ordinance in 1951 empowering the
authorities to punish any agitational publications. Under the Treasonable Offenses
Ordinances, any person who intended to "deprive or depose the Queen of the
United Kingdom" or to "levy war against Her Majesty" could be sentenced to life
imprisonment. The Sedition Ordinance outlawed "an intention to bring into hatred
or excite disaffection against the Hong Kong government, to raise racial or class
discontent, or to incite violence." The Public Ordinance, passed after the 1967
riot, forbade the press to print any news about an unlawful assembly, defined as a
"gathering of 10 or more persons in a public place without a police permit." These
restrictive ordinances were not pursued rigidly, but not for lack of trying. The
colonial regime had to back down under strong pressure from Beijing when it
applied these ordinances to subjugate the communist press in the early 1950s and
during the 1967 riot. Besides, no compelling need existed to subject the media to
overt control because Hong Kong had no indigenous political parties and had
only weak labor unions; moreover, since the media were not structurally integrated
with these institutions, they did not pose any threat to the colonial power (Chan &
Lee, 1991, pp. 9–10).

Many of these vague and arbitrary ordinances have been repealed since 1985,
partly out of the fear that China might use them after 1997. Of the more than 40
revised ordinances, six specifically restrict the arbitrary executive power over
freedom of assembly, emergency situations, public order, broadcasting, and
telecommunications (including the government's authority to revoke licenses on
security grounds and to censor films or pre-broadcasting TV content). Most
importantly, the colonial government passed the Bill of Rights in 1991, only to
have it scrapped by the China-appointed Provisional Legislature in 1997. The
future of the Bill of Rights and the Freedom of Information Act is also dubious.
Most ominous is Article 23 of the Basic Law that authorizes the SAR government
to enact laws to prohibit acts of "treason, secession, sedition and subversion against
the Central People's Government or theft of state secrets." But on the question of
theft of state secrets, the colonial regime contradicted itself when it transplanted—
with the PRC's consent but contrary to public demand—the highly inhibiting
Official Secrets Act from Britain to Hong Kong without modification, a law that
may have serious negative implications for press freedom (Lee, 1997).

6.2 Broadcasting

Although the government has set some limits on the publication of pornographic and politically sensitive material, the government's interference in content is minimal in practice. Without an explicit and elaborate cultural policy, Hong Kong is a free port for information as no strict control exists over the flow of media in and out of Hong Kong. Although the SAR government is expected to enact laws to prohibit sedition, separatism, and the stealth of national secrets, most signs seem to indicate that Hong Kong will continue its open policy.

Hong Kong has been following a world trend toward de-regulation driven by both technology and market needs. In September 1998, the government announced a package of proposals to further liberalize TV broadcasting and program services. The new policy would allow the Fixed Telecommunication Network Service (FTNS) licensees to convey and provide TV program services, including pay television and video-on-demand. The policy would allow satellite broadcasters to offer pay TV services in Hong Kong, and require Cable TV to open up its broadband network for use by other TV and telecommunication service providers. The policy would also relax the restrictions on ownership and investment of licensees to facilitate diversification and cross-fertilization of the telecommunication and broadcasting markets. If all these proposed policies were to be implemented, Hong Kong will witness the emergence of a relatively unified TV market, enhanced competition and media convergence.

Another policy trend is to differentiate carriers from program or service providers. Technological development and program production each have a different logic of operation. Carriers are concerned with speed, resolution, and capacity whereas program providers focus on moral consensus, political bias, and entertainment values. Under the new policy proposal, the government plans to replace the existing transmission-based licensing and regulatory regime for TV services with a technology- and transmission-neutral regime under four categories of services: domestic free, domestic pay, non-domestic, and other licensable TV program services.

To strike a balance between local interest and the need to establish Hong Kong as a regional broadcasting center, Hong Kong's media regulators have been making an effort to separate the local from the regional. To ensure the local commitment of TV broadcasters, the existing regulations set a limit on the foreign ownership of broadcasting corporations. Previously, foreign ownership of a satellite-broadcasting license was restricted to a maximum of 49 percent of aggregate holding of shares. To attract investment and enhance Hong Kong's status as a regional communication center, the SAR government relaxed the foreign ownership restriction for regional broadcasters in 1998. In addition, the government also released the requirement that the majority of directors of a satellite broadcasting company be ordinary residents of Hong Kong. The government is likely to be motivated by its desire to strengthen Hong Kong's position as a regional broadcasting center in setting its future broadcasting policy.

7. MAIN ISSUES

● Political and legal pressure

Media self-censorship was a matter of long concern when the political transition to China was near its end. After the handover, however, the press has continued to be more vocal than most people had envisaged. It remains to be seen whether, in the long run, this desirable trend will continue. A threat to press freedom in recent years has been the many libel suits filed against media organizations and critics. This, in effect, may dampen the critical exchange of ideas and public monitoring of the press (Chan et al., 1997; HKJA, 1998).

● Publishing economics and media ethics

The recent economic downturn and the fierce market competition started partly by the entry of the successful *Apple Daily* have raised another issue. As a matter of survival, many newspapers have lowered their editorial standard to attract the largest possible number of readers by offering vulgar content. Under the name of market-driven journalism, yellow journalism has become the order of the day for the popular press, as well as for some so-called "info-tainment" type of TV programs (Chin, 1998; Lee, 1997). The decline in media ethics is evident in the growing number of complaints that people have lodged with the government monitoring body. The intense market competition may also lead to folding of a few newspapers that will further narrow the spectrum of opinion.

● Convergence and the broadcasting industry

The changing government policy toward de-regulation and the trend of media convergence brought by the advancement of communication technologies will affect the broadcasting industry. In 1998, radio stations began to test-run digital broadcasting, which enables the audience to receive high-quality audio and visual signals. Commercial Radio has already teamed up with Interactive TV (ITV) to provide instant radio-on-demand. Cable TV has voiced its desire to become the third wireless TV stations to offer free, over-the-air programs. Telephone companies, the traditional channel providers, can easily become content providers using their digitized fiber-optic networks (Granitsas, 1998). One company jointly owned by Richard Li (the son of Hong Kong billionaire Li Ka-shing) and US computer giant Intel is actively exploring the possibility of offering Internet-based interactive TV in the near future. The disappearing distinction between telecommunications, broadcasting, and computer networks is likely to make the broadcasting market much narrower as more companies try to get into this chaotic field. It will take some time before a new order emerges.

● The unresolved status of RTHK

The SAR government has left the status of RTHK unresolved. RTHK's corporatization effort was aborted when China opposed it during the political transition. It was even denied an independent cable TV channel. Some have urged the re-evaluation of these issues in light of the societal needs of Hong Kong so that RTHK could corporatize itself and become eligible to run independent channels over the air and through the cable network. How the SAR government will resolve the status of RTHK will provide an important signal of the future of Hong Kong's press freedom.

8. STATISTICS

General Profile

Exchange rate (1999)	US$ 1 = HK$ 7.77*
Population (mid-1999)	6.8 million
Population density	6,270 per sq km
Number of households	2.04 million
GDP per capita (PPP)	US$ 21,830
Geographical size	1,092 sq km

Source: * OANDA Historical Currency Table (http://www.oanda.com/converterer/ cc_table?lange=en); Census and Statistics Department, Hong Kong; *Asiaweek*, February 11, 2000.

Table 1
Press

Title	Established	Nature	Circulation*	Readership**
Oriental Daily News	1969	mass	*	2,551,000
Apple Daily	1995	mass	406,666	1,780,000
The Sun	1999	mass	*	*4
Ming Pao Daily News	1959	elite	85,699	285,000
Sing Pao Daily News	1939	mass	*	241,000
South China Morning Post	1903	elite, English	117,563	206,000
Hong Kong Daily News	1959	mass	*	157,000
Tin Tin Daily News	1960	mass	*	158,000
Sing Tao Daily	1938	elite	59,338	118,000
Hong Kong Economic Times	1988	elite, business	68,123	101,000
Hong Kong Economic Journal	1973	elite, business	63,120	62,000
Wen Wei Po	1948	pro-China	*	*
Ta Kung Pao	1938	pro-China	*	*
Hong Kong Commercial Daily	1952	pro-China, business	*	*
Hong Kong Standard	1949	elite, English	*	*

Source: * Hong Kong Audit Bureau of Circulation (ABC) Ltd (July–December 1998 figures). Those marked by an (*) were either not members of ABC or did not report figures; ** *ACNielsen media index Hong Kong mid-year report* (1999). Those marked by an (*) were below one percent average issue readership (aged 9+) which was the cutting point adopted by ACNielsen.

Note: *The Sun* claimed that its readership just surpassed 1 million one week after its launch and ranked third among all newspapers. The scenario was obviously a result of its price-cutting strategy to sell at HK$ 2 per copy. *Apple Daily* and *Sing Pao Daily News* correspondingly slashed their regular retail price from $5 to $3. *Oriental Daily News*, its parent company also owns *The Sun*, followed suit and reduced its price from $4 to $3.

Table 2
Broadcasting

Number of TV stations	3 (ATV, TVB, HKCTV [formerly Wharf Cable])
Number of TV channels	4 (terrestrial), 35 (cable)
Number of radio stations	3 (CR, MR, RTHK)
Number of radio channels	13 (3 by CR, 3 by MR, 7 by RTHK)

Table 3
Origins of Television Programs, 1969–96

Program origins	1969		1975		1985		1995–96	
	RTV %	TVB Jade %	RTV %	TVB Jade %	RTV %	TVB Jade %	ATV Home %	TVB Jade %
Local	71.6	62.7	65.4	61.7	78.0	80.2	76.0	82.5
Foreign	19.8	33.8	24.8	17.3	21.5	19.3	23.9	17.5
Others	8.6	3.5	9.8	21.0	0.5	0.5	0.0	0.0
Total %	100.0	100.0	100.0	100.0	100.0	100.0	99.9	100.0
(Weekly transmission hours)	(101)	(97)	(101)	(101)	(138)	(166)	(163)	(167)

Source: Adapted from Lee & Yung, 1990, and BA, 1997.

Table 4
Weekday Prime Time TV Ratings (TVRs)

Year	TVB Jade ratings	ATV Hong Kong ratings
1985	43	8
1987	45	4
1989	36	8
1991	31	10
1993	29	9
1995	24	12
1997	30	9
1999	26	11

Source: SRG ACNielsen.
Note: In 1998, one TVR=1% of total TV audience (aged 4+) = 60,450 individuals.

Table 5
Household Media Equipment

Households with TV sets	99%
Households with VCR	73%
Households with cable TV	20%
Households with satellite TV	19%
Households with home computer	36%
Households with Internet connection	16%
Number of mainline telephones per 100 people	56.5
Number of cellular telephones per 100 people	54.4 (November 1999)

Source: ACNielsen 1998 Establishment Survey; Howlett, 1998; OFTA.

Note: Other surveys put the figures of households with home computer, as well as Internet connections much higher. For example, some studies estimate that over 50 percent of Hong Kong households had computers at home in 1998. The Office of the Telecommunications Authority puts the number of personal computers in Hong Kong at 1.5 million in 1998.

Table 6
Advertising

Advertising earnings	(HK$ '000)	(US$ '000)	%
Press	8,606,593	1,107,670	36
Magazine	2,755,255	354,602	12
Radio	915,257	117,794	4
Television	10,691,461	1,357,992	45
Others	682,092	87,785	3

Source: Hong Kong Adex, 1999.

Table 7
Advertising Revenue by Media, 1972–97

Year	TV	Newspaper	Magazines	Radio	Others	Total %	Annual Ad-spend in HK$ millions
1972*	34.0	54.7	3.7	5.5	2.1	100	222
1974*	41.0	49.1	3.3	4.6	2.0	100	239
1976*	53.8	39.2	3.0	2.7	1.3	100	280
1978*	58.5	31.8	5.4	3.4	0.9	100	460
1980*	49.0	38.4	7.7	4.6	0.3	100	939
1985**	60.2	23.5	9.6	3.7	3.0	100	2,871
1987**	57.4	26.4	10.4	2.5	3.3	100	3,865
1989**	50.5	28.7	12.9	3.8	4.1	100	5,529
1991**	50.4	27.7	12.8	4.7	4.4	100	7,532
1993**	42.9	36.3	10.8	6.0	4.0	100	11,395
1995**	49.2	28.9	11.9	6.5	3.5	100	15,116
1997**	46.9	32.9	11.9	5.3	3.0	100	20,400
1999**	45.2	36.4	11.6	3.9	2.9	100	23,651

Source: * Marketing Research Department, HK-TVB Ltd; ** HK Adex, SRG

Table 8
Estimated Mass Media Penetration

	Radio receivers		TV receivers		Daily newspapers		
	Number ('000)	Per 100 people	Number ('000)	Per 100 people	Number	Circ'n ('000)	Per 100 people
1990	3,800	66.6	1,550	27.2	38	4,250	74.5
1995	4,200	67.5	1,750	28.1	46	4,500	72.3
1996	4,300	67.6	1,790	31.9	52	5,000	78.6
1997	4,450	68.4	1,840	28.3	...	...	....

Source: UNESCO, 1999.

9. USEFUL ADDRESSES

Apple Daily
No. 8 Chun Ying St.
TKO Industrial Estate West
Tsueng Kwan O, Hong Kong
Telephone: 852-2990 8388
Fax: 852-2741 0830
URL: http://www.appledaily.com.hk

Hong Kong Economic Journal
22/F, North Point Industrial Building
499 King's Road, North Point, Hong Kong
Telephone: 852-2856 7567
Fax: 852-2811 1070

Hong Kong Economic Times
6/F, Kodak House II
321 Java Road, North Point, Hong Kong
Telephone: 852-2565 4288
Fax: 852-2811 1926

Ming Pao Daily News
15/F, Block A
Ming Pao Industrial Center
18 Ka Yip St., Chai Wan, Hong Kong
Telephone: 852-2595 3111
Fax: 852-2898 3783
E-mail: mingpao@mingpao.com
URL: http://www.mingpao.com

Oriental Daily News
Oriental Press Centre
7 Wang Tai Road
Kowloon Bay, Kowloon, Hong Kong
Telephone: 852-2795 1111
Fax: 852-2795 2299
E-mail: odn@oriental.com.hk
URL: http://www.orientaldaily.com.hk

Sing Tao Daily
3/F, Singh Tao Building
1 Wang Kwong Road
Kowloon Bay, Kowloon, Hong Kong
Telephone: 852-2798 2323
Fax: 852-2795 3022
URL: http://singtao.com

South China Morning Post
29/F, Dorsct House
979 King's Road, Quarry Bay, Hong Kong
Telephone: 852-2565 2222
Fax: 852-2516 7478
URL: http://www.scmp.com

Asia Television Ltd (ATV)
Television House
81, Broadcast Drive
Kowloon Tong, Kowloon, Hong Kong
Telephone: 852-2992 8888
Fax: 852-2338 6469

Cable Television, Wharf Cable Ltd
4/F, Wharf Cable Tower
9 Hoi Shing Road
Tsuen Wan, N.T., Hong Kong
Telephone: 852-2112 5541
Fax: 852-2112 7844
URL: htt://www.cabletv.com.hk

Television Broadcasts Ltd (TVB)
TV City
Clearwater Bay Road
Sai Kung, N.T., Hong Kong
Telephone: 852-2335 9123
Fax: 852-2358 1300
URL: http://www.tvb.com.hk

Hong Kong Commercial Broadcasting Company Ltd
3 Broadcast Drive
Kowloon Tong, Kowloon, Hong Kong
Telephone: 852-2336 5111
Fax: 852-2338 1354

Metro Broadcast Corporation Ltd
(Metro Radio)
Basement 2, Site 6
Whampoa Garden
Hung Hom, Kowloom, Hong Kong
Telephone: 852-2123 9888
Fax: 852-2123 9876
E-mail: newsroom@metroradio.com.hk
URL: http://www.metroradio.com.hk

Radio Television Hong Kong (RTHK)
Broadcasting House
30 Broadcast Drive
Kowloon Tong, Kowloon, Hong Kong
Telephone: 852-2339 7774
Fax: 852-2794 1137
URL: http://www.rthk.org.hk

10. REFERENCES

ACNielsen. (1998). *ACNielsen Internet survey.* Hong Kong: ACNielsen.

ACNielsen. (1999). *ACNielsen weekly TV audience survey.* Hong Kong: ACNielsen.

Breakthrough. (1998). *Research on Net behavior of youth in Hong Kong.* Hong Kong: Breakthrough.

BA (Broadcasting Authority). (1996). *Hong Kong broadcasting authority, 1994–1995.* Hong Kong: Hong Kong Government Press.

BA (Broadcasting Authority). (1997). *Hong Kong broadcasting authority 1995–1996.* Hong Kong: Hong Kong Government Press.

BA (Broadcasting Authority). (1998). *Broadcasting in Hong Kong: Television broadcasting* [Online]. Available: ⟨http://www.hkba.org.hk/english/broadcasting/telbroadcasting.html⟩.

Chan, J.M. (1996). Television development in Greater China: Structure, exports, and market formation. In J. Sinclair, et al. (Eds.), *New patterns in global television: Peripheral vision* (pp. 126–160). Oxford: Oxford University Press.

Chan, J.M. (1997), Media internationalization in Hong Kong: Patterns, factors, and tensions. In G. Postiglione & J. Tang (Eds.), *Hong Kong's reunion with China: The global dimensions* (pp. 222–238). Armond, NY: M.E. Sharpe.

Chan, J.M., & Lee, C.C. (1991). *Mass media and political transition: The Hong Kong press in China's orbit.* New York: Guilford.

Chan, J.M., & Lee, P.S.N. (1992). Communication indicators in Hong Kong: Conceptual issues, findings and implications. In S.K. Lau, et al. (Eds.), *The development of social indicators research in Chinese societies* (pp. 175–204). Hong Kong: Hong Kong Institute of Asia-Pacific Studies, Chinese University of Hong Kong.

Chan, J.M., Ma, E.K.W., & So, C.Y.K. (1997). Back to the future: A retrospect and prospects for the Hong Kong mass media. In J.Y.C. Cheng (Ed.), *The other Hong Kong report 1997* (pp. 455–481). Hong Kong: Chinese University Press.

Chang, K.S. (1982) Hong Kong. In J.A. Lent (Ed.), *Newspapers in Asia: Contemporary trends and problems* (pp. 78–94). Hong Kong: Heinemann Asia.

Chin, F. (1998, December 17). Learning self-control: Hong Kong's media are torn between ethics and profits. *Far Eastern Economic Review, 161,* 24–25.

Clayton, C.C. (1971). Hong Kong. In J.A. Lent (Ed.), *The Asian newspapers' reluctant revolution* (pp. 55–64). Ames, Iowa: Iowa State University Press.

Everest, F.A. (1978). Hong Kong. In J.A. Lent (Ed.), *Broadcasting in Asia and the Pacific: A continental survey of radio and television* (pp. 74–97). Philadelphia: Temple University Press.

Granitsas, A. (1998, September 17). Changing channels: Hong Kong tries to reclaim spot as Asia's media hub. *Far Eastern Economic Review, 161,* 50.

Ho, M.C. (1975). *Hong Kong broadcasting industry in the past twenty-five years* (in Chinese). Unpublished undergraduate thesis, Department of Journalism and Communication, Chinese University of Hong Kong.

HKJA (Hong Kong Journalists Association). (1997). *The die is cast: Freedom of expression in Hong Kong on the eve of the handover of China.* Annual report. Hong Kong: HKJA.

HKJA (Hong Kong Journalists Association). (1998). *Questionable beginnings: Freedom of expression in Hong Kong one year after the handover to China.* Annual report. Hong Kong: HKJA.

HKLC (Hong Kong Legislative Council). (1950). *Hong Kong Hansard: Reports of the meetings of the Legislative Council of Hong Kong.* Hong Kong: Government Printer.

Hongkong Telecom IMS. (1998). InteracTVe [On-line]. Available: (http://www.hkitv.com).

Howlett, B. (Ed.). (1988). *Hong Kong—a new era: A review of 1997.* Hong Kong: Government Services Department, Hong Kong Government.

ITBB (Information Technology and Broadcasting Bureau). (1999, March 3). *$13 billion Cyberport project announced* [On-line]. Available: (http://www.info.gov.hk).

ITU (International Telecommunication Union). (1999). *Challenges to the network: Internet for development.* Geneva: ITU.

Lau, S.K. (1982). *Society and politics in Hong Kong.* Hong Kong: Chinese University Press.

Lau, T.Y., & Ang, P.H. (1998). The Pacific Rim. In A.B. Albarran & S.M. Chan-Olmsted (Eds.), *Global media economics: Commercialization, concentration and integration of world media markets* (pp. 310–327). Ames: Iowa State University Press.

Lee, C.C. (1997). Media structure and regime change in Hong Kong. In M.K. Chan (Ed.), *Hong Kong's reintegration with China: Transformation and challenge* (pp. 113–138). Hong Kong: Hong Kong University Press.

Lee, C.C. (1998). Press self-censorship and political transition in Hong Kong. *Harvard International Journal of Press/Politics, 3* (2), 55–73.

Lee, C.C., & Chan, J.M. (1990). Government management of the press in Hong Kong. *Gazette, 46,* 125–139.

Lee, P.S.N., & Yung, D. (1990, January). *The program problems of cable television in Hong Kong and its policy implications.* Paper presented at the 12th Annual Conference of the Pacific Telecommunication Council, Hawaii.

Lent, J.A. (1982). Freedom of the press in East Asia. In J.A. Lent (Ed.), *Newspapers in Asia: Contemporary trends and problems* (pp. 20–30. Hong Kong: Heinemann Asia.

Li, Y.L. (1983). *Hong Kong newspaper distribution system: An exploratory study* (in Chinese). Unpublished undergraduate thesis, Department of Journalism and Communication, Chinese University of Hong Kong, Hong Kong.

Ma, E.K.W. (1992). *The warring states of television* (in Chinese). Hong Kong: Subculture Press.

OFTA (Office of the Telecommunication Authority). (1999). *Fact sheet 1998* [On-line]. Available: (http://www.ofta.gov.hk/index_eng1.html).

Pomery, C. (1988). Hong Kong. In M. Alvarado (Ed.), *Video worldwide: An international study* (p. 106). London: UNESCO.

RTHK (Radio and Television Hong Kong). (1988). *Sixty years of broadcasting in Hong Kong.* Hong Kong: RTHK.

Seymour-Ure, C. (1974). *The political impact of mass media.* Beverly Hills, CA: Sage Publications.

So, C.Y.K. (1996). Pre-1997 Hong Kong press: Cut-throat competition and the changing journalistic paradigm. In M.K. Nyaw & S.M. Li (Eds.), *The other Hong Kong report 1996* (pp. 485–505). Hong Kong: Chinese University Press.

So, C.Y.K., Lee, C.C., & Fung, A.Y.H. (1996, December 5). How do media workers view press credibility? (in Chinese) *Ming Pao Daily News,* p. C6.

So, C.Y.K., Chan, J.M., & Lee, C.C. (1999, January 4). The change of media credibility in the nineties (in Chinese). *Ming Pao Daily News,* p. E9.

To, Y.M., & Lau, T.Y. (1994, July). *The sky is not the limit: Hong Kong as a global media exporter.* Paper presented at the International Communication Association Convention, Sydney, Australia.

UNESCO (United Nations Educational, Scientific and Cultural Organization). (1999). *Statistical yearbook.* Paris: UNESCO.

Vanden Heuvel, J., & Dennis, E.E. (1993). *The unfolding lotus: East Asia's changing media.* New York: Freedom Forum.

◆

20

MACAU SAR (CHINA)

Clement So, Joseph Man Chan, & Chin-Chuan Lee

1. NATIONAL PROFILE

1.1 Geography

A narrow isthmus connects the Special Administrative Region of Macau, located at the mouth of the Pearl River Delta in southeastern coast of China, with the mainland. Macau SAR, just 70 kilometers southwest of Hong Kong SAR, has a total area of 21.45 sq km, comprising the Macau peninsula and the islands of Taipa and Coloane. Two bridges link Taipa to the peninsula. An isthmus connects Coloane with Taipa. Hot and humid summers bring in tropical storms.

1.2 People

In 1999, Macau had a population of 437,312 representing a density of 20,387 per sq km—one of the highest in the world. It has experienced an annual population growth rate of almost 4 percent over the last two decades. More than 20,000 people visit Macau daily by boat from Hong Kong. Almost 50,000 mainlanders also work in Macau. While 69 percent of Macau residents are Chinese nationals, 27 percent are Portuguese in nationality. However, 96 percent speak Chinese, compared to only 2 percent who speak Portuguese, as the first language. The literacy rate is 75 percent and life expectancy 76 years. Urbanization is 94 percent (*Asiaweek*, February 11, 2000).

1.3 Government and Politics

The Lisbon Protocol and the Treaty of Commerce and Friendship, signed respectively in 1887 and 1888, ceded sovereignty over Macau to the Portuguese. China, however, took effective control of Macau after the 1966 riot. Following 13 years of tension, China and Portugal resumed diplomatic relations in 1979. They signed a joint declaration in 1987 recognizing Macau as a Chinese territory under

Portuguese administration. They agreed to create the Macau Special Administrative Region on the principle of "one country, two systems"—following the Hong Kong model. The joint declaration states that the current social and economic systems, as well as the way of life, will remain unchanged. All the rights and freedoms will be guaranteed and protected by the Basic Law, which came into force on December 20, 1999, when China assumed sovereignty over Macau (Macau Government, 1998).

The governor and the legislative assembly constituted the executive and legislative arms of Macau under Portuguese rule. A local chief executive appointed by the government of China replaced the governor when Macau became a SAR. The legislative assembly has 23 deputies—eight elected by popular vote, eight by indirect vote, and seven appointed by the chief executive. Members serve four-year terms.

1.4 Economy

Macau's gross domestic product at purchasing power parity was at US$ 7.8 billion in 1999. Its per capita income about US$ 17,500. It exported merchandise valued at US$ 2.1 billion in 1999, and its reserves stood at US$ 2.3 billion (*Asiaweek*, February 11, 2000). The economy is based largely on the tourism and casino business. In 1997, it had 7 million visitors who were mostly (63 percent) from neighboring Hong Kong. Because it borders Zhuhai, a Special Economic Zone in Guangdong, Macau has been able to develop a mutually beneficial economic relationship with the mainland. Macau has a manufacturing industry dominated by textiles and clothing. Its principal markets include the United States, the European Union, Hong Kong, China, and Japan. It has invested heavily in infrastructure improvement, particularly on the airport and the container port projects. Pataca, Macau's currency, is attached to the Hong Kong dollar.

2. THE PRESS

2.1 History and Development

Macau was developed much earlier than Hong Kong but sunk into relative insignificance. The Jesuits established the first Chinese church there in 1560. Macau became a center of East–West cultural exchange, from where Western priests published religious messages and reached out to potential constituencies in China, Korea, Japan, and Southeast Asia. The inception phase of Macau's press history is marked by the birth of Portuguese newspapers such as the *Abelha de China, Gazeta de Macau*, and *Chronica de Macau*. Eight Portuguese newspapers appeared from 1822 to 1840, but their influence was small. Many of these newspapers did not last long either for political or economic reasons. On the contrary, the English newspapers published in Macau during this period had greater impact (Lo & Tam, 1996; *Macau handbook*, 1993; Wong & Ng, 1996). The *China Repository* is a good example. Like Hong Kong, Macau was also a place where contending Chinese political forces waged their propaganda wars, but on a smaller scale. These forces published Chinese-language newspapers such as *Kang Hai Chung Pou, Ji Sin Pou*, and *Ho Kang Pou*. Since 1842, the neighboring Hong Kong has overshadowed Macau. Macau's press, like its economy, could never catch up with Hong Kong's, but was for a long time better developed than the press in the Pearl Delta zone (including Guangzhou).

Macau's press began to flourish after 1911. The more notable titles included *Journal Informacao, Tempo de Macau, Diario de Macau, Journal Actualidade Popular, Jornal "Tai Chung,"* and *Jornal "Va Kio."* Many Macau newspapers closed after the outbreak of the Pacific War in 1941 (Lo & Tam, 1996). Although Macau did not come under Japanese occupation, the authorities permitted the operation of only those newspapers sympathetic to the pro-Japan authority in China. However, all the pro-Japan newspapers folded after the war.

When the Chinese Communist Party (CCP) defeated the Nationalist Party in mainland China, some pro-Taiwan elements withdrew to Macau where they set up newspapers (Hoi, 1993). Given Macau's marginality vis-à-vis Hong Kong, the Chinese communists did not establish the *Macao Daily News* as their mouthpiece until 1958. The 1966 riots marked a watershed in the development of Macau's press. The pro-China forces sparked the riots as an extension of mainland's Cultural Revolution. The riots resulted in the rise of China's political influence and the decline of the authority of the Macau government, which agreed to stop the pro-Taiwan forces from operating. The press structure reflected the shift in political power. The pro-Taiwan newspapers ceased, and the other newspapers realigned in favor of the CCP. Concerned primarily with Lisbon's politics rather than local affairs, the highly partisan Portuguese press exerted little influence on the majority Chinese community in Macau (Lent, 1982; Lo & Tam, 1996).

2.2 Structure and Organization

The press structure in Macau is comparatively simple. The SAR has eight Chinese dailies and 10 weeklies. The most influential is the communist organ *Macao Daily News*, which claims a circulation of 100,000 copies. This daily, which reaches some coastal cities in Guangdong as well, is a "semi-official" paper reflecting the views of the Chinese government. The *Jornal "Va Kio"* is a more objective non-party newspaper with a circulation of 35,000 copies. The other newspapers include *Jornal "Tai Chung," Si Man Pou, Seng Pou, Cheng Pou, Today Macau Journal*, and *Correio Sino-Macanese* (which ceased to publish in January 2000 due to a labor dispute. Some Hong Kong newspapers are also shipped and sold in Macau every day.

The eight daily newspapers for a small population begs an explanation. Hoi (1993) suggests three reasons for this unusual situation:

- The low operating costs for newspapers in Macau favor their proliferation. The journalists' pay is low. Given a very limited newshole, the newspapers can readily fill the space with news. Some can even derive news from radio and TV news programs.

- Macau is a small place where the social celebrities know one another. Advertising based on personal relationship (*guanxi*) is a significant source of revenue for small newspapers. Advertising placed by the corporations representing China's economic interest in Macau is also significant. Such advertising serves "co-optation."
- The Macau government provides a monthly subsidy to newspapers (since 1985) in addition to providing government advertising. For some newspapers, this is a reliable source of income (Wong & Ng, 1996).

Three Portuguese morning dailies (*Gazeta Macaense, Macau Hoje*, and *Futuro de Macau*), one afternoon daily, *Jornal de Macau*, and five weeklies serve a small expatriate community of fewer than 20,000 people (Wong & Ng, 1996). Even the most popular Portuguese daily is in financial debt because its circulation does not exceed 2,000 copies. In 1985, the government decided to subsidize the Portuguese press. Later, it extended the same privilege to the Chinese press. All Portuguese papers were aligned editorially with the political parties in Lisbon. Inasmuch as Portuguese citizens in Macau could take part in presidential and parliamentary elections in Portugal, press attacks on opposition parties or candidates had been customary (Lo & Tam, 1996).

Protected by Portugal's constitution, Macau's press had been free from government interference in terms of editorial position, operation, and management. The only regulatory agency was the Government Information Services. It distributed government information, coordinated the press, accepted press registration, and issued licenses to journalists. The agency also provided services to the press ranging from subsidies (newsprint, power, and telecommunications) to journalist training classes. However, the agency's power was quite limited and, given Macau's political environment, had even less coercive power on the press. It was primarily a service agency and the government's public relations arm. Because the majority of Macau's press was already pro-communist, little has changed since Macau reverted to China in December 1999.

3. BROADCASTING

3.1 Development and Structure

3.1.1 Radio

Macau's radio broadcasting dates back to 1933 when some amateurs started Radio Macau. The station provided news and music programs in Portuguese for two hours each day (Lo & Tam, 1996; Wong & Ng, 1996). The Macau government took over the radio operation in 1948. In 1982, the government handed the management of the radio station to the Teledifusao de Macau (TDM), a body appointed by the government.

Macau has two radio channels, one broadcasting in Portuguese and the other in Cantonese, both owned by Teledifusao de Macau (Everest, 1978). Both channels provide 24-hour radio programs. The Macau government, under the Portuguese, exercised little interference with the Cantonese channel because of the unfamiliarity with the language.

Another broadcasting station, Radio Vila Verde, launched in 1950, was once very popular because of its entertaining programs. At first, it provided musical programs in Cantonese and Portuguese and became well known for its broadcasts of dog racing in the 1960s. From 1964, it only maintained Cantonese programming and became a commercial station. It stopped operation in 1995 (Wong & Ng, 1996).

3.1.2 Television

The Macau government established its first television service in 1984. Although the government financed the service, an independent public body ran the operation. Poor management and financial losses forced the government to sell 49.5 percent of the station's registered capital (50 million Patacas) to a consortium comprising five private financial groups in 1988. The government and the consortium signed a 15-year exclusive deal in 1990, with registered capital increased to 100 million Patacas (*Macau handbook*, 1993). At the beginning, it had only one channel that broadcast from 6 p.m. to 11 p.m., alternating the use of Portuguese and Cantonese.

In 1990, Teledifusao de Macau started to carry two channels, one each in Portuguese and Cantonese. Currently, the Portuguese channel is on air 12 hours per day, and the Cantonese channel broadcasts a total of 10 hours of programs per day in three separate time slots. About half of the programs on the Cantonese channel are either dubbed or imported from Hong Kong, Taiwan, Japan, or China, whereas about 80 percent of the Portuguese programs are imported from Portugal.

With the exception of news program, Hong Kong television, which reaches the Macau SAR, has dominated the Macau TV scene (Chan & Ma, 1996). However, Macau's radio audience has a more even distribution, with ratings split among Macau's two radio channels, Radio Television Hong Kong, and Hong Kong's commercial radio. In 1987, the Macau government wanted to privatize the TV station and boost its power to enable its signal to reach Hong Kong. Teledifusao de Macau had to abort the expansion plan because of opposition from the Hong Kong government. In 1993, another attempt to privatize Teledifusao de Macau failed because of opposition from China.

4. NEW ELECTRONIC MEDIA

4.1 Internet and On-line Media

Macau DDN, the territory's digital data network, came into operation in September 1991. The territory's three Internet service providers—CTM-Internet Services,

Fls (Unitel), and Macau Web Ltd—had 3,037 subscribers at the end of 1996. ITU (1998) estimated that the territory had 40,000 computers in 1996. The number increased to 6,033 at the end of 1997. The introduction of ISDN took place in April 1997 (APT, 1998). The January 1999 Network Wizard's survey estimated that Macau had 143 Internet hosts (a density of 3.41 per 10,000 people), while the July 1999 survey of the Internet Software Consortium (www.isg.org) estimated the number at 155 or 3.5 per 10,000 people.

4.2 Telecommunications Infrastructure

In 1998, Macau had 173,900 mainline telephones, a telephone density of 40.91 per 100 people. It also had 75,500 cellular subscribers, a density of almost 17.75 per 100 people (ITU, 1999). Macau Posts and Telecommunications (CTI-Macau) is the authority responsible for planning, regulating, and promoting telecommunication services in the territory. In 1981, Macau privatized the telecommunications network by giving a 20-year concession to a franchised company called Companhia de Telecomunicacoes de Macau (CTM), which now operates a fully digitized network and two satellite earth stations (APT, 1998). Macau joined the SEA-ME-WE 3 submarine cable project in January 1998 (APT, 1999).

5. MAIN ISSUES

● Media diversity

The main issues faced by the media in Macau are quite different from those in Hong Kong. Because the Chinese newspapers in Macau have for long been aligned with Beijing, a problem of self-censorship or legal threats after the 1999 departure of the Portuguese did not arise. The competition among the press is not strong. Now that Macau has reverted to China, the remaining few Portuguese newspapers will further lose significance and may even fold. The major issue, however, may be the lack of diversity in the press, which consequently limits its ability to offer a larger spectrum of opinion and to accommodate the views of the public.

● Television

As for the television industry, Macau is too small a place in terms of both audience and advertising revenue to support a commercial television station with adequate local program productions. The situation is compounded by the availability of free and high-quality TV programs not only from neighboring Hong Kong but also from mainland China. The relationship between Macau and Hong Kong is somewhat like that between Canada and the United States. To some extent, Macau suffers from a form of "media imperialism," although not many citizens in Macau seem to have any complaints about it.

6. STATISTICS

General Profile

Exchange rate (1999 average)	US$ 1 = 7.99 Patacas*
Population	437,312
Population density	20,387 per sq km
GDP per capita	US$ 17,500
Geographical size	21.45 sq km

Source: * OANDA Historical Currency Table (http://www.oanda.com/convereterer/ cc_table?lang=on); *Asiaweek*, February 11, 2000.

Table 1
Press

Title	Established	Circulation*
Macao Daily News	1958	100,000
Jornal "Va Kio"	1937	35,000
Jornal "Tai Chung"	1933	16,000
Si Man Pou	1944	12,000
Today Macau Journal	1987	2,000
Seng Pou (Jornal Estrela)	1963	*
Cheng Pou	1978	*
Correio Sino-Macaense	1989	*

Source: *Editor & publisher international yearbook*, 1999.
Note: * Figures not available. The total circulation adds up to about 165,000. However, Wong & Ng, 1996, have estimated the total circulation of the eight Macau dailies at about 50,000 or 60,000; and the Macau circulation of the Hong Kong dailies at 13,000.

Table 2
Broadcasting

Number of TV channels	4	Canal Portuguese (2 channels), Canal Chines (2 channels)
Number of radio channels	2	Radio Macau, Ou Mun Tin Toi

Table 3
Household Media Equipment

Number of mainline telephones per 100 people	41
Number of cellular telephones per 100 people	17.75

Source: ITU, 1999.

Table 4
Estimated Mass Media Penetration

	Radio receivers		TV receivers		Daily newspapers		
	Number ('000)	Per 100 people	Number ('000)	Per 100 people	Number	Circ'n ('000)	Per 100 people
1990	120	32.2	30	8.1	8	240	64.5
1995	145	33.7	45	10.5	9	250	58.2
1996	155	35.2	47	10.7	10	200	45.5
1997	160	35.6	49	10.9	...	...	....

Source: UNESCO, 1999.

7. USEFUL ADDRESSES

Cheng Pou
Av. Da Praia Grande, No. 63
1-E, F. Edf. Hang Cheong, Macau
Telephone: 853-965976
Fax: 853-965741

Correio Sino-Macaense
Av. Venceslau de Morais, No. 221
Edf. Ind. Nam Fong
2a Fase, 15-E, Macau
Telephone: 853-717569
Fax: 853-717572

Macao Daily News
Rua Pedro Nolaso Da Silva, 37, Macau
Telephone: 853-371688
Fax: 853-331998
URL: http://www.macaodaily.com

Seng Pou (Jornal Estrela)
Travessa Da Caldeira, No. 9, Macau
Telephone: 853-574294
Fax: 853-388192

Jornal "Va Kio"
69 Rua Da Alfandega, Macau
Telephone: 853-345888
Fax: 853-580638

Jornal "Ta Chung"
Rua Dr. Lourenco P. Marques
No. 7A, 2, Macau
Telephone: 853-939888
Fax: 853-934114

Si Man Pou
Rua Dos Pescadores, Edf. Ocean,
2a Fase, 2B, Macau
Telephone: 853-722111
Fax: 853-722133

Today Macau Journal
Patio Da Barca 20, Macau
Telephone: 853-215050
Fax: 853-215322

Teledifusao de Macau, SARL
TV Channel
Rua Francisco Xavier Pereira
157-A, Macau
Telephone: 853-519188
Fax: 853-519423

Teledifusao de Macau, SARL
Radio Channel
Av. Dr. Rodrigo Rodrigues, 223–225
Edif. "Nam Kwong", 7 Andar, Macau
Telephone: 853-335888
Fax: 853-343220

8. REFERENCES

APT (Asia-Pacific Telecommunity). (1998, 1999). *The APT yearbook*. Bangkok: APT.

Chan, J.M., & Ma, E.K.W. (1996). Broadcast and TV industries in Hong Kong and Macau. In *The changing mass media enterprises in Hong Kong and Macau* (in Chinese) (pp. 97–134). Taipei: Government Information Office.

Everest, F.A. (1978). Macau. In J.A. Lent (Ed.), *Broadcasting in Asia and the Pacific: A continental survey of radio and television* (pp. 87–91). Philadelphia: Temple University Press.

Hoi, T.W. (1993). *The political economy of the Macau press: A case study of the 1992 Legislative Assembly election* (in Chinese). Unpublished M.Phil. thesis, Department of Journalism and Communication, Chinese University of Hong Kong, Hong Kong.

ITU (International Telecommunication Union). (1998, 1999). *World telecommunication development report*. Geneva: ITU.

Lent, J.A. (1982). Macao. In J.A. Lent (Ed.), *Newspapers in Asia: Contemporary trends and problems* (pp. 151–152). Hong Kong: Heinemann Asia.

Lo, K.C., & Tam, C.K. (1996). The news media in Hong Kong and Macau. In *The changing mass media enterprises in Hong Kong and Macau* (in Chinese) (pp. 5–47). Taipei: Government Information Office.

Macau Government. (1998). [On-line]. Available: (http://www.macau.gov.mo/).

Macau handbook (in Chinese). (1993). Macau: Macao Daily News.

UNESCO (United Nations Educational, Scientific and Cultural Organization). (1999). *Statistical yearbook*. Paris: UNESCO.

Wong, H.K., & Ng, C.L. (Eds.) (1996). *Macau overview* (in Chinese). Macau: Macau Foundation.

◆

21

JAPAN

Shinichi Saito

1. NATIONAL PROFILE

1.1 Geography

Japan is made up of a chain of some 7,000 islands. These are situated to the east of the Asian continent, between the North Pacific Ocean and the Sea of Japan. Comprising an area of 377,835 sq km, Japan is slightly smaller than California. It has four major islands: Hokkaido, Honshu, Shikoku and Kyushu. The country is, in the main, rugged and mountainous. Its climate varies from subtropical in the south to subarctic in the north. Fujiyama (Mount Fuji), at 3,776 meters, is the highest peak in Japan (*World factbook*, 1999).

1.2 People

Japan's estimated population in mid-1999 was 126.2 million (US Census Bureau, International Data Base, 1999).[1] It is a densely populated country, averaging 334 people per sq km and 46.8 million households in 1999. Life expectancy was 77 years for males and 83.3 years for females in 1999. More than 40 percent of the population live in three urban centers: Tokyo, Osaka, and Nagoya. Tokyo is the capital.

The population growth rate in the 1990s was 0.2 percent. The birth rate has been declining of late, and this trend is expected to continue into the early 21st century. The population is expected to decline to 100.5 million in 2050 (http://www.stat.go.jp/16.htm). Most of the population speaks Japanese. According to the *Religion yearbook*, issued by the Agency of Cultural Affairs (1998), 49.2 percent of the people observe Shintoism and 44.1 percent follow Buddhism. Christians account for about 1.5 percent and other religions for 5.2 percent.[2]

---

[1] Japan demographic indicators (http://www.census.gov:80/cgi-bin/ipc/idbsum).

[2] The *Religion yearbook*, 1997 edition, which contains data provided voluntarily by religious organizations, states that Japan had some 208 million members of religious organizations in December 1996. This number, however, is more than 1.6 times the country's total population.

1.3 Government and Politics

Japan is a parliamentary democracy within a constitutional monarchy. The Diet is the country's legislative organ; the cabinet, the executive organ; and the law courts, the judicial organ. These three branches of government are separate. The bicameral Diet, or *Kokkai*, consists of the *Sangi-in* (House of Councillors or the Upper House) and the *Shugi-in* (House of Representatives or the Lower House). The term of office in the *Shugi-in* is four years, although it has been dissolved for elections every two-and-a-half years, on average. The term of office in the *Sangi-in* is six years, with half of the members being elected every three years.

The Liberal Democratic Party (LDP), the largest political party, has governed the country since 1955. The LDP lost its postwar political dominance for the first time in nearly four decades after the general election of July 1993. This defeat was "one of the most epoch making events in Japanese postwar politics" (Takeshita & Mikami, 1995, p. 27). The LDP returned to power in June 1994 in an unwieldy alliance with its long-time rival, the Social Democratic Party (SDP). The LDP regained a simple majority in the Lower House through defections from the opposition. In recent years, the LDP has occasionally teamed up with smaller parties. The Hashimoto cabinet, for example, formed in January 1996, was a coalition of the LDP, the SDP, and the *Sakigake*. Likewise, the 1999 Obuchi cabinet was a coalition of the LDP, the Liberal Party, and New Komeito.

1.4 Economy

Japan is a highly industrialized country and a powerful economic force in Asia. In 1999, Japan's gross domestic product, at purchasing power parity, was US$ 2,968 billion with the corresponding per capita GDP of US$ 23,480. Its nominal per capita GNP stood at US$ 30,340. Exports were valued at US$ 389 billion in 1999, and its reserves stood at US$ 271.6 billion (*Asiaweek*, February 4, 2000).

Japan experienced spectacular overall real economic growth for three decades. This growth averaged 10 percent in the 1960s, 5 percent in the 1970s, and 4 percent in the 1980s. The rate of growth slowed considerably in the first half of the 1990s. This was largely attributable to the aftereffects of over-investment during the late 1980s, and to domestic policies designed to reduce speculative excesses in the stock and real estate markets. Although growth picked up in 1996, largely because of stimulatory fiscal and monetary policies, the Asian financial crisis of 1997 had a negative effect on Japan. In early 1999, output had started to stabilize (*World factbook*, 1999).

2. DEVELOPMENT OF PRESS AND BROADCASTING

2.1 Brief Early History

As Komatsubara (1971) has pointed out, "it was not until just before the Meiji restoration [beginning 1868] that anything resembling a newspaper appeared in

Japan" (p. 65). Nevertheless, long before newspapers appeared, news media such as *kawaraban* (tile engraving), had existed in Japan (Ito, 1990). *Kawaraban*, similar to *flugblatt*, or news sheets, in Europe, first appeared in 1615, and they continued to appear until modern newspapers replaced them. Ito (1990) maintains that the *kawaraban*s were the precursors of the modern newspaper, because they "provided the masses in traditional Japanese society with news, entertainment and often criticism of government policies" (p. 424).

The *Batavia Shimbun*, published in 1861 by the Tokugawa Shogunate, is regarded as the first Japanese-language newspaper (Komatsubara, 1971, 1982). Another early newspaper was the *Kaigai Shimbun*, established in 1865 and published once or twice a month (Komatsubara, 1971). English-language newspapers also emerged during the 1860s. The *Nagasaki Shipping List and Advertiser*, published in 1861, was the forerunner of these English-language newspapers. According to Komatsubara (1971), 13 English newspapers appeared in the 1860s. The first Japanese daily newspaper, the *Yokohama Mainichi Shimbun*, was published in 1871. The *Tokyo Nichi-ninchi Shimbun* (1872) was the first daily newspaper in Tokyo.

Two types of newspaper existed in the early part of the Meiji Era (1868–1912): the *Oh-shimbun* (big paper) and the *Ko-shimbun* (small paper). Both the *Yokohama Mainichi Shimbun* and the *Tokyo Nichi-nichi Shimbun* belonged to the first category, which targeted intellectuals and dealt with political issues. The second category, smaller in format (tabloid) but much larger in circulation, offered an entertainment-oriented content. Their target was the general public, that is, those who had little interest in politics and scant knowledge of *Kanji* (Chinese characters). The *Yomiuri Shimbun*, which began publishing in 1874, is an example of this "small newspaper" type.

The number of dailies increased until the 1930s. In 1937, Japan had about 1,200 daily newspapers. This number decreased to a mere 54 in 1942, because of government restrictions on news content and newsprint, and its "one daily per prefecture" policy. Komatsubara (1971) says that "as the pursuit of war inevitably entailed the shortage of newsprint, by August 1938 the government reacted by reducing dailies by two to four pages" (p. 77). In 1944, newspapers terminated their evening editions and became one-sheet (two-page) papers (Haruhara, 1985). During World War II, "Japanese newspaper organizations were forced to merge into one organization per prefecture by the Newspaper Business Control Ordinance introduced in 1941 under the military government" (Hirose, 1994, p. 67).

Radio broadcasting in Japan began in March 1925. In 1924, the government decided to establish three stations as public corporations by persuading private interest groups to join the venture. Thus, the semi-government-sponsored Tokyo Broadcasting Station emerged, followed by the Osaka and Nagoya stations. The Ministry of Communications merged the three stations in August 1926 to form the Nihon Hoso Kyokai (the Japan Broadcasting Corporation, known commonly as NHK). Since its inception, radio broadcasting has been under the strict control of the government. (From 1925 to the end of World War II, the Wireless Telegraph Act of 1915 brought radio under government control.) During World War II, radio broadcasting served as a tool for military propaganda. After the end of the war in 1945, however, radio broadcasting emerged as a more democratic medium.

2.2 Developments since 1945

2.2.1 Press

After Japan's defeat in August 1945, the General Headquarters of the Supreme Commander for the Allied Powers (GHQ) supervised the press. This supervision extended to three sectors: the Civil Censorship Department of the Civil Intelligence Section; the Labor Department of the Economic and Scientific Section; and the Civil Information and Education Section (Komatsubara, 1982). GHQ took steps to remove those associated with the imperialist government from the media. Komatsubara comments:

> In the light of the propaganda role that the Japanese press had played during the war, it was only natural for the Allied powers to eliminate collaborators from the media to institute freedom of speech and press, enabling the Japanese people to be liberated from the constraints of Japanese imperialism and militarism. (p. 112)

With the advent of the Cold War, GHQ banned the communist newspaper, *Akahata*, and asked the mass media to expel all communists from their editorial offices. Although GHQ's censorship operations generated journalistic hostility, the press freedom gained after the war had, by 1946, encouraged 126 new newspapers to emerge (Komatsubara, 1982). Newspapers have flourished since the end of World War II. The growth in the total circulation of newspapers has roughly paralleled the growth of Japan's population (Figure 1).

The number of pages per newspaper has also increased steadily since the end of the war. Data from the Japan Newspaper Publishers and Editors Association (*Nihon Shinbun Kyokai* or NSK) shows the average number of newspaper pages increasing from 16.8 in 1970 to 19.2 in 1980, and to 26 in 1990. This figure had risen to 28.3 in 1997 (NSK, 1998). Circulation wars on a grand scale ensued with the lifting of newsprint controls in 1951. As Komatsubara (1982) points out, economies of scale led to Japan's newspaper publishing returning to a pattern of "concentration and monopolization, with the big national newspapers dominating the entire nation and the local dailies monopolizing their respective areas of circulation" (p. 115).

2.2.2 Radio

After World War II, GHQ restructured the Japanese broadcasting system. From 1945 to 1950 Japan's broadcasting system was guided by the radio code that GHQ had established. GHQ dismantled the existing monopoly system and replaced it with a competitive one, based on the American model.

A new phase of Japan's broadcasting history opened with the enactment of the following three laws in 1950: the Radio Law, the Broadcast Law, and the Radio Regulatory Commission Establishment Law. From 1950 to 1952, a Radio Regulatory Commission—an independent government agency patterned after the FCC—oversaw the broadcasting system (Dashiell, 1997; Tadokoro, 1978). The commission licensed 16 commercial radio broadcasting stations in April 1951, and the first commercial broadcasting began in September of that year, thus ending the NHK's monopoly. In 1952, the Japanese government delegated the authority for the regulation of broadcasting to the Ministry of Posts and Telecommunications (MPT), which now oversees the broadcasting and the telecommunciations industry.

Radio broadcasting enjoyed its golden age during the 1950s. The number of NHK receiver contracts (subscribers) peaked in mid-1950s.[3] The advent of television, however, dramatically affected radio. The number of radio listeners declined substantially in the 1960s. Cooper-Chen (1997) notes that "[p]eople used to listen to radio three hours a day in 1950, but the figure declined to 90 minutes in 1960, then to 30 minutes in 1965" (p. 126). Listening to the radio was restricted to about 26 minutes a day on weekdays in 1995 (NHK BCRI, 1996), far less than it was at its historic peak. NHK's data also show that fewer than 20 percent of Japanese have listened to the radio in recent years. As a counter-measure against television, radio has targeted specialized audiences and has survived mainly as a medium for music, sports (professional baseball, above all), and news.

2.2.3 Television

Television broadcasting in Japan started in 1953, when NHK went on the air in February. NTV, the first commercial station, followed in August. NHK's initial subscribers numbered only 866. At the early stage of television development, the price of a TV set was twice the average annual income of a college graduate. Thus, television was a luxury for most people.

The general public began to have access to ownership in the late 1950s. Hagiwara (1998) says, "With economic development and lowered prices made possible by domestic mass production, television sets soon found their way into every corner of Japanese society" (p. 171). In addition to rapid economic growth and lower prices, events such as the marriage of the present emperor in 1959 and the Tokyo Olympic games in 1964 also contributed to the rapid diffusion of TV sets among the general public. Color television was introduced in 1960. Today, nearly every Japanese household owns at least one television set. Many have two or more. In terms of the time spent watching, television is the dominant mass medium. It represents about three-quarters of the population's total media exposure (NHK BCRI, 1996).

Until the mid-1980s, television meant terrestrial broadcasting for most people. However, since then, a variety of new communication technologies, such as cable television and satellite broadcasting, have emerged. These developments have changed the terrestrial broadcasting situation. The development of multichannel Cable TV and CS (communications satellite) digital broadcasting has provided Japanese viewers with a wider selection of channels. It will take some time,

---

[3] The Japanese had to pay reception fees for NHK's radio broadcasting until the late 1960s.

however, before multichannel cable TV and satellite broadcasting can compete with the terrestrial broadcasters in Japan (NACBRI, 1997).

Cable television began in 1955 as a re-transmitter of airborne signals to remote areas. The so-called "urban-type cable TV" featuring multiple channels, however, did not develop until the late 1980s.[4] Multi-channel cable TV has made slow progress. The market penetration of urban-type cable TV was only 6.8 percent of total households in 1996.[5]

Japan has two types of satellite broadcasting. One type uses broadcasting satellite (BS), and the other uses communications satellites (CS). NHK started testing BS-TV in May 1984, and commenced a 24-hour service on two channels in June 1989. Japan Satellite Broadcasting (JSB) initiated the country's first commercial BS service known as WOWOW in November 1990. Today, four BS-TV channels are in operation: NHK's BS 1 and BS 2; JSB's WOWOW; and a test broadcasting of HDTV known as Hi-Vision. All BS channels, which currently broadcast in analog format, are expected to go digital in 2000, with BS analog broadcasting service ending in 2007.

Although the initial goal of NHK's BS broadcasting was to improve reception for NHK's terrestrial services in the remote parts of Japan (Kaifu, 1998), BS channels now provide services that are clearly distinct from terrestrial broadcasting channels. As of March 1999, about 9.5 million subscribers received NHK's BS-TV service, and JSB had about 2.5 million subscribers.

In 1992, two agencies—Japan Satellite Systems Inc. (SKYPORT TV) and Space Communications Corporation (CS-BAAN)—began a broadcasting service via communications satellites (CS-TV) in analog format. Until March 1998, 14 CS analog broadcasting channels (program-supplying broadcasters) were operating. However, CS-BAAN terminated its analog CS-TV service in March 1998, and SKYPORT TV followed suit in September 1998. Thus, Japan's brief history of CS analog broadcasting ended. Most of those who supplied CS analog programs continue their services with digital systems.

CS digital broadcasting has flourished in recent years. PerfecTV (run by Japan Digital Broadcasting Service) started Japan's first CS digital service in October 1996, followed by DirecTV Japan in October 1997. Initially, JskyB (Japan Sky Broadcasting) was scheduled to start its own service independently, but JskyB merged with PerfecTV in July 1998 to become Sky PerfecTV. As of January 2000, Sky PerfecTV had about 1.66 million subscribers, while DirecTV had about 400,000. "Japan Digital Broadcasting Services Inc. and Direct TV Japan Management Inc. have entered final negotiations for a merger that would sweep the nation's communication satellite broadcasting under one umbrella, industry sources said today" (*Asahi Evening News*, February 29, 2000).

---

[4] The urban-type cable TV is the term applied to multichannel large-scale facilities featuring (*1*) more than 10,000 drop terminals, (*2*) self-originated broadcasting with five or more channels, and (*3*) broadband and two-way communication.

[5] The MPT ceased using this term from 1997. The MPT now uses the term "original-programming cable TV" (cable companies offering their own television programs via cable) to distinguish it from cable TV whose purpose is merely to improve reception. The penetration of original-programming cable TV was about 15 percent of total households in 1998.

3. THE PRESS

3.1 Policy and Legal Framework

After Japan's defeat in World War II, "the Allied occupation forces, in an effort to demilitarize Japan, abolished many prewar laws and regulations restricting the press" (Hirose, 1990, p. 466). Although Japan has no press law that exclusively regulates newspapers at present, it has many legal provisions that relate to newspapers, unlike broadcasting. For example, Article 21 of Japan's Constitution, written with close American involvement, states, "No censorship shall be maintained, nor shall the secrecy of any means of communication be violated." Nevertheless, Article 175 of the Criminal Code restricts obscene material, while Article 21 of the Customs Standards Law bans the importation of pornographic material. The Copyright Law protects authorship rights and promotes publishing and printing businesses, and the Anti-Monopoly Law exempts the resale-price system for copyright items, including newspapers, from the application of the law. These are just a few of the legal provisions that relate to newspapers.[6]

Furthermore, Vanden Heuvel and Dennis (1993) point out that the National Public Employees Law allows for the prosecution of those who leak secrets. Burks (1985) adds that although a 1969 Supreme Court decree (*kettei*) recognized "the right to know" as an integral part of freedom of expression, the court had already held, in a 1959 case, that of freedom expression did not include freedom of news-gathering.[7]

What governs the Japanese press, first and foremost, is the Canon of Journalism formulated by NSK in 1946, and revised in 1955. This moral charter, in its own words, "stresses the spirit of freedom, responsibility, fairness and decency" and constitutes a standard that should "govern not only news and editorial writers but to an equal extent all persons connected with newspaper work" (quoted in Venkateswaran, 1996).[8] The canon stipulates "that the fundamental rule of news reporting is to convey facts accurately and faithfully and that reporters' personal opinions should never be inserted in reporting news" (Hirose, 1990, p. 470).

3.2 Financial Aspects: Circulation, Advertising, Marketing Strategies

3.2.1 Circulation

The *Yomiuri Shimbun*, the world's only newspaper with a daily circulation exceeding 10 million copies, broke through the 10 million mark in 1994. The *Asahi*

---

[6] Freedom House (Sussman, 1999) gave Japan a press restriction score of 19 out of 100 and placed it in the world's "free press" category.

[7] The Supreme Court held that the right to a fair criminal trial took precedence over freedom to gather and report news when four TV stations appealed a district court order to submit their films showing alleged police brutality against radical students at Hakata Station, Kyushu.

[8] An English translation of the Canon of Journalism is available: (http://www.pressnet.or.jp/).

Shimbun, the second largest daily in the world, has a circulation of about 8.3 million copies. Three other national papers also have large circulations (see Table 1 and Section 3.3). National newspapers account for more than 50 percent of total newspaper circulation in Japan. (The Japan Audit Bureau of Circulation has audited the circulation of major newspapers since 1961.) The three block newspapers (see Section 3.3) enjoy a large market share in their specific regions. The *Hokkaido Shimbun* boasts the largest circulation in the Hokkaido region, the *Chunichi Shimbun* in the Chubu region, and the *Nishinippon Shimbun* in the Kyushu region. The prefectural papers (see Section 3.3) enjoy a large market share in their own prefectures, although the national and block newspapers command an oligopolistic market as a whole.

3.2.2 Advertising

Japanese newspaper companies depend heavily on advertising revenue (Table 2). Although one-half of their total revenue comes from sales, nearly 40 percent comes from advertising. The proportions, of income from the sale of copies and from advertising differs slightly from year to year. The proportions were about equal in the early 1990s. For example, the revenue proportions in 1991 were 50.3 percent from advertising and 49.7 percent from sales. Sales revenues, however, have exceeded advertising revenues since 1992.

3.3 Structure and Organization

Japan is a newspaper-rich country. The total circulation of the 121 NSK-affiliated daily newspapers was about 53.7 million (1.16 copies per household) in 1998 (NSK, 1999). This figure counts morning and evening editions as a single copy. (Many Japanese newspapers publish both morning and evening editions under the same name and sell them as a set.) When morning and evening editions are counted separately, the total stood at 72.4 million. This figure corresponds to a newspaper penetration of 57.6 copies per 100 people.

Japan has five newspapers circulated nationwide: the *Yomiuri Shimbun*, the *Asahi Shimbun*, the *Mainichi Shimbun*, the *Nihon Keizai Shimbun*, and the *Sankei Shimbun*. In addition, Japan has many prefectural papers, which are distributed and read within each of the 47 prefectures. (Prefectures are political/administrative units, somewhat like the US states.) Each of the prefectures, with a few exceptions, has a local newspaper. (Some prefectures have more than one, while Shiga prefecture has none.) Also, Japan has three publications known as block newspapers: the *Hokkaido Shimbun*, the *Chunichi Shimbun*, and the *Nishinippon Shimbun*. These newspapers circulate across prefectural boundaries, but not nationally.

As Hasegawa (1998) points out, "the market structure of Japan's commercial media industry is oligopolistic, which is especially prominent in the news media" (p. 289). Japan has large media conglomerates owning businesses across different media and other industries (Akhavan-Majid, 1990). For example, the Asahi Shimbun group comprises many affiliated companies and collaborating organizations, whose activities cover a wide range of industries and interests. These interests include newspaper publishing and printing, TV and radio broadcasting, cultural activities, and advertising. They also extend to property management, insurance, and the travel business. Another example of a large media conglomerate is the Fujisankei Communications Group (FCG), of which the *Sankei Shimbun* and *Fuji Television* are core companies. The FCG, which comprises about 100 companies, is involved actively in all forms of print and electronic media.

Japanese journalism operates under a unique press-club system. The Press Club (*Kisha Kurabu*) is "a nationwide social association with which executives and editors of almost all major Japanese newspapers and broadcasting organizations are affiliated." Furthermore, "this system has been an essential element of Japanese journalism for many years" (Hirose, 1994, p. 63). The press-club system facilitates the flow of news from sources to news organizations everyday. It functions "as an efficient channel to distribute public information from news sources to the public" (Hirose, 1994, p. 66). Nevertheless, the system has come under severe criticism for many years because it discourages thoroughness in journalists and reduces them to being message carriers, thereby creating uniformity of content.

Vanden Heuvel and Dennis (1993) observe that Japan has "perhaps the best overall media system in East Asia, in terms of the amount, scope, accuracy and sophistication of information and entertainment" (p. 88). They also point out that although "the typical Japanese journalist is perhaps the best-informed journalist in the world" (p. 89), he or she hesitates to break corruption stories because of closeness to his or her news sources through the 400 or so nationwide press clubs, which foster a "pro-establishment style of journalism" (p. 83).[9]

3.4 Quality and Popular Press

Newspapers can be classified into several categories depending on their content. General newspapers cover a variety of domestic and international news including politics, the economy, culture, society, and sports. All national papers, block papers, and prefectural papers have the characteristics of general papers. Unlike the quality papers in the United States or in European countries, these newspapers, especially the nationals, have large circulation figures; yet, they provide high-quality, serious news.

Specialized newspapers (trade or business papers) focus on specific topics, for example, industry trends. Japan's top three financial newspapers are the *Nikkei Sangyo Shimbun* (226,360 copies in 1998), the *Nikkan Kogyo Shimbun* (533,145 copies in 1998), and the *Nihon Kogyo Shimbun* (411,732 copies in 1998). They

[9] The exact number of press clubs is not known. Hirose, 1994, refers to more than 700 press clubs, while Cooper-Chen, 1997, refers to more than 1,000.

provide the latest information on both domestic and international industry, with up-to-date, insightful analysis of economic and industrial trends.

Newspapers defined by the term "popular press," or tabloids, also compete in the market. Sports newspapers provide comprehensive coverage of sports (professional baseball, above all) and carry stories on show business, gambling, and leisure. They also cover some serious news, but with a sensational gloss. Evening newspapers, which differ from evening editions of general papers, are characterized by a smaller format and feature entertainment news (sports, soft pornography, and the like), as well as hard news (politics, the economy, and the like). Evening papers such as the *Nikkan Gendai* and *Yukan Fuji* are sold mainly at railway station kiosks (newsstands) or convenience stores. They target business people returning from their offices.

3.5 Distribution

A home delivery system distributes about 93 percent of daily newspapers (general papers) directly to the households in the country. About 6 percent of daily newspapers are sold at railway station kiosks, and convenience stores. Mail delivery accounts for less than 1 percent of the total. Newspaper delivery agents also distribute about 66 percent of sports papers directly to households, while newsstand and convenience store sales account for the remaining 34 percent (NSK, 1998).

4. BROADCASTING

4.1 Policy and Legal Framework

Broadcasting shares the print media's constitutional guarantee of freedom of speech and expression. At the same time, however, the 1950 Broadcast Law and the 1950 Radio Law regulate Japanese broadcasting while the 1972 Cable Television Broadcast Law regulates cable TV broadcasting.[10] The underlying reasons for regulating broadcasting are, first, the limitations of the radio wave resources; and, second, the enormous social impact broadcasting has on the general public.

The government enacted the Radio Law for promoting "public welfare through the impartial and efficient utilization of radio waves" (Article 1). The law deals with technical matters; it regulates the establishment and operation of radio facilities, including the licensing necessary for establishing a radio station. The Broadcast Law deals with policies that cover the broadcasting system framework and the editorial, management, and operational areas of programming. The Broadcast Law prescribes the establishment and operation of NHK. Some critics argue

[10] The English translations of these laws are available at (http://www.mpt.go.jp/policyreports/english/laws/index-e.html). See Otsuka, 1996, for an account of the revision of the Broadcast Law and a general review of the legal framework.

that these laws make it easy for the government to control the broadcasters (for example, Watanabe, 1997).

In 1989, when Japan launched its first commercial communications satellites (JCSAT-1 and SUPERBIRD-A), the government revised the broadcast and radio laws to enable broadcasting services via communications satellites to operate legally in Japan. The reform of the license system made possible the separate licensing of broadcasting stations and programming operations. The revised Broadcast Law provided for the separation of facility-supplying broadcasters and program-supplying broadcasters. Kaifu (1998) says, "The former can own and operate transponder space on a communications satellite, and the latter can provide broadcasts by leasing use of transponder space. This provision has made it easier for CS broadcasters to enter the market" (p. 8).

4.2 Structure and Organization

A dual broadcasting system functions in Japan, consisting of the public broadcaster (NHK) and commercial broadcasters. NHK is Japan's sole public broadcaster. It broadcasts nationwide and has a network of 54 domestic stations. Most of the commercial broadcasters, licensed for regional or local broadcasting, are affiliates of nationwide networks (see below). Commercial broadcasters derive their revenue predominantly from advertising. As Tokinoya (1996) points out, well-balanced competition between NHK and commercial broadcasters "has brought about today's development in Japanese broadcasting" (p. 248). In addition to NHK and the commercial broadcasters, the University of the Air Foundation operates one TV and one FM channel, covering a large part of the Kanto region. The University of the Air started broadcasting in 1985. Financed by tuition and government subsidies, it aims to provide educational programs leading to college credits.

4.2.1 Radio

NHK operates two medium-wave AM radio services (Radio 1 and Radio 2) and an FM radio service. NHK's Radio 1 offers a 24-hour broadcasting service (primarily news and lifestyle) that includes local programming of about 2.5 hours per day. Radio 2 offers educational programming, and it broadcasts the same program throughout the country for 18.5 hours per day. FM radio primarily offers music programming for 24 hours a day (NHK BCRI, 1999). NHK also transmits shortwave broadcasts overseas.

As of 1998, Japan had 99 commercial radio broadcasting stations: 47 medium-wave, 49 FM, 1 shortwave, 1 BS, and 1 CS. Most medium-wave stations are affiliated with both the Japan Radio Network (34 stations) and the National Radio Network (40 stations), with the exception of three wholly independent stations. Most FM stations are affiliates of the Japan FM Network (35 stations) or the Japan FM League (five stations), with the exception of nine independents (NHK BCRI, 1999). According to MPT's basic policy, at least one medium-wave channel and one FM channel are available throughout the whole of Japan. (For both medium-wave and FM broadcasting, two or more channels are available in major metropolitan areas.) (NHK BCRI, 1998, 1999).

4.2.2. Television

NHK has two terrestrial network channels. One offers general programming while the other provides educational broadcasts. Besides the terrestrial, general and educational channels, NHK also operates two satellite channels: Channel One (BS-1), and Channel Two (BS-2). BS-1 specializes in worldwide news and sports while BS-2 provides entertainment and cultural programs. NHK also operates an HDTV service known as Hi-Vision.

As of September 1998, Japan had 126 commercial broadcasting companies. Most (118) belonged to one of the five nationwide networks centered on Tokyo's key stations (Table 3): the Nippon News Network (NNN) centered on Nihon Television (NTV); the Japan News Network (JNN) centered on the Tokyo Broadcasting System (TBS); the Fuji News Network (FNN) centered on Fuji Television; the All-Nippon News Network (ANN) centered on TV Asahi; and the TX Network (TXN) centered on TV Tokyo. Tokinoya (1996) points out that "networking takes the form of a business arrangement in which powerful Tokyo-based television stations supply news and programs to regional commercial stations" (p. 240). Thus, regional commercial stations rely heavily on the networks to supply programs. Such programming makes up more than 80 percent of regional broadcasting time.

The number of available commercial TV channels differs with each prefecture. As of April 1999, about 90 percent of total households in Japan were able to receive four or more terrestrial commercial channels (MPT, 1999). Both NHK and the commercial stations broadcast more than 20 hours a day.

All the key commercial stations have ties with the major newspaper companies. Nihon TV is allied with the *Yomiuri Shimbun*, TV Asahi with the *Asahi Shimbun*, TBS with the *Mainichi Shimbun*, Fuji TV with the *Sankei Shimbun*, and TV Tokyo with the *Nihon Keizai Shimbun*. A recent trend has been the formation of alliances between the major American and Japanese TV networks. Major Japanese networks are now tied up with ABC, CBS, NBC, and CNN.

The cable TV industry has grown slowly but steadily. The number of cable subscribers has increased in recent years. The MPT began de-regulating the cable market in 1993 "for fear of getting technologically behind other countries in building terrestrial media distribution systems.... The 1993 deregulation policy permits not only multiple system operators (MSO) but also easier entry into telecommunications services" (Hasegawa, 1998, pp. 287, 288).

At the end of 1993, original-programming cable TV stations had about 2.4 million subscribers. The number increased to 3.6 million in 1995, to 5 million in 1996, and to 6.7 million in 1997. By the end of 1997, Japan had 973 original-programming cable TV facilities in operation. However, with competition from CS digital broadcasting providing a much wider selection of channels to viewers, CATV has to find new strategies for the future. Some cable TV companies have started Internet services. The first Internet service via cable commenced in October 1996. By May 1999, 52 cable TV companies provided Internet services (IAJ, 1999).

4.3 Program Policies

The Broadcast Law guarantees freedom of broadcasting. It states that "broadcast programs shall never [be] interfered with or regulated by any person, except in the cases where it is done through invested powers provided by law" (Article 3 of the Broadcast Law).

With regard to the production of domestic broadcast programs, the Broadcast Law requires broadcasters to follow certain directives: (*1*) to not disturb public security, good morals and manners; (*2*) to be politically impartial; (*3*) to broadcast news without distorting facts; and (*4*) to clarify the point of issue on controversial matters from as many angles as possible (Article 3-2). In the compilation of broadcast programs for television broadcasting, Article 3-2 of the Broadcast Law also requires the broadcaster to "maintain harmony among the broadcast programs, except those provided in accordance with a special business project, by providing general cultural or educational programs, as well as news and entertainment programs."

Nishino (1994) says that to maintain such a balance, "the government stipulates the minimum ratios that broadcasters should maintain in the programming of educational and cultural broadcasts" (p. 129). No special stipulations exist with regard to news and entertainment. Nishino says both NHK General and commercial broadcasters are "obliged to fulfill educational and cultural functions by assigning no less than 10 percent of broadcasting time to educational programs, and a minimum of 20 percent to cultural programs" (p. 125). The NHK Educational channel has to assign 75 percent or more of broadcasting time to educational programs, and 15 percent or more to cultural programs. Table 4 shows that entertainment programs (about 39 percent) dominate the commercial TV stations, while news (about 41 percent) dominates the NHK general service.

Article 3-3 of the Broadcast Law requires the broadcaster to "establish the standards for the compilation of broadcast programs." Thus, each broadcaster has standards for broadcast programs. Japan's National Association of Commercial Broadcasters, a private, non-profit corporation representing commercial broadcasting, sets the broadcasting standards.[11] Most of the program standards for commercial broadcasters are based on the NAB standards. NHK, on the other hand, sets its own standards for broadcast programs. In September 1996, NBA and NHK collaborated in establishing General Principles of Broadcasting Ethics.

[11] Available at (http://www.nab.or.jp/htm/english/estandards.html).

4.4 Ownership and Financing

Nihon Hoso Kyokai (NHK) is considered unique among public broadcasters in the world because it is independent of both government and corporate sponsorship and relies almost entirely on its household reception fees (NHK BCRI, 1998). On the other hand, commercial broadcasters derive their revenue predominantly from advertising. In 1998, television's share of the total advertising revenue was 44 percent, compared to newspapers' 28 percent, magazines' 10 percent, radio's 5 percent, and outdoor's 14 percent (WAN, 1999). (Also see Section 4.2.)

5. NEW ELECTRONIC MEDIA

Japan started *johoka* or *informatization* in the mid-1960s in an attempt to catch up with the more advanced industrialized countries (Ito, 1994). In the past 10 years, new communication technologies such as cable television, digital broadcasting, the Internet, and mobile telecommunications have developed rapidly in Japan. The traditional media are facing competition from the new electronic media.

5.1 Internet and On-line Media

Today, as in other industrial countries, the Internet has boomed in Japan. The estimated number of Internet users increased from 1.3 million in December 1995 to 5.7 million in February 1997. The number reached 10 million by February 1998 and exceeded 15 million in February 1999 (IAJ, 1999). As of March 1999, Japan had 3,395 Internet service providers.

The penetration rate for personal computers was 32.6 per 100 households in 1998 (MPT, 1999). The January 1999 Network Wizard's survey estimated that Japan had 1.69 million Internet host computers, a host density of 133.6 per 10,000 people, while the July 1999 survey of the Internet Software Consortium placed the figure at 2 million (164.2 per 10,000 people).[12] Businesses accounted for almost 59 percent of the domains, while educational institutions accounted for 14 percent (APT, 1998, 1999).

The newspaper industry is trying to come to terms with the new electronic environment. Major newspaper organizations are providing information on-line. For years, news flashes and databases have been available on commercial on-line services such as NIFTY-Serve. More notably, as the Internet began to expand, the newspaper industry rushed to create on-line versions of their papers. This rush was motivated by the possibility that the Internet may become a mass medium in the near future (Morris & Ogan, 1996) and may begin to compete with traditional media, such as newspapers and television, to provide news, information, and entertainment. To survive in cyberspace, the major Japanese newspaper companies are experimenting with their own on-line products. By February 1998, some 77

---

[12] Available at (http://www.nw.com/zone/www/top.html) and (www.isg.org) respectively.

newspaper companies had launched their own sites on the World Wide Web (NSK, 1998).

Although most of the on-line newspapers are available free of charge, some pay-services have also started, for example, services that deliver "personalized" electronic newspapers to computer users or provide database searches. Unquestionably, the newspaper industry has entered a new era for delivering news content, although the general public is not yet using on-line newspapers widely.

5.2 Telecommunications Infrastructure

The Public Telecommunication Law allowed the Nippon Telegraph and Telephone Public Corporation and the Kokusai Denshin Denwa Company to monopolize the telephone industry in Japan. NTT was the exclusive provider of domestic services and KDD the exclusive provider of international services. In 1985, two new laws—the Telecommunications Business Law and the NTT Corporation Law—superseded the old law, and NTT was privatized. Both NTT and KDD lost their legal monopoly in the telecommunications industry. The new legislation, identified as the "First Telecommunications Reform," classified telecommunication carriers into Type I and Type II. Type I carriers were those that provided both basic and enhanced services with their own communication equipment. Type II carriers were those that provided enhanced services through Type I carriers' networks. The law did not permit Type II carriers to own communication equipment. Further de-regulation occurred in 1997, when the government revised the 1985 legislation to remove all restrictions on foreign ownership of Type I carriers, except for NTT and KDD. The revision also broke down the division between the international and domestic telecommunications operators (APT, 1998). By May 1999, Japan had 183 Type I carriers and 6,663 Type II carriers.

In 1990, the number mainline telephone in Japan was 54.5 million, signifying a penetration rate of 44.1 per 100 people. By 1996, the number had increased to 61.5 million (48.9 per 100 people). Then the number declined to 60.4 million in 1997 (47.9 per 100 people) and further declined to 59.6 million in September 1998 (ITU, 1999; MPT, 1999). On the other hand, the number of subscribers to mobile telecommunication services has increased dramatically in recent years. Most notable is the rapid expansion in cellular telephones. The number of subscribers to cellular telephone services soared from 2.1 million in 1993 to 20.9 million in 1996, and to 36.5 million in September 1998 (MPT, 1999). (ITU, 1999, contends that the number stood at 47.2 million in 1998).

Personal Handy-Phone Systems (PHS) services were inaugurated in July 1995 in Sapporo and in the Tokyo metropolitan area. In September 1995, this service had only 132,500 subscribers, but the number increased to 1.5 million by March 1996 and jumped to 7.1 million in September 1997. The number of subscribers, however, began to decrease after late 1997. By September 1998 subscribers numbered 6.3 million (MPT, 1999).

Japan has promoted the construction of its own information and communication infrastructure for the emerging multimedia society. This development is expected to be primarily a product of private-sector initiative, but the public sector also plays a significant role. The MPT has set 2010 as the target year for completion of a nationwide fiber-optic cable network as the basis for the multimedia society. This information network, which is expected to make significant advances by 2005 (MPT, 1998), will link computers, TV sets, and telephones at corporations, schools, government agencies, and homes across the nation. To this end, the MPT is implementing various specific policy measures. Late in 1996, KDD announced plans to lay a Japan Information Highway submarine fiber-optic cable; and communication satellites operated by Japan Satellite Systems Inc. and Space Communications Corporation have expanded their data transmission services (APT, 1998).

6. POLICY TRENDS FOR PRESS AND BROADCASTING

6.1 The Press

The review of the policy relating to the resale price maintenance system (or the price-fixing system) has caused concern in the newspaper industry. Since 1953, the government has exempted copyright items, including newspapers, from the application of the Antimonopoly Act. The basis for such protection was "a national policy on the promotion of culture designed to ensure a system for the dissemination of diverse copyright items nationwide" (FTC study group, 1998, p. 8). The resale price maintenance system has enabled anyone to buy the same paper at the same price anywhere in Japan.

The government's de-regulation policy, however, caused the Fair Trade Commission (FTC) to examine this policy from a broader perspective and to specify the scope of copyright items protected by statutory measures. In an interim report released in July 1995, the Subcommittee on Resale Price Maintenance—an arm of the Study Group on Government Regulations and Competition Policy, and a private advisory body to the FTC—concluded that no special reasons existed to maintain the resale price maintenance system for all the copyright items under protection. Simultaneously, the Subcommittee on De-regulation of the Government's Administrative Reform Council, which was also handling this issue, released its final report in December 1997. This subcommittee also concluded that it could find no special reasons for keeping the resale price maintenance system intact, and recommended the adoption of appropriate action after thorough discussion aimed at reaching a public consensus (No decision reached, 1997). These reports, however, drew strong criticism from the industries concerned.

The FTC asked the study group to further examine the question of the resale price maintenance system. In March 1998, the FTC announced its decision not to repeal the system for copyright works for the time being. The study group's final report stated that few reasons justified the retention of the resale price maintenance system for copyright items. To promote a policy of competition, it suggested the eventual abolition of the system. From the cultural and public interest standpoint, however, the resale price maintenance system has served the role, albeit indirectly, of protecting copyright holders, as well as the distributors of copyright works (Resale price maintenance system, 1998). The FTC concluded that the issue of the resale price maintenance system needed further examination before arriving at a suitable resolution in the future.

6.2 Broadcasting

The MPT has been promoting the digitization of all broadcasting media by 2000 as a part of the development of Japan's information and communication infrastructure. Broadcasting in the analog format allowed the use of only a limited number of channels. This was the basis for the legal regulation of broadcasting. Digitization will bring about significant changes in broadcasting. A broadcasting revolution will occur with the digitization of the entire system, including terrestrial and cable television.

The advisory committee on digital terrestrial broadcasting, a personal advisory agency under the director of the Broadcasting Policy Bureau of the MPT, completed its final report in October 1998. It recommended the following schedule for digital terrestrial broadcasting (Yamada, 1998):

- The beginning of test broadcasts in the Kanto metropolitan area in 2000, and the commencement of a full-scale service by the end of 2003.
- The extension of full-scale broadcasting to the Kinki and Chukyo areas by the end of 2003. (Thus digital terrestrial broadcasting is expected to start by the end of 2003 in the three metropolitan areas.)
- The implementation of full digitization in all other areas by the end of 2006.

Terrestrial broadcasting services in the analog format will end in 2010 provided (*a*) household penetration rate of receiving equipment exceeds 85 percent, and (*b*) digital broadcasting has completely covered the same target areas as those of present analog broadcasting. However, based upon the diffusion of terrestrial digital broadcasting in each target area, the time to discontinue analog broadcasting is to be reviewed every three years. Regarding the allocation of channel frequencies, new broadcasters will be allowed an opportunity to participate after the closure of analog broadcasting services. A major problem with the digitization of terrestrial broadcasting is whether local commercial TV stations can bear the huge plant investments necessary for conversion to digital broadcasting.

7. MAIN ISSUES

- Abrogation of the newspaper resale price maintenance system

Although the newspaper industry gave qualified credit to the FTC for the position it took on this issue from the cultural and public-interest standpoint, the industry criticized the FTC for not adequately understanding the significance of the system for newspapers (Resale price maintenance system, 1998). The industry argued that price-fixing for copyright works was inevitable for the maintenance of the current distribution system built on the premise of the resale price maintenance system—a system that remains a crucial issue for the newspaper industry.

● The V-chip

This issue has received considerable attention in recent years. In May 1998, the MTP organized the Study Group on Broadcasting and Young People, to deliberate on "what the relationship between broadcasting and young people should be, and the future direction of policy related to young people from the view point of broad-casting in the 21st century" (Report on the "Study on Broadcasting," 1998, p. 1). The group, which compiled its report in December 1998, recommended seven measures, including the improvement of media literacy, information disclosure of broadcasting programming, and the use of the V-chip to block video program-ming. The study group concluded that the issue of the V-chip needed further deliberation, based on the implementation status of the group's recommendations and on trends in digital technology. The broadcasting industry and academic circles have argued strongly against the introduction of the V-chip. The MPT established an expert group in December 1998 to clarify the details on the early implementation of the recommendations of the 1998 MPT study group. The V-chip remains a crucial issue.

8. STATISTICS

General Profile

Exchange rate (1999 average)	US$ 1 = 113.74 Yen⁺
Population (mid-1999)	126.2 million (March 1999)
Geographical size	377,835 sq km
Population density (1999)	334 per sq km
Number of households	46.8 million (March 1999)
Number of daily newspapers (NSK affiliated companies)	121 (1998)*
Daily newspaper circulation per 100 people	57.6 (1998)*
Monthly subscription rate of the leading national dailies (Yen)	3,925 (1998)*
Radio (AM)	
NHK	1 (350)**·
Commercial stations	47 (259)**·
Radio (FM)	
NHK	1 (519)**·
University of the Air	1 (2)**·
Commercial stations	50 (257)**·
Commercial stations (community FM)	118 (127)**·

Table contd

TV (terrestrial)
  NHK   1 (6,902)**·
  University of the Air   1 (3)**·
  Commercial stations   127 (8,262)**·

Number of main telephone lines per 100 people (September 1998)	47.3^X
Number of cellular telephones per 100 people (September 1998)	29.0^X
Number of fax machines per 100 people (1997)	12.7^X
Number of PCs per 100 households (1998)	32.6^X
Number of Internet hosts per 10,000 people (January 1999)	133.6^X
Number of the Internet users (February 1999)	15 million^X
Number of Internet service providers (March 1999)	$3,395^X$

Source: ⁺ OANDA Historical Currency Table (http://www.oanda.com/converterer/cc_table?lang=en); * NSK, 1999; ** MPT, 1999 (· number broadcasting stations, including translators are in parenthesis); ^{X} MPT, 1999; IAJ, 1999; Network Wizards Survey, January 1999.

Table 1
Circulation of National and Block Newspapers in May 1999

Newspaper title	Morning edition	Evening edition
National Newspapers		
Yomiuri Shimbun	10,240,812	4,248,459
Asahi Shimbun	8,284,486	4,117,875
Mainichi Shimbun	3,962,917	1,768,369
Nihon Keizai Shimbun	3,012,890	1,652,241
Sankei Shimbun	1,973,650	909,354
Block Newspapers		
Chunichi Shimbun	2,673,210	754,209
Hokkaido Shimbun	1,229,167	743,380
Nishinippon Shimbun	840,470	189,230

Source: *Japan audit bureau of circulations' monthly report.*

Table 2
Newspapers' Revenue Make-up in the 1990s

Year	Sales revenue %	Advertising revenue %	Other business revenues %	Non-operating revenues %	Special profits %	Sales revenue + Advertising revenue=100%	
						Sales	Ad
1990	43.1	43.4	9.4	2.4	1.7	49.8	50.2
1991	42.5	43.1	10.2	2.9	1.4	49.7	50.3
1992	45.5	40.8	10.8	2.3	0.6	52.7	47.3
1993	48.0	36.1	10.7	1.6	3.6	57.1	42.9
1994	50.8	34.9	11.0	1.4	1.8	59.3	40.7
1995	51.3	35.2	11.7	1.4	0.5	59.3	40.7
1996	50.7	36.2	11.4	1.4	0.4	58.3	41.7
1997	49.6	37.2	11.4	1.3	0.5	57.2	42.8

Source: NSK, 1999, p. 83.

Table 3
Commercial Broadcasters' Networks, Key Stations, and the Number of Affiliated Stations

Network name	Key station	Affiliated stations
NNN	Nihon Television	30
JNN	Tokyo Broadcasting	28
FNN	Fuji Television	28
ANN	Television Asahi	26
TXN	Television Tokyo	6

Source: *NHK data book 1999: The world's broadcasting* (NHK, 1999).

Table 4
Breakdown of TV Programs by Content Type

	Hours per day (%)		
Program type	Commercial stations*	NHK General**	NHK Educational**
News	4 hrs. 07 min. (19.6)	9 hrs. 27 Min. (40.8)	33 min. (3.0)
Educational	2 hrs. 34 min. (12.2)	2 hrs. 39 min. (11.8)	14 hrs. 08 min. (77.0)
Cultural	5 hrs. 23 min. (25.6)	6 hrs. 45 min. (29.1)	3 hrs. 40 min. (20.0)
Entertainment	8 hrs. 11 min. (38.9)	4 hrs. 20 min. (18.7)	0 hrs. 0 min. (0.0)
Others	46 min. (3.7)	———	———
	21 hrs. 1 min. (100)	23 hrs. 11 min. (100)	18 hrs. 21 min. (100)

Source: MPT, 1999.
Note: * The average broadcasting time of 126 commercial TV broadcasting stations (from October 1998 to March 1999); ** Data for 1997.

Figure 1
Circulation and Population

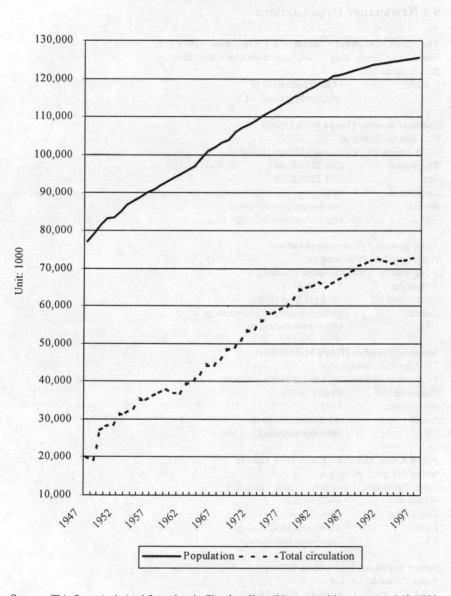

Source: This figure is derived from data in *Shimbun Keiei* (Newspaper Management), *142* (1998, p. 67).

9. USEFUL ADDRESSES

9.1 Newspaper Organizations

The Japan Newspaper Publishers & Editors Association
Nihon Press Center Bldg., 2-2-1 Uchisaiwai-cho, Chiyoda-ku
Tokyo, Japan 100
E-mail: editor@pressnet.or.jp
URL: http://www.pressnet.or.jp

Yomiuri Shimbun **(Tokyo Main Office)**
The Yomiuri Shimbun
1-7-1, Ote-machi, Chiyoda-ku, Tokyo 100-8055
Telephone: (03) 3216-8744
Fax: (03) 3216-8749
Established: 1874
E-mail: webmaster@yomiuri.co.jp
URL: http://www.yomiuri.co.jp

Asahi Shimbun **(Tokyo Main Office)**
Asahi Shimbun Publishing Co.
5-3-2, Tsukiji, Chuo-ku, Tokyo 104-8011
Telephone: 03-3545-0131
Established: 1888 (1879 in Osaka)
E-mail: newsroom@emb.asahi-np.co.jp
URL: http://www.asahi.com

Mainichi Shimbun **(Tokyo Main Office)**
The Mainichi Newspapers
1-1-1, Hitotsubashi, Chiyoda-ku, Tokyo 100-8051
Telephone: 03-3212-0321
Established: 1872
E-mail: mdn@mainichi.co.jp
URL: http://www.mainichi.co.jp

Nihon Keizai Shimbun **(Tokyo Main Office)**
Nihon Keizai Shimbun Inc
1-9-5, Ote-machi, Chiyoda-ku, Tokyo 100-8066
Telephone: 03-3270-0251
Established: 1876
E-mail: webmaster@nikkei.co.jp
URL: http://www.nikkei.co.jp

Sankei Shimbun **(Tokyo Main Office)**
Sankei Shimbun Co. Ltd
1-7-2, Ote-machi, Chiyoda-ku, Tokyo 100-8077
Telephone: 03-3231-7111
Established: 1950 (1933 in Osaka)
E-mail: webmaster@sankei.co.jp
URL: http://www.sankei.co.jp

9.2 Electronic Media Organizations

The National Association of Commercial Broadcasters in Japan
3-23 Kioi-cho, Chiyoda-ku, Tokyo 102-8577
(International div.) Telephone: 03-5213-7727
Fax: 03-5213-7730
E-mail: webmaster@nab.or.jp
URL: http://www.nab.or.jp

Nihon Hoso Kyokai (NHK)
Japan Broadcasting Corp.
NHK Hoso Center, 2-2-1, Jin-nan, Shibuya-ku
Tokyo 15-8001
Telephone: 03-3465-111
Established: Radio 1925, TV 1953
E-mail: webmaster@www.nhk.or.jp
URL: http://www.nhk.or.jp

Japan Cable Television Association
2nd Floor, SDI Gotanda Bldg.
7-13-6, Nishigotanda, Shinagawa-ku, Tokyo 141-0031
Telephone: 03-3490-2022
Fax: 03-3490-2575
Established: 1980
E-mail: renmei@catv.or.jp
URL: http://www.catv.or.jp

9.3 Commercial Television Stations (Key Stations)

Fuji Television Network Inc. (CX)
2-4-8, Daiba, Minato-ku, Tokyo 137-8088
Telephone: 03-5500-888
Established: 1959
URL: http://www.fujitv.co.jp/jp/index.html

Nippon Television Network Corp. (NTV)
14, Nibancho, Chiyoda-ku, Tokyo 102-8004
Telephone: 03-5275-1111
Established: 1953
E-mail: admin@ntv.co.jp
URL: http://www.ntv.or.jp

Asahi National Broadcasting Co. Ltd. (TV Asahi)
2-1-1, Roppongi, Minato-ku, Tokyo 106-8001
Telephone: 03-3587-5111
Established: 1959
E-mail: www-adm@tv-asahi.co.jp
URL: http://www.tv-asahi.co.jp

Tokyo Broadcasting System Inc. (TBS)
5-3-6, Akasaka, Minato-ku

Tokyo 107-8006
Telephone: 03-3746-1111
Established: Radio 1951, TV 1955
E-mail: www@tbs.co.jp
URL: http://www.tbs.co.jp

Television Tokyo Channel 12 Ltd (TV Tokyo)
4-3-12, Toranomon, Monato-ku, Tokyo 105-8012
Telephone: 03-3432-1212
Established: 1964
E-mail: webmaster@tv-tokyo.co.jp
URL: http://www.tv-tokyo.co.jp

10. REFERENCES

Agency of Cultural Affairs. (1998). *Religion yearbook* (in Japanese). Tokyo: Gyosei.

Akhavan-Majid, R. (1990). The press as an elite power group in Japan. *Journalism Quarterly, 67* (4), 1006–1014.

APT (Asia-Pacific Telecommunity). (1998, 1999). *The APT yearbook.* Bangkok: APT.

Burks, A.W. (1985). Japan: The bellwether of East Asian human rights? In J.C. Hsiung (Ed.), *Human rights in East Asia: A cultural perspective* (pp. 31–53). New York: Paragon House.

Cooper-Chen, A. (1997). *Mass communication in Japan.* Ames, IA: Iowa State University Press.

Dashiell, E.A. (1997). Law and regulation. In A. Cooper-Chen, *Mass communication in Japan* (pp. 175–192). Ames, IA: Iowa State University Press.

FTC study group negative on immediate repeal of resale system. (1998, March). *NSK News Bulletin, 21* (1), 8.

Hagiwara, S. (1998). Changing roles of foreign programming in Japanese television. In A. Goonasekera & P.S.N. Lee (Eds.), *TV without borders: Asia speaks out* (pp. 171–203). Singapore: AMIC.

Haruhara, A. (1985). *A history of Japanese newspapers* (in Japanese). Tokyo: Shinsensha.

Hasegawa, K. (1998). Japan. In A. Albarran & S.M. Chan-Olmsted (Eds.), *Global media economics: Commercialization, concentration, and integration of world media markets* (pp. 284–296). Ames, IA: Iowa State University Press.

Hirose, H. (1990). The development of discussions on journalism in postwar Japan. *Media, Culture & Society, 12* (4), 465–476.

Hirose, H. (1994). The press club system in Japan: Its past, present and future. *Keio Communication Review, 16*, 63–75.

ITU (International Telecommunication Union). (1999). *Yearbook of statistics: Telecommunication services 1988–1997.* Geneva: ITU.

IAJ (Internet Association of Japan). (1999). *Internet white book 1999* (in Japanese). Tokyo: Impress.

Ito, Y. (1990). Mass communication theories from a Japanese perspective. *Media, Culture & Society, 12* (4), 423–464.

Ito, Y. (1994). Japan. In G. Wang (Ed.), *Treading different paths: Informatization in Asian nations* (pp. 68–98). Norwood, NJ: Ablex.

Kaifu, K. (1998, spring). Digitization of Japan's satellite broadcasting. *NHK Broadcasting Culture & Research, 3*, 7–9.

Komatsubara, H. (1971). Japan. In J.A. Lent (Ed.), *The Asian newspapers' reluctant revolution* (pp. 65–87). Ames, IA: The Iowa State University Press.

Komatsubara, H. (1982). Japan. In J.A. Lent (Ed.), *Newspapers in Asia: Contemporary trends and problems* (pp. 95–125). Hong Kong: Heinemann Asia.

MPT (Ministry of Posts and Telecommunications). (1998, 1999). *White paper: Communications in Japan* (in Japanese). Tokyo: The Printing Bureau of Finance.

Morris, M., & Ogan, C. (1996). The Internet as mass media. *Journal of Communication, 46* (1), 39–50.

NACBRI (National Association of Commercial Broadcasters' Research Institute). (1997). *A vision of broadcasting in the year 2005* (in Japanese). Tokyo: NAB Research Institute.

NHK BCRI (NHK Broadcasting Culture Research Institute). (1996). *Living hours of the Japanese in 1995* (in Japanese). Tokyo: NHK.

NHK BCRI (NHK Broadcasting Culture Research Institute). (1998, Summer). Broadcasting in Japan (excerpts from NHK data book 1998: The world's broadcasting). *Broadcasting Culture & Research, 5,* 13–16.

NHK BCRI (NHK Broadcasting Culture Research Institute). (1999). *NHK data book 1999: The world's broadcasting* (in Japanese). Tokyo: NHK.

Nishino, Y. (1994). Diversity in TV programming in Japan. *Studies of Broadcasting, 30,* 115–130.

No decision reached on disputed resale price maintenance system. (1997, December). *NSK News Bulletin, 20* (4), 4.

NSK (Nihon Shimbun Kyokai). (1998). *Japanese newspaper handbook* (in Japanese). Tokyo: Nihon Shimbun Kyokai.

NSK (Nihon Shimbun Kyokai). (1999). *The Japanese press 1999.* Tokyo: Nihon Shimbun Kyokai.

Otsuka, H. (1996). The legal framework for media and channel multiplication in Japanese broadcasting. *Studies of Broadcasting, 32,* 175–204.

Report on the "Study on broadcasting and young people." (1998, December). *MPT News, 9* (19), 1–2.

Resale price maintenance system survives FTC review. (1998, June). *NSK News Bulletin, 21* (2), 3.

Sussman, L.R. (1999). *Press freedom 1999: News of the century.* New York: Freedom House.

Tadokoro, I. (1978). Japan. In J.A. Lent (Ed.), *Broadcasting in Asia and the Pacific: A continental survey of radio and television* (pp. 60–73). Philadelphia: Temple University Press.

Takeshita, T., & Mikami, S. (1995). How did mass media influence the voters' choice in the 1993 general election in Japan? A study of agenda-setting. *Keio Communication Review, 17,* 27–41.

Tokinoya, H. (1996). Japan. In A. Wells (Ed.), *World broadcasting: A comparative view* (pp. 235–249). Norwood, NJ: Ablex.

Vanden Heuvel, J., & Dennis, E.E. (1993). *The unfolding lotus: East Asia's changing media.* New York: The Freedom Forum Media Studies Center.

Venkateswaran, K.S. (Comp.) (1996). *Media monitors in Asia.* Singapore: AMIC.

Watanabe, T. (1997). Japan's media at present. *Social Science Review, 55,* 1–40.

WAN (World Association of Newspapers). (1999). *World press trends.* Paris: WAN.

World factbook. (1999). Washington, DC: Central Intelligence Agency [On-line]. Available: (http://www.odci.gov/cia/publications/factbook).

Yamada, O, (1998, summer). Development of Japan's digital terrestrial broadcasting *NHK Broadcasting Culture & Research, 5,* 5–7.

Yamamoto, F. (Ed.). (1995). *A history of mass communication in Japan* (Rev. ed.) (in Japanese). Tokyo: Tokai Daigaku Shupankai.

◆

22

NORTH KOREA

Shelton A. Gunaratne & Shin Dong Kim

1. NATIONAL PROFILE

1.1 Geography

The Democratic People's Republic of Korea (or *Choson minjujuui inmin konghwaguk*) comprises the northern half of the Korean Peninsula bordering the Korea Bay and the East Sea (Sea of Japan), between China and South Korea. Its total area, 120,540 sq km, is slightly smaller than Mississippi. It shares land boundaries with China (1,416 km), South Korea (238 km), and Russia (19 km), and it has a coastline of 2,495 km. Deep and narrow valleys separate its mostly hilly and mountainous terrain; and its coastal plains are wide in the west but discontinuous in the east. The highest point is the 2,744-meter Paektu-san. The country has a temperate climate (*World factbook*, 1999).

1.2 People

North Korea had an estimated mid-1999 population of 21.4 million (US Census Bureau, 1999 [http://www.census.gov/cgi-bin/ipc/idbsum]) of whom 61 percent to 64 percent lived in urban areas. The country is racially homogeneous with the exception of a small Chinese community and a few ethnic Japanese. Buddhism and Confucianism comprise the predominant religious make up. Some Christianity and syncretic Chondogyo also exist. The country's estimated literacy rate is 95 percent, and life expectancy is 71.6 years.[1] UNDP (1998) placed North Korea 75th in rank in its human development index (HDI).

---

[1] US Census Bureau's international data base (http://www.census.gov/cgi-bin/ipc/idbsum) placed a North Korean's life expectancy at 70.1 years and the population's rate of natural increase at 1.4 percent.

1.3 Government and Politics

Korea was a security concern for Russia from the time of the tsars. The disposition of Korea was a main issue in the Russo–Japanese War (1904–5). Because Korea had one of the oldest communist movements in Asia, the Soviet Union trained Korean guerilla fighters to resist the Japanese occupation of the peninsula (1910–45). Following the defeat of the Japanese, the United States proposed the establishment of a multilateral trusteeship in Korea. However, in August 1945, the United States unilaterally decided to make the 38th parallel the dividing line between the Soviet and US zones and established the US Army Military Government in Korea (1945–48) in the southern zone. The Korean resistance leaders set up an interim "people's republic," sparking a civil war in the south until a plebiscite resulted in the establishment of the Republic of Korea in May 1948 (Savada, 1994).

The Soviet troops, who had occupied the northern zone, worked with a coalition of communists and nationalists until January 1946. In February 1946, an Interim People's Committee led by Marshall Kim Il Sung became the first central government. The North Korean Workers' Party merged with the Korean Communist Party to become the dominant force in the country. Soviet influence was especially strong in the media, with the major organs staffed by the so-called Soviet-Koreans trained in the Soviet Union (Savada, 1994). The Democratic People's Republic of Korea was formally established as a communist state in September 1948, three years after the partition of the Korean Peninsula. Kim Il Sung based his rule on a philosophy of *Juche* (I myself) that combined Stalinism with economic self-reliance. Three years after his death in mid-1994, his son Kim Jong Il formally assumed the country's top leadership post (as general secretary of the Korean Workers' Party) in October 1997 (Freedom House, 1998). The premier, elected by the legislature, is the head of the government.

The 687-seat Supreme People's Assembly (SPA) (*Ch'oego Inmin Hoeui*) is the country's unicameral legislature. Elections were held in July 1998 for a new SPA, which amended and supplemented the socialist constitution of the Democratic People's Republic of Korea (DPRK) on September 5.[2] The previous legislature was elected in April 1990 by popular vote for a five-year term. However, it was not convened after the death of Kim Il Sung in mid-1994 thereby causing a four-year legislative vacuum.

1.4 Economy

More than 90 percent of this command economy is socialized. Agricultural land is collectivized; and state-owned industry produces 95 percent of manufactured goods. Economic growth during the period 1984–88 averaged 2 percent to 3 percent, but

[2] DPRK Socialist Constitution revised (http://www.korea-np.co.jp/pk/59th_issue/98090703.htm).

output declined by an average of 4 percent to 5 percent (or more) annually during 1989–97 because of systemic problems and disruptions in economic and technological links with the former USSR and China. A critical shortage in the energy sector has caused interruptions in industrial production. Manufacturing is centered on heavy industry (*World factbook*, 1998).

North Korea's estimated gross domestic product at purchasing power parity in 1998 was US$ 21.8 billion with the corresponding per capita GDP at US$ 1,000 (*World factbook*, 1999)[3] even though UNDP (1998) estimated it at US$ 4,058 in 1995 for deriving the HDI. The APT (1999) estimate of the country's 1996 gross domestic product was US$ 20.9 billion, with the per capita GDP at US$ 479.

2. DEVELOPMENT OF PRESS AND BROADCASTING

2.1 Brief Early History

The media are one of many subsystems in a society. These subsystems or sectors are organically interrelated rather than autonomous. Understanding this interrelationship is helpful when examining the media system in North Korea. From a Western liberal perspective, the North Korean media system may appear to be an extremely closed system that only serves the interests of a ruthless dictatorship. From the social and political perspective of North Korea, however, the system is "democratic" in the context of the roles assigned to the various components of the system.

The role of the mass media under the classic Marxist-Leninist concept of the press is to function as an agitator, a propagandist, and an organizer. The media in North Korea adhere to this model. The history of the country's mass media is an organic part of the history of the country's communist regime. The fundamental characteristics of the North Korean media emerged during Kim Il Sung's armed struggle for national liberation from Japanese colonialism, which ended in 1945. Kim Il Sung's method—the "anti-Japanese guerilla method" as North Korean authorities describe it—still continues as a principle of the press, which all journalists in the country follow (Kang, 1997, pp. 24–25).

Kim's "anti-Japanese guerilla method" has three components applicable to the press: popular journalism, popular mode of expression, and revolutionary spirit of writing. Popular journalism requires journalists to work on and with the people to reflect the people's needs and level of understanding. Popular mode of expression requires a brief and lively writing style. Revolutionary spirit of writing requires an active and aggressive manner of reporting.

Two newspapers laid the foundation of North Korea's print media system prior to the division of the Korean Peninsula: *Chongno*, the organ of the North Korean

---

[3] These figures are very close to those reported in *Korea annual*, 1998: GDP of US$ 21.4 billion and per capita GDP of US$ 910 for 1997—"the seventh negative growth year in a row" (p. 268).

Communist Party; and *Chonjin*, the organ of the Sinmin (New Democracy) Party. The Pyongyang Radio Broadcasting Station introduced radio to North Korea during the Japanese occupation.

2.2 Developments since 1945

Press freedom had ceased to exist in the North by the end of 1946, with all newspapers—central and local, communist and noncommunist—carrying essentially the same news, with some local coloring thrown in. Furthermore, Soviet-aligned Koreans tended to predominate in the cultural organs; all three of the editors of the party journal were "Soviet-Koreans" (usually meaning Koreans who had lived in the USSR, or followed the Soviet lead) in 1945–50. (Cumings, 1997, p. 231)

The history of the North Korean mass media falls into three periods under the Kim Il Sung regime (Kim & Lee, 1991). First is the Democratic Construction Period from the National Liberation on August 15, 1945, to the start of the Korean War on June 25, 1950. The *Rodong Sinmun* published its first issue on September 1, 1946, after merging *Chongno* and *Chonjin*, the organs of the Communist Party and the Sinmin Party respectively. In August 1945, the South Pyongan Province People's Committee began publishing the *Pyongyang Ilbo*, which changed its name to *Minju Choson* in June 1946, when it became the organ of the then North Korean Provisional People's Committee. The central committee of the League of Socialist Working Youth started publishing the *Minju Chongnyon* (later renamed *Rodong Chongnyon*) on November 1, 1946. Another significant development was the establishment of the Korean Central News Agency on December 5, 1946, under the direct control of North Korean Provisional People's Committee, which ceded its control to Administration Council on October 12, 1948. Seven of the current 11 provincial dailies also began publishing during this period: *Pyongbuk Ilbo* (November 27, 1945), *Hamnam Ilbo* (November 15, 1945), *Hambuk Ilbo* (October 1, 1945), *Chagang Ilbo* (March 11, 1949), *Kangwon Ilbo* (December 28, 1945), *Hwangnam Ilbo* (September 6, 1945), and *Hwangbuk Ilbo* (September 6, 1945).

The Korean Central Broadcasting Station began on October 14, 1945, with a broadcast on a Pyongyang rally to welcome Kim Il Sung's homecoming (Korea, Ministry of Unification, 1995). It used a 500-watt transmitter. Kim and Lee (1991) point out that during this period, the regime used the media to educate and mobilize the people for building a new socialist nation. The media were on the front in criticizing old ideas of capitalist society and in creating and spreading socialist thoughts nationwide.

The second is the "Liberation War Period" (from the outbreak to the end of the Korean War on July 27, 1953). Two more provincial dailies, *Pyongnam Ilbo* (December 12, 1950) and *Kaesong Sinmun* (March 26, 1952), began during this period, when the media had to serve in full force for the victory of the so-called

National Liberation War. The command of the People's Army strictly controlled the media for the publicity of the Army's victories on the front.

The third is the "Socialist Construction Period", which lasted until the death of Kim Il Sung in 1994. Two other provincial dailies emerged during the early part of this period: *Pyongyang Ilbo* (June 1, 1957)[4] and *Ryanggang Ilbo* (January 1, 1955). On May 17, 1964, the *Minju Chongnyon* changed its name to *Rodong Chongnyon*. Following the war, North Korea strove desperately to rebuild the national economy. To construct the foundation of the socialist nation, the media had to effectively mobilize the people by operating as propagandist, agitator, and organizer. By 1976, North Korea had 11 dailies (An, 1983).

During this period, the Kim Il Sung regime gave priority to restore the radio broadcasting services destroyed between 1950 and 1953 (Nam & Lent, 1978). Soviet assistance enabled the Central Broadcasting Station to increase its transmission power to 150kW on April 9, 1955, and later to 300kW. The authorities also laid a network of cable for radio broadcasting, linking the central station in Pyongyang to some 4,300 broadcasting booths in factories, offices, and cooperative farms nationwide. A push for improving broadcasting equipment and technology in 1957 resulted in upgrading the transmission power in Sariwon, Kanggye, and Hyesan stations. The clandestine radio station for "liberation of the South" went on the air in March 1967. In December 1967, the Central Broadcasting Station was split into Station No. 1 (300kW) for domestic broadcasting and Station No. 2 (500kW) for external broadcasting. In 1970, North Korea instituted a new four-pronged broadcasting structure under the control of the Central Broadcasting Committee: Broadcasting No. 1 (which became *Choson Joongang Bangsong* on November 10, 1972). Broadcasting No. 2, TV broadcasting, and external broadcasting. A music channel, Pyongyang FM, also began operating to entice the youth of South Korea (Korea, Ministry of Unification, 1995).

The introduction of television took place with pilot programs televised in March and April 1963. Soviet assistance enabled the completion of the Central TV Station (5kW) in Pyongyang in April 1969, when it began regular black-and-white programming. Kaesong TV Station opened on April 15, 1971, as a propaganda channel targeting the South. At Kim Il Sung's behest, North Korea pursued the goal of nationwide TV reach by building relay towers in Masikryong, Hwanghae, Wonsan, and Chagangdo. Korean Central TV began color TV broadcasting on April 15, 1974. By 1976, the country had 13 radio stations and two TV stations. There were 110,000 TV sets and 1.8 million radio sets (An, 1983). Mansudae TV Station began operating on December 1, 1983, primarily as a weekend channel for sports and movies (Korea, Ministry of Unification, 1995; Koreascope, 1998).

The decade of 1960s was crucial for the two Koreas (North and South) as both raced hard to achieve industrialization. A series of seven-year development plans transformed the North from an agricultural socialist country to an industrialized socialist one. During the decade, the media basically performed the roles of cultural

---

[4] *Pyongyang Ilbo* was also the founding name of *Minju Choson*.

educator, indoctrinator, mobilizer, organizer, and propagandist. In the late 1960s, the media also played an important role in establishing and promoting *Jucheism*,[5] which eventually became a principle of media practice until Kim Il Sung's sudden death. *Jucheism* emphasizes the importance of developing the nation's potential, and of using its own resources and reserves of human creativity. It legitimizes cultural, economic, and political isolationism by stressing the error of imitating foreign countries or becoming excessively "international" (Savada, 1994, p. 69; Kim, 1993).

3. THE PRESS

3.1 Policy and Legal Framework

Chapter 5 of the country's revised 1998 Constitution deals with the fundamental rights and duties of citizens. Article 67 states: "Citizens are guaranteed freedom of speech, of the press, of assembly, demonstration and association. The State shall guarantee conditions for the free activity of democratic political parties and social organizations." Article 68 states that "Citizens have freedom of religious beliefs," while Article 79 states that "Citizens are guaranteed inviolability of the person and the home and privacy of correspondence."[6]

However, freedom of the press is only guaranteed to the extent that it "[h]elps the masses participate even more vigorously in the construction of socialism" (Choi, 1998, p. 48). Freedom House (1998) reported: "The government denies citizens all fundamental rights in what is one of the last totalitarian societies in the world. As such there are not even rudimentary elements of civil society.... The Criminal law subjects citizens to arbitrary arrest, detention and execution for 'counterrevolutionary crimes.'... In practice these can include...criticism or even a slight to the leadership, and listening to the BBC or other foreign broadcasts" (p. 315). The role of the press is "to explain, disseminate, advocate and help accomplish Kim Il Sung's instructions and Kim Jong Il's policies, and to further strengthen the proletariat dictatorship, as well as to strengthen politico-ideological unity and solidarity among the people" (Koreascope, 1998). In November 1995, Kim Jong Il urged all news media to intensify their functions of indoctrination and control to help solidify the country's regime (Korea, Ministry of Unification, 1995).

The US Department of State (1999) reported that:

> The constitutional provisions for an independent judiciary and fair trials are not im-
> plemented in practice. The regime subjects its citizens to rigid controls. The state
> leadership perceives most international norms of human rights, especially individual
> rights, as illegitimate, alien social concepts subversive to the goals of the state and

---

[5] Article 3 of the constitution stipulates that the government shall make *Jucheism* the guiding principle for all its actions.
[6] DPRK's socialist constitution (full text) (http://www.korea-np.co.jp/pk/61st_issue/98091708.htm).

party. The Penal Code is draconian, stipulating capital punishment and confiscation of all assets for a wide variety of "crimes against the revolution," including defection, attempted defection, slander of the policies of the party or state, listening to foreign broadcasts, writing "reactionary" letters, and possessing reactionary printed matter.

The government prohibits freedom of speech, the press, assembly, and association, and all forms of cultural and media activities are under the tight control of the party. Radios sold in North Korea are constructed to receive North Korean radio broadcasts only; radios obtained from abroad must be altered to work in a similar manner. Under these circumstances, little outside information reaches the public except that approved and disseminated by the government. The government restricts freedom of religion, citizens' movements, and worker rights.[7]

Youm (1991) points out that North Korea does not have specialized press laws as such. No such laws are necessary because the press is an organ of the state. However, several statutes, including a number of articles in the Criminal Code,[8] relate indirectly to the press. No documentary evidence exists to show how these indirect press laws affect the country's press. Youm concludes: "The impact of the statutes upon the North Korean press is negligible in that the press does not [or to be precise, need not] feel any statutory constraint. This is because there is no room for conflict between the North Korean press and law enforcement authorities" (p. 86).

Specifically touching on North Korea's freedom of speech and press framework, the US State Department (1999) elaborated that articles of the constitution that required citizens to follow "socialist norms of life" and to obey a "collective spirit" took precedence over individual political or civil liberties. Although the constitution provided for freedom of speech and the press, the government prohibited the exercise of these rights in practice. The regime permitted only activities that supported its objectives. Choi (1998) asserted that the role of the DPRK press was to function as "an advertiser, instigator and organizer for the KWP designed to help achieve its goals" (p. 48). Publications inculcated communist ideology and fulfilled their organizational role as instigators of the revolution. All publications, including literary and artistic works, supported *juche* ideology and the leaders' unitary ideological system.

The government strictly curtailed freedom of expression. In the early 1990s, no evidence existed of any *samizdat* or underground literary or cultural movements such as those in the former Soviet Union or in China. The central committee of the KWP exercised control over culture through its agitprop and culture departments (Savada, 1994). The authorities punished individuals for criticizing the regime or its policies by imprisonment or "corrective labor." One defector reported in 1986 that a scientist, whose home was bugged through his radio set, was arrested and executed for statements made at home critical of Kim Il Sung. In another case,

---

[7] DPRK: *Country report on human rights practices for 1998.* (http://www.state.gov/www/global/human_rights/1998_hrp_report/northkor.html).

[8] Articles 76 (on treasonous acts), 77 (on sedition), 99 (on lies and rumors), 146 (on libel and slander), and 245 (on obscenity).

Amnesty International reported that a family formerly resident in Japan was sent to a "re-education-through-labor" center because one member of the family allegedly made remarks disparaging the government (US Department of State, 1999).

The government has control over all information. All mass media are subject to censorship before and after publication/broadcast. It carefully managed the visits of Western journalists. In 1996, the Cable News Network was allowed to broadcast live, unedited coverage of the second-year memorial service for the death of Kim Il Sung. The regime had recently allowed foreign journalists to report on the food situation. Foreign journalists also were allowed to report on the Korean Peninsula Energy Development Organization (KEDO) light-water reactor groundbreaking at Kumho in 1997. Although more foreign journalists have been allowed into North Korea, the government still maintains the strictest control over the movements of foreign visitors. It enforces strict censorship over the domestic media and tolerates no deviation from the official government line. Moreover, the government places severe restrictions on academic freedom and controls artistic and academic works (US Department of State, 1999). Freedom House assigned North Korea the maximum restrictive score—100 out of 100—based on all four criteria (within the framework of Article 19 of the Universal Declaration of Human Rights) used to determine press freedom: laws and regulations that influence media content, political pressures and controls on media content, economic influences over media content, and repressive actions against journalists and journalism (Sussman, 1999).

3.2 Financial Aspects: Circulation, Advertising, Marketing Strategies

UNESCO (1999) estimates show that in 1995 North Korea had 11 dailies with a circulation of 5 million—a penetration of 22.5 copies per 100 people (Table 2). However, North Korea's economic crisis, which has intensified since the mid-1990s, may have slashed newspaper circulation significantly. UNESCO estimates for 1996 show only three dailies—the three central newspapers—in operation, indicating that the provincial newspapers no longer appear on a daily basis.

One of the most visible characteristics of the North Korean newspapers is that they do not carry any advertising except a handful of government notices. Because mass media are a subsystem of a communist state, neither private ownership nor market competition and advertising exist. Competition among newspapers is possible only in showing their loyalty to the party and Kim Il Sung, or to his son, Kim Jong Il.

3.3 Structure and Organization

All media in North Korea are organs of the Korean Workers' Party, the government and its agencies, and various social organizations. The Propaganda and Agitation Department of the Central Committee of the KWP exercises ultimate control over the format and content of the media. At the apex of the newspaper hierarchy are the three central newspapers: *Rodong Sinmun* (Labor Daily), organ of the central committee of the KWP; *Minju Choson* (Democratic Korea), organ of the government (Administration Council); and *Rodong Chongnyon* (Working Youth), organ of the party youth league. Additionally, each provincial party committee publishes a local newspaper—11 in all. Every factory or enterprise publishes its own news bulletin. College newspapers are also published.

The mission of *Rodong Sinmun* is "to restructure society and human beings as requested by Kim Il Sung's and Kim Jong Il's revolutionary thought and *Juche* ideology" (Koreascope, 1998). The party's agitprop department controls all its editing activities. Its editorial and opinion pages present the regime's position on current issues. The editor-in-chief[9] of *Rodong Sinmun* simultaneously serves as president of the Journalists Union of North Korea. He has the assistance of three vice editors-in-chief (see Figure 1). The newspaper's editorial department has 12 desks, which include the party history and indoctrination desk, the revolutionary education desk, the party life desk, the foreign news desk, and the South Korea desk (Korea, Ministry of Unification, 1995).

Because *Minju Choson* serves as the newspaper of the administration, it publishes more news on administrative affairs than about the party. It too aims to spread *Jucheism* and Kim Il Sung's revolutionary thoughts among the populace and to mobilize workers to execute party policies. Its editor-in-chief also has the assistance of two or three vice editors-in-chief and an editorial department of 12 desks, which include the people's administration desk and the culture and arts desk. It depends on the Central News Agency and the foreign desk of *Rodong Sinmun* for most of its news (Korea, Ministry of Unification, 1995).

The *Rodong Chongnyon* aims to promote *Jucheism* in society and to contribute to the triumph of *Jucheism* in world history. It attempts to achieve that objective through the indoctrination of the next generation of revolutionaries and by encouraging the youth to struggle hard to realize party policies (Korea, Ministry of Unification, 1995).

The major goal of the 11 provincial newspapers (see Section 2.2) is to motivate the provincial residents to remain true to the guiding policies of Kim Il Sung and to carry out party policies. To do so, these newspapers highlight the achievements and experiences of Kim Il Sung and the party as the occasion arises, based on instructions from the party, as well as the Administration Council's General Bureau of Publication Guidance (Korea, Ministry of Unification, 1995).

Commissions of the Administration Council also publish their own organs, which include *Teachers News, Transportation News*, and *Construction News*. The other newspapers include *Choson Inmingun* (People's Army), organ of the army; *Kunroja* (The Worker), theoretical organ of the party central committee; *Rodongja Sinmun*, organ of the General Federation of Trade Unions; and *Pyongyang Sinmun*, organ of the Pyongyang Municipal Administration (Korea, Ministry of Unification, 1995; *Korea annual*, 1993).

---

[9] *Korea annual*, 1998, lists two people, Chong Chun-ki and Kim Ki-nam, both members of the central committee of the Workers' Party, as editor-in-chief of *Rodong Sinmun* (pp. 819, 828).

The Korean Central News Agency (*Choson Joongang Tongsinsa*), a subsidiary organ of the cabinet, is the sole distributor of news (An, 1983). It speaks for the Workers' Party and the DPRK government. Its mission is "to turn all Korean constituent members of the society into self-reliant communist revolutionaries, who are permanently loyal to Kim Il Sung and Kim Jong Il, and contribute to the realization of a restructured society imbued with *Juche* ideology or the idea of self-reliance" (Koreascope, 1998). Although the agency has a general director as the head, a political bureau actually administers and controls the agency. A vice director is in charge of the local and foreign bureaus of the agency. The editor-in-chief and two deputy editors supervise the writing and editing of news. KCNA also has a separate South Korea department (Korea, Ministry of Unification, 1995). The agency transmits news to other countries in English, Russian, and Spanish. It is responsible for uniform delivery of news and other information to the country's mass media. It has cooperative relations with foreign news agencies.[10] The Korean Central News Agency (KCNA) publishes the daily *Choson Joongang Tongsin* (Korean Central News), *Sajin Tongsin* (Photographic News), and *Choson Joongang Yonbo* (Korean Central Yearbook). It issues daily press releases, which are available on-line.

The Foreign Languages Press Group (FLPG) publishes the general-interest monthly *Korea Today* and the English-language weekly *Pyongyang Times*, the first issue of which came out on May 6, 1965. *Tongil Sinbo* is another general-interest weekly. The FLPG also publishes special-interest monthlies such as *Foreign Trade, Korea* (pictorial), *Korea Trade Unions*, and *Women in Korea*. Kim Song Youth Publishers' *Youth & Students* is another special-interest monthly (UN, 1995).

3.4 Quality and Popular Press

The distinction between the quality and the popular press has little meaning within the framework of the North Korean communist media system. If the importance attached to newspapers is a characteristic of their quality, then the country's two major "quality" dailies are the *Rodong Sinmun* and the *Minju Choson*. Typically, they allocate a high proportion of their news coverage (about 60 percent) to foreign relations. Coverage of economic and industrial affairs, domestic politics, and socialist ideas comes next. The KWP and the KCNA provide about 65 percent of the news (Yu, 1992).

Economics has forced the DPRK newspapers to publish only a limited number of pages. The *Rodong Sinmun*, for example, is limited to six pages. The first page carries the editorial, as well as fixed columns devoted to Kim Jong Il's activities. The second page contains party propaganda and features on communist enlightenment. The third page focuses on the domestic economy while the fourth page highlights domestic and foreign news. The fifth page contains articles critical

---

[10] Korean Central News Agency (http://www.kcna.co.jp/index/intro.htm).

of South Korea, and the sixth page carries anti-imperialist articles critical of the West (Koreascope, 1998). The *Minju Choson* publishes four pages except on Tuesdays, Fridays, and on special occasions when it publishes six (Korea, Ministry of Unification, 1995). Each provincial daily also consists of four pages.

The newspapers carry considerably long reports with simple editing. They do not carry news on accidents, disasters, crimes, and such other major staples of news so familiar to Western readers. Nor do they carry advertising. Headlines make good use of verbs.

3.5 Distribution and Technology

North Korea does not allow individual newspaper subscriptions except for high officials in the party. The government postal service delivers newspapers to factories and various other organizations on the basis of collective subscriptions. Some claim that foreigners can buy newspapers on sale at recognized hotels or at major railway stations (KPI, 1997).[11] However, the Asia Foundation representative to Korea, Kenneth Quinones, who has visited North Korea 13 times from 1992 to 1997 as a US State Department official, says foreign newspaper are not available in North Korea. Quinones could not buy any newspaper whatsoever at department stores in Pyongyang when he visited the city in 1997. Domestic newspapers are usually delivered directly to the party members at home. The regime allowed no exposure to foreign mass media—newspapers, magazines, radio, or television broadcasts (C. K. Quinones, interview with S. D. Kim, June 8, 1999).

Jucheism has prevented the adoption of advanced technology befitting the "Information Age." Absence of market competition, as well as government ownership of the media, has stifled wider distribution of the print media and the search for innovative strategies.

4. BROADCASTING

4.1 Policy and Legal Framework

An annual white paper on human rights in North Korea (Choi, 1998) explained the significance the regime attached to broadcasting thus:

> Broadcast networks function as the "most incisive and combative, mobile weapon" among the "ideological weapons" of the class struggle. As Kim Il Sung pointed out, broadcast networks "[e]xplain and publicize the party line and party policies; they are a powerful advertising and inducement means to mobilize the masses to revolution and socialist construction." Broadcasting is responsible to "[i]nstigate strongly the fight against class enemies such as the Americans and the construction of socialism while upholding absolute confidence in the victory of the masses as a whole." (p. 48)

---

[11] Also see Joong-Ang Ilbo (http://www.joongang.co.kr).

The broadcast media, just as much as the press, are devoted largely to the propagation of the personality cult of the chief of state. Foreign broadcasts are excluded because the dials of many radio receivers are fixed so as to receive only domestic programming under the control of the Korean Central Broadcasting Station (Vanden Heuvel & Dennis, 1993). Senior party cadres, however, have good access to the foreign media (Savada, 1994). The party has strict control over broadcasting, which is basically a subsystem of the party. The US Department of State (1999) also asserts that the regime prohibits people from listening to foreign media broadcasts and subjects violators to severe punishment. Radio and television sets are built to receive only domestic programming. Those who obtain receivers from abroad must submit the sets for alteration to operate in a similar manner (Section 3.1). Quinones (interview with S. D. Kim, June 8, 1999) says that as a foreign visitor he could only listen to BBC shortwave at a designated place in Pyongyang. Korea historian Bruce Cumings has claimed that during his 1981 visit to North Korea, he "listened to group of professors in Seoul discuss the demerits of communism on Seoul radio" (cited in Youm, 1991, p. 77).

The annual white paper on human rights in North Korea (Choi, 1998) described the situation as follows:

> Pyongyang blocks the flow of information. All radio dials are fixed to the DPRK official broadcasting service channels and sealed. An official of the MPS visits each home every three months; if a seal is found broken the person concerned is assumed guilty of listening to South Korean or other broadcasting services and treated as a political criminal. In areas near the DMZ all television sets have their channels fixed. Chinese TV programs as well are blocked in border regions. (p. 50)

4.2 Structure and Organization

A dual system based on two axes—the party and the Administration Council—manages broadcasting in North Korea. Although, ostensibly, the Korean Central Broadcasting Committee, which comes directly under the Administration Council (politburo), operates domestic broadcasting, it does so under the guidance and supervision of the social and cultural department of the Korean Workers' Party. The party appoints the committee chairman, who belongs to the politburo, and it controls the program content and the appointment of broadcasting executives. Under the KCBC come the provincial or city broadcasting committees, under which come the military broadcasting committees, which supervise the cable broadcasting relay centers. The KCBC's primary concern is with domestic broadcasting. The Pyongyang Broadcasting Committee guides and coordinates the external broadcasting of Pyongyang Television (Korea, Ministry of Information, 1995). Figure 2 shows the organizational structure of the North Korean broadcasting system.

4.2.1 Radio

The Radio and Television Broadcasting Committee (KRT) runs the Korean Central Broadcasting Station (*Choson Joongang Bangsong*); the Pyongyang FM Broadcasting Station (*Pyongyang Yuson Bangsong*); the Pyongyang Broadcasting Station (*Pyongyang Bangsong*), which handles the foreign/external service called Radio Pyongyang (Table 4); and the clandestine Korean People's Democratic Front Radio, known as the Voice of National Salvation.

The Central Broadcasting Station has both medium-wave and shortwave stations in Pyongyang, Chongjin, Hyesan, Wonsan, and Hamhung. It has medium-wave stations in Wiwon, Kaesong, Shinuiju, Hwangju, and Haeju, and shortwave stations in Sariwon, Pyongsong, and Kanggye. The majority of the stations carry both central and regional programs. The Pyongyang FM Broadcasting network has stations in 14 areas of the country (*World radio TV handbook*, 1998).

The Pyongyang Broadcasting Station has shortwave stations in Pyongyang and Kanggye; medium-wave stations in Chongjin, Kangnam (the key station serving Pyongyang area), Samgo, Sepo, Hwadae, and Sangwon; and FM stations in Pyongyang and Kaesong (*World radio TV handbook*, 1998).

The North Korean Workers' Party United Front Department in the Hungbudong area of Pyongyang directs the Korean People's Democratic Front Radio (KPDFR), which has a transmission station on Mount Namsan in Haeju, on the 38th parallel, close to the South Korean border. The KPDFR professes to be a dissident voice coming from South Korea, where the station has provided inspiration for a leftist group called the "*Juche* Ideology Faction" (Koreascope, 1998).

UNESCO (1999) has estimated that in 1995 North Korea had 14.6 radio receivers per 100 people. The number of radio receivers stood at 3.36 million.

4.2.2 Television

The Korean Radio and Television Broadcasting Committee (KRT) runs the Korean Central TV Station (*Choson Joongang TV*), which operates 38 TV transmission stations each with an effective radiated power exceeding 10kW, including the 700kW Channel 12 in Pyongyang. KRT also runs three other TV services (Table 6): Kyoyuk Munhwa Television, which runs education and culture programs; Mansudae Television, which runs Channel 5 Pyongyang during the weekends; and Kaesong Television, which runs Channel 8 in Kaesong and Channel 9 in Pyongyang (*World radio TV handbook*, 1998).

UNESCO (1999) has estimated that in 1997 North Korea had a television penetration of 5.2 receivers per 100 people. The number of receivers stood at 1.2 million.

4.3 Program Policies

4.3.1 Radio

The program policies of the domestic service of the Central Broadcasting Station (*Choson Joongang Bangsong*), as well as of the external service Radio Pyongyang (*Pyongyang Bangsong*), reflect the agitprop function of the media subsystem. Nam and Lent (1978) elucidated, "North Korean broadcasting is the voice of the party and government, reflecting the thinking, to the minutest detail, of a handful of leaders" (p. 59).

The programs of the central station focus on promoting party lines and policies, the cult of Kim Il Sung and his son, the merits of socialism, and other related areas. Radio Pyongyang targets the external/overseas listeners, including the South Koreans, with programs depicting the "supremacy" of the North Korean system. Even though music entertainment dominates FM Radio Pyongyang (*Pyongyang Yuson Bangsong*), the guiding theme of all broadcasting is "allegiance to the party and indoctrination of its tenets" (Nam & Lent, 1978, p. 58). The FM station, which targets the South Korean youth in particular, functions as another tool of psychological warfare against the South. Its serial drama programs praise the North Korean leadership and criticize South Korea and the United States (Koreascope, 1998).

Radio Pyongyang, KRT's external service, broadcasts in Arabic (three hours), Chinese (four hours), English (seven hours), French (six hours), German (three hours), Japanese (eight hours), Korean (seven hours), Russian (five hours), and Spanish (six hours) (*World radio TV handbook*, 1998). Nam and Lent (1978), who described the situation two decades ago, wrote that in external broadcasts, North Korea placed "major emphasis on efforts to unify Korea through whatever means at its disposal" (p. 59).[12]

The KPDFR or the Voice of National Salvation also presents *Jucheism* as the basis for a worldview. It advocates the reunification of Korea on the basis of a confederacy through a determined struggle to achieve "independence from the United States." It calls for the removal of US troops from Korea and the overthrow of the government in the South (Koreascope, 1998).

4.3.2 Television

The program makeup of the television services also reflects a heavy dose of agitprop (Table 9 and Table 10). Television broadcasting is a means for the regime to propagate the party line and to carry out party policies (Koreascope, 1998).

---

[12] Although the two Koreas agreed in principle in 1972 to achieve unification peacefully without foreign interference, they have differed substantially on the practical methods to accomplish it. The two sides signed the Agreement on Reconciliation, Non-aggression, Exchanges and Cooperation on December 13, 1991 (Savada, 1994).

The basic task of the Central TV Station is to embody *Jucheism* and Kim Il Sung's revolutionary thought in its programming. The Mansudae TV Station specializes in televising cultural programs—art performances, movies, sports, and the like—for Pyongyang citizens and foreigners on weekends only. The Kaesong TV Station uses the NTSC transmission system to exclusively target South Korea with propaganda programs tantamount to psychological warfare. The Education and Culture TV Station, which started operation on February 16, 1997, televises programs on education, science and technology, physical education, general knowledge, and the like (Koreascope, 1998).

Compared with commercial TV programming in capitalist societies, North Korean television has some peculiar characteristics. First, television programming is very irregular. North Korean television does not use typical strategies of block programming or strip programming, which commercial TV stations use to construct the audience's viewing habits. Second, TV programming is devoid of advertising. What appear between successive programs are songs and publicity releases. Third, cultural programs—such as music, dance, films, and literary works—take up a large proportion of TV programming.

5. NEW ELECTRONIC MEDIA

5.1 Internet and On-line Media

Because of under-investment in telecommunications (Section 5.2), the Internet and on-line media have not received adequate emphasis in North Korea. No data are available on the number and penetration of personal computers or on the number of Internet hosts. The US Department of State (1999) reported that the government has set up an Internet website, based in Tokyo for propaganda purposes and that very limited Internet access might exist in North Korea for government officials. The state-run Korean Central News Agency operates the website from the Korean News Service in Tokyo under the banner *Korean News* (http://www. kcna.co.jp/). This site provides a link to the on-line newspaper *Choson Sinbo* (http://www.korea-np.co.jp/pk/) available in Korean, Japanese, and English. The English edition is titled *The People's Korea*.

5.2 Telecommunications Infrastructure

North Korea had an estimated 1.1 million main telephone lines in 1997—a penetration of 4.9 telephones per 100 people. This represented a compound annual growth rate of more than 5 percent from 1990 in terms of the number of lines (ITU, 1998). APT (1998) reported that North Korea's telephone density had increased to 5.2 per 100 people in October 1997, although its rural telephone density was only 1.7 per 100 people. The APT reported: "Development in the field of telecommunications has suffered due to serious underinvestment and slow introduction of new technologies" (p. 37).

The telecommunications department of the Ministry of Posts and Telecommunications is in charge of the development and maintenance of the infrastructure. APT (1998) reported that successive natural disasters had reduced the usable number of main telephone lines to about 650,000. Only 5 percent of the total exchange lines are digital. So far fiber-optic lines have been laid between Pyongyang and each provincial city. A digital gateway exchange in Pyongyang serves the international traffic. Two earth stations operating on an Intelsat (Indian Ocean) satellite and an Intersputnik (Indian Ocean Region) satellite provide international connections. Other international connections are possible through Moscow and Beijing. Plans are afoot to set up another earth station to access a Pacific satellite.

The US State Department (1999), however, reported that private telephone lines operated on an internal system that prevented making and receiving calls from outside the country. International phone lines were available under very restricted circumstances.

6. POLICY TRENDS FOR PRESS AND BROADCASTING[13]

Choi (1998) says neither press freedom nor human rights conditions in North Korea are likely to improve in the foreseeable future. In mid-1998, South Korean news media rushed to North Korea following the newly elected government's "sunshine policy" toward Pyongyang. This rapprochement enabled the South Korean news media to report on historic and cultural sites in North Korea, giving valuable insights to historians and archaeologists. But no paper reported on the famine or the human rights violations lest North Korea would end the visiting privileges.

Defector Kang Chul-hwan, who testified on North Korea's human rights in December 1998 at the Asian Democratic Conference in Paris, said the country had no basic freedom of expression. It had 12 concentration camps. In 1997, North Korea was shaken by the defection of the highest-ever-ranking Communist Party member—Hwang Jang-Yop, 74, a communist ideologue. He repeatedly stressed the need for North Korea to open its economy and reform its political system.

Choi (1998) further points out that in August 1997, when a UN subcommittee, at a meeting in Geneva, raised North Korea's failure to report to the United Nations for the past 10 years on the country's implementation of the Covenant on Civil and Political Rights, Pyongyang took the unprecedented decision to withdraw from the Covenant, which it had signed in 1981. Amnesty International visited the country in 1995 but the regime did not allow the team to undertake independent monitoring.

North Korea's troubles began in 1995, when floods wiped out the staple crops— maize and rice. Pak Dong Tchoun, North Korea's ambassador to UNESCO, commented in July 1997 that his country was "extremely reticent" about opening its doors to the Western press, "which says it is equitable, but writes horrible

---

[13] This section summarizes the 1998 and 1997 IPI press freedom reports on North Korea.

calumnies about our regime the minute they leave the country. The Korean people do not want to receive journalists who have bad intentions. We want journalists who show good will and want to promote friendship between peoples, not subvert our regime and sovereignty. We do not want shortcomings reported. The [Western] mass media must not write articles that are not encouraging." Pak even attacked the French communist daily, *Humanite*.

Late in 1997, the government published threats against the South Korean media for criticizing North Korea's leadership. The first instance was in response to a South Korean newspaper editorial; the second in reaction to a television drama about life in North Korea (US Department of State, 1999).

The central committee of the (North) Korean Journalists Union (KJU), in a statement on July 9, 1997, declared: "The people and press men in the northern half of Korea are getting angrier by the day at the vicious provocation committed by the treacherous group of the puppet *Chosun Ilbo* to slander and insult the digni- fied system in the North. In fact, *Chosun Ilbo* pulled the trigger of war against the North, agitating for the 'overthrow of the system of the North.'" The KJU statement went on to say it regarded *Chosun Ilbo's* comments as "an open declaration of war against the North." The paper, it said, "should apologize to the nation and ex- plode itself [*sic*]." In November 1997, Radio Pyongyang began broadcasting threats to blow up the KBS building and to kill its drama producers, after the South Korean public television network announced it planned to air, from December 1, a drama about North Korean life, "Till the Azaleas Bloom." The drama is based on a book written by Shin Young-Hee, wife of a former North Korean diplomat, Choi Se- Woong, who defected with his family to Seoul via London in December 1995.

North Korean leader Kim Jong Il explained the propagandistic role of his country's media during a visit to the studios of the broadcasting service in May. "Equipped with the most modern technology and facilities, our television broad- casting has up-to-date scientific achievements and is highly consistent in ideological content and artistic value, and has thus became a close friend, which is an inextri- cable party of our people's lives and is actively contributing to their ideological cultural indoctrination," he said.

North Korea opened its first site on the World Wide Web in January 1997. Dis- patches in English from the official Korean News Agency (KCNA) were made available to all Internet users. "Up to 18 news items will be made available on the Internet each day," said an official from the Korea News Service, which acts as Japanese agent in Tokyo for the Pyongyang news agency.

7. MAIN ISSUES

● *Jucheism*

This state philosophy has isolated the country in an era of global interdependence. Koo (1992) points out that the philosophy of economic self-reliance has hindered economic growth and driven the economy into a morass. *Jucheism* has hampered international cooperation, as well as introduction of foreign capital and advanced technology. The mass media, as an organ of the communist political and social structure, cannot but promote this state philosophy.

● Political and economic change

Byun (1990) wrote that although North Korea had carefully followed China's method of opening to the world, it had stepped up the *Juche* ideology. Byun surmised that the gradual adoption of Gorbachev's policy of perestroika was inevitable in North Korea in the near future. Hara (1996), however, argued that North Korea was failing in its attempt to adopt a Chinese-style reform. The country's leaders were hardly in a position to democratize their political system without fear of their own well-being. Therefore, these leaders were unlikely to adopt serious reform if such reforms were likely to lead to their own suffering. The survival of the current regime and reform seemed incompatible. Thus press freedom is unlikely to emerge in North Korea in the near future.

8. STATISTICS

General Profile

Exchange rate (1999)	US$ 1 = 2.20 North Korean Won (fixed rate)
Population	23.9 million❶
Population growth rate	1.6 percent❷
Population density	198 per sq km
Life expectancy (1998)	71.6 years❸
Literacy (1995)	95 percent
Real GDP per capita (PPP) (1995)	US$ 4,058❹
Urban population	61.2 percent

Source: UNDP, 1998; *UN statistical yearbook*, 1998.
Note: ❶ ❷ ❸ See Section 1.2 for other estimates. ❹ See Section 1.4 for other estimates.

Table 1
Provincial Newspapers

Newspaper	Date of establishment
Hwangbuk Ilbo	September 6, 1945
Hwangnam Ilbo	September 6, 1945
Hambuk Ilbo	October 1, 1945
Hamnam Ilbo	November 15, 1945
Pyongbuk Ilbo	November 27, 1945
Kangwon Ilbo	December 28, 1945
Chagang Ilbo	March 11, 1949
Pyongnam Ilbo	December 12, 1950
Kaesong Sinmun	March 26, 1952
Ryanggang Ilbo	January 1, 1955
Pyongyang Ilbo	June 1, 1957

Note: Average circulation of the provincial newspapers is 40,000–50,000. The three national dailies are *Rodong Sinmun, Minju Choson,* and *Rodong Chongnyon.*

Table 2
Estimated Daily Newspaper Circulation and Penetration

	Number of dailies	Circulation	Per 100 people
1980	11	4 million	22.6
1985	11	4.5 million	23.8
1990	11	5 million	24.4
1995	11	5 million	22.5
1996	3	4.5 million	19.9

Source: UNESCO, 1999.

Table 3
Estimated Data on National Dailies

	Established	Circulation
Minju Choson (Democratic Korea)	1946	200,000
Rodong Sinmun (Labor Daily)	1946	1,500,000
Rodong Chongnyon (Working Youth)	1946	N.A.
Choson Inmingun (People's Army)	1948	N.A.

Source: *Editor & publisher international yearbook*, 1999.

Table 4
The Radio Services: Channels and Broadcast Time

Stations	Broadcast time per channel
Domestic service	
Choson Joongang Bangsong	3 medium-wave channels and 4 shortwave channels; total 22 hrs/day
Pyongyang Yuson Bangsong	
Pyongyang FM Bangsong	14 regions, 25 stations
Foreign/External service	
Pyongyang Bangsong	23 hrs 30 minutes/day
Voice of National Salvation	1 medium-wave channel and 4 shortwave channels; 16hrs/day

Source: Kang, 1997.

Table 5
Estimated Radio Penetration

	Number of receivers	*Receivers per 100 people*
1980	1.25 million	9.9
1985	2.00 million	10.6
1990	2.60 million	12.7
1995	3.00 million	13.4
1996	3.30 million	14.6
1997	3.36 million	14.6

Source: UNESCO, 1999.

Table 6
Television Services

Stations	*Transmission*	*Broadcast time*
Choson Joongang TV	PAL	Weekdays (excepting Wed.) 15:00–22:00 Sunday 09:00–12:00, 15:00–22:00 Wednesday 09:00–12:00, 15:00–22:00
Kyoyuk Munhwa TV	–	Weekdays 19:00–22:00 Sunday 12:00–22:00
Kaesong TV	NTSC	Weekdays 19:00–23:00 Saturday 16:00–23:00 Sunday (no service)
Mansudae TV	PAL	Viewable in Pyongyang area only on Saturday and Sunday

Source: Koryo taehakkyo sinmun bangsong yon'guso, 1997.

Table 7
Estimated Television Penetration

	Number of receivers	*Receivers per 100 people*
1980	130,000	0.7
1985	200,000	1.1
1990	330,000	1.6
1995	1,050,000	4.7
1996	1,090,000	4.8
1997	1,200,000	5.2

Source: UNESCO, 1999.

Table 8
Pyongyang FM's Program Mix

Types of program	Minutes	Percentage
Domestic art music	235	52.2
Foreign music	160	36.6
Radio drama	55	12.2
Total	**450**	**100.0**

Source: Kang, 1997.

Table 9
An Example of Choson Joongang TV Programming

Time (PM)	Program
6:05	News
6:15	Pre-school children program <Blossoming talents under the sun light>
6:34	Song lesson <Let's sing our blossoming life>
6:40	News documentary <Nicolai Causescu of the Romania Socialist Republic Visits our country>
7:10	Propaganda movie <Transport! Produce!>
7:13	Local news <A battlefield full of the passion of loyalty>
7:18	Documentary <The creation of '80's speed' according to the Party's appeal>
7:45	News film <Resource base that produces silver>
7:49	Sports <Party's 40th anniversary republic handball championship>
8:29	News film <Threshing field is busy threshing>
8:33	News film <The party leads a whole new change of a tourist resort>
8:48	News film <The constructiveness of socialism and exhibition hall>
9:00	News
9:35	Unforgettable story <Taking a memorial picture together>
9:53	News interpretation <Thresh frugally>
10:00	News interpretation <Watching the Juche country, Joson>
10:02	Opera drama <from the revolutionary opera 'Blood Sea'>
10:53	Common sense <Aqua resource and the prospect of its use>

Source: Kang, 1997.

Table 10
An Example of Mansudae TV Programming

Time (PM)	Program
4:11	Foreign movie <Soviet art film: The Death of a Stamp Collector>
5:28	The performance of the Mansudae Art Company
5:45	World Tour <Egypt>
6:00	News
6:10	World Wrestling Competition
7:04	Revolutionary Opera <from the 'Flower salesgirl'>
7:40	Movie <Soviet art film: All Alone without Arms>
9:00	News
9:30	World competition of field and track

Source: Kang, 1997.

Figure 1
Organizational Structure of the *Rodong Sinmun*

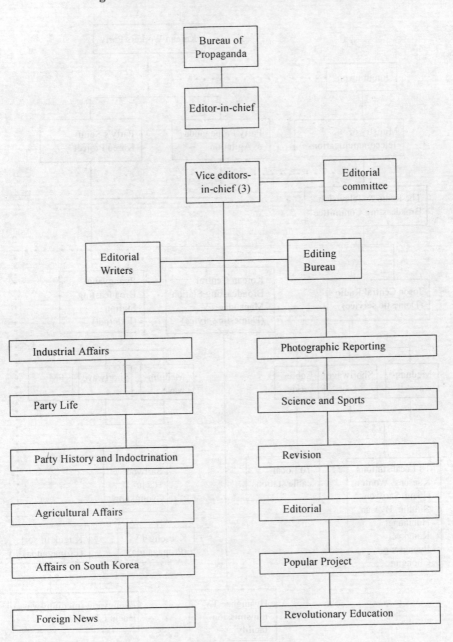

Source: Koryo taehakkyo sinmun bangsong yon'guso, 1997.

Figure 2
Organization of North Korea's Broadcasting System

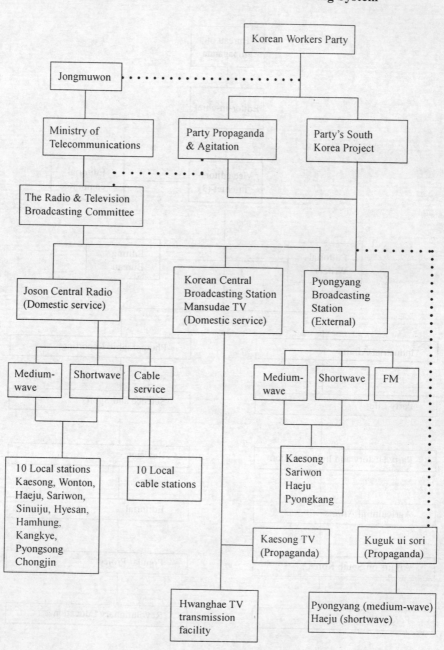

Source: Kang, 1997.

9. USEFUL ADDRESSES

Ministry of Posts and Telecommunications
Central District
ˉOe-Song Dong, Pyongyang
Telephone: +850 23 813 180
Fax: +850 23 814 418

Korean Central News
Pyongyang-dong 1, Potonggang
Pyongyang
Fax: +850 23 812 421

Korean Central Broadcasting Station
Moranbong District
Pyongyang

Rodong Sinmun/Minju Choson/Rodong Chongnyon
Junggu District
Pyongyang

10. REFERENCES

An, T. S. (1983). *North Korea: A political handbook*. Wilmington, DE: Scholarly Resources Inc.
APT (Asia-Pacific Telecommunity). (1998, 1999). *The APT yearbook*. Bangkok: APT.
Byun, D. H. (1990). *North Korea's foreign policy of "juche" and the challenge of Gorbachev's new thinking*. Unpublished doctoral dissertation, University of Miami, Miami.
Choi, E. C. (Ed.). (1998). *White paper on human rights in North Korea*. Seoul: Korea Institute of National Unification.
Choi, K. W. (1998). North Korea. *World press freedom review* [On-line]. Available: (http://www.freemedia.at/archive97/norkor.htm).
Cumings, B. (1997). *Korea's place in the sun: A modern history*. New York: W.W. Norton & Co.
Editor & publisher international yearbook. (1998, 1999). New York: E&P.
Freedom House Survey Team. (1998). *Freedom in the world: The annual survey of political rights and civil liberties, 1997–1998*. New York: Freedom House.
Hara, O. (1996). *The future of North Korea: Its structural constraints and alternatives*. Unpublished doctoral dissertation, University of Hawaii, Hawaii.
ITU (International Telecommunication Union). (1998, 1999). *World telecommunication development report*. Geneva: ITU.
Kang, H. D. (1997). *Pukhan maes medio ron* (Mass media in North Korea). Seoul: Nanam.
Kim, Y., & Lee, B. (1991). *Pukhan ollon ui iron kwa silch'on* (Theory and practice of the North Korean mass media). Seoul: Nanam.
Kim, S. H. (1993). *The juche ideology of North Korea: Sociopolitical roots of ideological change*. Unpublished doctoral dissertation, University of Georgia, Georgia.
Koo, B. H. (1992). *Political economy of self-reliance: The case of North Korea, 1961-1990*. Unpublished doctoral dissertation, University of Cincinnati, Cincinnati.
Korea annual. (1993, 1998). Seoul: Yonhap News Agency.-
Korea, Ministry of Unification. (1995). *Introduction to North Korea: Press and publication* [On-line]. Available: (http://www.unikorea.go.kr/eg/load/D43/int/int53.htm).
KPI (Korean Press Institute). (1997). *Segae-ui media* (World media). Seoul: KPI.

Koreascope. (1998). *North Korea today* [On-line]. Available: (http://www.koreascope.org/english/sub/2/ks2.htm).

Koryo taehakkyo sinmun bangsong yon'guso. (1997). *Tongil ul taebi han ollon ui yokhal (The role of mass media in preparation of national unification)*. Seoul: Korea University MCRC.

Lent, J. A. (1982). Democratic People's Republic of Korea. In J. A. Lent (Ed.), *Newspapers in Asia: Contemporary trends and problems* (pp. 126–129). Hong Kong: Heinemann Asia.

Nam, S., & Lent J. A. (1978). Democratic People's Republic of Korea (North Korea). In J. A. Lent (Ed.), *Broadcasting in Asia and the Pacific: A continental survey of radio and television* (pp. 55–60). Philadelphia: Temple University Press.

Savada, A.M. (Ed.). (1994). *North Korea: A country study.* Washington, DC: Federal Research Division, Library of Congress.

Sussman, L.R. (1999). *Press freedom 1998: News of the century.* New York: Freedom House.

UNESCO (United Nations Educational, Scientific and Cultural Organization). (1999). *Statistical yearbook.* Paris: UNESCO.

UN (United Nations). (1995). *World media handbook.* New York: UN Department of Public Information.

UNDP (United Nations Development Program). (1998). *Human development report 1998.* New York: Oxford University Press.

US Department of State, Bureau of Democracy, Human Rights, and Labor. (1999, February 26). *Democratic People's Republic of Korea: Country report on human rights practices for 1998* [On-line]. Available: (http://www.state.gov/www/global/human_rights/1998_hrp_report/northkor.html).

Vanden Heuvel, J., & Dennis, E. E. (1993). *The unfolding lotus: East Asia's changing media.* New York: The Freedom Forum Media Studies Center.

World factbook. (1998, 1999). Korea, North [On-line]. Available: (http://www.odci.gov/cia/publications/factbook/kn.html).

World radio TV handbook. (1998). Amsterdam: Billboard Books.

Youm, K. H. (1991). Press laws in North Korea. *Asian Journal of Communication,* 2 (1), 70–86.

Yu, J. C. (1992). *Pukhan ollon ui silsang (The truth of the North Korean press).* Seoul: Minjok T'ongil Hyobuihoe.

♦

23

SOUTH KOREA

Chul Heo, Ki-Yul Uhm, & Jeong-Heon Chang

1. NATIONAL PROFILE

1.1 Geography

South Korea covers the southern half of the Korean Peninsula located between North Korea and Japan. With an area of 98,480 sq km, it is slightly larger than Indiana. It has a 238-km border with North Korea and a coastline of 2,413 km. The 1,950-m Halla-san is the highest point. The terrain is mostly hilly and mountainous, with wide coastal plains in the west and the south. It has a temperate climate and heavier rainfall in summer than in winter (*World factbook*, 1999).

1.2 People

The country's 46.9 million people form an ethnically homogenous group, excepting some 20,000 Chinese. Life expectancy is 74.3 years, adult literacy is 98 percent, and urbanization stands at 84 percent. The religious distribution is 47 percent Buddhist, 49 percent Christian, 3 percent Confucian, and 1 percent others (NSO, 1998, 1999). The population has grown 2.3 times since 1949. Korean is the country's national language. In terms of the human development index, South Korea ranked 30th with a value of 0.852 in 1997 (UNDP, 1999).

1.3 Government and Politics

South Korea is a republic with a unicameral National Assembly or *Kukhoe*, which has 299 seats. Members are elected by popular vote to serve four-year terms. The president, who is elected by popular vote for a single five-year term, appoints the prime minister. The country's administrative divisions comprise nine provinces and six special cities (Yonhap Tongshin, 1998).

South Korea is in transition. *Han-kook*, as South Koreans generally refer to their country, has moved from a society dominated by dictatorial-military-authoritarian mindsets and behaviors toward a more capitalistic, democratic system after the nationwide pro-democratic movements in 1987 and particularly after the establishment of the civilian government in 1992. The country's socio-political changes have expedited the decentralization process, causing dramatic transformations in its body politic and culture, as well as changes in the media landscape.

1.4 Economy

South Korea's gross domestic product at purchasing power parity stood at US$ 578 billion in 1999. The per capita GDP at purchasing power parity was US$ 12,455 while the nominal per capita GNP was US$ 6,810. The country exported merchandise valued at US$ 144 billion in 1999, and its reserves stood at US$ 66.1 billion (*Asiaweek*, February 4, 2000). Its major exports are electronic and electrical equipment, semiconductors, machinery, steel, automobiles, and ships; textiles, clothing, and footwear; and fish. Its major trade partners are the United States, the European Union, and Japan (*World factbook*, 1999).

2. DEVELOPMENT OF PRESS AND BROADCASTING

2.1. Brief Early History

The first Korean newspaper, *Chobo* (Court Gazette), appeared in 1392 during the Chosun dynasty (Lent, 1974). The Royal Court published and circulated it "irregularly" until 1895 (Cha, 1987; Youm, 1996). The first modern Korean newspaper, however, which met Otto Groth's "universally applicable" standards for a "true" newspaper (Youm, 1996, p. 8), was *Hansung Sunbo*; it appeared on October 1, 1883, as the Chosun dynasty court's official newspaper printed in Chinese characters. *Hansung Chubo* (weekly), which used both *Hangul* and Chinese characters, replaced it in January 1886 (Cha, 1987; Youm, 1996). The first private Korean newspaper was *Tongnip Shinmun*, which appeared thrice a week, beginning April 7, 1896. Although numerous other titles appeared between 1898 and 1899, the first Korean daily, *Maeil Shinmun*, appeared only on January 26, 1898 (Kim, 1971; Nam, 1982).

Contemporary media in South Korea reflect the dramatic socio-historical changes that have influenced Korean society since the second half of the 19th century. After the Japanese annexed Korea in 1910, they closed all newspapers except three—the Korean *Maeil Shinbo*, the English *Seoul Press*, and the Japanese *Keijo Nippo*, which became their mouthpieces (Cha 1987; Youm 1996). The resistance movement for independence, which began on the eve of King Kojong's funeral on March 1, 1919, led the Japanese colonizers to adopt a policy of appeasement rather than suppression in an effort to mitigate anti-Japanese sentiments among Koreans. Two of today's top Korean newspapers—*Chosun Ilbo* and *Dong-A Ilbo*—emerged in 1920 (Youm, 1996). The Japanese authorized the publication of these two, along with *Sisa-Shinmun, Sidae Ilbo*, and *Choongweo Ilbo*; but they suppressed the private newspapers again in 1940 to stifle anti-war sentiments. *Maeil Shinbo*, with a printrun of 500,000 copies, re-emerged as the mouthpiece of the Japanese occupiers until Korea's liberation in 1954 (Cha, 1987; Kim, 1971).

The Japanese set up the first Korean broadcasting entity, Kyung-Sung radio station (JODK), on February 16, 1927. Established as a public institution, it took the form of a Japanese-style BBC model that placed great power in the hands of the state. They established local stations and relaying facilities across the Korean peninsula during the 1930s and early 1940s. The national coverage of radio boosted the audience and increased the number of receivers from 20,419 in 1932 to 277,281 in 1942 (Chung, 1992; Nam, 1982). They used Korean and Japanese alternatively as broadcasting languages. Early radio had ongoing financial difficulties because of dependence on license fees. It had no government support or commercial sponsorship (Chung, 1997; Chung, 1992).

2.2 Developments since 1945

A series of historical events that followed the Japanese occupation shaped the development of the mass media: the US military occupation from 1945 to 1948, the Korean War, the April 1960 (Students') Revolution against Syngman Rhee's dictatorship, the 1961 military coup, the establishment of the 1972 *Yushin* Constitution, the 1980 military coup, the 1987 nationwide pro-democratic movement, the 1992 election of a civilian government, the 1997 election that transformed the power structure, and the current phase of economic austerity caused by the Asian economic crisis and the IMF demands.

2.2.1 Press

The history of the Korean press was a struggle against systematic suppression and control even though those organs that served as "mouthpieces" received special financial support and perks. After World War II, two major themes shaped the rulers' press policies: anti-communism and modernization. The US military, as well as the succession of authoritarian governments, implemented policies that aimed to control and suppress those elements of the press that questioned the rulers' political legitimacy and criticized their socio-economic agenda.

The US Army Military Government in Korea (USAMGIK), during its three-year rule from 1945 to 1948, placed the Korean press under the control of its Department of Public Information. A conservative, right-wing media culture developed under strict governmental control within this structure (Kim & Shin, 1994). When the ideological confrontation between the rightist and the leftist forces intensified, however, the USAMGIK used a series of ordinances (Nos 55, 72, and 88, in particular) to license the press—especially to regulate the leftist publications. One could argue that USAMGIK's press policies, in effect, contradicted its own political and ideological commitment to liberal democratic principles (Youm, 1996). During this period, two more national dailies appeared—*Maeil Shinmun* (later titled *Seoul Shinmun*, and now called *Daehan Maeil*) in 1945 and *Kyunghyang Shinmun* in 1946 (KPI, 1998a).

Successive dictatorial governments adopted the USAMGIK's press policies to suppress leftist publications and, later, to regulate progressive and critical ones as well. Using the slogan "Anti-communism in defense of democracy," Syngman Rhee's government (1948–60) even deprived the citizens of their basic civil rights through the 1958 National Security Act. It faced stiff criticism from three major national dailies—*Kyunghyang Shinmun, Dong-A Ilbo*, and *Chosun Ilbo*—which blamed Rhee's dictatorship (Kim & Shin, 1994). Meanwhile, in 1954, the Chang Ki-young family had established another national daily, the *Hankook Ilbo* (Korea Daily).

When Rhee's 12-year authoritarian rule came to an end after the April 1960 Students' Revolution, the South Korean press experienced freedom for the first time in its history. The Second Republic (1960–61) led by Premier Chang Myon and the democratically elected parliament guaranteed freedom of the press. The government replaced the licensing system with a registration system. This resulted in the explosive growth of media outlets: within a year, the number of daily newspapers grew from 41 to 112; news agencies from 14 to 274; weeklies from 136 to 476; and monthlies from 400 to 470 (Kim, 1991). Often characterized as "chaotic," this *laissez faire* era, however, came to an abrupt end with the May 1961 military coup led by Gen. Park Chung Hee.

During the 1960s, the government established the structural preconditions for the monopolistic growth of the newspaper industry in the 1970s. In 1965, the Lee family, the owners of the Samsung group and the Tong-yang Broadcasting Corporation (TBC), established *Joong-ang Ilbo*, the sixth national daily. *Kyunghyang Shinmun* established the Munhwa Broadcasting Corporation (MBC) in 1969, and the Korean Broadcasting System (KBS) merged with *Seoul Shinmun* (Won, 1991a). These media conglomerates maintained a close relationship with the Park regime throughout the 1970s by supporting the regime in exchange for monopolistic market privileges. This contributed to the growth of the media conglomerates and the cultivation of submissive journalism.

The system of suppression against the press extended to encompass basic human rights. In the early 1970s, the Korean press fared worse than in the 1960s. Starting with Martial Law Decree No. 1 in December 1971, Park issued nine presidential emergency decrees to "safeguard national security and public order." He also revised the Criminal Code to prohibit Koreans from criticizing the president and his government through foreign media. He forced the media to support the government in the interest of "national development" and "national security" (Kim & Shin, 1994, pp. 53–55). In 1972, the Park regime consolidated several newspaper companies and cancelled licenses of regional newspapers such as *Taegu Ilbo, Taegu Kyungje Ilbo, Hankook Kyungje Ilbo, Taehan Ilbo*, and *Honam Maeil Shinmun*. The number of regional newspapers went down from 22 to 14, leaving only one or two newspapers in each province (Won, 1991a).

A very short period of liberalization of journalistic practices and media ownership followed Park's assassination. Chun Doo Hwan's "new military" soon pressured the media into discharging more than 1,200 newsworkers; cancelled the registration of 172 periodicals; and forced mergers of wire services, newspapers, and broadcasting stations. The number of wire services went down from six to one, and newspapers from 28 to 11. The Chun regime enacted the 1980 Basic Press Act, an "all-inclusive net of control measures designed to blight the press to death" that emphasized press responsibility than its freedom and rights (Chung, 1997, p. 21; Kim & Shin, 1994, p. 56; Youm, 1996, pp. 59–63).

The media became more profit-oriented and prospered under monopolistic market domination and various government subsidies. Major print and broadcast media routinely made the list of the nation's 100 largest firms. Just as the rapid economic growth of the 1970s allowed the development of an advertising market, the 1980s allowed the emergence of the industry on an even larger scale, based on monopolistic capital. Having become a monolithic leviathan, the media gradually showed a "paradoxical decrease" in their submission to political power, especially during the first half of 1987, when student-led pro-democracy resistance movements began to spread. In June 1987, Roh Tae Woo, Chon's "would-be" successor, made an eight-point pledge to mollify the students who, backed by the middle class, led nationwide, student-led anti-government demonstrations for democratization. Among other things, Roh pledged to revise to constitution, to allow direct presidential elections, and to establish freedom of the press.

In November 1987, the Act Relating to Registration of Periodicals (Periodicals Act) and the Broadcast Act replaced the "notorious" 1980 Basic Press Act. The new law allowed the media to break away from the "authoritarianism-for-development" paradigm (Kim & Shin, 1994, pp. 57–59). As a result, Koreans witnessed the establishment of four more national dailies—*Hankyoreh* (1988), *Kook-min Ilbo* (1988), *Segye Ilbo* (1989), and *Minju Ilbo* (1989–1991). The Hyundai group established another national newspaper, *Munhwa Ilbo* in 1991 when *Minju Ilbo* went bankrupt. By the end of November 1994, the number of daily newspapers, both regional and national, had increased more than threefold, from 32 to 99 (KPI, 1998a; Youm, 1996).

The contemporary Korean media have been freer than ever to criticize the government and to cover issues they previously avoided (Vanden Heuvel & Dennis, 1993). Press unions, which have emerged in almost all news media organizations, have launched movements for the independence of editorial rights and for the practice of fair reporting. The 1997 Asian financial market crisis, however, has placed economic hardship on the Korean media, which are in the process of organizational downsizing and restructuring.

2.2.2 Radio

The US military government (1945–48) played a key role in promoting the Americanization of radio broadcasting. In 1946, it restructured the Korean Broadcasting

System into specific divisions such as the "continuity section," the "production section," and the "news and special event section." It separated the duties of producer, editor, and reporter for the first time (Chung, 1992). It required KBS to air American popular music for one hour a day (Chung, 1994, p. 303), thereby promoting American programming formats and marketing strategies. KBS adopted the commercial model of broadcasting, including audience participation programs and survey-based programming that encouraged entertainment. On the other hand, US officials censored the KBS radio news programs and promoted anti-communist discourse (Chung 1992).

A dual broadcasting structure emerged in 1954, when the Korean National Christian Council established the first private radio station, the Christian Broadcasting System (CBS). The first commercial radio station, Pusan MBC, started broadcasting in 1959 (Kang & Kim, 1994). The eventual proliferation of commercial broadcasting companies—Seoul MBC radio (1961), Dong-A Radio (DBC, 1963), and Tongyang Radio (TBC, 1964)—contributed to the development of a mass consumption culture in the 1960s and the 1970s. FM services began in 1965 with the Seoul FM Broadcasting Company followed by three other FM stations in 1970—Seoul MBC-FM, Pusan MBC-FM, and Taegu Korea-FM. As Korea's national economy grew, the radio industry became a major advertising medium. Radio receivers increased sharply from 706,491 in 1963 to 3 million sets in 1970 (Kang & Kim, 1994).

Confronted by television, radio began to lose a large number of listeners and advertisers throughout the 1970s and 1980s. Television forced radio stations to position themselves through specialized programming including classical music, Western pop music, and minority-oriented programs. In particular, commercial radio stations, such as MBC, DBS, and TBC, made an effort to survive by exploring new program formats and introducing the concept of niche programming (Kang & Kim, 1994). A 1990 revision of the 1987 Broadcast Act triggered more specialization of radio stations. In the early 1990s, five new radio stations appeared: the Buddhist Broadcasting System (BBS), the Pyonghwa Broadcasting Corporation (PBC), the Traffic Broadcasting System (TBS), the Educational Broadcasting System (EBS), and the Seoul Broadcasting System (SBS) (KPI, 1996; MCRCKU, 1998).

2.2.3 Television

Television came into the country in May 1956 when Korea RCA Distribution company, KORCAD, established HLKZ-TV as part of RCA's international marketing strategy to sell more TV sets in developing countries (Yoon, 1994). This station ceased operation after one year because of insufficient advertising and low TV penetration—a mere 3,000 TV sets in the country. However, it played a key role in infusing American commercial and cultural values among the elite who could afford TV sets. The American Forces Korea Network, AFKN-TV, continued the infusion of American values during its four-year TV monopoly from 1957 to 1961. AFKN commanded a bigger audience with TV penetration reaching

7,000 receivers by 1960 (Yoon, 1994). Thus, an uneasy mixture of commercialism and state influence emerged. State-controlled broadcasting pursued commercial interests under this set-up.

In December 1961, the Park Chung Hee regime established the first full-scale television network, KBS-TV, as a state-owned system that charged a compulsory license fee from TV set owners and permitted commercial breaks between program blocks. Two privately owned TV networks followed. Joong-ang Ilbo, a newspaper company of the Samsung group, established the first commercial TV network, TBC-TV, in 1964. Kyunghyang Shinmun, a newspaper company of the Foundation of Chung-Soo Scholarship, established the second commercial network, MBC-TV, in 1969. But these two commercial networks were under government control because the 1963 Broadcasting Law required them to report summaries of their broadcast programming to the state. The result was an overemphasis on entertainment at the expense of news. The media became dramatically commercialized as the advertising market grew in response to the increasing affluence of the 1970s. TV penetration increased as the numbers of receivers skyrocketed from 379,564 in 1970 to 6.3 million in 1980 (Kang & Kim, 1994; KPI, 1998a).

The Chun military government established a public broadcasting system by consolidating six of the 29 broadcasting stations into the state-run KBS, including TBC-TV. As a result, no commercial broadcasting existed during the 1980s. During the Chun regime, the Korean television industry functioned as a political mouthpiece of the government and as a purveyor of consumer culture (Chung, 1997; Youm, 1996).

The de-regulation of the broadcasting industry occurred with the amendment of the Broadcast Act in April 1990. The Seoul Broadcasting System (SBS-TV), owned by 39 private companies, received a license in December 1990. The National Assembly also enacted a cable television law in December 1991 that enabled the establishment of cable TV for the first time in Korea in 1995, when four private TV stations—KBC-TV, TBC-TV, TJB-TV, and PSB-TV—started operation. In 1997, the government allowed the establishment of four more commercial TV stations—UBC-TV, ITV-TV, JTV-TV, and CJB-TV (Yonhap Tongshin, 1997).

3. THE PRESS

3.1 Policy and Legal Framework

The 1987 Act relating to Registration of Periodicals (Periodicals Act) and the Broadcast Act—which replaced the Basic Press Act of 1980—are the basis of the current legal structure of the press. Moreover, the country's constitution outlines the fundamental principles relating to freedom of the press, rights of the individual, and national security. The Act provides for the reader's right to demand, within a month of publication, a correction of any false statement that has injured the individual, a corporation, or the government (Article 16). It established a Press Arbitration Commission to deal with complaints and requests for the redress of injuries to reputation and with alleged infringement by the press of individual rights (Article 17) (KPI, 1998a).

The Freedom House (Sussman, 1999) has placed South Korea in the "free" press category with a restriction score of 28 out of 100. On laws and regulations that influence media content, it scored 2 out of 15 for broadcast and 4 out of 15 for print. On political pressures and controls on media content, it scored 7 out of 15 for broadcast and 9 out of 15 for print. On economic influences on media content, it scored 5 out of 15 for print and zero for broadcast. Finally, it scored 1 out of 5 on repressive actions on print media. Thus, only political pressures and controls stand as the major obstacles in attaining further press freedom.

3.2 Financial Aspects: Circulation, Advertising, Marketing Strategies

The number of dailies increased steadily before the Asian financial market crisis (Table 2). At the end of 1997, South Korea had 115 registered daily newspapers, a four-fold increase from 28 in 1987 (KPI, 1998a). As of March 1999, the country had 108 regional and national dailies (Table 3). The national dailies are published in Seoul, a city of more than 10 million people (MCT, 1999).

The country's top dailies are *Chosun Ilbo* (circulation, 2.35 million; readership, 3.9 million), *Dong-A Ilbo* (circulation, 2.2 million; readership, 3.4 million); *Joong-ang Ilbo* (circulation, 2.1 million; readership, 4.2 million); *Hankook Ilbo* (circulation, 1.4 million; readership, 1.8 million); and *Kyunghyang Shinmun* (circulation, 1.2 million; readership, 1.4 million). *Hankyoreh* had a circulation, 0.5 million (Shim, 1998; WAN, 1999). In terms of revenue, however, *Joong-ang Ilbo* topped the other dailies with US$ 359 million in 1997, followed by *Chosun Ilbo* (US$ 319 million), *Dong-A Ilbo* (US$ 255 million), *Hankook Ilbo* (US$ 229 million), and *Daehan Maeil* (US$ 153 million). *Hankyoreh*'s revenue (US$ 51 million) recorded the highest growth, 14.6 percent in 1997 (KPI, 1998b).

Newspapers have the largest market share of the total advertising revenue. Although their revenue decreased in 1997 by 8.3 percent and in 1998 by 36.8 percent after the IMF bailout (Table 4), advertising is still the main source of income for South Korean newspapers (KPI, 1998b). Newspapers generated US$ 533 million in advertising revenue from January to March in 1999 (Lee, 1999), indicating a recovery from some of their financial losses as the national economy recovered.

All major national dailies, except *Hankyoreh*, target the elite and the conservative class. In particular, *Chosun Ilbo* and *Daehan Maeil* (formerly *Seoul Shinmun*) have positioned themselves to represent the far right-wing readership. Other national dailies, including *Dong-A Ilbo, Hankook Ilbo, Joong-ang Ilbo*, and *Kyunghyang Shinmun*, also aimed to reach the conservative elite (*Hankyoreh*, February 8, 1999).[1] Only *Hankyoreh* has positioned itself to target progressive

---

[1] *Hankyoreh* (http://www.hani.co.kr).

intellectuals and working-class readers. Claiming to be the "most critical above-ground" newspaper in Korea, it has served as a progressive alternative to the largely pro-business, pro-government, and conservative newspapers.

Promotional competition among newspapers intensified, especially after *Joong-ang Ilbo* became a morning paper on April 15, 1995. In 1995, *Joong-ang Ilbo* spent US$ 3.5 million to produce public relations material and advertising through television, radio, and magazines (KPI, 1996). The total advertising expenditure of the South Korean newspapers reached US$ 7.8 million in 1995, a 92.8 percent increase from 1994 (KPI, 1996). The fierce competition for readership triggered these national dailies to increase the number of pages published and distributed from eight (during the pre-1987 era) to 12 (during the late 1980s and the early 1990s), and finally to 20 (during the mid-1990s until the IMF bailout) (KPI, 1998a; Won, 1991b). Their more aggressive marketing strategies have included delivering free papers to non-subscribers almost "forcefully," and not just a trial basis (KPI, 1998a, p. 64).

Responding to this excessive competition among newspapers, in 1997, the Korean Newspaper Association created a Fair Competition Appraisal Committee to apply "voluntary standards for fair competition" (KPI, 1998a, p. 58). As a result, newspapers have refrained from offering free coupons and sweepstakes. "Forceful" delivery of free papers, however, continues, constituting 90 percent of the 1,743 complaints received by the KNA in 1998. Reports also indicate that 70 percent of these "unfair" competitive practices involved the top three newspapers—*Chosun Ilbo, Dong-A Ilbo*, and *Joong-ang Ilbo* (Yonhap Tongshin, 1997; MCT, 1999).[2]

3.3 Structure and Organization

South Korea has 10 major general-interest national dailies, 64 local dailies, five economic dailies, four sports dailies, five teen dailies, 11 specialty dailies, and four foreign-language dailies, all of which are privately owned (MCT, 1999). The only exception is the state-run *Daehan Maeil* (formerly *Seoul Shinmun*) (KPI, 1998a). The 10 major national dailies are the *Kyunghyang Shinmun, Kook-min Ilbo, Dong-A Ilbo, Munhawa Ilbo, Daehan Maeil, Segye Ilbo, Chosun Ilbo, Joong-ang Ilbo, Hankyoreh*, and the *Hankook Ilbo*; the five economic dailies are the *Naeway Kyungje Shinmun, Maeil Kyungje, Seoul Kyungje Shinmun, Jaeil Kyungje Shinmun*, and the *Hankook Kyungje Shinmun*; the four sports newspapers are *Ilkan Sports, Sports Seoul, Sports Chosun*, and *Sports Today*; and the four foreign-language newspapers are *Korea Herald, Korea Times, Asian Wall Street Journal*, and *Han-Joong Ilbo* (MCT, 1999).

Old media families own three of the "Big Four" national dailies—*Chosun Ilbo* by the Bang family, *Dong-A Ilbo* by the Kim family, and *Hangkook Ilbo* by the

---

[2] MCT (http://www.mct.go.kr).

Chang family (KPI, 1998a; Vanden Heuvel & Dennis, 1993). The Samsung group, one of the largest conglomerates, owned the fourth—*Joong-ang Ilbo*, which became an employee-owned daily on March 2, 1999. Until recently, the conglome-rates—the Hyundai group and the Hanwha group respectively—owned the smaller *Munhwa Ilbo* and *Kyunghyang Shinmun.* When the two conglomerates relinquished their ownership of the two newspapers after the 1997 economic calamity, the newspapers' own employees took over ownership and operation (KPI, 1998a).

Religious organizations also own Seoul-based national newspapers. A funda-mentalist Protestant religious group led by Rev. Yong-Ki Cho established *Kookmin Ilbo* after the enactment of the 1987 Periodicals Act. Also, the church organization of Rev. Sun-Myung Moon publishes the *Segye Ilbo*, often giving away its copies for free.

Hankyoreh (One Nation Daily, formerly *Hankyoreh Shinmun*), on the other hand, exhibits an atypical ownership pattern (Han, 2000). The paper started in 1988 with an original capital of US$ 7 million amassed by more than 60,000 small shareholders through a nationwide campaign for an alternative source of opinion and information. A group of progressive journalists dismissed by the establishment newspapers during the Park and Chun administrations founded it in December 1987. Even though national security agents raided its newsrooms and succeeded in sending its advertising manager to prison in May 1989, *Hankyoreh* received donations exceeding US$ 17.7 million from its readers and supporters to expand its facilities (Youm, 1996).

Newspapers in South Korea are going through a painful transition to "slim down" and to minimize the decline in profits. Most are returning to the pre-1987 organ-izational framework. The most obvious structural change is the reintegration of similar functions and operations under bigger umbrella departments, thereby merging sectionalized editorial functions as well. Major newspapers have merged the general affairs and projects-and-plans departments and brought together advertising and business branches to maximize marketing potential. They have either closed down foreign correspondent bureaus or fused them into a few major posts. Such structural transformation has resulted in massive layoffs (KPI, 1998b).

3.4 Quality and Popular Press

Korean journalists are collectively often referred to as a social "tocsin," literally, a wooden gong that monks use in prayer. Historically, this image of journalists is related to that of "off-court" Confucian scholars of the Chosun Dynasty: anti-establishment intellctuals with a vocational calling to awaken and educate the general populace. Nam (1982) characterized Korean newspapers "as a press with a political mission" that "assumed the leadership role" (p. 134). This tradition has attracted highly educated and critical intellectuals to journalism (Vanden Heuvel & Dennis, 1993, p. 20).

From this perspective, three national dailies—*Dong-A Ilbo, Chosun Ilbo*, and *Hankyoreh*—may well qualify as "quality newspapers. Although political influence or commercial interests have swayed many journalists, those at *Dong-A Ilbo* and *Chosun Ilbo* strove to live up to the "tocsin" image during the Japanese occupation and through the subsequent series of dictatorial governments. Thus, they joined the Free Press Movement of the 1970s. To evince their concern for journalistic integrity, a number of courageous journalists who worked for other major national dailies joined *Hankyoreh*, which has struggled to maintain independence from both governmental influence and commercial interests since its establishment.

Considering their influence on public opinion, one can classify newspapers such as *Joong-ang Ilbo, Hankook Ilbo, Kyunghyang Shinmun, Munhwa Ilbo, Kookmin Ilbo*, and *Daehan Mail* as the second-tier quality press.

The popular press is generally sensational and profit-driven to a higher degree. Established major newspaper companies publish a number of popular publications (Won, 1991b): *Feel, Ilkan Sports, CALLA, Sports Seoul, Sunday Seoul, News & People, Jookan Chosun*, and *Ilyo Shinmun*.

3.5 Distribution and Technology

Home delivery is the dominant form of newspaper distribution in Korea. In 1998, home deliveries accounted for 91.5 percent of daily newspaper sales; single copy sales, 7.3 percent; and postal deliveries, 1.1 percent (WAN, 1999). On the other hand, newsstands sell more than one-half of sports newspapers while home delivery and mail take care of the rest (Yonhap Tongshin, 1995).

Since 1991, national newspapers such as *Kyunghyang Shinmun, Dong-A Ilbo, Chosun Ilbo, Joong-ang Ilbo, Hankook Ilbo*, and *Daehan Maeil* started simultaneous printing and same-day distribution through their regional printing plants to reduce transportation costs (KPI, 1998a; Won, 1991b). In the 1970s and 1980s, the big four dailies—*Chosun Ilbo, Dong-A Ilbo, Joong-ang Ilbo*, and *Hankook Ilbo*—had expanded their distribution overseas to Los Angeles, New York, Singapore, and Sau Paulo using the Tele-press system, which sends computerized page layouts via satellite (Won, 1991b).

By the mid-1980s, most newspapers replaced typesetting machines with offset printing presses. With the advent of free-market competition in 1987, newspaper publishers invested heavily to expand their businesses with new office buildings, printing plants, and high-speed and high-capacity presses. Major newspapers adopted the computerized typesetting system to speed up the process of information input and output. *Chosun Ilbo* and *Joong-ang Ilbo* have used CTS since 1992 and *Dong-A Ilbo* since 1994 (Won, 1991b). Now all major national dailies use CTS technology enabling field reporters to use personal computers linked to the central computer in their companies (KPI, 1998a).

Maeil Kyungje has served its readers by providing stock information through MEET on the Internet since 1988. *Hankook Kyungje Shinmun* and *Joong-ang Ilbo* have operated KETEL and Joong-ang JOINS service, respectively, as their database systems since 1989 (Won, 1991b). Most major newspapers have established their own databases, which the readers can access freely on the Internet. These include World Net (*Kyunghyang Shinmun*), Korea NewsNet (*Daehan Maeil*), Digital Chosun (*Chosun Ilbo*), Internet Hankyoreh (*Hankyoreh*), and MIDAS Dong-A (*Dong-A Ilbo*).

4. BROADCASTING

The economic crisis of 1997 set the wheels in motion to open the mass media industry to wider competition, both domestic and foreign. The year 2000 is the key transitional point into the era of free-market competition. Traditional players can no longer count on an oligopolistic media market.

4.1 Policy and Legal Framework

Three laws have allowed the Korean government to control the ownership and programming of the country's broadcasting industry: the 1987 Broadcast Act (as amended in 1989, 1990, 1991, 1995, and 1998), which covers the overall broadcasting industry; the 1987 Korea Broadcasting System Act (as amended in 1989 and 1990), which covers the state-owned broadcasting system; and the 1980 Korea Broadcasting Advertising Corporation Act (as amended in 1982, 1989, 1990, and 1993), which makes KOBACO the exclusive sales agent of broadcast advertising under the supervision of the Ministry of Culture and Tourism (MCT). Under these laws, MCT has the authority to draft and execute basic policies governing Korean broadcasting in general. The Ministry of Information and Communication (MIC) deals with administrative duties related to broadcast technologies and licensing. The Korean Broadcasting Commission (KBC) determines the operational and programming aspects. The KBC consists of nine members appointed by the president for three-year terms. The president appoints six of them from nominations received from the speaker of the National Assembly and the chief justice of the Supreme Court (KPI, 1998a).

The KBC supervises "quality" programming, "impartiality," and "public accountability." Programming content must meet with its approval. It screens TV movies, animation films and video, foreign programming (excluding sports and news), and advertising. It can take punitive action against broadcasters who violate KBC standards, through warning or by seeking a clarification, correction, retraction, or apology, as well as by cancelling the violating program or suspending a performance. Violators must broadcast the full text of the KBC decision within seven days of receiving the order. The 1997 Act relating to the Protection of Minors empowers the KBC to order broadcasters to air only after 10 p.m. those programs that are deemed harmful to minors (KPI, 1998a).

4.2 Structure and Organization

4.2.1 Radio

South Korea has four national radio networks (KBS, MBC, CBS, and EBS), five specialized radio broadcasting companies (PBC, BBC, FEBC, ABS, and TBS), and six local commercial radio stations (SBS, PSB, TBC, TJB, KBC, and K-FM).

4.2.1.1 The national radio networks: The Korea Broadcasting System (KBS) operates seven radio channels (Radio 1, Radio 2, FM 1, FM 2, Radio Korea International, Voice of Love, and Liberty Program Service) with 26 regional stations. Munhwa Broadcasting Corporation (MBC) provides three radio channels (AM, FM, and Standard FM) covering 96 percent of the Korean peninsula through 20 "owned and operated" local stations. Christian Broadcasting System (CBS) operates a national network service through seven AM stations and three FM stations. Although Educational Broadcasting System (EBS) lacks its own regional stations, it serves national listeners by utilizing the relaying and transmitting facilities of KBS.

4.2.1.2 The specialized broadcasting companies: The Buddhist Broadcasting System (BBS) operates five FM stations as a religious radio network. The Peace Broadcasting Corporation (PBC), a Catholic enterprise, operates three FM stations. Two overseas Christian radio services, the Far East Broadcasting Company and Asia Broadcasting Station, operate three FM stations (FEBC) and one AM station (ABS). The Traffic Broadcasting System (TBS) operates three FM stations that specialize in traffic issues and information.

4.2.1.3 The local commercial radio stations: Providing an FM service in specific localities are the Pusan Broadcasting (PSB), Taejeon Broadcasting (TJB), Taeku Broadcasting (TBC), Kwangju Broadcasting (KBC), and Kyungki FM (K-FM). These local stations have contracted a program relay agreement with Seoul Broadcasting System (SBS) to receive parts of SBS radio programming (KPI, 1998a; MCRCKU, 1998).

4.2.2 Television

South Korea has two public broadcasting networks (KBS and MBC), one commercial network (SBS), and eight local private broadcast stations (KBC, TBC, TJB, PSB, UBC, ITV, JTV, and CJB). It also has one government-owned educational broadcasting network (EBS) and cable television companies (77 system operators, 29 program providers, and 20 network operators). Contemporary Korean viewers enjoy about 45 television channels including five terrestrial broadcast channels (KBS1 & 2, MBC, SBS, and EBS), 30 cable channels, four satellite channels (KBS1 & 2 and EBS1 & 2), and six foreign satellite channels (KPI, 1998a; MCRCKU, 1998, p. 33).

4.2.2.1 Public broadcasting networks: The Korean Broadcasting System (KBS) operates two television channels (KBS-1 and KBS-2) with 23 regional stations. KBS has 931 relaying and transmission facilities with 97 percent nationwide coverage. It has three subsidiaries under its management: the KBS Cultural and Video Business Group, KBS Facility Maintenance Company, and KBS Art Vision. (In 1998, the KBS Production Team, a KBS subsidiary, separated from its mother company and privatized itself.) KBS is organized under six departments: programming operations, news and sports, television, radio, broadcasting, and engineering and administration.

Munhwa Broadcasting Corporation (MBC), another leading broadcasting network, also combines both public and commercial characteristics. It operates one television channel and three radio channels (AM, FM, and Standard FM) covering 96 percent of the Korean peninsula through 19 "owned and operated" local stations. It has six subsidiary companies including MBC Production Corporation, MBC Media Tech Company, MBC Academy, MBC Art Center Company, MBC Art International and MBC Adcom (KPI, 1998a).

4.2.2.2 Commercial network: Seoul Broadcasting System (SBS) is the only private commercial network in Korea. Owned and operated by 31 private companies, it has one television channel and two radio channels (AM and FM) primarily covering the vicinity of Seoul, though expanding to nationwide coverage through a programming alliance with eight private local stations. Advertising is the only source of SBS funding. SBS is organized into seven divisions (news, production, planning and programming, media events, sports, radio, and administration) and five branch companies (SBS Art & Technology, SBS News Service, SBS Production, SBS Broadcasting Academy, and SBS Culture Foundation).

4.2.2.3 Local private broadcast stations: Since 1995, eight private television stations have served local audiences in eight provinces. All these stations are independent companies but they occasionally join programming alliance with SBS network in Seoul. Only ITV in Inchon province is capable of filling 100 percent programming through in-house production.

Cable television took off in March 1995—after four years of experimental service (Youm, 1998)—to meet the high demand for advertising time. Korea has 77 system operators, 29 program providers, and 20 network operators offering 30 cable channels (Table 5). Tongyang Group is a major player in this field operating three channels through its Orion Cinema Network—DCN, BTV, and Tooniverse. With the removal of legal restrictions on foreign investment in 1999, the Korean cable industry has undergone dramatic changes in ownership. One million households subscribed to cable TV in 1999 (Yonhap Tongshin, 1998; Korea Cable Television Association, 1999).[3]

---

[3] Korea Cable Television Association (http://www.kcta.or.kr).

4.3 Program Policies and Trends

Korean broadcast programming was geared toward national and political interests until the 1980s. In the 1990s, ratings and competition among major broadcast networks have determined the programming. Because all three networks (KBS, MBC, and SBS) rely partly or mainly on advertising, extreme competition is at play to attract larger audiences. With the introduction of SBS (1991), cable television (1995), local private stations (1995), and satellite broadcasting (1996), Korean broadcasting has become extremely commercialized. Entertainment programming, especially prime time drama and mini-series, leads the change. The four networks are engaged in head-to-head competition for prime time supremacy. The present competitive situation is expected to be even fiercer with the restructuring plan for market-driven liberalization.

In terms of radio programming trends, the Broadcasting Act mandates AM broadcasting stations to balance "news," "entertainment," and "culture and education." Thus, most AM stations carry comprehensive programming while FM channels have specialized programming strategies (Table 6). For example, KBS FM-1 focuses exclusively on classical music while KBS FM-2 concentrates on popular music (MCRCKU, 1998).

Variety shows, sitcoms, news, melodrama, and comedies mostly fill the prime time slots of Korean television. In particular, serial drama and music variety programs are popular genres targeting mainly women and teenagers. Three TV networks produce more than 80 percent of their programming in-house to fill 14 hours of airtime a day (early morning: 6 a.m.–11 a.m., early evening: 4 p.m.–7 p.m., prime time: 7 p.m.–10 p.m., late night: 10 p.m.–1 a.m.). To transform the monopoly structure of network production and encourage independent TV productions, the government, in 1998, designated that 18 percent of the networks' airtime be allotted to "bought-in" domestic programming (Kang & Kim, 1994; MCRCKU, 1998).

The three networks have attempted to mollify critics by declaring an end to rating-competition and a reduction in entertainment programs. However, they have never implemented these promises in concrete form. In particular, the decrease of advertising revenue after the economic crisis (Table 4) has created more commercialized programming with networks attempting to attract advertisers. In this environment, the networks have introduced more programs that require lower production costs, such as talk shows, newsmagazines, and situation comedies.

4.4 Ownership and Financing

The ownership structure of the Korean broadcasting industry has experienced various changes since 1945: the government-owned system (1945–54), the cohabitation of the government-owned and private-owned systems (1955–73), the cohabitation of the public system and commercial systems (1973–80), the public broadcasting system (1980–91), and the cohabitation of the public broadcasting system and the commercial systems (1991 to the present). Rapid economic growth and the monopoly market structure made broadcasting a profitable enterprise. Broadcasting makes up the biggest portion in terms of scale of industry (US$ 1,546 million) compared with the video industry (US$ 577 million), cable television (US$ 223 million), and the film industry (US$ 200 million) (IKBD, 1998).

The major TV and radio networks in Korea, KBS and MBC, are public corporations. KBS receives funds from a mandatory TV subscription fee (KBS-1 TV, 100 percent; and KBS-2 TV, 39 percent) and advertising fees from radio and television (KBS-2 TV and KBS Radio-2, 61 percent) (KPI, 1998a). The Foundation for Broadcasting Culture, which the government created through the 1987 Act, owns 70 percent of MBC stock while the private Foundation for Chung-Soo Scholarship owns the remaining 30 percent. MBC relies on advertising for 95 percent of its revenue. Although KBS and MBC serve as public broadcasters, they operate like private business corporations because they depend partly (like KBS) or primarily (like MBC) on advertising. The Ministry of Education operates the EBS network (KPI, 1998a). In 1998, MBC received the biggest share of advertising revenue—US$ 474 million or 43.6 percent, followed by KBS (28.9 percent) and SBS (19.4 percent) (*Hankyoreh*, February 19, 1999).

Major religious institutions own and operate broadcasting services, such as ASIA, FEBC, PBC, BBS, and CBS. They also depend heavily on advertising. Other broadcasting stations are privately owned: the SBS network, KBC, TBC, TJB, PSB, UBC, ITV, JTV, and CJB. Advertising is their only source of funding. By law, *chaebols* or local conglomerates are prohibited from owning broadcasting business but they participate in the cable industry indirectly through their branch companies.

The Korea Broadcasting Advertising Corporation, a government agency that sets the advertising rates, has maintained a monopoly over the entire broadcast advertising industry in Korea since its establishment in 1981. By law, both local and foreign advertisers must deal with KOBACO to buy broadcasting airtime. The Broadcasting Act limits advertising time to 10 minutes per hour and prohibits the insertion of advertisements, except within sportscasts. This law has created a shortage of available airtime for small advertisers and international companies because fewer than 10 Korean companies control 95 percent of the limited commercial time (Yoon, 1994 [http://www.koreaherald.co.kr/kh1021/m1021619.html]).

5. NEW ELECTRONIC MEDIA

5.1 Internet and On-line Media

Use of personal computer communication and the Internet has exploded in South Korea. PC communication has been extremely popular since 1995, though DACOM established its first service, Chollian I, in 1986 and Chollian II in 1988. ITU (1999a, 1999b) has estimated that South Korea had 7.2 million PCs in 1998, a penetration of 15.68 PCs per 100 people. The country had an estimated 388,256 Internet hosts in July 1999, a density of 8.28 per 1,000 people (Internet Software Consortium, 1999 [www.isg.org]). On-line services over PC communication had 5,275,900 customers by February 1999 (Table 7). According to the Ministry of Information and Communications, the country had 37,364 registered domains on the Internet by July 1999.

The growth of Internet users has caused all broadcasting networks—KBS, MBC, and SBS—to provide "intercast" services that allow viewers to access interactive broadcast programming on the Internet: simultaneous broadcasting, video-on-demand, and news-on-demand. SBS created 20 episodes of the animation series *Boong-ka-Boo* and offered them exclusively on the Internet. A number of newspapers—including *Chosun Ilbo, Ilkan Muyok* (Daily Trade News), *Dong-A Ilbo, Joong-ang Ilbo, Korea Herald, Korea Times, Hankyoreh, Munhwa Ilbo, Daehan Maeil, Hankook Ilbo, Segye Ilbo*, and *Kyunghyang Shinmun*—publish on-line editions as well.

Since Internet TV, an on-line broadcasting company, established its first service in 1997, Koreans have had access to some 30 Internet-casting sites. Most such sites—Korea Music, Korea Internet Broadcasting for Teens, Muchapyul, Cintelcast, Christian TV, Christian Internet Broadcasting, and GBN—offer music, entertainment, or religious programs (*Joong-ang Ilbo*, January 10, 1999).[4] Also, *Digital DDanji*, a cyber journal that satirizes the traditional press, has gained extreme popularity among young "netizens."

5.2 Telecommunciations Infrastructure

In 1998, South Korea had 23.8 million main telephone lines—an overall telephone density of 51.7 per 100 people. Also, by February 1999, the country had 16 million mobile phone subscribers (Table 8)—a penetration rate of 35.5 percent (NSO, 1999). The network has the benefit of several submarine links, including the fiber-optic link around the globe (FLAG) and SEA-ME-WE-3 cable system. It is also linked to KoreaSat system. Two Korean earth terminals are under construction to link the low-earth orbit satellite system (LEO) with existing communication facilities (APT, 1998, 1999).

Another development was the launching of KoreaSat, Korea's first multipurpose, commercial broadcasting and communication satellite, in 1995. Currently, Korea has three KoreaSats (1, 2, and 3) covering the East Asia service area for telecommunication and digital broadcasting. Officially, no Korean-owned satellite broadcasting service is in operation because KBS-2 channel is only running trials on a limited basis. Financial problems in the cable industry and the lack of legal foundations have caused KBS and EBS to delay offering a full satellite-broadcasting service, which may become a reality if the National Assembly were to enact a

---

[4] *Joong-ang Ilbo* (http://www.joongangilbo.co.kr).

unified law on broadcasting and telecommunication in 1999 (*Hankyoreh*, February 12, 1999).

Korean broadcasters will offer digital broadcasting in 2001 after conducting test runs in 2000. They have already developed related technologies for HDTV operation through alliances with various research institutes. For the terrestrial digital TV broadcasting service, Korea has adopted the advanced television system committee (ATSC) standard of the United States (*Korea Herald*, May 18, 1998).[5]

6. POLICY TRENDS FOR PRESS AND BROADCASTING

Korean media face a series of radical changes as they get enmeshed in "liberalization," "competition," and "globalization." The Korean government has encouraged the self-reformation of the press within the framework of a liberal market economy. Backed by the emerging groups of civil society, as well as the press unions, the government has pushed for the independence of the press from *chaebols*, media barons, and political pressure. In 1999, plans were introduced to revise the Periodical Act in order to de-regulate the industry and allow greater competition (*Hankyoreh*, February 26, 1999; *Korea Herald*, February 27, 1999).

The government announced an ambitious five-year plan in 1998 to reconstruct the cultural infrastructure of the nation to boost five "strategic" cultural industries— video production, computer games, animation, music records, and film production—through governmental subsidies and a unified law de-regulating visual-entertainment industries (*Korea Herald*, October 21, 1998). In 1999, the Broadcasting Reform Committee (BRC), a temporary consulting committee to the president, announced its reformation plan to guarantee public interest and political independence of broadcasting while boosting the visual-entertainment industry (*Hankyoreh*, February 26, 1999). Kim (1996) has argued that "the Korean public broadcasting system has actually never been a public system" because, despite continuing emphasis on "publicness," it had amassed "a large amount of capital by exploiting the state-protected duopoly" for more than a decade (p. 93). To avoid this uncanny mixture of "public" and "commercial" interest, the BRC has proposed the elimination of advertising from KBS and the privatization of MBC (*Hankyoreh*, February 26, 1999). In particular, the proposed unified law will provide a legal framework to cover broadcasting, cable television, satellite television, and the broadcast advertising market. If the National Assembly were to pass this legislation, it would wrap up more than a decade of debate since 1987 among the government, scholars, media industries, and social organizations. In the tug of war to maintain or extend each party's interest, the Korean media have gone through trial and error throughout the 1990s, stuck precariously between "political interest" and "commercial interest." The new legislation would mirror the outcome of consistent tension among these interests. Thus, it would set the legal framework to prevent any form of monopoly power in the culture industry—a response to the long history

[5] *Korea Herald* (http://www.koreaherald.co.kr).

of authoritarian government control, on the one hand, and extreme commercialism, on the other.

7. MAIN ISSUES

● Massive layoff and union movement

Media organizations had laid off about 4,150 employees between the IMF bailout in December 1997 and April 1998 (*Hankyoreh*, May 14, 1998; KPI, 1998b). Because of continuing economic difficulties in the media industry, more layoffs are likely in the process of organizational downsizing and restructuring. The Korean Federation of Press Unions, as well as civil rights organizations, have taken up cudgels against the layoffs. In 1998, various labor unions and citizens' groups formed the *Ul-Ron-Kae-Hyuk Simin-Nyun-Tae* (the Citizens' Alliance for a Better Press). It pledged to fight for the reformation of the press through changes in legal and media structures, media education, and a push for alternative media. In particular, the alliance aims to establish editorial independence by de-linking it from the management and to fight against monopoly ownership by big capital and media families (*Hankyoreh*, February 26, 1999; Shim, 1998).

● Legal and ethical issues

Youm (1998) points out that "the Korean press now confronts more legal and ethical issues than ever before" (p. 188). People have been suing the news media "in explosive frequency" for defamation and breach of rights to privacy. Although such recourse to law has become a "a new weapon against critical news coverage," it also reflects the public concern about the responsibility of the press inasmuch as "envelope journalism, plagiarism, and press clubs have changed little" since the authoritarian period (p. 189).

● The BRC report

In February 1999, the Broadcasting Reform Committee—made up of government officials, scholars, politicians, and representatives of the broadcasting industry—released its report on restructuring the broadcasting industry. To ensure the independence of the Korean Broadcasting Commission from political influences, it proposed the funding of KBC with public assets and the nomination of three of the nine commissioners from citizens' groups. It also proposed permitting *chaebols*, media organizations, and foreigners to own up to 33 percent of satellite and cable companies. It suggested empowering media consumers and media professionals to ensure viewers' rights, editorial independence, and creative control. It also proposed an end to the 18-year monopoly of KOBACO in the advertising market, the elimination of advertising from KBS, and the privatization of MBC. Moreover, it proposed the establishment of EBS as an independent public institution, as well as the establishment of a Unified Committee for Broadcasting and Telecommunication (*Hankyoreh*, February 26, 1999).

● Import of Japanese cultural artifacts

The Korean government has decided to lift a 52-year-old prohibition against the import of Japanese comic books, magazines, and award-winning movies as the first step towards opening up to Japanese pop culture. Products of the Japanese pop culture are banned officially because of the deep animosity of Koreans towards their former colonial rulers. This governmental decision has generated hot debate. Japanese broadcasting has been made available from early 2000 (*Korea Herald*, October 28, 1998).

● Prospects

The proposed media reformation in Korea will create new tensions between freedom and the public responsibility of the press. It will focus attention on the issue of quality in respect to the electronic media: whether the new environment will bring genuine diversity, or just new channels for the audience. As Korean media history testifies, the politics of the pendulum will apply again some years later. If the Korean media simply join the global homogenization toward entertainment business without promoting its uniqueness, the globalization and liberalization of the media will be reduced to another trial and error from which it will be hard to recover.

8. STATISTICS

Table 1
General Profile

Exchange rate (1999 average)	US$ 1 = 1,189 Won*
Population (mid-1999 estimate)	46.9 million**
Population density (1999)	477.5 per sq km
GNP per capita (nominal) (1999)	US$ 6,810
GDP per capita (PPP) (1999)	US$ 12,445
Geographical size	98,480 sq km
Urban Population	84 percent
Literacy rate	98 percent
Cellular subscribers (March 1999)	16 million

Source: (http://www.nso.go.kr/majorecono/13.htm); * OANDA Historical Currency Table (http://www.oanda.com/converterer/cc_table?lang=en); ** US Census Bureau, International Data Base (http://www.census.gov/cgi-bin/ipc/idbrank.pl); *Asiaweek*, February 4, 2000.

Table 2
Estimated Mass Media Penetration

	Radio receivers		TV receivers		Daily newspapers		
	Number ('000)	*Per 100 people*	*Number ('000)*	*Per 100 people*	*Number*	*Circ'n ('000)*	*Per 100 people*
1980	36,000	94.4	6,300	16.5	30	8,000	21.0
1985	41,000	100.5	7,721	18.9	35	10,000	24.5
1990	43,350	101.1	9,000	21.0	39	12,000	28.0
1995	46,000	102.3	15,000	33.4	62	17,700	39.4
1996	47,000	103.7	15,258	33.6	60	...	...
1997	47,500	103.9	15,900	34.8	...	...	...

Source: UNESCO, 1999.

Table 3
Number of Registered Periodical Publications (March 1999)

Type	Number
Daily	108
Weekly	2,423
Monthly	2,522
Bimonthly	477
Quarterly	874
Biannual	255
Total	6,659

Source: MCT (http://www.mct.go.kr/tonggye/ml.htm).

Table 4
Yearly Trends of Advertising Revenue by Medium

	Revenue (million US$)			Growth rate (%)		
	1996	*1997*	*1998*	*1996*	*1997*	*1998*
Television	1,322	1,290	855	21.8	−2.5	−33.7
Radio	176	192	114	22.1	9.3	−40.7
Newspaper	1,932	1,772	1,120	8.3	−8.3	−36.8

Source: KOBACO, 1999 July; KPI, 1998a.

Table 5
Cable TV Program Genre and Program Provider

Type of programming	Channel/Owner
Public Service	K-TV (National Film Institute) OUN (Broadcasting University) Arirang TV (International Broadcasting Exchange Foundation)
News	YTN (YTN Incorporated)
Business News	MBN (Maeil Kyungje TV Incorporated)
Movies	DCN (Orion Cinema Network Incorporated) Catch One (Samsung Trading Incorporated)
Sports	Sports-TV (Foundation for the Betterment of People's Sports)
Culture	Q Channel (Joong-ang Ilbo) CTN (Centry TV Incorporated)
Entertainment	HBS (Hyundai Broadcasting Incorporated) Drama-Net (Home-Shopping Television Incorporated)
Education	Jae-neung-seu-sev-ro Broadcasting (Jae-neung Education Incorporated)
Golf	Golf Channel (My TV Incorporated)
Medicine/Health	DASOM (Dasom Broadcasting Incorporated)
Music	M.Net (Music Network Incorporated) KMTV (Korea Music Broadcasting Incorporated)
Children	Dae-Kyo Broadcasting (Dae-kyo Incorporated)
Women	DTV (Dacom Inter-park Incorporated) GTV (GTV Incorporated)
Traffic/Travel	Living TV (Traffic Safety Institute)
Religion	PBC-TV (*Pyonghwa* Broadcasting Corporation) BTN (Buddhist Television Incorporated) KCTS (Christian Television Incorporated)
Cartoon	Tooniverse (Orion Cinema Network Incorporated)
Padook	BTV (Orion Cinema Network Incorporated)
Home Shopping	LG Home Shopping (LG Home Shopping Incorporated) 39 Shopping (Home-Shopping Television Incorporated)
Art	Yaeshool-youngwha TV [Artistic Film TV] (Kolon Sporex Incorporated)

Source: MCT, July 1999; Park, 1999.

Table 6
Program Types of Korean Broadcast Networks (Spring 1999)

		News (%)	Cultural/Educational (%)	Entertainment (%)
KBS-1 (100%	1-TV	32.2	46.1	21.7
license fee)	Radio-1	37.4	42.2	20.4
	1-FM	0.0	0.8	99.2 (Music)
KBS-2 (61% adv.)	2-TV	47.0	53.9	35.7
	Radio-2	12.2	48.3	39.5
	2-FM	0.0	6.3	93.7 (Music)
MBC (95% adv.)	TV	22.9	36.7	40.5
	AM	16.0	65.0	19.0
	FM	0.0	58.0	42.0
SBS (100% adv.)	TV	11.8	41.2	47.0
	AM	35.0	40.0	25.0
	FM	0.0	38.1	61.9

Source: Korean Broadcasting Commission, 1999.

Table 7
Number of PC Communication Subscribers

Provider/Owner	Market share (%)	Subscribers
Chollian (DACOM)	28.6	1.51 million
Hitel (Korea PC Telecom)	23.4	1,232,000
Unitel (Samsung SDS)	22.6	1,193,000
NowNoori	16.7	881,200
Netsgo (SK)	8.7	459,100

Source: Ministry of Information and Communication, 1999.

Table 8
Mobile Phone Market (March 1999)

Provider	Market share (%)	Subscribers
SK Telecom	42.0	6,530,000
Korea Telecom Freetel	17.2	2,675,200
Shinsegi Telecom	15.1	2,348,200
LG Telecom	14.8	2,306,500
Hansol PCS	10.9	1,691,300

Source: Ministry of Information and Communication, 1999.

9. USEFUL ADDRESSES

9.1 Major Daily National Newspapers

Dong-A Ilbo
139 Choong-chung-ro-3-ka
Seo-dae-mun-ku, Seoul, Korea
Telephone: (82-2) 361-0114
Fax: (82-2) 361-0444
URL: http://www.dongailbo.co.kr

Chosun Ilbo
61 Tae-pyung-ro-1-ka
Choong-ku, Seoul, Korea
Telephone: (82-2) 724-5114
Fax: (82-2) 724-5109
URL: http://www.chosun.com

Joong-ang Ilbo
7 Soon-hwa-tong Choong-ku
Seoul, Korea
Telephone: (82-2) 751-5114
Fax: (82-2) 751-9809
URL: http://www.joongang.co.kr

Hankyoreh
116-25 Gong-deuk-tong
Mapo-ku
Seoul, Korea
Telephone: (82-2) 7100-114
Fax: (82-2) 7100-210
URL: http://www.hani.co.kr

Hankook Ilbo
14 Joong-hak-tong, Chong-ro-ku
Seoul, Korea
Telephone: (82-2) 724-2114
Fax: (82-2) 739-5928
URL: http://www.korealink.co.kr

9.2 News Agencies

Yonhap News
85-1 Soo-song-tong, Chong-ro-ku
Seoul, Korea
Telephone: (82-2) 398-3114
Fax: (82-2) 738-0820
URL: http://www.yonhap.co.kr

9.3 Broadcasting Networks

KBS (Korea Broadcasting System)
KBS-TV 1&2, Satellite 1&2, AM 1&2, FM 1&2
18 Yoido-tong
Youngdungpo-ku
Seoul, Korea
Telephone: (82-2) 781-1000
Fax: (82-2) 781-4179
URL: http://www.kbs.co.kr

MBC (*Munhwa* Broadcasting Corporation)
MBC-TV, AM, FM
31 Yoido-tong
Youngdungpo-ku
Seoul, Korea
Telephone: (82-2) 780-0114
Fax: (82-2) 784-0880
URL: http://www.mbc.co.kr

SBS (Seoul Broadcasting Corporation)
SBS-TV, AM, FM
10-2 Yoido-tong
Youngdungpo-ku
Seoul, Korea
Telephone: (82-2) 780-0006
Fax: (82-2) 780-2530
URL: http://www.sbs.co.kr

EBS (Educational Broadcasting System)
TV, FM
92-6 Woomyun-tong
Seocho-ku, Seoul, Korea
Telephone: (82-2) 522-8020
Fax: (82-2) 598-9530
URL: http://www.ebs.co.kr

10. REFERENCES

APT (Asia-Pacific Telecommunity). (1998, 1999). *The APT yearbook.* Bangkok: APT.

Cha, B.K. (1987). *Communication hak gae-ron I.* (Introduction to mass communication). Seoul: Saeyung.

Chung, J.C. (1994). Mass culture, media and the popular cultural movement in modern Korean society. In C.W. Kim & J.W. Lee (eds.), *Elite media amidst mass culture: A critical look at mass communication in Korea* (pp. 297–315). Seoul: Nanam.

Chung, R. (1997, February). Hankook bangsong 70 nyeon-sa (Seventieth anniversary of Korean broadcasting), *Broadcasting and the Audience,* 20–27.

Chung, S. (1992). *Hankook Ullron II* (Korean press II). Seoul: Korean Press Institute.

Han, D.S. (2000). The middle classes, ideological intention and resurrection of a progressive newspapers: A South Korean case. *Gazette,* 62, 61–74.

IKBD (Institute for Korean Broadcasting Development). (1998). *Bangsong Hyeonwhang Boko* (A report of Korean broadcasting industry). Seoul: IKBD.

ITU (International Telecommunication Union). (1999a). *Yearbook of statistics: Telecommunication services 1988–1997.* Geneva: ITU.

ITU (International Telecommunication Union). (1999b). *Challenges to the network: Internet for development.* Geneva: ITU.

Kang, J.G., & Kim, W.Y. (1994). A survey of radio and television: history, system and programming. In C.W. Kim & J.W. Lee (Eds.), *Elite media amidst mass culture: A critical look at mass communication in Korea* (pp. 109–136). Seoul: Nanam.

KBC (Korean Broadcasting Commission). (1999, March). *Bangsong Pyunsung Bogo* (A report on broadcasting programming). Seoul: KBC.

KBAC (Korea Broadcasting Advertising Corporation). (1999, July). *Wol-byul Kwang-ko Yung-up Shil-jeok* (Monthly Report of Broadcasting Advertising). Seoul: KOBACO.

Kim, B. (1971). Korea. In J.A. Lent (Ed.), *The Asian newspapers' reluctant revolution* (pp. 88–104). Ames: The Iowa State University Press.

Kim, D.C. (1991) Legal and ethical issues in Korea. (In Korean) In *Hankook Ullron I* (Korean press I) (pp. 158–186). Seoul: Korean Press Institute.

Kim, D.K. (1996). Expansion of the Korean television industry and transnational capitalism. In D. French & M. Richards (Eds.), *Contemporary television: Eastern perspectives* (pp. 91–112). New Delhi: Sage Publications.

Kim, C.W., & Shin, T.S. (1994). A half century of controls, suppression, and intermittent resistance. In C.W. Kim & J.W. Lee (Eds.), *Elite media amidst mass culture: A critical look at mass communication in Korea* (pp. 43–64). Seoul: Nanam.

KPI (Korean Press Institute). (1996, 1998a). *Hankook Shinmun Bangsong Nyeon-kam* (Korean media yearbook). Seoul: KPI.

KPI (Korean Press Institute). (1998b, July). *IMF-wha ullron-sa byeonwha* (IMF and the change of Korean Press). Seoul: KPI.

Lee, S.H. (1999, May). Kwang-ko Shi-jang: Shinmun (Current advertising market of newspaper). *Shinmun-kwa Bangsong,* pp. 3–14.

Lent, J.A. (1974). A reluctant revolution among Asian newspapers. In A. Wells (Ed.), *Mass communication: A world view* (pp. 112–134). Palo Alto: Mayfield Publishing.

MCRCKU (Mass Communication Research Center at Korea University). (1998, December). *Tong-il Daebi Bangsong Che-jae Koo-chuk* (A report on the broadcasting structure of reunified Korea). Seoul: Korea University.

MCT (Ministry of Culture and Tourism). (1999, April). *Jeong-ki Kan-hang-mul Deung-lok-hyun-whang* (A report of periodicals). Seoul: MCT.

Nam, S. (1982). Republic of Korea. In J.A. Lent (Ed.), *Newspapers in Asia: Contemporary trends and problems* (pp. 130–149). Hong Kong: Heinemann Asia.

NSO (National Statistical Office). (1998). *Tongae Nyunkam Bogo* (Annual report of Korean statistics). Seoul: NSO.

NSO (National Statistical Office). (1999, June). *Tongae Bogo June* (Monthly report of Korean statistics). Seoul: NSO.

Park, M. J. (1999, June). Cable TV Tonghap Jinhaeng Hyunwhang-kwa Jeon-mang (Current status of Korean cable television ownership). *Shinmun-kwa Bangsong,* pp. 30–38.

Shim, J. H. (1998, November 5). Watching the watchdog. *Far Eastern Economic Review,* p. 24.

Sussman, L. R. (1999). *Press freedom 1999: News of the century.* New York: Freedom House.

UNDP (United Nations Development Program). (1999). *Human development report 1998.* New York: Oxford University Press.

UNESCO (United Nations Educational, Scientific and Cultural Organization). (1999). *Statistical yearbook.* Paris: UNESCO.

Vanden Heuvel, J., & Dennis, E. E. (1993). *The unfolding lotus: East Asia's changing media.* New York: Freedom Forum Media Studies Center.

WAN (World Association of Newspapers). (1998, 1999). *World press trends*. Paris: WAN.

Won, W. H. (1991a, fall). Hankook shinmun kyongyung-euy silsangkwa kwa-jae (A report on the management of Korean newspaper industry). In *Kaey-kan Sa-Sang* (pp. 147–176). Seoul: Nanam.

Won, W. H. (1991b). Korean press industry. (In Korean) In *Hankook Ullron I* (Korean press I) (pp. 188–240). Seoul: KPI.

World factbook. (1999). Washington, DC: CIA [On-line]. Available: (http://www.odci.gov/cia/publications/factbook).

Yonhap Tongshin. (1995, 1997, 1998). *Yonhap Nyeon-kam* (Yonhap Yearbook). Seoul: Yonhap Tongshin.

Yoon, Y. (1994). Political economy of television broadcasting in South Korea. In C. W. Kim, & J.W. Lee (Eds.), *Elite media amidst mass culture: A critical look at mass communication in Korea* (pp. 191–213). Seoul: Nanam.

Youm, K. H. (1996). *Press law in South Korea*. Ames: Iowa State University Press.

Youm, K. H. (1998), Democratization of the press: The case of South Korea. In P. H. O'Neil (Ed.), *Communicating democracy: The media and political transitions* (pp. 171–193). Boulder, CO: Lynne Rienner.

◆

24

MONGOLIA

Barry Lowe & Shelton A. Gunaratne

1. NATIONAL PROFILE

1.1 Geography

Mongolia is located in central Asia between Russia in the north and China in the south. It has a land area of 1.56 million sq km, making it slightly smaller than Alaska. Its vast area embraces several distinct geographic zones: desert, mountains, forest, permafrost, and grassy plains. The landlocked country has a harsh continental climate with a long and cold winter in which temperatures fall to minus 50 degrees Celsius. The summer is short and warm. Rainfall is low, and constant strong winds contribute to a generally dry climate. The highest point is the 4.374-meter Tavan Bogd Uul. The Gobi Desert lies to the southwest of Mongolia.

1.2 People

Mongolia had a mid-1999 population of 2.6 million, giving it the lowest population density in Asia (US Census Bureau, International Data Base). (A larger population of Mongolians, about 4 million, lives in the Chinese province of Inner Mongolia with smaller populations in Manchuria, Buriyat [Russia], and on the Volga.) Ethnically, more than 90 percent of the population is Mongolian. They speak an ancient Altaic language—Khalkha Mongol. Others include a small community of Kazhaks (4 percent), Chinese (2 percent), and Russians (2 percent). The country's literacy rate is 84 percent and life expectancy 65.8 years (UNDP, 1999).

During the Soviet era, Cyrillic replaced the Mongolian script, a vertical script similar to the now extinct Manchurian written language. Popular support has emerged for a return to the native script. Prior to the Soviet intervention, most Mongolians were adherents of the Tantric or Tibetan sect of Buddhism, which they followed with great devotion. Almost one-third of the male population was cloistered in monasteries. A minority observed the older faith of shamanism, common to a number of communities in Siberia. The communists savagely repressed and largely stamped out religious practice. A strong religious revival has resulted in the building of monasteries and temples around the country (Lowe, 1998b, p. 185). Muslims constitute about 4 percent of the population.

Mongolia has a long history as a sovereign state. It once controlled the largest empire ever known in human history, stretching from the east coast of China to central Europe. The zenith of the Mongol Empire was from the 13th to the 15th centuries. This was, however, followed by a long decline that led eventually to Chinese and Russian dominance. China annexed southern or Inner Mongolia and occupied northern or Outer Mongolia for two centuries until the overthrow of the Qing dynasty in 1911, when a new independent Mongolian state, ruled by a hereditary leader, was proclaimed. Chinese domination returned in 1919 until a Marxist revolt in 1921, when Mongolia regained independence (Freedom House, 1999). But in 1924, a Moscow-backed communist revolt against Mongolia's feudal government gave the Soviet Union virtual control over the new state. The Mongolian People's Revolutionary Party (MPRP) ended the monarchy when the last king of Mongolia died powerless (Williams, 1995). The new regime brutally purged the aristocracy and destroyed nearly all of the powerful Buddhist monasteries. Under the dictator Choibalsan, the country went through a period of terror. An estimated 30,000 monks were slaughtered. Mongolia's population had declined to 600,000 at the beginning of Soviet control (Lowe, 1998b, p. 185).

1.3 Government and Politics

Mongolia became a republic under the 1992 Constitution. It has a unicameral legislature—the *State Great Hural*—comprising 76 members elected by popular vote to serve four-year terms. The president, nominated by parties in *Hural*, is elected by popular vote for a four-year term. The *Hural* also appoints the cabinet and elects the prime minister (*World factbook*, 1999). For administrative purposes, the country is divided into 18 provinces (*aymguud*).

In the wake of the anti-communist revolts that swept Eastern Europe in the late 1980s, Mongolia discarded its socialist government in a peaceful uprising in 1990. However, the ruling Mongolian Peoples Revolutionary Party won a majority of seats in the first free election after adopting a program of free-market reforms. An alliance of democratic parties, which promised to hasten reforms aimed at transferring control of the economy to the private sector, ousted the MPRP in the 1996 parliamentary election. These reforms, however, led to massive job losses and a sharp fall in living standards.

1.4 Economy

The economy is dependent on agriculture with more than half the workforce involved in raising livestock and processing animal products. Despite the importance of the rural economy, urbanization in Mongolia stands at 62 percent with a third of the population living in the capital Ulaanbaatar and another third living in provincial cities and towns. Industrialization began only recently. Many enterprises established by Soviet advisers have collapsed since the overthrow of communism. The country is rich in mineral reserves, including gold, copper, and coals. A number of international mining companies are prospecting for mine sites. Mongolia's exports in 1999 were a mere US$ 0.5 billion, and it had reserves of only US$ 0.1 billion (*Asiaweek*, January 28, 2000).

The elimination of social welfare safety nets has condemned many Mongolians to extreme poverty. Foreign aid, amounting to more than US$ 500 million since 1991, has somewhat offset the trauma that economic restructuring has caused. Mongolia has become the world's biggest per capita recipient of foreign aid. Despite this assistance, the country's gross domestic product in 1997 was about 20 percent below that of 1989, the last year of communism (UN, 1997). The current GDP at purchasing power parity is US$ 3.6 billion with the corresponding per capita GDP at US$ 1,520. The nominal GNP is about US$ 396 (*Asiaweek*, January 21, 2000).

2. DEVELOPMENT OF PRESS AND BROADCASTING

2.1 Brief Early History

Prior to Soviet intervention, Mongolia was a backward, isolated nation with a primitive communications infrastructure. The country had to wait until 1911 for its first mass medium, a short-lived weekly newspaper called *Shine Tol* (New Mirror), which served a small circle of readers in Ulaanbaatar with mainly official news provided by the new government. For most Mongolians, mass communication was not a familiar concept when the new Soviet-inspired regime introduced a mass media framework that conformed to the socialist propaganda model. The organs of the ruling party and other state institutions became the mouthpieces of the new revolutionary government. These media promoted the ideals of socialism. Because literacy was low at the time, the new mass media reached only a small audience comprising educated residents of the capital. *Unen* (Reality/Truth), originally established in the Soviet city of Irkutsk on November 10, 1920, was the first communist-era newspaper, which continued to operate well into the overthrow of the communists 70 years later. The communists started other newspapers and magazines during the first two decades of their rule that closely followed the Soviet model, including the *Namyn Amdral* (Party Life), which began in 1923 as the theoretical organ of the party's central committee; and *Ulaan-od* (Red Star), which began in 1924 as the army newspaper (Urjinbadam, 1982, p. 155). Radio was established in Mongolia in 1934 as another mouthpiece of the party (Williams, 1995). This framework remained intact until the end of the communist era.

2.2 Developments since 1945

2.2.1 The Press

At the close of the Soviet era, the Mongolian press consisted of the following:

- *Unen* (Reality/Truth), official organ of the ruling Mongolian People's Revolutionary Party;
- *Zaluuchudiin Unen* (Reality/Truth for Youth), established in 1924 as the official organ of the Mongolian Revolutionary Youth League;
- *Hudulmuur* (Labor), established in 1947 as the official organ of the Mongolian Trade Union Federation;
- *Ulaanbaataryn Medee* (Ulaanbaatar News), official organ of the capital city administration;
- *Utga Zokhiol Urlag* (Literature and Art), newspaper of the Mongolian Writers' Union
- *Ulaan-od* (Red Star), official organ of the Mongolian Defense Ministry;
- *Pioneeriin Unen* (Reality/Truth for Pioneers), established in 1944 as the official organ of the Young Pioneer Organization; and
- *Sportyn Medee* (Sports News), newspaper of the National Sports Committee.

The titles of these newspapers indicate how closely they mirrored the Soviet press system. They were tightly controlled to project a strict party line and reflected an austere form of communism closer to the Stalinist model than to that of other Eastern Bloc countries in the 1980s. Newspaper publication also reflected the political division of the country, with two levels of newspapers corresponding to the two levels of government: the national government and the *aimak* or provincial governments. Each *aimak* center published its own newspaper, usually a weekly. Darkhan was the only other city apart from the capital to have its own daily newspaper. The country had 23 national and 19 regional newspapers with a combined circulation of about 750,000 (Urjinbadam, 1982, pp. 155–159). In 1990, Mongolia had 45 periodicals nationwide with a combined circulation of 6.36 million (Williams, 1995).

2.2.2 Broadcasting

Mongolia's other media units under communism were the state-owned Mongol Radio-TV network and Ulaanbaatar TV operated by the Ulaanbaatar city administration. Television was established in Mongolia in 1967 (Williams, 1995). Both the radio and TV networks included regional services based in the *aimak* or provincial capitals. These provided local news and factual programming broadcast in conjunction with networked programming provided by the main studios in Ulaanbaatar. Lent (1978) reported that in 1975 Mongolia had 20 city and provincial radio stations, in addition to the single national radio station. Williams (1995) noted that by the time of the democratic revolution, the country had 12 AM stations and one FM station. With regard to television, Lent (1978) reported that the Soviet Union supplied two TV programs via satellite to Mongolia's government-run TV channel. In 1974, Mongolia had an estimated 148,000 radio receivers. It also had 34,000 TV receivers in 1973 (Lent, 1978).

These broadcast institutions, just like the press, reflected a rigorous propaganda approach to public information. Their news bulletins defined the news agenda according to the ruling party's priorities of maintaining social control and promoting acceptance of the party's infallibility. A major emphasis was on education, particularly in relation to imparting socialist values. Fostering social responsibility was a fundamental objective of radio and TV broadcasts. The only foreign content on Mongolian television was program material provided by other "fraternal" socialist nations, deemed suitable for Mongolian audiences in terms of its ideological message.

2.3 Developments since the End of Communism

The overthrow of the socialist regime in a peaceful revolution in 1990 brought immediate demands for the liberalization of the mass media. The first postcommunist government immediately lifted restrictions on private ownership of media outlets and introduced a simple registration system that granted newspaper-publishing licenses on "a no-questions-asked" basis. The response was a virtual stampede of private interest groups applying to register new publication titles. By 1994, Mongolia had some 30 "principal" periodicals, not including three English-language magazines, distributed from the capital (Williams, 1995). However, two years later, some 584 newspaper and magazine titles had been registered. Many ceased publication after only a few issues; others developed small niche markets. Some, however, became mainstream publications, their profitability depending more on reader support than on advertising (Lowe, 1997b, p. 78).

Proprietors of these newspapers included members of a new breed of Mongolian entrepreneurs who saw the business potential of mass media outlets as vehicles of commercial activity. Others included supporters and promoters of the new democratic political parties and journalists who wanted the editorial control that came with running their own publications. However, the motivation for the biggest group of proprietors was profit, pure and simple, and many of the Mongolian newspapers launched in recent years have sought to build circulation on a simple formula of sleaze and sensation. Revenue from newspapers was based, until very recently, on newsstand sales. Advertising is only just becoming a factor in profitability for some of the larger circulation titles. The concept of advertising is still new for Mongolians who had, until the end of communism, lived in a world where even basic display advertising, such as shop signs, were absent. Communists had espoused a severe brand of socialist theory that saw advertising as a pernicious attribute of capitalism (Lowe, 1998b, p. 183).

The evolution of the post-communist Mongolian press as a highly fragmented and uniquely diverse media market is the result of a number of factors:

- A tradition of newspaper reading. Mongolians are a highly literate people with a strong attachment to reading. Their harsh winters encourage this activity.
- Dissatisfaction with the party organs of the communist era. This created a powerful thirst for Western-style newspapers and magazines.
- Popular support for the concept of a free press. This encouraged people to consume newspapers.
- Low distribution costs. Almost 62 percent of Mongolians are urbanized, and most newspaper readers live in the capital and the major provincial cities.
- New access for commercial interests to media ownership. Mongolia's new entrepreneurs are investing in media outlets.
- Low expectations of newspaper quality. Readers have little exposure to quality newspapers. They are, therefore, less critical of low production and content standards.
- Many journalists who worked under the communist system were inspired by the advent of a free press to launch their own newspapers.
- Newspaper production is supported by newsstand sales, not advertising. This makes it much simpler to establish a newspaper because no prior need exists to sell advertising space.
- The cost of production is very low compared to international standards. A newspaper can be launched with a capital outlay of a few hundred US dollars (Lowe, 1997a, p. 46).

3. THE PRESS

3.1 Policy and Legal Framework

Chapter 2 of 1992 Mongolia's Constitution guarantees human rights and freedoms. Article 16 guarantees "freedom of thought, free expression of opinion, speech, press, peaceful demonstration and meetings" (Clause 16) and the "right to seek and receive information except that which the State and its bodies are legally bound to protect as secret" (Clause 17). Because Mongolia had no specific law governing ownership of publishing houses, the Company Law of Mongolia regulated those publishers who had their own presses—Ardyn Erkh, Ulaanbaatar, and Unen. Those who did not have presses had to register as public organizations with the Ministry of Justice (WAN, 1999). No law prohibited foreign ownership of media.

Between 1995 and 1998, the Ministry of Justice had registered 800 newspapers, one for every 3,225 people, but only 304 of those were published in 1998. About 10 percent of these were no more than organizational newsletters. These figures indicate the volatile nature of the Mongolian newspaper industry (WAN, 1999).

On August 28, 1998, the parliament passed the Law on Freedom of Media to create the legal basis to guarantee media freedom and promote democracy and pluralism. The law is founded on the following concepts:

- Both state (official) and public information should be open to the public.
- The public media should be free and independent of the state, its organizations, and officials.
- The state should not control or censor public information.
- State organizations should provide the public with official information and use a press brochure of their own to publish official original texts and explanations of official activities and decisions.

Article 1 of the Law says that its purpose "is to guarantee the rights of Mongolian citizens, stipulated in the Constitution of Mongolia, to freely express opinions, speak and publish." Article 2 forbids the parliament to pass "any laws that limit freedom of media and independence of media outlets." Article 3 says media outlets should bear the responsibility for the information they publish or broadcast while there should not be any control or censorship of public information. This Article also stipulates that the state should not finance the establishment and activities of the organizations that control information published and broadcast by media outlets. Article 4 forbids state organizations from having their own media organizations.

The parliamentary resolution to implement this "Freedom of press and information law" stipulated the following actions when the law came into effect on January 1, 1999 (Press law [On-line]. Available: [http://www.soros.org/mongolia/prelaw98.html]):

- The dissolution of the two state-owned dailies—*Ardyn Erkh* (The Peoples' Right) and *Zasgiin Gazriin Medee* (The Government News)—and of the radio and TV stations, as well as the newspapers and magazines controlled by the provinces (*aymguud*) and governor's chancelleries in the capitals, ministries, agencies, and similar organizations. The resolution prohibited these media from using their original names for the next five years.
- The dissolution of the Department of the Radio and TV Affairs (the State Radio and Television) and the Montsame agency as government coordination agencies and their reorganization as national public media organizations.
- The reorganization of the radio and TV operation under the governor's office in Bayan-Ulgiy Province (in the northwest) as a national public media organization.

The law enacted on January 1, 1999, aimed to unshackle from government control those newspapers, radio and television stations, and other media not already in private hands. Until then, although government policy was to encourage the establishment of a free-market press, government institutions remained prominent in the press industry. This reflected the gentle pace of transition from communism to democracy—a transition that allowed the ruling party, the MPRP, to remain in power until 1996 after it voluntarily discarded its socialist ideology and adopted free-market policies in response to demands for democratic reform. Thus, government media outlets did not retain a strong association with the communist past and became acceptable institutions in the new democratic era.

Under communism, independent media outlets were simply not possible, as all mass communication was subservient to the requirements of the state. No laws were needed to proscribe or prevent alternative media voices so media laws were not considered necessary. After the fall of communism, a vacuum in media regulation remained. With the rapid evolution of Mongolia's freewheeling post-communist press, both the national and local governments began to see a need to provide a legal framework for press regulation. Freedom House (1999) reported the availability of "scores of private newspapers representing diverse viewpoints" (p. 326). Until the first press law was drafted, media regulation was often done on an ad hoc basis. For example, in 1997 the mayor of Ulaanbaatar reacted to complaints about the number of pornographic publications being sold on the city's streets by issuing an ordinance restricting the sale of pornographic newspapers to the precincts of the main Ulaanbaatar post office (Lowe, 1997c).

3.2 Financial Aspects: Circulation, Advertising, Marketing Strategies

A 1997 survey of Mongolian media consumers (PIM, 1997) found that readers supported a wide range of newspapers. The 567 respondents named 89 different newspapers as their newspapers of choice (only 433 respondents said they read newspapers regularly). However, only 24 of these newspapers had been read by more than 10 people from the sample. The remainder had an average of only four readers in the sample. The survey showed a strong preference for the government-owned newspaper *Ardyn Erkh* (People's Right)[1] with 91 percent of respondents saying that they read this newspaper regularly compared to 53 percent for the *Zasgiin Gazriin Medee* (Government News),[2] and 36 percent for the independent *Onoodor* (Today). The most popular of the "yellow" tabloids was *Seruuleg* (Alarm) with 15 percent of respondents claiming to be regular readers. In answer to whether there was a need to choose from a great range of newspapers, 69 percent answered in the affirmative.

Circulation figures for Mongolian newspapers need to be treated with caution (Table 2). The volatile state of the press industry—with new titles appearing and old titles disappearing almost every month—makes it difficult to gauge a single newspaper's readership over a sustained period. Newspapers tend to go in and out of fashion very quickly. Rivals imitate successful titles. With the plethora of titles available on newsstands, readers are tempted to try out new publications. Circulation figures thus tend to vary widely from month to month. Furthermore, no audited circulation figures exist. Government statistics are based on printruns and are woefully out of date.

---

[1] Since January 1, 1999, this newspaper has undergone several changes in name. It now has the title *Udriin Sonin* (Daily News). The newspaper began in 1990 as *People's Right* before the press law took effect on January 1. Afterwards, it was registered as the *National Right* and later became the *Daily Mirror*. But a court instructed the Justice Ministry to withdraw registration under that name, ruling that the newspaper's management had illegally solicited subscriptions and advertising using the name and market position of its state-owned predecessor. The court fined the newspaper US$ 200 and allowed its publication as *Daily News*.

[2] Since January 1, 1999, this newspaper has changed its name to *Zuunii Medee* (Century News).

Circulation figures provided by the Press Institute of Mongolia (PIM, 1998)—estimated from the publishers' claims and data provided by printing houses—indicated sustained support for the two government-owned broadsheet dailies: *Ardyn Erkh* (People's Right) and *Zasgiin Gazriin Medee* (Government News). The Associated Press (AP, 1999) reported that the *National Right* (*People's Right* under government ownership), had 15,000 subscribers, as well as street sales of about 3,000 copies, since the transfer of ownership from the government to the newspaper's employees—down from the previous year's circulation of 30,000. Now known as *Udriin Sonin* (Daily News), its circulation stands at 16,000 although its editor, Jambal Myagmarsuren, has hopes of raising the circulation to 50,000. Both *Udriin Sonin* and *Zuunii Medee* (Century News), which was called *Government News* under state ownership, were up for sale after April 1, 1999, under the provisions of the press law.

The only other daily newspaper *Onoodor* (Today), founded in 1996 after democrats took power from the former communists in national elections, trailed a distant third in the newspapers-of-record stakes. The newspaper with the highest circulation was the weekly *Seruuleg* (Alarm), which sells about 51,000 copies—26,000 subscriber copies and 25,000 newsstand copies (AP, 1999). In 1998, more than 71 percent of the newspaper sales were from single copy sales compared to 28 percent from postal deliveries. This is a change from 1995, when 42 percent of the sales came from postal deliveries (WAN, 1999).

Apart from industry estimates of dubious reliability, no recent data exist on total newspaper circulation. UNESCO (1999) data for 1996 show newspaper sales of 2.7 copies per 100 people—a decline from 10.6 per 100 people in 1980. WAN (1999) estimates show circulation figures of 61,300 for 1995; 55,800 for 1996; 59,000 for 1997; and 50,000 for 1998. Thus, in 1998, newspaper penetration stood at 2.1 percent. The Mongolian Publishers Foundation said the 1998 fall in circulation was the result of non-publication of special promotional papers in a "non-election" year.

Advertisers spent an estimated 962.2 million Tugrik in 1998 compared to 720 million in 1997 (WAN, 1999). The advertising revenue share of newspapers was 48 percent in 1998 compared to 61 percent in 1997. Most of the revenue went to the five dailies, leaving 171 other regular newspapers with just 19 percent of the newspaper advertising market. In 1998, television received 44 percent of advertising revenue compared to 30 percent in 1997. The balance 8 percent in 1998 went to radio—1 percent less than in 1997.[3]

Now that the benefits of media advertising are beginning to be understood, entrepreneurs are realizing that newspapers can be vehicles of profit, as well as of ideology. While some of the successful tabloids have generated solid returns for their investors purely from sales, an increasing demand for advertising space by burgeoning enterprises has created a new economic base for newspaper production. Ringle (1994) reported that Mongolian newspapers had no advertising specialists.

---

[3] The data are from the Central Statistical Department of Mongolia.

Low-paid reporters sold advertisements on the side to earn extra money. More than 80 percent of the revenue of newspapers came from selling copies.

3.3 Structure and Organization

In 1998, Mongolia's top 10 publishing companies, ranked by total copy sales, were Ardyn Erkh, Zasgiin Gazriin Medee, Mongol News, Seruuleg, Tsenkher Delgets, Ulaanbaatar, Huviin Amydral, Shar Sonin, Deedsiin Hureelen, and Unen. In 1998, of the five regularly published dailies, four were national and one local. Of the 15 non-dailies, 10 were national and five local. The regular publications also included four Sunday editions and 132 free papers (WAN, 1999). The important new publications in 1998 were *Mongoliin Medee*, a daily started in December by Erel Company Ltd; *TV Medee* of Mongol Television; *Onoodor—Weekend* of Mongol News Company Ltd; *Zavsarlaga—Time Out* of Tsenkher Delgets; *Nogoodor*; and *Shine Medee. Ulaanbaatar* changed its name to *Ulaanbaatar Times*.

Although state organizations dominated both the print and broadcasting sectors until the end of 1998, media ownership has become increasingly diversified over the recent years. Access to newspaper ownership in Mongolia has become relatively easy, and individuals or small groups of people with relatively modest capital outlays have established many newspapers. However, a recent trend was for fledgling corporations to acquire media outlets and for cross-media ownership. For example, the Mongol News Company, a new mass media consortium (Mongolia's first) owns *Onoodor*, an established and reputable daily broadsheet. This consortium also owns and operates a new FM radio station and a TV channel, Channel 25. As far as free market business practices are concerned, Mongolia is still at the lower end of the learning curve. However, a recent development in media ownership is the interest shown by new Mongolian capitalists who have succeeded in other business ventures. Until recently, most private investment in the mass media was in the broadcasting sector where equipment costs required substantial outlays. However, local entrepreneurs are currently showing interest in acquiring new printing technology, thus indicating a shift in investment priorities.

3.4 Quality and Popular Press

Challenging Mongolia's pre-1999 state-owned press for market share is a long list of newspaper titles that displays a broad range of publishing standards in terms of quality and credibility. At the top end of the independent spectrum are serious daily broadsheets like *Onoodor* that are beginning to acquire the look of capital city newspapers. At the bottom end of the spectrum are eight-page, A-4 size "yellow" newspapers, printed on grainy, gray paper with smudgy type and foggy photographs and filled with gossip and smut.

Although papers like *Onoodor* are striving to raise standards, the majority of outlets in the independent sector collectively display the following characteristics:

- Lack of regular frequency: Many newspapers are published sporadically with no regular pattern of frequency. They go to print when they have sufficient articles to fill them or when sales returns from the previous issue are sufficient to pay for a new printrun.
- A large proportion of the content is sourced overseas and loosely translated for Mongolian readers.
- Many stories are not current. They are chosen for their sensationalism rather than their relevance to contemporary issues in Mongolia.
- Externally sourced news material is used without permission of the copyright holder.
- Most carry very little advertising. Revenue comes largely from newsstand sales.
- The smaller tabloids are often one-or-two-person operations relying partly on freelancers for copy.
- Little variety or originality exists in design and layout.
- Photographic reproduction is generally poor.
- Newspapers are produced on old and primitive technology.
- They make no distinction between straight news and opinion. The two are often mixed in the same story.

Most Mongolian tabloids are not tabloid in size. The market leader *Seruulug* is a broadsheet, as are most of the other well-established weeklies such as *Deedsin Hureleen* (High Society) *Jigshuurt Hereg* (Crime), and *Khumus* (People). Mongolia has no daily tabloids—the only daily newspapers are three relatively sober broadsheets. The tabloids are all weekly or of an even lesser frequency. Many of the less popular titles are published sporadically.

In the battle for readers, magazines and newspapers with names like *Top Secret* and *Long Ear* have filled pages with gossip and scandal. Some publications carry photographs of scantily clad women. The government in 1996 closed one of the most famous newspapers, *Hot Blanket*, for printing pornographic advertisements. With a circulation of 80,000, the newspaper, which came out every 10 days, was one of the most widely read. Its founder, S. Bayarmonkh, a self-styled rebellious journalist known for scoops, has started another newspaper. *Five Rings* covers sports, *Blue Spot* follows Parliament, *Wolf* is full of sex stories, and *Yesterday, Today,* and *The Day After Tomorrow* prefer straight news. From newsstands, Mongolia's news media look to be as free as can be (AP, 1999).

3.5 Distribution and Technology

The continuing market dominance of the pre-1999 government press outlets is also a reflection of the relatively slow growth of the independent press. The independent outlets have had to battle for circulation growth in a weak economy in which the popular enthusiasm for the emergence of a free press has not been matched by market realities. But perhaps the main reason for the resilience of the government-owned media sector in the face of competition from new independent outlets has been the issue of expertise. Until this decade, no organizations or individuals outside of state organs had any experience of operating media outlets in Mongolia. The government newspapers already existed, and the people read them because they were used to reading them. Mongolia's isolation from the rest of the world meant there was little help, or even inspiration, from outside to promote independent media outlets. Of the large amounts of foreign aid that has poured into Mongolia during the last few years, surprisingly little has been earmarked to support mass media reform and development. One exception is a project by the Danish International Development Agency or DANIDA to support the establishment of a media training institute, the Press Institute of Mongolia, and an independent printing house (Ringle, 1994).

Technology for media production in Mongolia is primitive, even by the standards of the developing world. Most of the smaller newspapers are still printed on hot metal presses and newspaper layout is still done manually. Many media establishments are distinguished by their complete lack of computers. The only substantial foreign investment in mass media to date has been in the broadcasting sector, which also suffers from a lack of modern technology. Ringle (1994) reported that only a few newspapers reached the areas outside Ulaanbaatar. Those that reached were not at all timely because of the poor postal service. The local party organizations tended to dominate the weekly newspapers of the provincial centers, thereby weakening those media.

4. BROADCASTING

4.1 Policy and Legal Framework

Under communism, only state organizations could operate broadcasting outlets. The 1998 Media Law (see Section 3.1) stipulated the dissolution of state broadcasting in 1999. Since the transition to democracy, the government has encouraged private interests to enter the broadcasting market. Legal restrictions do not exist on who can establish a broadcasting network, on foreign ownership, or on cross ownership (simultaneous ownership of both print and broadcasting outlets). This framework has enabled foreign interests, South Korean and American, with links to fundamentalist Christian organizations to participate in the establishment of the new Eagle TV network. Lack of regulations on broadcasting standards has allowed another new independent network, Channel 25, to broadcast using the low-quality amateur video format, Super VHS. Freedom House (1999) reported that the "state broadcast media...generally offer[ed] pluralistic views" (p. 326).

4.2 Structure and Organization

4.2.1 Radio

With the recent establishment of three independent radio networks, the state broadcaster, Mongol State Radio, lost the monopoly status that it enjoyed under communism. However, it still enjoys the loyalty of the biggest radio audience. Because no restrictions exist on who can establish a radio network and because of the relatively low cost of the technology required, more independent radio stations are expected to open to cater to a rising demand for broadcast time by advertisers.

Williams (1995) reported that a 1,900-km radio relay from Ulaanbaatar in the north-central part of the country to the extreme western provincial capitals of Altay and Olgii provided radio, television, and direct-dial telephone links. Radio relay lines also ran from the national capital to far eastern provincial capitals of Choybalsan, Sukhbaatar, and Saynshand.

Williams (1995) also observed discrepancies in data relating to the number of radio receivers in use. One set of data showed a decline from 226,200 in 1988, to 222,500 in 1989, to 205,600 in 1990, to under 186,000 in 1995. Another set of data showed a higher number of sets in 1991—some 297,000, which increased to 360,000 in 1993, excluding 443,200 wired radio outlets in urban areas. UNESCO (1999), however, reported 360,000 receivers in 1997—a density of 14.2 per 100 people compared to 10.5 per 100 people in 1985.

4.2.2 Television

The International Telecommunication Union (ITU, 1999) estimated that Mongolia had 150,480 TV receivers in 1997—a penetration of 6.3 per 100 people. In 1990, Mongolia had some 137,400 TV receivers, which declined to 135,705 in 1993. UNESCO (1999) data, however, showed 118,000 TV receivers in 1997 (4.7 sets per 100 inhabitants)—a dramatic increase from 1980 when only three people in a thousand owned TV sets. The penetration of cable television services has been accelerating in recent years, from 1,500 in 1993 (APT, 1999) to 25,800 in 1997 (ITU, 1999). In 1998, more than 30,000 households subscribed to cable television (APT, 1999). Mongolian TV sets received broadcasts from local transmitters or provincial repeaters. In the mid-1990s, these transmitters received their signals from relay lines, landlines, or AsiaSat (Williams, 1995). The Asia-Pacific Telecommunity (APT, 1999) reported that Mongolia's Intelsat earth station uplinked the domestic TV programs to the country's remote TV receivers and also down-linked a variety of regional satellite TV channels for programming in Ulaanbaatar.

4.3 Program Policies

Until recently, the primary language of broadcasting was Mongolian with some special programs in Russian. Williams (1995) wrote that the government-controlled Ulaanbaatar or Mongol Radio (Mongol Yaridz) broadcast two national programs in Mongolian and external services in English, Chinese, Japanese, Kazakh, and Russian. Mongol broadcasting has dropped most of the Russian programs to cater for a new interest in English. Private "English-as-a-second-language" colleges have been proliferating in the population centers to cater to a demand for tuition in English for business; and broadcasters have been increasingly mobilized to support the new focus on English as Mongolia's second language.

Historically, Mongolian TV and radio emphasized educational and informational programs that enshrined the virtues of social responsibility. Traditional culture—Mongolian music, dance, and sports—made up most of the arts content. News programs are now much shorter, and they are becoming more and more objective and critical of governing institutions. Arts program continue to focus on indigenous Mongolian culture—the Mongolian wrestling broadcast by Mongol TV has a consistently high rating—despite an increasing predominance of Western feature films and sitcoms in evening programming schedules.

Williams (1995) wrote that Mongolia received Russian TV programs transmitted via the Molniya satellite and the Orbita ground station in Ulaanbaatar and by the Ekran satellite system. The far western province of Bayanolgiy, where a substantial Kazakh minority lived, received Kazakh television. Satellite TV, such as STAR channels, were available in selected sites, such as "luxury" hotels.

4.4 Ownership and Financing

A 1998 survey (PIM, 1998) showed that the two government TV stations remained the market leaders despite the introduction of private stations. Mongol TV, the state network, had a regular audience of 63 percent, while UB TV, the Ulaanbaatar municipal government's station, had a regular audience of 37 percent. Channel 25, the new commercial station, had 29 percent of the market share. The next most popular broadcaster was Mongolia's cable network with 22 percent regular viewers, followed by the other private free-to-air station, Eagle TV, with 8 percent regular viewers. Mongol State Radio, the state broadcasting service's radio arm, was the market leader among radio listeners with 22 percent regular listeners. The three commercial stations—FM 102.5, Durvun Uul, and FM 107—followed in order of preference.

The government has been injecting some US$ 36 million (3.2 billion tugriks) annually to run the state television and radio broadcasting services, which generated an annual commercial income of about US$ 110,000 (100 million tugriks). From 1999, public funds are being channelled to these services through a self-funding national public broadcasting system.

Approaches to programming are changing rapidly in the broadcasting sector. Under communism, the emphasis was on didactic values and socialist ideology. The only foreign content came from countries with the same approach to broadcasting. TV stations are now showing a large proportion of programming sourced from Western countries, particularly Hollywood feature films. One undesirable outcome of this newfound interest in Western television programming is a tendency towards piracy by local broadcasters who have been known to steal programs from subscription satellite services and to broadcast from videotapes without the permission of the copyright owner.

5. NEW ELECTRONIC MEDIA

5.1 Internet and On-line Media

Mongolia is one of many developing countries that hopes to leapfrog into a prosperous future by adopting new information technology. However, despite the official rhetoric proclaiming the country's commitment to the Internet revolution, adoption of on-line technology and services has been slow. According to the July 1999 survey of the Internet Software Consortium (www.isg.org), Mongolia had just 20 Internet host computers. In 1998, the number of Internet users stood at 3,200 (APT, 1999)—mostly in the NGO, government, and academic sectors. DataCom, established in 1994, is the primary Internet service provider. The government, which is setting up an Internet network for government and public organizations, has not attempted to impose control over Internet service providers. Issues such as access to politically or morally questionable sites have not yet arisen.

Several Mongolian newspapers now publish on-line editions. The first to launch a website was the independent daily *Onoodor* (http://www.MOL.mn/eneeder.htm). The top-circulation former-government paper *Ardyn Erkh* (http://www.MOL.mn/udur_toli), now renamed *Odriin Toli*, soon followed. *Zuunii Medee* (Century News) also has a Web edition (http://www.MOL.mn/zuunii_medee/). Mongolia's two English-language newspapers, *Ulaanbaatar Post* (http://www.MOL.mnub_post.htm) and the *Mongol Messenger* (http://www.MOL.mn/montsame/messenger.htm), both launched their on-line editions in 1997. The *Post*, however, has not updated its Web edition since December 1998.

5.2 Telecommunications Infrastructure

In accordance with the Telecommunications Act promulgated in November 1995, the government established the Communication Regulatory Council to "create an efficient and fair competitive environment" in the telecommunications industry (APT, 1999, p. 296). In December 1997, the government set up an advisory group to coordinate the development of national information and communication technology. The state-run Mongolian Telecommunications Company (MTC) operates the telephone system with about 96,000 subscribers in its network (APT, 1999). International calls are connected via the Intersputnik satellite, which covers the Indian Ocean region. Effective from January 1999, the principle of open competition applied to the manufacturing and installation of telecommunications equipment and networking facilities. However, MTC retains its monopoly on international telecommunication services.

In 1998, Mongolia had 4.1 telephone lines per 100 people (61.6 percent residential), showing a compound annual growth rate of 4.7 percent since 1990, the last year of communism, when there were only 3.2 lines per 100 inhabitants (ITU, 1999). However, the waiting list for new lines remains relatively high at 445,373 people. The number of public payphones has increased from 60 in 1993 to 200 in 1998 while the number of cellular subscribers has increased from 1,200 in 1996 to 5,300 in 1998, a density of 0.22 per 100 people (APT, 1999). ITU, 1999, however, places the cellular subscriber density at 0.08 per 100 people. Access to telefax services also increased dramatically in the first half of the decade, from 350 outlets in 1990 to 5,300 in 1996 (ITU, 1998).

6. POLICY TRENDS FOR PRESS AND BROADCASTING

The Mongolian government has been committed to a policy of privatizing media industries by transferring ownership and control of state-owned media outlets to the private sector. The *Great Hural* has been considering a press law since 1991. A committee of the *Hural*, the Standing Committee for State Structure, began in 1998 to draft a set of media laws and regulations. A major objective was to disengage the state from media ownership. Options considered included transferring control of state-owned media entities to staff, offering the entities for sale to all bidders, or simply closing down the entities and selling their facilities to investors interested in starting new mass media outlets. The committee also considered regulations governing foreign ownership of media entities. At present, for example, South Korean and American interests are majority shareholders in the Eagle TV network (PIM, 1997).

Some journalists have praised the 1998 Media Law as a likely stimulus to competition, but others point to loopholes that they say could pose difficulties for the country's news media. Odsuren Banbab, deputy editor of the state-controlled news agency, has described the law as "good for journalists" because "there will be more competition" (Mower, 1998). Opponents, however, maintain that the press law provides no protection for journalists from harassment or libel suits. Currently, journalists must pay court costs even if they win a lawsuit. They also note that the press law fails to address, specifically, the issue of journalistic access to government information.

Under provisions of the press law, the two state-owned daily newspapers have moved into private ownership without receiving government subsidies. The papers' physical assets (reportedly valued at less than US$ 400,000) were turned over to a State Property Committee, for subsequent auctioning. The government-run television, radio, and news agency will continue to receive public funds, but will come under a self-funding national public broadcasting system modeled on Western examples like the BBC (Mower, 1998). The law, which forbade state ownership of news media and required newspapers to be privatized, immediately caused changes in media outlets that once were mouthpieces of the Communist Party. The law also required them to change their names for at least five years. The *Hural* must yet decide how to implement the Media Law, which requires that 40 percent of the assets of the former state-run newspapers are to be distributed among employees. The law also requires the remaining 60 percent to be auctioned only to buyers having publishing experience. The application of this provision is open to dispute because this may allow former editors and managers of the state-owned enterprise to regain control.

T. Ochirhuu, a member of the *Hural* who helped draft the legislation, has explained that the Media Law would not affect media outlets in the countryside because local governments would decide whether to continue funding publications. A potential problem with the law was that newspapers, radio, and other news-gathering organizations outside the capital city would remain under control of local governments. The absence of a developed advertising and circulation base makes it difficult to envision local newspapers raising adequate revenues without government support.

Although the prevailing philosophy guiding government policy on economic reform is the nurturing of a free market, the Mongolian government has yet to embrace this concept fully in relation to its policy toward media industries. This is not from lack of commitment to these ideals but more from a lack of concrete ideas about how the transfer of government media outlets to the private sector should be managed. The belated progress on this issue also reflects the fact that the national government has other more pressing priorities to deal with, such as the increasing unemployment rate and the widespread poverty and homelessness in the urban centers.

The Media Law was also expected to address other issues, such as anti-monopoly measures, whether to permit cross media ownership (ownership of newspapers and broadcasting outlets in the same market), and whether to regulate the professional practice of journalists. This last issue fueled intense debate within the media industry. On the one hand, there was increasing public concern about ethical standards in the media since the focus of newspaper development has been on an increasingly strident and scurrilous tabloid sector. On the other hand, journalists (represented by the Mongolian Association of Free Democratic Journalists) had protested that any laws to control their activities and their output would be a step back to the dark days of communism, when journalists were controlled rigorously by the state to the detriment of press freedom.

In January 1999, the state news agency reported that, in connection with the ratification of the Media Law and related parliamentary resolutions, the working group of the State System Standing Committee had worked out draft regulations for the amendment of various laws and rules, the properties of media organizations, and the hierarchical structure of media organizations (Montsame [Mongolian News Agency], January 15, 1999). Furthermore, the report said that the standing committee would submit to the *Hural* plenary session the draft rules relating to radio and television, Directing Council of the Mongolian Radio and Television, and the Montsame (Mongoliin Tsakhigaan Medie) national news agency.

The Media Law, despite its critics, is regarded as one of the most important reforms in Mongolia's nine-year effort to dismantle its communist legacy and build a substantial free-market democracy. Supporters of the law have pointed out the state media were not free enough. Others say that little has changed with the new law. *Century News* was given a splash of color for a few days, then reverted to black and white. *Daily News* looks the same as before (AP, 1999). The former state-owned media now have to find buyers. They face a market crowded with publications, most of them private. D. Undraa, an employee of the national news agency Montsame, said, "They will make their money off their prestige and accurate reporting. There is no need for these papers to resort to scandalous press" (AP, 1999).

Freedom House (Sussman, 1999) has placed Mongolia in the "free" press category giving it a restriction score of 30 out of 100. On the criterion of laws and regulations that influence media content, Mongolia received 7 out of 15 for print and 6 out of 15 for broadcast. On the criterion of political pressures and controls on media content, it received 6 out of 15 for broadcast and 3 out of 15 for print. On the criterion of economic influences over media content, it received zero for broadcast and 8 out of 15 for print. On the final criterion of repressive action, it received zero out of 5 for both media.

7. MAIN ISSUES

● The transformation of the Mongolian press from a propaganda mill to a vehicle of free thought and expression is still not complete despite the 1998 Media Law. Freedom of the press is the official policy, but mass media entities remain in the control of state organs. Although these entities no longer have the look of propaganda outlets, they still tend to reflect favorably on the policies and actions of their government controllers.

● Related to the issue of media ownership is the need for more capital investment in the mass media industry, particularly in new technology to modernize media production methods. So far, the only substantial capital investment from abroad has been the South Korean and American money invested in the Eagle TV network. However, the broadcasting networks still have to rely on relatively primitive analog equipment. For example, one of the new networks, Channel 25, uses the SVHS amateur format for broadcasting. The very basic and outdated print technology prevents improvements in production standards.

● Advertising is a relatively new concept for media proprietors in Mongolia. Its adoption will inevitably change the market fundamentals of media production in the country. Newspapers need to give priority to marketing advertising space to enable them to reduce their dependency on newsstand sales. Currently, many newspapers do not even employ advertising sales staff.

● Another crucial issue facing the Mongolian media, particularly the press, is standards and ethics (Lowe, 1998a). In its rush to develop a free and popular press, Mongolia has embraced a hands-off approach toward regulating or critically monitoring media content. Little public concern exists about the garish headlines and lurid photographs that scream sex, crime, and scandal from the front pages of the many tabloids competing for attention on newsstands. An exasperated mayor of Ulaanbaatar recently ordered the most blatantly pornographic newspapers off the streets of the capital to be sold only from the news kiosk in the central post office building. The government, however, clearly wants to avoid regulation of media content lest it would be seen as acting like its communist predecessors.

● A related issue is the professional standards of journalists. During the communist era, journalists were discouraged from taking a critical approach to their work. Their output was based on work practices that most now see as incompatible with the current emphasis on the watchdog function of the press. A number of organizations, particularly the Press Institute of Mongolia, are supporting the efforts to re-train journalists in Western approaches to newsgathering.

● A final issue that is just emerging pertains to the script used for Mongolian newspaper publication. Until recently, all Mongolian newspapers used Cyrillic, introduced by the Soviets during their 70 years of hegemony, for newspaper production. Efforts to revive the traditional Mongolian script, a vertically written script, broadly similar to Persian, have come to the fore during the past few years. Some newspapers are now printing mastheads and headlines in the Mongolian script. Soon, entire articles, sections, or pages are likely to appear in the traditional written language.

8. STATISTICS

Table 1
General Profile

Exchange rate (1999 average)	US$ 1 = 990.84 Tugrik
Population (mid-1999 est.)	2.62 million
Population density	1.6 per sq km
GDP per capita (PPP)	US$ 1,520
GNP per capita (nominal)	US$ 396
Human Development Index ranking	119 (out of 174)
Adult literacy (1997)	84 percent
Urban population	62 percent
Geographic size	1.56 million sq km

Source: *Asiaweek*, January 21, 2000; *World factbook*, 1999; UNDP, 1999; OANDA Historical Currency Table (http://www.oanda.com/converter/cc_table?lang=en).

Table 2
Estimated Circulation Data by Newspaper (1998)

State-owned until end of 1998	
Ardyn Erkh [People's Right/National Right/Daily Mirror/Daily News]. Former publisher: Parliament of Mongolia	25,000* (daily)
Zasgiin Gazriin Medee [Government News/Century News]. Former publisher: Government of Mongolia	13,500* (daily)
Njamgarig [Sunday]	9,000
Private	
Onoodor [Today] Publisher: Mongol News Co.	6,000* (daily)
Mongoliin Medee Publisher: Erel Co. Ltd	3,000* (daily)
Seruuleg [Alarm]	45,000–51,000
Il tovchoo [Open History]	N.A.
Deedsin Hureleen [High Society]	21,000
Shar Sonin [Yellow Paper]	13,000–15,000
Bi, Bi, Bi [Me, Me, Me]	12,000
Hoh Tolbo [Blue Spot]	8,000–12,000
Mongoliin neg udur [Mongolian Day]	10,000
Khumuus [People]	10,000
Jigshuurt Hereg [Crime]	12,000
Others	
Ulaanbaatar Times (UB Municipality owned)	3,500* (daily)
Unen [Reality] (MPRP: party-owned)	5,000–6,000

Source: *WAN, 1999; PIM, 1998.

Table 3
Radio Broadcasting (1998 Estimate)

Station	Market share
Mongol State Radio	39 percent
FM 102.5	35 percent
Durvun Uul	18 percent
FM 107	8 percent

Source: PIM, 1998.

Table 4
TV Broadcasting (1998 Estimate)

Station	Market share
Mongol State TV	35 percent
UB TV	22 percent
Channel 25	19 percent
Cable TV	15 percent
Eagle TV	9 percent

Source: PIM, 1998.

Table 5
Telecommunications and the New Media

Number of telephones per 100 people (1998)	4.1
Number of fax machines per 1,000 people (1997)	2.5
Number of Internet host computers (1999)	20
Number of Internet subscribers (1998 estimate)	3,200
Electric power capacity (1995)	900,000kW

Source: ITU, 1998, 1999; APT, 1999.

9. USEFUL ADDRESSES

A longer list of media contacts is available on the Web at: (http://www.soros.org/mongolia/mongcont.html).

Press Institute of Mongolia
P.O. Box 46/600
Ulaanbaatar, Mongolia.

Montsame (Mongolian news agency)
C.P.O. Box 1514
Ulaanbaatar-13, Mongolia

Mongolian Free Democratic Journalists' Association
P.O. Box 36/236
Ulaanbaatar-210136, Mongolia.

Onoodor (daily newspaper)
Ekh toiruu, Ulaanbaatar-20, Mongolia.

10. REFERENCES

AP (Associated Press). (1999, February 5). Bevy of publications emerges as new media law takes effect in Mongolia. *The Freedom Forum* [On-line]. Available: (http://www.freedomforum.org/international/1999/2/5mongolia.asp).

APT (Asia-Pacific Telecommunity). (1998, 1999). *The APT yearbook*. Bangkok: APT.

Freedom House Survey Team. (1999). *Freedom in the world: The annual survey of political rights and civil liberties, 1998–1999.* New York: Freedom House.

ITU (International Telecommunication Union). (1998, 1999). *World telecommunication development report.* Geneva: ITU.

Lent, J. A. (Ed.). (1978). *Broadcasting in Asia and the Pacific: A continental survey of radio and television.* Philadelphia: Temple University Press.

Lowe, B. (1997a). Mongolia's bid for free media is stifled by a lack of standards. *Media Development, 44* (3), 44–66.

Lowe, B. (1997b). Mongolia's media at the crossroads. *Nieman Reports, 51* (3), 78–79.

Lowe, B. (1997c, March 18). Fledgling free press threatened by its own zeal. *Gemini News Service.*

Lowe, B. (1998a). *Ethics training for Mongolian journalists* (Report submitted to the Freedom Forum in Hong Kong). Hong Kong: City University of Hong Kong.

Lowe, B. (1998b). Of mushrooms and Mongolia. *Index on Censorship, 28* (2), 181–187.

Mower, J. (1998). Mongolian press law approved; provisions divide journalists. *The Freedom Forum* [On-line]. Available: (http://www.freedomforum.org/international/1998/10/19mongolia.asp).

PIM (Press Institute of Mongolia). (1997). *Mass media survey of Mongolia.* Ulaanbaatar: Press Institute of Mongolia.

PIM (Press Institute of Mongolia). (1998). *Survey on media advertisement.* Ulaanbaatar: Press Institute of Mongolia.

Ringle, W. (1994). *A hope still unfilled: Free press in Mongolia—a report for the Freedom Forum* [On-line]. Available: (http://www.freedomforum.org/freedomforumtextonly/resources/international/asia/mongolia/mongolia.html).

Sussman, L. R. (1999). *Press freedom 1999: News of the century.* New York: Freedom House.

UN (United Nations). (1997). *Statistical yearbook* (42nd issue). New York: United Nations.

UNESCO (United Nations Educational, Scientific and Cultural Organization). (1999). *Statistical yearbook.* Paris: UNESCO.

Urjinbadam, D. (1982). Mongolian People's Republic. In J.A. Lent (Ed.), *Newspapers in Asia: Contemporary trends and problems* (pp. 153–157). Hong Kong: Heinemann Asia.

Williams, J.W. (1995). *Mass media in post-revolution Mongolia* [On-line]. Available: (http://userpage.fu.berlin.de/~corff/im/Landeskunde/john.html).

WAN (World Association of Newspapers). (1999). *World press trends.* Paris: WAN.

World factbook. (1999). Washington, DC: CIA [On-line]. Available: (http://www.odci.gov/cia/publications/factbook).

◆

25

TAIWAN

Georgette Wang & Ven-Hwei Lo

1. NATIONAL PROFILE

1.1 Geography

Taiwan, also known as Formosa ("the beautiful isle"), is an island situated about 160 km off the southeast coast of mainland China. It was one of the 35 provinces of the Republic of China's before 1949. However, when the Nationalist government lost mainland China to the communists in a civil war and retreated to the island, Taiwan and a few small, scattered islands—including Pescadores, Matsu, and Quemoy—were all of the territory that was left of the country. With a land area of 36,140 sq km, Taiwan is slightly more than half (55 percent) the size of Sri Lanka (Gunaratne, 1997). The eastern side of Taiwan is mostly rugged mountains while the west has flat-to-gently-rolling plains. The highest point is the 3,997-meter Yu Shan.

1.2 People

The Chinese began to settle in Taiwan in the 7th century, but large-scale immigration from southern China did not begin until the 17th century. The latest significant influx started in the late 1940s and continued in the early 1950s when the communists took control of the mainland and the Nationalist government, accompanied by some 2 million refugees from every mainland province, moved to Taiwan.

Today, 84 percent of Taiwan's mid-1999 population of 22.1 million comprises Taiwanese descendants of the early Chinese immigrants; 14 percent mainland Chinese who fled the communists since 1949; and 2 percent aborigines, the earliest inhabitants, whose origin can be linked with the other ethnic groups in the South Pacific. Taiwan's population density is 685.4 per sq km—one of the highest in the world (US Census Bureau, 1998). The greatest density is in the western coastal plains and basins. It has an urban population of 58 percent concentrated in four large cities: Taipei, Kaohsiung, Taichung, and Tainan. About 93 percent of the people observe a mixture of Buddhist, Confucian, and Taoist religious practices while 4.5 percent follow Christianity and 2.5 percent follow other beliefs (*World factbook*, 1999).

The adult literacy rate is 93.2 percent (*Asiaweek*, January 21, 2000) and life expectancy 77.5 years (US Census Bureau, 1998). Education is compulsory for those between the ages of 6 and 15. About 91 percent of junior-high-school graduates went on to senior-high-school, and 59 percent of senior-high-school graduates went on to higher education (GIO, 1998a). In 1997, Taiwan had 139 tertiary education institutions, including 38 universities, 40 colleges, and 61 junior colleges (GIO, 1999).

1.3 Government and Politics

Politically, Taiwan was de facto a one-party state before 1987. The Nationalist party, known as the Kuomintang (KMT), monopolized power in the government and the military. Under martial law, the KMT was Taiwan's only active legal political party, although it allowed independent candidates to run for public office in elections at various levels. But as literacy and economic conditions improved, Taiwan's society gradually became heterogeneous, and the pressure for political reform grew.

In 1987, President Chiang Ching-kuo oversaw the lifting of the Emergency Decree, the legal basis for the enforcement of martial law in Taiwan. Thereafter, new political parties emerged, and Taiwan moved rapidly towards a full-fledged democracy. In 1997, Taiwan had 84 registered parties (GIO, 1999), of which only two, the Democratic Progressive Party and the New Party, were able to challenge the KMT in both local and national elections.

On March 23, 1996, Taiwanese elected their president in the first direct presidential election. Lee Teng-hui, the KMT candidate and incumbent president under the old system, was the winner with 54 percent of the total vote. Peng Ming-min, the DPP candidate, received 21 percent. In the 1990s, Taiwan continued on a complex and difficult transition from an authoritarian political system dominated by a mainland-Chinese elite to a localized democratic system. Meanwhile, the relationship with China remained delicate.

Until the late 1980s, the Nationalist government claimed to be the sole legitimate government in China, including Taiwan and the mainland. The communist Chinese government also claimed jurisdiction over Taiwan, insisting on unification as the only way to end the conflict between the two sides. Since the lifting of martial law in 1987, the Nationalist government has adopted a more "realistic approach" vis-à-vis China by recognizing the limits of its own "effective rule" to Taiwan and the surrounding islands. China, however, is unshaken in its claims. Although trade, tourist, and cultural exchanges have become quite common since the late 1980s, the Chinese government refuses to renounce the use of military force to bring about unification. For those living in Taiwan, the test of missile fires targeted at

Taiwan's coast during the island's 1996 presidential election was a loud reminder of Chinese intentions.

Taiwan has five *yuans* (governing bodies): legislative, executive, control, judicial, and examination. The executive *yuan* is responsible to the legislative *yuan*, which submits proposals to the national assembly. The Taiwan Provincial Council was responsible for the general administrative affairs of the island, but since 1998 other government offices have largely replaced its function as part of a plan for more effective management.

1.4 Economy

During the past three decades, Taiwan's real growth in gross national product averaged about 9 percent a year. In the early 1950s, the country was a poor, rural society with a per capita GDP of less than US$ 200. In the 1990s, Taiwan has evolved into a highly urbanized and industrialized society. Its gross domestic product at purchasing power parity now stands at US$ 381 billion with a corresponding GDP of US$ 17,495. The nominal per capita GNP stands at US$ 12,040. Rapid export growth has veered the country toward industrialization. Agriculture contributed less than 3 percent to GDP, down from 35 percent in 1952. Its major exports in 1997 were machinery, electrical equipment, and electronic products (36.5 percent); information/telecommunication products (12.8 percent); and textile products (11.6 percent). In 1999, it exported merchandise valued at US$ 118 billion and had reserves of US$ 106.2 billion (*World factbook*, 1999; Gold, 1996; *Asiaweek*, January 21, 2000).

2. DEVELOPMENT OF PRESS AND BROADCASTING

If, as Pang (1998) has observed, the Taiwan press is modeled after that of the Western world, perhaps the reference must be to some special genre of the Western press. Vanden Heuvel and Dennis (1993) characterized Taiwan's media as "stridently partisan" (p. 45), a feature which James Chu, the then director for cultural affairs of the KMT, described as "[a] phase, a natural part of the democratization process" (p. 45). By the end of the 20th century, the partisan flavor of Taiwan's media may have faded, but the fundamentals of a free and responsible press are still under serious challenge, with new threats coming from commercialism.

2.1 Brief Early History

China ceded Taiwan to Japan in 1895 when China's ruling Ching dynasty lost the Sino-Japanese War. During the 50 years of Japanese occupation, the colonial government completely controlled the publication of newspapers. In 1944, Japan's colonial governor ordered the merger of all six existing newspapers into a single publication, *Taiwan Hsin News*. When Japan returned Taiwan to China after the former's surrender in 1945, *Taiwan Hsin News*, renamed *Taiwan Hsin Shen News*, (New Life Daily News) was the island's only newspaper (Clayton, 1971).

The history of radio broadcasting in Taiwan goes back to the colonial period. The Japanese colonial authorities established the first radio station, the Taiwan Radio, in 1925. Six years later, in 1931, they completed an island-wide network, which they placed under government control (Hsu, 1978). When Japan returned Taiwan to China in 1945, five radio stations were in operation with an estimated 97,000 radio receivers throughout the island (Tien, 1989).

2.2 Developments since 1945

2.2.1 Press

After the restoration of Taiwan, the Nationalist government abolished news censorship and monopoly, and the number of newspapers increased to 28 by early 1947 (Lee, 1973). When the communists won the mainland in 1949, the Nationalist government of President Chiang Kai-shek retreated to Taiwan and declared martial law. In 1951, claiming a newsprint shortage, the government froze applications for new newspaper licenses and set a ceiling on the number of pages in existing newspapers. For the next 37 years, the number of daily newspapers remained at 31, and the number of pages allowed for each issue was limited: from eight in 1957 to 10 in 1966, and 12 after 1971 (Lo et al., 1999).

Through the newspaper ban, the government effectively restricted freedom of the press and prevented newspaper ownership from falling into the hands of the opposition (Lee, 1993). This strategy resulted in the government, the KMT, and the armed forces owning 14 of the 31 daily newspapers (Cheng, 1988). Although the two largest dailies, the *United Daily News* and *China Times* were privately owned, both their owners sat on the KMT's Central Standing Committee. Before 1987, the *Independence Evening Post* was the only opposition newspaper on the island. In the name of national unity and security in the face of the communist threat, the press had to manage with limited freedom, and it rarely challenged government authority openly.

The government lifted the freeze on newspaper license applications in 1988, soon after the revocation of martial law. Since then, the number of newspapers has increased from 31 in 1987 to 360 (of which 179 are dailies) in 1998, although only 40 have a wide readership (GIO, 1999).

Immediately after the lifting of the newspaper ban, the two largest newspapers, the *United Daily News* and *China Times*, doubled their pages from 12 to 24 per issue (Lay & Schweitzer, 1990). In the early 1990s, the number of pages for the largest dailies had increased from 30 to 50 per issue, and was often more than 50 on the weekends (Rampal, 1994a).

The democratizing movement in Taiwan led to a growing liberalization in news reporting and commentary (Rampal, 1994a; Wei, 1998). In the face of fierce competition —especially from the new pro-opposition party newspapers such as *The Capital Morning Paper*—those with a pro-government and pro-KMT editorial policy, including the *United Daily News* and the *China Times*, began to take a more liberal, neutral stand (Lo, 1994).[1]

At the end of 1990s, newspapers in Taiwan have adopted a lively, colorful layout. Their content is more diverse and their approach to reporting more balanced, with greater emphasis on public opinion. For example, letters to the editor, which used to be tucked away in corners, now occupy a full page in a majority of newspapers. The larger daily newspapers publish local editions, offering extensive coverage of local politics and society in addition to sports, arts, and culture, and "particularly extensive and sophisticated" business reports (Vanden Heuvel & Dennis, 1993, p. 48). Special sections on lifestyle, book reviews, and science appear on different days of the week.

2.2.2 Radio

When China got back Taiwan in 1945, radio was hardly a "mass" medium. The entire island population had an estimated 97,000 receivers—an average of 1.5 sets per 1,000 people. In the 1950s, Taiwan's economic growth began to take off; and, by the end of 1956, the number of receivers exceeded 249,000. In 1959, the government imposed a freeze on radio licenses, thus limiting the number of stations to 33, although the number of receivers continued to grow. By 1974, Taiwan had become one of the leading countries in radio penetration, with about 26 receivers per 100 people.

The government lifted the freeze on new radio licenses in 1993. From then up to 1997, the authorities approved applications for 118 radio frequencies. By mid-1998, the number of radio stations had increased to 80 while another 65 stations were under construction (GIO, 1999). In the early 1990s, radio broadcasting reached almost every household with about 18 million receivers in the country (Rampal, 1994b). By mid-1998, about 99 percent of Taiwanese homes owned at least one radio with the majority (82 percent) owning two or more (Chiu, 1999).

2.2.3 Television

Television arrived in Taiwan in 1962, when Taiwan Television Enterprise inaugurated its service. TTV completed its island-wide relay system in 1965; and two other companies, China Television Company (CTV) and the China Television System (STS), later joined the competition (Hsu, 1978). These three companies dominated the Taiwan television market for more than three decades until the authorities released more frequencies to license applicants in 1993. In the late 1990s, Formosa Television (FTV) and Public Television joined the TV market.

Over the years, TV receivers have turned from a luxury to a general appliance item in the households. In 1997, Taiwan had an estimated 7.1 million TV receivers, a penetration of 32.6 per 100 people (ITU, 1999). In 1998, less than 1 percent of

---

[1] The *Capital Daily* was forced out of competition in 1990.

the households in Taiwan did not have a TV receiver. Despite fierce competition from cable and satellite channels, terrestrial television remains a lucrative business. In 1989, for example, two years after the lifting of martial law, the advertising-revenue share of the three terrestrial TV stations stood at 29.4 percent of the total advertising revenue, showing a 24.5 percent growth from the previous year (*ROC advertising yearbook*, 1989–1990). In 1993, the share of television stood at a high of 33.4 percent, which declined to about 30 percent in the subsequent years. Although television was second to newspapers in advertising market share, some television channels have attracted a great deal more advertising.

3. THE PRESS

3.1 Policy and Legal Framework

Article 11 of the Constitution of the Republic of China (Taiwan) guarantees "freedom of speech, teaching, writing and publication." But Article 23 subjects this freedom to a number of restrictions "to prevent infringement upon the freedoms of other persons, to avert an imminent crisis, to maintain social order or to advance the public welfare" (Clayton, 1971, p. 110).

Before 1987, martial law permitted the government to infringe the constitutional protection of freedom of speech and press. The Publications Law—written in 1930 and revised in 1937, 1952, 1958, and 1973—required the licensing of newspapers. It also gave the government the right to implement post-publication censorship (Parker, 1982, p. 854). Although the government seldom censored the newspapers, it had made clear that certain topics were taboo: calling for Taiwan's independence, glorifying mainland China and communism, or criticizing the president (Parker, 1982).[2]

Magazines in Taiwan, unlike the newspapers, never had a freeze on licenses. Consequently, at times, magazines became the favorite medium of political dissidents. Despite the famous case of *Free China* in 1960, when the authorities made several arrests on sedition charges, dissident magazines flourished in the 1980s as democratization began to take shape. Dissident magazines never died—despite arrests, confiscation of issues, and order to shut down businesses—until the lifting of martial law liberalized the media and took away their market.

Since the lifting of martial law, the press has acquired a freedom that it never enjoyed before. In 1992, the government amended the Sedition Law to cover only direct advocacy of violence. It legalized the promotion of political independence from China. With most of the controlling measures getting outdated, the Publications Law lost its raison d'être, causing the government to abolish it in early 1999.

The press in Taiwan is now free to release information or comment on the performance of any government official or public figure, provided it does no irreparable

---

[2] Taiwan's independence here refers to Taiwan being an independent country without mainland China having jurisdiction over it. Hence, it implies here that Taiwan is not a part of China as both the Nationalist and the Communist governments claim.

harm to national security. In 1999, Freedom Forum (Sussman, 1999) ranked Taiwan as a "free" press country with a restriction score of 25 out of 100. In relation to laws and regulations that influence media content, Taiwan scored 5 out of 15 for broadcast and 2 out of 15 for print. In relation to political pressures and controls that influence media content, the score was 6 out of 15 for broadcast and 4 out of 15 for print. In relation to economic influences over media content, the score was 4 out 15 each for broadcast and print media. It had a zero score on repressive action.

The major concern among critics of the media is no longer the lack of press freedom but the increasingly confused ethical principles. As Pang (1998) points out in a review of press freedom in Taiwan, attacking the mass media has become a campaign strategy during elections. Gangsters can physically attack reporters, who can also be fired by media owners unhappy with them. On the other hand, the line between press freedom and the invasion of privacy has become increasingly indistinguishable (Wang, 1998), as are the boundaries separating fair media access, the public's right to know, and trial by press. For example, an already accepted practice among journalists in Taiwan is interviewing criminals after, or even before, their arrest.

3.2 Financial Aspects: Circulation, Advertising, Marketing Strategies

Chu (1982) wrote that it was "impossible to compile accurate circulation figures for newspapers in Taiwan" (p. 61) because the country had no audit bureau and the newspapers exaggerated their sales to attract advertising. Even today, newspapers do not publish their circulation and sales figures. Estimated figures indicate that the three leading dailies are the privately-owned *China Times*, *United Daily News*, and *Liberty Times*. The first two have a circulation of over 1 million each. The three together shared more than two-thirds of the total daily newspaper circulation in Taiwan (Anon, 1998).

The morning papers, which have a 10-to-1 edge over their evening counterparts, account for more than 90 percent of all newspapers sold in Taiwan. Because the morning dailies have traditionally dominated the market, they have garnered 95 percent of newspaper advertising as well (Anon, 1998). The total circulation of newspapers stood at 7 million in 1995—with 33 out of every 100 people buying a newspaper (Jing, 1996). Newspaper readership is normally higher than the circulation figures because people share newspapers with others. A 1998 survey of 1,920 randomly selected respondents in Taiwan indicated that 87 percent "occasionally" read a newspaper (Chiu, 1999). The survey also found that about 82 percent of the respondents above the age of 18 read a newspaper at least once a week, while 64 percent read one almost every day.

In recent years, newspapers have faced a declining share of advertising revenue. In 1975, newspapers had a 46 percent share of the advertising market. In 1995, this share had dropped to 36 percent (GIO, 1998b). The *United Daily News* and the *China Times* continued to dominate the market and advertising revenue. In

1997, the *China Times* generated an advertising income of US$ 240 million, followed by the *United Daily News* with US$ 200 million; and the *Liberty Times* with US$ 120 million (Anon, 1998). Table 5 provides an analysis of the share of advertising expenditure (Adspend) by the major media categories.

3.3 Structure and Organization

Two family-owned newspaper groups have dominated Taiwan's daily newspaper market. The United Daily News Group, owned by the Wang family, is the largest. It also publishes a business daily, an evening daily, a leisure- and sports-daily, and four overseas Chinese-language newspapers. The China Times Group, owned by the Yu family, also publishes a business daily and an evening daily. In 1997, these two groups shared 60 percent of the nation's daily newspaper circulation and more than 75 percent of newspaper advertising (Anon, 1998). The *Liberty Times*, a daily owned by the real estate tycoon Lin Rong-san, managed to reach the top category with aggressive and, often, controversial promotional strategies, including the offering of lottery prizes to new subscribers.

Next to the two private conglomerates in the scale of newspaper ownership is probably the government, although most of the government-owned newspapers have suffered serious financial difficulties and limited circulation. They include the KMT-owned *Central Daily News* and *China Daily News*, the Taiwan Provincial Government-owned *Taiwan Hsin Shen News* and *Taiwan Shin Wen News*, and six other papers owned by the Ministry of Defense.

3.4 Quality and Popular Press

Reflecting the situation in the early 1980s, Chu (1982) wrote that "the Chinese newspapers usually focussed on one or two crimes to attract readers" (p. 70). Indeed, compared with what is available today, Taiwan newspapers in the 1980s and 1970s might have looked rather monotonous. The situation, however, has undergone drastic changes since then (as described in Section 2.2.1).

Contemporary newspapers in Taiwan show variety and heterogeneity. Despite the criticism of superficial reporting, the majority of the mainstream national newspapers are quite similar in quality. The Western distinction between the quality and the popular press is less relevant in Taiwan, where what is more pertinent is the difference in style and appeal between the national and the local newspapers. Local newspapers, limited by their market size, are noticeable for their sensational news reporting and rampant advertising. They carry advertising that promotes gambling, superstition, and prostitution, a practice for which they are criticized frequently.

3.5 Distribution and Technology

According to the findings of communication and information behavior surveys (Chung et al., 1989; Wang et al., 1991; Wang et al., 1994), a close relationship exists between newspaper readership and place of residence. The more urbanized the place of residence, the higher the newspaper readership usually is, a correlation that can be attributed to the differences in average educational background of the residents.

The educational barrier cannot be overcome by improving the means of distribution. However, as the number of newspaper readers decreased at a rate ranging from 1 percent to 5 percent every year since 1991 (Chen & Chen, 1997), the press began to experiment with electronic newspapers or information services. The *China Times* group's on-line services (http://www.chinatimes.com.tw), for example, started operation in 1995; and the group became financially independent within two years (Chen & Chen, 1997). Although some critics remained unconvinced about the future of on-line information services, more newspapers, including *China Times' major* competitor *United Daily News*, have announced plans to join the race.

4. BROADCASTING

4.1 Policy and Legal Framework

The two laws governing electronic media in Taiwan are the Radio and Television Broadcast Law and the Cable Television Law, both stipulating licensing procedures, requirement on company structures, and program and advertising codes. Also related to communication and information media are the Copyright Law, the Consumer Protection Law, and the Telecommunications Law.

The Government Information Office, an agency under the executive *yuan*, has been the major regulatory body.[3] Officially, the GIO is the most influential government office in setting the course of development for Taiwan's communication industry. However, the formulation of policies and execution of rules and regulations often involve a process entangling political forces and economic interests.

Ownership limitations apart, TV programs in Taiwan are regulated in content as well. The Radio and Television Broadcast Law stipulates that, except for news, all programs are subject to prior censorship. The Cable Television Law does not exempt cable TV programs from censorship, although the censorship in this case is more lax in nature and is implemented only upon viewers' complaints following the program. The ceiling for programs originating in foreign countries is set at 30 percent for broadcast television and 80 percent for cable systems.

4.2 Structure and Organization

4.2.1 Radio

The government started radio broadcasting and kept it under its control in the initial phase of development. Under martial law, the government closely monitored

[3] The executive *yuan* is the executive branch of the government in Taiwan.

radio broadcasting and, for 34 years, kept the number of radio stations at 33. The ruling KMT, the government and the armed forces owned 12 of these stations (Rampal, 1994b). The largest was the KMT-owned BCC, which had four island-wide domestic networks, an overseas service, and a mainland China service.

In 1993, the government approved additional frequencies for applicants. Many of these frequencies covered only small-to-medium broadcast ranges, and private community radio stations started to flourish, bringing significant changes to an industry dominated till then by nationwide or metropolitan radio stations. In comparison to their well-established competitors, the new genre of community radio stations paid closer attention to local affairs. At the same time, they also became more global in perspective as many entered into alliances with other radio networks, or even cable and satellite TV services to achieve economies of scale.

4.2.2 Television

Although television arrived in Taiwan some 30 years later than radio, the two electronic media followed a similar path of development. At the outset, the government closely monitored television and kept its operation largely in the hands of the triple alliance of the government, the armed forces, and the ruling KMT (Lee, 1993). The Taiwan Provincial Government had a controlling 49 percent stock ownership of Taiwan Television Company (TTV), the first TV station on the island. The KMT owned 68 percent of the stock of China Television Company (CTV) established in 1969. The Ministry of Defense, with 72 percent of the stock, and the Ministry of Education with 10 percent of the stock, controlled the Chinese Television System (CTS) established in 1971 (Lo et al., 1994). This ownership structure enabled the government-KMT-military monolith to exercise control over the TV industry's major appointments, finance and content (Lo et al., 1998).

In 1993, the government lifted the 22-year ban on new TV stations (Peng, 1994). The fourth terrestrial TV station, Formosa Television (FTV), came into existence in 1997. With strong financial backing from the major opposition party, the Democratic Progressive Party, Formosa TV served as a balancing chip in Taiwan's government-dominated TV broadcast ecology. The last terrestrial television station, Public Television, went on air in 1998 after a long and winding legal process. It was an extension of the two-hour public TV program broadcast daily over the three TV channels, and the only one that survives on public funding.

At the turn of the century, the convergence of telecommunication services and cable television networks has become an issue debated frequently in Taiwan. As early as 1979, some entrepreneurs in the plumbing business had started to offer Japanese wrestling programs at street-corner tea-houses by using cables to connect their video-cassette recorders with subscriber's TV sets (Wang, 1984). In its primitive form, cable television offered only one or two channels. However, over the years, significant growth in channel capacity and penetration occurred despite government efforts to stamp out unlicensed operations. In 1994, a year after the legalization of cable television, about 42 percent of Taiwan's total TV households were subscribing to cable TV services (Liu, 1994). By 1998, that number had soared to nearly 80 percent (Lee, 1998), with many operators offering more than 90 channels of information and entertainment programs.

Mergers reduced the number of Taiwan's cable-system operators from more than 300 in the 1980s to 140 in 1998, with two conglomerates, Tung-seng and He-hsin, emerging as the major competitors. By the end of the 1990s, cable-system operators, who were not allowed to offer value-added services before, had begun experimenting with cable modems. Meanwhile, feuds between program providers and cable-system operators were likely to cause cut-throat competition as the former turned to direct-to-home (DTH) transmission to ensure outlets for their programs. With an 80 percent growth in advertising revenues in 1996 itself, it is likely that Taiwan's cable communications market will remain one of the most lucrative (and also an extremely sensitive one) for some time to come.

4.3 Program Policies

Hsu (1978) has pointed out that Taiwan's radio and television programs are primarily oriented towards entertainment. Radio stations went through a process of program diversification when television became popular in the late 1960s. The "Traffic Report on the Police Networks," a program still popular today, was one example (Hsu, 1978).

By the early 1990s, political groups and entrepreneurs who were impatient with the current pace of opening up radio frequencies for new stations, introduced a new style of presentation format to Taiwan's radio broadcasting. During the highly competitive 1994 mayoral and gubernatorial elections, 14 unlicensed radio stations went on the air before the government accepted applications for new radio licenses (Wang, 1998). These unlicensed radio stations relied heavily on call-in programs not only to attract listeners but also to cope with the shortage of professional broadcasters and to maximize public support for their political causes. The down-to-earth, daring comments made by hosts and listeners, usually on highly controversial topics, soon turned call-in programs into a fashion that lasted until after the elections.

If radio programs were entertainment-oriented, television was not much different for two good reasons: avoiding politically sensitive material (Lo et al., 1994) and possible violation of taboos, and generating greater profits. TTV in 1973, for example, had as much as 78 percent of its telecast time allocated to entertainment (Hsu, 1978). In 1998, CTV was the most watched TV channel followed by TTV, CTS, and FTV, according to the ACNielsen survey. The most popular TV program was the CTS variety show "Super Sunday," followed by several drama series—CTV's "A Ching Princess," TTV's "A Heroic Couple," FTV's "Parent's Kind Heart," and CTS' "Judge Shih's Cases." The CTV variety show "Red & White Victory" came next (Anon, 1999).

Although entertainment remains a major part of Taiwan's radio and TV programs, the broadcast industry, in general, entered a new phase of development since the lifting of martial law that forced open the market to cable and satellite television. Unprecedented competition from both within and outside of the national borders has resulted in greater content diversity, notable increase in public participation in current affairs programs, and freedom in news coverage. Competition, however, also brought commercialism, which will remain unchanged unless the broadcasters pay enough attention to public interest.

4.1 Ownership and Financing

Although the government, the army, and the KMT owned the majority of terrestrial television stations and a significant number of radio stations, many of these stations have become commercial in nature. As Taiwan began to democratize, the heavy concentration of media resources in the hands of a few became the frequent target of criticism, and the pressure to privatize the two government- and one ruling-party-owned broadcast television companies has mounted.

The China Television Company was the first to respond to such calls. Since 1996, the KMT has sold 19.7 percent of its shares to reduce its holding to less than 47 percent, and in 1999, CTV made another bold move, releasing 6.7 percent of its shares on the market. CTV's change in ownership structure, in the face of fierce competition from the popular liberal satellite channels such as the Hong Kong-based TVBS, reflects a positive response to calls for decentralization of resources. It also reflects the authorities' willingness to relax controls on terrestrial television, which they now perceive more as a business than as an instrument for ideological control.

Advertising is the backbone of broadcasting. Television's share of advertising expenditure rose from US$ 990 million in 1997 to US$ 1.2 billion in 1998. CTV was the most profitable, while TTV and CTS have been going through mixed fortunes of late. The opposition-backed FTV is way behind the other three in ratings (Anon, 1999).

5. NEW ELECTRONIC MEDIA

Improved economic conditions and rising audience expectations have turned Taiwan into a fertile ground for new media despite stringent government controls placed on the traditional media.

5.1 Internet and On-line Media

Computer networks did not achieve significant growth in Taiwan until the 1990s but, once started, the speed of growth was comparable to that of many high-income countries. ITU (1999) reported that in 1997 Taiwan had an estimated 2.57 million computers, a density of 11.8 computers per 100 people. In January 1997, Taiwan also had 34,877 Internet host computers, which increased to 177,382 one year later. This meant the country had 6.9 Internet hosts per 100 computers. The January 1999 Network Wizards' survey estimated that Taiwan's Internet hosts had increased to 309,523, producing a density of 142.75 per 10,000 people, while the Internet Software Consortium estimated the number of Internet hosts in July 1999 as 424,209, or 191.80 per 10,000 people. Taiwan has a dozen private companies offering Internet access, but the state-owned Chunghwa Telecom,[4] the island's principal domestic and international telecommunications operator, remains the largest ISP, with 1.8 million paid subscribers and another 1.2 million users on school campuses (Baum, 1999).

Similar growth has occurred in the number of commercial websites, which increased from 333 in early 1996 to 1,951 in mid-1997 (Chen & Chen, 1997). Gunaratne (1997) wrote that highly literate small countries like Sri Lanka had much to learn from Taiwan's rapid entry to the information age. As getting on-line became both a necessity and a fashionable hobby, the "Net" slashed into the audience, as well as the advertising revenue, of the other media, which themselves had to go on-line to compete. By 1998, almost all major media in Taiwan had crossed into the network business. Considering that few had made substantial profit and many still defined it as a service to the audience, it is difficult to predict how this service will play out.

Chunghwa Telecom has completed the backbone for the National Information Infrastructure, with the aim of making Taiwan an Asia-Pacific Regional Operations Center—an Asian Internet hub. Its target was to increase the number of Internet users to 3 million within three years. The NII high-speed backbone network for public data communication includes eight asynchronous transfer mode (ATM) backbone switches and 11 ATM access switches covering the entire island. The NII project comprises a broadband communication network, HiNet expansion, and ISDN (www.dgt.com.tw).

5.2 Telecommunications Infrastructure

Telecommunications had been a major element of the nation's development plans since 1979. By the late 1990s, all of the trunk communication cables were in optic fiber; and plans were afoot to digitize all communications media by 2006. As in the case of mass media, telecommunication had a modest beginning in Taiwan. In 1952, the country's mainline telephone density was 0.39 per 100 people. In the 1970s, telephone penetration grew at an average annual rate of 25 percent (Chung

---

[4] Baum, 1999, says that Taiwan government remains committed to selling two-thirds of its shares in the 100 percent state-owned Chunghwa Telecom by the end of 2001 as part of a decade-long privatization drive. In mid-1998, Chunghwa had assets valued at NT$ 445 billion, and its after-tax profit in the year to June 1998 was NT$ 58 billion (US$ 1.8 billion).

et al., 1989). In 1988, the mainline telephone density stood at 26.8 per 100 people. In 1998, Taiwan had 11.5 million main telephone lines with a density of 52.5 per 100 people, slightly behind Hong Kong and Singapore (ITU, 1999).

Mobile communication also achieved rapid growth in Taiwan. Cellular subscribers, for example, averaged 0.19 per 100 people in 1989, increasing to 2.57 in 1983 and to 6.86 in 1997. State-owned Chunghwa Telecom dominated the telecommunication market until January 1998, when liberalization permitted six cellular competitors—Pacific Cellular, FarEasTone, KG Telecom, Mobitai, Tuntex, and TransAsia—to enter the field. Thus at the end of 1998, the number of cellular subscribers leaped to 4.7 million or 21.6 per 100 people (ITU, 1999). Apart from building a mobile communication network, Chunghwa is also involved in implementing a synchronous digital hierarchy (SDH) transmission network and an advanced common channel signaling No. 7 (CCS-7) network (http://www.cht.com.tw/). In August 1998, Chunghwa also launched the ST 1 communication satellite, jointly owned with Singapore Telecom (APT, 1999).

Under the 1958 Telecommunications Act, the Directorate General of Telecommunications (DGT) regulated and operated almost all telecommunications activities and services in Taiwan. The government envisioned turning Taiwan into an Asia-Pacific Regional Operations Center over a 10-year span by making information technology more competitive. Thus it promulgated a three-pronged telecommunication law on February 6, 1996 comprising the new Telecommunications Act, which replaced the 1958 Act; the Organizational Statute of the DGT and Chunghwa Telecom Co. Ltd Statute.

The Telecommunications Act separated the old DGT into two units: Chunghwa Telecommunications Corporation (CHT), a fully state-owned operating company; and the DGT as the regulatory body reporting directly to Ministry of Transportation and Communications (MOTC). The two statutes legalized the organization of the respective units. Chunghwa Telecom took over the business operation of the DGT on July 1, 1996. The law entrusted Chunghwa to operate both domestic and international telecommunications and to invest in or operate telecommunications-related and other businesses approved by the MOTC. The 1996 Act defined two categories of Telecom operations: Category I operations that require provision of Telecom switching and infrastructure, such as fixed network, long distance, international, mobile, paging, and the like; and Category II operations that require operators to rent or lease existing infrastructure from the Category I service provider, such as X.25, Internet, messaging, S&F fax, private leased circuits, and the like. The deregulation of wireless services began in 1997. Under the three-phased liberalization plan, Chunghwa's monopoly on fixedline telephone services will end in the first half of 2000; and the leading contenders for the new licenses are KG Telecom and Rebar Telecommunications, both owned by groups that own Taiwan's two largest cable-TV operators (Baum, 1999).

6. POLICY TRENDS FOR PRESS AND BROADCASTING

As mentioned earlier, the Government Information Office has been the single most important government office in formulating communication policies in Taiwan. However, this situation could change as Taiwan enters a new phase of media development.

A factor leading to the new phase is social and political development. When democratization began to gather momentum, the need for an autonomous regulatory body also became pressing. To allow for greater objectivity in major licensing and penalty decisions, the authorities introduced the idea of an "independent" committee into all major communication regulations. The committee, constituting academics, experts, and politicians of major political parties, became the major decision-making body, and the Government Information Office was left with the responsibility of implementing committee decisions. The committee approach, however, has failed to work effectively because members could seldom afford the time and energy demanded. Even when they made decisions, the rather insignificant weight they carried in the political hierarchy sometimes made it difficult to implement such decisions, especially when the cases involved powerful media groups.

Technological development has also challenged the regulatory framework for electronic media, a typical example being cable regulation. In the 1980s, cable television spread throughout the island causing several problems. Because the Radio and Television Broadcast Law contained no clause on cable licensing, cable-system operators could not apply for licenses. When they had to operate without a license, no incentive existed for them to respect other regulations regarding television; they filed no taxes, they indulged in piracy, and they often showed violent and pornographic material. Because of technical difficulties involved in stamping out these unlicensed cable systems, they were able to prosper until the GIO decided to legalize them in order to make it possible to apply some form of regulation. The Cable Television Law came into effect in 1993, more than a decade after the introduction of cable television in Taiwan (Peng, 1994).

By the late 1990s, it was becoming obvious that the existing legal framework was no longer adequate. Difficulties in regulating the industry arose when technological convergence and business integration increasingly blurred the distinctions between the media, telecommunications carriers, and computer systems. With technological standards set by the Telecommunications Law, and licensing and content regulation set by laws governing individual media, a need would arise not only for a new law each time a new medium appeared, but also for a team of experts to decide which law should apply in each individual case.

In 1998, the government announced plans to undertake a major overhaul of its communications regulatory framework. The new design, which may incorporate the idea of an independent Communications Commission at the ministerial level, will probably take years to come into shape and to be put to work. The ever-changing media scene, however, continues to test the wisdom of communications policy makers.

7. MAIN ISSUES

● The increasing market dominance of conglomerates, especially cable and satellite television, has hampered fair competition among media.

● The respect for professional ethics has waned as the media often justify questionable performance in the name of competition. For instance, reporters turned a kidnapping case, as it took place, into an action drama.

● Policy formulation has often overlooked public interest; and effective execution of regulations is difficult because interest groups and legislators who themselves are owners of media businesses heavily influence the legislative body.

8. STATISTICS

General Profile

Exchange rate (1999 average)	US$ 1 = NT$ 32.22
Population (mid-1999)	22,113,250
Geographical size	36,140 sq km
Population density (1999)	685.4 per sq km
Number of households (1998)	6,355,469

Table 1
Press: 1998

Number of newspapers	360
Number of dailies	149
Number of non-dailies	211
Households with newspapers	59.7%

Table 2
Most Frequently Read Dailies

Newspapers	1991		1998		1998 Circulation of
	Number	Percent	Number	Percent	top dailies (est)
United Daily News	264	30.3	42.9	25.6	*1.2 million
China Times	262	30.1	454	27.1	*1.2 million
Min Sheng Daily	93	10.7	91	5.4	*600,000
Commons Daily	54	6.2	32	1.9	
Taiwan Times	48	5.5	34	2.0	*400,000
Liberty Times	34	3.9	370	22.1	*1.2 million
United Evening News	16	1.8	42	2.5	*450,000
China Times Express	15	1.7	20	1.2	*420,000
Taiwan Shin Wen News	14	1.6	–	–	
Independence Evening Post	13	1.5	3	0.2	
Independence Morning Post	11	1.3	2	0.1	
Economic Daily News	9	1.0	31	1.9	
Central Daily News	9	1.0	17	1.0	
Taiwan Shin Shen News	6	0.7	5	0.3	
Commercial Times	2	0.2	27	1.6	
China Daily News	2	0.2	29	1.7	
Taiwan Daily News	2	0.2	16	0.9	
Great News	2	0.2	26	1.6	
Others	15	1.7	45	2.7	
Total	**871**	**99.8**	**1673**	**99.8**	

Source: The 1991 data are from Lo, 1993; The 1998 data are from Chiu, 1999; *WAN, 1999.

Table 3
Television: 1998

Number of terrestrial TV channels	4 private, 1 public
Households with TV sets	99.84%
Licensed cable TV system operators	103
Number of cable TV channels	96
Households with cable TV	79%

Table 4
Radio: 1998

Number of radio broadcast companies	80
Households with radio receivers	99.1%
Households with stereo sets/CD players	77.3%

Table 5
Share of Advertising Expenditure by Media, 1994–98
(Compound Annual Growth Rate of Adspend from 1990–97 = 13%)

Year	Total Adspend (NTS$ millions)	Newspapers	Magazines	Television	Radio	Outdoor
1994	73,153	43	6	37	5	9
1995	80,976	47	6	36	5	6
1996	91,024	50	7	33	4	6
1997	105,221	46	7	37	4	6
1998	128,480 (est.)	44	7	40	4	5

Source: WAN, 1999.

9. USEFUL ADDRESSES

United Daily News
No. 555, Sec. 4, Chung-Shiao E. Road, Taipei
Telephone: 886-2-27615142
Fax: 886-2-27568526
URL: http://www.udngroup.com.tw

China Times
132 Dali St., Taipei
Telephone: 886-2-23087111
Fax: 886-2-23044375
E-mail: service@it.chinatimes.com.tw
URL: http://www.chinatimes.com.tw/main.htm

The Liberty Times
137, Sec. 2, Nanjing E. Road, Taipei
Telephone: 886-2-25042828
Fax: 886-2-25094136

Taiwan Television Enterprise
10, Sec. 3, Bade Road, Taipei
Telephone: 886-2-25781515
E-Mail: ttvc@email.ttv.com.tw
URL: http://www.ttv.com.tw/Default.htm

China Television Co.
120 Chungyang Road, Nangang Area, Taipei
Telephone: 886-080012258/886-27838308
URL: http://www.chinatv.com.tw/know/know1.html

Chinese Television Service
100 Guanfu S. Road, Taipei
Telephone: 886-2-27510321
URL: http://www.cts.com.tw

Formosa Television
14F, No. 30, Sec. 3, Bade Road, Taipei
Telephone: 886-2-25702570
Fax: 886-2-25700752
E-mail: webadm@mail.ftv.com.tw
URL: http://www.ftv.com.tw

Public Television Service
100, Lane 75, Sec. 3
Kangning Road, Neihu Area, Taipei
Telephone: 886-2-26349122/886-2-26329533
E-mail: rnd5003@mail.pts.org.tw
URL: http://www.pts.org.tw

Television Business Satellite
23, Sec. 1, Bade Road, Taipei
Telephone: 886-2-23579988
Fax: 886-2-23210606
URL: http://www.tvbs.com.tw

Summon Television Network Company
7F, No. 53, Dungshing Road
Shinyi Area, Taipei
Telephone: 886-2-27472757
Fax: 886-2-27654464

Eastern Broadcasting Company
13F, No. 4, Sec. 1, Jungshian W. Road, Taipei
Telephone: 886-2-23118000
Fax: 886-2-23821707
URL: http://www.ettv.com.tw

Videoland Enterprise Co. Ltd
3F, No. 57, Dungshing Road, Taipei
Telephone: 886-2-27472757
Fax: 886-2-27472767
URL: http://www.videoland.com.tw

Willging New Spread Enterprise Company
3F, No. 51
Dungshing Road, Taipei
Telephone: 886-2-27492888
URL: http://www.startv.com

Broadcasting Corporation of China
53, Sec. 3 JEN-AI RD, Taipei
Telephone: 886-2-27710151
Fax: 886-2-27218509
URL: http://www.bcc.com.tw

UFO Radio
25F, No. 102, Sec. 2, Luosfu Road, Taipei

Telephone: 886-2-23938880
Fax: 886-2-23688833
URL: http://mail.ht.net.tw/~amoeba/home.htm

Public Radio System
17 Guangion St., Taipei
Telephone: 886-2-23888099
Fax: 886-2-23756567
URL: http://www.prs.gov.tw

International Community Radio Taipei
#8-1 Chung Yung 2nd Road
Yang Ming Shan
Taipei 111, Taiwan
Telephone: 886-2-28612280
Fax: 886-2-28613004, 886-2-28613863
E-mail: Doc Casey, General manager, dcasey@icrt.com.tw
URL: http://www.icrt.com.tw/en default2.asp

Happy Communication
8-3F, No. 63, Sanduo 4th Road
Kaohsiung
Telephone: 886-7-3350053
Fax: 886-7-3350448
E-mail: behappy@mail.keynet.com.tw
URL: http://www.happyradio.com.tw

10. REFERENCES

Anon. (1998). Advertising revenue of Taiwan newspapers in 1997. *Brain, 266*, 58–60.
Anon. (1999, April 6). Country profile: Taiwan. *ASIACom*, pp. 5–8.
APT (Asia-Pacific Telecommunity). (1999). *The APT yearbook*. Bangkok: APT.
Baum, J. (1999, June 17). Calling all investors: Deregulation will create Taiwan's first pure telecoms play. *Far Eastern Economic Review, 162* (24), 59–61.
Bureau of Telecommunications. (1995). *Telecommunications white paper*. Taipei: Bureau of Telecommunications.
Chen, S.M., & Chen, P.L. (1997). *The impact of NII on communications media*. Unpublished research report in Chinese, The Institute for Information Industries, Taipei.
Cheng, J.C. (1988). *Mass media*. Taipei: Commonwealth.
Chiu, H.Y. (1999). *The basic survey project of Taiwan area's social change*. Taipei: Academia Sinica.
Chu, J.C.Y. (1982). Republic of China (Taiwan). In J.A. Lent (Ed.), *Newspapers in Asia: Contemporary trends and problems* (pp. 54–76). Hong Kong: Heinemann Asia.
Chung, W.W., Wang, G., & Shen, V. (1989). *A study of informatization and cultural change in Taiwan*. Unpublished research report in Chinese, National Science Council, Taipei.
Clayton, C.C. (1971). Taiwan. In J.A. Lent (Ed.), *The Asian newspapers' reluctant revolution* (pp. 105–114). Ames: The Iowa State University Press.
GIO (Government Information Office). (1998a). *The Republic of China yearbook 1998*. Taipei: GIO.
GIO (Government Information Office). (1998b). *The Republic of China yearbook*. Taipei: GIO.
GIO (Government Information Office). (1999). *The Republic of China publication yearbook, 1999)*. Taipei: GIO.

Gold, T.B. (1996). Taiwan society at the fin de siecle. *The China Quarterly, 4* (148), 1091–1114.
Gunaratne, S.A. (1997). Sri Lanka and the third communication revolution. *Media Asia, 24,* 83–89.
Hsu, C.S. (1978). Republic of China (Taiwan). In J.A. Lent (Ed.), *Broadcasting in Asia and the Pacific: A continental survey of radio and television* (pp. 12–21). Philadelphia: Temple University Press.
ITU (International Telecommunication Union). (1998, 1999). *World telecommunication development report.* Geneva: ITU.
Jing, C.J. (1996). Newspapers. In *The 1996 ROC news media yearbook* (pp. 34–64) Taipei: The Chinese News Association.
Lay, Y.J., & Schweitzer, J.C. (1990). Advertising in Taiwan newspapers since the lifting of the bans. *Journalism Quarterly, 67,* 201–206.
Lee, C.C. (1993, April). Sparking a fire: The press and the ferment of democratic change in Taiwan, *Journalism Monographs, 138.*
Lee, C.L. (1998). Taiwan's media miracle. *Brainstorming, 262,* 4–48.
Lee, T. (1973). *A history of world journalism.* Taipei: National Chengchi University.
Liu, Y.L. (1994). *Cable television management and programming strategies.* Taipei: Cheng-Chun Publishing.
Lo, V.H. (1993). *News media credibility.* Unpublished research report in Chinese, National Science Council, Taipei.
Lo, V.H. (1994, July 20–24). *Press coverage of the 1992 National Assembly election in Taiwan.* Paper presented to the International Association for Mass Communication Research, Seoul, Korea.
Lo, V.H., Cheng, J.C., & Lee, C.C. (1994). Television news is government news in Taiwan. *Asian Journal of Communication, 4* (1), 99–110.
Lo, V.H., Neilan, E., & King, P.T. (1998). Television coverage of the 1995 legislative election in Taiwan: Rise of cable television as a force for balance in media coverage. *Journal of Broadcasting & Electronic Media, 42* (3), 340–355.
Lo, V.H., Wu, H., & Paddon, A. (1999). Front page design of Taiwan daily newspapers: 1952–1996, *Mass Communication Research, 59,* 67–90.
Pan, C.C. (1995). *Communication behavior of residents in Taiwan.* Unpublished research report in Chinese, The National Science Council, Taipei.
Pang, K.F. (1998). Taiwan. In A. Latif (Ed.), *Walking the tightrope: Press freedom and professional standards in Asia* (pp. 173–182). Singapore: AMIC.
Parker, E.S. (1982). Taiwan (Republic of China). In G.T. Kurian (Ed.), *World press encyclopedia, Vol. 2* (pp. 851–859). London: Mansell Publishing.
Peng, B. (1994). The regulation of new media in Taiwan. *Asian Journal of Communication, 4* (2), 97–110.
Rampal, K.R. (1994a). Press and political liberalization in Taiwan. *Journalism Quarterly, 71,* 637–651.
Rampal, K.R. (1994b). Post-martial law media boom in Taiwan. *Gazette, 53,* 73–91.
ROC advertising yearbook. (1989–1990). Taipei: Taipei Advertisers Association.
Sussman, L.R. (1999). *Press freedom 1999: News of the century.* New York: Freedom House.
Tien, H.M. (1989). *The great transition: Political and social change in the Republic of China.* Taipei: SMC Publishing Inc.
US Census Bureau. (1998, December 28). *International data base summary data* [On-line]. Available: ⟨http://www.census.gov/cgi-bin/ipc/idbsum⟩.
Vanden Heuvel, J., & Dennis, E.E. (1993). *The unfolding lotus: East Asia's changing media* (pp. 40–53). New York: The Freedom Forum.
Wang, G. (1984). *The fourth channel.* Unpublished research report in Chinese, The National Science Council, Taipei.
Wang, G. (1998). Communication ethics in a changing Chinese society. In C. Christians & M. Traber (Eds.), *Communication ethics and universal values* (pp. 225–243). Thousand Oaks, CA: Sage Publications.

Wang, G., Chung, W.W., & Chi, J.Y. (1991). *A study of cultural values and information behavior*. Unpublished research report in Chinese, National Science Council, Taipei.

Wang, G., Wu, S., & Chen, P.L. (1994). *The importance of cognition and values to information literacy*, Unpublished research report in Chinese, National Science Council, Taipei.

Wei, R. (1998). Press developments in Taiwan and the changing coverage of the Taiwan-China relationship. In B.T. McIntyre (Ed.), *Mass media in the Asia Pacific* (pp. 67–71). Clevedon, PA: Multilingual Matters.

WAN (World Association of Newspapers). (1999). *World press trends*. Paris: WAN.

World factbook. (1999). Washington, DC: CIA [On-line]. Available: (http://www.odci.gov/cia/publications/factbook).

◆

About the Editor and Contributors

EDITOR

SHELTON A. GUNARATNE is currently a professor of mass communications at Minnesota State University Moorhead. A specialist in international communication, he is the author of *The taming of the press in Sri Lanka* and *Modernization and knowledge: A study of four Ceylonese villages*. His authoritative essay "Old wine in a new bottle: Public journalism, developmental journalism, and social responsibility," was featured in *Communication Yearbook 21* (1998). Another of his essays, "Convergence: Informatization, world system, and developing countries," will appear in *Communication Yearbook 25*. Professor Gunaratne is also on the editorial advisory boards of *Gazette* and *The Journal of International Communication*. Born in Sri Lanka, he worked as a journalist in Colombo from 1962 to 1967, and has since taught journalism and international communication at several universities in Australia, China, Malaysia, and the United States.

Mass Communications Department, Minnesota State University Moorhead, 1104 Seventh Ave. S., Moorhead, MN 56563, USA.
E-mail: gunarat@mhd1.moorhead.msus.edu ♦ gunarat@mnstate.edu

CONTRIBUTORS

OWAIS ASLAM ALI is secretary-general of the Pakistan Press Foundation (PPF), an independent media research, documentation, and training center. He is also chairman of Pakistan Press International (PPI), the country's independent news agency. Mr Ali is a member of the International Press Institute's Experts Committee on News Agencies as well as of the Commonwealth Association for Education in Journalism and Communications (CAEJC), and an associate member of ORBICOM, the UNESCO network of chairs and associates in communications. He was elected convenor of the International Freedom of Expression Exchange (IFEX), a worldwide network of organizations for freedom of expression for the year 1998–99.

Press Center, Shahrah Kamal Ataturk, Karachi, Pakistan
E-mail: owais.ali@ibm.net

PENG HWA ANG teaches media law and management at Nanyang Technological University, Singapore, where he is vice dean of the School of Communication Studies. A lawyer by training, he holds a Doctorate in mass media from Michigan State University. His research is in legal and policy issues in the media, covering such areas as copyright, censorship, and content-regulation on the Internet.
School of Communication Studies, Nanyang Technological University, Singapore 639798
E-mail: TPHANG@ntu.edu.sg

SERAJUL I. BHUIYAN is an associate professor at the Department of Communications, Alcorn State University, Mississippi. Professor Bhuiyan received his Doctorate in mass communications from the University of Wisconsin, Madison, and subsequently, was a research assistant at the Nanyang Technological University, Singapore. He has authored a book and over three dozen research papers. These have been published in various journals including *Journal of Development Communication, Media Asia, Bangladesh Journal of Training and Development*, and *Bangladesh Journal of Extension Education.* He has also been a guest columnist for several newspapers in Bangladesh, Japan, and America, and has received an award from the Bangladesh government for investigative reporting.
Department of Communications, Alcorn State University, 1000 ASU Drive # 269, Lorman, MS 39096, USA
E-mail: bhuian_58@hotmail.com ♦ sibhuiyan@yahoo.com

KALYANI CHADHA currently manages the Hubert Humphrey Fellowship Program in journalism at the University of Maryland. She has a Doctorate in mass communications from the College of Journalism, University of Maryland. Dr Chadha has worked on several international-oriented media research projects, ranging from an analysis of national policy responses and global media flows in Asia to studies of the cultural and ideological function of television news broadcasts in India. She has presented papers at annual conferences of the ICA and the AEJMC.
College of Journalism, The University of Maryland, College Park, MD 20742, USA
E-mail: kchadha@wam.umd.edu ♦ kchadha@jmail.umd.edu ♦ fvl9umailsrv0. umd.edu

JOSEPH MAN CHAN is currently a professor at the Department of Journalism and Communication, Chinese University of Hong Kong, and president of the Chinese Communication Association. He has published several essays in books and journals on international communication and political communication, and has co-authored *Mass media and political transition* and *Hong Kong journalists in transition.* Professor Chan has also been a Harvard-Yenching Scholar and a member of the Hong Kong Broadcasting Authority.
Department of Journalism and Communication, The Chinese University of Hong Kong, Shatin, Hong Kong

JEONG-HEON CHANG is a Doctoral student in the mass media program at Michigan State University where he also works for the Visiting International Professional Program as a preceptor. As a group leader, he works with professionals from advertising agencies, broadcasting companies, and dailies from several foreign countries. His main research areas include public opinion, political campaigning, and voting decisions.

Michigan State University, Mass Media Ph.D. Program, 309 Comm. Arts & Science Building, East Lansing, MI 48823, USA
E-mail: changjeo@pilot.msu.edu

JUDITH CLARKE is a former Indo-China correspondent and editor of *Asiaweek* who now teaches journalism at Hong Kong Baptist University. She recently completed her Doctoral thesis on the history of international news coverage of Cambodia.

Department of Journalism, Hong Kong Baptist University, Kowloon Tong Kowloon, Hong Kong
E-mail: jlc@hkbu.edu.hk

C.J. CONLON has a Master's degree in journalism from the University of Technology, Sydney, where she currently lectures on on-line journalism. She is also the editor of *Communications Update*, a monthly magazine of the Communications Law Center, Sydney. Ms Conlon's interest in South Asian politics and media is inspired by her strong personal connection with the region and draws on her work in London with specialist publishers of works on Tibet, Sikkim, and Bhutan.

Australian Center for Independent Journalism, University of Technology, Sydney, 755 Harriss St. (cnr Broadway), Ultimo, PO Box 123, Broadway, NSW 2007, Australia
E-mail: cjconlon@sydney.net

YEN DO is the founder and publisher of *Nguoi Viet*, based in California. He served as its editor-in-chief until 1995. In Saigon, he was the administrative editor of *Dai Dan Toc*. He also worked as a war correspondent until 1975.

14891 Moran St., Westminster, CA 92683, USA

DARADIREK EKACHAI is an associate professor at the Department of Speech Communication, Southern Illinois University, Carbondale, from where she obtained her Doctorate in journalism. Dr Ekachai has published works related to public relations education and the practice of public relations in Thailand, intercultural communication, and mass media and cultures.

Department of Speech Communication, 2002 Communications Building, Southern Illinois University, Carbondale, IL 63901-6605, USA
E-mail: ekachai@siu.edu

CHUL HEO is a television producer, theorist, and teacher, and is at present a doctoral candidate in the Communication Studies Department at the University of Iowa where he teaches courses in ideology and TV aesthetics, television production, and broadcast management. The University of California at Berkeley has distributed his award-winning documentary "Between Two Worlds." His other video works have been broadcast nationally on PBS stations in the United States and the MBC network in Korea. Chul Heo's research interests include media technology and modernity, television production and popular culture, and production of identity and class.

University of Iowa, Department of Communication Studies, 105 Becker Comm. Bldg., Iowa City, IA 52242, USA
E-mail: cheo@blue.weeg.uiowa.edu

NASWIL IDRIS is a member of the Board of Expert MASTEL (Indonesia Tele-communication Society), Jakarta, and the chairman of the Educational Laboratory. Universitas Terbuka (The Indonesian Open Learning University), Jakarta. He holds two Master's degrees—in international development and international communication, respectively—from the School of Education and school of communication, Stanford University, Palo Alto, and a Doctorate in educational technology from the Institute of Educational Science, Jakarta. Naswil Idris is also an active member of AMIC (Asian Media Information and Communication Center) Singapore, IDLN (International Distance Learning Network), and PRAI (Public Relations Association of Indonesia). In the last three years he has been a speaker and panelist at several national and international conferences on media and communication in Indonesia and abroad.

Universitas Terbuka, Bukit Pamulang Indah Blok A4 No. 7, Pamulang Timur, Ciputat 15417, Jakarta, Indonesia
E-mail: hendri@indosat.net.id

KAVITA KARAN is an associate professor at the Department of Communication and Journalism, Osmania University, Hyderabad. Earlier she was chairwoman of the Board of Studies in the same department. She obtained her Doctorate from the London School of Economics and Political Science and specializes in political communication. Dr Karan has presented papers at several international seminars and conferences. Her interests include advertising and market research, communication and social groups, and health communication.

Department of Journalism and Communication, College of Arts and Social Sciences, Osmania University, Hyderabad 500 007, India
E-mail: pranava@hdl.vsnl.net.in

ANANDAM P. KAVOORI is an associate professor of telecommunications at the College of Journalism and Mass Communication, University of Georgia. His research interests are in trans-national cultural studies, television news, media ethnography, and tourism. He has published essays in leading international journals including *Critical Studies in Mass Communication Media, Culture and Society, Journal of International Communication,* and *The Journal of Communication.* He is the co-editor of *The global dynamics of news.*

College of Journalism and Mass Communication, The University of Georgia, Athens, GA 30602, USA
E-mail: akavoori@arches.uga.edu

SHIN DONG KIM is an assistant professor in communication at Hallym University, North Korea. He received his Bachelor's and Master's degrees in journalism and mass communications from Korea University and a Doctorate in mass communication from Indiana University. His research and teaching interests include media policy, media globalization, culture and communication, and social/cultural impacts of new media technologies. Dr Kim has been a visiting assistant professor in the East Asian and Middle Eastern Studies Program at Dartmouth College and has published various articles.

School of Communication, Hallym University, Okchon-dong 1, Chunchon 200-702, North Korea
E-mail: kimsd@sun.hallym.ac.kr

BHARAT KOIRALA began his career in journalism in 1965 as the chief reporter of a prominent English Daily, *The Rising Nepal.* In 1974 he became editor of *The Gorkhapatra,* the first and largest daily newspaper in Nepal. He has been executive chairman of Gorkhapatra Corporation and was elected secretary-general of the Nepal Press Institute after serving as its executive director for almost 15 years. Mr Koirala is associated closely with many media organizations and with innovative programs in the print and broadcast media.

Nepal Press Institute, P.O. Box 4128, Kathmandu, Nepal
E-mail: bdkoirala@npi.wlink.com.np

EDDIE KUO is the founding dean of the School of Communication Studies, Nanyang Technological University, Singapore. He was formerly head of the sociology department, and director of the Center for Advanced Studies and of the Mass Communication Program at the National University of Singapore. A sociologist by training, Professor Kuo's research interests include communication policy and planning, information technology and information society, cultural policy and national integration, and the sociology of multilingualism. He is the founding co-editor of the *Asian Journal of Communication* (Singapore) and serves on the advisory boards of *Journal of Asia-Pacific Communication* (USA), *Journal of Development Communication* (Malaysia), and *Journal of International Communication* (Australia).

School of Communication Studies, Nanyang Technological University, Singapore 639798
E-mail: CYKUO@ntu.edu.sg

CHIN-CHUAN LEE is a professor of journalism and mass communication at the University of Minnesota. He has previously been a professor of journalism and communication at the Chinese University of Hong Kong and a visiting professor at Academia Sinica. His major research interests include political communication and international communication in general, and Chinese communication in particular. Professor Lee has written and edited five books in English and eight in Chinese. He received his Doctorate from the University of Michigan and was the founding president of the Chinese Communication Association.
Department of Journalism and Communication, The Chinese University of Hong Kong, Shatin, Hong Kong

VEN-HWEI LO is a professor of journalism at the National Chengchi University, Taipei. He holds a Bachelor's degree in journalism from National Chengchi University, a Master's degree in journalism from the University of Oregon, and a Doctorate in journalism from the University of Missouri-Columbia. Previously, Professor Lo was a reporter for the *China Times* and the *China Post*. He is the author of four books and numerous articles about the performance of the news media and the effects of mass media.
Department of Journalism, National Chengchi University, Taipei, Taiwan 11623
E-mail: vhlo@hotmail.com

ERIC LOO, is the head of the Graduate School of Journalism, University of Wollongong. He has worked as a financial journalist, features editor, and production editor, and has conducted media training workshops in Malaysia, Laos, Hong Kong, and Australia. His current research interests include a study of the impact of the Internet on the concepts and practice of conventional journalism, as well as reporting across cultural and political boundaries. He is the founding editor of the refereed journal, *Asia Pacific Media Educator*.
Graduate School of Journalism, University of Wollongong, NSW 2522, Australia
E-mail: eric_loo@uow.edu.au

BARRY LOWE is an associate professor at the City University of Hong Kong, where he teaches journalism and multimedia authoring. He also conducts media training courses in various Asian countries, including Mongolia. He has a background in journalism and formerly worked as a foreign correspondent in Southeast Asia and Eastern Europe. His main research interest lies in documentary production.
Department of English, City University of Hong Kong, Kowloon Tong, Hong Kong
E-mail: enbarry@cityu.edu.hk

CRISPIN C. MASLOG, a writer and editor, has been a professor of communication since 1967. He has authored or edited 20 books in communication and communication education and has lectured internationally on communication. A former journalist and university publications director, Professor Maslog is an experienced editorial and communication consultant, and senior vice dean and dean of the Graduate School, Asian Institute of Journalism and Communication, Metro Manila.

Institute of Development Communication, UP Los Banos, College, Laguna 4031, Philippines
E-mail: crismas@csi.com.ph

FRANK MORGAN has worked extensively in broadcasting and media development in Asia and the Pacific for more than 25 years. A television producer and documentary film maker, he was the deputy director of the Australian Film Television & Radio School (1981–86) and has been a professor in the Department of Communication & Media Arts at the University of Newcastle, Australia, since 1988. He first worked in Laos in 1991 under the AIBD-Australia Media Program. Currently, he is president of the Professional Education Section of IAMCR, and of JOURNET, the UNESCO Global Network for Professional Education in Journalism and Media.

Department of Communication & Media Arts, The University of Newcastle, NSW 2308, Australia
E-mail: fmorgan@mail.newcastle.ed.au

ZENY SARABIA PANOL is an assistant professor at Southwest Texas State University, where she teaches advertising and public relations at both the graduate and undergraduate levels. She obtained her Bachelor's degree in journalism from Silliman University, her Master's degree in communication from the University of the Philippines at Diliman, and her Doctorate in mass communication from Oklahoma State University.

Department of Mass Communication, 204 Old Main, Southwest Texas State University, 601 University Drive, San Marcos, TX 78666, USA
E-mail: ms16@swt.edu

SANDHYA RAO is assistant chair and associate professor at the Department of Mass Communication, Southwest Texas State University. Her research areas include international communication and new communication technologies. In recent years, her research has focused on new technologies in India and the Asian region. She has presented papers at numerous international and national conferences and published essays in international journals including *Gazette, Media Asia,* and *ICCTR Journal.* She has also contributed chapters to several books, including *International satellite broadcasting in South Asia* and the forthcoming *Critical issues in communication: Looking inward for answers,* of which she is also the co-editor.

Department of Mass Communication, 118 Old Main, Southwest Texas State University, San Marcos, TX 78666, USA
E-mail: sr02@swt.edu

H.M. SAFAR is an associate professor at Universiti Kebangsaan Malaysia, where he teaches journalism and international communication. He has a Doctorate in communication from Universiti Kebangsaan Malaysia and a Master's degree in mass communication from the University of Minnesota. He was a Bernama journalist and foreign correspondent for more than 12 years, prior to joining academia. Dr Safar has written four and translated eight books and has published numerous articles in journals. His current research interest is on Internet usage in Malaysia.
Department of Communication, Universiti Kebangsaan Malaysia, 43600 UKM Bangi, Selangor Darul Ehsan, Malaysia
E-mail: msafar@pkrisc.cc.ukm.my ◆ msafar@ukm.my

SHINICHI SAITO is an associate professor at the Department of Communication, Tokyo Women's Christian University. He received his Doctorate from the Annenberg School for Communication, University of Pennsylvania. His research interests include the effects of mass media, the social impact of new communication technologies, international communication, and quantitative research methods. His most recent publications include essays in the *Asian communication handbook* (1998) and in *Images of the U.S. around the world* (1999), as well as articles in several journals.
Department of Communication, Tokyo Women's Christian University, 2-6-1 Zempukuji, Suginami-ku, Tokyo 167, Japan
E-mail: philly@parkcity.ne.jp

ASIAH BINTI SARJI is an associated professor at Universiti Kebangsaan Malaysia, where she currently teaches broadcasting. She obtained her Master's degree from Syracuse University, USA, and her Doctorate in communication from Universiti Kebangsaan Malaysia. Her research is concentrated on issues related to broadcasting development and strategies. Dr Sarji is involved in consultation activities with governmental organizations and NGOs on broadcasting and film development. She has recently co-authored two books—*Professionalism in film industry in Malaysia* (1999) and *Issues on script writing and film industry in Malaysia* (1999).
Department of Communication, Universiti Kebangsaan Malaysia, 43600 UKM Bangi, Selangor Darul Ehsan, Malaysia

CLEMENT SO is an associate professor at the Department of Journalism and Communication, the Chinese University of Hong Kong. He received his B.S.Sc. (sociology) and M.Phil. (communication) from the Chinese University of Hong Kong, and a Doctorate from the Annenberg School for Communication, University of Pennsylvania. Dr So has worked as a marketing researcher for a television station in Hong Kong, as well as a reporter and editor for two newspapers in Canada. His major research interests include the sociology of news, developments in the field of communication, citation study, and new communication technology.

Department of Journalism and Communication, The Chinese University of Hong Kong, Shatin, Hong Kong
E-mail: clementso@cuhk.edu.hk ◆ 6068759@mailserv.cuhk.edu.hk

KI-YUL UHM is a doctoral candidate at the School of Journalism and Mass Communication and a Seashore Dissertation-Year Fellow at the University of Iowa. He was the editor of the *Journal of Communication Inquiry* in 1995, and has edited a special issue on "Critical Communication Law and Policy."

University of Iowa, Journalism and Mass Communications, W615, Seashore Hall, Iowa City, IA 52242, USA
E-mail: kiuhm@blue.weeg.uiowa.edu

K. VISWANATH, who has a Doctorate from the University of Minnesota, is on the faculty of the School of Journalism and Communication at Ohio State University. He also holds appointments in the School of Public Health and the Center for Health Outcomes, Policy, and Evaluation Studies. Dr Viswanath is interested in using macro-social approaches to the study of mass communication and has published extensively in different journals. With Dave Demers he has co-edited *Mass media, social control and social change* (1999).

School of Journalism and Communication, The Ohio State University, 242 West 18th Avenue, Columbus, OH 43210, USA
E-mail: vish+@osu.edu

GEORGETTE WANG is professor and dean of the College of Social Sciences, National Chengchi University, Chiayi. She holds a Doctorate from Southern Illinois University, Carbondale. Professor Wang has worked as a research associate at the Communications Institute, East–West Center in Honolulu, Hawaii, and has taught in universities in Hong Kong and Taiwan. Her major publications include *Globalization, localization or something else: The emerging communications landscape* (forthcoming) and *Informatization in Asia*, both of which she has edited, as well as *Information society: A retrospective view*, which she co-authored with Herbert S. Dordick.

Department of Journalism, National Chengchi University, Taipei, Taiwan 11623
E-mail: telgw@ccunix.ccu.edu.tw

CHANUKA LALINDA WATTEGAMA obtained his Bachelor's degree in electronics and electrical engineering from Karnataka Regional Engineering College, affiliated with Mangalore University, India. He currently works as the systems engineer at the Central Bank of Sri Lanka. A frequent contributor to the local media on communication and issues related to information technology, he has more than 10 years' experience as a freelance journalist. He has twice won the award for the best Science Writer in Sri Lanka presented by the Sri Lanka Association for the Advancement of Science.

22, Jayanthipura, Battarmulla, Sri Lanka
E-mail: chanu@sltnet.lk ◆ cbslitd@slt.lk

LIQUN YAN, originally from China, is an associate professor of journalism in the Department of Communication, Tennessee State University. She holds a Bachelor's degree in English language and literature from China, and a Master's degree and Doctorate in journalism from the University of Missouri's School of Journalism. Dr Liqun Yan worked at the *Beijing Review* before going to the United States. She has previously co-authored a book and published numerous essays, professional as well as academic, in English and Chinese.

Department of Communication, College of Arts and Sciences, Tennessee State University, 3500 John A. Merritt Blvd, Nashville, TN 37209-1561, USA
E-mail: yanl@harpo.tnstate.edu ◆ YanL@tnstate.campuscwix.net

YUSSOF LADI is an information officer at the Department of Information, under the Prime Minister's Department, Brunei Darussalam. He holds a Master's degree in Communication from Universiti Kebangsaan Malaysia. His other qualifications include a Bachelor's degree in economics from the University of Brunei Darussalam, a Diploma in tourism studies, and a Master's degree from the Dorset Institute of Higher Education, UK.

Department of Communication, Universiti Kebangsaan Malaysia, 43600 UKM Bangi, Selangor Darul Ehsan, Malaysia

SUBJECT INDEX

AUTHOR INDEX